TORY RADICAL

THE LIFE OF RICHARD OASTLER

RICHARD OASTLER, AT THE AGE OF 48

Tory Radical

THE LIFE OF RICHARD OASTLER

Cecil Driver

NEW YORK

Oxford University Press

1946

Preface

THIS BOOK tells the story of a personality whose name was once a household word among the English common people: a 'character' in the Dickensian sense, whose disturbing enthusiasms caused him to be execrated by some but beloved by many.

From the very nature of his labors, however, the narrative of this man's life amounts to something more than a biography. It becomes a chapter in the unfinished story of the development of the public conscience. For Richard Oastler, despite his limitations (or perhaps because of them), belongs indisputably to the fretful and troublesome company of those whose imagination having once been shocked into a sense of finer possibilities in social ordering cannot thereafter walk peaceably alongside complacency.

By their efforts to impart their consuming convictions, such men invariably make a nuisance of themselves to the administrators of the established pattern, as Oastler assuredly did. Yet none the less, as in this case too, they may serve as the agencies whereby the prevailing standards of acquiescence become gradually transformed into the conditions of a richer accomplishment. But only in the perspective that time confers can their achievements be adequately assessed.

This may explain, in part, why Oastler's biography has not before been written. The phrase he used to symbolize his hopes—*the social State*—was anathema to most of his contemporaries: today it is a catchword heard on every hand.

In order that the reading of the narrative may not be impeded, the notes and technical discussions have been relegated to the back of the book. They are not in any sense complete: their main purpose is to validate the more significant or more controversial phases of the narrative, and at the same time to suggest possi-

bilities for future research into what is a largely unexplored territory of working-class history. In the bibliography I have given a
comprehensive indication of all the sources used.

Yale University,   CECIL DRIVER
6 August 1946

Contents

I.	The Ancient Ways	3
II.	The Making of an Evangelical	13
III.	The Making of a Tory	25
IV.	Oastler's Awakening: 'Yorkshire Slavery'	36
V.	The Great Controversy Begins	49
VI.	The Reply of the Mill Owners	58
VII.	The Dilemma of Whiggery	71
VIII.	The Workers Organize	81
IX.	Parliament Refuses to Interfere	90
X.	Philanthropy Becomes Politics	100
XI.	Oastler's First Debate	118
XII.	Oastler Discovers His Power: The First Rousing of the North	125
XIII.	Propaganda Becomes Necessary	140
XIV.	The Pilgrimage to York	154
XV.	Sadler's Ten Hours Bill	164
XVI.	Reform Bill Excitement	178
XVII.	The General Election of 1832	191
XVIII.	The Second Rousing of the North	206
XIX.	The North Receives the Royal Commission	222
XX.	Climax and Defeat: The Passing of Althorp's Factory Act	237
XXI.	Aftermath: Disunion and Deflation	251
XXII.	The Problem of the Poor Law	269
XXIII.	Toryism Reconsidered	292
XXIV.	The Third Rousing of the North	307
XXV.	The North Repudiates the New Poor Law	331
XXVI.	Defiance Becomes Turbulent	351
XXVII.	The Mobilization of Protest	364
XXVIII.	The Farewell to Fixby	378
XXIX.	Chartism	390
XXX.	Trial	410
XXXI.	Life in Prison	415
XXXII.	The Faith of a Tory	424
XXXIII.	'The Ransomed Patriot'	438

XXXIV.	The Ten Hours Movement Revives	450
XXXV.	Interlude of Misfortune: 1844–6	459
XXXVI.	Triumph At Last: 1847	463
XXXVII.	The Struggle for Law Enforcement	478
XXXVIII.	The Fight for a Declaratory Act	493
XXXIX.	Proclaiming Tory Democracy	507
XL.	The Closing Years	516

ADDENDA

Acknowledgements	521
Notes	523
Appendices	547
Bibliography	563
Index	585

List of Illustrations

Richard Oastler, at the age of 48 — *frontispiece*

Fixby Hall, near Huddersfield, c.1830 — *facing page* 22

Richard Oastler, at the beginning of his public career — *facing page* 23

Michael Thomas Sadler — *page* 116

George Stringer Bull ('Parson Bull of Bierly') — *facing page* 230

One of the posters calling for the great Wibsey Low Moor demonstration on behalf of the Ten Hours Bill, 1 July 1833 — *facing page* 231

Joseph Rayner Stephens — *facing page* 342

Richard Oastler, 'the Factory King,' after his dismissal from his stewardship — *facing page* 343

William Busfield Ferrand — *page* 449

Oastler's employer: Thomas W. Thornhill, Squire of Fixby — *facing page* 470

TORY RADICAL

THE LIFE OF RICHARD OASTLER

The Ancient Ways

No county in England abounded in more vivid contrasts than did Yorkshire a century ago.

Its very landscape was a panorama of contrasts: of peak and moorland as well as valley and park; of expanding cities and lonely, remote hamlets. It was the home, moreover, of treasures old and new. Within its borders stood two of the wonders of the North—Fountains Abbey in its twelfth-century grandeur and the Leeds Cloth Halls in their eighteenth-century pride. There too, side by side, could be seen the village cottages of the old domestic industries—lingering reminders of a medieval economy—and the rapidly spreading textile mills. Growing wealth and grinding poverty walked the streets together; and while the comfortable residences of the prosperous were going up in the suburbs, the cellar-dwellings of the indigent were multiplying in the slums.

The spirit of Yorkshiremen was no less beset with contradiction. The county was the cradle of militant evangelicism and sectarian fervor as well as the field for ruthless acquisitiveness and hazardous speculation. And between the Pennine uplands and the coast was spread the entire range of social attitudes that Englishmen had ever held, from the resentments of the swelling proletariat to a feudal regard for the nobility whose great estates lay scattered over the countryside. It was, as a foreigner once observed, the fit setting for paradox.

No man from that county was more completely the embodiment of paradox than Richard Oastler. He was the Anglican who held to his Faith with evangelical intensity; the defender of aristocracy who sacrificed the best years of his life for the workers; the zealot for the Constitution who incited the masses to di-

3

rect action. One of the most-feared yet best-loved figures of his generation, he was the Tory who brought politics to the people and the man who created that most striking of all English paradoxes—the conception of Tory Democracy.

Few in their day have had so many contradictory labels attached to their names. During a famous speech in the House of Lords, the Lord Chancellor of England denounced Oastler as a criminal incendiary; while The Times *in a memorable editorial called him the providential organ of the oppressed and suffering poor. The Liberal journals, led by the* Manchester Guardian, *said that he was a dangerous socialist; while the Radical journals were warning the Forces of Progress that he was a supple and reactionary Tory, of greater danger to their cause than more definable enemies.*

Even modern scholars have achieved little more concurrence in their judgments. Recently an American economic historian pronounced Oastler an irresponsible humbug; yet only a few years since one of the most erudite of Frenchmen credited him with a beneficence that Englishmen have insufficiently honored.

Richard Oastler was essentially a romantic: and in his passionate efforts to shape the things that were to come he was inspired largely by his own dreams about the things that once had been. Local story and family tradition gave the materials out of which those dreams were fashioned. When, therefore, in the anger of his protest against the consequence of economic change, he recounted the legend of happier days, there were thousands who found in his words something of the universal sense.

¶ 1

RICHARD OASTLER, the turbulent champion of social reform, was born at Leeds in the West Riding of Yorkshire five days before Christmas, 1789. Of his mother's family, named Scurr, little is known save that they were devout and respected middle-class folk who had been established in Leeds for a good many years. But about his father's family much more has come to light.

The Oastlers, as their standing gravestones still testify, were Yorkshire yeomen farmers who for generations had held their freehold and exercised their franchise in the North Riding of the county. Their property lay well away from the main road in the parish of Kirby Wiske, a small, secluded village which has as its sole claim to distinction the fact that it was the birth-place of the famous Tudor scholar Roger Ascham, who became tutor to Queen Elizabeth.

Here Richard's father Robert was born in the year 1748. His upbringing was in no wise different from that of any other child similarly situated, and had it not been for the Wesleyan revival he might have succeeded in due time to the family farm and lived out his inconspicuous days in the manner of his forebears. When the boy was about 16, however, he embraced the Methodist faith with intense ardor—an ardor, indeed, which was to be sustained in remarkable fashion for over 50 years. This led to a quarrel with his father; the domestic situation soon became intolerable, and the boy was finally forced to leave home.

He went to the near-by market town of Thirsk, where he had two uncles of considerable standing who had both recently received the same inner call and were energetically devoting themselves to the promotion of its cause. His uncle John, the elder of the two, virtually adopted the boy, and in his home Robert grew to manhood. Nor was this the only consolation he found, for he soon got to know the great evangelist himself. Wesley came to Thirsk in April 1766, to open the new chapel which the uncles had built. (In its deeds 'John Oastler, gentleman,' and 'Samson Oastler, yeoman,' are named as trustees.) This proved but the first of many meetings. The acquaintanceship, we are told, 'ripened into a more than common friendship.' In later years, whenever Wesley went to that part of the country he stayed with Robert Oastler; and on his last visit to Yorkshire Robert was his host.

For some 25 years Robert remained at Thirsk. At first, apparently, he helped on his uncle's estate; then he set up on his own as a grocer. It may be that he did a little trading in cloth as well. Certainly he prospered, and as lay-preacher and church worker became one of the pillars of Methodism in the North Riding. Eventually he married Miss Sarah Scurr of Leeds, a lady whose piety and philanthropic energy matched his own in every respect, and who bore him seven children in the course of the next ten years.

Sometime during the late seventeen-eighties he decided to abandon the quiet life of a country town in order to become a cloth merchant in the West Riding. At that time the cloth business was booming; markets were expanding, output was being almost doubled every decade, and money seemed to come easily, as the Riding appropriated to itself a steadily increasing proportion of the country's woolen and worsted industry. Already a migration to the textile towns was well under way when Robert Oastler joined it in his early forties.

He took his family to Leeds, settling in St. Peter's Square close to the new Methodist Chapel. And there was born his eighth and last child, whom they named Richard.

¶ 2

This region in which Richard grew up was one of the most distinctive areas in all England. Without an adequate understanding of that fact, the true significance of Oastler's career can scarcely be appreciated: for his lifetime saw the West Riding swept by a series of industrial and commercial changes which were to make it the greatest cloth-manufacturing district in the world, and his career was largely a running commentary by word and deed upon the unforeseen implications of that upheaval.

Here on the bleak slopes and in the intersecting valleys of the Pennine Hills was to be found one of the ancient homes of the English woolen industry: an industry which for centuries had ranked second only to agriculture in the economic life of the nation, and which at this time accounted for almost a third of the country's exports. Still largely hereditary in its personnel, the calling, the craft, and the weekly routine had been handed down from father to son with very little change for generations, so that the industry had gathered about itself something of the conservatism that envelops all venerable institutions.

It was here above all the counties of eighteenth-century England that the real home of domestic industry was to be found. The scene was still much the same as Defoe had depicted it a generation before. Few big producers had yet appeared. The large majority of men in that society were still independent craftsmen working in a small way in their own homes with family labor (and maybe a journeyman or two), just as their ancestors had done in the days of the Tudors and beyond: men, as they described themselves in a petition to Parliament in 1794, who 'with a very trifling capital, aided by the unremitting labor of themselves, their wives and children united under one roof, decently and independently have maintained themselves and their families.' Independence was the very warp of their character: an independence begotten of a certain measure of security and a deep attachment to the old organization; but an independence that might easily become inverted into militant resentment when confronted with the changes that lay in the years ahead.

These small 'working clothiers' of the West Riding, with whom Robert Oastler had come to deal and who still had in their hands the bulk of the industry, were the industrial counterparts of the yeoman farmers. Although most of them worked with a very small capital and had but a small turnover, yet they owned their own tools, bought their own materials, and were in a real sense their own masters. A conspicuous feature of the Riding—one, indeed, on which no visitor failed to comment—was the very large number of little enclosed properties into which the whole region was divided. Each of these clothiers had his cottage or farmhouse around which might be anything from 3 to 15 acres of land, used chiefly as pasture for keeping a cow or two, a pony or donkey, and maybe a few chickens and pigs. But the ownership of their freehold was a bulwark of their independence, in a political as well as in an economic sense, for with it they had the parliamentary vote. Such men still constituted the majority of the West Riding electorate, and on occasion could even bring pressure to bear upon the County Members. Perhaps nowhere else in the provinces was there to be found a more vivid political consciousness or a fuller realization of the possible relevance of Westminster. A Yorkshire county meeting, they used to say, gave the political tone to the whole Kingdom.

In all these homes around Leeds and to the west the routine was much the same. The father would get his weekly supply of wool from the local dealer, and set his household to work preparing it for spinning. The processes were many and tedious. The raw wool had to be sorted and cleaned, oiled, and beaten; then 'carded' to work it into a flossy mass. Only after a good many hours of hard work was it ready for the women and children to spin into yarn. For the smaller clothiers this domestic spinning might be sufficient to keep them supplied; for those in a bigger way of business operating with more than one loom, outside help might be necessary. In that case the work would be given out to the women in the cottages roundabout, for the spinning wheel was found in every home. The biggest and most prosperous clothiers put out their spinning over a very wide area.

When the yarn was spun the clothier could prepare his warp, fix it on the loom, and start the laborious work of weaving his 'piece.' That completed, he had to carry the cloth to the fulling mill down in the valley, where the miller scoured and felted it in the stocks with pounding hammers driven by a water-wheel. Then the clothier fetched it back home to be stretched and dried on the tenter-frame outside his cottage.

It was then ready for sale, for most of these people sold their cloth in the rough, unfinished state. The clothier loaded the bale on his pony or donkey and took it off to the weekly market in one of the Cloth Halls—at Leeds or Bradford, Halifax or Huddersfield. These Halls have been called 'the Shrines of the Domestic System.' There each clothier who could afford it had a cupboard and stand for the display of his wares; and if he could not afford a regular rental he could hire a stand at sixpence the 'piece.' When the bell rang for the opening of the market, the clothiers were all standing in rows with their cloths spread on the counter before them, while the merchants walked to and fro examining, bargaining, and making their purchases. When the sale was completed the clothier carried his bale to the merchant's inn or warehouse and took cash payment to keep him going for the next week or two.

The relationships in such an established scheme of things tended to take on a personal quality throughout the industry. Good feeling prevailed to a conspicuous degree, for it was comparatively easy for a journeyman to set up on his own account: the amount of capital required was not excessive, and wool dealers were always ready to give credit to young men of good repute. Considerable differences did exist, of course, both in the size of the various concerns and the amount of hired help employed; but the open-market system of the Cloth Halls did much to keep the little man on terms of something like equality with his bigger neighbors. The majority of the families, however, did things on a small scale with very slender margins. Some managed to get a couple of pieces to market in a week: many only one. The standard of living was pretty low: only long hours, hard work, and strict frugality ensured anything like a reasonable competence. Yet in the dark times that lay a generation ahead, these men and their children after them grew more and more disposed to look back upon the old days with longing, to forget their bleak reality, and to think of them only as a dream of blessedness which had once actually existed—a 'merry England' of which they had been dispossessed.

The towns—with Leeds above all the rest—were more finishing centers than places of manufacture. The 'piece' which the merchant had bought in the Cloth Hall was by no means ready to be sold to the tailor or shopkeeper. It still had to be 'finished,' that is, given a proper surface by having its nap raised and then sheared; and perhaps it had to be dyed too. All these skilled processes were undertaken by independent master-finishers, who specialized in them in their own building, employed their own journeymen, and did the work put out to them by the merchants at so much a cloth. They were all town occupations, or at least conducted as near the town as possible; but they were still manual crafts wherein the slow skill of the hand had not as yet been displaced by the speedy precision of the machine. Most of the shops were small, and the master still supervised the whole of the work himself. These Yorkshire 'croppers' were as proudly independent as the clothiers, and it was from their ranks that there came 20 years later the bitterest opposition to the introduction of the new machinery.

¶ 3

Robert Oastler became one of the cloth merchants of Leeds at a time when the town had entered upon a remarkable phase of development. Since the beginning of the century it had been growing continuously. Direct communication with the ports of east and west had been opened up by river improvements and canal construction. Barges and sloops came and went in ever-increasing numbers, and great warehouses were going up along the banks of the waterways. In the second half of the century this expansion became prodigious. Public works and philanthropic enterprise altered the whole appearance of the town, making it one of the most progressive in the country. Lighting and sanitation were improved, streets were widened, large open squares were laid out. An infirmary and a public library were built; charity schools, Sunday schools, and a free grammar school were established. Nonconformist chapels of every sect began to multiply in extraordinary fashion, so that Leeds came to be regarded as the headquarters of British nonconformity. New and larger Cloth Halls were built to replace old ones that trade had outgrown. Roads were extended, the coach services were multiplied and speeded up: 8 coaches a day now left for London, covering the 186 miles in 20 hours. And men came from afar—even Royal visitors from Europe—to see these marvels of a modern town.

It is not surprising, therefore, that an intense civic consciousness should have developed, or that the city fathers, exulting in the manifestations of this abundant enterprise, should have passed their famous resolution in January 1793 demanding the abolition of all governmental restrictions and the complete freeing of trade. Out of their well-to-do optimism came an enhanced political aggressiveness, sustained and stimulated by the local newspapers. Nowhere outside London was there a more lively press warfare than that which the Tory-Anglican *Leeds Intelligencer* and the Whig-Nonconformist *Leeds Mercury* had been waging weekly for over 30 years.

Yet in this very prosperity and release of new energies there were being generated forces deeply inimical to the conservative routines of the countryside. Prosperity spelled the slow but steady triumph of the big man: the man with large reserves who could take risks, cater for a distant market and afford to wait a long time for his returns: the man who was able to stand the initial cost of installing the latest inventions in his workshop. Such enterprises might in time come to undermine entirely the old-fashioned independence of family craftsmanship. Already some of the wealthier merchants were invading the producing business and becoming large clothiers on their own account. They operated in various ways. Some short-circuited the Cloth Market by putting the country weavers to work on materials which they supplied, to be woven according to specification, thus gradually making the weavers into their own employees. Others built large sheds in the town and equipped them with twenty or thirty of their own looms, which they hired weavers to come and operate, while women and children in an adjoining shed were working up the necessary wool and spinning the yarn with instruments the master had provided. Yet others bought up (or built their own) finishing shops and so became their own dressers as well. And the mightiest merchants did all of these things. The most significant portent of the 'nineties was the erection of Messrs. Wormald and Gott's establishment just outside Leeds, in which the whole process of clothmaking was undertaken from the first carding of the wool to the last dressing of the cloth.

Such concerns, however, were as yet auguries only; the little clothier was still the typical figure of the industry. Yet the rate of change was clearly accelerating at the time of Oastler's birth, and no man could foresee the consequences. 'Fifty years ago he was thought a great clothier that made 2 pieces a week,' said a witness to the Parliamentary Committee of 1806, 'and now if he makes 6 or 8 or 10 he is not the largest by far. Some make 2 in a week and some make 20.'

And if it was true of the cloth industry that power was getting increasingly concentrated in the hands of the big producers, it was even more conspicuously so in the case of worsted, the manufacture of which centered upon Bradford some ten miles to the west of Leeds. These two branches of the woolen textile industry differed in important respects, both in regard to processes and organization.[1] The making of worsteds, for centuries associated

[1] There were two main branches of the woolen textile industry, namely (a) the cloth or woolen trade and (b) the stuff or worsted trade. The two fabrics differed in numerous respects. For cloth, *short* wool was used and

with the county of Norfolk, had been introduced into the West Riding only in the later seventeenth century, but since then had undergone a remarkable expansion. From the outset it had been predominantly capitalistic in structure and obviously less restricted by conservative traditions. In consequence, the new machinery and the factory system were introduced earlier and more readily than was the case with its older rival, with the result that the domestic system disintegrated there much more speedily.

In more than one sense, then, a child born in the year of the French Revolution stood between two worlds. And within the arena of his own personality, hope and apprehension and a medley of things both old and new were set by circumstance to struggle for mastery.

---

was 'carded' into a fluffy mass before it was spun; for worsted, *long* wool was used and was 'combed' instead of 'carded' to make a different kind of yarn. Furthermore, after being woven, cloth was thickened and felted through sundry fulling and finishing processes, whereas this was not necessary in the case of worsteds, which had a smooth surface.

CHAPTER II

The Making of an Evangelical

O N the first of May 1790, John Wesley came to Leeds on his
last visit. He stayed overnight with the Oastlers and before
he left took the eight-months-old Richard in his arms and blessed
him. Richard's entire upbringing was conducted in the spirit of
that blessing, for from the moment of his birth he was breathing
the air of deepest piety. His mother he adored: 'kindness and
gentleness itself,' he called her. And for his father he grew to
have an almost boundless admiration.

¶ 1

One feature that nowadays seems so impressive about so many
of these first-generation Methodist families is the astonishing
energy they displayed for organized endeavor and works of well-
doing. The Oastlers are a good example. Sarah Oastler brought
up her children to visit the poor and the sick, to help with the
distribution of food and clothes, and to be ever-conscious of the
ministry of service to which they were called by their Master.
Robert Oastler spent all his time outside his business day in every
manner of philanthropic undertaking. He preached regularly in
Leeds and the district roundabout; he helped to get new chapels
started; he founded various young men's clubs and debating
societies; and he worked zealously for the Anti-Slavery movement. There was ample truth in what the *Leeds Mercury* said of
him after his death, that 'his fervent piety to God was ever shown
in his active benevolence to man.'

Yet he was a man of the stoutest independence. In his early
days he had been a Tory: then gradually he changed. Probably
it was living amidst the vigorous and confident bustle of Leeds
that altered him, for the atmosphere of the Leeds Cloth Hall was

the atmosphere of 'progress' and the new liberalism. In the doctrine of 'freedom of enterprise' the merchants readily found the program for their own furtherance. Eventually, therefore, Robert became a reformer and even a 'Tom Painer,' as did so many others of the growing commercial class, advocating 'liberty,' reading his *Leeds Mercury,* and bringing up his family in the doctrine of equality of opportunity.

In some respects he was more 'advanced' than his fellow-Methodists, as he twice clearly proved. The first occasion was when his oldest boy was tragically killed in a fire at his place of work. Contrary to all custom, Robert wanted the boy buried by a chapel preacher in chapel ground, instead of in the parish churchyard. But no Methodist preacher could be found daring enough to make such an innovation in defiance of the Establishment. Robert was determined to have his own way, however, and eventually found a Baptist minister who was willing to conduct the service. And so, according to local tradition, the custom began for Wesleyans to have their own burial rites for interments in their own ground. This grave, in fact, became a family plot, and in it lie buried Robert and his wife, two of their children, and two grandchildren.

The following year he showed himself prepared to apply liberal principles even to Methodism. When Wesley died, the organization he had created changed from a benevolent autocracy to an oligarchy which left little place for the participation of the laity. Led by a fiery young evangelist named Alexander Kilham, a radical party soon arose demanding a democratic reorganization of the whole Wesleyan system. Their proposals were summarily rejected by the Conference, however; Kilham was expelled from the Society; and in August 1797 the first Methodist secession took place. At its inception, the 'New Connexion,' as it called itself, was only a very small sect—some five hundred members in all. But Robert Oastler went with them, believing that the action of the Conference had been 'arbitrary and tyrannical.' He was one of the few men of substance to do so; and to the new organization he gave the same unflagging devotion he had given to the old. Indeed, until the sect was well established, the effort he put forth was greater than ever.

¶ 2

By his own account, Richard's childhood was one of uneventful happiness. To the end of his life he was fond of recalling in letter and conversation memories of those days, and of the domestic trivialities that always seemed to have for him a peculiar fragrance. Doubt cast no shadow over the regularity of that household. The confidence that comes from certitude about ultimate things was his from the beginning, and the naïve vigor that seems to thrive in an atmosphere of assured affection. Almost everyone who came to know him in later years remarked upon his fearlessness. It is not surprising they should have done so, for all the formative circumstances of his childhood went to its making.

The spontaneous and outflowing disposition which was to be the dominant trait of his character matured naturally. As he grew up he came to have an eager delight in the larger life around him. His father inducted him into a consciousness of local and sectarian politics. He got to know the idiom and accent of the weavers who came in from the countryside. He mingled with the crowds on market days, and watched the sloops that came and went from the seaports. He became familiar with the mysteries of wharf and warehouse. All these experiences and countless more went to the fashioning of what was one day to become an ardent local patriotism, and provided him with an enduring store of imagery which was to enhance his oratorical power with a homely and appealing vividness.

When Richard was 9 years old he was sent to the Moravian boarding school at Fulneck, outside Leeds, and there he stayed for the next 8 years. This school was part of a self-contained little village colony which the Moravian Brethren who came over from Germany had originally established as a headquarters and training center for the evangelizing mission they conducted in collaboration with the Wesleyan Movement.[1] In its day it was reck-

[1] The Moravian Church was a protestant sect which had been founded in the fifteenth century. Almost eliminated during the Thirty Years' War, it underwent a considerable expansion in Germany during the eighteenth century. It was a Moravian Brother, Peter Bachler, who had converted both John and Charles Wesley. Moravian missionaries came to England in the seventeen-forties and took an active part in the Evangelical Revival. Their doctrines were essentially the same as those of the Methodists.

oned a 'progressive' school, anticipating in some respects the principles that Dr. Arnold was later to introduce at Rugby. Unlike many pietistic sects, the Moravians had set a high value upon intellectual ability ever since the time of their great philosopher Comenius. They were inspired by a genuine educational philosophy and a clear sense of their objectives. Two features in particular stand out as distinctive in their system: one an emphasis on character building, and the other a curriculum exceptionally broad for the age. It was, one of Fulneck's founders declared, 'not a school to teach children what is politeness and good breeding,' but rather a place for training children in conscious personal integrity and stimulating their interests. The aim was so to deal with the pupils 'that instead of dreading school they may rejoice, and think it too short when 'tis over.'

Doubtless they had no greater measure of success than any other educational reformers have had. But Richard certainly 'rejoiced' in his 8 years at Fulneck, and continued to do so in retrospect for the rest of his life. He was particularly fortunate in being sent there at a time when the school was undergoing considerable expansion: new buildings had recently been added; trained teachers had been brought over from German academies to inaugurate a kind of tutorial system; and geography, bookkeeping, and nature study had been added to the syllabus. But his greatest good fortune, he always used to say, was in having as his tutor Henry Steinhauer, son of the Principal, who had recently come back from 6 years' training on the continent.[2] Steinhauer left a deep impression upon Oastler. Besides being a man of real religious feeling, he appears to have been an enthusiastic exponent of Moravian educational ideals. So the training that had been begun at home was confirmed and completed at Fulneck. Until the day he died Oastler strictly observed the routines of

[2] Henry Steinhauer had himself been a pupil at Fulneck and had afterwards been sent to a teachers' training academy at Barby, Prussia. He came of Moravian families on both sides, his mother's father being a bishop in the Church. After leaving his tutorship at Fulneck he was put in charge of a seminary for the training of students for the ministry. In 1815 he became Principal of a girls college at Bethlehem, Pennsylvania. Soon afterwards he was elected member of the American Philosophical Society and contributed to its *Transactions*. He wrote a number of hymns, some of which appear in the church hymn book. He died in 1818.

prayer, and public worship, and Bible reading: not out of any artificial sense of conformity or filial obligation, but simply as one treasures the proved contrivances of one's own fulfilment.

¶ 3

One day when Richard was 11 years old his father rode over to Fulneck to take the surprising news that he intended giving up the cloth business and starting a new career.

The curious reason he gave for this sudden change was the growing use of 'gig mills' in the cloth-finishing trade.[3] Machines of this sort had been invented as early as the Tudor period, though Parliament had hastened to forbid them. As the eighteenth century advanced, however, enterprising cloth finishers had begun using them again. The expansion of the industry in the 'nineties only served to extend their use, particularly in the clothing districts of the southwest. Undoubtedly they were a profitable investment for those who adopted them, for it was estimated that a man and a boy working with one of these machines could do in 12 hours the work it had formerly taken a skilled cropper over 80 hours to perform.

This naturally aroused the resentment of the croppers, who saw in the continued application of the new inventions only the prospect of permanent unemployment for themselves, with all their own skills thrown into the discard. And to begin with, at least, this resentment received a striking measure of sympathetic endorsement from the general public. Robert Oastler's disquiet was thus by no means unique. Only a short while after he had decided to go out of business, for instance, when disturbances broke out in the West Country, the Home Office began getting letters of complaint reporting 'the disgust at the introduction of machinery' evinced by the people in that region, and their refusal to serve as special constables to keep the peace. Ten years later reports

[3] There were two main stages in the cloth-finishing process: first a nap was raised on the cloth, and then it was cut to a smooth surface with the huge cropping shears. Originally the nap had been raised by brushing the cloth with teasels. The *gig-mill* was a machine that did this work by means of a rotating cylinder. The *shearing-frame* (which was being adopted simultaneously) was an apparatus that carried several cropping shears across the cloth at a time, thus greatly expediting the shearing of the nap.

of a similar kind, and just as emphatic, were to come in from the West Riding as well.[4]

A long-drawn-out struggle followed. There was rioting and sabotage in some parts; secret organizations were formed to combat the introduction of the machines; and two parliamentary committees sat to investigate the problem. Despite all this, the forces of 'free enterprise' eventually triumphed, even though in some areas they were temporarily hindered.

Robert Oastler left the cloth trade before that unhappy story had begun. He fully sympathized with the attitude of the croppers and regarded the use of machinery, we are told, 'as a means of oppression on the part of the rich and of corresponding degradation and misery to the poor.' Since he could not walk at peace with his own conscience, therefore, he was going to abandon business altogether.

Before going to Fulneck to take his boy the news, Robert had already found himself a new job. He was about to become steward for a big landowner named Thomas Thornhill, who had a beautiful estate at Fixby, just outside the neighboring town of Huddersfield; at the age of 53 he was going back to the land. Some of the family were vexed by this, Richard tells us in his memoirs. They thought he was demeaning both himself and them by accepting such a post. But Robert's mind was made up and nothing could shake it.

¶ 4

Richard was rising 17 when he left Fulneck and the question of his future arose. One ambition had already somehow caught his fancy: that was to become a barrister. Unquestionably he had the temperament and talents that might have made him a great pleader; but his father simply would not listen to the suggestion. Robert had a Quaker's sensitive scruples about the law, believing

---

[4] General Grey, commanding officer of the troops being used to keep order in the West Riding, wrote in April 1812, to inform the Home Office 'how much the opinion and wishes of even the more respectable part of the inhabitants are in unison with the deluded and ill-disposed populace with respect to the present object of their resentment, Gig Mills and Shearing Frames, and this extends also to persons having mills of a different description employed in the manufacturing branch.'

it to be an ungodly profession which exploited the follies and misfortunes of mankind. So Richard had to look about for something else: he did not much care what.

They apprenticed him to an architect at Wakefield. He served four years of his time and was just beginning to like the work, when eye trouble compelled him to give it up. Barren though those years may have been from a professional standpoint, however, they were not without their significance for his general development, since it was at Wakefield that Oastler had his first personal experience of electioneering and found the first public cause to which he could give his adolescent enthusiasm. In 1807 there took place one of the most bitterly contested elections in West Riding history, with William Wilberforce, the great leader of the movement for the abolition of Negro slavery, running as a Tory along with Viscount Lascelles against Lord Milton, representing the Whig interests. From his father and from Fulneck, Oastler had learned to abhor slavery; and though he had been brought up in Whig surroundings, his humanitarian sympathies overcame all political considerations and led him to throw himself heart and soul into Wilberforce's campaign. He worked zealously on the emancipator's behalf, speaking at many meetings. Once when on the hustlings he was hit by a brickbat intended for the candidate—an occurrence of which he continued to boast for many years.[5]

The interest thus awakened in the emancipation question survived the election excitements and proved enduring. Oastler went on working locally for the cause until abolition was finally achieved 26 years afterwards. Indeed, his wholehearted admiration for Wilberforce and his enthusiastic participation in the long-sustained anti-slavery campaign was to have a deep influence upon his life in a manner that became apparent only when he reached middle age. This famous campaign was something new in British political life. It was the first time that a group of dis-

[5] It is interesting to observe that though Wilberforce was returned, his running-mate, Lascelles, was defeated. Lascelles was reputed to be opposed to the continuing agitation against the use of gig-mills—the matter that had caused old Robert Oastler such heart-searchings. One of the reasons given for his defeat was the resentment of the clothiers at his attitude towards the new machinery.

interested men had sought to effect a great social reform by means of organized propaganda deliberately designed to bring upon Parliament the full pressure of an aroused public opinion. By assisting in the demonstrations and helping with the distribution of propaganda, Oastler was thus getting more than a training in public affairs and the skills of the platform: he was serving an apprenticeship in the art of agitation, the lessons from which he was to put to remarkable use a generation later.

On leaving the architect's office in 1810, Oastler found himself a job as a commission agent, acting as a sort of middleman between the wholesale houses of Leeds and the retailers in the towns and villages of the Riding. The trade directories listed him as a 'drysalter, oilman, general dealer and chapman.' All through his twenties he kept this business and prospered at it. 'It was not long,' says one of his friends, 'before he ranked among the principal merchants in Leeds, respected for his sterling integrity and honour and considered as one whose superior talents for business would shortly raise their possessor to affluence and distinction.' Such expectations were not surprising. Oastler was endowed with native vigor and capable of great assiduity; moreover, he was decidedly personable: broad shouldered, fresh complexioned, and well over six feet tall, abounding in joviality and health.

His business by no means absorbed all his energies. Strong within him, whatever its source, was the impulse to do good on behalf of his fellow-men. He was possessed of a strong conviction that if Christianity meant anything at all, it meant a call to service, and that he who would follow the Master must take the Master literally by going out into the by-ways to minister to the needy. In Leeds he found two other people who felt as he did and shared his beliefs. One was Michael Thomas Sadler, 9 years older than himself, who came from a prominent Leeds family of linen merchants and bankers. The other was a young man his own age, named Joseph Dickinson. With these he co-operated in all kinds of social welfare work. It was apparently Sadler who first invoked his help. Soon after Oastler returned to Leeds, the town was ravaged by a terrible typhus epidemic, which carried off hundreds and created something near panic among the poorer

classes. Michael Sadler, whose piety sprang from the same
evangelical source as Oastler's, strove to mitigate the horrors of
the pestilence as far as his personal efforts availed. 'That great
and good man,' says one admirer, 'went into the filthiest and
most loathsome hovels of the poor, forsaken outcasts whom their
own neighbours and relations were afraid to approach,' and there
ministered to the sick and dying. Richard heard of these exertions and joined his services to Sadler's. Together they 'performed
every office of attendant and nurse' and brought in others to do
the same.

These experiences came as a great shock to Oastler, as he often
afterwards confessed. For the first time in his life he caught a
glimpse of the depths of suffering among the underprivileged.
As yet, however, he still thought of the problem mainly as a
personal and ethical challenge. There is not the slightest indication that he considered it as a general social question to be treated
by Parliament on a national scale. Rather was it a call to the
devout and generous to volunteer for service in the cause of
practical charity.

He himself certainly served. He was already a local preacher
for the Methodists. In addition, he became a visitor for the Bible
Society, went regularly to the local Infirmary, and continued his
labors with the Emancipation Movement. Along with his friend
Joseph Dickinson he also worked for the Strangers' Friend Society—a body that can claim to be the first district visitors' association in Britain.[6] With the ending of the Napoleonic war and
the onset of the grave post-war depression, the calls upon his
conscience became more numerous and insistent. For many hundreds of families in Leeds the winter of 1815–16 brought stark
tragedy, and all the resources of civic philanthropy had to be
utilized to relieve the distress.

One evening his friend Joseph Dickinson came round to see
him and they fell to talking about the unemployment and the
misery in the town. Oastler has left an account of what happened.

[6] The Strangers' Friend Society was a Methodist organization established
in each of the principal towns for the purpose of helping distressed and
needy strangers. The first societies were started in Bristol, Dublin, and London about 1790.

We were bemoaning the case of the poor, and were sorrowing that we had not the means of relieving the distress which we saw around us. I said to Joe: 'Let us kneel down, Joe, this moment, and ask God how we are to act—it is of no use sorrowing and weeping about it—there's something to be done, and let us ask God what it is; and how we are to do it?' We did kneel down—we prayed. God saw us, heard us, and answered us. When we rose from our knees, I said to Joe, 'I think, Joe, I can pity the poor £5, can you?' He said 'Yes, I can.' We were not rich but we did what we could. Well, we set down that £10 to spend for the poor of Leeds. Joe and I then sat down to determine on a plan of operation, and resolved to do this—to go to a respectable butcher and to ask him if he would take our cards for 1 lb., 8 lbs., or 16 lbs. of meat; to a potato merchant, to ask him if he would receive our cards for a firkin, or half a firkin, or two firkins of potatoes, to be settled with every week. We did so, and they agreed to receive any number of our cards, and supply the bearer with what was stated thereon. Though we were both engaged in business (we worked long hours then, visiting the poor before and after business hours), during that winter we relieved more than fifteen hundred poor persons. Some families were relieved many times. We were not niggardly, we opened our hands wide. We never stopped until the distress was over, and how do you think we were enabled to meet the demand upon our purses? We had faith in God. We never asked anybody for a shilling, the people brought the money to us. They heard what we were doing, and they brought us their £1, £5, £10 and £20, and during that winter, through the blessing of God, we had put into our hands upwards of £840.

Into Leeds and the villages around they went together: into hovels and cellars where whole families were perishing without food and without hope. In Oastler's reminiscences it reads like a chapter from one of the realistic novels with which Mrs. Gaskell was to shock a complacent world a generation later. It is not to be wondered at, therefore, that when the Luddites started their machine-breaking again he was unable to feel the horror that the well-to-do felt, but rather a deep pity. He knew only too well the misery that begot such violence. When fear of revolution seized the town, he considered it his duty as a citizen to serve in the Leeds Watch and Ward establishment; and he did Ward service at Fixby, too, when the Luddites were reported to

Fixby Hall, near Huddersfield, c.1830

RICHARD OASTLER, AT THE BEGINNING OF HIS PUBLIC CAREER

be drilling on the moors at night in preparation for an attack on the Hall. Nevertheless he still believed that alleviation and not repression was the only real remedy. For the repressive measures wherewith Lord Liverpool's ministry sought to curb discontent he had nothing but contempt.

¶ 5

In October 1816 Richard married. His wife, Mary Tatham, was a Nottingham girl, who came of a prominent Wesleyan family very similar to his own. Her father was in the lace business. Her mother was as remarkable a character as old Robert Oastler: just as wholeheartedly dedicated to the Wesleyan cause, and for over 40 years a vigorous class leader in the Society. Of Mary herself, several who knew her have left their impressions and all speak in the same terms. 'Mrs. Oastler,' said a Lancashire journalist, 'was of a delicate frame.'

Her manners were gentle, unassuming and retiring; but in the cause of truth she was bold and unflinching, entirely divested of self-seeking. She was affectionately devoted to relieving the despised and neglected poor, and secured the love of all who knew her . . . deceit, malice, or jealousy had not any place in her breast. She was frank, generous, sincere and confiding; never so happy as when, at any sacrifice to herself, she could increase the happiness of others. Her religion was unostentatious, 'pure and undefiled'; and so her faith and trust in God never failed.

As the sequel shows, when the great days of her husband's political work came, she proved that she had a courage and a tenacity that could match his own.

For two and a half years they lived happily. Then a series of misfortunes befell them. First a daughter was born in January 1819, and died almost immediately. The following December a son was born, and he, too, died within a few days. Out of their grief they struggled to summon the resignation that came from their acknowledgment of the will of God. Then two months later Richard went into bankruptcy.

The circumstances of this bankruptcy are obscure. We have little more to go upon than the statement of his friend, the Reverend J. R. Stephens, but we are told that Oastler came to his decision in spite of all the efforts made by his friends to induce him to continue in business.

He refused all their offers of credit and assistance. He was in no want of either money or credit at the time, but did not think he could —and therefore would not as an honest man—run the slightest risk at the expense of others. It is still fresh in the memory of many at Leeds and will never be forgotten, we are persuaded, by those who at that time became acquainted with the facts of the case. Mr. Oastler has much to be proud of in his singularly eventful history; but were we asked to point to any one circumstance of his whole life as illustrative of the mental and moral grandeur of the man, we should single out his bankruptcy.

He paid his creditors in full and then quit business altogether. Whatever may be the story lying behind the episode (and 1819 was a year of many bankruptcies in the West Riding), this much at least can be said in confirmation of Stephens' eulogy: that 12 years and more later, when Oastler had drawn upon himself the vehement animosity of almost the entire business world of the West Riding and was being roundly aspersed through press and platform, only a single obscure reference was ever made to his bankruptcy. Many another episode of his career was used for his belaboring, but not this.

The following summer his father died at the age of 71, active to the last. Only the previous August he and young Edward Baines (son of his friend, the proprietor of the *Leeds Mercury*) had been sent by the Guardians of the Poor at Leeds to investigate conditions at Robert Owen's experimental village of New Lanark. Leeds was still suffering acutely from the 1819 depression and the Guardians were willing to consider anything that might relieve the distress. The deputation came back enthusiastic for what it had seen, and published its joint report as a pamphlet. There is a suggestion that the long journey, followed by his continuous exertions all the following winter, proved too much for the old man. 'He wore out his strong constitution in the service of the poor,' said his son. 'A more benevolent and excellent man,' declared the editor of the *Mercury*, 'this country has not produced.'

CHAPTER III

The Making of a Tory

H IS father's death brought an unexpected change in Richard's fortunes. Thomas Thornhill, the squire of Fixby, summoned him for an interview and offered him the stewardship of the Fixby estate at a salary of £300 a year. Richard, of course, was delighted and accepted without hesitation. It was just the kind of work that suited his temperament. After two professional misfortunes and nine years in a business that did not really attract him, it seemed that at last, at the age of 31, he had found a career to which he could devote his full energies. 'Mr. Oastler,' Thornhill said, 'your situation will be a very important one. I am in some measure compelled to leave my name as well as my property in the hands of my Yorkshire steward.' No appeal could have been more calculated to call forth Richard's earnestness.

¶ 1

The Fixby estate was large and very diversified, with a rent roll that came to something not far short of £20,000 a year. Nearly a thousand tenants of one sort or another lived on the property, ranging from small cottage weavers to substantial farmers. In addition there were 4 collieries and 25 quarries on the estate, besides sundry turnpike roads in which Thornhill had invested. So Oastler's new position involved plenty of responsibility.

It was an old and wealthy family he was now called upon to serve. Eighteen Thornhills in the male line had held the manor since the middle of the fourteenth century. None of them had attained any national eminence, but all had been active in the affairs of the Riding. From the days of Elizabeth they had been Justices of the Peace. They had fought in the Royalist cause, given High Sheriffs to the county after the Restoration, established a local grammar school under Anne, and prospered with the agricultural changes under the Georges. They were, in fact, a line of Sir Roger de Coverleys. The previous owner, 'old Squire Thomas,' who had held the estate for 45 years and been High Sheriff too, was almost as notorious for his vigorous idiosyncrasies as Sir Roger himself. The present incumbent was also an odd individual. He was at this time just over 40: a man of huge proportions and so corpulent that a semicircle had to be cut out of his dining table to enable him to sit there in comfort. Good living, the London season, and horse racing were his main preoccupations. Twice in the previous three years he had run the Derby winner. Unlike his father, however, he was not a popular landlord and had shown little of the paternal interest which the village expected of its squire. Moreover, he had become involved in more than one scandal, which had put him out of favor with the local gentry. In 1808 he had quit Fixby and gone to live on another of his estates at Riddlesworth in Norfolk. The Hall was let out to tenants and the management of affairs left entirely in the hands of his steward.

¶ 2

Fixby Hall, where Oastler was to spend his next 18 years, was the typical country seat of an affluent Georgian gentleman. As refashioned according to the current convention a couple of generations earlier, it lacked nothing becoming to that station of life either in appointments or surroundings. Beautifully situated on the uplands overlooking the town of Huddersfield from the north, it stood in simple Augustan elegance as the monument of an assured social order. Four imposing gateways at each point of the compass gave on to the drives which meandered past copse and plantation up to the house. Around the Hall itself were broad lawns and formal gardens, and beyond those the rhododendron walks and bluebell dells, once the pride of earlier Thornhills. The inevitable little lake was there, and the orangery built like a Greek temple. But its greatest glory was the superb panorama from its windows which commanded hill and vale as far as Wakefield's spire, 20 miles away.

At first Oastler continued living in Leeds as his father had done, riding over to Fixby once or twice a week to attend to business. But it was a long journey—16 miles each way—and the work seemed heavy. Moreover, he began to feel that Fixby really needed a resident steward if Hall and estate were to be kept in reasonable condition. The twelve years' absence of its owner had unquestionably harmed the place. He therefore proposed that he should live there. Thornhill readily agreed; so on 5 January 1821 the Oastlers moved in.

On the day they arrived, Richard tells us, the two of them knelt down in the cheerless, deserted hall to pray that they might be made useful in the new position to which they had been called. Richard had large ideas about what that position should imply.

Ever since his childhood Fixby had been to him a place of delight, appealing to his imagination. Moreover, he had for the countryside an unaffected love; and, as is so often the case, with that feeling was mingled a keen sense of the continuity of life and of institutions: a sense which perceived in Hall and park, farmstead and cottage, something beyond the obviousness of economic facts. He saw Fixby as the setting of a long unfolding story, the home of successive generations of squires spanning the centuries with their traditions. And in the very conception of 'gentleman' he saw a wealth of significance. It connoted ancient things and the security of accepted ways; it implied duties and responsibilities and leadership; it involved, in fact, the whole complex of personal relationships that make up the pyramid of society. And to Oastler all these intangibles seemed to find their embodiment in these gracious acres.

Now that he had come to live here, he felt, these things were in some measure entrusted to his keeping. It was the idea of trusteeship that so appealed to him: both the trust he held for the Thornhill line, and the obligations it carried towards their tenants. He deplored the absence of the squire, who should have been a father to his people. Clearly he intended to make himself the squire's deputy. Stories of the earlier glories of Fixby in 'the good old days' still lingered in the village. Oastler was resolved that as far as in him lay those good old days should be made to return. Fixby, as he said, should 'once more be recognized as the mansion of a fine old English gentleman.'

¶ 3

The first two years meant hard though exhilarating work. Oastler dropped all his outside activities and gave himself over entirely to the business of the estate. He learned its different boundaries and studied the problems of conflicting rights and overlapping jurisdictions. He delved into the old records and read up local history. He visited all the tenants and came to know them personally. Soon he had at his fingertips every tale and tradition of Fixby as if it were his own. With his overflowing enthusiasm he completely identified himself with the place.

Gradually he revived old customs. Rent day, for instance, was resuscitated and made an occasion for entertainment and conviviality, as it had been in former times. Before long the villagers came to regard him as a friend. They brought him their difficulties, discussed their personal problems, and argued with him about local politics and national affairs. Out of his own pocket he disbursed charity among the poor cottagers. Those who were sick were relieved with medicine and food, while those who fell in arrears of rent always found him to be considerate and accommodating.

One who knew him intimately—a political opponent—has given us a glimpse of those days. Oastler's every effort, he said,

was turned to the endeavour to make the tenantry on his employer's estate comfortable and happy, and also to observe the true interests of his employer. When the tenantry sought advice of him they had no fees to pay, though it was well known that in this way the stewards on some estates contrived to amass from the tenantry large fortunes. He kept up the hospitality of an old English mansion. The poor were never turned empty away from his gates. Whoever sought him on business had never to regret his conduct towards them. Whenever refreshment was required, it was always there to be had.

Compared with his previous standards, it was of course an expensive life. The whole of his salary went in keeping up his position as he thought it should be maintained. Fortunately he had

several small legacies left him, so he had no difficulties. But he
was unable to put anything by for the future.

Under his continuous watchfulness the estate prospered. He
soon had the dilapidations of the Hall repaired. Friendly relations
were established with neighboring stewards, with the result
that nagging litigation, so common a feature of eighteenth-century life, was entirely obviated. He even began to be consulted
on valuations and arbitrations in the district, and in that way
was able to make a little extra money. And every year, the week
after Christmas, he went to stay at Riddlesworth to render his
account. Everything he did was fully reported to Thornhill, and
Thornhill heartily approved, though he never came near the
place.

By the end of three years Oastler had established a routine
which worked smoothly, leaving him more time for himself;
time to visit and entertain, and time to take up once more the
philanthropic enterprises he had been compelled to drop. The
Bible Society, foreign mission work, and the slavery-abolition
Movement still claimed his lively interest. And he started a school
in the village 'for all the children of the poor who chose to come,
where they were taught reading, writing, sewing, knitting, and
useful domestic occupations: and above all, where they were
trained as good Christians to venerate the Church, and to honour
the clergy and their superiors.'

¶ 4

As the years went by, Oastler's outlook gradually changed.
He had been brought up in an atmosphere of Radicalism and
Wesleyanism; now he moved over to Toryism and Anglicanism.
No record survives of that inner transformation, yet it is not difficult to see how it came about. The change from the town to the
country, from Leeds' commercial clatter to the placidity of a
country estate, would be certain in any case to work its own
alchemy. His admiration for Wilberforce, his loyalty to Thornhill, his deep regard for the Tory Michael Sadler: all three
patently colored his disposition. Then, too, the people amongst
whom he was moving were conspicuously different from those of
his early days—farmers and stewards and country gentry whose

point of view he now grew to appreciate. Moreover he became intimate with several of the local clergy, some of whom were to remain his friends for life.

But the greatest factor of all was the fulfilment of his own temperament. In Fixby he found himself. He was averse from trade and had no interest in money-making. On the other hand, he had a curious sense of the continuity of history, and really felt, in a kind of poetical way, the bloom of charm that lies on ancient things. Partly sentimentality and romanticism it may have been, yet beneath that was something deeper and more significant: the conviction that there is a destiny divinely willed. Had Oastler known his Burke (which apparently he did not) he might have recognized his own elusive sense of history in that daring definition of it as 'the known march of the ordinary providence of God.' Steeped in evangelicism though he was, he had no difficulty in bringing these feelings into harmony with his religious views. It is only one half of the evangel of mystic experience that seems to betoken militant individualism. The other half, with its emphasis upon resignation and the quiet acceptance of the will of God, implies just the opposite. The essential Tory doctrine of 'my station and its duties' can be sustained, indeed, only by a faith in some inexorable Purpose that is being worked out in the hearts of men, such as Oastler had learned at Fulneck. So the evangelical Toryism of the son had as religious a logic behind it as the evangelical Radicalism of his father.

In some indefinable way, the demands of Fixby and the process of identifying his own ambitions and energies with its larger purposes wrought in Oastler the silent conversion. In the place and in his work he discovered his own capacities. And in that discovery lay the making of a Tory.

Throughout his public life Oastler emphatically proclaimed himself a Tory. That was a proud affirmation, not an affectation. But Toryism is an ambiguous term. Few words in the whole vocabulary of politics have been more variously used, and none more frequently in a derogatory sense. But several difficulties hinder the appreciation of its true meaning. One is that 'Tory' is not primarily a term of intellectual analysis at all; another that it belongs to a bygone age and has lost its relevance for us today;

and still another, that between the widely diffused Tory sentiment in the nation at large and the party that bore the name
in Parliament, the relationship was imprecise and variable.
Toryism, in fact, is as much a term of social psychology as it
is of politics. The things it connotes came from the country
village, from the days when England was still predominantly
rural before the village had become the moribund society to
which it degenerated in the latter nineteenth century. Its source
is to be found in the attitudes and sentiments of men living as
parts of an established order: in an awareness, that is to say, of
the organic nature of society begotten of the immemorial routines
—plowing and sowing, hayzel and harvest—as well as in a feeling
for the continuity of institutions maintained by the very loyalties
they evoke. The whole emphasis of the Tory was upon the going
concern as the legacy he had inherited from history. And this
in turn involved a stress upon the concreteness of duties and
obligations which that inheritance implied. The Tory thus viewed
the State as the ultimate totality of a myriad social cells. But his
immediate attention was focused upon the nearer communities of
village, shire, and guild, wherein were developed those attitudes
of acceptance that are the deposit of the years: a particular notion of neighborliness and a tacit assertion of the 'proper' gradation of men and classes. That is why Newman could define Toryism as 'loyalty to persons'—a definition with which Oastler would
have heartily concurred: one, indeed, which he virtually formulated himself.

It is thus apparent why Toryism was hostile to 'individualism'
and deeply skeptical of all theories and ideologies, even its own.
Its skepticism sprang from a conviction that the concreteness of
actual life cannot be reduced to the generalization of formulas.
Its antipathy to 'individualism' as a political creed was the natural
result of its emphasis upon community, group, and family. Individualism implies social mobility, and the acceleration of social
mobility weakens the coherence of the group, thus sapping the
psychological foundations of Tory power. This was to be the
recurrent theme of scores of Oastler's discourses.

There is one further consideration that has to be stressed because of the intimate bearing it was to have upon Oastler's public

career. As has just been indicated, Toryism is, so to speak, a
mold of thought or a psychological matrix. But the ethical spirit
with which such a matrix may be filled can vary enormously from
person to person. Into it may be poured the disturbing ardor of
the philanthropist no less than the defensive apprehensions of
the satisfied. No political creed possesses a monopoly of social
righteousness, even though each claims it. To identify a particular administrative convenience with the imperatives of the
moral sense is liable to issue in some strange conclusions, as the
party history of the nineteenth century so amply proves. This
helps to explain why Toryism has so often been at war within
itself: for if assent to yesterday's acceptances breeds the complacency of the obtuse, the nostalgia for remoter days may gener-
ate the protest of the rebel.

When Oastler declared himself a Tory, he was proclaiming
some such outlook as that just described. Attachment, obligation,
custom—for him these things were gradually transposed from
social facts to social ideals. Later in life circumstances forced
him to expound and elaborate them in hundreds of pages of
writing, and to give them a moral significance which was to
startle many who claimed the name of Tory. At the moment,
however, the thing he called Toryism remained only a cluster
of intuitions, strong though barely articulated. Central to them
all was clearly his delight in his Fixby work. In this respect, as
far as his life from the age of 30 to 40 was concerned, Oastler
exemplifies with more than usual appositeness the element of
truth in Bagehot's remark that 'the essence of Toryism is enjoyment.' Anyone who dips into Oastler's many effusions concerning
these years cannot fail to see the relevance of that aphorism in
his case, or to appreciate the pertinence of the economist's other
observation, that 'over the cavalier mind the world passes with
a thrill of delight; there is an exultation in a daily event, zest in
the regular thing, joy at an old feast.' Despite his Puritan upbringing, Oastler's was essentially a cavalier mind, so that the
other things followed as a matter of course.

As he grew into this mood, his prejudices against trade hardened, his suspicion of left-wing nonconformity deepened, and
he became increasingly apprehensive about all those forces of

the age that seemed to be weakening the established bonds. The Whigs, he believed, were playing a dangerous game in stirring up discontent for party advantage. He therefore campaigned vigorously for the Tory candidates at county elections, and protested sharply in letters to the papers against emancipation of the Catholics.

¶ 5

In view of this change in his outlook, it is ironical that Oastler should have first come prominently before the public of the West Riding as the leader of a tithe war. Yet this was the case.

Tithes were an ancient institution from which the principal revenues of the Church were derived. They were a direct charge upon the land according to which the parson was entitled to collect 'in kind' from the farmer each year one-tenth of the natural yield of his fields: a primitive custom as vexatious to the cultivator as it was discouraging to agricultural improvement. But the law attending it was a tangled undergrowth of prescription, legislation, and court decision, which had grown steadily more complicated since the upheaval of the Reformation. Some farms were entirely tithe-free; for some the payment had been 'compounded' as a fixed annual payment; while in other cases part of the tithe was paid and the rest of the claim had fallen into disuse. During the latter part of the eighteenth and the early years of the nineteenth century resentment against the whole system had become general and undignified quarrels over particular situations were numerous.

The village of Fixby came within the parish of Halifax, to which a new vicar, the Reverend Charles Musgrove, was appointed in the spring of 1827. This gentleman was on the make. In his previous parish he had successfully revived claims to forgotten dues, and soon after coming to Halifax he showed that he intended to do the same thing there. Within six months of his arrival the leading property owners received a circular letter informing them that their vicar had enquired into the rights of his living, that he had consulted legal authorities in London, and that he was desirous of putting before them the results of his researches.

That started a struggle which continued many months. When the delegates from the various townships met the parson and his lawyer, they were informed that in addition to Easter offerings, surplice fees, and mortuaries they were being asked for one-tenth of all

milk or cows—agistment—foals—calves—pigs—poultry or eggs—pigeons if sold—potatoes—turnips—gardens—herbs—small seeds—rape—flax—hemp—fruits of trees—bees, honey and wax—corn mills.

The claim was so sweeping and unexpected that the assembled representatives decided they had better report back to their respective townships and convene again the following week.

Oastler, as the delegate from Fixby and representative of the largest landowner in the parish, immediately became the leader of resistance. He could see there might be a case for increasing the vicar's salary, but not by these means. 'Since Fixby was a township,' he told the second meeting, 'no such payments have been made; since Halifax was a vicarage, till now, they have never been demanded.' And in the vicar's presence he persuaded the 46 delegates to pass unanimously a resolution to resist the claims to the limit. The parson's answer was to send round an ultimatum giving his parishioners fifteen days in which to compound with him over the claims, either individually or collectively. What he was really trying to do, of course, was to bluff them into some sort of compromise. But in this he was prevented by Oastler's tactics.

Oastler succeeded in getting the parish to establish a strong organization for resisting every move the vicar might make. Each township set up a local committee, and each of these committees sent a delegate to a central body, which was to conduct the campaign, levy dues on the townships to pay expenses, and lobby against any private bill the vicar might try to get through Parliament. Finally he had a legal deed drawn up, by which the townships jointly and formally made themselves responsible for their share in the struggle.

It is unnecessary to relate the details of the story. On the vicar's side there was much coming and going in furtive cabals, still with the hope that the recalcitrants might be induced to com-

pound; and on the part of the opposition, one public meeting
after another at which Oastler repeatedly showed he had a native
talent for fluent speechmaking of a particularly boisterous and
satirical kind. The local newspapers reported him fully. As the
struggle became more talked about, the *Mercury* was devoting
two and a half columns to it by the end of October. The Anglican
Intelligencer singled out Oastler for special denunciation, sneer-
ing at him as a 'radical' and a 'servant scarcely out of livery.'
But such abuse only made him more caustic and aggressive in
reply. In a pungent pamphlet called *Vicarial Tithes,* which he
published at the beginning of December 1827 to give the public
the inside story, Oastler showed that his pen was as facile as his
tongue in respect of caustic invective.

All the vicar's efforts failed to break the fighting organization
Oastler had created. No one was persuaded to compound. And
when the vicar went to the limits of bluff by putting every township in the Exchequer, the organization still held. Eventually the
parson was forced to accept the terms Oastler had proposed at the
very beginning of the contest—an increase of £750 in his salary.
The original claims, it was estimated, had amounted to more
than twenty times that figure.

The episode cost Oastler an enormous amount of energy and
not a little expense. But it had ended in a personal triumph. He
had added considerably to his prestige and made himself a man
to be reckoned with in local politics. His prospects seemed
brighter than at any time since his bankruptcy. Capitalizing on
the notoriety he had gained, and with Thornhill's permission, he
and a friend opened a land agent's office at Halifax during the
summer of 1830. Twice a week he rode over from Fixby to spend
the day there. Business soon began to come his way, and by the
autumn he was making a substantial addition to his salary.

CHAPTER IV

Oastler's Awakening: 'Yorkshire Slavery'

IN the last week of September 1830, Oastler received an invitation to visit his friend John Wood, a prominent worsted spinner who lived at Horton Hall just outside Bradford.

This chance visit was to prove the turning point of Oastler's life, putting in train a series of events that would make of him a national figure. In order to understand the dramatic developments that followed, however, it is first necessary to appreciate certain general matters of which Oastler himself at this time was almost wholly ignorant.

¶ 1

During the half century or so that had passed since Richard's father first came into the West Riding, numerous far-reaching changes had overtaken the Yorkshire textile industries, which had expanded and thrived upon the Army contracts resulting from the Revolutionary and Napoleonic wars. As the new inventions had been improved and perfected, machinery had been adopted in one manufacturing process after another; the concentration of power had continued apace with the growth of the bigger men and the extension of their control; and the structure of the industry had become greatly altered in consequence. Increase in the scale of operations as well as technical change had gone a long way towards destroying the primitive simplicity of organization that Defoe had noted. The three primary units—clothier, miller, and merchant—were no longer as distinct as they once had been. Enterprising merchant-manufacturers were amalgamating the three branches into single vertical organizations; and that meant hierarchy, subordination, and a new social outlook.

Weaving was still a domestic occupation performed on the handloom in the weaver's own home. But in the past generation there had been an enormous extension of the putting-out system, whereby the more prosperous clothiers in the countryside, as well as the merchants operating from the towns, gave out their work to the craftsmen in their cottages. This inevitably furthered the concentration of power, as well as resulting in an increase in the numbers of the wage-earning class. At the time of Oastler's visit to his friend Wood, the overwhelming majority of weaving families in the Riding were 'outworkers' for such employers, and their lot had greatly deteriorated since the days of their high prosperity during the French war.

It was in spinning and the various other processes preparatory to weaving, however, that the really revolutionary changes in technique had taken place. These processes had now ceased to be domestic occupations and were universally undertaken in mills equipped with special machinery. To begin with, the machines had been installed in the old fulling mills standing by the streams in the valleys, and had been driven by the water power. After the turn of the century, when steam engines first supplemented and then eventually came to supersede the water-wheel, such mills had multiplied rapidly. No longer dependent upon the streams, they could now be built nearer the towns and that made them the pivot for all kinds of fresh developments which would change the industry still further.

This mechanical revolution affected several stages in the preparation of the yarn, though not all the new contrivances were power driven. But one general result was an increased demand for women and children to tend the machines. The work could be easily learned and did not require the muscular strength of grown men. 'The grand object of the modern manufacturer,' explained Dr. Ure, the optimistic publicist of the new capitalism, 'is, through the union of capital and science, to reduce the task of his workpeople to the exercise of vigilance and dexterity,— faculties, when concentrated to one process, speedily brought to perfection in the young. . . . It is, in fact, the constant aim and tendency of every improvement in machinery to supersede human labour altogether, or to diminish its cost by substituting the in-

dustry of women and children for that of men.' Children, particularly little girls, were used as 'fillers' to feed the raw wool into
the machines, and as 'pieceners' to join the slivers into a continuous roving. There was nothing novel, of course, in the use
of child-labor, except in regard to the kind and location of the
work. Under the domestic system, children were set to work
just as soon as they could be of use to the family. Defoe had
considered it a matter for gratification that in Yorkshire 'there
was hardly anything above four years old but its hands were
sufficient to itself.' Nevertheless a few discerning people were
already beginning to feel in a vague sort of way that this haphazard congregation of children in the mills was posing a new
kind of problem: one involving the whole complicated question
of the status of the child in an industrial society and the issues
of public policy to which that gave rise.

All these changes had affected both the wool and worsted
industries, but it was worsted that had led the way. There the
concentration of capital and the power of the big man had always been greater than in the case of wool. As a result, the development of worsted mills had proceeded more rapidly. The
introduction of power spinning into Bradford in 1794 had provoked a riot, but by 1810 hand-spinning was clearly declining
and 20 years later it was dead. Weaving by power-looms followed more tardily. The first power-loom factory in Bradford
dates from 1826. Once again innovation was met by riot and
protest that came to nothing. The general adoption of the new
inventions followed here, too, in the course of the next generation.

For centuries the cloth industry of England had been an object of parliamentary concern and governmental control. But
the old idea, which had inspired Elizabeth and her ministers,
that it was one of the legitimate functions of the State to regulate
industrial enterprise was long since outmoded. This great transformation in the early nineteenth century had thus taken place
without any kind of supervision whatever. To those hard, shrewd
men who were exploiting the new technology in a hazard to
make themselves rich and their country the workshop of the
world, the very suggestion that the State had any right to regulate

their affairs was anathema. And the economists told them that
their convictions were soundly based.

¶ 2

John Wood, whom Oastler had come to visit, was an unusual
character. His father as quite a young man had settled in Bradford, where he started a hair-comb manufacturing business which
prospered so remarkably that eventually he became the largest
comb manufacturer in England. When he died in 1832 he was
said to be worth half a million pounds. This son John had been
apprenticed to the worsted trade. Then in the year of Waterloo
he had set up on his own with a spinning mill in Bridge Street,
Bradford. At that time Bradford was expanding rapidly. In the
course of a single generation, the coming of the steam engine
had transformed it from a quiet little market town, on which
the country clothiers of the surrounding districts used to converge, into the humming center of the entire Yorkshire worsted
industry. Since the beginning of the century its population had
increased fourfold.

Wood was in the front rank of the new factory owners. He was
a spinner on the largest scale, in whose mill every operation was
carried on from the first sorting of the wool to the final packing
of the yarn. Evidently he had inherited his father's commercial
acumen, for his business had increased uninterruptedly in spite
of the post-war depression. He was able to install all the latest
inventions, and before 10 years were past had built an even
larger and more up-to-date mill, which was one of the wonders
of the town. In it were employed over 500 hands, mostly women
and children operating the spinning machines. In 1828 he made
further improvements and extensions, so that by 1830 he was reputed the largest worsted spinner in the country. And he had signalized his prosperity by purchasing Horton Hall, a stately mansion on the outskirts of Bradford, standing like Fixby on a hill
overlooking the town.

Yet in several respects Wood was very unlike the conventional
literary figure of a north-country businessman thrown up by the
industrial revolution. He was a sensitive, somewhat retiring person; a Tory in politics, devoutly attached to the Church of

England and given to charitable works. And in spite of all his prosperity he was disquieted. Some of the consequences attendant upon the changes sweeping the neighborhood worried him greatly, especially the long hours women and children were compelled to work. Five years earlier, he had got together two other prominent master-spinners, Matthew Thompson and John Rand, and had talked over the matter with them. They had agreed that 10 hours a day was the maximum that workers ought to spend in the mills. But when they sounded out the other masters, they were met with nothing but opposition. Reluctantly, therefore, they had to let the matter drop. It was out of the question for three men alone to make the quixotic gesture of reducing hours when the rest of the industry refused to do the same. Nevertheless Wood continued to be worried by the problem; and he was still pondering it when Oastler came to visit him.

That Tuesday evening when tea was over, Wood brought the matter up as they sat talking. Oastler has left his own account of what happened and his words still convey something of the vividness of the original experience.

'I wonder you have never turned your attention to the factory system,' Wood said.

'Why should I?' asked Oastler. 'I have nothing to do with factories.'

'That may be,' replied Wood. 'But you are very enthusiastic against slavery in the West Indies; and I assure you there are cruelties daily practised in our mills on little children which, if you knew, I am sure you would strive to prevent.'

'Cruelties in mills!' exclaimed Oastler. 'I don't understand you. Tell me.'

Wood then unburdened himself of all that was on his mind and all that he knew from first hand experience. He told of the condition of things in his own mills: how quite small children worked from six o'clock in the morning until seven o'clock in the evening the year round, with only a single noontime break of 40 minutes out of a thirteen-hour day. He told Oastler that even this interval was 10 minutes longer than any other mill owner in the town gave, and that some mills had no break at all, the children having to snatch the food they had brought with them as best they could while the machinery was running. He hinted at even worse things: at the strapping of the children by bullying 'overlookers'—children who came late to work, or who fell asleep in the late afternoon, or who did not tend the broken threads on the spindles quickly enough. He told him, too, that such things went on even in factories belonging to reputedly pious men: men who were known to be keen advocates of temperance, of foreign missions, and chapel building, to say nothing of political reform. Bradford, he said, was tolerating in its midst things that were a fundamental denial of all the humanitarian protestations in which the town abounded.

Oastler was astonished. He could hardly believe what he was hearing. Moreover, he had a feeling that in some sense he himself was being convicted. For 10 years he had lived a spacious and prosperous life in the very heart of a manufacturing district. From his windows at Fixby there was a clear view of the whole of Huddersfield. He had watched the town growing and observed the factories spreading. Yet he had never given the matter more than a passing thought. He had taken it on trust that all this expansion was a proof of England's prosperity and had cheerfully gone on with his estate work and his advocacy of slave-emancipation while all the time a new kind of slavery was being developed before his own eyes. Now on a sudden he was learning something of the implications of this prosperity, and the shock was great.

Next morning he had to leave soon after four o'clock, but when he was called the valet brought a message that Wood would like to see him. He went into his friend's room to find Wood reading the Bible by the light of a couple of candles.

On my advancing towards the side of his bed, he turned towards me, reached out his hand and in the most impressive manner pressing my hand in his he said: 'I have had no sleep tonight. I have been reading this Book and in every page I have read my own condemnation. I cannot allow you to leave me without a pledge that you will use all your influence in trying to remove from our factory system the cruelties which are practised in our mills.' I promised I would do what I could . . . I felt that we were each of us in the presence of the Highest and I knew that that vow was recorded in Heaven.

The promise made in that bedroom just before dawn on 29 September 1830 was the real beginning of Oastler's career: it was to prove to be an important date in English social history as well.

¶ 3

That evening when Oastler returned to Fixby after a long day's work, he wrote to the *Leeds Mercury* a letter which he deliberately superscribed with the challenging words 'Yorkshire Slavery.' It was eventually to rank as one of the most famous letters of the nineteenth century:

YORKSHIRE SLAVERY

To the Editors of the Leeds Mercury

'It is the pride of Britain that a slave cannot exist on her soil; and if I read the genius of her constitution aright, I find that slavery is most abhorrent to it—that the air which Britons breathe is free—the ground on which they tread is sacred to liberty.' *Rev. R. W. Hamilton's Speech at the Meeting held in the Cloth-hall Yard, September 22d, 1830.*

Gentlemen,—No heart responded with truer accents to the sounds of liberty which were heard in the Leeds Cloth-hall Yard, on the 22d instant, than did mine, and from none could more sincere and earnest prayers arise to the throne of Heaven, that hereafter slavery might only be known to Britain in the pages of her history. One shade alone obscured my pleasure, arising not from any difference in principle, but from the want of application of the general principle *to the whole empire*. The pious and able champions of *negro* liberty and *colonial* rights should, if I mistake not, have gone farther than they did; or perhaps, to speak more correctly, before they had travelled so far as the West Indies, should, at least for a few moments, have sojourned in our own immediate neighborhood, and have directed the attention of the meeting to scenes of misery, acts of oppression, and victims of slavery, even on the threshold of our homes.

Let truth speak out, appalling as the statement may appear. The fact is true. Thousands of our fellow-creatures and fellow-subjects, both male and female, the miserable inhabitants of a *Yorkshire town*, (Yorkshire now represented in Parliament by the giant of anti-slavery principles) are this very moment existing in a state of slavery, *more*

horrid than are the victims of that hellish system *'colonial slavery.'*
These innocent creatures drawl out, unpitied, their short but miserable
existence, in a place famed for its profession of religious zeal, whose
inhabitants are ever foremost in *professing* 'temperance' and 'reformation,' and are striving to outrun their neighbors in missionary
exertions, and would fain send the Bible to the farthest corner of the
globe—aye, in the very place where the anti-slavery fever rages most
furiously, her *apparent charity* is not more admired on earth, than her
real cruelty is abhorred in Heaven. The very streets which receive the
droppings of an 'Anti-Slavery Society' are every morning wet by the
tears of innocent victims at the accursed shrine of avarice, who are
compelled (not by the cart-whip of the negro slave-driver) but by
the dread of the equally appalling thong or strap of the over-looker,
to hasten, half-dressed, *but not half-fed,* to those magazines of British
infantile slavery—*the worsted mills in the town and neighborhood of
Bradford!!!*

Would that I had Brougham's eloquence, that I might rouse the
hearts of the nation, and make every Briton swear, 'These innocents
shall be free!'

Thousands of little children, both male and female, *but principally
female,* from seven to fourteen years of age, are daily *compelled* to
labour from six o'clock in the morning to seven in the evening, with
only—Britons, blush while you read it!—*with only thirty minutes
allowed for eating and recreation.* Poor infants! ye are indeed sacrificed
at the shrine of avarice, *without even the solace of the negro slave;*
ye are no more than he is, *free agents;* ye are compelled to work as
long as the *necessity* of your needy parents may require, or the cold-
blooded avarice of your worse than barbarian masters *may demand!*
Ye live in the boasted land of freedom, and *feel* and mourn that *ye are
slaves,* and slaves without the only comfort which the negro has. He
knows it is his sordid, mercenary master's interest that he should *live,*
be *strong* and *healthy.* Not so with you. Ye are doomed to labour from
morning to night for one who cares not how soon your weak and
tender frames are stretched to breaking! You are not mercifully valued
at so much per head; this would assure you at least (even with the
worst and most cruel masters) of the mercy shown to their own
labouring beasts. No, no! your soft and delicate limbs are tired and
fagged, and jaded, at only *so much per week,* and when your joints
can act no longer, your emaciated frames are cast aside, the boards
on which you lately toiled and wasted life away, are instantly supplied with other victims, who in this boasted land of liberty are
HIRED—not sold—as slaves and daily forced to hear that they are free.

Oh! Duncombe! [1] Thou hatest slavery—I know thou dost resolve that 'Yorkshire children shall no more be slaves!' And Morpeth! who justly gloriest in the Christian faith—Oh, Morpeth! listen to the cries and count the tears of these poor babes, and let St. Stephen's hear thee swear 'they shall no longer groan in slavery!' And Bethell, too! who swears eternal hatred to the name of slave, whene'er thy manly voice is heard in Britain's senate, assert the rights and liberty of Yorkshire youths. And Brougham! thou who art the chosen champion of liberty in every clime! oh bend thy giant's mind, and listen to the sorrowing accents of these poor Yorkshire little ones, and note their tears; then let thy voice rehearse their woes, and touch the chord thou only holdest—the chord that sounds above the silvery notes in praise of heavenly liberty, and down descending at thy will, groans in the horrid caverns of the deep in muttering sounds of misery accursed to hellish bondage; and as thou sound'st these notes, let Yorkshire hear thee swear, 'Her *children* shall be free!' Yes, all ye four protectors of our rights, chosen by freemen to destroy oppression's rod,

> 'Vow one by one, vow altogether, vow
> With heart and voice, eternal enmity
> Against oppression by your brethren's hands;
> Till man nor woman under Britain's laws,
> Nor son nor daughter born within her empire,
> Shall buy, or sell, or HIRE, or BE A SLAVE!'

The nation is now most resolutely determined that negroes shall be free. Let them, however, not forget that Britons have common rights with Afric's sons.

The blacks may be fairly compared to beasts of burden, *kept for their master's use;* the whites, to those *which others keep and let for hire.* If I have succeeded in calling the attention of your readers to the horrid and abominable system on which the worsted mills in and near Bradford is conducted, I have done some good. Why should not children working in them be protected by legislative enactments, as well as those who work in cotton mills? Christians should feel and act for those whom Christ so eminently loved, and declared that 'of such is the Kingdom of Heaven.'—I remain, yours, etc.,

A Briton

Fixby Hall, near Huddersfield, Sept. 29, 1830.

[1] Duncombe, Morpeth, Bethell, and Brougham were the Yorkshire County Members of Parliament.

¶ 4

It was only Wednesday and the *Mercury* was not published until Saturday, so there was ample time to get the letter into the next issue. The following day, therefore, Oastler rode over to Leeds to take it to the *Mercury* office. He happened to run into Wood in the town and showed him what he had written. Wood approved it all except one phrase which Oastler, nevertheless, decided to retain. Then he went to call on his father's old friend Edward Baines.

Baines, now in his fifty-seventh year, was by this time one of the most prominent figures in the West Riding. He had originally come to Leeds as a printer's apprentice, shortly after old Robert Oastler had settled in the town. Through one of his various young men's clubs Robert had come to know the boy, and impressed by his energy and intelligence had made a friend of him. In his early days Baines was often at the Oastlers' home for a meal or a chat, railing at Pitt and the war, and praising Whiggery, Liberty, and Mr. Fox. He was soon doing well for himself as a publisher and before long had embarked on the career that was to make one of the big success stories of his generation. In the year that Robert Oastler gave up the cloth business, Baines had bought the *Leeds Mercury* with the help of a few friends and had begun editing it himself. Since then his 30 years' proprietorship had turned the paper into one of the most important provincial journals in England, while his personal influence had grown proportionately. His assiduity was extraordinary. He believed ardently in the principle of equality of opportunity, and therefore vigorously advocated free trade and parliamentary reform. He encouraged chapel building, pressed for the establishment of local Mechanics Institutes, and backed the temperance movement. Long before the days of Samuel Smiles he was already a noted exponent of the gospel of self-help. And wherever there was a movement for attacking privilege, Anglicanism, or the landed gentry, Edward Baines was to be found on its platforms. He was on terms of intimacy with all the big manufacturers of the county, for he was the complete embodiment of their prejudices and point of view. The *Mercury* had thus become a

powerful engine of public opinion on behalf of the middle classes
and of all those causes to which Baines was so deeply attached.
He was now a reasonably wealthy man, increasingly devoting
himself to public affairs. Rumor said that he might stand for
Parliament in the not distant future. But he still continued to
edit the *Mercury* personally, though he now had his eldest son
Edward as associate editor.

Oastler found Baines in his office and gave him the letter.
He explained what it was about and told Baines to alter it as he
saw fit. Baines read it through twice and appeared nonplussed.
He expressed his surprise at the facts it contained and asked what
Oastler's authority was for such statements. Oastler told him,
but Baines remained skeptical and said he thought Oastler must
be mistaken. Anyway, he added, Oastler must sign his own name
and not use a *nom-de-plume*. Baines, of course, fully realized the
serious nature of the letter. It was a damaging attack on the
very classes with which he was most intimately identified and
whose mouthpiece the *Mercury* was. Yet he could scarcely refuse
to publish it: Oastler was an old friend, and Baines, according to
his lights, was a sincere man. He had himself become an advocate
of slave emancipation in recent years, and all his life had professed the cause of 'the people.' Were not the influence and circulation of the *Mercury* entirely built up on such a profession?
Besides, if he did not accept the letter, his rival, the *Intelligencer*,
probably would. It would be a great scoop for the Tory paper
to take a letter which a 'liberal' journal was afraid to publish. So
he was in a quandary and would do nothing for the moment but
temporize. Oastler had to be content, therefore, with vague
promises.

But the letter did not appear in the following issue; nor in the
issue after that. Baines (as Oastler afterwards learned) was
making enquiries. On 9 October, however, there appeared a
strange editorial in the *Mercury*, relevant to nothing that had
gone before. 'It is alleged,' said the article, 'that some of the
labouring class in this country are subject to a great degree of
toil, and to severe privations, as well as the slaves in our colonies.
This is doubtless true.' But it went on to say that circumstances
in the two cases were entirely different and that all comparisons
between 'white slaves' and 'black slaves' were nothing but 'a

mere empty jingle of words.' The fact was that the two Baineses, having made their enquiries and having discovered the essential truth of Oastler's statements, had finally realized that they could not exclude his letter. They were therefore trying to prepare their readers for its reception by discounting its significance in advance.

A week later the letter appeared. There appeared also a second editorial commenting upon it, obviously written by the editor himself to define his own position. Baines admitted Oastler's sincerity, but regretted the 'undue warmth' of its expression. He went on to say that if the allegations were true (and he implied they were) the evil was a real one. The general rule of public policy should be the complete freedom of industry. But children were not free agents, since they were subject to both parents and employers. Yet neither employers nor parents were blameworthy; child-labor was essential to each: without it the capitalist would be ruined by foreign competition and the parents would be reduced to poverty. It was all the fault of the law, or rather the absence of law on the subject. So Oastler ought not to charge a 'respectable class of manufacturers' with hypocrisy and oppression, but should promote petitions to Parliament to get a law passed to settle the matter. It sounded reasonable enough to the casual reader, but while preserving a tone of bluff common sense it was discreetly vague about the nature of the remedies to be applied.

Oastler, indeed, had no idea what a hornets' nest he was stirring up when he took his letter to the *Mercury* office. He was a man of essentially unsophisticated character, temperamentally enthusiastic and animated by an unequivocal moral code. His upbringing and education made him think in terms of simple categories, of the struggle of Right against Wrong, so that he believed the issues of life could be clearly defined in terms of black and white. When he wrote his letter, therefore, he never doubted that the bulk of the public would be on his side. He thought that like himself they had simply been ignorant of these things and only needed to be shown the truth in order to acknowledge it. He knew, of course, that there would be (as he afterwards put it) 'a few mercenary, irreligious, immoral characters' who would oppose him. But he fully expected that most people would back him enthusiastically, especially since the whole of the West Riding was humming with evangelical fervor and with a multitude of societies and sects devoted to good works. Every week's issue of the newspapers bore fulsome witness to these numerous philanthropies. What could be more reasonable, then, than to suppose that a public subscribing so handsomely to foreign missions, Bible societies, and Sunday schools, to the anti-slavery movement, to soup kitchens and parochial charities, as well as to the building of new churches and chapels and mechanics institutes, would be both ready and enthusiastic to remedy an evil at its very doors? In writing his letter he had no thought of personally conducting a campaign, for he fully expected that someone with more first-hand experience than himself would arise to lead an awakened public opinion.

Yet the challenge Oastler had made was to prove immensely more far-reaching than he could possibly have imagined when he wrote his letter. His indignation had concerned itself with the single fact of long hours in the worsted mills. But he was very soon going to learn that numerous other counts could be added to his indictment, and not for worsted manufacture alone, but for the woolen and flax industries as well. At present he knew next to nothing about the details of factory life. He did not know, for instance, that he had understated the hours worked in a good many of the mills, particularly in those in the outlying districts. He knew nothing about overtime working, or the continuous labor of 'rush seasons,' or the dishonest manipulation of factory clocks. He was unaware of the system of fines used in most mills or of the custom of 'truck payment' still practiced in some places. And even Wood had not told him all that was yet to be discovered about the cruelty of many of the 'overlookers' in punishing the children working under them. The one thing Oastler knew was that the hours children worked seemed to him shockingly long. Now that the storm had burst, however, there were thousands in the Riding who would tell him of these and other matters too. And thus what had begun as the condemnation of a specific evil was eventually to become a generalized protest against the new industrialism which would embrace other considerations than those of the children's welfare.

CHAPTER V

The Great Controversy Begins

¶ 1

ALL over the West Riding Oastler's letter created the sensation Baines had feared it might. Some were shocked, more were alarmed, and thousands were encouraged. Partly this was due to the content and style of the challenge, partly to the moment of its appearance; for it had come at a time when public opinion was already turbulent and confused with many pressing issues.

The great economic depression of the later 'twenties had not yet lifted. For many months, now, the newspapers had been reporting grave unemployment and distress. The previous winter had been terrible, and relief associations had been formed in every township to assist the parish officers in raising funds. A committee of Huddersfield workmen had called upon the chief master-manufacturers of the town to beg them do their utmost to mitigate the general suffering. As a result a series of investigating committees had been formed, each surveying an allotted district, to assess needs and plan relief. The picture they gave in their reports is pitiful in the extreme: hundreds of families living on a single daily meal of potatoes or gruel, and many on not as much as that; clothes that were the merest rags; no fires through the winter; furniture sold up piece by piece to pay for food and rent; and even, in the final abandonment of hope, the selling of tools and loom. Charity alone kept many alive, while in thousands of other homes the two shillings a week which the children got in the spinning mills was all the family budget. At a public meeting in Huddersfield called nine months earlier to launch a new soup-kitchen scheme for the district, the Reverend Drawbridge of Honley had confirmed this dark picture from

his own experience but had declared his conviction 'that the evil
has come upon us by the permissive providence of Almighty
God.'

The workers, however, could find little consolation in such theology and went over in their thousands to the Radical cause of
parliamentary reform. 'Give us the vote,' they cried, 'and we will
end the exploitation that makes such suffering possible.' In the
towns and on the moors they held their meetings weekly to proclaim the salvation that lay in manhood suffrage and the abolition of sinecures. When the radical Cobbett toured the Riding
in January they were roused to a delirious frenzy; even the Tory
Intelligencer gave him six columns. And when the July revolution in France achieved its bloodless success it seemed a prelude
to their own triumph; every town in the industrial districts held
its public celebration.

Other concerns were agitating men's minds too. Everyone of
any worth was on the platform of the anti-slavery meetings, which
grew in frequency and enthusiasm as the year wore on. Morpeth
and Baines and Brougham thundered forth their sympathies for
the Negroes. Religious Tract Societies of the various denominations multiplied steadily and raised surprising amounts of money.
So did the innumerable missionary societies. And in the early
autumn an extensive campaign was launched to establish Temperance Associations in every town and village in the county. A
fervent young thirty-one-year-old parson named George Stringer
Bull, recently returned from the African mission field, was the
chief figure in this movement, quickly making himself the fiercest
foe of the gin shop and the laudanum traffic which had prospered
in the despair of the depression.

Emotions in the West Riding were thus already running high
when Oastler's challenging letter appeared. Its publication could
scarcely have been better timed. In workshop and factory and
public house men began talking about it, for here seemed a
measure of hope that all could share, whatever their ideas about
parliamentary reform. 'I remember my father reading it when it
first came out,' said one of the mill hands later. 'It did make a
stir among the factory folk! I was then a factory girl working
14 hours a day, and tired as I was when my father was reading

it my heart was lifted up to think that somebody felt for us.'

It is true the letter referred merely to children, and only to those in the worsted industry at that. But most of the workers who read it, or had it read to them in the public houses, saw in it an indictment of the whole industrial system. They read into it, indeed, many of their own grievances, including things Oastler knew nothing about. They felt that the regulation of child labor might be made the beginning of an improvement in their own lot. They did not reason or analyze but simply took the letter for what it was—a protest against inhumanity; and they felt their own fate was covered by that. One of the Radical booksellers in Leeds quickly had the letter printed as a broadsheet, which was plastered all over the town and hung in the public houses; and only three days after its publication, at yet another public dinner held to commemorate the recent French Revolution, someone proposed amidst much enthusiasm 'the health of Mr. Richard Oastler of Fixby Hall, and thanks to him for his very able letter in favour of white slaves, both male and female, young and old, in England!' There was no doubt about the stir; Oastler's local reputation and his status at Fixby Hall were sufficient assurance of that. One of the leading manufacturers who hastened to answer the charges did so, he said, because he was 'convinced of the effect produced by the letter emanating from so respectable an individual.'

¶ 2

Public controversy broke out at once, and for the next six weeks raged by letter and counter-letter in the local press. Though the *Leeds Mercury* had been the first to air the question, the other papers soon realized its import, so that within a month every Yorkshire journal was engaged in the controversy through its correspondence columns and editorials. Before Christmas two camps had defined themselves: the one led by the *Leeds Intelligencer*, which soon became enthusiastic in support of Oastler, the other led by the *Mercury*, which gradually grew more hostile. Within twelve months, echoes of the struggle were being heard in the London dailies.

An immediate reply to Oastler appeared the following Thursday in the *Intelligencer* (for that paper was published two days ahead of the *Mercury*). It was from Simeon Townend, who was to make himself in the course of the following months the outspoken apologist of the masters and the most vigorous of Oastler's opponents. Townend was a prominent local figure in the vanguard of industrial enterprise; only two years earlier he had set up the first power looms to be run in Thornton valley and had met with so much opposition from the villagers that he had been compelled to fetch workers from Lancashire to operate them. His letters are veritable essays in Podsnappery, in which the reader can find lucidly expounded all the ideas and sentiments inspiring the new industrial leaders who had made Leeds and Bradford what they were.

He would have ignored a letter from anyone else, he said, but Oastler was in a special position, being 'an individual whose attainments were above mediocrity and whose display of aptitudes had been often justly acknowledged.' He paid tribute to the disinterestedness of Oastler's motives, and frankly admitted that the hours of work for the children were just as Oastler said they were, from six in the morning until seven in the evening. But he was indignant at the 'violent and undeserved attack' Oastler had made on the Bradford spinners, declaring that the comparison with Negro slavery was preposterous. In the first place little girls were necessary for the spinning machines, because they were quick and clean in their work. Moreover, though their day was long their work was 'far from laborious.' And by going to the factories the children received a splendid training: they learned regularity and discipline, they acquired the virtues of early rising, and they became self-supporting; 'the attainments of their labouring infancy place them generally in a sufficient capacity to undertake piece-work; this procures them a little to supply their own gratifications, besides paying for their maintenance.' Moreover, families having children who went to work in the mills were the envy of families who had none. So Oastler's onslaught was entirely unjustified, especially as the Bradford worsted spinners were noted for their 'humane and charitable actions.' In cotton mills the case was different. There regulation was certainly necessary; but not in worsted.

Two anonymous letters in the *Mercury* the next Saturday rang the changes on the theme that the factory provided a fine training for children and that the burden of the hours had been exaggerated. One was from a man signing himself 'Verax,' who claimed to have lived in Bradford nearly 20 years and to have been on the committees of all the societies mentioned by Oastler in his letter. According to his experience, he declared, the children were 'not only content but cheerful in the sphere which Providence has allotted to them.' Oastler afterwards learned that 'Verax' was a prominent nonconformist minister in the town, a discovery which came as a painful surprise since he had reckoned on unanimous evangelical backing for his plea.

It was to be expected that opposition would come first; but the following number of the *Mercury* brought strong support, and much more, from someone signing himself 'X.' This writer expanded the indictment by showing that Oastler had erred on the side of moderation. The majority of children in Bradford, he said, worked at least 14 hours a day, not 13, and that in rooms heated from 20 to 30 degrees above ordinary temperature. The children were utterly untaught; and even if they were capable of going to school after such a day in the factories, Bradford had not enough schools to cope with them. Factory life fostered ignorance and contaminated morals, as everyone knew. In fact, Oastler had been too restrained in his analogy: conditions were actually worse in Bradford mills than they were on the West Indian slave plantations, because the masters did not have to maintain the children: they only had to pay them two to three shillings a week without any sort of obligation to provide for them when they were prematurely worn out and useless.

Oastler followed this up with a second letter running to a column and a quarter of the *Mercury* on 30 October. It was scarcely less sensational than the first, and certainly harder hitting, for he vigorously underlined all the admissions made by his critics and supplemented his original charges by facts he had learned in the interval. He rejoiced that the *Mercury* admitted the 'evil was a real one.' Nobody could accuse him of exaggerating, for he might have said 14 or even 16 hours 'in many, nay in most mills.' Nor had he made sufficient mention of the thrashing of the children, or of the foul atmosphere in which they worked, or of overtime. It was significant, moreover, that his critics had defended factory conditions in precisely the same terms that the West Indian slave owners always used, stressing the happy and contented lot of their victims. No wonder he had roused the hostility of 'certain individuals who were quietly pocketing the profits of the children's excessive labour and were soothed by the hope that the public knew not of their oppression!' But it was not individuals he was going to attack, it was the whole system. Now that he had extorted these damning admissions from his opponents, nothing would stop him from pressing his case to the limit.

This second letter was written in a markedly different tone from the first and shows the change of mood Oastler had undergone in the space of a month. It was not just an appeal to philanthropy but a gage of battle. It revealed to a surprised public that there had arisen in the north a born controversialist of considerable power who was not easily going to be put down: one, moreover, who was using no mere scholar's rapier but a stout, old-fashioned quarter-staff, whose bludgeoning use the masses could readily appreciate.

So vigorous was the letter, and so great the storm Oastler had raised, that the *Mercury* deemed it expedient to run in the same issue an editorial of almost the same length. It was an important pronouncement, and while it provided Oastler with polemical material for months to come it must have perturbed not a few of the manufacturers by its moderate tone. The Baineses were feeling their way carefully, for even though they had one eye on their friends among the wealthy classes they had the other on their circulation and the *Intelligencer's* competition.

Their admissions doubtless surprised many a complacent reader. They conceded that Oastler and 'X' had brought forward facts the public ought to know. They acknowledged there were 'real evils affecting a numerous class of helpless beings who not only have a right to the sympathy of the humane, but whose health, morals, and intellectual character cannot be injured without that injury affecting the whole body of society.' They went further. Oastler had denounced the thirteen-hour day with but a single half-hour's break. Yet this was the normal day in only the best Bradford mills. In the worst establishments, said the *Mercury,* it stretched at least to 14 or 15 hours. And in the remoter villages the normal day was from five in the morning until nine at night, not counting the time taken in going to and from the factory. Nor was this condition of things confined to Bradford (as Oastler had seemed to suppose); it was general 'throughout the manufacturing district.' Its consequences were there for all to see in widespread immorality, irreligion, and illiteracy. The *Mercury* accordingly proposed three remedies. First, there must be some kind of parliamentary regulation, such as the extension of the acts already regulating the hours in cotton mills to cover wool and worsted mills as well. Legislation was essential, Baines thought, since the benevolent attempts by Wood and the others in 1825 had shown how futile merely individual effort was: competition would always kill it. Secondly, the masters ought to promote philanthropic undertakings, such as evening schools, in their own mills; Owen's experiments at New Lanark had already shown how rewarding such schemes could be. Lastly, boys should be separated from the girls in the factories.

The *Intelligencer* was not behindhand in its support. Its editor announced that he had instituted enquiries of his own and had been able to corroborate all that was said about the hours of children's labor. He therefore urged the Bradford owners to reorganize voluntarily: otherwise 'the public will take the matter up' and then legislation would be inevitable. 'But we know the Bradford manufacturers too well,' he concluded, 'to suppose that an act of Parliament is necessary to induce them to act with common humanity.'

The workers were delighted at the way things were going. At a mass meeting of Radicals held at Huddersfield two days later, Oastler's name was joined with Cobbett's and O'Connell's as a champion of the people, and a unanimous vote of thanks was passed to 'Richard Oastler Esq. for his able and manly letters to expose the conduct of those pretended philanthropists and canting hypocrites who travel to the West Indies in search of slavery, forgetting that there is a more abominable and degrading system of slavery at home.'

There was now no gainsaying the fact that public opinion was stirred. Oastler's aggressive and devastating second letter had served to heighten the effect that the first had created, and a mass of confirmatory evidence was quickly forthcoming to support all he had said. Three big manufacturers and an independent gentleman publicly came out on his side in the next few days.

First of all John Wood brought corroboration in a letter that particularly stressed the tension imposed upon the children by the nature of their work, and the insufficient time allowed them for taking meals.

The operations of the machinery ought to be suspended to allow its wearied attendants to take meals—at the same time affording relaxation from their long supported 'attention and quickness.' It is this unvarying closeness, when stretched as it is by established custom from six in the morning to seven in the evening—*very often* to eight, and sometimes even to nine at night with but one brief interval of *thirty minutes,* that constitutes what I think Mr. Oastler has *justly* designated 'Slavery' . . . The necessity of an allowance of proper times for meals is more evident, when it is considered, that the employment almost constantly requires the children to be in a standing position.

A week later Wood's friend and neighbor Matthew Thompson wrote to the *Mercury* saying that the abortive reform efforts in Bradford five years before had made him 'perfectly satisfied that no effective change would come without legislative interference.' He was therefore ready to meet and discuss plans with any owners who were of his way of thinking, and hoped that Wood's and Oastler's letters would induce the trade generally to do 'an act of justice to the offspring of the labouring classes.'

At the same time John Halliley, a spinner employing a large number of children in his mills at Dewsbury, published an open letter to Oastler praising him for his two 'invaluable papers' on white slavery and confirming the evils they had made public. At rush seasons, he added, children as well as adults had to work one or two hours overtime 'for months in succession.' The only possible remedy was legislation, since nothing but a uniform law for all would protect the more benevolent masters from their unscrupulous rivals. He therefore gave his hearty blessing to Oastler's 'truly pious and benevolent interposition.'

A similar letter appeared the following week from Richard Webster of Halifax. Hitherto nearly all attention had been concentrated on Bradford, but according to Webster, the conditions in Halifax were even worse than those in Bradford. No mill there worked for less than thirteen and a half hours: some went on until eight-thirty or nine o'clock at night; and none allowed any time off for breakfast or tea—only a half-hour break at midday. Anyone visiting Halifax, said Webster, 'if he were a man, would blush to see the degradation to which those children were brought by the avarice of their employers.'

I do not mean to charge this epithet upon all the manufacturers of this town . . . I know there are honourable exceptions. But at the same time there are individuals who would not care to exact labour from them both day and night, consequently those who are possessed of more humanity are obliged, however reluctantly, to follow the same rule.

This is the more significant in view of the fact that it was from Halifax there was to come the most ruthless and unqualified opposition to Oastler's efforts. Nevertheless Webster deplored the idea of parliamentary intervention to deal with the matter: 'to have recourse to the Legislature upon a subject like the present stamps upon them the most palpable disgrace.' What he wanted was a voluntary compact of the best masters to 'shame the rest into compliance.'

So striking had been Oastler's attack, and so explicit the corroboration, that it seemed as if results would follow quickly.

CHAPTER VI

The Reply of the Mill Owners

WITHIN six weeks of the publication of Oastler's first letter, a meeting of Bradford mill owners had agreed to press for legislation to regulate the working day for children. Within six months a bill to that end was actually before Parliament and the struggle for its passage had begun. Events could hardly have moved more rapidly.

¶ 1

It was Wood, Thompson, and Rand—the same three who had sought to improve conditions five years earlier—who started things moving. Thompson had said in his letter to the newspapers that he was willing to discuss plans for reform with any other manufacturers who felt as he did on the question. The result was seen in a placard bearing the endorsement of 24 firms, which soon appeared throughout the Bradford district, calling for 'the attendance of the trade generally' at a meeting in the Talbot Inn on 22 November. Wood sent the poster to Fixby along with a cheerful note advising Oastler to stay his hand from replying to the recent attacks upon him until after the meeting was over. 'I send you this,' he added, 'as proof of the general disposition to meet the question. The signatures annexed include almost every Bradford spinner. I hope I am not too sanguine in saying that so far as we are concerned the wished-for object is sure of being accomplished.'

The meeting seemed to justify such optimism. Some forty mill owners foregathered at the Talbot under the chairmanship of John Rand, 'the father of the worsted business,' and displayed a remarkable degree of uanimity. Thompson cited the admitted

facts which had been brought out in the newspaper correspondence and explained that while he believed industry should be
left 'free for free agents,' he thought that children could not fairly
be said to fall into that class. They obviously needed protection
and required 'the fostering care of legislative enactment.' So his
proposal was that the meeting should press for a bill which would
limit the work of all children under 15 to 11 hours a day (exclusive of two hours for meals) and 8 hours on Saturdays; in other
words, a sixty-three-hour week. The discussion showed, however,
that while most of the owners present were in favor of some such
reform, they felt 15 was too high an age at which to fix regulation. Thompson therefore modified his proposal to end with the
fourteen-year-olds.

Simeon Townend, who had already criticized Oastler so sav-
agely in the newspapers, was the only one to introduce any real
discord into the meeting. In a long, aggressive speech he argued
that the establishment of a definite sixty-nine-hour week was all
the protection the children needed, though he also made it
abundantly clear that he preferred no regulation whatever. He
thought the fourteen-year-old limit was absurd, the allowance
for mealtimes excessive, and the proposed shortening of the day
suicidal. Since Oastler's first letter appeared, he said, he had been
in communication with the recently formed Lancashire Cotton
Spinners' Association to find out what the factory owners there
felt about regulation. For a decade, now, the cotton industry had
had experience of regulation. Under Peel's Act [1] children between
the ages of 9 and 16 were limited to twelve hours' work a day.
But the cotton masters, Townend told the meeting, were seriously
dissatisfied with the working of the Act: it harmed the industry
and inconvenienced the organization. Some of them were therefore about to press for its repeal. The worsted trade ought to take
warning by that. If it rashly invited parliamentary interference,

[1] Peel's Act was passed in 1819 largely as a result of the humanitarian
endeavors of Robert Owen, though it fell far short of Owen's original proposals. The Act applied only to the cotton industry. It (a) forbade child
labor under 9 years; (b) forbade children between 9 and 16 to work
more than 12 hours daily, exclusive of mealtimes; and (c) left enforcement to the Justices of the Peace. It was working very badly and its intentions were being circumvented by sundry kinds of evasion.

he said, it would gratuitously bring upon itself similar disabilities and gravely hamper initiative.

Many a time later, both inside and outside the House of Commons, this line of argument was to be advanced. But at the moment Wood and Thompson had no difficulty in answering it, or in carrying their proposal for an eleven-hour day for children. Thereupon the meeting agreed to ask Lord Morpeth, Member for the Riding, to present a petition to this effect in Parliament. At the same time a committee of manufacturers was set up to promote the necessary legislative action.

When the meeting finally closed, after various tributes had been paid to Oastler for publicizing the matter in the first place, it really seemed as though something worth while had been accomplished. The facts had been proclaimed and confirmed, public interest had been roused, and an important body of masters had pledged themselves to see the evils eliminated. The *Mercury* next week came out with an enthusiastic editorial in the course of which it said:

Without in any degree altering the opinion we expressed at the time of Mr. Oastler's first letter, we feel that it is due to that gentleman to say that the public are indebted to him in a high degree for his humane exertions in favour of those who, by reason of their tender age and dependent situation, could not speak for themselves. The most appropriate reward he can receive, will be that meed of gratitude to which he is entitled. The manufacturers of Bradford are also doing themselves great honour, and we trust that their laudable example will be generally followed.

The editor of the *Intelligencer* commented in like vein.

In spite of this, Oastler was not satisfied and wrote a third long letter to the *Mercury* explaining why. The Talbot Inn meeting had disappointed him in two ways. In the first place, he thought it should never have agreed to lower the age for protection from 15 years to 14. Furthermore, it had overlooked one crucial problem altogether: the age at which child labor might begin. No child, he felt, ought to be allowed to work in a factory until ten years old. Children younger than that had not the strength to walk to work before six o'clock in the morning, spend 13 hours in the mill, and then walk a mile or two home after seven in the evening. Yet no one had brought up this question at the Talbot, though it would obviously have to be settled before any parliamentary action could be taken.

One cannot read this third letter of Oastler's, however, without getting the clear impression that it was not the matter of details that was bothering him so much as the general tone of the whole discussion, and all the qualifications and hesitancies that seemed to constrict it. From the moment of his sudden awakening, Oastler had thought of the question as a perfectly simple ethical issue on which good men would take one stand and bad men the other. Instead of which he found the discussion proceeding on two completely different planes. While he was talking about moral obligation, others were showing a disconcerting tendency to argue whether or not it involved a violation of 'freedom' to prevent children from overworking; whether industry would 'suffer' if working conditions were improved; or whether in any circumstances Parliament ought to 'interfere' in economic matters. The continued silence of the evangelical nonconformists puzzled him, too. With no little bitterness, therefore, he denounced and satirized the catchwords his critics were using in defense of existing conditions. He was obviously afraid lest the issue should get befogged with current clichés, and a substantial measure of reform be whittled down by a trivial discussion of nicely calculated less or more. The paramount consideration, as he saw it, was not one of calculation at all, but of the picture of society men entertained in their minds.

The skill and ingenuity of man is now made to destroy the happiness and comfort of many merely for the gain of a few; it might be made instrumental to every man's increase in comfort and happiness. The factory system is necessary, but it is not necessarily an evil; it is conducive to the misery of many—it might be made advantageous to all. It is a system which drags in the train of the remorseless tyrant the man of benevolent mind; it compels the kindhearted master either to relinquish business altogether, or in some measure to copy the cruelty of the oppressor. The system which impoverishes, enslaves and brutalizes the labourer can never be advantageous to any country. The nation's strength and stability is built, if built for perpetuity, on the solid basis of a contented and happy population. The constitution of this country and the present factory system cannot long exist together; their principles are as opposite as light and darkness.

That was an important statement, for it was the first time Oastler had made any kind of generalization about society. He made it in an effort to elucidate his own uneasiness. Eventually it was to become the major premise of a coherent political philosophy which events would compel him to articulate in full.

That he was justified in being uneasy was made plain when next week's papers appeared. In a second attack on Oastler, Simeon Townend wrote to say there was far less agreement among the worsted masters than the Talbot meeting had led people to believe. Various mill owners, he declared, had since told him they regretted voting for the reform proposals; so he was organizing a counter-petition to Parliament in opposition to the one Lord Morpeth would present. This would call for a sixty-nine-hour week, with no regulation at all after the age of thirteen.

A clear issue was thus joined. Oastler's three letters were forcing the Yorkshire masters to answer three straight questions:

At what age should children be allowed to start working in factories—10 years or earlier?

At what age should regulation end—15 years, 14 or 13?

How many actual working hours daily should they be permitted—11, or more?

¶ 2

Public controversy on the factory question ceased for a while after the Talbot meeting, though much was going on behind the scenes. Lord Morpeth duly presented the petition to Parliament; and John Cam Hobhouse, the Radical member for Westminster, had agreed to introduce a bill on the subject at the earliest opportunity. During the ten weeks' lull, the various interested parties were organizing their supporters and maneuvering for position. All kinds of rumors in regard to the terms of Hobhouse's Bill spread about the Riding, and all manner of advice was tendered its author about what those terms should be, but no official statement was forthcoming until early in March.

Meanwhile the outward scene was one of violence and agitation concerning other matters which were not without some bearing upon the factory controversy. All that January and February 1831, public opinion throughout the north was becoming more seething and the mood of the workers more militant. The effects of the depression were still being acutely felt; the excitement evoked by the July Revolution in France was still running strong; and the coming to power of the Whigs after the fall of Wellington and the Tories in mid-November was causing the hopes of Radicals to soar. A big strike of cotton spinners was in progress at Manchester; strikes of equal bitterness broke out among the woolen workers of Leeds and Wakefield. Mysterious fires razed several newly erected worsted mills, including one owned by a close friend of Oastler's a few hundred yards from Fixby. The general belief voiced in the newspapers was that they were all 'wilfully occasioned.' And a wave of horror swept the northern counties at the murder of Thomas Ashton, son of the biggest mill owner at Hyde, whose men were on strike and were suspected of being implicated in the crime. Attempts at murder were also made on two other masters noted for their animosity to trade unions, both of whom were engaged in lock-outs at the time.

Political associations were everywhere being organized to press for parliamentary reform now that the Tories were out of office at last. The cause they advocated was given a spectacular impetus by Orator Hunt's remarkable victory over Lord Stanley at a Preston by-election. A mammoth Radical dinner was held at Leeds to celebrate the event, before Hunt set out on his triumphal march to London. At the same time, the West Riding Irish started an O'Connell Fund to help 'the Liberator,' and boasted of being the first in England to send the Catholic Rent to Ireland. A government bill to sweep away the crazy and outworn electoral system of Britain was expected in the immediate future, along with a substantial democratizing of the political process. The middle classes began to organize as well as the workers; and Edward Baines with the help of his friend John Marshall (the man whose enterprise had made Leeds the center of British flax-spinning) was already forming an Association for the Return of Liberal Members to Parliament.

It was within this hubbub and commotion that the campaign for improving the lot of factory children had to be conducted: a campaign that both confused and was confused by all the other pressing problems, and which on that account was all the harder to get before the public as a separate issue.

¶ 3

Though slow to start, Townend's opposition to Oastler and the projected reforms quickly gathered momentum after the turn of the year. With the help of William Ackroyd of Otley, a manufacturer as ruthlessly uncompromising as himself, Townend succeeded in completely breaking the apparent unanimity of the Talbot gathering. At successive meetings held at the same inn on 27 January and 3 February, these two managed to persuade another 40 mill owners to carry unanimously a series of resolutions in outspoken condemnation of the earlier agreement, on the ground that the November decisions were 'not borne out by the facts or supported by sound arguments.' Pity had nothing to do with the question, they declared. It was the hard facts of foreign competition and burdensome taxation that made much shortening of a child's working day unthinkable. Parliamentary interference would only put another burden upon the industry. 'No legislative enactment can effectually protect innocence from the fraud and tyranny of the unprincipled,' affirmed the eleventh resolution:

Viewing the question in a comprehensive point of view as affecting Men as well as Masters, the sweeping and dreadful effects it will infallibly produce are more to be deprecated than the abuses and evils which it is believed always will exist in such a wide-spread manufacture.

Oastler, of course, was appropriately castigated. The precise terms of the indictment are revealing:

This meeting censures with the strongest terms the inflammatory and unwarrantable language of parties who arrogate for themselves the exclusive possession of humanity and integrity as tending to the destruction of social order, and who blindly stigmatize the worsted spinners of this district as the authors of the excessive labour to which the lower classes are subjected, instead of that actual necessity for voluntary and daily labour under which they were born . . .

Even Townend's first proposal of eleven-and-a-half hours was considered too generous. What these forty masters now called for was an unqualified seventy-two-hour working week. 'We think twelve hours a day is little enough,' said Ackroyd, 'and we are also of the opinion that there are no grounds for the accusations against the trade made by the gentlemen of Bradford.' In confirmation of which statement several masters took the opportunity to deny reports which were being circulated to the effect that they worked their children 16 hours a day. They had never done such a thing, they indignantly declared, without paying the children overtime.

Two similar meetings were held at the Old Cock Inn, Halifax, in the course of the next four weeks. Fired by an indignation as great as that of their Bradford colleagues, the Halifax worsted spinners deplored with equal emphasis 'that a portion of the trade should have been frightened from their propriety by Mr. Oastler's inflammatory and enthusiastic letter which, divested of its flourish, contains nothing to warrant such proceedings.' Just before the second of these gatherings, the terms of Hobhouse's Bill had been made public. The fact that the bill really seemed designed to impose definite restrictions upon the freedom of mill owners, slight though the interference was, put venom into the speeches and comments made at the adjourned meeting on 5 March. In a string of 14 comprehensive resolutions prepared in advance by a special sub-committee, the men of Halifax utterly and unanimously repudiated Hobhouse's proposals.

So vigorous and so explicit are these resolutions that only the *ipsissima verba* can do them justice.[2] They delineate the picture of society in the mind of the average northern manufacturer more completely than can be found anywhere else at this time, their very source precluding the charge of caricature. Moreover, they have a direct bearing upon Oastler's career. The unfolding of his own humanitarian Toryism in the course of the next few years was largely engendered by the dialectical effort to formulate an effective answer to the ideology they proclaim.

Two cardinal ideas underlay the Halifax declaration. One was that existing conditions were 'in no way injurious to the health and comforts of this class of operatives'; and the other, that pre-

[2] They are given in Appendix A.

vailing economic circumstances would make the limitation of the working day disastrous for the country. The younger children were not the real problem, they declared, but the adolescents. (It was a plea that was to have a singularly important legislative history in the coming decades.) 'The period between fourteen and twenty-one is the most critical period in the life of those employed . . . Those of the ages between seven and fourteen are more capable of undergoing long continued labour than those of the ages before named.' As for the economic consequences of Hobhouse's proposals, the Halifax masters came near to suggesting that a major depression would ensue if they were put into effect. Wages would fall *pari passu* the shorter working day; unemployment would grow; the workers' family budget would shrink; the home market would collapse; the farmer would lose an outlet for his wool; and finally, foreign competitors would seize the rich opportunity thus gratuitously offered. As long as a reactionary government maintained the existing taxes and restraints on trade, such results would follow inexorably. Therefore the seventy-two-hour working week must be maintained at all costs.

Extensive publicity was given to these resolutions as well as to those from Bradford and other towns. They were inserted as advertisements in the newspapers; they were reprinted as a circular and sent to every mill owner in the Riding; they were mailed to Members of Parliament. Petitions to implement their conclusions were left for signature in each of the Cloth Halls. And in both Bradford and Halifax steering committees were formed to press the case they advocated and frustrate Hobhouse's intentions.

¶ 4

The bill that had aroused such resentment among the Halifax masters had four main provisions applicable to all the textile industries. First, it declared that no child might enter a factory before the age of 9. Secondly, that no one between the ages of 9 and 18 should work for more than eleven-and-a-half hours daily, or eight-and-a-half on Saturdays: that is, 66 actual working hours a week. Thirdly, that in addition to these times there must be a break of half an hour for breakfast and another of an hour for dinner. Lastly, that no one under 18 should be allowed to do night work, defined as the time between 7 P.M. and 6 A.M. This was hardly a revolutionary measure. Indeed, it legalized the very length of day against which Oastler had first protested, namely, from six in the morning to seven in the evening, though it did mitigate some of the other things that had shocked him.

The draft of the bill reached the *Mercury* office just as the issue for 5 March was going to press. There was only time for Baines to indicate brief, tentative approval. 'We should be glad,' he added, 'to hear the opinions of *practical* men whether any serious objections lie to any part of the Bill.' The response was immediate and emphatic: drastic criticisms poured in throughout the week. Summarizing them in his next editorial, and associating himself with them completely, Baines now declared it was obvious that the proposed bill had been drawn up by men 'totally ignorant of the subject' and therefore stood unreservedly condemned.

What enraged the mill owners more than anything else was the proposal to forbid nightwork for all young operatives under 18. The men who had framed the bill could have had no idea what the implications of that clause were, the *Mercury* asserted. Its immediate result would be to stop the uninterrupted use of the plant, since machines could not be kept running without the children to tend them. Yet in some branches of the industry it was imperative to keep the machinery working for long periods at a stretch. Fulling and milling, for example, sometimes required unbroken attention for 24 hours or more at a time. To break that continuity would be disastrous. Similarly with 'rush orders.' These often required long stretches of work if they were to be met on time; but such work would not be allowed under Hobhouse's scheme. Moreover, there was the problem of accidents, breakdowns, and other stoppages. Strict application of the proposed rule would make it impossible to exact the customary overtime to compensate for these delays. And as for the mills driven by water power, they would be ruined, since their operation was not determined by any fixed schedule but was conditioned, day or night, entirely by the fluctuations in the volume of the stream. The conclusion drawn by the 'practical men' was unhesitant: 'prohibition of night work would either compel many masters to make a very great outlay in additional buildings, or to give up half their amount of business.'

The *Mercury's* emphatic condemnation of Hobhouse's Bill in the same issue that carried the Halifax Resolutions proved to be a major event in the development of the factory question for a number of reasons. By transforming a debate about general principles into a fight over specific proposals, it sharpened the alignment of parties to the controversy and thus made conspicuously more evident the disposition of forces in the Riding. The newspapers, for instance, were now compelled to declare themselves on one side or the other. A hardening of determination resulted all round. And this intensification of militancy inevitably led to organization and planned effort on a scale neither side had hitherto contemplated. That was to bring Oastler to the fore again: this time, however, not just as a controversialist in the correspondence columns but as a leader.

This onslaught by the *Mercury* also had a result of another kind, though one that was not so immediately apparent: it contributed to the dissipation of an illusion. The excitement over the Whig Government's long-awaited Parliamentary Reform Bill was just then at its height.[3] Lord John Russell had introduced his epoch-making measure the previous week, and the *Mercury* was giving it almost hysterical endorsement. For a generation past, that journal had been proclaiming itself the true champion of democracy while denouncing all Tories as enemies of 'the people,' and thousands of Yorkshire operatives and craftsmen had accepted it at its own valuation. But in this hour of climax Baines found himself compelled by circumstances to define his attitude to the social question, and this he had done uncompromisingly in the terms of the 'practical men.' On a sudden it was thus revealed that 'democracy' meant the vote for the 'ten-pound householder'

[3] The Reform Bill, introduced into the House of Commons on 1 March, 1831, was designed to achieve two main objectives, viz: (1) To rearrange parliamentary representation and make it more rational: to which end seats were to be taken away from the old, corrupt nomination boroughs and redistributed among the large towns hitherto grotesquely unrepresented. (2) To broaden the franchise: to which end the vote was to be given uniformly in electoral boroughs to every inhabitant whose house was rated at a ten pound rental. The country franchise was somewhat extended too. Under 'the Bill,' Leeds, Huddersfield, and Halifax would all return members.

only; that 'reform' spelled the entrenchment of the capitalists; and that as far as the daily lot of the working-classes and their children was concerned, 'liberal' policy was to be enunciated in the idiom of the Halifax masters. It was all very confusing. Yet even more confusing was the fact that the Tory *Intelligencer* was wholeheartedly supporting Hobhouse's Bill, and that the bill itself had emanated from a chain of circumstances initiated by an avowed Tory. Such confusion put many in the mood for reconsidering their objectives. Out of it Oastler was soon to attempt the fashioning of a Tory Democracy.

¶ 5

The tone and the substance of the mill owners' response to Oastler's denunciations are indicative of more things than appear on the surface.

Oastler supposed he was fighting hard-hearted men. To a considerable extent that was true. Large numbers of the mill owners were self-made men who had come from humble origins. They were not people of much education or refinement of taste; most of them were crude, forceful men with wits and energy above the average, which alone made possible their survival in a fierce competitive struggle. The chance to get rich seemed to be there for the seizing, and they seized it without a squeamish concern for the welfare of those in their employ. Such considerations as regard for the human capital of the nation at large lay entirely beyond the range of their reckoning. Time tempered this ruthlessness in many instances. It is a highly significant fact that almost all the employers who came to Oastler's help at the outset were second-generation men like Wood, Walker, Rand, and Whitacre, while in nearly every instance the bitterest of his opponents were men of the first generation, like Ackroyd and Townend.

But Oastler was fighting something more than hardness of heart, though it was many years before he came to realize it. He was fighting fear, too. Wars, revolutions, foreign speculation, and a defective banking structure made business very much of a gamble. There were wild price fluctuations, so that it was perilously easy to fall into the abyss of bankruptcy as scores did every year. For a century after 1760, not a decade passed without at least one general and spectacular collapse of credit. In these circumstances, the proposal to cut down the length of the working day seemed ominously like adding to the burden of risk. That conviction made for the writing of the Halifax Resolutions fully as much as did crass pitilessness. No estimate concerning efforts for reform can have much validity, therefore, unless it takes into recognition the specter of apprehension that attended every consultation in the counting house after the depression of the 'twenties.

There were other reasons for the mill owners' animosity too. These rising men were sullenly hostile towards an aristocracy that dominated both central and local government in which they themselves had no share. They were 'outsiders,' socially and administratively. They were acutely aware of the fact and most of them resented it strongly. Moreover, they were enraged at the suggestion that a privileged class knowing nothing about industrial affairs should presume to regulate *their* affairs, and in furtherance of that end should propose to haul them before a Bench of Magistrates drawn from the 'gentry' to whom they had to justify their conduct.

To appreciate these things is not to endorse the mill owners' stand: it is merely to affirm that much inhumanity is socially conditioned and that the history of its reform is not a mere recapitulation of the plot of an old-time morality play. Child-labor was unquestionably an evil, but it was parasitic upon standards of acceptance without which it could never have been sustained. This was an age of considerable violence and tolerated cruelty, and the regard for life was light. Flogging of fantastic brutality was still a normal punishment in both the Army and the Navy; hanging and transportation were notorious features of a ferocious criminal code; the condition of prisons was still a national disgrace. The reform of these things was distressingly slow and in every case the effort to effect it ramified far beyond the expectations of its promoters. But in each instance the process began with an angry sense of finer possibilities being entertained by a few disinterested souls: a sense which reached the obsessive intensity that alone enabled them to endure the obloquy heaped upon those who challenge their day with the morrow's standards.

CHAPTER VII

The Dilemma of Whiggery

IN the midst of the public excitement over the Parliamentary Reform Bill, Oastler wrote his fourth letter on 'Yorkshire Slavery' in reply to the Halifax Resolutions. Its result was to strain to the breaking point his relations with the Bainses, and to carry him another definite stage forward towards the assumption of an unexpected role.

Oastler abstained from all participation in the raging controversy over the Reform Bill, not from lack of interest but of set policy. Personally, he was vehemently opposed to the Whig measure. To him it was nothing less than a revolutionary proposal to desecrate a constitution which the centuries had hallowed: a desecration devised for the advantage of none but the moneyed classes. He was quite incapable of thinking about the franchise question in terms of abstract ideas. He always considered it in concrete and personal terms. In his opinion 'reform' meant simply the overthrow of the Howards, the Lascelles, and their like, and the substitution for them of the Marshalls, the Baineses, and the Townends: a change which he emphatically refused to believe could be for the better. Its only result, he repeatedly declared, would be that a dangerous uniformity would replace a healthy diversity in Britain's constitutional arrangements: that the rich variety of national interests fortuitously gathered together and harmonized in Parliament would be destroyed by the calculated triumph of a single interest— industrial capital.

But though he ardently believed these things, he was even more deeply convinced that he must do nothing that might jeopardize the cause of the factory children. Here was one issue standing apart from all others to be adjudged solely by humani-

71

tarian standards. He must not risk complicating it by entangle-
ment with even so momentous a matter as constitutional reform.
On the other hand he realized that every effort would be necessary to keep the question prominently before the public and
prevent its being forgotten in the excitement of the hour. In the
middle of March, therefore, he broke his long silence by sending
the *Mercury* a full commentary upon the factory controversy to
date.

¶ 1

It happened that the elder Baines was in London when Oastler's letter arrived, and that the editorial chair was being occupied
by his son. That was unfortunate, for between Oastler and young
Edward was a temperamental hostility which nothing could
reconcile. This Baines, now 30 years old, was a veritable model
of the second generation of a self-made family. Brought up in
comparative affluence, expensively educated and moving in the
most prosperous circles of the county, he was inspired with a
strong sense of his own worth and had cultivated that tone of
quiet reserve which is the hall-mark of social assurance. He
thought Oastler crude: a well-meaning but rather irresponsible
zealot. Oastler for his part considered young Baines a conceited
humbug and a social climber.

Oastler's letter was extremely emphatic and very long, so
Edward 'cut' it for publication by about half. He also added some
pungent editorial comments. The letter was of 'such unmerciful
length,' he said, that it could not be printed in full. By its violence
and 'brimstone rhetoric' it outraged judgment and exceeded the
bounds of reason. And even though Oastler's humane intentions
could be admitted, it was regrettable they were 'connected with
infirmity.'

Nevertheless, the substance of the letter did actually appear on
19 March. It has several interesting features, but as far as Oastler
himself is concerned the most important thing about it is the clear
evidence it contains of a conspicuous maturing of his social re-
flections. He had begun his advocacy with a simple humanitarian
plea. The ardor of that appeal was in no way lessened by what
had been said during the previous five months. But to it were

now added other considerations which went far beyond his original intentions, and were obviously capable of being elaborated still further.

Hobhouse's Bill, he said in effect, would in some measure rationalize the industry and put limits to the anarchy of reckless competition. In this way it would give workers and masters alike a fairer chance than they were able to get under existing conditions. Restricting the hours of labor as the bill proposed would distribute available work more equitably and more regularly, as well as prevent glutting of the market. Furthermore, by making necessary the building of additional mills (as opponents claimed it would) it would help reduce unemployment and so increase purchasing power. These are significant arguments: soon the share-the-work idea would be heard from a hundred platforms. At the moment, however, to anyone detachedly watching the development of the controversy, their chief interest lay in the open declaration they made of Oastler's expanding horizons. He was at last beginning to see that effective regulation of child-labor might entail indirect limitations upon adult labor too. That had not at first occurred to him. Yet unlike the overwhelming majority of manufacturers in the Riding he was not shocked by the implication. Confident in the validity of his major premise, he was willing to follow the argument wheresoever it might lead.

Another notable feature of the letter was the use it made for the first time of Dr. C. T. Thackrah's recent book on *The Effects of the Principal Arts, Trades and Professions on Health and Longevity.* The author was one of the physicians at the Leeds Infirmary, a man of wide experience and considerable professional distinction. Oastler had come to know him soon after the controversy started and had received his assurances of full support in the struggle to restrict child labor. 'The employment of children in *any* labour is wrong,' Thackrah said.

No man of humanity can reflect without distress on the state of thousands of children, many from six to seven years of age, roused from their beds at an early hour, hurried to the mills and kept there with an interval of only forty minutes till a late hour at night; kept moreover in an atmosphere impure not only as the air of a town, not only as defective in ventilation, but as loaded also with noxious dust

. . . Recreation is out of the question; there is scarcely any time for meals. The very period of sleep so necessary for the young is too often abridged. Nay, children are sometimes worked even in the night . . .

Coming from such a source, those words were like a tonic to Oastler. Henceforward Thackrah's book was a bible among the factory reformers.

Right conduct, Oastler went on to say, was not just a variable conditioned by one's ability to defray its cost. The moral law was immutable; before it all purely economic considerations must yield. Sweeping aside the technical arguments of the Halifax masters, Oastler reduced the meaning of their notorious Resolutions to half a dozen satirical propositions:

1st. God's laws must bend and break at the call of avarice and self interest!
2nd. Money is of more value than principle, morality and religion!
3rd. Government is no longer of any use, because it is unable to protect the innocent and weak against the rapacity of the guilty and strong!
4th. The state of the trade of this country is really such, that its very existence depends upon excessive application and overworking on the part of the operatives!
5th. It is better that the labouring classes should live by the excessive and overpowering toil of their infants, than that the parents should labour for the support of their offspring!
6th. The exorbitant taxes which we are obliged to pay, the loss we sustain by the East India monopoly, the corn laws, and every other abuse, as a matter of clear right and justice, must and ought to be paid and borne out of the blood, bones and sinews of our infantile population!

That was a debating trick Oastler was often to employ later: challenging expediency with the ethical imperative, piling up data about existing conditions, and then leaving the moral sense of his audience to make its own judgment.

¶ 2

Oastler was extremely angry at Edward Baines's handling of his letter. As soon as he saw what had happened to it he sent the full version to the *Leeds Intelligencer* accompanied by a vehement covering letter. The *Intelligencer* was delighted to get both, of course, and though they ran to a column and a half, the editor published them in full. All the hard things that had been said on both sides during the Halifax tithes dispute were now forgotten. From that moment on the *Intelligencer* was Oastler's paper. By taking the unexpurgated letter, the editor initiated an alliance which was to endure for almost a quarter of a century.

Baines, Oastler maintained, had no right to publish only part of the letter and then comment adversely on the rest. What 'improper' epithets had he used?

Let the sapient scribe enter the field in defense of these infamous resolutions. Let him support these 'practical' men whose opinion he so much covets and admires. Let him prove that they have their foundation in Religion, Morality, and Patriotism. If he should succeed in this charitable undertaking without 'outraging the judgment' and 'exceeding the bounds of reason and justice' he will be a more consummate casuist than ever his father was.

And who was Baines of all people to talk about 'brimstone rhetoric'? He was ready enough to use it himself when attacking the owners of West Indian slaves,

but the untaxed factory monger stands on hallowed ground! Not a hair of his head must be singed! His rights are sacred! His 'order' must be maintained! And infants' blood must be his food!—While I live I will oppose his tyranny. If I had the vocabulary of Hell, perhaps I might be able to paint his traffic in appropriate language. The language used on earth can ne'er describe the cruelty of this horrid system practised in 'this land of Bibles.'

The *Mercury* made much of the opinions of 'practical men.' Why then had its editors not referred to Thackrah's book? What trust could be put in the judgment of these 'practical men,' anyway? The flax spinners were trying to wriggle out of the terms of Hobhouse's Bill on the ground that regulation was not necessary in their case. The worsted masters had made it plain they did not think regulation was necessary for them either, though their fourth resolution affirmed that the flax industry needed supervision. Since each was so generously willing to concede that the other needed legislative control, could the word 'practical' be anything more than a synonym for self-interest?

Now that the full letter was published, it was seen that the parts young Baines had deleted were those commenting seriatim on the Halifax Resolutions. These Oastler had treated with the utmost scorn. 'Is it possible,' he asked, 'that avarice and self-interest can have such a bewildering effect on the mind of man? One cannot help thinking while one reads [them] of the fervor and disappointment depicted in the countenances of a gang of free-booters, whilst sharing their spoil, being suddenly alarmed by the approach of the King's officers. The tears and alarms of these worsted spinners are deserving of no more pity than the detected banditti.' As for the suggestion that the regulation of child labor would involve the catalogue of disasters which the Halifax men had prophesied, it was scaremongering nonsense:

Resolution 3 attempts to persuade the public that if the manufacturers are not allowed to continue their present cruelties, the children will be starved and unemployed, and that *as these poor little children are the main support of their strong and healthy parents*, why forsooth, the parents must starve too! That compelling the masters to treat their children better will REDUCE wages and, what is very singular, will *at the same time* RAISE the price of goods to the consumer. Thus destroying 'at one fell swoop' the maker, the buyer, the consumer—both the home and foreign markets will be lost—the agricultural and landed proprietor ruined—all this, say they, will be the consequence if poor little English children are protected from the cruelty and oppression of their worse-than-Egyptian taskmasters. Happy England whose very existence depends upon thy cruelty to infants! Brave and gallant nation who hast the magnanimity to throw all thy burdens on thy little ones! Nation of freemen—ah no!—the tyrant never yet was free! He who holds his child in bondage never knew what freedom meant. Self-interest and avarice and *not necessity* now goad thee on to ruin.

The *Intelligencer* added a cordial comment which its editor must have enjoyed writing. Though Oastler's diction was 'rather strong,' it said, he had been denied a fair hearing by the *Mercury* and subjected to a not very honest criticism. In the interests of freedom of speech and the success of a great cause, therefore, they were delighted to give him full publicity. The evils Oastler had described were hardly to be exaggerated. It was now being revealed that factory labor involved much more than long hours. Children sent to work at a tender age contracted all manner of disabilities hitherto overlooked: stunted growth, deformed limbs, and occupational diseases. So the *Intelligencer* hoped Hobhouse's Bill would be passed without any weakening amendments.

¶ 3

Two days later the *Mercury* replied in kind. It repeated its assertion that Oastler's good intentions were not to be doubted, but regretted that such an 'excellent cause as the not-overworking of children' should have 'so intemperate an advocate.' But even his foolish scurrility would not prevent their continuing to champion the cause of humanity, though in doing so they were anxious to avoid harming the country's industry by unnecessarily interfering with its freedom.

Clearly the *Mercury* was finding itself in a difficult position. The sort of philanthropic appeal Oastler was making might come to have great importance. It had obvious similarities to the Emancipation cause, now rapidly riding towards success, and might just as easily cut across party lines. Now that the *Intelligencer* had openly come out on Oastler's side, it was not inconceivable that a temporary fusion of purpose might be effected between Toryism and the Riding's abundant liberal humanitarianism. As the organ of Yorkshire nonconformity the *Mercury* would have to tread warily, particularly as there was now no longer any doubt that the large majority of masters were definitely opposed to Hobhouse's Bill.

The Baineses had therefore to prove to Yorkshiremen they were on the side of both business prosperity and true philanthropy simultaneously. To that end several editorial lines were available. One was to belittle Oastler by representing him as well-meaning but unbalanced; another, to press the 'practicality' argument; a third, to project the solution of the social problem into the future when circumstances would be more favorable. All three devices were used, but increasingly the Baineses found the last a particularly useful line to take. Once the corruptions and restrictions inherited from the decadent days of Tory rule were swept away, they said, the question of hours and wages would

solve itself in the resulting prosperity. Until then, men must bide
in patience.

By now it was evident that in the case of both the major issues
of the day—the franchise question and the factory question—the
Mercury was combating two enemies at once: the Tories of the
right and the Radical universal-suffrage men of the left. In each
instance it had to show that its own middle-class Whig position
was the only really sound and progressive one to adopt. Appo-
sitely enough, on the same day Baines's denunciation of 'silly
raving' appeared, the radical *Leeds Patriot* declared itself for
Oastler. From the first it had approved Hobhouse's Bill, though
it had been suspicious of Oastler himself; now it warmly commended his latest 'excellent letter.' It expressed regret, however,
that he had not sent his exposition to their columns also. Such a
hint Oastler was not slow to take. From now forward he had on
each flank a vantage point from which he could enfilade the
Mercury.

¶ 4

The introduction of Hobhouse's Bill and the publication of
Oastler's fourth letter resulted in a vigorous renewal of the debate
in the correspondence columns. Most of the old arguments were
traversed afresh, but little new was forthcoming. The only distinctive feature of this second battle of letters was the presentation of the masters' case by an anonymous 'Vindex' in a series
of pronouncements more crass and more extreme than anything
written hitherto.

The gist of Vindex's argument was that the factory masters
were realists and their critics a pack of ignorant fools. 'The body
of the trade of worsted spinners in this district do not pretend
to argue the question on what is falsely called the "humanity"
side of the question,' he declared, 'or on that partial and fanatical
argument which consults the present ease and convenience of the
labourer at the expense of his real and solid interests.' To regard
the freedom of children as in any way different from that of
adults was merely to introduce a 'jesuitical distinction'; moreover,
it involved 'a direct and gross violation of the liberty of the subject and an invasion of the rights of the poor man as master of

his house and family.' Complete and unqualified laissez-faire was
the only safe rule to adopt in economic matters. The whole movement, he protested, was nothing but a plot by the big masters
to crush their smaller rivals; Hobhouse had simply been imposed
upon by 'interested capitalists behind the scenes.' A little later,
this same Vindex gave an alternative explanation of the pother
which had so unnecessarily been raised. Oastler, he said, was
merely a 'hireling advocate' of the West Indian slave owners
employed to distract public attention from the Emancipation
movement.

❋   ❋   ❋

Meanwhile all the arguments that had been elicited in the
Yorkshire newspapers during the course of the past six months
were being brought to bear upon Members of Parliament in preparation for the debate on Hobhouse's Bill.

Textile masters from different parts of the Kingdom were
working hard to have the bill altered to suit their various interests. Hobhouse was plied with advice; Members were interviewed; reports and resolutions were distributed. The Scottish
manufacturers were especially active. Fearing the competition
of the up-to-date Yorkshire machinery with their own inferior
plant, they were loath to give up a single working hour and had
organized a separate protest movement. Baines wrote personally
to Hobhouse to convey the opinions of the 'practical' men, but
got back a surprisingly forthright reply. 'It would give me much
pain to see the Bill opposed by well-meaning and fair antagonists,'
said Hobhouse; 'but as to parties interested in upholding present
abuses, I not only am prepared for their attacks, but should think
I have attempted nothing useful if I did not encounter them.'

The pressure was too great to be completely withstood, however. In the end, even before the bill came before the House,
Hobhouse had to make some concessions. Apart from comparatively minor alterations, he had to modify it in four ways. The
definition of 'night time' was cut down by two hours, thus enabling employers to use their children anytime between five in
the morning and eight in the evening. Some parts of the woolen
industry (such as wool processing) were exempted from regula-

tion altogether. The silk industry was allowed to employ children from seven years of age, instead of nine. And owners of water mills were given permission to exact an extra half-hour daily to make up for delays due to loss of water-power.

The *Mercury* hailed all this with delight, claiming that 'the principal objections' to the bill had now been removed while its 'humane purpose' was left intact. True, a core of substance still remained in spite of these drastic amendments: the eleven-and-a-half-hour day for children in spinning mills was preserved. But the fate of even that was far from certain. The owners of water mills immediately started a new outcry that they were being unfairly treated. And early in April, in preparation for the definitive vote in the House, the executive committees appointed at the various protest meetings sent chosen representatives to London to start lobbying.

Within a fortnight, the newspapers announced that Hobhouse had further altered his bill to permit a twelve-hour day.

CHAPTER VIII

The Workers Organize

¶ 1

THE committees for action set up by the masters made the operatives see that they themselves must organize if Hobhouse's Bill was to become law.

Until the beginning of March, when the Halifax Resolutions were passed, there had been no sort of organization to press for factory legislation other than the little group that Wood and his colleagues had appointed at the first Talbot meeting. Oastler had written his letter in the simple belief that he merely had to shame the conscience of contemporaries to effect reform, never supposing that a 'movement' would result. It was purely a personal gesture. After that he had been quite content to leave the practical business in the hands of his Bradford friends. That there would be a general breakaway from the Talbot agreement never crossed his mind; the bitterness of his fourth letter is a measure of his astonishment at the turn events were taking. Even so he did not fully realize the pertinacity and strength of the interests he was challenging.

But some of the operatives did. Among them were hard-headed men who had a much shrewder idea than Oastler of the sort of opposition Hobhouse was likely to encounter. For the most part they were ardent Radicals, members of one or another of those political societies that had come into being to fight for manhood suffrage after the July Revolution in France; and nearly all were readers of the illicit, unstamped journals.[1] A few years earlier, a

[1] To combat Radicalism and sedition, Lord Liverpool's government in 1819 had imposed a tax of 4d. on all journals and pamphlets sold for less than sixpence. In defiance of this an extensive illegal press had come into

number of them had got together in various groups to press foi parliamentary regulation of the woolen and worsted industries, though nothing had come of their efforts. Others, working in the cotton mills of the Riding, were still members of local, self-appointed committees which had been formed to publicize evasions of the law that was supposed to regulate the cotton industry. None of them knew Oastler personally; but they saw clearly enough that, whatever his political convictions might be, the publication of his letters had created a situation highly favorable to the renewal of their own efforts.

Accordingly, soon after the details of Hobhouse's Bill were made public, some of these men began forming what they called Short Time Committees to help in promoting the passage of the measure. The movement was spontaneous and unco-ordinated. Huddersfield and Leeds each claimed the honor of being the first place to establish such bodies; but before the year was out similar ones were to be found in all the principal towns of the Riding. They were very informal affairs and in no sense exclusive. The initiative came entirely from the workers, most of whom already knew one another from their political or trade-union activity; but though spinners and weavers made up the bulk of the original membership, any sympathizer was welcome to join if he were willing to work with them. The Committee at Leeds, for instance, was composed almost entirely of representatives from each of the mills and workshops in the town, while that at Huddersfield included several small shopkeepers and the manager of the local co-operative store. In each instance, some local inn was adopted as a headquarters where meetings could be held and records kept.

Each committee followed its own line of action. Some wrote to Members of Parliament urging that Hobhouse's Bill be enacted; others concentrated on getting local support. But the most im-

---

being mainly under the leadership of Henry Hetherington and William Lovett. Refusing to pay the tax, these Radical publishers had built up an elaborate underground organization for the distribution and sale of their journals, despite the prosecutions and imprisonments with which the government sought to crush them. There was a marked increase in the numbers of these papers after the 1829 depression.

portant immediate outcome of this new phase of activity was
the publication by the Leeds group of a carefully reasoned reply
to the 'practical' opinions put forth by the *Mercury*. Sent in the
first instance as a private memorandum to Hobhouse, it was subsequently reproduced as an open letter in all the local newspapers
and then reprinted in pamphlet form for general distribution in
the Riding. It thus became for the Short Time Committees what
the Halifax Resolutions had become for the Masters—the definitive brief of their case.

The Leeds men agreed that eleven-and-a-half hours constituted
a reasonable working day for children; their chief concern was
to prevent Hobhouse from accepting wrecking amendments that
would lengthen it. Most of the arguments Oastler had already
developed were included in the brief. The humanitarian plea was
restated with dignity and vividness; the share-the-work theme
was elaborated with cogency; and the fallacies in the special-
pleading of the owners of water mills were lucidly exposed. But
the most striking thing about the document was its frank declaration in favor of regulating adult labor.

It has sometimes been said that the northern workers did not
begin openly advocating the regulation of adult labor until
several years later. This pronouncement by the Leeds Committee
effectively refutes that assertion: there is nothing ambiguous in
the wording whatever:

As the system stands at present, one adult and one child, and in
some branches one adult and several children, are employed together;
which, if the Bill pass, would cause the adults to give up work at the
same time with the children. Hence the objection of the manufacturer
and, so far as we are concerned, our support of the Bill.

It was the gradual realization of the truth of this proposition that
largely accounted for the confusion of public opinion on the factory question in the months that followed. Unquestionably the
workers' motives in supporting child-labor legislation were mixed
from the start: only a superficial cynicism would see anything
disparaging in such an admission. The operatives wanted shorter
hours and better conditions as much as anyone; the work of the
children was technically and inextricably bound up with that of

the adults; apart from any philanthropic considerations, therefore, the men would naturally support a cause that promised to redound to their own advantage also. It stands to the credit of the Leeds men that they said as much frankly.

For some weeks the *Leeds Patriot* kept urging the operatives to hold general meetings for the purpose of rallying public support and countering the much advertised pronouncements of the masters. Not until April, however, did the Short Time Committees deem it wise to follow this advice.

Bradford was the first to do so with a gathering of overlookers from the local worsted mills. Expressing their gratitude to Oastler for his 'manly and humane conduct,' they went on to pass a series of resolutions based upon their personal experience to prove the need for reform. The stark fact was unchallengeable, they declared, that most Bradford mills were working thirteen-and-a-half hours daily with only half an hour off for meals. Three days later the Leeds Committee held an even more important assembly at their Union Inn headquarters, attended by delegates from each of the wool, linen, flax, cotton, and silk mills of the district. Similar resolutions were passed, and a petition drafted for presentation to Parliament. Within a week over 10,000 signatures were obtained. Even the *Mercury* was impressed by the demonstration, which it conceded could only be 'regarded as impartial and disinterested.' Then Bradford went a step further with a more general meeting of 'the middle and working classes of the town and neighbourhood.' A third set of resolutions appeared in the Public Notices columns, and a third petition was transmitted to Westminster, bearing 4,000 more signatures in support of Hobhouse's Bill.

Both the Tory *Intelligencer* and the Radical *Patriot* waxed enthusiastic at all this. The latter had now completely shed its original suspicion of Oastler and become unreservedly complimentary. 'To Mr. Oastler,' wrote the editor after the third meeting, 'they owe much; and ultra-Tory though he is in name he possesses genuine Radical feelings, or in other words is a real friend to the best interests of the country.' And someone calling himself 'Observator' wrote to the *Intelligencer* confirming from recent investigation all the revelations Oastler had made, and likening him to St. Paul before Festus proclaiming 'temperance, righteousness and justice to come.'

¶ 2

Meanwhile the Parliamentary Reform Bill had been encountering heavy going in Commons. The second reading had been carried by a single vote, and shortly afterwards the Government had been defeated in Committee. Lord Grey asked for a dissolution. The King first hesitated, then acceded, and on 22 April Parliament was dissolved. The general election campaign began immediately.

Oastler at once issued a manifesto *To the Working Classes of the West Riding,* which he paid to have inserted in the newspapers along with the various election addresses. It is an important pronouncement in more than one respect and marks yet another distinct stage in his political development. There was no reference in it to the constitutional crisis which had occasioned the dissolution. Oastler's one purpose was to urge the operatives to make known to every candidate the facts about the factory system. They should try, he advised them, to get from each candidate a straight pledge in favor of a *ten-hour day.*

This was the first time Oastler had addressed himself to the working class. That in itself was significant. But vastly more so was his declaration in favor of a ten-hour day. Up to this point, he and his Bradford friends, as well as the members of the various Short Time Committees, had all been content to support Hobhouse's proposal for an eleven-and-a-half-hour day. Now Oastler suddenly abandoned such a petty and humble request. Ever since his second letter to the *Mercury* he had been growing more bewildered and more uneasy on account of the qualifications and sophistries in which he found himself getting entangled.[2] With this emphatic public gesture he rid himself of all those perplexities, and by so doing formulated the clear-cut objective and the ringing slogan that rally men to effort. The Ten Hours Movement had begun.

The consequences were incalculable, for British social politics as well as for Oastler personally. Never afterwards did he retreat

[2] See above, pp. 54 and 61.

from the position first enunciated in this manifesto. And that committed him to agitation, struggle, and a strange journey for the rest of his days.

*   *   *

The general election resulted in an overwhelming victory for the Whigs, who returned to Westminster with a large majority. The dissolution had automatically disposed of pending legislation. Hobhouse's Bill would thus have to be reintroduced and the struggle start all over again.

¶ 3

On a bright Sunday in June 1831, half a dozen operatives from the Huddersfield mills were to be seen trudging up the steep hill-road that leads to Fixby Ridge, making their way across the Park just as the church bells in the valley were beginning to ring for morning service. Their coming was a direct sequel to Oastler's recent election manifesto: the last of that series of events which brought him to leadership.

Although more than nine months had elapsed since Oastler had written his famous letter, he had still not had any personal contact with the operatives themselves. He was going his way with letter and manifesto, they were going theirs with the Short Time Committees. They were grateful for the dramatic eruption of his benevolence, of course, as their resolutions repeatedly declared; but until now neither they nor he had sought to bridge the gap that separated them. Yet the mill owners' concerted action, Oastler's widening knowledge and growing militancy—the whole trend of affairs, indeed, since the introduction of Hobhouse's Bill—made it inevitable that they should come together sooner or later unless they were prepared to submit to a defeat as complete as that of six years before. The organization that had already brought the masters such speedy success must be met with one equally united. The operatives were on their way to Fixby to find out whether the undertaking of such a union might not be begun forthwith.

They had decided on this the night before. Each week since its formation, the Huddersfield Short Time Committee had been holding regular Saturday night meetings in a back room of the Ship Inn, which served as their headquarters, and one of the items on the agenda for 18 June had been the question of getting into touch with Oastler. After some discussion they had agreed that a deputation of six should go to Fixby next morning to talk over the situation.[3]

Oastler was just about to set off for Woodhurst Church when they arrived. He was always punctilious in his church attendance, and when they explained what they had come for he told them he could not see them. Any other day in the week he would be only too pleased to meet them, he said, but not Sunday. They begged him to reconsider. Sunday, they explained, was the only day on which they could possibly get up to Fixby; the rest of the week they were at work from soon after dawn until late at night. Oastler pondered this for a few moments, went to consult his wife, and then (as he afterwards wrote) 'seeing it was clearly a work of charity' agreed to stay at home while the rest of the household went to church.

Many a time afterwards Oastler told the story of that memorable discussion; so did the operatives. For Oastler the conference was more revealing than anything that had happened since John Wood had first made him aware of the factory question. These operatives gave him the industrial picture from an entirely new angle, from the standpoint of the workers themselves, supplementing the paternalism of his ideas with the facts of their own lives. Then they asked that he would communicate with them freely, offering in return to co-operate as fully as they could in his efforts to get a decent factory bill passed. 'I heard all they had to say with great interest,' Oastler wrote:

I was struck with their intelligence and their civility. I had seen much of the poor when in sickness and distress at their homes, and in the workhouse and infirmary, but till that day I had never entered into communion with working men on matters relating to themselves as a class connected with their employers. A new field seemed open to me. Those men surprised me by the knowledge which they communicated and the sensible manner in which they conveyed that knowledge.

[3] Those who made up the deputation were: Lawrence Pitkeithly, John Hanson, James Brook, Joshua Hobson, John Leech, and Samuel Glendinning.

Still Oastler was hesitant about co-operating. He was a Tory
and a Churchman; they were Radicals and mostly Nonconformists. 'It will be better that we work separately,' he advised them,
'you taking your course and I taking mine.' But the men wanted
something more definite than this. Oastler could say and do
things they could not; he had more leisure, more contacts, and
more opportunities than they had. In short, they wanted him
as a leader in their own organization. Back and forth, therefore,
the talk ranged over the entire field of their differences. Finally
the deputation talked Oastler out of his doubts and got him to
agree to full co-operation on condition that both parties should
put aside as far as they humanly could all their sectarian and
political differences and work together for the single objective
to which they were all committed. That was the bargain which
was to be known to history as the 'Fixby Hall Compact.' Twelve
years afterwards, Joshua Hobson (a self-educated handloom
weaver who was later to become editor of the *Huddersfield
Chronicle*) was speaking for all of them when he declared:

At that meeting the foundation of the 'union' between Mr. Oastler
and the working people to effect practical good was laid. He stated to
the deputation frankly and freely what his political tenets were; he
ascertained what theirs were; and an understanding was come to that
on the Factory Question they would all work together totally irrespective of political or party considerations. In that spirit we commenced
to work; in that spirit we have continued to work; and in that spirit we
will work the matter out. The consequences of that meeting at Fixby
are not yet known. *There,* on *that day,* has a lever been forged which
has already heaved England to her centre, and which will set her
right at last.

Oastler now began to attend the weekly meetings at the Ship
Inn. Gradually a new relationship grew up between the operatives and himself. For their part, they kept him informed of factory news and workers' gossip, supplying him with facts with
which to answer the masters' arguments. In return they found
in him a personal friend and an inspiring leader. The loyalty
they came to have for him was remarkable. Years of effort,
frustration, and calumny were to try it as few such relationships
are tried, yet it held to the end of their lives.

The 'Compact' brought Oastler greatly increased power and soon made him the best-informed man on factory conditions in the West Riding. The number of his working-class friends increased rapidly. They put him in touch with the other Short Time Committees, and before long he was riding over to Leeds, Keighley, Bradford, and elsewhere to attend their meetings as well. These and other well-wishers to the cause began communicating with him directly. John Wood and his friends on the one hand, Hammond, Pitkeithly, and the rest of the workers' leaders on the other, were soon all keeping Oastler advised of their moves and intentions. Without any planning, Fixby Hall became the unofficial central office of the whole campaign. By the end of the autumn Oastler found himself the leader of a great movement.

CHAPTER IX

Parliament Refuses to Interfere

IN spite of the national excitement over the second Parliamentary Reform Bill, which the Government introduced immediately after its sweeping victory at the elections, Hobhouse lost no time in preparing a new factory bill. Its terms were much the same as those of his amended measure of the previous session: no child to enter a factory before the age of nine (but seven in the case of silk mills); 12 working hours a day, and nine on Saturdays, for all young persons under eighteen; such working hours to be taken between five-thirty in the morning and eight-thirty at night, with the provision of one-and-a-half hours for mealtime. It was a meager and shriveled thing, the more so since generous provision was made for the masters to exact overtime as compensation for delays resulting from accidents or the failure of water power. In the case of water mills, for example, it would become legal to maintain a sixteen-hour day between five in the morning and nine at night for six months in the year. The only novel feature—one which was to figure prominently in the agitation later—was the provision that a 'time book' should be kept for recording the actual running hours of mill machinery.

¶ 1

The Short Time Committees were greatly disappointed; so much so, in fact, that they took it for granted the bill would pass without much difficulty since it was hardly more liberal than the Halifax Resolutions. But at least it purported to remedy some of the more outrageous abuses which had recently been brought to light, so it was not to be entirely despised. In a spirit of resentful acquiescence, therefore, the operatives' committees continued their propaganda during the early autumn. Oastler too, dissatisfied though he was, was prepared to take what he could get as a first instalment and await a more opportune time to launch a new campaign after the Reform fever should have run its course.

Yet, in spite of Hobhouse's moderation, there were as many interested parties as ever to whom the very idea of such legislation was anathema: men whom no concessions would satisfy because they felt that any kind of regulation was (as one of them said) 'a most unjustifiable infringement on the liberty of British subjects and the Free Trade system.' Some wrote to the papers about it; and just as on the two previous occasions when effective action had seemed imminent, the correspondence columns were the arenas of weekly debate. At Westminster, in the meantime, all the pressures that had been brought to bear upon Hobhouse the previous March to persuade him to amend his bill were now renewed to induce him to abandon it altogether. It was reported that no fewer than 28 of the leading mill owners of Yorkshire and Lancashire had gone up to London to 'watch' the course of the bill through Parliament. All that torrid summer while the second Reform debate was in progress, personal lobbying and the presentation of hostile petitions continued.

Some interesting light on the tactics and attitudes of the mill owners is shed by a Huddersfield petition against the bill, which Lord Morpeth presented early in August. Signed by ten local firms and got up so secretly that few people in the town knew anything about it until after it was presented, it asked for outright rejection of the measure on the ground that 'all legislative interference in regard to the price of labour or the mode in which masters should employ their servants is injurious to the principles of sound commercial policy.' Conditions in cotton mills were bad, it admitted, and justified some deviation from this cardinal doctrine there. But work in the woolen industry was in no way harmful; on the contrary, it provided children with 'wholesome and comfortable employment.' Nor was 8 years too early an age for children to start learning the trade. The net result of the proposed law, it prophesied, would simply be a reduction in wages and the unnecessary impoverishment of working families.

Most of the opposition to reform had hitherto come from the
worsted industry around Bradford and Halifax. This was the
first time a protest had emanated from Oastler's own neighborhood. Perhaps on that account, as well as because of the furtive-
ness of the affair, Oastler was incensed when he heard about
it. He immediately wrote to Michael Sadler to find out the exact
terms of the document and the names of its signatories, and when
the required information came he and the Short Time Committees drew up a vigorous reply, which they sent along with
all the other particulars to the *Intelligencer* and *Patriot*. They
also asked the signatories to call a round-table conference on the
Petition, but all they got in answer was a curt letter from a lawyer
saying the firms 'did not consider that a meeting for discussion
would be profitable.'

A month later a curious communication arrived from one of
the firms, saying they had 'not read the Petition when it was
brought, being much engaged,' and that all they sought was
modification, not rejection, of the bill. To this John Leech, secretary of the Huddersfield Committee, sent a devastating reply.
No longer, he announced, were the men going to waste their
time higgling about amendments and compromises. The evils of
mill labor had now been so well attested that his Committee
was going to take its stand upon a ten-hour day and nothing
less. Many other trades had the six-to-six custom: the Committee
did not intend to rest until it had won that for wool and worsted
too.

The sting and forthrightness of this avowal were in striking
contrast to the deference that had characterized so many of the
operatives' declarations six months earlier. Oastler's hand was
plainly to be seen in it; yet that is not the only reason for the
altered tone. There can be little doubt that the mood of the
operatives was rapidly changing at this time. Disappointment
over the Whigs' Reform Bill, which gave the vote to the middle
classes and left the workers unenfranchised; bewilderment at
Hobhouse's vacillation; disgust at learning about the masters'
high-pressure lobbying at Westminster: all these things, besides
Oastler's vehement urgings, contributed to their growing militancy. The day was fast approaching when supplication would

altogether give place to campaigning. There was a substantial element of realism in the *Intelligencer's* remark apropos of this episode that the operatives 'seeing the delusion of *The Bill* have wisely resolved to attend to those points which really affect their interests instead of wasting their time and means on party politics to promote the objects of pretended friends who seize the earliest opportunity of trampling them under foot.'

¶ 2

Throughout the journey of the factory bill in the House, Oastler and Sadler were in close touch. Oastler sent him data, arguments, and advice, Sadler sent back strategical reports. 'I not only concur with Mr. Hobhouse's factory bill,' Sadler had written, 'but as I have expressed to him over and over again, I go much beyond it.' Indeed, much of the burden of countering hostile moves and petitions fell upon him: a task which proved to be a great strain to one with his sensitive temperament. 'My great loss is,' he confessed, 'that I have no energetic friend like yourself at my elbow to prompt and encourage me in these endeavours.'

I thank you most deeply for your concluding advice [he wrote on another occasion]. May my motives be kept single and my conduct upright and humble! Indeed, I have more temptations arising from despondency and want of confidence at this moment than vanity or pride, which would ill become me; having no pretensions whatever to anything that could make me proud. The happy medium is what religion alone can give. I have of this a little—may God increase it; that is His gift, and the most precious one He bestows.

The millowners, I am aware, are very powerful in Leeds. I meditate nothing but what I think would be for *their* interest, properly understood, if carried into full effect; nothing that I would not gladly submit to, were I one of them.

Adieu. Our objects are the same, and I hope I shall live to see some of them realized. In the meantime, allow me in great haste to subscribe myself, my dear Sir,

Your affectionate friend and fellow labourer,

M. T. Sadler

London, September 22nd, 1831.

But all the striving came to nothing. Late in the sitting of 28–29 September (after all the reporters had left the gallery) the bill came up on the report stage and Hobhouse accepted all the amendments which effectively emasculated the measure. By an irony of chance it was the anniversary of the day on which Oastler had written his first letter on 'Yorkshire Slavery': twelve months almost to the hour since he had stood by John Wood's bedside and made his solemn vow. The principles of the Halifax Resolutions triumphed and the House of Commons decided that children in the woolen and worsted industries needed no protection after all. In its final form the Act applied only to cotton, and even there it failed to provide any machinery for its enforcement. As the leading historian of the nineteenth century has said, it amounted to 'nothing more than a barren declaration of principles.' And a couple of years later a writer who knew what he was talking about was able to aver that its terms were unknown to many of the manufacturers and disregarded by the rest. So negligible was it, that even at the time the London press passed it by in silence.

¶ 3

A deepening of the operatives' anger was one immediate result of the emasculation of Hobhouse's Bill; a newspaper orgy of recrimination, explanation, and self-excuse over the fiasco was another. Both helped to prepare the way for a resumption of the struggle on such a scale and with such intensity that the factory question was transposed from a local to a major national issue.

For this reason the defeat of Hobhouse's original scheme was probably a good thing in the long run for the cause of social reform, though it was difficult to see the matter in that light at the time. If the pattern of later events is anything to go by, then it is almost certain that the passage of the unamended bill would have effectively prevented the renewal of the agitation for some while to come. Enthusiasm would have been dissipated; people would have said the act must be 'given a chance'; the cry that 'these people could never be satisfied' would certainly have been raised. As things were, this did not happen. A moderate measure had been defeated—so moderate that anything less would scarcely have been worth bothering about—and that mainly through the lobbying of men over whose mills the vaunted 'orange flag' of Reform was flying all those critical weeks. This was a dramatization of the issue that could not fail to provoke resentment or to bring home the lesson that success would come only by means of an organization capable of effectively engaging the one that had recently ridden so easily to victory. The frustration of low-pitched hopes may turn to more sullen anger than the disappointment of more exalted claims. So it was in this case, as the next six months were to prove.

Meanwhile the considerable concern felt in the Riding about the exact reasons for Hobhouse's unexpected abandonment of his bill found acrimonious expression in a post-mortem enquiry conducted over several weeks by all the local newspapers. The *Mercury* was plainly uneasy over the affair. All its editorials on the factory question reveal vexation at having the simple political struggle between Whig progressiveness and Tory reaction complicated by this unnecessary intrusion. Now to an already confused public mood was added the further complication of a sharp disappointment. The curtailment of the measure, wrote young Baines, was 'much to be deplored' and required explanation. Had not the *Mercury* itself declared the revised bill practicable, desirable, and humane? With an eye to future electoral consequences, therefore, both the Baineses were anxious to exculpate not only themselves but also Yorkshire Whiggery in general.

The *Intelligencer* said there was no mystery about the debacle. The bill had been ruined by the secret lobbying of the local mill owners backed by the Scottish master-spinners. The four Whig County Members were much too implicated in the interests of their wealthier constituents to make a stand against such a combination. Lord Morpeth, the most popular of those Members, at once expostulated. He regretted the 'wholesale curtailment' of the bill as much as anyone, and said he had protested to Hobhouse in private. But the unrelenting opposition of the Members from Scotland and of those from the southwestern woolen districts had made Hobhouse's position impossible. He hoped the cause would not be abandoned, though he warned that owing to 'the delicate and susceptible nature of trade' whoever undertook the responsibility for a new bill must have the advice of men with 'practical experience.'

Baines was sufficiently troubled to invite Hobhouse to send along his own explanation. The *Mercury* did not publish the full answer, but contented itself with quotation and summary. The main point that emerged was that the solid bloc of Scottish members had demanded that their constituencies be left out of the bill entirely. In this they had the support of Poulett Thomson at the Board of Trade; whereupon all the Members from the English industrial districts had said that if Scotland were given such special consideration they themselves would vote against the measure. The west-country woolen factors were bringing strong pressure to bear against it anyway, so Hobhouse claimed he had had no alternative but to accept the wrecking amendments and take what bill he could get.

Oastler, who had never doubted Hobhouse's good faith, was much dissatisfied with this summary, and believed the *Mercury* was trying to hold something back. So he wrote directly to Hobhouse, asking if he might have a copy of the letter.

Hobhouse's answer is very illuminating, alike for the information it conveys and the indication it gives of the sense of parliamentary possibilities entertained at this time by a generous-minded Radical. Rarely are the intangibles of political assumption so clearly revealed. Confirming the *Mercury's* report that the bitterest opposition to his measure had come from Scotland and the western counties, Hobhouse went on to warn Oastler against fostering among the workers hopes that were impossible of attainment:

I regret very much to perceive that the discussion on the factory system is mixed up with party politics in Yorkshire, and more especially of the town of Leeds—still more do I regret that the good operatives should have been so much deluded, either by very ignorant or designing men, as to promise themselves the accomplishment of what can never be realised. Those acquainted with the real state of the question, so far as parliament is concerned, know very well that nothing can be more idle than to talk of the possibility of limiting the hours of daily labour to ten for five days, and to eight on the Saturday—and I was, and am surprised to find, by Mr. Sadler's answer to the Huddersfield deputies, that the worthy member for Aldborough should appear to concur in views so extravagant, and which can only end in disappointment . . . The censures which, it seems, are passed upon those concerned in the recent Act, and more especially on myself, can proceed only from those altogether unacquainted with the circumstances of the case, and from those who know nothing of the difficulty of carrying a controverted measure through Parliament . . .

Should Mr. Sadler make the effort which he seems to contemplate, of limiting the hours of labour to ten, you may depend upon it he will not be allowed to proceed a single stage with any enactment, and, so far from producing any beneficial effects, he will only throw an air of ridicule and extravagance over the whole of this kind of legislation. I trust that, on mature reflection, that very respectable gentleman will adopt a more useful course of conduct, and in that case he may depend upon my exertions, such as they are, to second and encourage his honourable labour . . . I cannot conclude without hoping, that what I have thought right to impress upon your consideration may alter in some degree the opinions you have hitherto entertained as to the best mode of promoting the object which we have, I believe, mutually at heart.

Oastler replied to this with a letter scarcely less revealing which marks, so to speak, his political coming-of-age. After months of facile hope, he had at last learned that he had pitted himself against forces and attitudes far more powerful than he had originally supposed. The desired reforms, he now knew, would never come by the mere expectation of philanthropy. They would have to be fought for all the way; and that would mean campaigning and electioneering. Gradually, through the logic of events, Oastler was being driven to translate his old-world Toryism into a new Tory Democracy. It was only as the consequences of the defeat of Hobhouse's Bill made themselves apparent to him during the autumn of 1831 that he became aware of the process in which he was involved.

His letter was a token of that awareness. Instead of convincing him that the factory question had nothing to do with politics, he wrote, Hobhouse's explanations had had just the opposite effect. If the pressures from industrialists and economists had killed this bill, then the workers must create new pressures of their own:

I really think the 'good operatives' are quite as able to exercise a correct judgment on this question as they are on the very complicated one of 'parliamentary reform'; and you know the King himself and the government made that an 'electioneering question.' We are exhorted, I see, by Mr. Baines, to 'petition parliament.' This may be very right when we have secured good members; but if we are to have our petitions presented to a body of representatives, governed by 'the cold, calculating, but mistaken Scotch philosophers,' then I fancy we might as well save ourselves the trouble and expense . . . I have no doubt that a much more extensive measure will be adopted before many years are passed; and although, at present, the idea of working infants ONLY ten hours a day may appear ignorant, ridiculous, extravagant, idle, delusive, and impossible to the legislators of this country, I cannot doubt that, in a very short time, our legislators will hardly believe it was ever possible for a Christian parliament to refuse such an act.

The controversy dragged on into December. Three times Oastler joined the scuffle, on each occasion to assert that the Scottish and west-country interests were not alone responsible for Hobhouse's retreat. The Whig mill owners of Yorkshire had just as much to do with it as the others, he declared, so the self-righteous pose of the *Mercury* was an outrageous piece of hypocrisy. With the bitterest invective he had yet used he gave vent to the accumulated wrath of the last three months against young Baines, openly accusing that bland editorial writer of deliberate equivocation. None knew better than Baines, Oastler asserted, that Marshall, the Leeds linen magnate, and other of his friends had been working for weeks in London to destroy the bill. Yet all the while that the Baineses had been busy behind the scenes striving to make the proposed legislation as innocuous as possible, they had been proclaiming themselves in print as true champions of reform. In confirmation whereof, Oastler addressed to them 17 searching questions which he challenged them to answer on pain of self-conviction.

The *Mercury* made no attempt to answer the questions, of course; but it turned to castigate Oastler in equally vehement language. Long since had it stopped paying tribute to 'the sincerity of Mr. Oastler's motives.' Now it accused him of 'going on with the question' just in order to win votes for the Tory interest. The 'good sense' of the operatives was therefore invoked against his 'utopian project' of a Ten Hours law. Such a law would never be obeyed anyway, said one editorial; and if it were, it would ruin British industry.

This preoccupation with the next election is an increasingly marked feature of the *Mercury* after the debacle of September. Like Oastler, the Baineses were beginning to see that these social issues would erupt into the field of party differences to distort the conventional patterns. Philanthropy was becoming politics. It was therefore certain that when the next election did come it would be an affair of considerable bitterness.

CHAPTER X

Philanthropy Becomes Politics

D URING the autumn of 1831 England was in a state of contingent rebellion as a result of the rejection of the second Reform Bill by the House of Lords on 8 October and the proroga-
tion of Parliament eleven days later. After the overwhelming
Whig victory in the May elections, many had thought the passage
of 'the Bill' was assured. The disappointment of these hopes
caused a new fever of excitement to sweep the country. Tumultuous meetings in support of the Government were held in all
the big towns, the unprecedented popular demonstrations leading
in some instances to serious rioting.

Yet surprisingly enough there appeared to be no slackening
of interest in the factory question during those lurid weeks, but
rather the reverse. Several things accounted for this. One was
the enquiry that the northern journals conducted into the causes
of the recent fiasco; another, the increase in the number of Short
Time Committees and the wide extension of their propaganda
activities; a third, the feverish preparation by all parties (and
not least by the operatives) for the forthcoming general election, which the grave political situation seemed to make inevitable. In all these activities Oastler was extremely busy, behind
the scenes as well as publicly. The result was that by Christmas
everything was ready for launching a huge campaign on behalf
of a new factory bill.

¶ 1

While arguments and recriminations were following one another week after week in the local newspapers, the Short Time
Committees were quietly formulating their plans. Another factory bill would be brought forward in the near future: that much

could be taken for granted. The aim of the Committees, therefore, was to create a favorable public opinion in advance, just as Reform societies had prepared the way for the Whigs' franchise proposals. For this purpose two immediate possibilities offered themselves, and the Committees decided to make use of both; one was to build a special propagandist organization of their own, the other to enlist the help of such existing workers' associations as might be willing to co-operate.

Four effective Short Time Committees had come into being in the early part of the year, but apparently no more had been established until after the second reading of Hobhouse's Bill. From mid-August onwards, however, new groups began to form in one township after another. The hope was that a network of such committees might eventually cover the entire Riding so as to include every village and perhaps every factory as well. The pattern that the promoters had in mind was clearly the Wesleyan system of 'class meetings.'[1] It was a device already familiar to many of the operatives' leaders who (like the Huddersfield men) belonged to one or another of the Wesleyan sects. Oastler himself had grown up under the system; whenever he was confronted with problems of voluntary organization his thoughts immediately ran to the Wesleyan pattern, as he had shown when he created his anti-tithe organization to fight the Vicar of Halifax, and as he was to show again many a time later. The merit of the class-meeting system was its adaptability. It could be readily established in conjunction with any kind of neighborhood group, whether workshop or hamlet, chapel or public house. Throughout the autumn, therefore, Oastler was actively engaged in seconding the efforts of the Short Time Committees to get these cells started. Already he was beginning to have intimations of

[1] Every society in the Wesleyan Connexion organized these class meetings made up of a dozen or more of the faithful under a 'class leader.' They foregathered weekly at any available rendezvous—private house or hayloft, chapel or barn—for fellowship, devotion, and mutual help. Membership tickets were issued, a class roll was kept, and subscriptions of a penny a week were exacted. Above these was the Leaders' Meeting attended by all the class-leaders of the local society. Later in his career, Oastler consistently tried to make the factory reform organization approximate to this pattern more exactly, particularly by making it a 'membership' organization with formal enrollment and regular dues.

the dream that was afterwards to become almost an obsession with him: the creation of a huge fighting association composed of scores of these units co-ordinated by a central committee of resolute leaders determined on social reform.

But there were organizations already established whose help might be invoked too. At its regular Saturday night meeting at the Ship Inn at the beginning of October, the Huddersfield Short Time Committee decided to circularize all the trade unions, sick-benefit clubs, and friendly societies of the Riding, asking for their support. If only they could be brought into one comprehensive drive for a Ten Hours Bill the movement might assume an entirely different character. It was with a keen sense of this possibility, therefore, that the Huddersfield Committee sent out their circular letter:

TO THE FRIENDLY SOCIETIES AND UNIONS OF ALL DESCRIPTIONS.

Gentlemen,

Deeply impressed with the conviction that the working classes of this Empire owe a great duty to themselves, and especially to their children; and that Brotherly Associations etc. can do, and ought to do more than they hitherto have done in the cause of civilisation, and in the diffusion of knowledge, we earnestly and respectfully call upon you to operate, conjointly with each other and with us, in discharging this sacred obligation.

Behold the little slaves!—Is it not a shame and a disgrace that, in a Land emphatically called the Land of Bibles, children of a tender age should be torn from their beds by six in the morning, and confined, in pestiferous factories, till eight in the evening?—Why, the children of our colonial slaves are not so harshly treated; so toiled, nor so abused, as ours! Heaven forbid that such should be the case much longer!— Ten hours a day, with eight on Saturdays, and a Time Book is our motto—may it be yours. We do indeed hope, that our sentiments on the subject are alike—if so—let the expression of them be simultaneous! —A general Election is at hand; let no man over whom you have any legal control, enter the House of Commons, without having first pledged himself to bring in, or support a measure which shall abolish infantile slavery.

Gentlemen, let us rouse ourselves from Lethargy and Carelessness, and rally round the principles of humanity, with an irresistible voice, demand the immediate curtailment of the hours of Factory Labour!—

cry for the instantaneous emancipation of our little ones,—and thus accomplish this great and necessary Deed of National Mercy!

You are requested to send copies of this circular to your respective Lodges in other Towns.

I am, Gentlemen,

By order of the Short Time Bill Committee of Operatives,

Your most obedient Servant,

John Leech.

N.B. Any sum, however small, subscribed by you for this Cause will be gratefully acknowledged.

This meeting over which Oastler presided—it was 6 October 1831, the first Saturday since Hobhouse's defeat had become known—marked the opening of a new chapter. All these problems of organization and propaganda were discussed in detail and a general line of policy was agreed upon. From that night forward, the Ten Hours Movement really had a plan of campaign. Circumstances had destroyed the possibility that the operatives would be content with the kind of well-meaning compromise that had come out of the Talbot gathering only eleven months earlier. 'Ten Hours a day and a Time Book' was to be the slogan of the new campaign.

¶ 2

The following Monday Oastler inaugurated the new phase by writing the sixth, and in some respects the most impressive, of his letters on 'Yorkshire Slavery.' It caught the new mood exactly and was given even more publicity than the previous letters. It was reprinted as a broadside, cast into pamphlet form, pasted on walls, and distributed to public houses.

Appended as footnotes to the letter were descriptions of actual instances of overworking, which Oastler had been personally investigating in Huddersfield. All were taken from those mills whose owners had so furtively petitioned against legislation the previous August. It was the first time he had used the citation of concrete cases to support his theoretical arguments; after this he did so constantly, both in speech and pamphlet.

At one of these mills, . . . a boy about ten or eleven years of age
has worked for five months from SIX o'clock in the morning to TEN
o'clock at night—say FOURTEEN hours work per day, allowing two
hours for meals. This boy has very frequently been sick and ill when
he has been kept to his labour; nine days ago, however, he was
obliged to be laid up and has not yet returned to his work. About
FORTY boys have worked along with him. Now the master of this
mill is a strenuous petitioner against 'Negro Slavery' and at the same
time a practicer of, and petitioner for 'Yorkshire Slavery.' If he be
what he professes, he is also a very good Christian. Let him name
forty boys in the West Indies as cruelly treated as these boys of his
are, or, if he fail, let him blush, repent, and be just . . .

Another of these humane petitioners exacts the following fines from
children who earn from sevenpence to eightpence for TWELVE hours
work. If a child be five minutes too late, he pays THREE-HALFPENCE;
if fifteen minutes THREEPENCE; if forty-five minutes SIXPENCE. Some
of these children sleep miles from the mills, and everybody knows how
the millclocks are managed. The 'fine-Marker' pockets half the amount
for the purpose of sharpening his appetite . . .

At a mill near Huddersfield, where little children are worked
NIGHT and DAY, and where the internal arrangements are revolting
to morality and disgusting to human nature, a clergyman of the
Church of England, minister of the township, was wishful to 'see
with his own eyes and hear with his own ears' what this system was,
but the 'benevolent factory master' absolutely refused to let him visit
his flock. Now this millman is one of the greatest 'liberals' of the town
and would sign petitions for everlasting against 'Negro Slavery,' and
if a West Indian slaveholder were to refuse to allow a clergyman to
visit his slaves, this 'kind creature' would require no further proof
that the system was horrifying. In all the West Indies this man could
find no parallel for cruelty and misery to this sink of oppression under
his own nose; and caused by himself for his own profit; and yet he is
a 'real liberal.'

But take another anecdote or two from these Huddersfield mills. I
really think these masters would have been wiser had they not petitioned. They have provoked inquiry and inquiry is sure to lead to
exposure and exposure must produce disgrace. ——, aged about
eleven years, and —— about thirteen years old, live about three
miles from —— mill at which they work. Last Friday week these
boys began work at the mill at six o'clock in the morning and absolutely worked till five o'clock on Saturday evening, say thirty-five

hours, with only the following time for meals: at half-past eight
o'clock, half an hour; at twelve, an hour; at five, half an hour; at
twelve o'clock at night, an hour; at half past four on Saturday morning, half an hour; at half past eight, half an hour; at twelve o'clock
at noon, an hour. And then they work till five on Saturday evening
and walk home nearly three miles . . .

This is not Slavery, is it? The man is intemperate, is he, who exposes
this accursed system? I am not speaking of things afar off. This is no
West Indian cruelty. It is practised upon individuals who reside within
a mile from where I am writing. Practised by men called Christians,
by 'Liberals' of the 19th century. What are the ministers of religion
doing? Would that they would raise their voices and resolutely interfere for these their lambs.

This challenging manifesto was powerfully supplemented by
a forty-page pamphlet compiled by the Huddersfield Committee
and published early in December under the title *Humanity
Against Tyranny*. It was the first of a long series of such works
called forth by the factory movement, and so comprehensive in
scope that for the next several months it served as a kind of
speaker's handbook. For the first time it gave the public the
full story of the petition against Hobhouse's Bill from the ten
local firms, and reprinted all the correspondence. It cogently
presented the case for state regulation in terms of the three lines
of reasoning which had been gradually developed during the
newspaper controversy: that is to say, the humanitarian plea, the
share-the-work argument, and the underconsumption idea. It answered the masters' hostile petition item by item, and ended with
a superb appeal for social purposiveness to replace the policy of
laissez-faire.

Nowhere at this time is there to be found a more vivid or
succinct presentation of the theme of the 'two nations,' which
Disraeli was to make into a novel a decade later. 'While one
part of the community is rolling in the most excessive luxury,
starvation, yea destitution in all forms and in almost every degree are the lot of the poor . . . millions toil, not indeed for
use but for waste.' The root of the trouble, said the Committee,
was the unrestrained competition which led to repeated wage
cuts and the simultaneous intensification of labor.

How strange that machinery should have an inverted and continually diverging effect upon society, rendering the condition of those attendant upon it worse and worse while others are reaping its amazing productiveness in pernicious luxury.

What logic, they asked, could justify such a situation? Yet simply because Oastler had dared to challenge this paradox in the name of moral sense he had been jeered at and reviled:

Facts, authenticated not hearsays, numerous not isolated, facts hideous to think of, have been brought to light. The *Leeds Mercury* now asserts the system is 'monstrous' [2] though it still requires infants to labour longer per day than full grown men. And Marshall himself has become a convert to the Factory Bill!!! If this be true, who shall say good has not been effected? Our Cause must triumph, its advocates increase; their sublime appeals have reverberated through the recesses of cruelty. The Factory Child has shaken the foundation of Tyranny. Let us not faint till we have won our children emancipation.

It is certainly a striking document: the distillation of a year's wrangling in press, public house, and workshop. Few such pamphlets can stand the test of other than academic rereading, but this is one of the few. If the endorsement of another century be a tribute to social insight, then that little group in the back room of a Huddersfield inn command a measure of respect, for few today would care to deny their basic contentions.

¶ 3

Preparations for the expected general election served to publicize the cause of factory reform still more effectively.

No one knew, of course, when the election would come; as matters turned out, it did not occur until December of the following year. Yet a full fifteen months before then, the political organizations in most of the leading towns were seeking candidates of sufficient distinction to rally the interests of their respective parties. Rarely, indeed, has a British election campaign been

[2] See above, p. 54. The ironical comment upon the flax-magnate Marshall is in reference to an editorial in the *Mercury* of 19 November declaring that Oastler's strictures upon the 'liberals' were unjust, that all liberals—even so great a manufacturer as Marshall—favored sensible factory reform, and that they themselves had 'always advocated it.'

as protracted as that of 1832. Long before the climax of the Reform struggle was reached, electoral addresses were being issued, squibs were flying, counter-broadsheet was being pasted over broadsheet, and argument was growing steadily more acrimonious. Leeds was naturally one of the first places where the battle was joined, for according to the terms of 'the Bill' it would return two Members to a reformed Parliament. Nowhere in the country did partisans on both sides display greater bitterness than in the West Riding, largely because of the fact that nowhere else was the straight issue of Whig against Tory so complicated by a strong movement for social reform cutting across the old party lines.

It was taken for granted that one of the two Whig candidates would be the younger John Marshall, son of the famous Leeds flax spinner whose rise to fortune and a threefold alliance with the nobility made yet another of the big success stories of the industrial revolution. His fellow-candidate, it was soon learned, was to be Thomas Babington Macaulay, the brilliant scholar who had already created for himself a national reputation by his contributions to the *Edinburgh Review* and was at the moment sitting in Parliament for one of Lord Landsdowne's pocket boroughs. On the Tory side the obvious candidate was Oastler's old friend Michael Sadler, who held his present seat for Aldborough as a nominee of the Duke of Newcastle. Coming from a prominent local family of merchants and bankers and long identified with Yorkshire Toryism as Wilberforce's political agent, he was one of the few men who could be expected to put up much of a fight against the powerful combination the Whigs were running.

Marshall's return was certain; no one doubted that. The real fight would be between Macaulay and Sadler for the second seat. It was a strange chance that threw these two men into opposition, for a greater contrast of personalities it would be hard to find. The one was scintillating, erudite, and assured; the other introverted, pious, and diffident. Macaulay, the lionized conversationalist of Whig salons, aspiring to become the philosopher-statesman of Whig reform; Sadler, the Sunday-school superintendent wrestling with himself to achieve nameless victories in the world of the spirit. The former the lusty exponent of the gospel of progress; the latter yearning for a romanticized yesterday, 'when every cottager had a cow and every cottager's wife had a spinning wheel.' And to this clash of temperaments was added a measure of personal animosity too. In his book on the *Law of Population* Sadler had fiercely assailed the prevailing doctrines of Malthus, to which Macaulay had recently replied in two articles which rank among the century's masterpieces of literary invective. So this was no ordinary contest being staged at Leeds; and the fact that Macaulay had been brought in by the manufacturing interests whereas Sadler was the acknowledged champion of factory regulation served to enhance the dramatic quality of the struggle.

The campaign was opened in a curious but highly significant way by a Reverend Richard Watson. This Watson was one of the most prominent figures in the Wesleyan Connexion. For one thing, he was its Missionary Secretary; and for another, as the author of the *Institutes of Religion* he was the leading Methodist theologian of his day. His words therefore carried especial weight. In the middle of September 1831, he took it upon himself to write a letter from London to the superintendent of the Leeds circuit, espousing the cause of Macaulay (particularly on account of Macaulay's championship of slave emancipation) and belittling Sadler. The letter was read to the congregations in several of the chapels around Leeds and then, unfortunately, given out to the newspapers. The consequences were deplorable. A controversy of the utmost ferocity raged for weeks in press and pulpit as henchmen on both sides carried the vilification of their rivals to greater and greater lengths. The *Mercury,* of course, made itself the mouthpiece of the Watson-Macaulay party, while the Tory *Intelligencer* and the Radical *Patriot* joined their voices in defense of Sadler.

This episode would make an interesting case study for the sociologist. At first glance it may look like an ordinary, sordid electoral squabble, but closer examination shows it to have an importance much greater than that: one, moreover, with no little bearing upon the politics of the factory question. In reality it was part of a struggle for the unpledged Methodist vote, involving the whole question of the political implications of evangelicism.

Methodism at this time was in a peculiar position in relation to party alignments. The alliance of Toryism and the Church of England was firm and unquestioned: that went back to the seventeenth century. Equally firm was the alliance between Whiggery and Dissent—Congregational, Baptist, Unitarian, and the rest—which had been sealed by the Hanoverian settlement of 1714. But Methodism came somewhere in between the two. John Wesley, though himself a Tory, had sought to keep the Methodists free from party entanglements, and out of loyalty to their leader most of his followers had observed the no-politics rule during his lifetime. After his death in 1791, however, the leaven of democratic sentiment began to work within the Societies, particularly in Yorkshire. Kilham's secession, which Robert Oastler had supported, was only an extreme manifestation of this, and the establishment of his New Connexion meant an additional member for the Whig-Dissent alliance. Official Methodism nevertheless went on trying to keep clear of politics. In the period of reaction after Waterloo, when the ruling classes were obsessed with the phobia of revolution, it consistently proclaimed its loyalty to the established order and sought by every means in its power to free itself from all suspicion of 'radicalism.' But by 1831 things had changed greatly and the cloud of fear had lifted. The July Revolution in France, the overthrow of Wellington, the accession of the Whigs to office, and the introduction of the middle-class Reform Bill together transformed the national mood. As a result, the latent elements of liberalism inherent in both the psychology of Methodism and the personnel of its societies increasingly began to manifest themselves. Particularly was this the case in the Leeds district, where a rugged, self-assertive liberalism was clearly to be seen among the Methodist laity from Kilham's day onward. The process thus started took another two generations to complete, but by the end of the century in most constituencies in England the alliance of Wesleyanism with the Liberal party could be taken for granted.

So Watson's letter was explosive with meaning for West Riding politicians. Ten years earlier, perhaps even five, it could hardly have been written. Coming at that particular time, however, it stood for something stirring within Wesleyanism itself. Despite the official neutrality of the Wesleyan Conference, this was frankly an appeal to local Methodists to support the middle-class Whig cause. And the outcry it provoked was just as revealing as the letter. Sadler, too, was a Methodist. But whereas Watson sought to rally Wesleyan evangelicism to political liberalism, Sadler sought to rally it to humanitarian reform. The unsavory controversy thus brought out the deep cleavage in the ranks of Wesley's followers. 'The fact is,' as E. E. Kellett has so wisely reminded us, 'that within the small realm of Methodism there were, as in the larger realm of England, Disraeli's Two Nations: and there was between them the same misunderstanding as in the wider world.' In addition to its working-class membership, it embraced large numbers of manufacturers, tradesmen, and artisans who were rising in the social scale. Apart from their religion, there was little in common between the prominent Wesleyan mill owners, who had petitioned against Hobhouse's Bill and assented to the Halifax Resolutions, and the simple operatives who had joined the Short Time Committees and made the Fixby Hall Compact. The former gravitated inevitably towards the new Liberalism, which comported with all their economic and social aspirations; they could never have felt really at home in a Tory party that looked with suspicion upon 'trade.' The latter, on the other hand, were driven of practical necessity to seek amelioration of their lot through the radical hope of manhood suffrage as advocated by the *Patriot* and through regulatory reform as espoused by Sadler. This also explains Oastler's growing animosity towards the Wesleyans. Months earlier he had been astonished by the opposition or indifference which so many of the more prosperous Methodists had shown towards his plea. Later on he was to be even more shocked when, time after time, he was refused the use of their chapels for his meetings. From the Primitive Methodists [3] he invariably received

[3] The Primitive Methodists seceded from the parent body (mainly on matters of church organization) in 1811. Their membership was recruited chiefly from the lower classes of society to whom they preached a fervent evangelicism. It has been called 'pre-eminently a layman's church' on ac-

a hearty welcome, and for them he always retained a warm regard; but for Connexional Wesleyanism he came to have only a
deep contempt.

¶ 4

It was not the role of the Wesleyan voter, however, nor even
the dramatic quality of the fight between two such champions as
Macaulay and Sadler, that gave this famous Leeds election its
deepest significance. The real import of the contest lay in the
fact that a new pattern of political forces was in the making:
one, moreover, that might have a bearing upon the political con-
figuration of the rest of the country. This was clearly going to be
a struggle of the middle-class Whig interests against the rest;
and 'the rest' included both those who called themselves Tories
and those who professed to be Radicals. The open question was
whether Toryism and Radicalism could be brought into combination, not merely for temporary political advantage but as a permanent party with an intelligible purpose.

Oastler believed they could. Generalizing from the Fixby Hall
Compact between himself and the Huddersfield workers, he had
come to entertain the possibility of extending such an alliance
first to the rest of the West Riding and then to the country at
large. Furthermore, he had become passionately convinced that
such a consummation was imperatively necessary for the national
well-being. Unless some popular union of this sort were speedily
brought about, he was persuaded, Britain was going to be completely made over in the capitalists' interest. This was the identical conception that Disraeli was to make famous during the
next decade. The purpose of *Coningsby*, said its author in 1849,
was 'to vindicate the just claims of the Tory party to be the
popular confederation of the country.' Oastler was here setting
himself to make that same vindication 18 years earlier.

There was nothing inherently unrealistic in the idea of a fusion
between Toryism and Radicalism at that time. Shrewd contempo-

---

count of the markedly subordinate role which the ministers played in its
administration. The available evidence shows that the 'Primitives' were
enthusiastic supporters of Oastler. Many times when he was denied a forum
elsewhere he found one in the local Primitive Methodist chapel.

rary publicists in the Whig camp showed plainly enough by their comments that they were far from regarding such a move as beyond the bounds of possibility. It is only when considered in terms of preconceptions and alignments derived from a later age that the suggestion seems at all anomalous. Political energies were in an extremely fluid condition and there was no certainty about the molds in which they would finally become set. The working classes were as yet by no means conscious of their proletarian status: that could come only with fuller industrialization and the wider extension of factory discipline. Moreover, though the old deference-structure of society was perceptibly changing, it had in no sense vanished. Since the boundaries of affiliation were not fixed, genuine alternatives seemed available. Thus, to outward appearances at least, England in the eighteen-thirties seemed to contain almost as many possibilities of political nucleation as continental countries were to display later.

Other considerations that were to prove equally relevant to Oastler's future have to be taken into the reckoning, too. For one thing, an essential element in the Tory tradition was the principle of social control—a principle entirely at variance with the spirit of the new individualism espoused by the employers. That control, it is true, had hitherto been used in the interests of an aristocratic class. But was it expecting too much from the Tories to ask that they should show themselves far-sighted enough to respond to the contemporary challenge by putting into that formal principle a new, positive content appropriate to an age of industrial change? In other words, were they capable of enriching their conception of 'station and duties' with the guarantee of those minimal social decencies that alone can secure the healthy maintenance of any kind of hierarchical structure? Southey and Coleridge had already indicated their belief that such an adjustment was possible. And Oastler was soon to find there were many others who thought the same way.[4]

----

[4] A vigorous exponent of this line of thought was the Leeds Tory, Sir John Beckett. One paragraph from a speech Beckett made later Oastler went on quoting for years. Political matters are secondary to the question of social welfare, Beckett had said: 'That is an object which I think every Government ought to pursue with a steady and unflinching hand. If they can introduce regulations by which labor shall be better paid, for God's sake let

On the other hand, the motivation of working-class Radicalism
was the longing for better conditions of life. The demand for the
vote was primarily a demand for the means to achieve that end.
And not all who were racked with the longing had the doctrinaire
conviction that the vote was the indispensable means. Conceiv-
ably a leader with the right quality of appeal promising speedy
delivery of tangible benefits could rally this enormous mass of
the discontented to a mighty effort on behalf of social reform.
Certainly both the *Reviews* displayed an apprehensive faith in
the power of 'agitators' to fashion the allegiance of the mob.

In some respects Sadler was particularly well qualified for being the candidate of such a Radical-Tory fusion. Of his Toryism
there could be no doubt, while to the sincerity of his philanthropy, 25 years of selfless local service bore witness. From his
personal experience he knew only too well the appalling misery to
which the underprivileged in cellar, garret, and slum might be
condemned. And deeply did he feel the obligation laid upon him
to mitigate such suffering as he could. For him, as for Oastler,
Toryism was a creed of public obligations to be discharged no
less than of duties to be demanded, and in his own life he sought
to live forth that conviction. In the absence of an independent
Radical candidate, therefore, the circumstances at Leeds were
peculiarly propitious for testing the possibility of fusion politics,
for while Sadler in no sense represented the radicalism of manhood suffrage he did in a very real way embody the other radicalism of social reform. His fifteen-months-long electoral campaign
thus provides an illuminating commentary upon this emerging
ideology that was to have such an odd fate during the rest of the
century.

¶ 5

Oastler, who had as big a hand in shaping Sadler's campaign
strategy as the Baineses had in shaping Marshall's, did everything

---

them do it . . . As to superabundant labour, I don't believe in any such
thing . . . Peace at home means contentment at home; and unless we can
establish such a system of things as will afford men a fairer remuneration
for their labour and enable them to maintain themselves and their families
in comfort, there *can* be no peace at home; there never *will* be peace at
home; there never *ought* to be peace at home.'

in his power to dramatize the contrast between the rival candidates and their philosophies. On 13 October, Marshall's acceptance of candidature and statement of principles was published. It was a straightforward bourgeois pronouncement without mention of the factory question. On its positive side it called for public economy and the passage of the Reform Bill, and on its negative for the abolition of the corn laws, Negro slavery, and all monopolies. Three weeks later Oastler staged an answer. A deputation of workers from the Huddersfield Short Time Committee waited upon Sadler at his Leeds home to present him on behalf of the operatives they represented with an *Address* of gratitude for all his efforts, beginning as follows:

Honoured Friend—if by such an endearing appellation we may be allowed to address you. But we feel confident you will not consider us too presumptuous in calling you *our* friend notwithstanding the great disparity of condition and circumstances there is betwixt you and us;— and especially when we reflect upon your devotedness to the cause of suffering humanity and consider those noble and energetic and disinterested appeals you have so frequently made to the government in behalf of the poor of this country, we are encouraged not only to recognize you as a *friend* but also to look upon you as a *father* who is ever wishful to promote the welfare and happiness of his children. We are indeed fully convinced in our minds that your benevolent disposition, which seems so much delighted in doing all the good you possibly can to those who stand in need of help, will not be the less gratified by this familiar, friendly and grateful address which we, the Committee of Operatives of Huddersfield and its vicinity here present to you in the name and on behalf of our fellow workmen.

Sadler made an appropriately gracious reply the tone of which was set by the significant remark:

You have conferred upon me the ennobling appellation of being your *friend;* a friend to that class of the community which, however neglected or abused, *alone creates the wealth and constitutes the strength of this great and powerful Empire.*

This was the first move made to promote the Radical-Tory fusion, and all possible publicity was given to it. To the surprise of many, the manhood-suffrage champions greeted the gesture

with just as much enthusiasm as the Tories. The formerly suspicious *Patriot* gave the alliance its warmest blessing, reporting
the story prominently on its front page and running an eloquent
editorial upon it:

Never mind, Sir, the attacks of the wicked and malignant which, as
sure as darkness succeeds the day, will be levelled against you. The
money-getters and the money-changers will be in arms against you,
but these have been 'moved out of the temple' before by the greatest
friend of the friendless the world has yet beheld. And to the operatives of Huddersfield we would say: You have done yourselves great
credit. Continue to distinguish your real from your pretended friends,
and days of relief and enjoyment are not so far distant as some of the
oppressed ones may imagine.

Tory Democracy as an operative force in British politics must
be reckoned as beginning that first Saturday night in November
1831, when the Huddersfield men called upon Sadler to offer their
support. The owners of the *Mercury* showed that they realized
something of the implications of the move by instantly launching
a virulent attack on 'the contemptible trickery by which the Tories
of Leeds have attempted to wheedle the working classes out of
their principles.' For years to come, in the lack of any other topic,
complaint of such 'trickery' was to be a frequent theme in northern Whig newspapers.

But the creation of a new radical Toryism was going to be
no easy undertaking. Difficulties both of organization and psychology were involved, which not only hampered Sadler's efforts
at the moment but were also to handicap Oastler's work later.
For instance: was Sadler being supported by a temporary coalition of separate parties, or was he creating a new party? This
was no mere academic question, since it involved important consequences for his electoral tactics. Yet no definite answer was
forthcoming. The result was that throughout the campaign the
Sadler forces were operating with a confused symbolism which
could not fail to play into the hands of the other side. The Whigs
had a coherent set of slogans and a facile gospel of promise, while
over their bastions there daily flew the single orange flag of
'Reform.' But Sadler's men had none of these advantages. Their

symbols were still in the making; and at every meeting their platform had perforce to be adorned with two banners—the Tory blue and the Radical white—neither of which might be denied its place. To add to these difficulties, the very name Tory was a heavy liability to carry. Was it not ineffaceably associated with the horror of Peterloo and a policy of brutal reaction? An outstanding feature of this Leeds election struggle, therefore, is the continuous effort made by the Ten Hours men to combat the inhibitions associated with the label Sadler bore. Numerous correspondents wrote to the papers hoping (as one of them put it) 'that the people will no more be led away from the path of rectitude merely by the *name* or *colour* the individual may bear, as has too often been the case, and make their best friends the objects of popular vengeance.' One of the first election pamphlets given wide circulation through the constituency was devoted to the same theme. It was written by a Radical named Cavie Richardson, and took the form of *An Address to the Working Classes of Leeds and the West Riding.* 'Sadler is a Tory, Oastler is a Tory, Perring is a Tory, and Foster [5] is a Radical,' it said; 'but, noble-minded men, they lay aside their differences for a while to maintain the cause of the poor.' 'Recognise your own true friends!' should be the workers' watchword.

First and foremost in the front of the battle appears our matchless Oastler; yea, blessings on his heart; the poor innocents shall lisp his name; you shall make mention of his excellent acts, and you and your smiling happy (still not idle) children shall bless their Deliverer.

¶ 6

Meanwhile, plans for a new Factory Bill were going forward behind the scenes, and the hope was that it might be pushed through Parliament before the dissolution came. This time it was going to be no partial measure, but a real Ten Hours Bill. That meant Sadler would have to introduce it, since Hobhouse and Morpeth had both so plainly made known their conviction that the project was chimerical. The three leading Short Time Committees therefore entered into consultation and named a representative deputation to call upon Sadler to make the formal request that he would become their parliamentary champion. Oastler went with them, Sadler expressed himself strongly in favor of the idea, and after a gratifying conference the men came away with a promise that the bill would be brought forward at the first opportunity. Thereupon, in preparation for its introduction, the Leeds committee deliberately provoked a new correspondence controversy in the *Mercury* by writing to ask why that journal favored an eleven-hour rather than a ten-hour day.

[5] Perring was editor of the *Leeds Intelligencer;* Foster owned and edited the *Leeds Patriot.*

Oastler's First Debate

SOME TIME early in the new year, then, a Ten Hours Bill was really going to be introduced into Parliament. This meant that the Short Time Committees must immediately start mobilizing public opinion on its behalf to prevent the House of Commons from shuffling out of its responsibilities as it had done over Hobhouse's Bill. On that occasion not a single London newspaper had reported the course of the measure. Such crushing indifference could at least be shaken this time by the right kind of propaganda. What the Committees planned to do, therefore, was to hold a series of well-publicized preliminary meetings for the operatives in their respective districts, and then follow this up with a campaign of monster meetings to rouse the general public just before Sadler brought forward his bill. In that way Parliament would be compelled to give the factory question full and open consideration. As things turned out, the plan worked more effectively and dramatically than its promoters could possibly have foreseen.

The opening of the struggle, however, took the unexpected form of a public debate between Oastler and the two Baineses: an episode which was to have important consequences for the rest of the scheme.

The first of the operatives' meetings was planned to take place on Saturday night, 10 December, at the Union Inn headquarters of the Leeds Short Time Committee. Delegations from all the mills in the vicinity were asked to attend, and Oastler was invited as a matter of course. It was hoped to make the meeting the most representative gathering of workers that had yet been held in connection with the Movement.

Oastler rode over to Leeds late in the afternoon to help the

Committee complete its arrangements. When he arrived he found that that day's issue of the *Mercury* contained yet another attack upon him in the form of a letter purporting to come from 'A Friend to the Poor.' It was frankly a personal attack, hinting at strained relations between Thornhill and his steward over the factory question, and suggesting that the latter was guilty of rackrenting and maltreating the Fixby tenants; the writer drew the obvious conclusions regarding Oastler's sincerity. To which the editor had added half-a-column of supplementary jibes of his own.

When Oastler read this he was roused to fighting anger. As soon as the Committee assembled, he told them he wanted both the Baineses present at the meeting. If they could be induced to come, he would answer all their sneers and innuendos to their faces and force them to drop the equivocalities they kept resorting to in their paper. It was an opportunity he had been seeking for a long time.

A deputation at once went to the Baines home and brought back father and son. But for over an hour the audience was kept waiting while a wrangle went on in an adjoining room concerning the exact purpose of the meeting. The Baineses said they had agreed to come solely on the supposition that they were being asked to debate the Ten Hours issue, and that if they had been inveigled there for any other purpose they were not going to stay. The Short Time Committee had no intention of letting them leave, however, now it actually had them in its midst. A compromise was therefore reached. It was agreed that the formal proceedings should be confined to a consideration of the Ten Hours proposal; if there were any time left at the end, Oastler would make his reply to the *Mercury's* attacks and the Baineses could stay or go as they chose.

The large room of the Inn was packed to the doors. Over 300 operatives were crowded into the place, tense and expectant, and more than that number had already been turned away. Presiding over them was John Hammond, founder of the Leeds Committee, who had already made himself prominent by the part he had played in the newspaper controversy and particularly by his drafting of the workers' answer to the Halifax Reso-

lutions.[1] Proceedings were pitched in a high key of excitement
with the opening announcement that Sadler was about to bring
a Ten Hours Bill before Parliament. The news had been held
back for this particular occasion and its effect was electric as
the organizers had calculated. On top of that came a reading of
the latest controversy in the *Mercury* on the ten-hours-or-eleven
issue, which the Committee had recently precipitated; then
young Baines was called upon to present the case for an eleven-
hour day.

Baines gave his hearers the desiccated gospel of contemporary
economic orthodoxy. His main thesis was that the immutable
laws of economics could not be transgressed without bringing
disaster upon the whole community, and that a ten-hour day
would do just that. He was as much a friend of the workers as
anyone, he said, but he was a friend of the masters too. The
two interests were complementary and equally menaced by foreign competition. Britain's competitors were running her very
close; they did not restrict their working day, nor did they carry
the same enormous burden of debt and taxation. Injudicious
factory legislation would therefore be a final and fatal handicap to the nation. The economic sorites was clear: a restricted
working day would mean diminished output; diminished output
would lead to higher prices; higher prices would cause a con-
traction of the market, and that in turn would entail a further
decrease in production. The result would be wholesale unemployment. Masters running their mills 13 hours as at present
would immediately become bankrupt, for though the proposed
bill applied only to children, everyone who knew anything about
the industry fully realized that regulation of child labor was
tantamount to regulating adult labor as well. Moreover, the
operatives ought to remember that it was not only a matter of
the masters' bankruptcy; even if some concerns were able to
keep going, wages would have to be cut in direct proportion
to the cut in hours. An eleven-hour day thus represented the
very limit of economic possibility. Even that, the meeting was
given to understand, would bring the country uncomfortably
close to the abyss.

[1] See above, p. 83.

Whether it was the substance of Baines's speech that angered the audience, or his arrogance, we cannot tell, but angered they certainly were. Time after time groans and protests interrupted him, and only Oastler's vigorous appeal for fair play got him a hearing. Immediately he sat down Ralph Taylor rose to reply. Taylor, who had been on the Short Time Committee from its inception, was one of the ablest of the Leeds Radicals and had been largely responsible for the Tory-Radical fusion on behalf of Sadler. By inverting the whole of Baines's main argument, he made an effective debating rejoinder. Wages, he said, were not 'regulated by arithmetic or political economy'; to suppose they were was unrealistic. What determined wages was the supply of labor. If the working day were shortened, obviously the demand for labor would be increased. This increased demand would actually raise wages, not lower them, and that would naturally lead to an expansion of the home market which Baines's analysis had entirely ignored. The foreign-competition argument was nothing but a bogey raised by such men as the Leeds manufacturer near by that very inn, who was at that moment working his hands 16 hours a day without even intermission for meals. The point was taken with wild applause.

Then Oastler rose. It was the first time most of these Leeds men had seen him, and the first occasion at which he had been called upon to speak on behalf of the movement he had unwittingly initiated. He was not new to public speaking, of course. He had preached in Methodist chapels in his younger days and addressed many a missionary meeting and anti-slavery gathering; and during the Halifax tithes dispute he had had plenty of opportunity to develop his debating skill. But this was something different, at once more personal and more consequential than anything he had undertaken before.

With his opening words he refused even to examine the arguments of young Baines. This, he declared, was no mere matter of arithmetical calculation but a grave moral issue. 'I would ask, as a Christian, upon what authority and under what necessity is a parent compelled to act the part of a tyrant to his child?' Foreign commerce had nothing to do with the matter. 'Whatever the size of our trade, if it depend upon making infants work more than adults and upon supporting the most horrid system of slavery in the world, I would say: *sink your commerce, and rise Humanity, Benevolence and Christianity.*' These factory children were beings with immortal souls and an eternal destiny, but what opportunities did the factory system allow them for achieving any kind of spiritual worth at all? All over the Riding, as had now been conclusively demonstrated, they were being made to work under shocking conditions from 14 to 17 hours out of the 24. How was it possible for them to grow into decent citizens and God-fearing parents after such a start in life? Yet young Baines had been crass enough to introduce questions about taxation and the national debt! 'Is it to be borne,' Oastler thundered, 'that the expenses of government and the national debt should be paid out of the bodies and souls of poor infants? And have we really come to the pass that with the Bible in our hands, professing to be guided by its precepts, we act as if we thought it right to sell immortal souls for dirty gold?'

There was no question of setting men against masters, he went on, as the enemies of reform had alleged. This 'cannibal' system of cut-throat competition was ruining all alike, but men were blinded to the fact by the dreadful hold which a false economic philosophy had over their heads and hearts. 'Political economists are the natural enemies of the Bill,' he declared. No issue could be simpler: this was a straight fight between humanity and greed.

This speech was a remarkable performance; and by all accounts, to have heard it must have been a stirring experience. Nothing comparable to it had been heard in the Riding since Cobbett's last visit. The excitement of the audience became intense as the speech rolled on. Round after round of applause punctuated the argument as it swept forward, and when Oastler at last sat down after a telling peroration the crowd sprang to its feet cheering wildly.

For the elder Baines to follow was no easy task. It was evident to all present that he was considerably shaken, and it was equally clear that as a mere debate the affair was over. 'Quite a new light has been thrown upon my mind by Mr. Oastler's speech,' Baines admitted. If the masters could be brought to

agree to a Ten Hours Bill as well as the men, he said, 'then in
the name of God let them have ten hours.' As far as he was concerned, the matter could be left to the two parties involved. He
had defended the eleven hours' position only because Hobhouse
had assured him nothing better could be hoped for; if he had
been misinformed he was prepared to withdraw his opposition.
As to Oastler's general humanitarian argument, there was no
sort of disagreement between them. He himself had never once
dismissed a workman in the whole of his career, and he was as
anxious as anyone to see decency and security established in all
factories. The evil of overtime working he denounced almost as
vehemently as Oastler had done. Altogether it was a dignified
and impressive reply.

Oastler immediately rose to underline all the admissions Baines
had just made and to point out how effectively they invalidated
his son's arguments. Then he passed on to protest vigorously
against the malicious turn the controversy had taken in that
day's *Mercury*. What was published there was a tissue of lies.
He had kept the 'good old-fashioned aristocrat' Thornhill fully
informed of everything he had said and done, and the Squire's
only complaint had been that Oastler's letters were too long!
The charge of maltreating the Fixby tenants was a stupid calumny. He was prepared to submit the accusation to a commission of tenants under Baines's own chairmanship. Baines, however, declined the challenge, though he was gracious enough to
second the motion of gratitude to 'the operatives' friend Mr.
Oastler' which the meeting thereupon carried with a rousing
'three-times-three.'

Oastler had scored a resounding success. But the ultimate importance of the meeting lay in the fact that through it he had
stumbled upon the discovery of his unique oratorical talents: on
the eve of his forty-second birthday he had at last found his
'vocation,' as the old-fashioned pietists would have called it.
The consequences of his first letter fifteen months before had
been far-reaching; the consequences of his first speech were to
be even more so. For some weeks now, the Committees had been
talking about the mass demonstrations they were going to hold
in the New Year. By this triumph Oastler had made himself the

obvious leader of that campaign. Henceforth he was to be dedicated to the platform.

The debate was given remarkable publicity and was the talk of the district for days. The newspapers not only gave it a full report but ran editorials upon it as well. The *Intelligencer* issued a verbatim account as a free supplement to its next number, and a five-column broadsheet was made for the Short Time Committees to distribute in their various localities. Oastler's new social Toryism seemed to be making real headway at last.

Three days after the Leeds meeting, Sadler received leave to introduce his Ten Hours Bill into the House of Commons. The Committees at once began an intensive canvass of the mills in their neighborhoods. By Christmas all was ready for the big campaign.

Oastler Discovers his Power: The First Rousing of the North

THE TEN HOURS campaign was well timed. Or perhaps it would be more accurate to say that circumstances had made a mass movement of protest in Yorkshire inevitable, and that the Ten Hours campaign only served to canalize the surging energies of discontent which were there already.

The causes of this discontent were many and complex. As the old routines crumbled under the impact of spreading industrialism and the new mobility, the northern workers found themselves caught up in a psychological revolution of which they had little understanding. The multiplication of mills and factories, the lengthening of the working day, the mounting tensions of labor which the growing use of machinery involved generated a mass of half-formulated resentments seeking almost any promise of assuagement. In the countryside the condition of the handloom weavers was seriously worsening, while the rapid expansion of the towns was creating innumerable problems of overcrowding and demoralization.[1] During the previous 30 years, for example, the population of Leeds had more than doubled, while that of Bradford had expanded almost fourfold. The new generation of city dwellers cut off from the old loyalties found itself in a world of bewildering flux with few familiar institutions com-

---

[1] Housing conditions in the Riding were beginning to attract the attention of various philanthropists at this time, and occasional investigations were being undertaken. 'From a recent inspection of the eastern part of the town [i.e., Leeds] it appears that many of the streets are unpaved and without common sewers, and that for want of proper receptacles several of them . . . are almost filled with ashes and filth, which filth oozes into many of the cellar dwellings and renders them unwholesome.' (*Leeds Mercury*, 1 December 1831.)

manding any obvious allegiance. The exhausting stresses of re-
adjustment bore heavily upon these tired, ill-fed, and illiterate masses, as the wild oscillations of the trade-cycle swung
them between enforced unemployment and enforced overtime
throughout the 'twenties and 'thirties. The gin palaces flour-
ished for the oblivion they offered the majority, at the same time
that a resolute and far-seeing minority worked at the heartbreak-
ing task of building a militant unionism which could stand up
to the new generation of employers.

More immediate circumstances also tended to bring resentment to a focus. The national excitement over the Reform Bill
engendered a spirit favorable to demands other than the political, and thus helped to change men's ideas of social necessity.
By raising the cry of 'reform,' the Whigs were invoking a collective purposiveness that might easily be carried over from the
question of the franchise to that of social conditions. The shrewd
Whig wit Sidney Smith said that the Tory Mrs. Partingtons were
trying to push back the incoming tide of political reform with a
kitchen mop. But he was not quite perceptive enough to see
that most of his fellow Whigs were just as fervently hoping to
hold off social reform with piled-up volumes of political economy.

The sentiment, then, was there; all it required was articula-
tion and direction, and this Oastler was about to give it. A
strange unfolding had brought him to that situation: a story
compounded of piety, chance, and an aggressive temper. But
now at the beginning of his forty-third year he found himself
with the aspirations of thousands fixed upon him while he was
still only partly aware of all that he really stood for.

¶ 1

The explanation of the extraordinary hold Oastler was to exercise over these northern workers is not easy to formulate. It
must be sought in the convergence of several factors, involving
the personality of the man as well as the curious symbolic quality accidentally conferred upon him by the processes of change.

Of his physical attractiveness there can be no question. Innumerable contemporary reports speak of his commanding presence and imposing carriage: 'a picturesque, if it be not more

accurate to say a statuesque figure,' one diarist wrote on first
seeing him. The face, too, was immediately prepossessing. Several observers described it as handsome, and in his prime it
probably was, with its regularity of features and freshness of
coloring, though as he grew older the suggestion of heaviness
in cheek and jowl became more pronounced. The thick, curly,
sandy hair just beginning to recede from the temples, and the
wide-set, hazel eyes further contributed to his air of distinction.
Yet none could fail to see that there was something contradictory
about the face. The square jaw and set chin betrayed the pugnacity of the fighter, while the manifestly sensitive mouth suggested very different things. Everyone who ever tried to describe Oastler remarked upon the expressiveness of the mouth.
'The scornful curl of those lips was terrible,' wrote Anthony
Trollope's brother, and others said the same.

His oratorical power which came to its maturing in the ensuing months amounted almost to genius. Literally scores of
descriptions of this power survive, so that we are still able to
catch some authentic intimations of the spell he could cast. His
voice had the richness and compass essential to all great oratory.
He could modulate it at will to caress or inflame, and he was
master of all the range between. He developed an artist's consciousness in the use of these skills which set him apart from
most of the demagogues of his age. But perhaps the most impressive thing about him was his feeling for his audience. He had
in a supreme degree the gift of the born orator for identifying
himself with his hearers, enabling him to enunciate and give
back to them their own unformulated aspirations. And he was
endowed with all the requisite talents to do this: a delicate
sense of cadence, a wide variety of styles, and above all that
capacity for accurately judging emotional tension which alone
makes possible a mounting crescendo and the explosive climax.

He would usually start in a conversational way, fluent and
unsophisticated. He would rally his hearers with an ironic local
jest or two and convey the warm sense of a common endeavor.
He would be racy and terse in his sentences and concrete in all
his illustrations. There was never a hint of talking down to his
audience. Gradually he would pass into what may be called the

second movement of his discourse. He would remind his hearers of the happier times that once had been, and voice nostalgia with the vividness of simplicity. Then against this he would sharply set the ugly reality of the present. His sentences would lengthen and the cadence become richer as he passed into his third mood of somber hope and hardening resolution. As he did so his speech would become more and more reminiscent of the Old Testament prophets in phrase and tone and oblique reference, as though the piety of his own childhood were welling up from the depths. He brought to his listeners the sense of eternal verities lying beneath the flux of things and cast that sense in time-hallowed images of ancient potency. Invariably it was the moral appeal he stressed, and with it always went the suggestion of a merrier England lying somewhere at the heart of things waiting to be actualized.

Not that Oastler had any standardized pattern in his oratory: far from it. Indeed, the versatility of his skill was remarkable. But this at least typifies the sort of thing he could do with consummate power. Long before he was halfway through a speech he had his audience at his command and could fire them with his own passionate zeal, as Wesley could. He could make them laugh or cry, or convulse them with a sense of the wrath to come. By a dramatic gesture he could tense their muscles, and by a pitch of the voice, scald their eyes with tears of fervor.

Astonishing though his powers were, however, they do not entirely account for the sway he was able to exercise. As has been suggested, Oastler must be reckoned as a symbol as well as a personal force, and much of the influence he was able to exert is to be charted in terms of the effectiveness of that symbol. For eight years or so it was powerful, then its appeal began to diminish. As he gradually came to have less and less symbolic significance for the rising generation of operatives, so with his own advancing years his authority slowly waned and finally vanished.

What was it, then, that he symbolized? Perhaps we cannot get any nearer to it than to say 'the good old days'; and if those days are but a myth, we just have to admit that for a while Oastler was the embodiment of a folk-dream which had an especial

cogency in the days of transition to an industrial economy. Nevertheless it was a myth in which he himself believed with intense
conviction. He came from the land and he stood for the land.
The things he loved in his deepest being were the things he
symbolized—the ways of the perennial village. Homestead and
hall and the ordered society, craftsmanship and the venerable
harmony of functions: these things possessed his imagination
utterly.

For the factory workers and handloom weavers who flocked
in their thousands to hear him, therefore, Oastler came to stand
as both a token of the things that once had been and a promise
of the deliverance that should come. He would fight with them
against the unhappy consequences of unprecedented change.
He would be their deliverer against the acquisitiveness of all
who would pull down the pyramid of society in the scramble
for wealth. And until the time when a new ideology of protest
should be formulated, this idiom and this symbolism remained
singularly evocative.

¶ 2

The strategy of the campaign had been mapped out after
numerous consultations in the office at Fixby. 'The only way to
succeed,' said Oastler, 'is by legally, constitutionally and strenuously urging the question upon Parliament. The only way we
can do it is to let Parliament know what the factory system is,
for it is my opinion that they do not know half the cruelties
that are practised under that system. Let us, then, never relax;
and if we cannot get a bill this session, let us by the next.' So
six mass meetings were to be held in each of the big textile
centers of Yorkshire—Huddersfield, Bradford, Leeds, Keighley,
Dewsbury, and Halifax. The Chief Constable or some other
local dignitary was to be asked to preside, and opponents of
factory legislation as well as its advocates were to be invited to
state their case from the platform. It was one of Oastler's convictions that the only effective way to capture public opinion
was to bring the enemy into the open as fully and frequently as
possible. Forthright opposition and personal abuse never worried him; in fact he enjoyed a fight. What did trouble him was

intrigue and anonymity, and these he sought to combat by every means his ingenuity could devise. He had a deep faith in the conscience of the ordinary unsophisticated citizen. To his mind, therefore, the battle for the Ten Hours Bill would be a battle for publicity.

The first meeting was held at Huddersfield, the day after Christmas, 1831. Everything had been well prepared by the Short Time Committee, and good advertising as well as the wide reporting of the debate with the Baineses resulted in an attendance of well over a thousand people. Among those on the platform with Oastler were the six men who had made the Fixby Hall Compact, and the Reverend Richard Oglesby, a Nonconformist minister of the town who has the distinction of being the first clergyman of any denomination to come out publicly on behalf of the movement. This was the only meeting of the campaign at which none of its opponents was represented.

Half a dozen speakers took the floor in succession and presented the usual arguments for the bill with vigor and effectiveness. Then Oastler's turn came, and in a very few minutes he held the audience in his grip. He started disarmingly by emphasizing the non-partisan character of the cause. 'Let no feelings of animosity as politicians ever interfere in this question,' he pleaded; 'but let us be resolved as Tories, as Radicals, as Whigs, to join hand and heart till British infants are free.' He stressed, as always, the moral purpose of their endeavor, and repudiated emphatically the charge which had so often been leveled against him that he wanted to set masters and men at odds. Nothing could more grossly misrepresent his aim; the letters he cited in support of his stand from masters of every political hue proved that.

Do I then say that there should be no grades in society, that there are not to be servants and master? No! But I do say that servitude and labour ought not to be oppressive. I know from my own experience— for I am but a servant—that I have as much pleasure in serving my master as my master can have in receiving my services. No master has a right to demand the services of any human being unless the reward of those services will be a comfortable living. And that is, I verily believe, all the working classes want.

Things had not always been as bad as they now were. 'Gentlemen,' he declared, 'I am old enough to remember that there were thousands of respectable domestic manufacturers worth their £50, or £100, or £200, who were able to make their cloth at home and go to sell it in the market. But they are now reduced almost to pauperism, or to the class of common labourers. They were the best masters the workmen ever had: these were the strongest bulwarks of the state, but they are now mixed amongst the paupers and labourers in one common mass. I remember the time when there were happy companies upon a village green, as blithesome and as gay as lambs, and I have gambolled with them. But they are now all gone and disappeared. We see nothing of that sort now! We scarcely see the complexion of a boy or girl in a country place but they are black, blue, or brown. I remember the time when it was not so; but now they are locked up the live-long day in a loathsome factory. And when I know that the Almighty Creator of the Universe never intended them to be sent there, I feel that I am doing the work of God when I require the doors to be opened, and that these little ones should once more see the rising and the setting of the sun . . .'

It was not only the long hours he denounced, however, but the bullying and brutality in many of the mills as well—cruelties which had grown commoner with the spread of unsupervised child labor, and which it was nobody's particular duty to publicize or prevent. One little girl 7 years old had recently collapsed and died under the treatment she had received, and Oastler recounted her story with dramatic force. 'If "the Bell" had ceased to ring when she arrived with trembling, shivering, weary limbs at the factory door, there stood a monster in human form before her and as she passed he lashed her . . .' Here he struck the front of the platform with a long heavy strap. 'This,' he thundered, holding up the strap, *is no fiction*. It was hard at work in this town last week, and I have seen the effects of such instruments in black marks from the neck to the seats of children . . .' Then with his vibrant and measured emphasis which whipped the audience to passion, *'this system ought to be exposed, to be corrected . . .'*

Few who were present forgot this 'strap speech' as it came to be called. Fifty years later an old man writing his reminiscences for one of the local papers could still recall the lightning of Oastler's indignation that opening afternoon. Its consequences were great. With a single speech he captured the allegiance of the Huddersfield operatives as completely as he had won the hearts of the Leeds delegates a fortnight earlier. Henceforward the Huddersfield men were his to command, and for seven exciting years he led them as they had never been led before. Soon they were calling themselves 'Oastler's Own' and had formed themselves into a sort of personal bodyguard to accompany him at all the big demonstrations. They protected his hustings and policed his meetings; and before the story finally ended they had seen him through many a nasty scrape and several ugly riots.

Nor was this the only outcome of the speech. Before long Oastler found himself regarded by many of the poorer folk in the town as a champion and benefactor to whom they might bring their problems and sorrows. Cases of cruelty were quickly reported to him and whenever possible he investigated each one personally. Children whom mill-labor had sickened or deformed were brought to Fixby for help: here an application for leg-irons for withered limbs, there an appeal for a bed in the infirmary, and so on. In this way he quickly accumulated a vast store of detailed information which he was able to utilize in his speeches with overwhelming effect.

¶ 3

The next day Oastler went to Bradford for an even bigger demonstration. This time there was an impressive array of notables on the platform, including John Wood of Horton Hall, old John Rand, the 'father of the worsted trade,' and a number of local doctors.

Wood, who was one of the most popular masters in the town, spoke of the things he knew with a quiet impressiveness that roused the meeting to great enthusiasm. But he disclaimed all honor for himself at the way matters had developed. 'To whom but to Mr. Oastler are we indebted for this meeting?' he asked.

'It is to his exertions alone that we owe this large assemblage of masters and men; it is he who called our attention to the sufferings of the little things who work in our mills.' Others testified in like vein. Doctors Sharp and Macturk from the Bradford Infirmary painted horrible pictures of the deformed and exhausted childhood they were constantly being called upon to tend, and several of their colleagues corroborated what they said. John Rand was so impressed by this medical testimony that, in spite of the fact that he had come to the meeting still accepting the moderate position he had first taken at the Talbot meeting,[2] he now announced his conversion to the Ten Hours cause.

Then came Oastler, and in spite of a troublesome cold he was as successful as he had been the day before. 'Mr. Oastler at this meeting was himself,' declared one reporter; 'that is the greatest compliment the writer of these remarks can pay him. In the service of humanity, in unkennelling a slippery, fox-like opponent, in knocking down a sturdy antagonist or in sweeping away the sophistry of puling apologists for the right divine of doing wrong, he, Richard Oastler, is truly THE MAN.'

Apart from its publicity value, however, this Bradford meeting was a landmark in the progress of the movement on account of the new recruit who walked onto the platform just when the great ovation to Oastler was subsiding: a recruit whose name will be associated with the Ten Hours Movement as long as it is ever remembered—the Reverend George Stringer Bull. He and Oastler had never met before. From that day forward they were to be not merely brothers-in-arms but intimate personal friends, whose remarkable comradeship was to endure for almost 30 years.

Bull was a captivating little man now in his thirty-third year. On both his father's and his mother's side he was descended from a line of clerical families, and four of his seven brothers were Anglican clergymen too. At the age of 12 he had joined the Navy but had left it 7 years later to offer himself to the Church Missionary Society. Fever having ended his short career as a schoolmaster in Sierra Leone, he was invalided home. On his

[2] See above, page 58.

recovery he was ordained, and after holding curacies at Hull (where he got to know Michael Sadler) and Dewsbury, he was given the living of Bierly, just outside Bradford. He took his work very seriously, so that before long his energy and enthusiasm had won him considerable prominence in the Riding. The two causes that had been particularly engaging him during the past five years, were temperance reform [3] and children's education. He was tireless in his efforts for the promotion of both day schools and Sunday schools, and it was this work that had first drawn his attention to the problem of child labor in the Bierly mills.

In many respects Bull was a complete contrast to Oastler. He was rather shorter than average, thick set, and inclined to stoutness. He had what it was once customary to call an 'open countenance,' with prominent nose, broad forehead, and an exceptionally firm mouth and chin. His coloring was striking, for while his complexion was conspicuously florid, his short, fuzzy hair and mutton-chop whiskers were black. But the most impressive thing about him was something that altogether escapes the surviving stylized portraits; 'humorous shrewdness' would perhaps be the best name for it, though his friends described it in various other terms too. Wherever he went he seemed to radiate a breezy self-possession and downrightness which marked him out in any company in which he mixed. With his clear, sonorous voice he could capture an audience almost as completely as Oastler could, though his style was entirely different. His was the direct appeal to hardheaded common sense and the simple challenge to innate decency. He and Oastler thus made an ideal combination for platform work in such a movement.

This was the little man who came bustling onto the platform while Oastler was receiving his friends' congratulations. As an inhabitant of the district, he claimed his right to speak, and speak he did! In short, incisive sentences he told the meeting just why he was concerned with the question under discussion, and why from that hour he would be pledged to the Ten Hours cause. If factory conditions continued as they were, he said, an entire

[3] See above, page 50.

generation would grow to maturity deformed in mind as well as body, utterly unfitted for either parenthood or citizenship; he had 500 children in his charge, and he knew.

That the speech was an instant success the roar from the crowd showed. The seven most stirring years of Bull's life had begun.

¶ 4

Gratifying though the results of the first two meetings had been, publicity and good stage-management by the local Short Time Committee made the gathering at Leeds a fortnight later a still greater success. Even the *Mercury* considered it necessary to devote four-and-a-half columns to the affair, and echoes found their way into the London dailies too, for this was not merely a town meeting but a demonstration of the entire Leeds district.

On the day of the meeting, workers from the surrounding villages were arriving in the city from early morning. All the forenoon a band was parading the streets and by midday a crowd estimated at more than 12,000 had assembled. So great was the turn out, in fact, that at the last moment it was decided to hold the meeting in the Yard of the Mixed Cloth Hall instead of at the Court House. Thither the concourse marched, led by the band and preceded by three huge banners—the Blue of Toryism with the inscription 'Dwell in the Land and verily thou shalt be fed'; the Orange of Liberalism with the text 'Be merciful and thou shalt obtain mercy'; and the White flag of Radicalism, adorned with the painting of a factory child kneeling in supplication before Justice. On the platform was gathered the most distinguished array of representative eminence the movement had yet brought together, including the popular Leeds mayor, William Hey, who presided, Michael Sadler, Doctor Thackrah, the vicar of Leeds, the editors of the *Intelligencer* and *Patriot*, as well as the local trade-union leaders. Various opponents of factory legislation were there to speak as well, the most important of whom was John Marshall, the prospective Whig candidate.

Each of the speeches had a distinctive quality. They were all

impressively realistic in tone and remarkably free from sentimentality. One of the most forceful was that by Doctor Thackrah,[4] who cited the cases of some of his child patients in condemnation of the lack of regulation. Was it to be wondered at,
he demanded, if the rising generation was having its resistance to
epidemics and disease undermined by prevailing conditions?

Then came Oastler's turn, and for an hour or more he held the
throng spellbound by his comprehensive attack on the whole policy of laissez-faire: a policy that resulted in the public abnegation
of all social purposiveness by elevating economic anarchy into a
moral value and depressing child and adult alike to the status of
mere attendants upon the machine. 'How, then,' he challenged,
'shall our children be placed in a situation in which they will be
able to believe that they are born free, and that they are born
in a Christian land?'

This system, as it is natural it should have done, has destroyed that
feeling of reverence and affection amongst workmen towards their
employers which I remember existed when I was young. It has destroyed that profitable system which formerly obtained in this vast district . . . Instead of trying to get living profits, the whole system *now*
is a cut-throat system; and for the sake of meeting those demands which
this system has created, in many instances the children and work-
people are absolutely worked *against time.* Yes, the sinews of the
workmen and infants are now compelled, by excessive and destroying
labour, to make large quantities of goods by a given time in order to
meet the engagements which men without capital are liable to; thus
making the stock of *their* trade the bones and sinews of their labourers; thus creating an unnecessary glut in the market. For, mind you,
these men do not work 'to order' but from 'need.' Thus they lower the
prices by 'forced sales' and ruin themselves, their workpeople, and
their neighbours . . . *That machine which cannot afford good and
comfortable wages to the man who works with it is a curse to the
country.*

Then he went on to denounce some of the petty tyrannies and
trickeries of the neighborhood ('strapping' the children, for example, and manipulating the factory clock so as to lengthen the
working day). Time after time as his argument developed he was

[4] See above, page 73.

interrupted by a tremendous outburst of cheering; and when he sat down after a majestic peroration the crowd broke into a tornado of applause.

To this day one can sense in the printed version of the speech something of its original power. One is not surprised at the London *Standard's* glowing tribute to 'that "noble of Nature," Mr. Oastler, whose speech at the Leeds meeting is one of the finest specimens of eloquence that we have ever had the enjoyment of reading.' 'We observed,' wrote the editor of the *Intelligencer,* 'many a tear stealing down the care-worn cheeks of the elderly operatives. Of all Mr. Oastler's triumphs, this is his greatest.'

The meeting lasted until nightfall. The promoters were delighted with its success, as well they might be. Nearly every newspaper in the county gave it several columns in the next week's issue, and the resulting petition that went up to Parliament carried more than 18,000 signatures. People began to think that things were now really moving. 'The great work begun by Mr. Oastler in the columns of a newspaper,' wrote one pamphleteer, 'prosecuted amid all sorts of opposition, abuse and misrepresentation, advanced step by step, winning its way to the feelings and affections, despite of power, despite of self-interest, despite of the cunning artifices of needy slaves and unprincipled hirelings.'

¶ 5

The movement was gathering momentum with each successive meeting. At Keighley three weeks later Oastler took Bull with him for the first time and scored a success as sweeping as any that had gone before. At Dewsbury the week after he repeated the performance. But the greatest triumph of all seems to have been the one he achieved at Halifax on Shrove Tuesday, 6 March.

In Halifax were some of Oastler's bitterest enemies, the men who had drawn up the notorious Resolutions. There, too, were some of the worst conditions in the Riding, with the operatives reputedly apathetic. Rumor had it that Oastler dared not show himself in the place, but this only made him the more determined to go. The local Committee had emulated all the preparations of the Leeds men to build up a dramatic effect, so that in spite of

bad weather another huge crowd gathered to hear the new revivalist and watch the trouble that was so freely prophesied.

The course of the meeting ran to much the same pattern as
that of the earlier ones, but Oastler's speech was unlike any he
had yet given. The arguments, of course, were unchanged, but
the tone was entirely different. That afternoon he was not concerned to state a case; all his hearers knew the case by this time.
Instead, he was out to denounce the enemy in its own stronghold,
and for such an undertaking his armory was now immeasurably
better stocked than it had been when the campaign started eight
weeks before.

His central theme was the threat of retribution. For the first
time there crept into what he said a suggestion of the apocalyptic
mood which in later years came to possess him so completely.
Life avenges the frustrations that menace it, was his argument.
He contrasted the days of his youth, when masters lived near
their own mills or workshops and personally knew their own
workmen, with the present situation when 'the whole country is
decked with their stately mansions and their splendid equipages.'
Had the lot of the workers improved proportionately during that
time; had it not rather deteriorated? 'I would say deliberately
and advisedly,' he warned the masters, 'if you are anxious to keep
what you have got, help us to pass this bill.'

He gave some vivid pictures of distressing cases he had recently brought to light. He described the cruel system of fines
practiced more frequently at Halifax than anywhere else:

The other morning two little girls came to a mill in this town just
five minutes past six. The morning was dark, cold and wet. They had
a mile and a half to walk and were wet through. They were shut out
of the mill and refused entrance. They turned towards a boiler house,
intending to dry their clothes. There also they were rejected, and the
poor creatures had to seek a place of shelter, which they found about
half a mile off, where they were allowed to dry and warm themselves.
At nine they returned to the mill and had *half a day's wages taken off*
for being five minutes late . . .

As he continued, the indignation of his hearers mounted. They
immediately identified his various innuendos. 'Ackroyd, Ackroyd,' they shouted; 'Shame, shame . . .' But on he swept

whipping them to greater and greater fury. Never before had they heard anyone lash these hard-bitten masters as Oastler lashed them that day. It was not the 'system' he was attacking now, but evil men who profited by it and complacent men who condoned it. With such there could be no compromise.

Impressive as had been the effect Oastler had wrought at the earlier meetings, it was surpassed by what he did at Halifax. There was something more than a revivalist enthusiasm in this fervor: for the moment it was not far short of the revolutionary temper. When Oastler sat down, the throng hailed him with tumultuous applause.

Ten days later Sadler introduced his Ten Hours Bill into the House of Commons.

CHAPTER XIII

Propaganda Becomes Necessary

•

MASS meetings, however spectacular and successful, would not of themselves suffice to get a Factory Bill through Parliament: by now Oastler and his friends realized that clearly. Hobhouse's failure had served as a fine object lesson on the conditions governing a successful appeal to the legislature. Public opinion had not only to be aroused: it must be sustained and fortified. Sections of society hitherto unreached must be brought into the movement; misrepresentations must be answered; and then, when all was in readiness, pressures of a very direct kind would have to be brought to bear upon indifferent or unawakened Members at Westminster.

All this involved planning, organization, and expense undreamed of fifteen months earlier. Continuous staff work was essential. And circumstances had made it inevitable that the main burden of the work would fall upon Oastler's shoulders. Watching the unfolding of the elaborate schemes, one finds it impossible to resist the conclusion that Oastler was consciously making Wilberforce his pattern and exemplar. In the same manner that Wilberforce had fought for the black slaves, he would fight for the white.

¶ 1

The amount of work Oastler got through in the ensuing months was remarkable. By letter or personal contact he kept track of everything, so that his study at Fixby virtually became the information bureau of the movement. All the pamphlets and leaflets bearing upon either side of the factory question he carefully examined, annotated, and filed. Week by week he pasted into his scrap books all the relevant excerpts from the local newspapers. The secretaries of the local committees regularly sent him their various bulletins and posters, which were duly put away into a third collection. From Leeds to Manchester these same secretaries constantly sought his advice or endorsement for their sundry schemes. His correspondence, of course, grew enormously. And all the time he had to be prepared to ride off at a moment's notice to any place in the Riding that needed his help: here to address a meeting, there to preside at a committee, elsewhere to investigate a charge of cruelty or dismissal.

Only a strong constitution and the unflagging co-operation of his wife enabled him to endure the strain year after year. Mary Oastler's labors, indeed, anonymous though they were, were almost as great as his own. She not only ran the home but did most of his routine work on the Fixby Estate as well, and in addition taught herself to make her own handwriting indistinguishable from his, so that she could take upon herself some of the burden of his correspondence. One who knew them both intimately has left us his impression of what she meant to him.

In his labours for the factory children she more than sympathised, night and day cheering, helping and comforting him in the prosecution of his overwhelming labours. Writing for him, sometimes through the night, day by day when he was weary, exhausted, absent or sick, Mrs. Oastler never allowed the great work to stand still. She would take up his pen and continue his public and private correspondence where he left off. She would read back a few sentences, ascertain his thoughts, and then finish his argument or directions, none being able to detect that another mind or hand had been engaged, so entirely—as in all other things—were their style and handwriting one. Returning home late at night or at early morn, wearied and exhausted by his 'factory labours,' Mr. Oastler was sure to find his wife attending with every comfort and kindness, and when he was refreshed, she would listen with anxious attention to his report of proceedings . . .

¶ 2

The need for new and more effective kinds of publicity became increasingly apparent as the movement expanded in scope.

During the first few months, when the factory question was

still a non-party issue, the correspondence columns of the various
local newspapers had provided almost all the publicity that had
seemed necessary. At that time the suggestion of factory reform
had simply amounted to a philanthropic appeal to the benevolent,
so there had been no difficulty in getting communications printed.
Indeed, when the smaller journals saw the extent of the interest
that had been aroused, they began reproducing or summarizing
items from their more important contemporaries, and even invited the sending of reports direct to themselves.

By the time of the great campaign, however, all that was
changed: the factory question had now become inextricably entangled with party considerations. Oastler's deteriorating relations
with the Baineses served as a clear index of this transformation,
for the new phase had started about the time that young Edward
expurgated Oastler's counterblast to the Halifax Resolutions and
had become generally recognized when the *Mercury* editorially
accused Sadler of being a hypocritical Tory intriguer who deliberately sought to exploit social discontents for party advantage.
No longer, therefore, did the newspapers provide a forum that
could be relied on. As the Whigs grew more apprehensive at the
prospect of governmental 'interference' with industry, their journals became increasingly cautious about the sort of thing they
would publish, until eventually their columns were entirely closed
to the advocates of regulation. The Tories, of course, did not let
slip the opportunity to represent their 'liberal' rivals as fearful
of free criticism. Nor did the men on the left wing either: for it
has to be remembered that most of the Radical press was by now
supporting the Ten Hours Movement, even though treating it as
subordinate to the demand for manhood suffrage. So everywhere
north of the Trent, the Whig papers came to adopt a purely party
line against the simultaneous assaults of Radicals and Tories. And
when, after the campaign of public meetings, *The Times,* the
Standard and the *Morning Post* of London all began giving
Oastler their support too, a similar situation developed in the
metropolis.

To Oastler and his friends this alignment of the press could
not be other than a matter for regret. From the beginning, they
had sought to keep the question of child labor a non-party issue,

for they knew well enough that only so was there any hope for
effective legislation. If any substantial volume of public opinion
was to be won over, therefore, it was imperative for the Ten
Hours men to resort to independent propaganda of their own,
however expensive such an undertaking might be. Thus as the
year advanced the sheer pressure of events completely transformed the nature of the movement.

Various kinds of publicity were employed, designed to appeal
to different social classes. Broadsheets were the first and cheapest
device, having an obvious utility in appealing to the less literate.
Every pronouncement calculated to be of use was immediately
turned into a large sheet for public display—all Oastler's letters
to the press, for instance, medical testimony, and excerpts from
the London dailies. Large quantities were printed at a time and
sent to the local Short Time Committees, who distributed them
everywhere. They were pasted on walls and fences, hung in reading rooms and shop windows, and put up in the taverns where
operatives gathered.

Then there were the pamphlets which began to be regularly
used during the second year of the campaign. In all, nearly two
hundred were put out, of every conceivable kind: dialogues, open
letters, narratives, dialect stories, and sentimental verses. Parson
Bull was a particularly strong believer in the efficacy of the pamphlet for winning over the middle-class churchgoer, and from his
pen came some of the ablest appeals the movement produced.
Oastler himself wrote no fewer than 35 within 6 years, several
of which ran to over a hundred pages. Usually they were sold at
a penny or twopence apiece and bought by local sympathizers
who made their own arrangements for distribution. In some districts special committees were formed to give them out by house-
to-house visiting in emulation of the missionary societies.

A third device was the newspaper reprint. This appeared as a
direct outcome of the recent platform campaign. Each of the five
big meetings had been reported at great length by most of the
weekly journals, sufficient to fill the entire page of a modern daily.
It was an easy matter, therefore, to get a few hundred extra
copies run off at but slight cost. Rearranged in a four-page format,
such reprints had the size and appearance of tabloids and could

be used for a variety of purposes. They were sent to Members of
Parliament and the local clergy, for example; they were very
useful for keeping informed the officers of Trade Unions, Friendly
Societies, and Short Time Committees; and at certain critical
stages later on they had particular value in counteracting the
distorted reports of the hostile press.

Lastly, mention has to be made of the tiny tracts which were
put out by the thousand: another of the ideas borrowed from the
missionary and Bible societies. Specially useful for church meetings and similar public gatherings, they dealt with every manner
of theme—anecdotes of factory children, prayers for the social
awakening, hymns and rallying songs, and so on.

¶ 3

With the increased output of propaganda went an equally
significant expansion of organization. After the introduction of
Sadler's Bill into Parliament, this proceeded rapidly.

One obvious task was to press ahead with the original plan to
cover the whole of the textile districts with Short Time Committees. Already such groups existed in each of the big centers;
now sub-committees began to be established in the villages and
smaller towns too. The evidence shows that all through the spring
and early summer of 1832 these bodies were extremely active,
meeting twice a week, collecting information, distributing literature and posters, and reporting back to the leaders about conditions in their particular sector. To co-ordinate all this activity, a
Central Short Time Committee was set up at Leeds, composed of
representatives from each of the regional groups.

These were mainly working-class bodies. But Oastler and his
friends knew well enough that the movement could have little
hope of success unless its appeal were broadened. To this end
they set about establishing a parallel organization designed to
win middle-class approval as well. It was not just a matter of
increasing the volume of support, necessary though that was;
there was the other necessity of earning for the movement the
claim to 'respectability.' During the 'thirties and 'forties it was
essential for any cause to be able to make that claim, if results
were to be achieved by parliamentary means. At the back of

many people's minds there still lurked an uneasy fear of 'radicalism' and revolution, which could be called forth in opposition to reform all too easily. In denouncing Oastler as an 'incendiary' and a 'wrecker' who sought 'to set class against class,' the *Mercury* was deliberately exploiting this latent mood for its own purposes. To counteract such appeals was a constant concern of the Ten Hours men throughout the course of their struggle.

Once again Huddersfield led the way. In the new year a committee of ladies was formed to stir up interest on behalf of Sadler's Bill. Their main activity was to visit the homes of the wealthy, to distribute literature and solicit subscriptions. Soon other towns were following their lead.

By far the most important and elaborate of these bodies, however, was the one formed at Leeds under the presidency of the vicar. It called itself 'The Leeds General Committee for Promoting the Bill now before Parliament,' and was made up of a dozen very diverse members, including businessmen, gentry, and clergy, as well as the editors of both the *Intelligencer* and *Patriot*. Revealingly enough, the prospectus styled eight of them 'esquire' and four plain 'Mr.' They planned to go about their task in a big way. An office was rented, a lithographing service was arranged for, and to prevent overlapping of effort two secretaries were appointed. One was William Osburn, a Sunday school superintendent and trustee of the Leeds workhouse, who had recently been town overseer; the other, Ralph Taylor, who had founded the local operatives group and was already secretary of the Riding Central Committee.

The appeal was explicitly to the well-to-do: 'of late the sympathies of the operative classes especially have been awakened, and they respectfully call upon those whom Divine Providence hath placed in a more influential station to arise to their aid and that of their children.' As a first step, a carefully drawn circular letter, together with some of the recently published literature, was sent to every likely supporter in the neighborhood; and with that kind of direct personal appeal the Committee assiduously continued to occupy itself during the next 15 months.

Early in April a similar society was started in London, known as 'The Society for Improving the Condition of Working Children.'

This signalized the first direct impact of the movement upon the metropolis and thus may be considered an important landmark in the transformation of the factory question from a local to a national issue. William Allen, the Quaker philanthropist, was its moving spirit, and Samuel Hoare, the well-known city banker, served as Treasurer. But impressive though it was on paper (the Duke of Sussex was its patron, and a strange assortment of notabilities made up the Committee) it does not appear to have contributed to the cause nearly as much as its counterparts in the north.

This expansion of organization inevitably raised the question how the enterprise was to be financed. At the outset there had been no such problem, since the leaders had defrayed all their own incidental expenses. Now, however, it had obviously become a matter of serious consideration, and when the struggle shifted from the provinces to Westminster, the need for funds became urgent.

From first to last the movement financed itself entirely from the individual donations of members and sympathizers, each local group being left free to raise what it could in its own way. Committeemen went the rounds of their mills or workshops, while ladies visited in the suburbs; collecting boxes were left in taverns and reading rooms, and personal appeals were sent by mail. Almost always the plate was passed around at the public meetings. When the movement was at its height, two full-time agents were engaged by the Leeds Committee to tour the country from Derby to Newcastle to raise money.

There was never any attempt to establish a single fund for the organization as a whole. Not only did the London and Leeds societies have their separate accounts, each administered by a prominent banker as treasurer, but each local Short Time Committee had its own fund, too, which it disposed of at its own discretion. The typical quarterly balance sheet of the Manchester operatives reproduced on page 152 well illustrates both the nature of their activities and the sort of procedure they followed throughout the struggle.

The most important of all the funds, however, was the one Oastler controlled himself. This was not a public account, as the others were, but remained a private affair of his own. As nearly as one can estimate, Oastler was disbursing from it something around £2000 a year, at least until 1834. Apart from his own contributions (and he gave the movement not only all his savings but a substantial part of his income as well), it was mainly derived from intimate personal friends who put their donations unreservedly at his disposal. Without doubt the bulk of it came from John Wood of Horton Hall. Although Wood kept himself so completely out of the public eye and has received little notice from historians in consequence, his generosity sustained over seventeen years was without stint. It has been estimated that from first to last he spent more than £40,000 for the cause.

Thus it came about that all this expansion of organization actually strengthened Oastler's leadership rather than weakened it. In fact if not in name, he was general co-ordinating secretary, as well as figurehead and symbol. His peculiar mediating position in relation to the various classes and interests involved gave him a special authority which no one else enjoyed. The fact that he also controlled a substantial purse only added to his power. The General Committee, for example, was never able to meet all its expenses, and so had to apply to Oastler constantly. When bills had to be paid, the Chairman of the Leeds Society sent the creditors to Oastler with their accounts duly endorsed, and Oastler would settle out of his private fund.

¶ 4

So far, the impetus for factory reform had come entirely from Yorkshire: that is to say, from the wool, worsted, and flax industries. Now, with the actual introduction of Sadler's Bill into the House of Commons, the demand for regulation spread to the cotton operatives of Lancashire as well.

During the eighteen-twenties there had been the beginnings of such a movement, though it had come to nothing. Indeed, says Philip Grant, one of the later leaders, at that time 'any meddling with the subject was unpopular even amongst the masses, and was attended with risk and imminent danger to the situation of any workman that took part in it.' The energies of Lancashire had been otherwise absorbed. Here, under the indefatigable leadership of John Doherty, a militant trade unionism had been developing since 1826. Doherty it was who had led the spinners in their prolonged but unsuccessful resistance to the drastic wage reductions during the 1829 depression. Then, realizing the weakness that lay in merely local unions, he had secured the creation of a general union of Operative Spinners of the United Kingdom. Heartened by this success he had embarked upon a still bigger project. Under the influence of Robert Owen's teaching, he sought to federate all the unions of the country into a National Association for the Protection of Labor, for the purpose of establishing a new social order based on co-operative principles.

Doherty, who himself had begun work in an Ulster cotton mill at the age of ten, gave the Yorkshire movement his hearty support and carried the Lancashire workers with him, even though he envisaged the shorter working day as but a single item in a much more comprehensive scheme of national reconstruction. His relations with Oastler became extremely cordial. 'Mr. Oastler is a Tory in politics,' he told one of his Manchester audiences that spring, 'but when, we ask, will any of your boasting "liberals" or professing Whigs contribute a tithe of service which Mr. Oastler has rendered to the cause of suffering humanity?'

By the early part of 1832, therefore, a separate Lancashire movement was well under way. A number of Short Time Committees were already vigorously at work in different parts of the county. A Central Committee had been set up at Manchester with the same general functions as its counterpart at Leeds, and its secretary, Thomas Daniel, was in regular correspondence with Oastler. Posters and pamphlets were being printed in bulk for distribution by the local groups. And in March a campaign of public meetings was launched.

But support was by no means confined to the workers. George Condy, proprietor and editor of the Tory *Manchester Advertiser,* brought it his talented advocacy both on the platform and in pamphlets as well as through his newspaper. Various clergy and gentry joined at the outset, too, some of whom had previously been members of an earlier association which had been formed to prosecute offenders against the child-labor laws already on the Statute Book. But the most eminent supporters of all were the

three big master cotton spinners, Charles Hindley, Joseph Brotherton, and John Fielden, who were to remain connected with the
movement for the next 15 years. They were a strange trio, though
they had certain qualities of piety and disposition in common.
All three were self-made men, calling themselves Radical-Liberals
and shortly to become Members in the new reformed Parliament.
Two of them—Brotherton and Fielden—had worked in the mills
as children. And all three were intimately associated with nonconformist religious groups. Hindley had been educated by the
Moravians at Fulneck; Fielden was a noted Unitarian; and
Brotherton, whose untiring philanthropic exertions remind one
so forcibly of Oastler's father, was one of the leading figures in
a little sect known as the Bible Christian Church.

There were two features of this Lancashire movement, however, that distinguished it from the one in Yorkshire, and both
arose from the fact that for the past twelve years child labor
in the cotton industry had nominally been under parliamentary
regulation. One was its pre-occupation with the problem of law
enforcement, and the other its greater insistence upon the need
to regulate the working hours of adults as well as of children.

Lancashire men knew from experience what a farce the mere
statutory enactment of a reform could amount to in practice.
According to Peel's Act of 1819, supplemented by Hobhouse's
meager measure of 1831, children between the ages of nine and
eighteen in the cotton industry were limited to a sixty-nine-hour
week (exclusive of meal times). But the means for enforcing the
law were hopelessly inadequate: in consequence evasions were
common and brazen. This was admitted on all sides. The only
way to improve matters, according to general Lancashire opinion,
· was to direct the regulation to the *machines* rather than to the
hands that operated them: in other words, to control the hours
during which the engines might be run. So while the slogan of the
Yorkshire campaign had been 'ten hours a day and a time book,'
the Lancashire cry became 'ten hours a day and restriction on
motive power.'

Even the masters were coming round to this way of thinking.
Most of them, of course, would have preferred no regulation at
all; but seeing that some sort of new parliamentary interference

appeared inevitable, they wanted it at least to be a uniform
burden for all. This was expressed in a very forthright manner at
a meeting of the leading Manchester mill owners called to consider what they should do in view of the new Ten Hours demand.
Having been told by one of their number just back from London
that he had heard the Cabinet strongly disliked Sadler's Bill but
believed 'the feeling out of doors was so great in its favour that
they could not well oppose it,' these masters drew up a petition
to Parliament declaring that 'whatever measure be adopted, it
ought to be made equal and effectual in its operation, and that
from an accurate and attentive examination of the working of the
last act we are convinced no measure can be made effectual
which does not place *the restriction upon the power by which
the machinery of mills and factories is propelled.'*

There was no fundamental difference of purpose between the
Lancashire and Yorkshire movements: both were striving for
exactly the same goal. Yet in this Lancashire insistence upon
workability and enforcement there lay the possibility of diver-
gences and complications later. A changed political situation
might lead some of the Lancashire men to judge it worth while
to take what they could get in the form of a practical partial
measure rather than hold out for a full demand that might prove
unworkable. If the existing twelve hours' law was so flagrantly
evaded, could the Ten Hours cry be taken too seriously? Even
at this stage, one can detect slight hints of hesitation in some
quarters about the apparent intransigence of the Yorkshire men
on that question. One group of Manchester clergy and gentry sent
a delegate named Whittle to confer with Oastler on the real policy
of the West Riding movement. Oastler bluntly told him, he reported, that they all stood solidly for 'a ten hours bill for children
or none at all.' Nevertheless, the Manchester group could not
bring itself to any such definite commitment despite its strongly
proclaimed sympathies.

Clearly, however, such considerations had no practical bearing
on the immediate future. Sadler's Bill had only just been tabled
and a long, hard struggle lay in the weeks ahead. Any sort of
reform at all would have to be fought for through every stage
of the legislative journey.

¶ 5

Meanwhile the masters had been just as busy as the Ten Hours men. For them, too, the introduction of Sadler's Bill was the signal to extend their organization and intensify their propaganda; but since most of their planning went on behind closed doors it is not now possible to reconstruct the full story. Local Short Time Committees, however, as well as Tory newspaper reporters set themselves to unearth as much as they could of these 'hole and corner meetings' and to give them the widest publicity. Intrigue, Oastler kept saying, had been the masters' chief weapon in destroying Hobhouse's intentions: publicity was the only way to circumvent it this time. Proclaim from the housetops every gathering of masters, he told his followers; broadcast their petitions and refute their claims, for they alone need fear publicity. The truth about factory conditions was its own trumpeter.

Whenever possible the operatives followed his advice with vigor. The Keighley masters, for instance, met with the utmost secrecy outside the town, but somehow the local Committee got to know about it. The very next morning the place was plastered with posters:

TO THE INHABITANTS OF KEIGHLEY

To warn you that a Hole and Corner meeting was holden yesterday at Bingley, to frustrate the designs of Humanity and Justice.

BEWARE

A TEN HOURS BILL IS OUR BILL: A TWELVE HOURS BILL IS THEIR BILL.

Everywhere the other Committees did the same sort of thing.

By the end of February after innumerable meetings, agreement on policy had been secured among the masters and an extensive scheme of collaboration set up. The general demand was in accordance with the Halifax resolutions: a twelve-hour day, exclusive of meal times, for all children over ten years old. Petitions to that effect were sent to Westminster and delegates appointed

BALANCE SHEET

of the

MANCHESTER SHORT TIME COMMITTEE

published April 28, 1832

Dr.

	£	s.	d.
A Friend	1	0	0
Ditto	0	5	0
Ditto	0	2	6
C. Hindley, Esq.	1	0	0
T. Cook, Esq.	1	0	0
T. Townend, Esq.	1	0	0
C. Hindley, Esq, from a Friend	2	0	0
Our Yorkshire Friends	4	0	0
T. Fielden, Esq.	2	0	0
The Editor of the Manchester and Salford Advertiser	1	0	0
James Turner	1	0	0
Mr. Brooks	0	5	0
The Mechanics, Card-room hands, Spinners, Dressers, & others in the Hope Mills	8	16	3
Messrs. M'Connell's Old Mill Spinners	1	0	0
Mr. William Carruthers' Spinners	0	10	0
Messrs. Hargreaves and Higginbottom's Collecting Book	1	9	0
Messrs. Burrow and Moore's Collecting Book	0	5	7
Messrs. Brierley and Co's Collecting Book	0	9	2½
Mr. Lawton's Collecting Book	0	0	6
Mr. Farrall, Farrier	0	0	6
	£27	3	6½
Contributions from the Card-room hands, Spinners, Dressers, Weavers and Overlookers	35	14	4½

Cr.

	£	s.	d.
Meeting at the Mechanics' Institution	3	6	0
A number of Meetings held in the town and neighbouring districts	4	19	10½
Delivering Circulars calling Meeting	0	7	6
Petition Sheets and Ruling Paper, etc.	1	3	1½
Delegations and lost time	13	7	0
Subscription Books for Collectors and Letters	0	12	5
Lent Money	1	0	0
Printing Petitions, Address Bills calling Meeting, Bill for Ashton Meetings, Address for Stockport, Address to Workmen, Bill for Petitions, and Advertisements	12	16	0
Secretary 7 weeks	1	10	0
Expenditure	39	1	11
Balance in hand	23	16	0

152

to lobby among Members. Indicative of the unanimity displayed is the fact that only 3 of the 56 firms in the Huddersfield area refused to sign their local petition. In Lancashire the Master Cotton Spinners Association levied on its members a uniform impost of sixpence per horse power 'to defray the expenses of watching the bill through Parliament.'

On 16 March 1832, Sadler's Ten Hours Bill came up for the second reading.

CHAPTER XIV

The Pilgrimage to York

SUCCESSFUL in every sense though the campaign of public
meetings had been, Oastler had no intention of just waiting
upon events. If it were really true what they were saying in the
Manchester counting-houses, that though most of the Cabinet
disliked Sadler's measure, 'the feeling out of doors was so great
in its favour that they could not well oppose it,' then it was imperative that this pressure should be kept at its maximum until
the bill was safely on the statute book. Members of Parliament
must this time be made to hear above the whispers of the lobby
the shouts that came from the Pennine valleys.

What better for the purpose than a spectacular demonstration
by the entire county? Not a mere town meeting, but a county
gathering that would make the whole of England talk, demon-
strating the high resolve and solidarity of the Ten Hours men
and shaking the easy complacency of those four Yorkshire Members who were all too apt to take the voice of Marshall for the
voice of the West Riding.

The county meetings of freemen had often enough in the past
been an Englishman's boast, and Yorkshire meetings in particular
had on occasion been more than local episodes, being written into
the very history of the land. The old Castle Yard at York was a
shrine of political memory: 'the very cradle of Reform,' as one
modern historian has called it. Thither at each election time had
gathered successive generations of freeholders, Oastler's ancestors
among them, to listen to orgies of oratory and mount the hustings
to return the county Member. There Wilberforce had achieved
his first great victory in 1784: there Oastler had been with him
when he won his equally dramatic victory in 1807. And not so
long ago this same independent county had led the vanguard in

154

another national cause. It was only 52 years since that other
sturdy Yorkshireman, the Reverend Mr. Wyvil, had presided over
the memorable gathering of gentry, clergy, and freeholders that
had initiated the great campaign for 'economical reform': the
meeting that contemporaries believed was 'such as perhaps never
assembled in the same manner in this nation.' If one county meeting could shake vested interests to their foundation, a second
might do the same. This time, however, it should not be the
assembly of a single class but of all classes: operatives should be
there as well as gentry, shopkeepers as well as freeholders, the
unemployed as well as the politicians. Indeed, it would be something more than a county meeting: it would be a pilgrimage.

Such were Oastler's large imaginings in the days that followed
the conclusion of his campaign. Gradually the idea took shape.
As soon as it was clear in his own mind he got into touch with
Sadler and Wood, discussed with them the details, and then
unfolded the project to the leaders of the Short Time groups.
All were enthusiastic. They decided the meeting should be held
on Easter Tuesday, 24 April, and began at once to make the
necessary preparations. The appropriate constitutional forms
were carefully observed. A numerously signed requisition from
gentry and clergy was presented to the High Sheriff; his permission was duly given; the requisition was published; and by mid-
April everything was ready. In Holy Week, therefore, Oastler
issued a manifesto which appeared in every public place throughout the Riding, bidding the operatives appear in York,

> and in one loud, long thundering Voice let
> Yorkshire and all England hear you Swear
> OUR CHILDREN SHALL BE FREE!!

The most careful preparations were made, the whole project
being organized on a scheme of graded responsibility. The Central Committee for the Riding made the general plan; upon the
Short Time Committees of each district devolved the particular responsibilities for their areas; and they in turn delegated the more
detailed work to the sub-committees of village and factory under
their direction. Every division was to be led by the officers and
members of its own Short Time Committee. The route and the

massing of the various contingents was worked out in the same way. The smaller places were to converge upon the larger and the regiments so formed were to move in three main columns— from Bradford, Halifax, and Huddersfield—to Leeds. Thence they would all advance upon York, pausing only at the race-course just outside the city to take refreshment and get into their positions for making a spectacular grand march to the Castle Yard with bands playing and flags unfurled.

The Central Committee arranged to have rest stations all along the line of march. It would take the greater part of three days to get all the demonstrators from their homes to York and back again; and some who came from the remoter villages upon the western moors would have to walk nearly 120 miles before they had finished. Even the Huddersfield men would have to do a good 46 miles each way with rough going—literally up hill and down dale—the whole time. So barns and warehouses were temporarily taken over at different points; straw was got in; inns were notified; and arrangements were made to supply each contingent with bread and cheese and beer at appointed places. A few days in advance the Committees drew up lists of those who intended to come and gave each man a food ticket to be exchanged on the journey. Special arrangements were made for the unemployed, who were to march together in a single body.

It was scarcely to be wondered at that such a project should occasion a good deal of alarm. Farms on the route would be plundered, people said; ricks would be burnt and flocks slaughtered, and York was sure to be sacked. Even the High Sheriff seems to have grown somewhat apprehensive as the day drew near, so that Oastler had to go personally to pledge his word that no untoward incident would occur. The opponents of Sadler's Bill, of course, lost no opportunity to spread the panic and pour ridicule on the scheme. And in an unlucky moment the *Mercury* accused Oastler of delusions of grandeur, saying that his arrogance had grown so overweening that he imagined himself to be a king. The title immediately caught the humorous fancy of the operatives. With remarkable speed its use spread through the industrial districts of Lancashire and Yorkshire and within a few weeks Oastler was everywhere known as the Factory

King. It was a curious phenomenon of social psychology. Oastler's significance as a public figure had suddenly become crystallized into a sardonic symbol of affection and to the end of his days the name stuck. There are still some in those parts who remember hearing their grandfathers talk about 'the old King.'

The first movements began at dawn on Easter Monday. The Huddersfield division, 'Oastler's Own,' assembled in the market place at five o'clock, there to await the coming of the other divisions from Holmfirth and Honley and the surrounding hamlets. Several of the districts brought their own bands and all came bearing banners and devices of every conceivable kind which they had been busy making during the previous week. As the clock chimed six there went up a mighty shout, the banners were raised, the bands struck up the National Anthem, and with Oastler walking at the head along with John Leech and Lawrence Pitkeithly, Samuel Glendinning and John Hanson, this strange battalion of the underprivileged set off along the road to Leeds.

At the same hour other divisions were moving out of Heckmondwike, Dewsbury, Keighley, and Bingley, while Parson Bull was leading forth the men of Bradford. Some of the men who had no shoes of their own had borrowed a pair for the journey; others tramped the whole way in their clogs. The fortunate had got the loan of a coat from their neighbors as well, while the rest made do with a well-greased woolen 'piece' or blanket. Hundreds decided to come at the last moment, and in some districts even the women suddenly caught the thrill and joined the procession too.

The streets of Leeds were early crowded with thousands of sightseers who had turned out to watch the various divisions come in. The peals that echoed from the steeple of the old parish church added to the gala spirit (the vicar was the president of the General Committee and was going to be on the platform at York). One by one the contingents arrived and marched to their rendezvous at the White Cloth Hall Yard, where refreshments were provided. Then they were led off to their assigned warehouses to rest for a few hours before starting on the all-night march to the capital.

The Cloth Hall Yard that Easter Monday afternoon presented

a spectacle unique in its history. The forest of colored banners;
the clatter of countless clogs; the thousands of operatives and of
unemployed in their coarse and ragged clothes already stained
with the dust of the march; the orderly conduct and self-discipline
of the men under their own local leaders as detachment after
detachment debouched upon the Yard; the expectancy on those
drawn and poverty-lined faces—these were things that would not
soon be forgotten.

The last division was due at the White Cloth Hall by four
o'clock in the afternoon. Some while before then, however, the
day which had begun with sunshine grew overclouded, and in
the late afternoon the rain began to fall. It continued falling all
the evening. Patiently the men waited in the warehouses, but
there was no hint of a let-up. Hour after hour it poured, until by
eleven o'clock the leaders abandoned all hope of its clearing and
decided to carry on with their plans anyway. They were able to
hire a few carts and wagons, but not many: the majority would
have to go on foot. So just before midnight the first division
moved out of Leeds on its 22-mile march, and one after another
into the early hours the others followed. By that time a pitiless
storm was raging, and when the editor of the *Intelligencer* set
out in a gig soon after three in the morning, the rain was tumbling
down in torrents. Not until the first streaks of dawn did the storm
begin to ease. Nothing could have tested the men's morale more
severely, yet they responded splendidly. Singing old hymns and
folk songs, they trudged forward through the night with Oastler
and his 'own' division in the vanguard. Several people have left
us their impressions of that extraordinary march. 'The appearance
of the road was novel and impressive' says one who was present.

It resounded with cheers which were uttered by the Pilgrims at
those who passed them in carriages of various sorts. In some groups
there were torches composed of old ropes, and the undulations of the
road afforded many views of illuminated groups successively rising
over the hills and disappearing the next instant, leaving a loud, long
cheer behind as they sank out of view. It was indeed a moving scene.

At last, plastered with dirt, tired, hungry, and wet through,
they reached the race-course outside York, where the unemployed

were to have refreshment served to them in the Grand Stand. Here another disaster occurred: the beer had come, but none of the bread and cheese that had been arranged for. Quickly the hope that had sustained them during the night turned to resentment—soon it might grow into something worse. It was a critical moment. 'But for a good Providence and the magnanimity of King Richard there might have been havoc that day,' wrote one eye-witness.

Oastler had gone on into the city to the headquarters at the George Inn, where John Wood and the other organizers were to assemble. One of the Huddersfield men brought him news of the mischance out at Knavesmire and told him that rioting would soon start if something were not done immediately to calm the men. Oastler mounted his horse and galloped off at once. When he reached the race-course he found Pitkeithly haranguing the multitude, trying to appease them. Suddenly Pitkeithly saw him coming and shouted, 'the King, the King!' The mood of the crowd changed instantly. They cleared a passage for him to the Grand Stand and as soon as he stood up to speak gave him 'a three times three that rent the air.' He himself was wet through and bedraggled like the rest of them, having insisted on sharing all the discomforts of the marchers and refused to take advantage of any shelter on the way. Every sentence he poured forth, therefore, was vibrant with his deep feeling of unity with the folk he led; and they recognized the fact. Never did Oastler win a more timely triumph. He stayed the panic just in time. First he steadied, then consoled the huge crowd, and finally humored it back again into cheerfulness and animation.

Having got them all into their correct formation once more, he remounted his horse and, surrounded by band, bodyguard, and banners, led the procession through Micklegate Bar into the city. As the contingents took up their stations round the hustings in Castle Yard the sun began to break through the clouds. With the ready superstition of the fatigued, they took it for an omen, and for the next hour or two there was general gaiety while the leaders went about distributing the food they had been hastily buying up in the town. It was estimated that there were over 12,000 people within the Yard itself and just as many outside.

The proceedings of the meeting lasted five hours. Most of those who had been on the platforms during the big campaign were on the hustings, as well as some eminent new recruits. A surprising number of clergy were present, as well as several doctors. It made an impressive list in its political and professional variety: Captain Wood of Sandal, a country gentleman soon to be Huddersfield's Radical candidate for Parliament; Dr. Smith of the Leeds Infirmary; the Honorable William Duncombe, a former county Member who, as Viscount Feversham, was later to champion the cause in the House of Lords; George Strickland, the sitting Whig Member, who now more than made amends for his vacillation over the Hobhouse Bill by his emphatic declaration for the movement; and a dozen others just as eminent. Several of the operatives' officials spoke, and of course all the old leaders —Michael Sadler (sick man though he was), John Wood, Parson Bull, and Oastler. 'King Richard,' says one account, 'moved his audience into tears, into ecstasy, and into the firmness of immovable determination by his eloquence,' and the reception they gave him was thunderous.

The affair passed off without incident. 'Gentlemen,' said the High Sheriff in closing the meeting, 'I cannot let this opportunity pass without remarking upon the good conduct you have observed during the course of this day; a conduct which reflects credit upon yourselves, which should be held up as an example for the imitation of others, and which is worthy of the great county to which you belong.' The relief was general.

Just before dusk fell they began to move out of the city with Oastler again leading. Tadcaster was to be the first stop, 9 miles away, where stables, barns, and out-houses had been bespoken, but many never reached there that night. The rain had begun again and a heavy wind was blowing; most of the men were already worn out, and scores with blistered and bleeding feet could scarcely move. Hundreds of them dropped out along the way to beg what shelter they could get in taverns, cottages, and sheds. Probably Parson Bull's foresight alone prevented any fatality. Hastily hiring some covered wagons in York when the tempest broke, he and the rest of the Committee drove through the night picking up stragglers and administering restoratives.

Fortunately Wednesday morning dawned bright and dry. As the men left Tadcaster after a frugal breakfast, their spirits rose. Someone in the van started to sing the Doxology and in a moment it was taken up by those around and passed from division to division to the rear. The rest of the dozen miles to Leeds were covered in good humor. A couple of miles outside the town Oastler called a halt to let the rear-guard come up. Then having re-formed their ranks, the pilgrims made their orderly return to the White Cloth Hall Yard, while thousands lined the streets to watch their coming, some to cheer and a few to jeer.

A rest and some refreshment in the Yard, a farewell speech from Michael Sadler, and then the remaining divisions started for their respective towns. The market place was thronged when the 'King's Own' reached Huddersfield. It was an unexpected reception, and the Short Time Committee at once turned it to advantage by organizing an impromptu meeting. Some of the divisions, however, still had another two or three hours of walking before they reached home. Oastler himself did not get back to Fixby until long after dark. He had kept to his resolution to do the whole journey on foot both ways, and when he went to bed that night the skin of his feet peeled off with his stockings.

Not until Saturday was the bizarre chapter completed. That morning's issue of the *Mercury* was full of contempt for the whole business, pouring the ready vials of its scorn on Oastler and everyone else associated with the episode. The story was told in such a way that readers were led to suppose the organization had been chaotic and drunkenness general. The Leeds men who had been on the march were enraged. Early in the forenoon some two hundred of them marched through the town led by a man carrying the offending copy of the *Mercury* tied with black crape to the top of a pole. On reaching the *Mercury* office they set light to the paper amid the hisses and groans of the crowd. The Short Time Committee called for a more elaborate demonstration later in the day.

At about half-past eight that evening a procession set out from the Committee's headquarters at the Union Inn, bearing an effigy of Baines. On the front and back of the figure was the inscription 'The great Liar of the North'—the title that Cobbett had given

Baines in a recent number of the *Political Register*.[1] On its breast
the effigy bore the words: 'The *Mercury* is the Death of Thousands.' Preceded by a band playing 'The Rogue's March' and
bearing aloft the symbol of its wrath, the procession marched all
over the town. First they went to the office of the *Patriot* and
there gave three cheers for Radicalism. Then they went to the
Intelligencer office to give more cheers and make the effigy do
obeisance amidst roars of laughter from the crowd. Outside
Sadler's house, with bared heads, the crowd sang the National
Anthem; then on to the home of Dr. Smith, who had been at
York with them, for a lusty singing of 'Rule Britannia.' Finally
they brought up again at the office of the *Mercury*. By this time
the crowd had swelled to several thousands. The city authorities
were powerless. A huge bonfire was built, the dummy of Baines
was stuck on top, and amid the execrations and catcalls of the
mob he was burnt to ashes.

From its first dawning in Oastler's imagination until the last
echoes of that hilarious Saturday night had died away, the affair
was sheerest melodrama, though not the less significant to the
historian on that account. As symptomatic of pervasive discontents
it is far from being a negligible episode. Only a deep malaise in
the body politic can yield the emotional energies that may be
brought to such a focus. In Parliament and elsewhere, comment
testified to the apprehension it evoked, while in the memory of
those who took part it seemed to assume in retrospect a special
portentousness. A generation later Samuel Kydd, the lawyer who
wrote the history of the Factory Movement, could still speak of it
with evangelical intensity.

The journey, its objects, its circumstances [he said], will never be
forgotten. Generations yet unborn will learn with wonder that in a
professedly Christian land such a cause could exist for such a demon-

---

[1] Cobbett several times used this designation for Baines, the first occasion being on 12 November 1831. Three months before the pilgrimage to
York he had written apropos the Leeds election: 'This Babbington has the
support of one Baines, proprietor of the *Leeds Mercury*, who, in fact, put
Brougham and Vaux into Parliament for Yorkshire and who is, you know,
called the GREAT LIAR OF THE NORTH; a name, which on account of his
publications he most richly deserves.' *Cobbett's Political Register*: vol. 75,
No. 5 (28 Jan. 1832), p. 293.

stration . . . The happier firesides of our distant successors will be entertained with the legend of 'The Pilgrimage of Mercy,' and England's hearths and altars shall yet, we hope, record the downfall of infant slavery in every part of our island.

In Oastler's memory the affair became magnified to grandiose proportions, as though that day a Bastille had fallen. Certainly it was a red-letter day for him personally. In a sense, it placed a public seal upon the compact with the operatives, which he had entered into on Fixby lawn. The campaign of meetings had shown what he could do with an audience; this showed what he might do with the mob. It had put to the test the organization he had been building up in recent months and the test had proved successful; now his imagination began to range. Henceforward he grew more and more disposed to think in terms of even larger and more compelling demonstrations.

CHAPTER XV

Sadler's Ten Hours Bill

THE GOVERNMENT had given Sadler permission to bring
his bill to a second reading only on condition that it should
then be referred to a Select Committee of the House of Commons. *The Times* scoffed. 'To bend six hundred and fifty-eight
persons to lend themselves to private interests against the plain
dictates of justice and humanity is certainly a serious task,' it said
in a sarcastic editorial on 13 February; 'but to mould a small
committee of perhaps fifteen or twenty-three individuals principally selected from among the representatives of the manufacturing interests . . . would probably prove to the great mill
owners no very great task.' Two weeks later it felt obliged to
warn its readers anew that 'the manufacturers have arranged
themselves in formidable strength and are sparing no exertion
for the continuance of the existing system, notwithstanding the
melancholy proofs which are on record of its fatal effects upon
the lives, health and morals of the rising generation.'

Though disappointed, Sadler had no alternative but to agree
to the Government's condition, and on 16 March he duly moved
the reading. The terms of his bill were simple. They provided for
a ten-hour day for all factory operatives under 18 years old, with
8 hours on Saturdays, exclusive of meal times. Night work (defined as extending from seven in the evening until six in the
morning) was forbidden for all under 21; and no child was to
be allowed to enter a factory before the age of 9 years. The only
means of enforcement that the bill provided was the keeping of
a time-book in every factory.

¶ 1

Sadler's three-hour speech on behalf of his bill ranks as one
of the classics of British oratory in the nineteenth century. Moral

fervor and the simple pity that comes from somber realism were
fused in prose of rhythmic dignity. He admitted that legislative
interference with industry was an evil: but so was all legislation,
he said, to be tolerated only in order to prevent the development
of a greater evil. It was nonsense to oppose factory regulation
on the ground that workers were 'free agents.' In theory they
might be,

but practically I fear the fact is far otherwise, even regarding those
who are of mature age; and the boasted freedom of our labourers in
many pursuits will, on a just view of their condition, be found little
more than a name. Those who argue the question upon mere abstract
principles seem, in my apprehension, too much to forget the conditions
of society: the unequal division of property or rather its total monopoly
by the few, leaving the many nothing but what they can obtain by
their daily labour; which very labour cannot become available for the
purposes of daily subsistence without the consent of those who own
the property of the community. Hence it is clear that . . . the employer and the employed do not meet on equal terms in the market of
labour; on the contrary, the latter, whatever his age and call him as
free as you please, is often almost entirely at the mercy of the former.

If this were the case with adults, how much more was it so with
children?

Disposing thus of the current clichés derived from the economists, he went on to describe actual conditions in mills and factories. He told of the long hours and night work, the fetid atmosphere and deadening monotony. He showed the House the thongs
that were used for flogging children. He read to them part of a
memorandum which John Wood had specially prepared for him,
and cited the evidence of doctors with practical experience in
local infirmaries, such as Thackrah and Smith. He particularly
stressed the long-range consequences of these things for society
as a whole: the growth of a debilitated and demoralized proletariat. Against such a case the mill owners were putting forward
the same specious arguments as those advanced by the owners
of West Indian slaves against the abolitionists. Yet the Government had repeatedly rejected such reasonings in the latter instance
while listening to them in the former. What an irony thus lay in
the famous Orders-in-Council of the previous November: orders

which so far 'interfered' with the liberty and property rights of
slave owners as to restrict the working day of slaves in the Colonies from 6 to 6. Those were exactly the hours that Sadler's bill
was claiming for British children.

Viscount Althorp, Leader of the House, gave the answer on
behalf of the Government. It sounded ominous and created such
an unfavorable impression among the operatives in the north that
immediately the figure of Althorp came to stand for them as the
particular symbol of opposition: the villain in the parliamentary
drama. That was decidedly unfair to Althorp. He was certainly
no villain, but only an aristocrat with a limited range of imagina-
tive sensibility and an unusual taste for statistics, whose cautious
acceptance of an emerging orthodoxy was credited to him for
common sense. His reply to Sadler revealed as much. Sadler, he
said, had presented only one side of the question and might unwittingly have exaggerated. In such matters 'the utmost caution'
was necessary, for otherwise children might cease to be employed
in factories altogether: 'Now I appeal to the honourable member
whether a measure which would prevent children from obtaining
any employment in factories would not be more injurious than
beneficial to the labouring classes.' And to the moral fervor of
Sadler's challenge, he merely answered with the blandness of
apparent impartiality. 'I am not prepared to pledge myself in any
way with respect to the measure,' he said; 'even if the Committee
should report favourably of the bill, I will not pledge myself,
before the report be made, to support a measure of such vast
importance. I do not feel myself justified in saying that, whatever
the opinion of the Committee may be, I will abide by their
decision.'

Sixteen other members spoke during the debate: 5 in favor of
the bill and 5 against, while the rest merely put on record their
benevolent dispositions and expressed relief that the matter was
going to be properly investigated by what they hoped would be
an impartial tribunal.

The arguments advanced against the measure contained nothing new, being merely a restatement of the points that had been
elaborated in the Yorkshire newspapers eighteen months before.
The two recurrent themes were the menace of foreign competi-

tion and the danger of a flight of capital to countries where there was no such interference with human liberty. 'If you limit the hours of labour,' said Mr. J. T. Hope, 'you will to nearly the same extent reduce the profits of the capital on which the labour is employed.' So, either prices would have to be raised or wages would have to be lowered. In the one case England would lose her foreign markets: in the other, the workers would be grievously harmed.

The most striking feature of the debate, however, was the extraordinary spirit of fatalism about social matters voiced in so many of the speeches. 'Undoubtedly the system which is pursued in these manufactories relating to the working of young children is a great evil,' the member for Carlisle frankly declared; 'but it appears to me that the remedy which the honourable gentleman proposes to apply is worse than the disease. There appears to me to be only a choice of evils—the children must either work or starve. I say, therefore, that it is the least evil of the two to go on with the present system.' This spirit of fatalism extended to the matter of law enforcement as well. It seemed to be the general conviction of the opposition that such a drastic bill could never be implemented. Hobhouse's last Act had 'proved totally inoperative' because of evasions, said one member from the north; how, then, could it be expected that a much more sweeping measure would be observed?

It was apparent, therefore, that the impetus for change would have to come from the efforts of Sadler and his Committee, and that little help could be expected from the Government in getting the bill through Parliament.

¶ 2

The sending of Sadler's Bill to a Select Committee aroused great resentment among the Yorkshire operatives. They could see no other purpose in the maneuver than a subtle attempt by the Government to side-step the agitation and defeat the measure. 'Why a select committee should be required to ascertain whether or not it be right and proper to confine infants of seven, eight, nine, or ten years of age more than twelve hours a day, at unremitting labour, in the atmosphere of a factory,' said *The Times*, 'is beyond our imagination.' It was also beyond the imagination of the operatives. Their attitude was one of suspicion and bewilderment: intrigue had defeated Hobhouse's Bill, and now they felt that a procedural device was being invoked to defeat Sadler's. The ministry had not used a select committee when it had wanted to legislate on such matters as Negro slavery or the condition of jails, they argued; why, then, should it be necessary in this case? 'I do not think that any measure that has ever been adopted since I knew anything about public matters has so much dissatisfied the operative classes of the West Riding of the County of York as this very measure with respect to the Select Committee,' Oastler told that body when he came to give evidence; 'they have not sense enough to know why they should be put to such expense to prove that which is self-evident, and which every Member of Parliament must know to be true; but they do say that it is for the purpose of making it so expensive that they will not be able to bear it and that they will be beaten on account of the expense.' Witnesses would have to be sought out to give evidence: men and women with little experience of life outside their own circumscribed routines, many of them illiterate, who would now have to face the frightening embarrassments of coming to London and undergoing cross-examination by the great ones of the land. It seemed preposterously unnecessary, the more so as there was the obvious risk of victimization when they got back home. When Althorp's pronouncement was reported, therefore, many a member of the Short Time Committees was disposed to regard the whole thing as a farce which ought to be boycotted, though eventually Oastler and Sadler managed to overpersuade the dissenters.

A vast amount of preparation had to be put in hand straightaway, for the first hearing was going to be held on 12 April. Before that date evidence had to be organized, witnesses selected, and money raised. For three weeks Oastler and the West Riding Central Committee were in a flurry of activity. The first thing they did was to mail a lithographed letter to all supporters, explaining the circumstances and urgently appealing for funds to pay for sending the witnesses to London. Special collectors were named for each district. At the same time every Short Time Committee put out in the form of a standardized poster an 'Address to the Inhabitants' of its locality, making the same appeal.

But the most important task of all was the selection of the witnesses and the correlation of their evidence. Only through intimate co-operation between the Central Committee at Leeds and the various local Committees could this be done. Nothing more clearly demonstrated the efficiency of the organization that Oastler had built up than the speed and precision with which this co-operation was secured. The Central Committee planned and classified the general nature of the testimony to be submitted. It indicated the kind of information that would be sought by the members of the Select Committee and the points on which witnesses must be prepared for cross-examination. This scheme it transmitted to each of the Short Time Committees. Their work was to assemble the local evidence, sift and verify it, and then forward it to the Central Committee for comparison and coordination with the returns from other districts. In all the communications from the central body the utmost emphasis was put upon the necessity for Committees and witnesses alike to speak to only such things as they were familiar with from actual personal experience. Oastler had long ago learned what strength he commanded as a result of being absolutely sure of the facts he cited, and he impressed that lesson upon the Short Time Committees as earnestly as he possibly could. In this way, all the witnesses who were finally chosen to go to London had their credentials carefully tested, so that by the time of the first hearing the organizers could contemplate the thought of public cross-examination with tolerable confidence.

The thoroughness of all these preparations is vividly illustrated by one of the documents recently found among Oastler's papers. A confidential memorandum which he apparently drew up on behalf of the Central Committee, it specifies in questionnaire form the kind of information considered desirable to have presented at the hearings. Each local committee received a copy (though this one alone now survives), using it as a directive for assembling and collecting the evidence, while the central body utilized it in making the overall plans. A careful examination of the document lends added interest to the reading of Sadler's eventual report, for the questions it contains are the very questions that were put to the witnesses day after day as they came up to testify. Obviously Sadler and his friends had copies with them during the interrogations.[1]

¶ 3

The Select Committee under Sadler's chairmanship sat on 43 days between 12 April and 7 August. Its personnel was very mixed. Among its 37 members were the two Yorkshire county Members, Morpeth and Strickland; outright opponents of factory legislation, such as Poulett Thomson, president of the Board of Trade, and Gisborne, the big colliery owner of Duckenfield; skeptics such as Hobhouse; uncertainties, like Peel; and avowed sympathizers, such as the downright die-hard Tory, Sir Robert Inglis. Eighty-seven witnesses were called, including 60 workers of various ages (three of whom were women), 21 doctors, and two clergymen.

The main burden of the investigation fell upon Sadler personally, who took his responsibilities with the utmost conscientiousness. At the sittings of the Committee he had to keep firm control over the sequence of question and answer, watching for misinterpretations and putting supplementary questions to unravel ambiguities. He had to supervise the formulation of the findings, mastering the data and sometimes spending the entire night correcting the shorthand reports. Letters poured in from all quarters and had to be dealt with, and deputations had to be given an audience. Even a normally healthy man would have found it a considerable tax upon his strength; Sadler was suffering from heart trouble before it began and the extra burden strained him to exhaustion. His friends soon began to notice a change in his appearance. Several times a doctor had to be called in, but he would not think of giving up. 'It is God's work and therefore it must be done,' he kept saying. Within two years he was dead, and one can hardly doubt that the effort of these months helped to hasten his end.

The *Report* which the Select Committee completed in August has become one of the best known British State Papers of the

[1] This document is reproduced in Appendix B.

nineteenth century. Its 982 folio pages present a symposium of
sordid wretchedness, the evidence adduced exceeding anything
that Oastler had written in his letters on Yorkshire Slavery. Obviously the question of factory regulation could not now be
shelved as it had been the previous September. The investigation 'revealed a state of misery which even Sadler had not disclosed,' says the conservative historian Spencer Walpole; 'the
Committee, merely reporting the evidence without comment of
its own, made a bill of factory reform a necessity.' Even that
acidulous individualist Harriet Martineau was constrained to say
that 'by guilty neglect we had brought ourselves into an in-
extricable embarrassment.'

The power of the *Report* lay in the comprehensiveness and
vivid realism of its detail; only a reading of the document itself
can recreate the effect which that produced. Yet the general pattern of the findings stands out conspicuously enough. Children
were found to enter the mills and factories at any age from 6
years up, though 8 or 9 appeared to be the commonest. The
hours they worked varied greatly. The nominal regular day in
most districts was from six o'clock in the morning until seven
in the evening; but this was no more than nominal since refusal to
work overtime was out of the question. Rush seasons might see
these hours indefinitely extended, and the fifteen-hour day was
not uncommon. Even such a popular master as Halliley of Dewsbury worked his mill from five a.m. to ten p.m. during busy seasons. Night work was frequently compulsory, and if the children
would not go into the night shifts they were forthwith dismissed.
In some places at rush times the hands were kept in the factory
for forty-eight hours or more at a stretch, with occasional spells
off for rest on straw or sacking thrown down in some corner of
the mill. The intervals for meals were of the briefest. In many
mills only 30 or 40 minutes were allowed for midday dinner:
breakfast and tea had to be snatched while the machinery was
running. All the witnesses said that the food they took to eat
during the day became filthy when unpacked, because of the
dirt and fluff in the rooms. Often even the midday interval was
abridged for cleaning the machines.

Conditions of work were as deplorable as the hours were long.

Most of the witnesses complained of the evil atmosphere in which they had to labor. The air was full of impurities, particularly in the flax mills where the dust and fluff and fibers made it difficult to breathe. The rooms became exhaustingly stuffy as the day wore on. Close confinement in hot rooms and the odor of sweaty bodies made the air noxious anyway; to that was added the stink from the oil and grease of the machines, and in winter the gas from the lamps.

One thing they all complained of was the continuousness of the work, especially in the spinning mills. The little 'pieceners,' for example, were on their feet almost the whole day, going to and fro along their 'frame,' watching the bobbins and joining the broken threads without let-up. And repeatedly the older witnesses testified that during their lifetime there had been a continuous speeding-up of one process after another and a general increase in the intensity of labor. All of them spoke in their particular ways of the nameless and growing nervous tension that resulted.

But that was not the worst. The positions in which these 'piecener' children had to work were shockingly disabling. One witness after another brought this home to the Committee, in many cases their own deformed bodies giving sad corroboration to what they said. This is how one overlooker explained it:

[Q.] Will you describe to the Committee the position in which children stand to 'piece' in a worsted mill, as it may serve to explain the number and severity of those cases of distortion which occur?

[A.] At the top of the spindle there is a fly goes across, and the child takes hold of the fly by the ball of his left hand, and he throws the left shoulder up and the right knee inward; he has the thread to get with the right hand, and he has to stoop his head down to see what he is doing. They throw the right knee inward in that way, and all the children that I have seen, that I could judge, that are made cripples by the practice of piecening worsted, invariably bend in the right knee.

[Q.] Have you remarked that cases of deformity are very common in Bradford?

[A.] They are very common. I have the names and addresses of, I think, about two hundred families that I have visited myself, that have all deformed children, and I have taken particular care not to put one single individual down to whom it had happened by accident, but all whom I judge to have been thrown crooked by the practice of piecening, and of throwing up the left shoulder and bending the right knee.

Growth was stunted and deformity frequent, as one would expect from this overlooker's evidence. Poor health was common, bad chests and asthmatical conditions being often reported, and the general debility resulting from exhaustion. Moreover, fatigue helped to increase the number of accidents arising from ill-protected or unfenced machinery, for towards the end of the day the children were working in a daze.[2]

On no subject, however, was the testimony more impressively unanimous than on the question of cruelty. The thrashing of children to keep them awake in the late afternoon, or to punish them for mistakes, appeared to be general. Several of the older men said bluntly they did not see how the work could be kept going without it, since the children would otherwise fall asleep in front of the machines. And worse things were told of: it was said that seduction of the older girls by the foremen or even (in the smaller mills) by the masters was far from rare.

In view of all this there was hardly need to stress the lack of secular and religious education or the widespread prevalence of immorality among the mill hands. The evidence on these points

[2] Frances Trollope, the novelist, toured the factory districts of Yorkshire and Lancashire five years later. What she saw for herself confirmed much of the evidence presented to the Committee. The following is an instance:

'The ceaseless whirring of a million hissing wheels, seizes on the tortured ear; and while threatening to destroy the delicate sense, seems bent on proving first, with a sort of mocking mercy, of how much suffering it can be the cause. The scents that reek around, from oil, tainted water, and human filth, with that last worst nausea, arising from the hot refuse of atmospheric air, left by some hundred pairs of labouring lungs, render the act of breathing a process of difficulty, disgust and pain. All this is terrible. But what the eye brings home to the heart of those who look around upon the horrid earthly hell, is enough to make it all forgotten; for who can think of villainous smells, or heed the suffering of the ear-racking sounds, while they look upon hundreds of helpless children, divested of every trace of health, of joyousness, and even of youth! Assuredly there is no exaggeration in this; for except only in their diminutive size, these suffering infants have no trace of it. Lean distorted limbs—sallow and sunken cheeks—dim hollow eyes, that speak unrest and most unnatural carefulness, give to each tiny, trembling, unelastic form, a look of hideous premature old age.' *Michael Armstrong*, p. 80.

was overwhelming. Parson Bull was no more emphatic than the other witnesses when he explained that he had become an advocate of the Ten Hours cause because he saw a growing menace to the whole of society in the expansion of a stupid, fatigue-sodden populace morally isolated from the rest of the community.

Sadler took care to elicit from the witnesses ample corroboration of that absence of 'freedom' on which he had dilated in his speech to the House. The workers had to take what work they could get, or starve. Conditions varied little from one factory to another; furthermore, in many of the villages a single mill owner commanded all the available labor and so was in a position to make what terms he chose. Besides, there were the violent fluctuations in employment. Hands might be worked on a fourteen- to sixteen-hour day for weeks at a time and then be put on part-time or stood-off altogether. What meaning could the economists' talk of 'freedom' have in such circumstances?

Many were the vivid glimpses the Committee got of what all this meant in human terms. The evidence of Abraham Whitehead, a clothier living near Holmfirth, is typical:

I have seen children during the last winter coming from work on cold dark nights between ten and eleven o'clock, although trade has been so bad with some of the mills that they have had nothing to do; others have been working seventeen or seventeen-and-a-half hours per day. This requires that the children should be awakened very early in the morning. I can tell you what a neighbour told me six weeks ago—she is the wife of Jonas Barrowcliffe, near Scholes; her child works at a mill nearly two miles from home, and I have seen that child coming from its work this winter between ten and eleven in the evening; and the mother told me that one morning this winter the child had been up by two o'clock in the morning, when it had only arrived from work at eleven; it had then to go nearly two miles to the mill where it had to stay at the door till the overlooker came to open it. This family had no clock; and the mother believed, from what she afterwards learnt from the neighbours, that it was only two o'clock when the child was called up and went to work; but this has only generally happened when it has been moonlight, thinking the morning was approaching. It is the general practice in the neighbourhood—and any fact that I state here can be borne out by particular evidence that, if required, I can point out.

¶ 4

As the Committee continued its probe it gathered a good deal
of supplementary information on matters other than factory conditions. It received further evidence, for instance, of the way in
which the masters in some districts were fighting the unions by
requiring their work-people to sign the 'document' forswearing
membership of any workers' organization. But the most glaring
of these incidental discoveries was the revelation of the way
in which factory petitions against Sadler's Bill had been got
up, especially in Lancashire. The case of Holland Hoole, a big
mill owner at Salford, provided a good example. Hoole had
earlier written a pamphlet for private circulation among M.P.s
to convince them that all was well with factory conditions. Just
before Sadler moved the second reading, Hoole followed this up
by submitting to Parliament a petition against the Ten Hours
Bill signed by 730 of his workpeople. The way in which it had
been compiled was revealed to the Select Committee when
James Turner of the Manchester Short Time Committee came
to give evidence, and what he said was amply confirmed by
others. Turner had made a particular point of getting the details, because he had been requested by some of the Salford
operatives to come down and make a special investigation on
their behalf.

He found that Hoole had first sent a foreman through the
various rooms of the factory to ask the hands whether they
were in favor of a ten-hour or a twelve-hour day. After a short
address by one of the managers, who pointed out what evil consequences would follow from the passage of Sadler's Bill, the
workers in each room were publicly lined up in two groups, for
and against, so that a count could be made. A considerable majority was found to favor Sadler's measure, so nothing more was
done for a few days. At the beginning of the following week,
however, one of Hoole's partners came into the mill with sheets
already ruled and ordered each of the operatives to come up
and sign. He would not say what it was for but simply told them
to put their names down. One of the men named Charles Aberdeen (who was later called to give evidence before the Com-

mittee) resolutely refused to sign until he was given some sort of explanation. When the manager eventually admitted that it was for a petition against the bill, Aberdeen declined to have anything to do with it. News of the affair got into a local newspaper and a few days afterwards Aberdeen was dismissed, though he had been with the firm for 7 years. The other workers were indignant but powerless. The only thing they could do was to hold a meeting of protest and appeal to the Manchester Central Short Time Committee, who sent Turner down to look into the matter. Turner not only discovered how things had been managed but also learned that if there were 730 names in the petition then it must have included every man, woman, and child in the establishment: which implied that all of them—from the 6 year olds upwards—could sign their names! When Turner came to give evidence before the Committee he fully exposed the fake and also explained that arrangements were being made to present to Parliament a counter-petition in favor of Sadler's Bill signed by every adult male in the Holland Hoole factory.

This was by no means a solitary case, for others told of the same kind of thing happening in their own towns. The more reckless masters used every sort of intimidation to get their workers to declare against Sadler's proposals. Nor was Aberdeen's dismissal an isolated instance. Several of the men who gave evidence before the Committee found they had lost their jobs when they got back home. William Osburn, the Leeds Poor Law officer and Sunday school superintendent, gave the Committee the names of 6 witnesses from his district alone who had been treated that way. Indeed, so serious did the matter become that Sadler brought it before the House on 30 July and announced that in view of the risk of victimization which workers incurred by giving evidence he had decided to call no more. The last fifteen witnesses were all doctors, whose testimony impressively confirmed what had already been told. 'To have succeeded in collecting that body of medical evidence,' said Sadler, 'is worth all my labour, anxiety and sacrifice.'

❊   ❊   ❊

When the Committee began its labors in April, it had been agreed among the parties that Sadler should call his witnesses first, after which the masters should call theirs. The first task was completed on 7 August 1832. Then came the adjournment of Parliament, which automatically suspended the investigation, whereupon the Committee decided to publish without comment the minutes of such evidence as it had already gathered. No objection was raised against this procedure at this time, though considerable criticism was voiced later.

The *Report* was not published for another five months. Before then, however, the expectations of the Ten Hours men had been dashed for a second time. They had dared to hope, even after the appointment of the Select Committee, that there might still be time to get a bill passed before the end of the session. But Parliament was prorogued in October and dissolved in December. Once more, therefore, the struggle would have to begin all over again: and this time it would have to be fought out in the reformed House of Commons elected under the new franchise law.

CHAPTER XVI

Reform Bill Excitement

IT was while Sadler's Committee was still sitting that the struggle over Parliamentary Reform reached its climax. During the critical 'days of May' it seemed to many as though England had come to the very brink of revolution. In the excitement, Sadler's labors were all but forgotten, for the gaze of the people was directed to a far more thrilling drama. The mob howled at the King, pelted peers, and spat upon bishops. Respectable businessmen vowed they would pay no more taxes until the Reform Bill was law. Rumors spread that the people were arming; the Court prepared for flight. For 9 hectic days Britain was without a government, while the country waited to see whether Wellington or any other Tory leader would be able to get together a ministerial team to frustrate the Whigs and their franchise proposals. Wellington's failure—which ensured the passage of 'the Bill'—was followed by an explosion of popular rejoicing throughout the country. Then everyone began thinking about the General Election which would have to be held as soon as the new register of voters had been compiled.

¶ 1

Yorkshire was as convulsed as the rest of England. With all political energies concentrated on the crisis, therefore, little could be done for several weeks to support Sadler's efforts at Westminster. This was the hour of triumph for the Baineses and their *Mercury*, and the mob was with them.

At the height of the fever, the 'Leeds Association for Promoting the Free Return of Fit Representatives to Parliament' (which Baines and Marshall had founded) decided to hold a mammoth demonstration as a warning to the Tories of the might of 'the people.' It took place on Monday, 14 May—the day London was placarded with Francis Place's famous poster inciting a run on the Bank of England. All the firms in Leeds and the villages around stopped work at noon so that the operatives could attend. From midday onwards the streets were thronged as the boisterous crowds bedecked in colored favors headed in the general direction of the Cloth Hall Yard. The Association had omitted nothing that might rouse the enthusiasm of the populace. Bands paraded the town, leading companies of the various political unions with flags and banners inscribed with all sorts of lurid slogans: 'The Bill and No Taxes'; 'Be Firm, Be United'; 'Earl Grey the man who resigned office for the Liberties of the People'; 'No Petticoat Government.' The yellow banner of Liberalism and the tricolor of revolution were indiscriminately mixed; French rosettes and cockades abounded. Many of the banners were menacingly swathed in black crape and the poles that bore them were surmounted by pikes. Everywhere the Crown was depicted upside down. One of the most conspicuous figures of the harlequinade was a man dressed as an executioner, complete with mask and axe.

By the time the tricolor was run up over the hustings to signalize the beginning of the meeting, nearly 30,000 people had assembled. From four until seven they listened to the spate of revolutionary oratory; then young Baines, who was presiding, asked for endorsement by 'the people.' Thunderous cheers rolled forth for Grey and Morpeth, for Brougham and Reform, and for all the other symbols of Whig virtue. Finally the execrations were called for and just as heartily given: three groans for Wellington, three for the Bishops, and three for the Queen. There was no mistaking the temper of the crowd, and the *Mercury* waxed rhapsodic. But young Baines was going to live to regret those groans he had called for against the Queen. In later years, when the fires of Chartist fervor were spreading through the land and Baines was preaching his weekly sermon on the dangers of revolutionary methods, the Chartist leaders sharply reminded him of his former antics, and readers of their journal, the *Northern Star*, were presented gratis with a picture of this day's doings at Leeds.

All this excitement and the final Whig triumph threw Oastler for a while into the depths of despair. He felt that the entire structure of established certitudes was collapsing. To him the whole thing was one vast swindle, which the capitalist class was perpetrating upon a befooled people. The wealthy, he feared, would now come to dominate the new House of Commons so completely that the chances of getting a factory bill through would be more remote than ever. 'It has given the poor into the hands of the highest and middle classes and shut out entirely the great mass, the wealth-producing class,' he declared; 'the people do not live in ten-pound houses.'

He conceded that a plausible case could be made out by the Radicals. Manhood suffrage would at least have allowed of a reasonable distribution of 'interests' in Parliament, which for Oastler was the paramount consideration. But for giving the vote to the ten-pound householder he could see no case whatever. If the franchise had to be altered at all, the change should have been made in such a way that a reasonable harmony of function could have been preserved in the central assembly; without that, Parliament would inevitably become merely an instrument of the privileged. The plan he himself had advocated (and he had written to several Ministers pressing its consideration) was the one that Sadler had suggested some months before, namely, that every constituency should have *two* members—one to be elected by the propertied classes and the other by 'the people.' Only thus, he believed, could a new democratic Toryism be established, now that industrial capitalism had upset the old balance of society. As the years went by, he grew increasingly convinced that the establishment of such a Tory democracy was imperative if England were to be saved from degenerating into a servile state.

For the masses who were so feverishly shouting for Reform, Oastler was certain that a bitter awakening lay in store. Until such disenchantment became general, little could be done on behalf of social regulation. One day during the crisis, he was in Huddersfield on the outskirts of a meeting at which the speaker was promising all manner of benefits which would follow when the bill had become law. Seeing him smiling sardonically as he listened, half a dozen operatives came up to ask whether he did not approve of what was being said.

'No,' he answered. 'They tell you the aristocracy have got a chain round your necks and have used you very ill. But if this Bill passes, the ten-pounders will get a chain about your bodies, and they will then help the aristocracy to twitch you still tighter.'

'Aye,' said the operatives, 'but don't you hear they promise if they get free they will help us to get our rights and vote for our candidates?'

'I could only reply by smiling at their simplicity,' Oastler said, when relating the incident later. 'At that time it really was dangerous to say anything against the Bill.'

So the high hopes he had entertained when Sadler first introduced the Ten Hours Bill completely vanished. For 18 months he had striven to keep the factory question apart from all other issues and to that end had denied himself participation in the party struggle. Now, for the moment at least, the cause had become entirely submerged beneath this vast flood of public excitement. Not until the flood subsided would he be able to resume his efforts. Apart from that he could see nothing clearly. A letter he wrote to a friend on the day the Reform Bill received the royal assent shows his bewilderment:

What am I now? A Tory? No. A Whig? No, no, no. A Radical? I don't know. Time proves all things. Strange changes will soon take place. Every man will have to raise his hand to his face before he can say his nose is his own.

What will it be? Sword, imprisonment and death? Or mere quiet yielding? If the former, on my word, what a go! If the latter, away goes King! (The Lords are gone). Old Parliamentary debt and Church will have a race off the stage with the King. Which will beat? I know not . . .

I'll look on a little and see what plans are purposed and without caring two straws for names will support every effort to feed the poor. I don't mean by charity, but to give them work and fair wages.

Nevertheless, the organization he had built up managed to hold together in spite of the prevailing hysteria. Though public demonstrations were out of the question, the Short Time groups had plenty of work to do as long as Sadler's Committee con-

tinued sitting. And there was always the stream of petitions
to be maintained: neither in Lancashire nor in Yorkshire was that
effort abated. Even as late as the day when the Lords rejected
the Reform Bill for the last time, Sheffield was placarded with
an appeal from its local committee calling for signatures in support of Sadler's measure. Throughout June these appeals were
being presented to the House. On the 27th, Lord Morpeth rose
from his seat holding one end of the county petition which had
been initiated at the York Castle meeting and now lay at his
feet, a huge roll of nearly 800 yards bearing more than 138,000
names. In 'presenting' it he confessed that 'he had been convinced
from what had already occurred before the [Select] Committee
that humanity demanded a speedy corrective of the evils to
which the petition referred'; and Strickland in a supporting
speech declared he felt the facts that had been revealed were
a reproach to the country.

¶ 2

From June to December 1832, the dominant thought in everyone's mind was the General Election under the new franchise.
That might determine England's destinies for the next seven
years. Indeed, for those ecstatic souls who had wholeheartedly
accepted the *mystique* of 'Reform'—with a credulity that now
seems fantastic—the bill had already determined an even greater
destiny. On Midsummer Day the *Sheffield Courant* published
Ebenezer Elliott's famous rhapsody:

> Mind's great charter! Europe saved!
> Man for ever unenslaved!

And the many who echoed this sentiment saw in the coming
election the first Milestone on the Road of Progress. But owing
to Oastler's agitation, there were thousands in Yorkshire who
did not regard the matter so simply. Whatever the issue might be
in the rest of the country, events of the last two years had ensured that in the West Riding constituencies the social question
was going to cut across the facile antitheses of the Whig apocalypse. During the next 6 months, therefore, Oastler's energies
were concentrated on two main objectives. One was to get as

many of the prospective candidates as possible to pledge themselves to support a full Ten Hours measure; the other, to make
sure that Sadler would be returned for Leeds so that he might
carry his work to completion.

The opportunity to seek the first pledge came sooner than
Oastler had expected. Immediately the Reform Bill was assured
of passage through the House of Lords, the Leeds Liberal Association decided to stage a second monster demonstration in celebration of the event. In reality, of course, it was to be the first
of the election meetings, as everyone well knew. Both Macaulay
and Marshall were to make their official debut and address
their constituents.

The gathering was to take place in the White Cloth Hall
Yard on the afternoon of Friday, 15 June. Everything was planned
in grand style to whip up party enthusiasm. All business was
suspended for the day. Orange flags flew from shops and warehouses; bands paraded the streets; bells were pealing from early
morning, and cannon boomed at intervals. The whole town
turned out to see the fun and was rewarded with as riotous a
farce as local electoral history has to show.

Oastler rode over to Leeds during the morning to make sure
that adequate arrangements had been made for questioning the
candidates. As he passed through the streets he saw Ten Hours
posters everywhere and on arriving at the White Swan Inn found
the Short Time Committee already long assembled. When they
learned that he proposed to stay the day, the Committee at once
asked him if he would come to the meeting with them and put
the questions on their behalf. Oastler jumped at the chance, but
suggested that in view of the general excitement it might be
wiser to meet the candidates beforehand and put the questions
privately. The Committee readily agreed, and several of them
went off with Oastler to consult the Whig managers. The latter,
however, were less than accommodating: they were openly
derisive, and told Oastler that as a non-resident he had no right
to attend at all.

Stung by such a rebuff, Oastler withdrew to the Market Place,
where some hundreds of Ten Hours men had forgathered at the
call of their Committee. Explaining what had happened, he

vowed to meet the candidates face to face whatever happened, and called on the men to follow him to the fray. After parading for a while with their banner, they made for the Cloth Hall Yard.

Inside the Yard disorder was already rife. The attempt the Liberals had made to reserve the place for their supporters proved entirely futile. While the registered members of the Political Union were enjoying themselves at a preliminary festive dinner in another part of the town, several thousands of their opponents had broken into the Yard and surrounded the hustings, ready to heckle the candidates when the meeting started. They were a mixed lot: some were dissident Whigs who hated the Bainesite Liberals for reasons of their own, but most were members of the Radical Reform Union, angered by the Government's refusal to establish manhood suffrage. The Liberal cheer-party, which had been stationed in the Yard an hour or two earlier, was hopelessly outnumbered. Now came the Ten Hours men to add to the confusion. The din of cheer and counter-cheer drowned every effort at impromptu speechmaking, and Oastler was howled down with the rest.

About five o'clock the main Whig procession arrived with bands and panoply, led by the president of the Political Union clad entirely in yellow and mounted on a white horse; then the general public was admitted. Since it was impossible to get anywhere near the hustings, however, the Whigs tried to start their meeting from the opposite end of the Yard, with a tub for a platform. This enraged the waiting dissidents, who could not now get at the speakers; shouting soon turned to fighting, the tub was overthrown, and for half an hour the Yard presented a scene of utter pandemonium, while the helpless candidates looked on from an upstairs room.

When the riot seemed somewhat to have spent its force, the Whig Committee had a local stagecoach (called 'The Invincible') drawn into the arena to serve as a makeshift hustings. Macaulay, Marshall, and Baines got up on top and the meeting formally began. Even so, the roar of the multitude was so great that Macaulay could not make himself heard. 'Our reporter was distant from him no more than five or six yards,' said one newspaper, 'yet could only catch a few words at intervals.'

An irate Oastler was meanwhile hemmed in at the far end of
the courtyard. Determined at all costs to confront Macaulay
personally, he called on his men to fight through to the Invincible. When they got within hailing distance an altercation
with Baines took place.

'Mr. Oastler has no business here; he is not an inhabitant,'
yelled Baines.

'Neither is Mr. Macaulay,' shouted Oastler.

'But he has been invited,' retorted Baines.

'And so have I,' Oastler rejoined. 'He has been invited by a
few of our rich ten-pounders, and I have been invited by thousands of the ten-hours men.'

Then Macaulay joined in. 'If you will ask me any question
I will answer it,' he called out.

'I shall not ask you any question till I am at the top of that
coach,' Oastler shouted. 'I can neither be seen by the people nor
be heard by them if I speak where I am, and I will be both seen
and heard by them when I ask the question.'

A free-for-all ensued. The Whig bodyguard round the coach
tried to hold Oastler off, but the Ten Hours men fought back
so fiercely that they managed at last to get him onto the box,
though with the back of his coat rent from top to bottom. While
Oastler was clambering up one side, however, Macaulay and
Marshall slid down the other and made off for the proper hustings
at the far end of the Yard, leaving the two Baineses and Oastler
on the roof of the Invincible, quarreling violently.

Eventually sufficient calm was restored for Macaulay himself to invite Oastler to put his question. Macaulay's reply was
dignified but cautious. He was in favor of 'the principle' of factory legislation for children, he said, but would not commit himself to details until the Sadler Committee should have reported,
'knowing nothing myself of the particular operation of the manufacturing system.' His intentions were benevolent. 'I wish them
[i.e. factory children] not to work one hour more than what
is for their own real advantage as well as that of the rich.' Then
Marshall's turn came. His reply was downright and uncompromising. He professed as much concern for the welfare of the laboring classes as any man: 'but I must answer Mr. Oastler's question

certainly in the negative. I cannot say I think it would be for the benefit of the labouring classes to fix so low a limit as ten hours.' More uproar followed this answer, but Oastler had accomplished what he set out to do and at once retired.

That evening the Leeds Short Time Committee drafted and published a warm letter of thanks to Oastler for what he had done. The next issue of the *Intelligencer* carried 12 columns on the affair, which were afterwards reprinted as an eight-page souvenir.

¶ 3

Under the new Reform law, Huddersfield like Leeds was to send a Member to Parliament for the first time in its history. Four days later, therefore, Oastler was seeking an electoral pledge there too.

The Whigs were running the son of Sir John Ramsden, a local magnate who owned a large amount of property in the town, including the famous ship canal that bore his name. As soon as the candidature was announced, Oastler wrote to young Ramsden asking for a statement of his attitude on the factory question. Back came an answer avowing uncompromising hostility to Sadler's Bill and declaring in favor of a twelve-hour day in accordance with the Halifax Resolutions. Nothing could have been more unequivocal.

No Tory was standing, but the Radicals were running their own man—a retired army captain named Joseph Wood, who had a small estate in the neighborhood. His committee was already actively at work and had made arrangements for him to address a general meeting of constituents on 19 June.

Oastler came down from Fixby to hear Wood's declaration of principles and to put the same question he had put to Macaulay. Much of the radicalism in Wood's speech he found it difficult to stomach; but here as in every other constituency his favor or opposition was going to be determined solely by the candidate's attitude to Sadler's Bill. Wood gave him the unhesitating promise of support he had hoped for, whereupon Oastler climbed up onto the platform and harangued the crowd at length. Displaying his torn coat and contrasting the treatment he had just received with what had happened at Leeds, he denounced the Whigs vehemently and urged the utmost support for Wood.

Thus in Huddersfield as in Leeds a union of Oastlerites and Radicals was effected. Whereas in the latter case it was the Tory candidate who was the beneficiary of the alliance, however, in the former it was the Radical. The Whigs began to show signs of alarm. Ramsden was hastily sent for and the following week made a public entry and counter-demonstration of his own. Significantly enough, it was against Oastler and not against Wood that he directed most of his invective, warning electors against the insidiousness of 'Tory trickery' in regard to the factory question.

¶ 4

In the last week of June, Oastler had to go to London to dispose of some Fixby matters with Thornhill. He was glad of the change; for the moment London offered far more opportunities for furthering the cause than Yorkshire did. Bull and several of the other leaders had already been there some weeks helping Sadler with his Committee, while John Wood was quietly pressing on with his lobbying, but there was still much to be done.

Oastler, who was Thornhill's guest at his Berkeley Square house, took the occasion to explain to the Squire all about the factory question. The growing might of the capitalists, he told him, was creating a grave social situation, 'the same power which has already ruined the hopes of the working classes,' he said, 'is now directing its aim and energies against the aristocracy, and if not restrained by law it will as surely destroy your order as it has banished the independence of the operatives.' Thornhill seemed to be impressed. He gave a donation of £20 to the Factory Fund and asked if Oastler would like to explain these matters 'to any of our leading men.' Oastler seized the chance gratefully.

The man above all others he wanted to talk to was the Duke of Wellington. Since boyhood he had had the greatest admiration for the Duke and still entertained the most exalted notions of Wellington's political capabilities. If Wellington's support could be enlisted, he believed, the battle would be half won. Thornhill promised that Oastler should have an interview, and

forthwith procured a letter of introduction from his friend the
Duke of Rutland. Two days later Oastler went to Apsley House.

The interview lasted for over an hour, during which Oastler
did most of the talking. He told Wellington about conditions
in the mills and the growing class war; he explained how the new
industrialists 'were pushing the old country gentlemen out of
their estates, making the people believe that the Aristocracy and
Clergy were their only tyrants'; and he strove to show how
gravely erroneous were many of the Aristocrats' ideas about the
workers:

'Your Lordship and your Lordship's order, the Aristocracy,
think that the working classes wish for the plunder of your
estates and to deprive you of your honours.'

'Aye,' said Wellington, 'it looks very like it.'

'My Lord Duke,' Oastler replied, 'it is only their enemies who
say so, the great manufacturing *millionaires* who have an interest
in keeping the working classes and the aristocracy at variance
that they may the more easily fleece both. It is they who traduce
the operatives.'

He then went on to expound his social philosophy at length.
'I assured him,' Oastler wrote afterwards, 'that the only way the
aristocracy and clergy could regain the affections of the people
and save themselves from ruin was that they should use their
powerful influence to rescue the working classes from the thral-
dom and delusion in which the money and steam powers held
them.'

What Wellington thought of all this is not recorded. His interest was at least sufficiently aroused to ask Oastler to come
back for another talk and to bring Bull with him: and when they
finally parted the Duke assured Oastler he would always be glad
to receive further information about the factory question.

Oastler was absurdly exalted by these interviews. For many
months he continued to hope that Wellington would emerge from
his retirement and prove himself the strong man who would
frustrate the knavish tricks of the capitalists. Only slowly did
that hope fade. Indeed, to the end of his days he went on dream-
ing, like Thomas Carlyle, of the great national Leader who would
come to put things to rights; nor were such dreams merely in-

cidental: they were integral elements in his character and outlook. He had no appreciation whatever of the nature of the
democratic process, and none of Burke's sense of the function of
party. He thought of government in essentially executive terms.
Possessed of an ideal of social welfare, he longed for the strong
ruler who could implement the dictates of his own conscience. A
British Bismarck would have commanded all his uncritical devotion, but Wellington proved to be no Bismarck.

In the weeks that followed his visit to Apsley House, however,
his hopes were at their highest. He plied the Duke with pamphlets and documents. During the winter he wrote him a series
of lengthy letters on social conditions. And several times in the
ensuing eighteen months he was granted further interviews
whereat he fervently elaborated his case. The Toryism of social
reconstruction pleaded with the Toryism of supine reaction; but
Wellington remained obstinately blind to the vision that Oastler
would fain have given him.

This was by no means the only interview with the great that
Oastler had during his visit. He called on a number of other
Peers, as well as on several members of the House of Commons,
and he was granted an audience at Kensington Palace with the
King's brother, the Duke of Sussex. The Prince expressed lively
interest in the factory question and promised to present a petition in favor of the Sadler Bill in the House of Lords. Oastler
was delighted and put out a eulogistic bulletin, which was widely
publicized in the north. Unfortunately for Oastler's regard for
royalty, however, the Prince failed to keep his word. The petition
was forwarded to him in due course and then never heard of
again.

On 9 July, for over two hours Oastler gave evidence before
Sadler's Committee. He told how he had first become involved
in the factory question and of the cruelties he had subsequently
discovered. He contrasted existing factory conditions with the
domestic industry he had been familiar with as a boy, when
'the villages about Leeds and Huddersfield were occupied by
respectable little clothiers who could manufacture a piece of cloth
or two in the week and always have their family at home.' But
suppose, someone interpolated, that in consequence of the falling

off of profits the mill owners should close down their concerns, 'would not the result be great distress in the neighbourhood?' 'There are many that have small property who would begin business,' Oastler retorted. 'It would introduce domestic manufacture, which would be the greatest blessing that could be introduced into Old England.' He went on to tell about the operatives' hopes and enthusiasms: the public meetings, the pilgrimage to York, the huge petitions and the general demand for 'ten hours and no compromise'; and he wound up with one of his characteristic platform declarations: 'I will never cease to apply for the Bill till I get it because I believe it to be founded in justice, and I believe that Jesus Christ Himself, if He were here, would not refuse it me.'

The following day, well satisfied with his trip and feeling more optimistic than he had felt for a long time, he returned to Huddersfield. The Short Time Committee staged a royal reception. With band and guard of honor they conducted him from the coach stop to Back-Green Field, where a concourse of workers straight from the mills had assembled. The ovation that greeted him was rapturous, and he responded with as exuberant a speech as he had ever given. Sadler's report, he told them, would have such an effect on public opinion when it was published that a decent factory bill would be inevitable. With just a little more pressure and persistence, waverers like Morpeth could be won over to the Ten Hours solution, but there must be no slackening of effort to get clear-cut electoral pledges.

Victory seemed very near that summer evening as Oastler moved to his sweeping peroration in the gathering twilight. And when at the close he called for three cheers for Wellington, the Arch-Tory, these Radicals responded with a readiness that caused the Whigs to wonder.

CHAPTER XVII

The General Election of 1832

OASTLER had come back to Yorkshire full of zest, determined to press the factory question vigorously in the intensifying election struggle. But almost immediately his easy optimism received a nasty shock. For the first time since he had come to Fixby, he began to have fears about his own professional security.

¶ 1

The trouble arose out of Ramsden's hasty visit to the constituency just after Oastler had gone to London.[1] The Whig Election Committee had regaled its candidate with stories about Oastler's influence in Huddersfield and the possible bearing that might have upon the chances of the Radical, Captain Wood. 'Oh!' young Ramsden was reported to have answered, 'I know how to silence *him*.' (The story spread quickly for several of the committeemen were injudiciously gleeful in their boasting.) So he wrote to his father asking Sir John to complain to Thornhill about the Fixby steward's activities. Thornhill acted promptly.

Four days after returning from London, Oastler was astonished to receive from the Squire this ominous note:

I have received a letter from Sir John Ramsden complaining that *you* had produced great excitement in our part of the county of York and that you were interesting yourself in Huddersfield to oppose him, Sir John Ramsden, and to support a radical candidate, Captain Wood. I wrote him for an answer 'that I was sorry you had interfered with him—and that I would not keep persons in my employ who supported *Radical* candidates—that as to the excitement produced, I was for Mr. Sadler's Factory Bill.'

[1] See above, p. 187.

The significance was obvious. A diplomatic exchange had taken place between a great Whig landowner and a great Tory landowner, and both had agreed to observe the political proprieties by outlawing the common Radical enemy. The new enfranchisement of the ten-pound householder was not to be allowed to upset the interests of the gentry, whatever political label they might bear.

Oastler immediately saw the implications and was profoundly disturbed. Not only was this a menace to his personal security, but also a shattering denial of his romantic notions about a spiritualized Toryism. Many Tories betrayed the faith that should have been theirs, as he knew well enough, but he had wishfully refused to reckon his master among them. This curt note pulled him up sharply. In vindication of himself, therefore, as well as to restate what he believed to be the practical consequences issuing from Tory philosophy, he sent to Thornhill a vigorous reply. As an expression of his sentiments the letter is particularly enlightening, though on account of its length only the more outspoken passages can be cited.

Surely Sir John has influence enough over this neighbourhood without striding over Fixby also. These are the men who have been crying down the Duke of Newcastle for saying 'he had a right to do what he liked with his own'—and now they would usurp the right of their neighbours also, and require *you* to help *them* to crush me . . .

Yes, I oppose Mr. Ramsden's return heart and soul, and I cannot help it; because he is a decided Whig, an enemy to the Ten Hours Factory Bill, a party to the Humbug, nonsense and mischief of the Reform Bill, a 'political economist,' a free trader, and an out-and-out supporter of that ministry which is fast bringing ruin to this country. Sir John is quite correct in saying 'that I support Captain Wood,' and I do it because he is a warm friend of the Factory Bill, a friend to a tax on machinery and the funds, a hater of 'political economy' and of the *present system* of free trade. They call him a 'Radical' and very soon they will call every Tory a 'Radical.' He himself in his address says he is of no party.

I hate Whig politics with a most perfect hatred, because I believe the Whigs to be the enemies of my country, and if not stopped that they will be the ruin of the nation. They are the great enemies of the Factory Bill—the great supporters of the Factory system—which is fast

destroying the *Landed interest* and the *Labouring classes*. If such
men as Ramsden are to be returned to Parliament, there is an end of
all my hopes for the benefit of my country; the working classes must
sink—the landed interest must follow—the fundholder and the owner
of machinery will rise, and afterwards confusion and anarchy will follow. The time is come when all must join against the political economists or this country cannot be saved.

I am indeed a poor man; but I love my Country and I love my
Master who is my best friend—nay, I say truly, as far as pecuniary
matters are concerned you, Sir, are my only friend I have in the
world . . . But if the principles which I have declared in this letter
and in many former ones, and frequently also in conversations, are
such as to prevent you any longer confiding in me, all I can say is, I
have not learned to abandon my principles and I hope I never shall.
No! though an ill-natured world lies before me, I will trust in that God
who sent a raven with bread to His Servant rather than suffer him to
perish.

Thornhill was apparently reassured—at least for the time being—and the matter was allowed to drop. But in Oastler's mind
there lingered a fear which he could not entirely dispel, despite
the histrionic declaration of that closing sentence. Though they
had failed this time, might not the Whig schemers triumph one
day?

Even the inordinately long letter to his master did not entirely
disburden him of his feelings. He had to tell Sadler all about
it and to enclose a copy of what he had written to Thornhill.
Sadler answered at once:

London, July 16th, 1832

My Dear Friend:

The Lord reigneth! Any slight or insult offered to the 'King' of our
Cause will be taken up by thousands. It would destroy your enemies,
secure the success of the Bill, and exalt *you* beyond what it would be
almost possible to bear. Nothing can possibly exceed your letter to
Mr. Thornhill. I admire the kind temperate manner of it—never for-
sake that for one moment, whatever be the result. Thousands will
rally round you and I will hold it the post of honour to be at your
side—a better man, John Wood, will be there: a greater than all—God!

Pray go on with the correspondence with Mr. Thornhill as you have

begun. If he has a heart and a conscience all is safe; but oh! what a
fellow is Ramsden!!

I could not refrain, though killed, writing this much.

In very deed, my dear friend, yours ever,

Michael Thomas Sadler.

Love to Mrs. Oastler, I need not say—be strong!—You were never
so great.

The same week, the *Mercury* started its own campaigning in
pugnacious earnest by launching a new attack on Sadler, lam-
pooning his 'sublime and beautiful measure, so replete with profound erudition, yclept the Ten Hours Bill, which ought to be
called a bill for the lowering of wages.'

¶ 2

As soon as his work on the Select Committee was ended, Sadler
went to Fixby for a short holiday with Oastler. He was far from
well and in urgent need of a rest, but the respite could only be
brief: his election committee was already meeting daily and the
demands upon him were increasing rapidly.

Sadler's reputation among the northern operatives had swelled
enormously in the course of the past 6 months. By this time he
was at the height of his popularity. Now that the excitement
over the Reform Bill had subsided, interest in the Ten Hours
Bill was quickly reviving, and for obvious reasons it was upon
Sadler that these rising hopes were fixed. At innumerable gatherings of operatives, votes of encouragement and gratitude for his
labors were being passed, and from all over the factory districts
invitations for him to attend demonstrations and address meetings
kept coming into Fixby.

Obviously Sadler would have to save most of his energies for
his own constituency. But Oastler, who considered himself his
friend's publicity agent, arranged for him to attend three big
regional gatherings before making his formal public entry into
Leeds as a candidate.

The first was a rally for the Huddersfield area, held in Fixby
Park under the auspices of the local Short Time Committee. By
this time the Ten Hours men had become expert in utilizing

their dramatic effects to fullest advantage. At five o'clock on a beautiful August afternoon a huge procession, many thousands strong, set out from Huddersfield for Fixby. Oastler received them at the Park gates and led them to the hustings where he introduced Sadler. The secretary of the committee, James Brook, then read an 'Address of Gratitude,' which had been voted at a public meeting in the town a fortnight earlier. Part eulogy and part election manifesto, it amply answered the latest onslaught of the Baineses. 'The time has arrived,' it declared in one striking passage, 'when the working classes begin to think for themselves and are not altogether such "fools, tools and puppets" as to be the satellites of the *Mercury*. No, sir; we can distinguish our friends from our enemies, and we are sure that were the working classes possessed of the elective franchise there is scarcely a borough in Yorkshire or Lancashire that would not return Michael Thomas Sadler as their representative in Parliament.' The numerous speeches that followed developed the theme at length. The Yorkshire appetite for oratory seems to have been insatiable in those days, and it was not until dusk fell that the meeting finally dispersed.

The second demonstration took place at Manchester on Saturday, 25 August. So elaborately was it organized by the Lancashire Central Committee that it proved to be the Lancashire counterpart of the pilgrimage to York, which as a public spectacle it probably surpassed.

The visitors went to the inn at Ardwick Green as arranged, and during the afternoon held an unofficial reception. Charles Hindley, the Radical candidate for Ashton, came out to greet them, as well as Turner, Daniel, and other Ten Hours leaders from the near-by towns. All the while the crowd was growing in the road outside as the various local lodges kept arriving with their bands and their banners. By five o'clock the assembly was immense. 'As far as the eye could reach,' wrote Perring, 'nothing was to be seen but banners, flags, green boughs and various other emblems.' Every banner bore a woven cartoon of some sort and a slogan of the cause: 'Sadler for ever,' 'Oastler our Champion,' 'No White Slavery,' 'Revere Oastler the Children's Friend,' and others of like tenor. Several thousand factory children came, too, carrying branches, mops, sprays, or anything else they could wave. Before the proceedings began, no fewer than seventeen bands were adding to the liveliness.

The Committee had planned things well. The huge procession was admirably marshalled and each detachment from each particular mill had its appropriate place. Just after five o'clock, Sadler and Oastler entered an open coach along with John Wood and Parson Bull, and the procession moved off towards the meeting ground at Camp Field with the bands playing a medley of popular songs. It took two hours to pass through the town, so great was the throng in the streets. Folk crowded round the carriage to shake hands and voice their blessings; women shrieked and men shouted. Windows along the route were filled with spectators and in some places people had even climbed onto the housetops to get a better view.

The scene at Camp Field was just as remarkable. So dense was the crowd, indeed, that it was not even possible for the procession to come up to the platform. The speakers just had to get as close to the center as they could, and conduct the meeting from their carriage. Oastler, Sadler, and Bull spoke in succession, but, as one eyewitness said, 'the buzz occasioned by the tremendous multitude, and the great pressure rendering a calm steadiness of position impossible, only a small portion of the persons present had any chance of hearing what was said.'

At the close of the meeting the visitors were taken off in another procession to the Temple Tavern, where the Short Time Committee had arranged a dinner in their honor to be attended by some 300 prominent supporters. Tickets had been sold in advance, but in spite of that there was a last minute rush to get in. The doors were besieged, passages and rooms were crowded, and as much as ten shillings was being offered for a seat by the time the meal started. It hardly required the mounting crescendo of the successive after-dinner speakers to create the tension that Oastler's passionate invective finally released.

At Bradford the following Monday evening there awaited them another great demonstration. To the strains of 'See the Conquering Hero Comes,' Sadler and Oastler were escorted through the town to Rawson's Fold, where Parson Bull presented Sadler with a second 'Address of Gratitude' to the accompaniment of similar frantic scenes. During the course of Oastler's speech he was hissed by a small group of workmen reported to come from the Ackroyd mills. This stung him to fury, and he turned upon the interrupters with passion:

> Silence ye hissers. I tell ye, ye cowards, and ye may go and tell the tyrants by whom ye are employed, that ye may do your worst—that the Bill is safe—that WE WILL HAVE IT—that IT SHALL PASS! (*Loud cheers.*) Tell me not of your hypocritical supporters. Look at Manchester and its hundred thousand or more. Look at this meeting—look everywhere. Who's for us? Every father, every mother, every Christian. I tell ye again that we will have it—God in Heaven is for it, and who have we against it? A few hissers here, who skulk back in the dark and are ashamed to show their faces. (*Cheers.*) Go back, ye contemptible hissers, ye vipers,—go back and tell your gang what I say.—Go back to your dens and there feed upon the blood of your own cruelty. (*Immense cheering.*) Did you see that banner today [i.e. 'Welcome your factory King, Richard Oastler']? Here I stand the Factory King, declared King by the most contemptible enemies of the Cause. Yorkshire is mine! (*Cheers.*) Lancashire is mine! (*Cheers.*) Scotland is mine! (*Cheers.*) All Christendom is mine! (*Cheers.*) WE WILL HAVE THE BILL . . .

Those feverish words betray the striking change of disposition that had come over Oastler in the months since he had first discovered his platform powers. Whether he possessed the tempered judgment to match the compelling facility of his invective, only the unfolding of events would show; but that at least a part of his personality found a dangerous delight in the thunders of the multitude it was now too obvious to doubt.

¶ 3

While the Ten Hours leaders were making this tour, Marshall and Macaulay had announced their intention of holding an open-canvass meeting in Leeds the following week. Such meetings were a recognized part of the election ritual. If he so desired, the opposing candidate had the right to attend along with his principal supporters, in which case the hustings were partitioned into two pens to accommodate the rival parties. After the opening speeches, the meeting usually resolved itself into a heckling contest between the partisans.

This was just the kind of boisterous affair Oastler enjoyed, and he had no intention of missing it. As soon as he learned of the Whigs' intentions, therefore, he drafted a flamboyant 'proclamation' to the operatives of Leeds, reminding them of the Cloth Hall Yard fracas in June, and calling upon them for adequate protection this time:

> I know that our determined enemy, Baines, will spare no cost to prevent me from being heard . . . I shall ask him some close questions respecting the barefaced falsehoods he has published about us . . . I will engage either to make him eat his own words, or prove, in your presence, that he deserves the name that Cobbett gave him . . . I shall be with you in good time on Tuesday next. I shall wear the coat that Baines presented me with, and in that coat I will once more conquer your enemies.

The purpose of this, as well as of all the other tactics Oastler resorted to during the next three months, was to ensure that the factory question should be kept in the forefront of the Leeds struggle.

The night before the meeting, Sadler made his public entry into the town. The Short Time Committee turned the event into another Ten Hours pageant, fully as impressive as anything staged at Huddersfield or Bradford. A mighty procession with five bands and all the usual paraphernalia went along the road to meet him. His horses were taken out of the shafts and the carriage was drawn through thronged streets to the meeting ground; and there, in the glare of a hundred flares placed around the rostrum, a third tribute of gratitude was presented on behalf of the local workers.

Next day, just as Sadler and his committee were about to set out for the big meeting, Oastler turned up wearing his torn coat and leading a company of Ten Hours men composed of representatives from every Short Time Committee in the West Riding. With this escort Sadler was conducted through the town up to the steps of the hustings. For a moment it looked as though rioting might develop, for a gang of 'orange' henchmen tried to prevent Oastler and his party from following Sadler onto the platform. This did not come amiss to Oastler: he and his men were spoiling for a fight and had come much better prepared than they had been on 15 June. When he found his way barred, Oastler simply announced at the top of his lungs that if he and his friends were not allowed onto the platform they would forthwith pull down everyone already up there. The Whigs soon yielded to the ultimatum and Oastler was permitted to take his place at Sadler's side.

The meeting that followed was a rowdy affair in the best Eatanswill tradition. Oastler again heckled Macaulay and again elicited from him outspoken condemnation of any measure that might interfere with the 'freedom' of adult labor.[2] Oastler retorted with vigor and Macaulay lost his temper. As the wrangle became heated, the Whig rowdies raised the cry, 'Pull Oastler down,' and made a rush for the platform. A fierce scuffle ensued, but the Ten Hours bodyguard this time managed to hold their own, while Oastler looked on, grinning with delight.

For Oastler and Sadler both, the days that followed were excessively busy. Sometimes together and sometimes separately, they were addressing meetings night after night. Soon the Tory campaign began to have the appearance of a popular crusade. Already the Short Time Committees were everywhere working zealously on Sadler's behalf; then, in the third week of September, the Leeds Radical Union formally pledged its support as well and threw all its resources into the struggle. Oastler's spirits soared. A letter he wrote at this time to Daniel, secretary of the Manchester committee, vividly catches his mood of evangelical ebullience:

I long for the time when we shall have all our efforts crowned with success. What we have now to do is to persevere—we shall reap in due time if we faint not. Don't be alarmed at difficulties, all obstacles must

[2] 'I can by no means admit that those topics which I have so often heard advanced on that subject have in them any soundness, and . . . I say that if the labouring classes expect any great or extensive relief from any practical measure of legislation, they are under a delusion. (Hisses). I believe they are confounding the symptoms with the disease . . . I believe that the overworking of children is not the cause but the effect of distress. (No, No) . . .' *Leeds Intelligencer*, 6 Sept. 1832.

and will give way—I am sure of it. Oh how delighted I am when the
Enemies of my poor babes abuse me and try to confound me. I never
feel more happy than when they are emptying their magazine of
calumny and slander at me—poor things—and they call themselves
Christians too, and kneel down at the foot of His Cross and the foot-
stool of His Throne whose especial love to Children and the Poor was
always manifest! Aye, and they can preach His Gospel, too!!!—and
encourage the most loathsome Oaths and curses against myself and
Sadler, because we pity the poor, injured enslaved Infants!! And this
they call Christianity—well may infidelity abound. No wonder God
is angry when such is the conduct of professing, preaching and praying Christians.—Their conduct more than anything convinces me we
shall conquer—because we need no proof that these wretches are the
Devil's allies.—I am delighted to think they hate me and my Cause.
Then I know God must approve and prosper me . . .

I have glorious news from Nottingham—they want a public meeting
there—I am going to it. We shall have a blaze in the centre of the
Kingdom soon—a fire of Benevolence, not of plunder. Well, let us
thank God—it's all His Work . . .

Sadler's cause prospers more and more in Leeds—I have no doubt of
his success.

¶ 4

The campaign at Leeds lasted another three months. As the
days went by the contest became excessively bitter and every
week the *Mercury* grew more vitriolic. There was now no doubting the fact that factory regulation was the paramount issue, so
the *Mercury* concentrated on discrediting Sadler's motives. Time
after time it kept saying that Sadler's concern for the factory children was nothing but 'convenient philanthropy' adopted solely
for election purposes.

In this ever-thickening atmosphere of invective, tempers soon
wore thin. Even Macaulay's urbanity disintegrated under the
strain. One of his cruder remarks made during the last week of
the campaign particularly enraged the Ten Hours men:

Without the slightest hesitation I venture to declare that I am a
fitter object for the choice of this great community than one who has
laboured to deprive that great body of their privilege—who will not
be deceived by the profession of a *convenient philanthropist*. Gentle-

men, we have heard—you have heard—of a certain wild beast called
the Hyaena who, when it wishes to decoy the unwary into its den, has
a singular knack of *imitating the cries of little children* . . .

Sadler's supporters retorted in kind. The Short Time Committee immediately plastered the town with a mock election address soliciting the votes of all capitalists whose wealth had obviously 'marked them out as the favoured of Heaven,' and signed
it *Thomas Babington Hyaena.* Bull followed with a vehement
open letter, which was widely publicized. The *Mercury* answered
in a scurrilous editorial denouncing the 'pugnacious parson' and
'the reverend bruiser.' Bull replied with a further scathing attack
on both Baines and Macaulay.

But the struggle had long since transcended local interest.
Concern for the outcome extended to every textile district in
the Kingdom. One of the extraordinary features of the contest,
indeed, was the encouragement Sadler received from operatives all over the country. Beginning in early October, *Addresses* passed at public meetings began coming into the constituency begging 'the Worthy, Free and Independent Electors
of Leeds' to return Sadler. Bolton's was the first, carrying more
than 2,000 signatures, and its appeal for the non-party vote set
the tone for all the others: 'When the physical and moral salvation of an immense portion of the rising generation is at stake
. . . do not suffer the detestable distinctions of Party and Faction to seduce you from the path of Mercy and Charity.' Mass
meetings at Coventry, Glasgow, Oldham, Dundee, Bury, and
many other industrial centers vociferously endorsed the same
sentiments; and just before polling day the biggest petition of
all arrived from Manchester, bearing over 40,000 names. It
goes without saying that all three organizations—the Tory Association, the Radical Union, and the Short Time Committee—
dramatized the significance of these documents to the fullest
possible extent.

By polling day, 12 December, Leeds had about reached the
limit of endurable excitement. For three months continuously
there had been meetings and processions, placardings and pam-
phleteering, canvasses and riots. Yet in spite of the mighty ef-

forts of his supporters, Sadler finally went down to defeat. Marshall headed the poll, as expected, with 2012 votes. But the outcome of the real contest was:—

Macaulay	1984
Sadler	1596
Majority for Macaulay	388

The result was conceded by everyone to be a grave blow to the Ten Hours Movement, and the complete defeat of Wood at Huddersfield only added to the mortification. The cause had lost its parliamentary leader in the very hour when he was most urgently needed. The Whigs had swept the country; the Select Committee's Report would appear in three weeks' time, yet there would be no one to press its findings in the new and exultant House. Hobhouse had defected; Sadler had been defeated; where could the Ten Hours men now find hope? Looking back upon these days in the tranquillity that came 15 years later, Parson Bull could still recall that 'at that crisis, all was confusion.'

¶ 6

All these weeks Oastler had been content to pour out his energies on behalf of Sadler, Wood, and the other candidates in Yorkshire who had given the Ten Hours pledge. But towards the end of November suggestions began to be made that he himself should consider standing for Parliament. Some Keighley friends pressed him to come forward as a county candidate for the West Riding, and several similar requisitions followed, signed by men of all shades of opinion and accompanied by offers to contribute towards his expenses. The Whig press grew satirical,[3]

---

[3] e.g. 'There is a paragraph in the last "Intelligencer" stating that Mr. Oastler has received several *invitations* to become a candidate for the West-Riding . . . The public were certainly not prepared for this: when it was hinted at before, it was believed to be in "joke;" and never till now was it for a moment imagined that this individual was seriously thought of as a member of Parliament . . . As Whigs, we have been accused of being levellers; but never did we contemplate the turning the House of Commons into an almshouse for decayed tradesmen. If this vaunted martyr to the cause of the ten hours' bill should really offer for the Riding—*of course after being qualified,* (and when can that be?)—it will be the duty of his friends immediately to petition the Chancellor to issue a commission of lunacy against him—Oastler a member!—My conscience!!!' *The Retort.* 8 Dec. 1832.

though Oastler at one time considered the suggestion seriously and even got as far as drafting an election address. He soon dropped the idea, however, ostensibly because there would be insufficient time to canvass the constituency; actually, no doubt, because he realized that he stood very little chance of success.

Nevertheless he went to the poll at Wakefield on 20 December, when these two were returned unopposed. Though it was a preponderantly Whig gathering, a sufficiently vocal section of the crowd started calling for him. With foolish alacrity he responded, despite Whig efforts to keep him down ('Take him to a madhouse,' young Baines kept crying); but the interruptions became so continuous that he had to give up. Before withdrawing, however, he announced that he would hold a meeting of his own elsewhere in the town that same evening.

Some hours later, to a packed house in the Mechanics' Institute he expounded the whole of his political philosophy and presented his own program. He denounced the delusions of Whiggery and the triumph of the ten-pounder; he explained his own scheme of a double-franchise for each constituency; he demanded a full investigation of the national debt 'to devise some method of paying it out of the individuals who borrowed it.' He advocated the cheapening of legal costs, the removal of taxes on newspapers, and the reform of the Church of England. He emphatically demanded the elimination of all indirect taxation and the substitution of a uniform system of direct property taxes, which should fall on machinery and land equally. He urged that waste lands should be reclaimed and settled by the unemployed as the first step in the creation of a national system of peasant proprietorship. Above all, he denounced the whole laissez-faire policy of those he called the 'philosophic politicians.' These men, he said, were merely the apologists for capitalism, whereas what he stood for was a revivified Toryism —a conception of society according to which the interests of no single class should be allowed to dominate the rest, and which alone could make possible the maintenance of Christian principles. His whole philosophy he condensed into a phrase which he had recently coined during one of Sadler's meetings—*The Altar, the Throne and the Cottage.*

It was the fullest statement of his political creed he had yet made. Personal experience and the political contacts of the past few months had compelled him step by step to amplify his social convictions and to restate them in the light of all the emerging new hopes. The fundamentals of the Tory position, he felt, were as valid as they had ever been; for him Toryism was eternally true, since it involved the essential conception of an organic harmony of legitimate interests. But Toryism was in urgent need of restatement—partly because so many of its leaders seemed to have forgotten their own fundamentals, and partly because the Whigs had so completely deluded the populace that 'the People' themselves needed to be enlightened. Long before Disraeli assumed the same responsibility, Oastler had come to the conclusion that one of the duties laid upon him was to help educate his own party. 'My object,' he told Wellington, 'is to unite the Aristocracy and the People, and thus to save them both.'

By Christmas Eve, 1832, on the threshold of the new year, the new Parliament, and the new era, he was fully conscious of all this and set it forth in the preface to one of his pamphlets:

Now Tories, what say you? Will you go back? You cannot. 'Stand still?' Impossible. Will you join the Whigs against the people? If so, you are a set of unprincipled knaves, and deserve to meet with the first reward of roguery. Will you go forward, then, hand in hand with 'the people' and thus save the nation from anarchy and blood—thus secure the rights of the nobles by giving comfort, peace, and contentment to the cottage? If you follow this plan, every patriot will join you, I care not whether he be Tory, Whig, or Radical, every man who loves his country will be on your side. Not a Bainesite will be found in your camp, so you need not be alarmed. That person's days of political influence are numbered.

He was utterly convinced that such a rejuvenated Toryism was the only alternative to disaster. Whiggery he saw as naked class rule—the empowerment of the capitalists and their dependents. If these remained in power, he believed, it was inevitable that the country would revolt, for the Whigs had made one supreme mistake. In order to achieve their own immediate purposes they had invoked that sleeping giant 'the People,' and the giant could never be put to sleep again or lose its new-found political awareness:

The People have now learnt their strength, the avalanche is descending and will crush their opponents. It is not too late to guide it—it *is* too late to oppose. It will not stand still to please the 'liberal' men who now laugh and chuckle over the 'People' whom they think they have so cleverly choused.

That, he felt persuaded, was the ultimate conclusion to be drawn from the shouting and the tumult of the recent upheaval.

CHAPTER XVIII

The Second Rousing of the North

B Y THE TIME the last election returns had come in, it seemed
to many of the factory reformers that they were back where
they started from. In January 1833, the prospects looked hardly
any brighter than they had in January of two years before, when
everyone in Yorkshire was eagerly awaiting news about the
scope of Hobhouse's Bill.[1] True, a large section of the public
had now been awakened to the urgency of the problem; but it
was equally true that the opposition had effectively hardened
and become better organized. Moreover, powerful members
of the Government had made plain their hostility to the whole
idea of factory regulation.

For the third time, therefore, the reformers would have to
work their way through the now familiar cycle of effort. Someone would have to be found to introduce a new factory bill;
another big campaign of meetings would have to be undertaken in the north to keep up the pressure of public opinion;
and all the while persistent lobbying would have to be continued at Westminster—this time in a new and exultant House of
Commons—to counter the formidable influence of the mill owners.

It was not the thought of the weary struggle confronting them
that troubled the Ten Hours men, however, so much as the fear
that their opponents might resort to some new and unsuspected
wrecking tactics for which they would be unprepared. Poulett
Thomson had persuaded Hobhouse to accept wrecking amendments for the first bill; Althorp had compelled Sadler to accept
a Select Committee for the second. Could there be yet a third
device which the Government might use to frustrate the hopes
of the reformers? That was the question Oastler and Bull kept

[1] See above, p. 62.

asking. And it was on that account they decided that the most pressing task at the moment was to complete the building of the fighting organization Oastler had first envisaged 18 months earlier.[2]

¶ 1

The *Report* on the evidence given before the Select Committee on Sadler's Bill was finally published in the first week of January 1833.

Whatever may be the present judgment of scholars upon the fairness or objectivity of that famous document, one thing is certain: it had an immediate and profound effect upon public opinion. Indeed, its publication marked the completion of the process by which the factory question was transformed from a local to a national issue. Appearing as it did during the lull that followed the election, it was given the widest publicity. The metropolitan newspapers printed extensive excerpts and ran editorials upon it, and the quarterlies followed with critical articles on the issues raised.

For many people the reading of these findings was the occasion of their first awakening to the reality of the social problem. There were probably scores of responsible citizens who felt as J. R. McCulloch, the eminent economist, did when he wrote to a friend: 'I look upon the facts disclosed in the late Report as most disgraceful to the nation; and I confess that, until I read it, I could not have conceived it possible that such enormities were committed.' Even the cautious Sir John Hobhouse told the House of Commons a month later that 'after reading the evidence already before the House, two opinions could not be entertained' in regard to the propriety of legislating on the subject. The London dailies were just as emphatic, particularly those in the Tory camp. 'Such a history of brutal—of worse than brutal—ferocity in the pursuit of gain was perhaps never before disclosed to the world,' said the *Morning Herald;* 'we can scarcely believe our eyes while we read, or trust our sense while we consider, the statements of the different witnesses. No passion but that of avarice could have perpetrated such enormities. If

[2] See above, p. 102.

Mr. Sadler had never done anything for society but the bringing to light of this monstrous and inhuman system, society would be largely his debtor. The evil cannot long outlive its exposure.' And *The Times* declared that 'the system pursued towards children in our factories is brutal and heartless beyond the endurance of any civilized legislature.' Even the *Morning Chronicle*, chief organ of the laissez-faire school, felt constrained to admit that the voluminous evidence was 'of such a nature to make a man almost loathe his species.'

But in some ways the most significant comments were those that came from the pen of the younger Baines, written (as he said) before he had had time to digest the *Report* fully. Cynics might say the *Mercury* was only trimming once more to meet the new wind of public opinion. Yet the fact remains that these remarks really were written by Baines—the leading editorial apologist of the Yorkshire mill owners who for the past two years had been so vigorously aspersing Oastler's motives and challenging his assertions.

Making every allowance for exaggeration, there remains an overwhelming and irresistible mass of proof that cruel overworking has in many places been practised, and that it has been excessively injurious to the health of the children, crippling their limbs, stunting their growth, and often shortening their lives. Nearly two years since we pronounced that the working of young children fifteen, sixteen and seventeen hours in a day, and working them all night, was horrible.[3] We repeat the expression. It is horrible, and an outrage on humanity and decency, to work children of 7, 8, or 9 years old such a length of time. And the fact that such overworking has been practised, and still may be practised, without the child's consent, for the joint benefit of the master and the parents, seems to us now, as it has always seemed to us, to call imperatively for legislative interference.

Depite this admission, the *Mercury* had not deemed it necessary to report that six Leeds men had lost their jobs for giving evidence before a Parliamentary Committee whose report was now helping to persuade the country at large to this very way of thinking.

[3] Apparently Baines was referring to the admissions in the *Mercury* that are cited on pp. 54–5. No other such admissions had been made during the intervening two years.

¶ 2

It was some weeks before the influence of the Sadler *Report* became clearly apparent in London. Long before then, Oastler's new campaign for rousing the north was in full swing.

There was every reason for haste. The new Parliament was to meet on 29 January, and already there were persistent rumors that the Yorkshire mill owners were about to make a determined effort to end the factory agitation once and for all by promoting an eleven-hours' bill. Lord Morpeth, it was being said, would sponsor such a measure; and this sounded the more likely since Morpeth had frequently indicated his belief that eleven hours would constitute a reasonable compromise. He was heartily tired of the controversy, and wanted nothing better (as he said during the election) than 'to reconcile all the leading parties and bring this afflicting subject to a close.' The Ten Hours men knew well enough, of course, that were such a bill to be actually introduced in the House, their own measure would stand no chance at all. So it was obviously going to be a race to see which party would reach the Order Paper first.

Immediately after Christmas, therefore, Oastler and Bull called for a general conference of Ten Hours men at Bradford to work out a plan of campaign that could be put into operation at once. It was the first such conference that had been held, and proved to be an important landmark in the development of the movement. All the Short Time Committees were invited to send delegates, and several prominent friends of the cause were asked to attend as well.

The deliberations began on Friday, 11 January, and lasted 4 days. Twenty people came in all: 14 accredited delegates and 6 visitors. But a number of Committees that had been unable to send delegates sent letters explaining their attitude and offering suggestions. So the meeting was actually more representative than the figures suggest. From the records surviving among Oastler's papers we learn that no fewer than 26 Short Time Committees had come through the excitements of the Reform Bill crisis intact and were still in active operation. One was in Nottingham, 2 were in Scotland, 11 were in Lancashire, and 12 in

Yorkshire.[4] In addition, both Lancashire and Yorkshire had Central Committees to co-ordinate the efforts of their respective counties.

Both socially and politically it was a mixed gathering. John Doherty, the Catholic trade-union leader, was there along with Bull, the Anglican parson; workmen such as James Turner of the Manchester Committee, as well as middle-class stalwarts such as William Osburn of Leeds. Sadler came for a while, and Oastler attended throughout. In the chair was William Halli- well, a master cotton spinner from Lees in Lancashire, who stood in much the same relationship to the movement there as John Wood did in Yorkshire. Tories, Whigs, and Radicals sat amicably side by side and unanimously elected Bull as secre- tary of their proceedings.

After lengthy discussion of every aspect of the situation, sev- eral important decisions were reached. First it was agreed that Bull should immediately go to London to try to find a suc- cessor to Sadler. If Morpeth's intentions were to be frustrated, it was imperative that a parliamentary leader should be found as speedily as possible. When that quest had been successfully accomplished, half a dozen delegates were to be sent to West- minster to help with the necessary lobbying and 'to watch and effectuate the progress of the Ten Hours bill' through Parlia- ment. Meanwhile another vigorous campaign of public meet- ings was to be launched throughout the northern counties for the double purpose of enlarging the existing organization and promoting a fresh stream of petitions. The new Parliament was to be bombarded with appeals as assiduously as the old one had been.

It was the question of enlarging the organization that took up most of the time. Oastler's imagination had long been cap- tivated by the idea of an irresistible fighting association made up from a myriad of local lodges covering all the textile districts. Now more than ever he was convinced of its necessity. In this he carried the Conference with him. They resolved that forthwith

[4] The Yorkshire Short Time Committees were found in Leeds, Bradford, Halifax, Huddersfield, Dewsbury, Keighley, Gomersal, Heckmondwike, Holmfirth, Horton, Bowling, and Stanningley.

'as many Short Time Committees as possible should be formed in the villages bordering upon large towns,' each responsible for holding meetings, distributing literature, promoting petitions, and generally rousing the public sentiment in its neighborhood. Where committees could not be started, 'missionaries might be profitably employed to lecture on the Factory Bill for the further promotion of the same object.' There was to be one important difference between this scheme and the one that had been mooted before the Reform Bill crisis, however. This was to be a *membership* organization. Only those who formally joined the association and paid their regular dues were to share in the determination of policy and tactics. On this basis, for instance, the proposed delegates to London were to be chosen. Each local Committee was to canvass its enrolled members for nominations and then forward to the Central Committee the names of the two it considered most suitable. When the Central Committee had assembled all the nominations, it was to send the complete list back to the lodges. 'Each subscriber,' the instruction ran, 'is then to be called upon to vote for such two of the persons so returned as he esteems fittest, the votes to be recorded and the results to be immediately sent by every Local Committee to the Central Committee.' The latter would then make the count and declare the result.[5]

Oastler was to be the pivot of the organization. This had been the case from the beginning, but now it was formally acknowledged by a resolution affirming 'that the Central and Local Committees in both Counties shall consider Richard Oastler, Esq., of Fixby Hall, the centre of communication.'

Its main work accomplished, the Conference concluded by drafting an appeal to the nation cogently presenting the case for a Ten Hours Bill: *An Address to the Nobility, Clergy, Gentry, Master Manufacturers, Agriculturalists and Operatives of the United Kingdom.* In the press, as a pamphlet, and as a placard,

[5] Whether the organization was thus carefully elaborated because there had been trouble in or between some of the Committees, we cannot now tell. Possibly it was. There is reason to suppose that difficulties had arisen. at Leeds, though no details survive. If so, it would account for a curious fact that the Conference was held at Bradford and not at Leeds, and that henceforth Bradford was the seat of the West Riding Central Committee.

this manifesto was given greater publicity than anything yet produced by the movement.

With remarkable *éclat* the new campaign was begun right away, while Parson Bull went off to London to hunt for Sadler's successor.

¶ 3

To find someone to take Sadler's place as parliamentary champion of a Ten Hours Bill was no easy task. Oastler knew the sort of man he wanted, and there can be little doubt that his preferences determined the direction of the quest. Even now, however, he was still hoping that the Duke of Wellington might be persuaded to assume the leadership. 'It is my belief,' he told the Duke the day before Parliament assembled, 'if this country is to be saved it will be through the instrumentality of your Grace.' But if the Duke could not be persuaded, someone must be found with a social philosophy as nearly like Sadler's as possible. It was not just a matter of getting a Member to introduce the proposed bill: that would have presented little difficulty. Oastler was hoping for someone who would lead the country in a great Christian crusade against the consequences of unregulated capitalism, and so too were John Wood and Parson Bull.

With introductions and advice from Sadler, Bull called upon a number of Members in succession, but all begged to be excused. Then he chanced to meet that strange Scottish Whig, Sir Andrew Agnew, an ardent sabbatarian who session after session assiduously sponsored a bill to prohibit all Sunday labor. Agnew listened sympathetically and suggested that Bull should approach young Lord Ashley, the devout and somber Tory member for Dorsetshire. 'I can perfectly recollect my astonishment and doubt and terror at the proposition,' Ashley wrote later. 'I recollect that in vain I demanded time for consideration. It was necessary, Bull replied, to take an instant resolution as Morpeth would otherwise give notice of a bill which would defraud the operatives of their ten hours measure by proposing one which should inflict eleven. I obtained, however, a respite till next morning and set myself to reflection and enquiry.' The following morning, 'after meditation and prayer,' he had decided to accede to the appeal. Thus, at the age of 31, the most eminent British philanthropist of the nineteenth century began his remarkable career of humanitarian service.

Bull was delighted. Several discussions followed, and on 5 February, immediately after the King's speech, Ashley gave notice of a motion for leave to reintroduce Sadler's Bill. Next day Bull wrote to the secretary of every Short Time Committee in the West Riding telling of the success of his mission and reporting that Ashley's notice 'was received with hearty and unusual cheers from all parts of a House of more than three hundred.' [6] The secretaries were directed to summon their committees to hear Bull's letter read. 'I have just left his Lordship,' Bull concluded; 'he says it is *your* cause; if you support him he will never flinch.' The Committees responded without delay by electing the delegates who were to be sent to London in accordance with the Bradford scheme. Oastler wrote Ashley a letter of greeting and encouragement, and received a humble but resolute reply: 'I greatly fear my ability to carry on this measure. I wish—most ardently I wish—that some other had been found to undertake the cause; nothing but the apprehension of its being lost induced me to acquiesce in Mr. Bull's request.' So once again the battle was joined.

¶ 4

Bull's mission had been accomplished only just in time. At that same sitting, soon after midnight, Morpeth announced his intention of introducing his own factory bill at the end of February. The comment of *The Times* was caustic:

It seems that the mill owners, unable to resist the strong tide of public opinion which the force of the evidence before the Select Committee, the result of Mr. Sadler's indefatigable labours, has set in motion, have resolved to dole out some niggardly measure of relief to the poor children by the hand of Lord Morpeth . . . His Lordship must have been somewhat forgetful of parliamentary courtesy when, after mid-

[6] The parliamentary correspondent of *The Times* likewise commented on this cordial reception. Evidently the leaven of Sadler's *Report* was already working.

night on Tuesday and when the House was all bustle, he announced his intention to bring in his—or rather the masters'—bill, and in doing so dated his motion for the 27th of February, although Lord Ashley's was previously given for the 5th of March. There can be but very little doubt which of the two propositions—that which comes from the sufferers and their friends or that which emanates from the inflictors of that suffering—will meet with most of public support.

Oastler was infuriated at Morpeth's tactics. In his wrath he dashed off the most vituperative letter he had ever written, denouncing Baines, Morpeth, and the Whigs. The whole affair was a plot of the mill owners directed by Baines, he said. Baines had been evasive enough up to the present, but now he had shown his hand. No sooner had the operatives found a champion 'pledged to tread in Sadler's steps' than

the sleek and oily Morpeth like Judas enters, and at his season too— the midnight hour—supported like his great and wicked prototype by bands of murderers (mill owners), and would betray the infants' sacred cause—like Judas, with a kiss.

The letter was published on 9 February and received immense publicity. Two days later Oastler followed it up with one even longer, in which for the first time he gave expression to a new fear. Morpeth's real intention, he suggested, was to make possible a relay system for children whereby the working day for adults could be actually lengthened even though the labor of children might be restricted. It was a fear that was to persist for years.

The day before Oastler's bitter attack was published, however, Morpeth made what was tantamount to a withdrawal of his notice. The comments of *The Times* had evidently stung him sorely. He wrote to Ashley disclaiming any discourteous intention and explaining his position; then he took an early opportunity to repeat the explanation to the House. The gist of it was that he did not feel another Ten Hours Bill had any chance of success, and that what he had sought was a measure that would 'obviate objections' to Sadler's proposals and thus 'suit the interests of all classes.' He indignantly repudiated the suggestion that he was a tool of the masters or that he was more concerned for the welfare of one class than another.

Later in the month he said this all over again when complaining to the House that Oastler had called him a 'Judas.' But Ashley did not waver. He sent Morpeth a courteous answer, saying he did not in the least mind who brought in the bill as long as it really was a Ten Hours measure, and that if Morpeth felt unable to sponsor such a bill he would go on with his original intention.

Morpeth was too amiable a man to make a good fighter. Two or three times he got his motion postponed and then, on 6 March, he finally abandoned it. Ashley's motion was thus left alone on the Order Paper, and the Ten Hours men had won the first skirmish.

¶ 5

Meanwhile the planned campaign was being pressed with the utmost vigor in the north, and enthusiasm in both Yorkshire and Lancashire was steadily rising.

These were weeks of activity surpassing anything the movement had yet undertaken. In the 18 days following the conclusion of the Bradford Conference, 15 public meetings were held in the Riding and at least a dozen new Short Time Committees were established.[7] Wherever Oastler went, crowds thronged to hear him and yielded themselves to his domination. Sometimes the whole township would turn out to conduct him the last mile or two of his journey with a torchlight procession. And while Oastler and his Huddersfield bodyguard were busy in one place, Bull and the other leaders were holding forth somewhere else. Rarely did a meeting end without cheers for 'the Factory King' and vociferous pledges of loyalty to him personally.

The meetings reported in the newspapers were only the most conspicuous. Dozens of others which the general public never read about were conducted in outlying villages by 'deputations'

[7] These were at Pudsey, Yeadon, Guisely, Baildon, Otley, Calverley, Farsley, Eccleshill, Idle, Shipley, Thornton, and Clayton. This brought the number of Short Time Committees in the West Riding up to 26 by 1 February 1833.

of committeemen from the larger towns. Throughout the spring
of 1833, scores of missionaries whose names are now lost were
pouring out their energies on behalf of the cause, addressing
gatherings wherever they could find a forum: in schoolrooms or
Primitive Methodist chapels, in assembly rooms or taverns. Week
by week the Short Time organization extended its reach, meeting little opposition.

The famous meeting at the City of London Tavern on 23
February was really part of the same campaign. It was the first
big demonstration promoted by the London Society for the
Improvement of the Condition of Factory Children, and served
as the public inauguration of Ashley as the new parliamentary
leader. No one could complain that the crowded platform was
not representative. Robert Owen, the humanitarian socialist, was
there with Torrens, the economist; Michael Sadler along with
Daniel O'Connel, the Irish 'liberator'; and many others scarcely
less eminent. Oastler and Bull came by special invitation, and
the Lord Mayor, Sir Peter Laurie, took the chair. For three and
a half hours the audience was regaled with oratory presented
in a remarkable variety of styles; and in every speech the shock
to conscience that Sadler's *Report* had administered could
clearly be perceived. The proceedings were brought to a climax
with Sadler's deeply moving plea for a new spirit of social
purposiveness to replace the policy of 'letting-things-alone.' It
was destined to be the last speech he was to make in London,
and proved to be one of the greatest of his career.

In the second half of March Oastler went into Lancashire
to conduct his first campaign in the cotton districts. Innumerable small meetings had been held there, both prior to Sadler's Bill and since the Bradford Conference, but no campaign
at all comparable to Oastler's rousing of the West Riding the
year before. The Manchester Central Committee had long
wanted to hold such a crusade, but Oastler had hitherto declined their invitations. Now, however, in a whirlwind tour of
eight days he addressed five gatherings every bit as impressive
as those of the previous winter.

But there was a marked difference between the two campaigns. At the beginning of the movement he was preaching

a gospel of pity and trying to shake his hearers out of their indifference to the social question. Since then the propaganda of the Short Time Committees had rendered that kind of mission less necessary. What was needed now was not conversion but mobilization. The Government and the masters must be given mass proof that public opinion was overwhelmingly on the Ten Hours side. Moreover, Oastler's own temper had changed in the interval. He crossed the Pennines in a fighting mood, both to give the call to arms and to utter a solemn warning. With all his inflaming power he told one audience after another that 'the present system has caused a chasm in society,' and that 'the children of the poor have a *right* to be protected by the law against the tyranny and murder of the rich. If not, they have no interest in the State—they are dissevered from the Commonwealth.' The hint of unpredictable retribution increasingly colored all he said, for he had now come to believe that the fate of the Ten Hours Bill would mark a turning point in Britain's destiny. To him the issue was clear: either the new Parliament of the 'reformed' era was going to admit that there was such a thing as the *general interest,* and so legislate in terms of a collective purpose; or it was going to let its policy be determined by a narrow conception of 'national wealth' and by the dogma of laissez-faire. If the latter, then, Oastler believed, the community was heading for a social convulsion which would be as disastrous as it was inevitable.

These Lancashire audiences received his gospel with the same fervor the Yorkshire crowds had shown: similar scenes were witnessed everywhere. And the whole campaign reached a dramatic finale in the theatre at Bolton at the end of March, when Oastler was presented with an inscribed silver bowl subscribed for by the local operatives. In a speech of acceptance, he solemnly vowed never to desert the Ten Hours cause for any compromise.

¶ 6

This intensive renewal of Ten Hours propaganda did not go unanswered, of course. As soon as Ashley gave notice of his motion, individual mill owners began putting out their own pamphlets and broadsheets. None said anything that had not been said with equal effectiveness in the original newspaper controversy two years earlier,[8] but all played variations on the theme that foreign competition would ruin British industry if Ashley's Bill were passed.

Some adopted an urbane tone, praising the heart while pitying the head of the would-be reformers. A certain K. Finlay of Glasgow, for example, in *A Letter to Lord Ashley* which was widely distributed, lamented the tactics of Oastler and his followers, 'whose benevolent feelings have been excited and who, in their amiable eagerness to suppress what they are persuaded is wrong, would adopt ruinous and impractical measures to the manifest danger of the comfortable existence of these young persons they mean to protect and assist.' He added the strange argument that since the Lancashire masters openly admitted the existing factory laws were evaded in the cotton industry, there was no hope that a more stringent measure could be enforced.

Others were much less urbane. 'A Scottish Mill owner' from Melrose, in a *Letter to Lord Althorp,* bitterly denounced the 'mawkish philanthropy' of the age which was leading to 'excessive legislation' and to the 'impolicy of interfering between master and servant.' He made no attempt to deny the overworking of children; on the contrary he fully admitted it. But he put it down to excessive taxation and profligate administration, as the framers of the Halifax Resolutions had done.

At Manchester an anonymous manufacturer placarded the town with a warning to his fellow-citizens that three-quarters of the town's trade would be lost if the Ten Hours men were to have their way. No moral issue was involved in the proposed bill, he declared: only the simple, practical question, 'can England successfully compete?' To this the Short Time Committee immediately replied with a counter-placard pasted alongside, developing the familiar arguments about underconsumption and sharing-the-work, which the Yorkshire men had been using ever since the publication of *Humanity against Tyranny.*[9]

[8] See above, ch. V.
[9] See above, p. 105.

So the controversy raged again in pamphlet, press, and poster, just as it had when the issue was first raised in the autumn of 1830. To every pronouncement of the masters, the local lodges at once replied with such resources as they could command; and to the multiplying Short Time groups of workers the masters responded in their turn by reviving those defense committees that had sprung into being when Sadler's Bill was imminent.[10] In the week when Oastler was touring Lancashire, a meeting of Manchester cotton spinners unanimously resolved 'forthwith to take vigorous measures' to oppose Ashley. Within a few days the masters in every sizeable town in the textile districts had taken the same resolution.

¶ 7

The petitions for a Ten Hours Bill which came into the House of Commons from mid-February on represented the harvest of the campaign. The Central Committees had stuck to the plan that Oastler had impressed upon the Bradford Conference, whereby the House was to be plied with many and frequent local petitions rather than three or four big ones. Every few days they were arriving, therefore, up until the final debate, testifying in striking fashion to the effectiveness of the tactics that had been used. Twelve thousand signatures came in from Bradford, 2000 from Dewsbury, nearly 5000 from Huddersfield, over 16,000 from Leeds. From Bolton and Halifax they came, from Manchester and Glasgow, Dumbarton and Norwich, as well as from innumerable smaller places, such as Pudsey and Batley, Eccleston, Thornton, and Renfrew. And several times their presentation provided the occasion for what was virtually an informal preliminary debate on the factory question.

The enemies of the bill were no less busy, and much talk was going on in corridor and common room regarding the best line for them to take. The editors of the *Mercury* were still hoping that Lord Morpeth would go on with his eleven hours' measure. Soon after the convening of Parliament, however, an entirely new project began to be talked about: a project seemingly emanating from Wilson Patten, Member for North Lancashire

[10] See above, p. 151.

and one of the ablest spokesmen for the masters in the House. This was that the factory question should be investigated all over again: not as before, by a Select Committee, but by a Royal Commission.

Historians have not yet laid bare the story lying behind the maneuverings that followed, though the outward events are clear enough. At first Althorp, the Leader of the House, advised Patten not to press his suggestion. Yet the idea gradually found increasing favor, and during the last ten days of March, petitions in its support were steadily arriving from the north. The arguments used are revealing. To begin with, Patten pleaded only for fair play: Sadler's Committee, he said, had heard only the operatives' case; the adjournment of Parliament had prevented the masters from giving their own evidence, which would have cleared their name of the dishonor imputed by the *Report;* so the masters must now be given a chance. But some of Patten's supporters were much less cautious. Soon they were openly saying in debate that they wanted a Royal Commission because factory regulation would ruin trade. In other words, they took it for granted that a new enquiry would somehow be used to kill the Ten Hours cause.

Ashley's followers vigorously attacked the proposal as nothing but another wrecking device thought up at the last moment, and several of the members of Sadler's Committee took the same line. G. R. Robinson of Worcester, for example, told the House that 'no Committee ever took more pains to arrive at fair and just conclusions and to obtain every requisite information,' and Strickland corroborated. 'The facts brought before the Committee were so strong and unanswerable,' he said, 'that although they might go into a long and extensive investigation on the other side and might prove that some of the master manufacturers were disposed to acts of kindness and humanity, that could never overturn the mass of fearful evidence which had been submitted.' Even the amiable Morpeth, opposed though he was to a Ten Hours measure, was unable to bring himself to support a plea backed by such egregious reasoning as some of the Lancashire members had used. When the time came, he honorably gave his vote against it.

But all these protests were in vain. On 3 April Wilson Patten formally moved his motion, and after a lengthy debate it was carried by a single vote in a comparatively scanty House, 74 members voting for a Commission and 73 against. The very thing the Ten Hours men had feared had thus come to pass. Despite their enormous efforts, they had been frustrated for the third time.

CHAPTER XIX

The North Receives the Royal Commission

WHEN OASTLER heard the news that a Royal Commission was going to make a new investigation of factory conditions he was deeply angered. All along he had feared the consequences of middle-class enfranchisement; this latest trick seemed to justify his fears. What was there now, he asked, to prevent the complete triumph of the capitalists and the final enslavement of the masses? Perhaps a revolution might be the best solution after all. As yet that was only a half-formed idea at the back of his mind, but it persisted. And once again he unburdened himself in another appeal to the Duke. 'If some measures are not adopted to release the people, and the aristocracy too, from the liberal money-and-steam interest,' he wrote, 'the sooner we have a regular blow up the better.'

There was little time to indulge such speculations, however. The Royal Commission was going to start work without delay, so the Ten Hours organization would have to decide its policy immediately. Emergency meetings of all the Committees were called, hasty consultations took place between the leaders, and eventually two things were agreed upon. One was that the campaign of public meetings must forthwith be resumed, and the other that a big general conference should be held at Manchester after district conferences had first sounded out operative opinion concerning the best course to follow.

¶ 1

Within a week of the fateful vote in the House, therefore, the Ten Hours organization was in full activity once more, engaged upon a campaign of mass protest more comprehensive than ever. It began at Halifax with a wildly enthusiastic meeting on Easter

Monday, when Oastler roused his hearers with his new militancy. Never had he been more vehement or more searing in
his denunciation of local conditions. That same night the Bingley Committee was holding its own meeting, and so great was
the crowd that assembled that they had to adjourn to a near-by
field. Bradford's protest was made next day, and although the
posters were not on the streets until one o'clock, an audience of
nearly 3000 had assembled by the time the proceedings began.
And while John Wood and Parson Bull were holding forth there,
Sadler was addressing another perfervid gathering at Leeds. In
a remarkably short while the whole of the north was ablaze with
resentment against the Government. Challenging posters adorned
walls and hoardings as huge meetings were held in Manchester, Glasgow, Preston, Bolton, Wigan, Dewsbury, and Keighley,
besides innumerable smaller ones in the villages roundabout.
On Saturday the 13th, Oastler was back in Huddersfield, conducting another spectacular demonstration. A Sabbath's rest,
and he was off again, as all through the ensuing week the local
delegates' meetings were being held.

The crucial conference to decide what policy the movement
would adopt towards the Royal Commission began at Manchester on 22 April. The delegates, who represented all the Short
Time Committees of England and Scotland, came to the meeting already convinced that the sole purpose of the Government's inquiry was to gather the necessary data to justify before Parliament some kind of compromise measure, such as an
eleven hours' bill. At the outset, therefore, they unanimously
decided to decline any invitation to co-operate that the Commissioners might issue. But mere passive resistance would not
do much good. The operatives must demonstrate their firm resolve to have a Ten Hours law whatever the Government might
propose, and in doing so they must discredit the procedure and
the findings of the Commissioners by every means in their
power. To this end, after four days of discussion, the Conference formulated a plan of action that was to give the 1833
inquiry a notoriety its promoters had never expected.

In brief, the plan was this. As soon as the traveling Commissioners arrived in a town, the local Short Time Committee was

to call upon them and present a written protest informing them that their mission was 'unnecessary, partial and delusive.' Every evening after the mills were closed the factory children with their fathers and mothers were to assemble outside the hotel or house where the Commissioners were staying and hold an indignation meeting, so that the men from Whitehall should be under no illusion as to local sentiment concerning the factory question. As the Commissioners went about their business they were to be shadowed by two or more 'intelligent, discreet and inflexible men of good character' specially appointed by the Committee. These sleuths were to find out everything the Commissioners did: the places they visited, the witnesses they examined, the people they dined with, and the pressures they encountered. At the same time close watch was to be kept on all the local mills to learn just how much they had been renovated or refurbished in preparation for their inspection, and how many of their sickly and deformed hands had been kept out of the way. All these things were to be carefully recorded in a journal which the Committee was to forward to Oastler or one of the other leaders immediately the Commissioners had left the district.

Detailed confidential instructions for carrying out the scheme were sent from the Conference to the secretaries of all the Short Time Committees in the country.[1] Various other tactics were agreed upon before the delegates separated. Bull was to go to the woolen districts in the west of England to organize resistance there, while a certain George Downs of Derby was to do the same in the midlands. An impressive *Address to All Ranks and Classes of the Land* was drawn up for nation-wide distribution; and Oastler was instructed to get a special memorial presented to the Queen praying for her sympathy and intervention.[2] The final act of the Conference was to confirm the decision taken at Bradford that Oastler be 'the centre of communication to the Short Time Committees generally.'

On the last night, the delegates adjourned to the Manor Court Room, where the Manchester group was holding the final meet-

[1] These instructions are reprinted in Appendix C.
[2] The *Address* is given in Appendix D.

ing of that intensive campaign which had now been in progress for more than 12 weeks. It proved to be an astonishing
affair. Sadler, Bull, Wood, and Oastler were the principal orators and they drew an audience that packed the hall. All four
spoke magnificently, as though, realizing that their cause was
entering its last critical phase, they had the conviction that their
words might contribute to the patterning of destiny. They spoke
as prophets, solemnly weighing their age in the balance of
righteousness and warning of the divine retribution that would
surely overtake the oppressor. Indisputably the greatest speech
was Oastler's. It was a denunciation of the tyranny of wealth
and of the social anarchy that uncontrolled industrialism would
beget. As he lashed the hypocrisy of the evangelicals and the
crass selfishness of the capitalists, his mood grew more and more
apocalyptic. Things could not go on much longer as they were
going now: there are limits to human endurance. 'If the mill
owners will drive me to use the word, let them—at their own
bidding and not at mine—let them dread *the dagger and the
torch* . . . I have ceased to reason.' The effect on the audience
was indescribable. They cheered, they groaned, they shuddered
and were convulsed with all those paroxysms usually associated
with revivalist meetings. When Oastler sat down, they jumped to
their feet to hail him with wave after wave of cheering until
they were exhausted.

So ended the second great rousing of the north. Next day the
Royal Commission officially began its work.

¶ 2

If the Ten Hours men were roused to anger by the creation
of a Royal Commission, they were filled with alarm by its personnel and procedure, for it was the very embodiment of a way
of social thinking entirely antithetical to everything Oastler
and the humanitarian Tories stood for.

The Commission was made up of 16 members, comprising a
Central Board sitting with a secretary in London, and 12 Assistants who undertook the field work. No one can doubt their
sincerity or their learned competence. They were models of
bureaucratic rectitude: clear-thinking, detached, and unemo-

tional. And almost all of them had drunk deeply of the distilled waters of Philosophic Radicalism. Both Edwin Chadwick and Southwood Smith, who were the dominating personalities of the Commission, had been personal friends of the great reformer Jeremy Bentham, as had their secretary James Wilson. They were implacable enemies of aristocratic domination, social drift, and administrative muddle. They saw themselves as disinterested technicians of the new science of social engineering, which their master had been teaching these many years. As such they were possessed by the vision of a democratically renovated State, tidily uniform and administratively centralized, which would elicit the maximum energies of its members under the guidance not of a philosopher-king but of an expert civil service. To their coterie modern Britain owes a debt that can scarcely be exaggerated; yet in their own generation they brought upon their heads the wrath of masters and workers alike.

Their preconceptions gave them an entirely new approach to the factory question. They did not think of it in terms of pity or of Christian ethics, but rather in terms of expediency and the conservation of the nation's human resources. Unlike Morpeth, therefore, they had no interest in devising a compromise between the 'restrictionists' and the 'anti-restrictionists.' Fully persuaded though they were that the State should in no way interfere with the normal activity of 'free agents,' they were equally convinced that if it could be proved that children ought not to be regarded as free agents, then the protection afforded must be real and substantial and not based on any catch phrase. Furthermore, they believed that the State should utilize any such principle of control to enforce some kind of educational provision for the children. And it was equally obvious to them that, whatever the terms of the final statute might be, some sort of central machinery for effective law enforcement must be set up. In all of which respects Ashley's Bill might be considered seriously defective, especially since it so blatantly slurred over the fundamental distinction between free adult and unfree child.

The procedure of the Commission was calculated to alarm

the Ten Hours men no less than its membership. For the purpose of the investigation the country was divided into four zones. Three Assistant Commissioners were to make the survey in each zone and send their findings back to the Central Board in Whitehall. But these itinerant officials were not going to hold open hearings and take down a verbatim record, as the Sadler Committee had done; they were going to keep the initiative in their own hands throughout, inviting only such evidence as they needed and making their own notes. Moreover, the inquiry was to be made in accordance with an elaborate set of instructions (17 printed pages of them, including the questionnaires) drawn up by the Central Board. These instructions enraged the operatives for a number of reasons, but particularly on account of the intimate personal questions the Commissioners were told to put to the women workers. 'Such a mass of impotent and stupid verbiage,' said *The Times* in a mordant commentary which the Ten Hours men immediately reprinted as a leaflet, 'it has seldom been our fortune to face.' [3] What the relevance of such details could be to the simple question whether a factory child should work 10 hours a day or not, the ordinary worker found it hard to understand. To him it seemed just an impertinent affront to his independence.

To a later generation the purpose of this procedure is plain enough. The amazing speed with which the Commission reported (the first draft was in the hands of the Government within 45 days) tells its own story. Clearly the Commissioners knew in a general way what they wanted to find before ever they went to look for it. No body of men, however competent, could possibly have made an impartial survey of all the British textile industries in only 6 weeks: to believe otherwise imposes too great a strain upon credulity.

[3] 'The instructions,' *The Times* continued, 'contain a diversity of plans for enquiring into questions but remotely connected with that for which the establishment of the Commission had arisen, and indeed, not entirely compatible with that wholesome dread of ridicule and anxious love of decency which ought to characterize the proceedings of such a body. We subjoin as a curiosity some of the queries to be made of married women:—Was your first child born within one year of your marriage? How many miscarriages? . . . How many of the births were difficult cases; requiring instruments; not requiring instruments?' etc. *The Times* 3 June 1833.

Both parties, in fact, were maneuvering with ulterior considerations. The Ten Hours men were pleading the cause of the
factory child, but they were hoping to get out of it a shortening of the working day for adults as well. There was no conceal-
ment of this hope: Oastler and Bull, Fielden and Wood had
stated it explicitly and repeatedly during the preceding two
years. The Commissioners, on the other hand, were unquestionably sincere in their desire to find out the unvarnished truth
about conditions in the mills, but they were committed in advance to the belief that any attempt to interfere with the free
agency of adults was an evil not to be tolerated. Nor is this
to be interpreted simply as a conflict of programs: it goes much
deeper than that. What was really at issue was the ultimate contrast between two views of society. Between Chadwick's philosophy and Oastler's there could be no compatibility.

¶ 3

For five weeks the Commissioners toured the northern counties, pursued wherever they went by the embarrassing attentions of the Short Time Committees operating according to the
Manchester plan. It was in the West Riding, however, under
the goading of Oastler's intransigence, that the most spectacular
opposition was shown.

The three officials assigned to Yorkshire were John Drinkwater,
Alfred Power, and Dr. Louden. Arriving unobtrusively in Leeds
on the evening of 13 May, they set to work with the utmost circumspection. They tactfully made a number of courtesy calls,
invited the Short Time Committee to an informal chat, which
considerably impressed the operatives, and summoned a general
conference on procedure to be attended by Sadler and the Ten
Hours men as well as by representatives of all the local firms.

Tact, however, could not bridge the chasm between such rival
purposes as this conference revealed. Drinkwater explained to
the gathering that he was anxious to establish a mutually agree-
able procedure. What he proposed, therefore, was that when any
evidence involving masters and men was being heard, two or
three Ten Hours leaders should attend along with the same number of mill owners. Both parties would be allowed to submit ques-

tions or make statements, and to inspect the Commissioners'
notes. But there was to be no publication of evidence while the
Commissioners were on circuit; nor was the procedure to apply
when they were conducting their independent investigations.

The mill owners were satisfied with this scheme, but not Sadler. He was much too distrustful of the Commissioners to accept
any procedure that left all the initiative in their hands and allowed them to select the facts they wanted to emphasize. His
idea was that they should first hear the independent testimony
of masters and operatives and then seek to verify it by open inquiry. Any other plan, he believed, would give too much scope
to the preconceptions of the investigators—and those were already
only too well known. He therefore suggested two modifications
of Drinkwater's scheme. One was that all proceedings should be
public; the other, that an independent shorthand writer should
take down the evidence, which should then be sworn-to by the
witness.

The Commissioners rejected both proposals on the ground that
they were unnecessary and cumbersome. A long wrangle followed, during which the masters who were present became particularly vehement against the suggestion that evidence should
be given on oath. In vain Sadler pointed out that the rejection
of that suggestion implied that the Commission was afraid to
submit the mill owners' evidence to the same rigorous scrutiny
that the operatives' testimony had undergone before the Select
Committee. The three officials would concede nothing. Thereupon Sadler washed his hands of the affair and went to report
to the Short Time Committee.

Before nightfall the town was plastered with posters calling
upon the factory children of Leeds to make the first demonstration the following evening. Accordingly, as soon as the mills closed
for the day, some 3,000 ragged and grimy children assembled in
the Free Market. Under the direction of the indefatigable Cavie
Richardson they marched in procession to the hotel where Drinkwater and his colleagues were staying. The Commissioners
deemed it expedient to receive a deputation, so Richardson went
in with half a dozen of the children and read out a scathing denunciation which the Short Time Committee had drawn up. Then

on a given signal the dense throng outside broke into the *Song of the Factory Children,* which George Condy had just put to a popular tune of the day:

> We will have the Ten Hours Bill,
>   That we will, that we will;
> Or the land shall ne'er be still,
>   Ne'er be still, ne'er be still;
> Parliament say what they will,
>   WE WILL HAVE THE TEN HOURS BILL.

After a speech or two from the leaders, they all moved off to Sadler's house and spent the rest of the evening parading.

Hardly had the throng dispersed before Oastler rode into the town. He was immediately recognized, of course, and another crowd quickly began to gather round him, but for once he had not come to make a scene. He had come to tell the Commissioners to their faces just what he thought of them. They received him courteously enough and expressed their regret that he was unwilling to co-operate. But Oastler retorted that co-operation was futile, both because the Commission was unnecessary and because its findings were a foregone conclusion since all its members were 'political economists.' Drinkwater assured him they would be as impartial as they could and begged him to reconsider. Oastler's determination to make a quarrel, however, was proof against all blandishments. Once more he went over all the arguments against the idea of a Commission, and nothing the trio said made the least difference. The investigation, he kept repeating, was simply a trick of the Government's, 'playing into the hands of their dear friends the capitalists.' The squabble was entirely profitless. Men who find elation in the raptures of crowded halls are rarely endowed with the grace that captivates bureaucrats. And in this case Oastler did not even get the satisfaction of making the parting shot. That was reserved for Drinkwater, who told the 'Factory King' as he left that his refusal to co-operate was *un-English.*

Next day the Commissioners began their inquiries independently, trailed wherever they went by the sleuths of the Leeds Short Time Committee.

GEORGE STRINGER BULL ('PARSON BULL OF BIERLY')

West Riding
MEETING.

FREINDS OF HUMANITTY, BE AT
YOUR POST!

Be in the *MARKET PLACE* on *Monday Morning* next
before 7 o'Clock, to meet your

'FACTORY KING'

And other **FRIENDS**, and proceed to *Wibsey Low Moor*,
to give the grand and final blow to *Factory Tyrants*, and

THE LAST LIFT TO THE

TEN HOUR BILL.

Our admirable friend **CAPT. WOOD**, is expected to be in attendance, and head the **HUDDERSFIELD** grand division to
the scene of action, under **Flags and Banners** with suitable
inscriptions, accompanied with **Music.**
 Returns have been made from all the Towns of the **WEST-
RIDING**, & many *Lodges & Unions, determining to attend.*

BRADFORD and its surrounding districts, is to pour out all her population; The men of KEIGHLEY are prepared to show off;
LEEDS, HALIFAX, DEWSBURY, &c. &c. &c. Then Man, Woman, and Child, prepare for the great the glorious day. Meet your
Brethren in Spirit, in Strength, and in Deep Resolve, and on the field with one accord, with one mighty voice, pledge yourselves NEVER
to relax your efforts until

TYRANNY be ANNIHILATED,
And INFANT SLAVERY ABOLISHED.

June 27th, 1833. PRINTED BY J. HOBSON, SWAN YARD, HUDDERSFIELD.

ONE OF THE POSTERS CALLING FOR THE GREAT WIBSEY LOW MOOR DEMON-
STRATION ON BEHALF OF THE TEN HOURS BILL, 1 July 1833

¶ 4

One cannot but feel that Drinkwater and his colleagues were guilty of some gross indiscretions in the course of their inquiry. Even outside the ranks of the Ten Hours men the Commissioners were widely suspected of being partial to the mill owners' point of view. Yet they repeatedly lunched or dined with prominent manufacturers and twice spent the weekend with the Marshall family. The shadowing Committeemen reported it all, even to the details of the food eaten, and the information only served to exacerbate the already dangerous feeling of resentment.

Throughout the following week Oastler and the Short Time Committee did all they could to fan the resentment. On Monday night, Oastler and Bull came over to address an open-air meeting in the market place, at which the wildest enthusiasm was displayed. Not since the turbulent Cloth Hall meeting had Leeds seen the like, only this time the Ten Hours banners waved over a throng that was militantly unanimous. Oastler was at his raciest. For days past details had been pouring into Committee headquarters about the preparations being made in the various mills to receive the Commissioners. Walls had been whitewashed and unsavory conditions temporarily remedied; ailing children had been excluded and the rest told to come to work in their best clothes. Oastler had a great time exposing it all, and the crowd roared its approval. Then they trooped off in procession to present another protest to the harassed officials.

But the Committee did not rest content with public displays. Protests were arranged for in every mill the Commissioners were likely to visit and every village they might pass through. Day after day fresh posters of denunciation were scattered about the town, and narratives of the doings at Leeds were sent as broadsheets to other West Riding towns to encourage them to emulation. London papers soon began to take notice of the Yorkshire happenings and *The Times* devoted over a column to a sympathetic version of the story. Moreover, the movement suddenly acquired a new supporter on the left, for Henry Hetherington's proletarian journal, *The Poor Man's Guardian,* now began giving the cause its endorsement.

On Friday the 24th Oastler sent the Commissioners the most notorious of all the protests, which was publicized by every means the organization could command:

To Messrs. Drinkwater and Co.

Sirs,—I solemnly protest against your Commission and against your proceedings: in the name of the Father, and of the Son, and of the Holy Ghost.—

1st. Because it is 'Un-English'; and in the absence of evidence, it implies the want of Common Sense or Honesty to raise a question on the proposition that a Child should be required to labour for a longer period than from Six in the Morning to Six in the Evening, and be deprived of reasonable hours for rest and meals.

2nd. Because it is 'Un-English' to rave against Slavery 5 or 6,000 miles off, and to encourage a more abominable and more cowardly system of Slavery at home, practised by those very individuals who are the most noisy in their opposition to the accursed system of West India Slavery.

3rd. Because it is 'Un-English' to refuse the innocent and industrious Children of the poor of Britain the same legislative protection which is already granted to the guilty Adult Felon and the unfortunate Adult Black Slave.

4th. Because it is 'Un-English' to use the Prerogative of the King of England for the continuance of oppression and Murder—His Prerogative is a Prerogative of Mercy . . .

And so on, through another 17 indictments.

For all its extravagance and indiscretion, this farrago is no less revealing of the prevailing mood of the movement than it is of Oastler's temperament. Both belong to a political climate only to be found on the thither side of the Victorian uplands.

The Commissioners were outraged; by this time their tempers had worn thin. Their clerk sent a curt note telling Oastler not to write again unless he had something useful to impart, in which case he was 'to make that information known without recourse either to the language of blasphemy or of sedition.' That only provoked another blast, which duly reverberated through the Pennine valleys along with all the others:

To Messrs. Drinkwater & Co.

Sirs,—Think not to alarm me; you are receiving Wages from my Labour, and I shall express my opinion of your appointment and your Dark and Secret proceedings in such terms as to me may seem good.

I am in the habit of saying what I mean—and I declare it to be my deliberate opinion that your appointment and your proceedings are 'Un-English' and Un-Christian.

Talk not then to me of Blasphemy and Sedition; you know, or you ought to know, that the King of England is the Father of His People; not the supporter of their destroyers; and that as for blasphemy, it is the climax of Impiety to 'forbid Little Children to come unto Christ.'

The Commission which you have undertaken was instigated by those who in the pursuit of gain are regardless of the lives and happiness of the Poor—and I tell you without fear—you may report as yourselves and your employers may think proper—and earn your wages in whatever way you please. The People of England,—no more than myself,—are neither *blasphemous* nor *seditious—but they will have the Ten-Hour Bill.*

Talk of Sedition, indeed! You are, as I know, in communication with the Camp of Sedition. Mr. Drinkwater told me 'he had applied to Baines for the Parliamentary Report,' and it is not many months since Baines and his party, at the instigation of the Prime Minister of the King, marched under the flag—'We will pay no more taxes.' The King, with his Crown and Sceptre falling, clothed in Petticoats,—and the Queen in Breeches—the Tri-coloured flag—the veiled Executioner, —and the Bloody Axe—aye, and Baines, the Friend of you, the pretended anti-Seditious and Loyal Commissioners, absolutely required the people of Leeds to give *Three Groans for the Queen of England!!!*

Sedition, indeed; never was I so disgusted, as when I received a letter sealed with the King's Arms, from the Commissioners of Child Murder—the Friends of Baines. Don't think to Humbug us Yorkshire folks—but as I said before 'Get Away, Get Away!' We *will* not sanction the Murder of our Children!!

I perceive you beg that I will 'refrain from again addressing you, &c.' Poor things, you don't know who you are writing to,—had it not been for *me*, you would have just now been waiting and *longing* unnecessarily for briefs and for fees—in your own domiciles. But for *me*, even without your sanction, Child Murder would have continued to be perpetrated in England by the 'pious and respectable Saints,' who shout everlastingly against Negro flogging. You are deceiving yourselves, but I know who you are, whether you know yourselves or not, and I know if you had been possessed of talents in your professions, you would not have been at this moment travelling the country at *my* expense, for the purpose of legalising the Murder of my Poor Factory

Children, forming an intimate connection with the notorious Baines.

If I think it needful to communicate with you again, (as I fancy I shall, when you pollute Huddersfield with your presence,) believe me, I shall tell you the truth, although you chuse to call Religion, Blasphemy; and Loyalty, Sedition.

Read the Constitution and read the Bible, both of which I revere, and learn to know that the Life of the Child of the Poor is of more value than the Money of the hoary capitalist.

You will gain nothing by shewing your airs and being in a passion with me. For the present I say, 'Fare ye well.'

RICHARD OASTLER

Leeds, May 25th., 1833

While this exchange was going on, an epistolary brawl of another kind was developing between the Commissioners and Sadler. The former chairman of the Select Committee was certainly irked by the cavalier way his suggestions concerning procedure had been treated by the Commissioners. At the request of the Short Time Committee, therefore, he published a cogent pamphlet explaining why he and his friends had refused to co-operate in the enquiry. Drinkwater and Power immediately produced a reply inordinately arrogant in tone, which Baines printed and published for them. Various metropolitan dailies reproduced the controversy, and *The Times* added a forthright editorial sharply commenting on the fact that the Commissioners' reply contained 'no attempt at a vindication of the unsatisfactory and suspicious course' they were pursuing. Thus encouraged, Sadler answered the misrepresentations of Drinkwater's pamphlet. The Commissioners replied a second time and Sadler again retorted; and so the altercation dragged on all the while the Yorkshire investigation lasted. Nothing came of it except a worsening of tempers on both sides and a deepening of the suspicion that the Commissioners' questionable procedure was in some way related to their preconceived intentions.

¶ 5

During the last week in May the Commissioners were undergoing the same sort of treatment in Huddersfield. 'Oastler's Own' were not going to be outdone by the Leeds men. There were more processions of factory children, more dense throngs milling in angry protest, and more minatory fulminations from Oastler.

On 4 June, the hated trio went to Bradford, where they were further drenched with execrations. The worsted spinners there were, if anything, more hostile than the Leeds operatives had been. On their own initiative, 700 of John Wood's work-people petitioned their employer not to allow the Commissioners inside his buildings, otherwise they would be 'most offensively treated.' For 11 days the demonstrations continued, this time with Bull as the organizer in chief. The greatest of them—probably, indeed, the greatest in the whole turbulent chapter—was the one on the evening of 6 June when all the resources of the Yorkshire Central Committee were put to the staging of a spectacle involving the entire worsted area. Newspapers variously estimated the crowd at between ten and twenty thousand people. Other meetings catered for special audiences: for children, parents, and over-lookers as well as for the general public. Petitions and maledictions were presented daily. And once during a dinner hour Drinkwater and Power were mobbed by several hundred children singing the Factory Song and had to seek refuge in the yard of a near-by mill, whence they were unable to emerge until the factory bell called the youngsters back to work.

Wherever they went the Commissioners continued to be shadowed, and since their itinerary was not known in advance special messengers were kept in constant readiness by the Short Time Committees to warn other districts of their coming. At the end of their Bradford visit Drinkwater and Power made an effort to shake off these attentions. They announced they were going to Keighley and had their coach tickets made out accordingly. The Committee had a horse already saddled. At the last moment, however, the Commissioners got into the night coach for Doncaster. Their trailers immediately reported the news, and within a very few minutes 'King Richard's Commissioner' was galloping along the Doncaster road hard on their heels. When, at two o'clock in the morning, Drinkwater and Power went to warm themselves by the fire of a wayside inn while horses were being changed, they found their shadow already waiting for them prepared to launch into another protest according to instructions.

It made a grand story for Oastler's next speech, and the whole Riding laughed.

These five weeks of continuous protest came to a febrile conclusion in Huddersfield with an open-air meeting held for the purpose of initiating a town petition to the House of Commons praying for the rejection of the Factory Commission's report. All the calculated skill the Short Time Committee now so well knew how to employ was brought to bear with impressive effect: the bands and the banners, the organized marching and the mass cheering in the evening twilight, the preliminary speeches with their iteration and reiteration of the familiar slogans; and then, at the appointed moment, 'King Richard' himself stepping forth in the full consciousness of his mastery. He dramatized the struggle with vivid imagery and stung his hearers to hot anger. Once again he explained how the Government's Commission was working for their enslavement in the interests of the privileged. He spoke of the hope of a fuller life that might be theirs if men would will it so. But the will of a few was evil. The crowd was lifted to a frenzy, for all its familiarity with Oastler's technique. And when he had finished, it turned in fury to hoot and yell while the effigies of Drinkwater and Power were burned at a bonfire in the Market Place.[4]

[4] Dr. Thomas Chalmers, the eminent Scottish divine, happened that evening to be staying at Huddersfield in the course of a tour through England. In a letter to his sister he described what he saw:

'On entering Huddersfield I found that in respect of fairs, I was out of the frying pan into the fire; for before my inn door, the George, there was a prodigious assemblage of people at a market; and I had to wait some time ere I could get a room for the evening. The crowd was vastly augmented by there being furthermore a political meeting in the open air, and the whole of the spacious market-place was filled with the multitude. Mr. Oastler held forth on the sufferings of the factory children, and was enthusiastically cheered. I saw from my window, but heard not. Then followed, to me an original scene, the burning of the Factory Commissioners, and Captain Fenton, one of their obnoxious members of Parliament, and another unpopular master-manufacturer, in effigy. The figures were fearfully like men; and being now dark, the conflagration lighted up the whole square, and revealed the faces of the yelling myriads, so as to give the aspect and character of Pandemonium to the scene. The burning figures were tossed ferociously into the air; and to renew their combustion were dashed into a bonfire from time to time. The spectacle I am sure is a depraving one, and fitted to prepare the actors for burning the originals instead of the copies.' W. Hanna: *Memoirs of the Life and Writings of Thomas Chalmers,* vol. III, p. 366.

CHAPTER XX

Climax and Defeat: The Passing of Althorp's Factory Act

WITH the departure of the Commissioners for London, the spotlight of attention shifted back to the House of Commons, where Ashley's Ten Hours Bill was due to come up for its second reading on 17 June. Thither, therefore, the representatives of both masters and operatives returned to resume their lobbying: and high pressure lobbying it was. Some indication of the pressure used may be gleaned from the fact that John Doherty, delegate of the Manchester Central Committee, himself interviewed no fewer than 200 Members of Parliament during the nine weeks he was on duty.

¶ 1

By this time, the general sentiment of the country was definitely running in favor of some sort of factory legislation. Even the die-hard masters realized that, their chief concern now being to prevent too drastic a bill from getting on to the Statute Book. At a meeting held in the Union Hotel, London, where Baines and 30 of the lobbying manufacturers were staying, the matter was thrashed out at length. Two alternative schemes were formulated, either of which, the masters informed the Government, they were willing to accept. Both provided for a twelve-hour day for operatives under 21. Under the first scheme, children were not to enter the mills until they were 11; under the second, until they were 10. In the latter case there would be a preliminary two-year period during which the children worked only 6 hours a day. It was a slight advance upon the Halifax Resolutions, but not much.

Meanwhile the Government was biding its time until the Royal Commission had reported. That was why little attention was paid to the second reading of the Ten Hours Bill, for everyone knew the Government would probably base its policy on the Commission's findings. A broad hint of what might be included in those findings was given to the House when Lord Althorp rose during the reading to announce that the *Report* would shortly be tabled. In some respects, he said, the Commission was prepared to go beyond Lord Ashley's proposals. For his part he was persuaded that regulation of juvenile labor was necessary and that eight hours' work a day was the maximum that was desirable for children under fourteen. He left the impression that he considered regulation unnecessary for workers above that age.

Consternation rapidly spread through the factory districts at this pronouncement, for there was no escaping its implications. Posters were immediately rushed out by the two Central Committees, warning the operatives that an eight hours' bill for children would mean a double-shift system and thus a sixteen-hour day for adults. If such a measure were passed, the last state of the adults would be worse than the first. At all costs, therefore, the operatives must fight to preserve the two clauses in Ashley's Bill that would prevent the possibility of a relay system, namely: the ten-hour maximum for those under 18, and the elimination of night work for those under 21. The 'last battle' for the Ten Hours Bill was about to begin, said one of the West Riding proclamations; 'it cannot now be a battle for hours, but it will be a battle for the limitation of ages.' That was the new issue in a nutshell, as both sides clearly realized. On the day that the Leeds operatives packed the Court House to condemn Althorp's eight hours' proposal vociferously and unanimously, a deputation of reassured manufacturers and northern M.P.'s waited upon the Prime Minister to ask that the Government would now take the factory question into its own hands.

Oastler held hurried consultations with several of the other leaders to discuss tactics. What they had to decide was whether to wait until the Government had made its full intentions known or whether to continue agitating. Oastler himself was all for the latter course. In his opinion, which he was never tired of expounding, the Reform Bill of 1832 would never have become law if the Whigs had not deliberately whipped up such a storm as to force the Government into action and paralyze the Tories with fear. That was the great open secret of the Whig success, he believed, and unless the Ten Hours men made use of it too they would never succeed. All his efforts of the past two years had been inspired by that conviction, and he pressed it anew now. As a result, it was agreed to hold one more spectacular gathering, like the pilgrimage to York: a gathering so impressive that it would make even complacency pause. This time, however, it was to take place at some more central spot that would not involve a lot of unnecessary marching, and should include not only the Short Time organization but also the Friendly Societies, the Trade Unions, and every other workers' association that could be persuaded to co-operate. The rendezvous they chose was one of the uplands outside Bradford known as Wibsey Low Moor, and the date, 1 July. Without delay the Committees started getting ready.

¶ 2

Just how many people came it is difficult to say, for estimates varied considerably. One newspaper put the figure at 60,000 and another at 150,000. *The Times* said 100,000.

Proceedings were closely modeled on those employed for the York Castle meeting. Everything had been carefully worked out in advance, and in spite of intermittent rain the affair went off without mishap. As before, the village contingents assembled at dawn and marched to the nearest big town. Thence, in six huge columns, they all advanced upon the Moor, each division to its appointed station, with a Tory on horseback leading the van. There were innumerable banners, flags, and streamers bearing all manner of slogans and devices, and a medley of insignia borne by Foresters, Druids, and other fraternal Orders. Many organizations brought their bands as well: one eyewitness counted 40 as he looked down from the hustings.

For more than five hours, speaker after speaker poured forth condemnation of Althorp's eight hours' proposal as nothing but a trick of the masters to lengthen the working day. There was angry unanimity on that score. In Oastler's speech, however, another chord was struck as well. Ever since the disappointment over Sadler's Bill, the apocalyptic mood had been growing upon him, as his public utterances had plainly shown. Now it all but possessed him. On Wibsey Moor he advanced to the very frontier that separates the social prophet from the social revolutionary: 'It is a question of blood against gold. Infants' blood has been sold for nought, but if we are despised now, *it shall be a question of blood in another sense* . . .' There were dangerous possibilities in such words. Were they bluff or incitement? Probably Oastler himself did not know: for the moment he was content with the endorsement of the multitude. Yet from this point forward the question obtrudes itself insistently in the mind of anyone seeking to penetrate the enigma of Oastler's ultimate intentions.

Apart from the impressiveness of the display and the vigor of the oratory, however, the day was to remain memorable as the occasion on which there entered into the leadership of the Ten Hours Movement a recent convert destined to play a part in its subsequent history hardly less strenuous than that of Parson Bull. This was William Busfield Ferrand,[1] a twenty-four-year-old country squire, who owned a beautiful estate just outside Bradford.

Ferrand is a quaint character from a vanished age. Of good county family, though entirely lacking in the suavity of Mayfair, he was as emphatically a man of the provinces as Squire Western. Ugly, square-jawed, and befringed with turbulent whiskers, he

---

[1] The circumstances of Ferrand's conversion to the Ten Hours cause were set forth in a letter he later wrote to the Duke of Newcastle. The episode apparently occurred sometime during the winter of 1832–3:

'At the hour of five on a winter's morning, I left my home to shoot wild fowl. On my road, I had to pass along a deep and narrow lane which led from a rural village to a distant factory. The wind howled furiously—the snow fell heavily, and drifted before the bitter blast. I indistinctly traced three children's footsteps. Soon, I heard a piteous cry of distress. Hurrying on, again I listened, but all was silent except the distant tolling of the factory bell. Again I tracked their footmarks, and saw that one had lagged behind; I returned, and found the little factory slave half-buried in a snowdrift fast asleep. I dragged it from its winding sheet; the icy hand of death had congealed its blood and paralysed its limbs. In a few minutes it would have been "where the wicked cease from troubling and the weary are at rest." I aroused it from its stupor and saved its life. From that hour I became a "Ten Hours Bill man" and the unflinching advocate of "protection to native industry!"'

usually wore the sultry scowl that made a contemporary call him
'Dantonesque.' And fully in keeping with the impression of
chronic pugnacity he always conveyed were his inveterate prejudices. He was a Church and King Tory of the deepest blue. An
enthusiastic farmer himself and a patron of agricultural improvements, he was firmly convinced that agriculture alone was the
foundation of national greatness and that where there is no longer
appreciation of that fact the people perish. Of mill owners he
entertained the dourest suspicions. Magistrate, chief constable
of his division, and officer in the Yorkshire Hussars; an autocrat
who was the soul of generosity and an aristocrat who detested
Manchester and London about equally—he was the almost complete embodiment of everything Oastler believed the country
gentleman should be. In stentorian tones he bellowed across the
moor his damnation of capitalism and all its crimes; and Oastler
(as he afterwards wrote) warmed to him immediately. It was
the beginning of a stout friendship which was to last until death,
and to bring Oastler succour beyond estimation.

'The moral effect of the Wibsey Low Moor meeting was great
throughout the country,' says one historian. That is assuredly an
overstatement; nevertheless to many northerners the gathering
seemed to have ominous significance. Disquiet spread, particularly in the woolen and worsted areas: a disquiet which the next
issue of the *Intelligencer* underlined with frankness:

If Government should be at once so dishonest and unwise as to defeat
the passing of the Ten Hours Bill, it will most assuredly sow the
whirlwind and must prepare itself to meet the storm. The meeting on
Monday embraced a mighty physical power which may easily be called
into adverse exercise and a deep responsibility lies on that man or set
of men who, by denying justice, gives an occasion for an attempt to
grasp it beyond the confines of law.

¶ 3

Consideration of the factory question had hung fire at Westminster during the sitting of the Royal Commission. Four days
after the big West Riding meeting, however, the parliamentary
struggle entered upon its final phase and rapidly reached a
denouement.

Having been allowed to pass its second reading, Ashley's Ten Hours Bill was now due to go to Committee. The report of the Commission was still not in Members' hands, though the Government knew what the findings were. Althorp therefore sought to play for time. What he proposed was that, instead of being sent to a Committee of the Whole (which would have been the normal procedure), the bill should be sent to another select committee with instructions to amend it to the Government's intentions. Surprisingly enough, the maneuver was defeated by 23 votes.

The Short Time Committees were elated, and their hopes rose. But many of the masters became alarmed. An emergency meeting of Manchester manufacturers voiced the alarm in resolutions that were not without an implied threat. Deeming it expedient, they said, to acquiesce in a certain amount of regulation for the purpose of ending this 'perplexing and injurious agitation,' they had been willing to accept proposals they really disapproved of. Should their 'hope of accommodation' be disappointed, they would feel compelled to 'withhold their co-operation.' Their lobbyists at Westminster were instructed to inform all Members accordingly: the implications were plain.

Their fears were premature, however. Before the lobbyists could get to work, the report of the Royal Commission was published. Immediately it wrought an overwhelming change in the spirit of the House: a change so complete as to ensure the Government the easiest of victories and to take all vigor and effectiveness out of the Ten Hours Movement for many months to come.

'No document,' it has been said, 'could have hit off the prevailing temper of Parliament with a more dexterous touch.' It did this by resolving the uncomfortable quandary in which a large number of Members found themselves. Many had unquestionably been perturbed by the recent revelations about factory conditions; on the other hand, they were no less troubled by the cogency of the foreign-competition argument. Sir James Mackintosh, philosopher and economist, had forcefully indicated the dilemma during the debate on Sadler's Bill. He was anxious, he said, 'to avow himself a political economist, but at the same time

. . . he would not allow even the principles of political economy
to be accessary to the infliction of torture.' Yet the idea of the
Government's interfering in the productive process was exceedingly distasteful. Furthermore, as several Members admitted,
they resented having had the issue forced upon their attention
by means of public agitation and the incitement of the masses.
Now at one stroke, all their perplexities were resolved by the
masterpiece of lucid assurance that was tabled in the second
week of July 1833.

The masters from Lancashire who had promoted the Royal
Commission in the hope of killing any factory legislation must
have been grievously disappointed by the findings. For all its
cautiousness and its insistence upon the wide variety of conditions to be found throughout the country, the *Report* made out
an incontestable case for parliamentary action. The majority of
children entered the mills at nine, it affirmed, but it was 'not
uncommon' to find them there at seven or eight. Everywhere they
worked as long as the adults, though nowhere was the labor they
performed 'proportional to their strength.' The practice of extending the normal day by paid overtime during rush seasons was
found to be general, sometimes reaching fantastic lengths. Evidence about thrashings was scarcely less emphatic than that
presented to Sadler's Committee. Conditions in many of the small
mills were represented as appalling. But what appeared to impress the Commissioners most were the grave effects, both physical and moral, such employment had upon the children.[2] In such
circumstances, the Commissioners argued, legislative protection
was justified, since children were not able to look after themselves and therefore could not be regarded as 'free agents.'

Over against these admissions, however, the Commissioners
enunciated the full gospel of current economic orthodoxy as it

[2] e.g. 'That the excessive fatigue, privation of sleep, pain in various parts
of the body, and swelling of the feet experienced by the young workers,
coupled with the constant standing, the peculiar attitude of the body, and
the peculiar motions of the limbs required in the labour of the factories,
together with the elevated temperature and the impure atmosphere in which
that labour is often carried on do sometimes ultimately terminate in the
production of serious, permanent and incurable disease, appears to be well
established.' *First Report* etc: p. 33.

applied to adults. The spirit of that gospel permeates the entire document. Impairment of free contract and the free labor market was assumed to be a social menace, whether it came from Parliament or from trade unions. 'The pernicious notion of the propriety and necessity of legislative interference to restrict the hours of adult labour' was treated with scorn. 'There is not one of the motives of persuasion which have been commonly urged by the friends of the ten hour bill,' said the Commissioners, 'which affords a colourable plea for extending the protection of the legislature to the labour of adults òr adolescents.' The Ten Hours Movement was largely organized hypocrisy, utilizing the figure of the factory child as a screen for ulterior purposes. It was represented as chiefly controlled by trade-union 'agitators,' whom 'the repeal of the combination laws [3] released from all restrictions in the disposal of their own property (labour), and who now seek to impose restrictions equally vexatious on the disposal of the property of others.' And the Ten Hours Bill itself was condemned both because it would entail an inevitable shortening of the adults' day and because the protection it afforded the child was inadequate.

Childhood—adulthood: these were the fundamental categories of analysis. On the one side, social regulation; on the other, the unimpeded operation of economic law. Where, then, did the transition from one to the other occur? The answer of the Commissioners was clear: at the age of 13. Then it is, declared the Report, that 'the period of childhood, properly so called, ceases'; after that, 'the same labour which was fatiguing and exhausting at an earlier period is in general comparatively easy.'

All this reasoning issued in certain explicit recommendations. No child, it was urged, should be employed in any factory until it was 9 years old. Between that age and its thirteenth birthday the child should work only 8 hours a day and none at all at night; afterwards it might work the same hours as other adults. Any scheme of protection for the child should include compulsory schooling for 3 hours a day. In addition, employers ought to be

---

[3] The 'combination laws' of 1799–1800, which made it a criminal offense for workmen to 'combine' in order to shorten hours of work or to keep up wages, had been repealed in 1824–5.

held responsible for faulty construction of their mills and for inadequately protected machinery, a provision that would entail a scheme for workmen's compensation. Lastly (since the existing laws were reported to be 'almost entirely inoperative'), it was recommended that a system of full-time State inspectorship should be adopted to see that these regulations were properly observed.

Most of the Tory press was vehement in its condemnation of the *Report*. 'It is certainly the most preposterous production that was ever offered to human contemplation,' said *The Times;* 'we surveyed it with surprise and indignation, and then could not resist an involuntary fit of laughter. But the 'Thunderer's' sardonic laughter could not stay the sweeping popularity of the document in the House. When the crucial debate occurred on 18 July, most of the Members were already in a mood to reverse the vote of only 13 days before. On Althorp's motion to substitute *thirteen years* for the *eighteen* of Ashley's measure, the Government carried the day by an overwhelming majority, 93 voting for the Ten Hours Bill and 238 against.

Ashley immediately resigned the matter into Althorp's hands, believing (as he wrote to Oastler next day) that the Government's proposals would 'produce tenfold misery and tenfold crime.' Thenceforth it was plain sailing for the Government.

To Althorp, then, must go the credit for the Government's new Factory Bill, which now went through Parliament with remarkable dispatch and received the royal assent within 6 weeks. The leader of the House was a cautious pragmatist by no means devoid of humane intentions, and his bill bore the stamp of its sponsor. He did not like the idea of factory legislation any more than did the rest of the administration, and he certainly felt that 'the senseless clamour out of doors' which had made all the trouble was pernicious. (Poulett Thomson, at the Board of Trade, frankly confessed that the bill was 'an evil forced upon the Government.') But at least he was determined that whatever bill was passed should remedy the more glaring evils and should be enforced. In essentials, therefore, his measure was based upon the Commission's recommendations, though one feature going beyond them he added himself: namely, the institution of an

extra category of 'young persons' between the ages of fourteen
to eighteen who were to be given a limited amount of protection
as well.

For the first time a law was enacted covering all the textile
industries, and not merely cotton: that in itself was an important
advance. Employment was forbidden in those industries until
the age of nine (except for silk). Children under 13 were not to
work more than 48 hours a week,[4] and were to attend school for
2 hours a day. Young persons under 18 were limited to a sixty-
nine-hour week, and for them as well as for children night work
was forbidden. Above all, a system of inspection was established.
The latter was, as the Hammonds have remarked, 'a principle of
supreme significance.' With it the State assumed a new function.
The old, futile system of leaving the matter to the local Justices
of the Peace was swept away, and upon the shoulders of 4 Government inspectors (armed with drastic powers of entry and
taking information) was now squarely placed the responsibility
for law enforcement.

Despite all the limitations which its operation soon made
apparent, the Act may rightly be considered a legislative landmark in two respects: both as initiating a serious experiment in
social regulation, and as tentatively beginning a national educational policy.

¶ 4

This, then, was the outcome of all Oastler's efforts of the past
3 years, but it brought him not a vestige of satisfaction. The fact
that he more than any one man was responsible for 'the senseless
clamour out of doors,' of which ministers had complained even
in the act of bowing to it, gave him no consolation. He was disappointed and bitterly angry: disappointed because he had failed
to implement his famous slogan; angry because he found himself
in a false position.

The very men who had opposed him so relentlessly from the
start now began saying he had been 'outbidden in humanity';

---

[4] This clause was to come into operation in three stages. After 6 months
it would apply to children under 11; a year later, to those under 12; and a
year after that, to those under 13.

and in a sense, of course, it was true. His awakening had come with his sudden discovery of the lot of the factory child; to improve that lot he had pressed his crusade for a ten-hour day, never supposing a still shorter one might be possible; and now, thanks mainly to his labors (and despite all the confident opinions of 'practical men' and 'economists' which had been constantly cited to confute him), an eight-hour day for children had actually been promoted by his enemies. The *Leeds Mercury* did not fail to rub salt into the wound which that irony inflicted.

But the irony and Oastler's resulting chagrin are both to be explained by the particular way the story had unfolded. As Oastler's experience of industrial conditions broadened, he developed a sympathy for the operatives such as he had never known before. Trade unionists, Radicals, and Co-operators taught him things of which he had been entirely ignorant, so that soon he had come to believe a ten-hour day would be good for adults too. Naively he supposed the two objectives might be attained by the one remedy. His first conversion had come suddenly in Horton Hall; his second had been less dramatic and more gradual, but was just as real. There was nothing concealed about his intentions. Ebullient extrovert that he was, he talked-out his thought processes in public with a fulsomeness few could surpass and a definiteness none could misunderstand. The charge of hypocrisy which the Commissioners so plainly imputed was entirely unjustified; Oastler's speeches of the previous two years are themselves a sufficient refutation. Unsophisticated he may have been, but he was temperamentally incapable of the duplicity that comes from reticence. And the audiences who responded with such fervor to his vision of a fuller life were largely made up of bewildered and frustrated men who were as simple as himself.

As a philanthropist he had partially succeeded, and his plea for the children had been heeded; but as a champion of labor he had been completely defeated, and the prospects for future success seemed slight indeed. To appreciate the significance of that fact, one has to remember that most educated men of the age, both within Parliament and without, were operating under an obsession with the dogmas of orthodox political economy, and that from the outset Oastler had been challenging that obsession. Any artificial interference by the State with the automatic operation of economic laws, it was believed, would be an invitation to disaster, so the suggestion of labor regulation was regarded as manifestly preposterous. Nothing but ignorance of these laws, said the Factory Commissioners, led the working classes to think that trade unions could do them any good; hence all the caustic remarks about 'agitators' in the *Report*. Only familiarity with the literature of the time can induce a sufficient realization of the pervasiveness of this spirit, yet without that realization the nature of the factory struggle cannot be justly appreciated. The limits of political possibility in any epoch are set by the prevailing sense of the preposterous. The inner meaning of Oastler's revolt is to be found in his effort to get that sense altered.

But he had failed to get it altered. All that had happened was that the Commissioners had completely outmaneuvered his muddleheadedness by restating the dogma of laissez-faire with a proviso. Then Althorp had turned the qualifying proviso into a statute, which salved the consciences of the perturbed. In so far as his wider expectations were concerned, therefore, Oastler was left publicly routed and humiliated. For the sake of historical perspective, however, it is well to remind ourselves that the values that were ultimate in his pleading are the values that few today would care to repudiate. If the Commissioners' *obiter dicta* about the nature of the social process were to be accepted, the entire working-class movement of Britain and America would stand condemned as gigantic folly.

For Oastler personally the galling thing was the false position into which he had now been pushed. Taunted by his traducers with the unction of their claimed philanthropy, he found himself the deflated champion of a demand that could not be revived on account of a commendable enactment that could not be assailed. For this predicament the Bradford Conference was responsible. In their decision to play no part in the Government's investigation, Oastler and his friends made a bad error of judgment. They sadly miscalculated the determination of the Government to see the matter through, just as they grossly overestimated the efficacy of mass protest. It was an error the Chartists were to repeat years afterwards. But men who experiment with the tactics of non-co-operation can scarcely complain of the futility of the outcome; the subsequent resort to self-righteousness yields but feeble solace.

¶ 5

The Short Time Committees were thoroughly bewildered by the sudden change in the situation which had occurred in the 18 days between the spectacular Wibsey Moor meeting and the overwhelming defeat of Ashley in the House. Being entirely unprepared for such an anti-climax, they had no idea what to do next. Day after day letters poured into Fixby from the industrial centers asking for Oastler's advice, and the only advice he could offer was to tell them to call regional conferences to discuss the matter.

Protest meetings were held at Bradford, Aberdeen, Glasgow, Preston, and elsewhere. Oastler himself attended a West Riding delegates' conference at Leeds on 1 August, and for a brief while fired the men once more with his own sultry anger. It was a plain incitement to direct action. Petition no more, for petitions are futile, was the burden of his message: 'if you would be led by me, you would demand the Ten Hours bill in a way that would make tyrants tremble':

Yes, yes: if governments are established in this land for the sole purpose of hoarding up large masses of gold and stamping down individual wretchedness, if *that* is the sole intent and sole object of our government, I declare myself to be a traitor to it, if I die tomorrow for using the word.

So he recommended them to take the law into their own hands and 'to join themselves together from one end of England to the other in a resolute determination not to work more than ten hours a day.'

But this was only beating the air, however formidable it sounded. The consensus of opinion among the leaders was that nothing effective could be done for some while to come. In the light of the various reports from the districts, Oastler, Bull, Sadler, and Ashley explored every possibility but could find no alternative to quiet submission. More mature reflection led them to believe that the Act would prove unworkable, particularly the clauses concerning education and the relay system, and that it would reveal itself 'alike injurious and vexatious to the operatives and to their employers.' When it had collapsed through its own impracticability, then the agitation could be begun again.

CHAPTER XXI

Aftermath: Disunion and Deflation

THE period following the passage of Althorp's Act was one of bewildering confusion for the Ten Hours organization, as it was, indeed, for the English proletarian movement generally. First of all, one of the members of the original Central Committee suddenly turned traitor out of personal pique and for many weeks sought to defame the movement and to smear Oastler's character. This affair had hardly been disposed of before a bitter by-election contest at Huddersfield threw the Radicals and reformers of that borough into a turmoil of discord, the echoes of which reverberated for months. And then, to complete the muddle, the men of Lancashire (albeit with the best of intentions) started a rival factory movement which not only split the reformers' forces in two but led its supporters straight into an ambush of disaster. After that the proletarian forces lapsed into a sullen apathy from which nothing could rouse them for over two years.

¶ 1

Althorp's Act had not been on the Statute Book a fortnight when John Foster started the unsavory controversy that was to drag on for more than four months.

Throughout the period of the factory agitation, Foster had been the owner-editor of the *Leeds Patriot*. Politically he was a Radical, advocating manhood suffrage and biennial elections and entertaining a hearty hatred of the Baineses and their capitalist friends. Soon after the publication of the first letter on 'Yorkshire Slavery' he had taken up the factory question with zest, and for three years had remained a strong supporter, heaping repeated eulogies upon Oastler's labors. He had been made a member of the West Riding Central Committee, had attended all the big

demonstrations, and during the General Election had vigorously
supported Sadler against Macaulay. Then suddenly he precipitated this quarrel.

The origin of the trouble was to be found some twelve months
earlier when Foster had been sued for libel by a Knaresborough
linen merchant named Thorpe. In the columns of the *Patriot*
Foster had cast some aspersions upon this man's treatment of
his work-people, and Thorpe had responded by claiming £1,000
for damages. The matter was so trivial that when it came up at
the York Assizes the judge laughed it out of court and persuaded
both parties to settle outside. But the editor found himself saddled
with costs, which he put at £200.

Oastler was sorry for him, feeling that it was really for the sake
of the movement that Foster had been put to all this worry and
inconvenience. At his own expense, therefore, Oastler inserted an
advertisement in the newspapers urging supporters of the Ten
Hours Bill to come to Foster's help by sending donations to Fixby.
The Tory *Intelligencer* cordially endorsed the appeal, the response was not unsatisfactory, and eventually Oastler was able
to hand over £141.

Unfortunately, a few weeks later Foster went bankrupt and his
Patriot expired. Thenceforward he was a bitter and jaundiced
man. He convinced himself that one of the reasons for his failure
had been his support of the factory movement and that therefore
the Ten Hours organization ought to have rescued him from his
embarrassments. When the Central Committee told him it did
not feel justified in disbursing any of its money for such a purpose,
Foster passed from private complaints to open demands and
started writing Oastler abusive letters. For weeks Oastler continued to treat him with courtesy and sympathy. 'I know no feeling towards you but that of friendship,' he wrote just before the
final break, 'and I have always endeavoured to find your excuse
in disappointment, vexation and distress.' But Foster was not to
be placated: his demands turned into menaces and finally ended
in a threat to 'expose' Oastler and the whole organization.
Whereupon Oastler told him to do his worst.

The storm broke at the beginning of September 1833. Foster
wrote a long, vague letter hinting at all kinds of financial scandal

in connection with the Ten Hours Movement, and sent it to the *Morning Chronicle*—the one London daily that had been hostile to Oastler from the beginning. The *Chronicle* published it at once, with appropriate editorial comment, and within a few days the correspondence columns of both London and provincial journals were echoing to the quarrel.

The substance of Foster's accusation was that Oastler had received £7,000 in donations, that considerably less than half this had been spent, and that some £4,500 still remained to be accounted for. Oastler replied by explaining just how the finances of the movement had been organized.[1] He himself had never handled any of the donations, he said: donations had all been paid over directly to Beckett, Blayd, and Company, the Leeds bankers, and the account had been drawn upon by none but the Central Committee of which Foster himself was a member. His own part in the financial transactions had been limited to assisting the Committee out of his own pocket and out of the sums that John Wood had privately entrusted to him.

Foster repeated and expanded his charges, Oastler again replied, and so the wrangle developed. As the weeks went by Foster's letters grew more prolix and more obscure, until eventually they became practically unintelligible. However sympathetically considered, they read like the outpourings of a thoroughly unbalanced man. But that did not deter the *Chronicle*, the *Mercury*, and their satellites from making the fullest use of them in belaboring the movement in general and Oastler in particular. Nor were the attacks confined to the Whig papers. Unfortunately Foster also persuaded the unstamped proletarian press of London to accept his version of the story. In its issue of 2 November, Hetherington's *Poor Man's Guardian* ran an editorial on the quarrel in the course of which it said:

We have long been accustomed to hear the changes rung on Oastler and Sadler, and Sadler and Oastler, *ad nauseam*. We at one time really fancied they were the philanthropists *par excellence* of the present generation; but after enquiries which we have held it our duty to make we are forced to believe them very selfish fellows. They have had the patronage of the Factory Exchequer; and all the swaddlers, the hum-

[1] See above, chapter XIII.

bugs, and the money-loving London press who, without any real feelings on the subject, but for the base purpose of courting popularity, have been loud in their applause of these *Wilberforces the Second;* whilst the man who really did the business of striking *home* to the feelings of the country—not only by his pen and his newspaper but by his energetic and eloquent appeals at every large public meeting in Yorkshire, namely Foster of the *Leeds Patriot,* has been betrayed, despised, misrepresented, and all but destroyed by the miserable *cankers* who have thrived by his talents and reputation.

But that version was so grotesque that Philip Grant, the radical Lancashire journalist and a noted supporter of the *Poor Man's Guardian,* was moved to reply with vigor. Foster's services to the cause had been greatly overrated, he said, and were in no way responsible for the man's bankruptcy. 'Philip Grant will have it,' reported Hetherington, 'that the chief glory belongs to Mr. Oastler; that the same is the opinion of every group of operatives in either county; that Mr. Oastler has acted with perfect fairness both towards Mr. Foster and the public; and, in short, that the best way to settle the matter is to refer it to the arbitration of some third person mutually agreed upon.'

In point of fact, more than two weeks before Grant's letter was published Oastler had declared his willingness to have the matter settled by arbitration. He had gone even further. He was prepared to accept as arbitrator, he said, any one of the three editors who had been defaming him: Henry Hetherington, John Black of the *Chronicle,* or the elder Baines. And when some weeks later the *Mercury* published a particularly vicious editorial on the dispute, Oastler wrote an indignant protest, which he paid to have inserted in the advertisement columns, reaffirming his willingness to have the whole question publicly investigated. But Foster ignored the challenge.

At last a strong reaction to all this vilification set in. During December Hetherington toured the northern counties in the promotion of his Radical gospel. Wherever he went he found outspoken hostility towards Foster and universal praise for Oastler. Gradually he was compelled to change his opinion. Finally, just before Christmas, he made a full *amende honorable* at a public meeting of Manchester operatives. Seconding a resolution

in commendation of Oastler, he unreservedly apologized for what
he had written in the *Poor Man's Guardian:* 'I came here,' he
concluded, 'to acknowledge the wrong which was done to that
gentleman'; and the applause of the audience left him in no doubt
about the popularity of his recantation. Shortly afterwards he met
Oastler in person and the friendship that followed remained
unbroken until Hetherington's untimely end.

By good fortune another emphatic repudiation of Foster the
same week virtually ended the episode. Foster's series of accusations had culminated in an enormous farrago running to more
than two columns of the *Morning Chronicle,* in which Oastler
was now entirely forgotten and Sadler was made the villain of
the north. This was too much for Sadler's friends. They held an
all-party meeting at Leeds, under the chairmanship of the venerable mayor, William Hey, at which they unanimously passed a
resolution declaring Foster's letter to be false in substance and
in particulars and asking Sadler's friends to treat it 'with silent
contempt.' The resolution was seconded by the very Whig gentleman whom Foster had cited as an ally competent to substantiate
his charges. It was published as an advertisement in all the West
Riding newspapers, after which the affair fizzled out. The repudiation of the charges had been so complete that even the *Leeds
Mercury* considered it unprofitable ever to refer to them again.

¶ 2

Nothing could better illustrate the confusion of social purposes
that existed in England in the months following the passing of
the great Reform Bill than the Huddersfield by-election of December 1833. By that time it had become apparent that the operatives
and lower-middle classes everywhere were hopelessly at odds
among themselves, both in regard to the ends they wanted to
attain and the means by which these could be achieved. Largely
this was the result of Whig strategy during the previous two
years. As with the Reform Bill, so with the Factory Bill: ministers
had divided in order to conquer. In the one case, they had been
swept into office on the flood tide of bourgeois and proletarian
hope, and had then enfranchised only a section of 'the People'
while ignoring the rest. In the other case, they had been com-

pelled by public opinion to yield to the demand for action, but had adroitly bisected that demand too, giving relief only to the children and leaving the lot of the adult unchanged. In both instances they had called forth the bitter resentment of the disappointed.

But how were the disappointed to find remedy? Some said through industrial action, others through peaceful persuasion; some said by more parliamentary reform, others by more social legislation; some urged a new Radical party, others a union of humanitarians from all parties. In every tavern and reading room each nostrum had its advocates, and as autumn passed into winter the debate waxed strong. Then at the end of November came news of the unexpected death of Captain Fenton, Huddersfield's sitting Whig member who had so overwhelmingly defeated Wood at the General Election the year before.

The farce of personal rivalries and tangled intentions that followed was only a local dramatization of the confusion prevailing in the country at large. The details are obscure, but the general pattern of discord is all too clear. That a strong Whig candidate would be sent to try to hold the seat was obvious. He turned out to be a popular lawyer of the northern circuit, named Blackburne, who stood high in the graces of the powerful Ramsden family. It was no less obvious that the only possible way in which a man of this sort could be defeated would be by pitting against him a union of all the opposition forces of whatever hue. The ensuing turmoil in the constituency arose out of the attempt to find a candidate who would be capable of bringing about such a union.

The logical choice was Joseph Wood of Sandal, who had twice previously contested the seat in the Radical interest. But there was some hesitation about selecting him this time because he had turned Roman Catholic since the last election. He knew of the hesitation, of course, and therefore declined the invitation when it was put forward. In a letter to William Stocks, Chief Constable of Huddersfield and a leading Radical, he explained his position without any ambiguity. Since he could not himself stand, he said, his suggestion was that his old supporters should do what the Leeds men had done, and run Michael Sadler as a popular anti-Whig candidate. Needless to say, almost the whole of the local Ten Hours organization warmly supported the idea. Placards in praise of Sadler began to appear immediately.

It soon became apparent, however, that by no means all the Huddersfield Radicals were going to accept such a plan. There were many Irish Catholics in the borough who could not bring themselves to support the evangelical Sadler, just as there were many ardent secularists unable to accept the converted Wood. One group persisted in its demand for Wood's candidature, therefore, while the other stood out for a full-blooded, manhood-suffrage Protestant. The anti-Whig forces were thus split into three quarreling factions, rending the air and adorning the hoardings with their mutual recriminations.

Oastler was approached by both the Sadlerites and the Wood-ites, but he refused to have anything to do with either. It was not that he had no opinion of his own: he very definitely had. He believed Wood was the only candidate the Radicals could put forward who stood any chance of success whatever. But he promised to work wholeheartedly for whichever man were chosen. If the factions could not agree among themselves and both men were invited, he was not going to take any part in the election at all. Nevertheless, he said openly and repeatedly that if Sadler wrote to ask for his opinion, he would advise against standing.

For several days there was much coming and going. Twice more Wood wrote in furtherance of Sadler's nomination. 'Unite for the public good,' he said, 'and cease efforts in my favour which can only tend to insure the victory of the common enemy.' The upshot was that the Radical Committee accepted his advice. Sadler was asked to come in as an Independent candidate, he accepted the invitation, and on 9 December formally opened his campaign with a public entry into the town.

Then confusion deepened. The day after Sadler's entry, the constituency was placarded with the announcement that the Woodite faction was going forward with the nomination of its man whatever happened. Wood was not going to campaign on his own behalf, the poster said, but he had promised to accept the seat if elected.

Oastler was astonished. Late at night he rushed over to Sandal to find out for himself what Wood's intentions really were. Wood categorically disowned the Committee working on his behalf, though he refused to put out any more public statements. His letters on behalf of Sadler, he said, were already declaration enough of his attitude and could not possibly be misinterpreted by anyone.

Meanwhile some 1200 operatives had signed another requisition asking Oastler himself to stand. The situation was rapidly passing from confusion to absurdity. Oastler became apprehensive on Sadler's behalf, for he saw that unless some measure of accord could be established quickly the certain outcome would be the humiliating defeat of his friend. He therefore made the requisition the occasion for a vehement appeal for unity. By speech and poster he put before the constituency the full story of the recent negotiations and showed how the spirit of faction was merely playing into the hands of the Whigs and the moneyed interests:

Till you have resolved to bury all Party distinctions under the altar of our common country, my advice is—'Wear your chains as meekly as you may,' nor attempt to break the power which has only strength to bind you so long as you are determined to be the willing slaves of party. When you have *resolved* to be free, if you cannot find a better man, I am your willing servant. But remember, no man deserves to be free who loves his party more than he loves his country.

The appeals accomplished nothing, however: many of the Radicals now took to abusing Oastler, while 'Captain Wood's Committee' went ahead with its campaign.

But the climax of futility was yet to come. On 30 December, without any warning, Captain Wood decided that he would run after all and issued a vigorous election address setting forth his Radical convictions. His change of mind is entirely inexplicable, for nothing could have been more emphatic than his various published recommendations of Sadler. The Ten Hours men were in consternation and Oastler was enraged. There was now not the remotest chance that Sadler would be returned: the anti-Whig forces were divided beyond all possibility of reunion.

A week later Huddersfield went quietly to poll and returned Blackburne on a minority vote. The final figures were:

Blackburne	234
Sadler	147
Wood	108
Blackburne's plurality	87

Thus was Sadler defeated in what was to prove his last political fight. It was a pity he ever consented to stand in disregard of Oastler's advice. The contest brought no advantage to the cause he had so closely at heart; the strain of the campaign was nothing but torture to an already sick man. As for Oastler, he was racked with vexation. He felt that the Radicals had betrayed to Whiggery the real interests of the masses and in doing so had inflicted a grievous setback to the prospects for Tory Democracy. Of all places that might have served as a citadel for that faith his own borough of Huddersfield had at one time seemed the most promising. Now that hope was shattered. In the pamphlet-war of recrimination that he waged with Wood during the next few months, he gave full vent to his angry disappointment.

Close upon this came a second blow almost as hard to take. Three days after the Huddersfield contest had started, Macaulay informed his Leeds constituents that he had been appointed to the newly reorganized Council of the Governor-General of India and would therefore have to resign his seat in Parliament. Without hesitation the Leeds Liberal Association chose the elder Baines as their candidate to succeed him. The Tories turned to Sadler again. Unfortunately, Sadler had just accepted the call to Huddersfield. After his defeat there the Leeds offer was renewed, but now he felt too ill to accept. The Tories therefore ran Sir John Beckett, head of the famous Leeds banking family, who had already served many years in Lord Liverpool's Ministry. It was a fierce and very close fight; at one point Beckett seemed almost certain of victory. But when the result was finally declared on 16 February, Baines had won by the narrow majority of 6 votes in a poll of nearly 4000. With Sadler permanently out, and the editor of the *Leeds Mercury* at last at Westminster, the hopes of the Ten Hours men reached their nadir.

¶ 3

Oastler was realistic enough to see that there was no chance
of any further parliamentary action on the factory question for
a long while to come. Yet the idea of quietly waiting upon the
slow change of public opinion before renewing his crusade
seemed intolerable. Three years of continuous activity had generated a nervous restlessness that had to have an outlet.

He therefore called a conference of representatives from all
the surviving Short Time Committees in the West Riding to consider the various possibilities for action. The meeting took place
at Birstall, near Bradford, the last week end of October. It was
a small affair which got little publicity, but out of the deliberations came the decision to start an entirely new organization to
be known as the Factory Reformation Society. There was no
thought of its replacing the old militant Short Time organization:
this was to have a purely educational purpose and its appeal
was to be directed mainly to the middle classes. Branches were
to be established in all the big towns; literature was to be distributed and lectures given; and a central council of elected delegates was to determine general policy. An *Address to the Friends
of Justice and Humanity* issued by the Conference explained the
scheme and restated the general case for a ten-hour day while
criticizing Althorp's Act as hopelessly impracticable.

The Society was destined to a short life, however. A few
branches were started in the Riding, and the *Address* was assiduously distributed. But on the other side of the Pennines there
was gathering a hurricane which was to sweep the Bradford plan
into oblivion before most people had even heard of it.

¶ 4

The autumn and winter of 1833-4 witnessed an astonishing
upsurge of proletarian hopes and utopian dreams. It was the
psychological aftermath of the grim economic depression of the
late eighteen-twenties, intensified and embittered by the disappointment of the working classes over the Parliamentary
Reform Bill.

It is by no means easy to grasp in its entirety the pattern of

British proletarian endeavor during the ten years preceding Queen Victoria's accession. The movement was so extensive, the objectives were so diverse, and the incidence of the various appeals was often so localized that even today the intricacies of the story cannot always be disentangled. Contemporaries saw it yet less clearly: participants frequently complained of a chronic lack of unity at the same time that the more comfortable classes were regarding it as a monstrous and pervasive menace.

Since 1829 there had been a conspicuous increase in trade-union activity, accompanied by numerous attempts to replace local with nation-wide unions. Simultaneously, Robert Owen and his disciples had been proclaiming throughout the land the gospel of co-operative socialism. Both movements had been expanding rapidly while the factory agitation was in progress, and both had contributed in no small measure to the energy and fervor of that campaign. Unless that fact is appreciated, the story of Oastler's efforts cannot be seen in perspective. And mingling with the major movements were all sorts of lesser causes, each evoking its separate enthusiasms and producing its own heroes: the struggle for a free press, the promotion of workers' education, the dissemination of secularism, the establishment of friendly societies and so forth. Boundaries were fluid. Many a northern operative professed to be a trade unionist, a radical, an Owenite co-operator, and a Ten Hours man all at the same time, actively serving (like John Doherty) in all four movements. There was thus a bewildering tendency for the various organizations to fade into one another: sometimes to vanish altogether and then reappear in another guise. That was what now happened to the factory movement, and that was what was again to happen several times afterwards.

Just as Oastler had started his Factory Regulation Society to promote the Ten Hours cause, a new project was launched in Lancashire having as its object the establishment of a national eight-hour day for all adult workers in industry. The promoter of the movement was John Fielden,[2] the big Todmorden cotton spinner, who now had a seat in Parliament as William Cobbett's fellow-member for Oldham. Fielden had been a strong supporter

[2] See above, p. 149.

of the Ten Hours cause all along. Like John Wood at Bradford, he had instituted a ten-hour day for his own mills. So strongly had he felt about Althorp's relay-system 'trick' that he had actually pressed an amendment to make the working hours of children ten instead of eight (as Althorp's Act provided) in order that adults might be protected as well. Large employer of labor though he was, he was nevertheless a consistent champion of the interests of the working classes and a firm believer in the desirability of a strong trade unionism. Althorp had once sarcastically remarked in the House that if the adults wanted to have their lot improved they should take matters into their own hands. In the autumn of 1833 Fielden judged the time was ripe for accepting this advice.

The significance of the new project cannot be properly understood, however, unless it is seen in relation to two other facts. One is that at this time the idea of a general strike was everywhere in the air; and the other, that these were the months when Owenite prophecy and practice reached their flood. Apart from those trends the Fielden scheme would have been an empty gesture.

The idea of a general strike to bring about the overthrow of capitalism and the emancipation of the workers was not a novelty. But it had recently been widely publicized in a pamphlet called *The Grand National Holiday*, written by one of Hetherington's friends, the London coffee-house keeper, William Benbow. In the atmosphere of disillusionment after 1832 it thrived remarkably. 'The People have had their hopes disappointed in the Reformed Parliament,' wrote Cobbett in commenting upon the new tendency; 'they are therefore casting aside all disquisitions relative to forms of government and political and constitutional rights and betaking themselves to the best method of insuring sufficiency of food and raiment.'

Furthermore, the idea had become an essential ingredient in the latest formulation of Owenism. By this time Robert Owen was fully convinced that the days of capitalism were numbered and the triumph of the 'industrious classes' was at hand. His plans became more grandiose as his infectious enthusiasm spread, until finally, under his influence, a workers' conference in London

resolved to form a gigantic and all-inclusive union for the immediate establishment of the new social order. Thus was created
the famous Grand National Consolidated Trades Union. The idea
swept the country; a period of feverish trade-union expansion followed, and in a short while the Grand National was claiming to
have an enrollment of over half a million.

Obviously the new enthusiasm would have sapped the remaining vitality from the Ten Hours Movement anyway. Now came
Fielden's scheme for adding the eight-hour day to the general
program of reconstruction. 'The plan is,' wrote Fielden in asking
Cobbett's co-operation, 'that about the 1st March next, the day
the said Bill (now Act) limits the time of work for children under
eleven years of age to eight hours a day, those above that age,
both young persons and adults, should insist on eight hours a day
being the maximum of time for them to labour; and their present
weekly wages for 69 hours a week to be the minimum weekly
wages for 48 hours a week after that time.'

The scheme immediately found prominent supporters. Cobbett
gave it his blessing and publicized it in the *Political Register;*
Robert Owen and John Doherty joined in, along with Fielden's
brothers and sundry philanthropists from the cotton districts.
What most surprised Oastler, however, was the adhesion of his
three friends who had captained the old Ten Hours Movement
in Lancashire: George Condy, the editor of the *Manchester
Advertiser,* Philip Grant, who had championed him against
Foster, and James Turner, secretary of the Manchester Short
Time Committee. All three were on the committee that launched
the scheme, and all did their best to get Oastler in on it too.

Oastler, however, was profoundly skeptical of the project. On
receiving the invitation to attend the inaugural public meeting
he consulted the other leaders in the Riding and after due consideration decided to stay away:

We are of opinion [he wrote] that our attending at Manchester on
Monday would do harm instead of good. We have no delegated powers.
Our Delegates' Meeting sanctioned the Ten Hours Bill, and our Local
Committees have done the same, and the only power to alter (as stated
àt Mr. Bull's on Monday) rests with the Public Meeting. If we were to
turn aside from the resolutions of the Delegates' and Committee meet-

ings, we should deservedly lose the confidence of the operatives. . . .
I shall never argue against an eight hours' bill, I have often declared
eight hours long enough, to the People at Public Meetings. I still think
so, and that children ought not to work at all. But the people must
drive me by their majorities at Public Meetings from the 10 to the 8
hours' Bill.

The promoters went ahead, nevertheless, and at the public
meeting held in Manchester on 25 November there formally
came into being the new organization calling itself the Society
for Promoting National Regeneration.

The Society operated at great pressure: action would have to
be very speedy if a national eight-hour day was going to be
instituted thirteen weeks later. The organizing committee had
therefore submitted complete and detailed plans to the inaugural
meeting for ratification. A central office was taken in Manchester;
missionaries (paid and unpaid) were appointed 'to communicate
the idea to others throughout the Kingdom' and 'to visit the
master manufacturers to recommend the regulation,' a subscription list was opened; literature was issued—notably a *Catechism
of the Society* explaining the paradox of want in the midst of
plenty; and branches were projected for all of the big towns. On
New Year's Day all the workers of the Kingdom were to serve
notice on their masters that the scheme would go into effect on
1 March. Finally it was resolved:

That Messrs. Oastler, Wood, Bull, Sadler and others be urgently
requested to desist from soliciting Parliament for a ten hours' bill, and
to use their utmost exertions in aid of the measure now adopted to
carry into effect, on the first of March next, the regulation of 'eight
hours' work for the present full day's wages,' and that the thanks of
this meeting are hereby given to the aforesaid gentlemen, for their long
continued invaluable services in the cause of the oppressed working
classes, and especially in the cause of their children and young persons
employed in factories.

Employers became considerably alarmed. Voicing their apprehensions, the *Morning Chronicle* denounced the scheme as 'deep,
subtle and malignant,' devised to 'inflame and madden' the prevailing discontent and calculated to 'widen the breach between

workers and employers so that it cannot be healed.' But the movement was not to be stopped by abuse; it spread with remarkable enthusiasm. Soon it was publishing its own journal: *The Herald of the Rights of Industry*. By the end of January, thirty branches of the Society had been started.

In its inception it had been entirely a Lancashire affair. At the beginning of February, however, the Society made a determined effort to win over Yorkshire too. Deputations toured the West Riding and met with astonishing success. At Leeds, for example, they gained a resounding triumph right at the outset by completely 'capturing' Oastler's Factory Regulation Society, which thereupon voted itself out of existence. A fortnight later a general meeting of Leeds workers unanimously passed the resolution:

that the operatives' Short Time Committees should discontinue their exertions in favour of a Ten Hour Bill and that they now co-operate with other Committees formed for the purpose of promoting the Regeneration System and the Eight Hours Plan propounded by Mr. Fielden.

So it went in the other towns as well. For three months the tide ran very fast.

Oastler played no part in this revival. He went over to the inaugural meeting at Bradford just as a spectator, but when the audience clamored for him to go up onto the platform he gave them his reasons for standing aside. The Society's whole project, he told them, was entirely impracticable. Recent events had convinced him, he said, that there were far too many schisms among the workers for such a pretentious scheme to succeed. Sect was divided from sect: intrigues developed within sects. From the outside, perhaps, it looked impressive and menacing, but behind the declamations was very little substance. As soon as the masters made a determined stand the thing would collapse completely. He hoped his judgment was wrong, but he greatly feared it was right: 'I should rejoice to see the day when the people of England would part with all their party prejudice and cursed selfishness, and be resolved to stand up as free men that they might have a fair day's wage for an easy day's work.' But that day was still a long way off because there was nothing approaching unanimity of purpose or agreement on tactics.

Such reasoning made not a particle of difference. The operatives turned against him at Bradford just as they had done at Leeds, Huddersfield, Halifax, and elsewhere, and one more branch of the National Regeneration Society came into existence.

There was more to Oastler's speech, however, than concern about strategy. The truth is that by this time he was overcome by a profound reaction to the strain of the past three years, disappointed with the results of all his efforts, and hurt by the recent attacks of the Radicals. 'I am sure as I am of my existence,' he wrote to the Duke of Wellington a couple of days later, 'that we shall, if we proceed, either have anarchy and then despotism, or we shall shortly see all the property of the country in the hands of the fund-holders and the money-changers.'

Parson Bull was feeling much the same way. Though he had presided at two meetings of the Regenerators in order that the scheme might be thoroughly discussed, he refused to have any part in it himself. Instead, he made it the pretext for one of the most pungent pamphlets of his career, *To the Friends of the National Regeneration Society*. Like Oastler, Bull heartily assented to the ideals of the new movement but was convinced the thing could not succeed. He excoriated the workers for their fickleness: they were 'a rope of sand,' he said, jealous of one another and mistrustful of their best friends. Their obsession with mere political Radicalism blinded them to reality, distorting their judgment and preventing their seeing that it was primarily a social problem they were faced with. Tyranny and long hours, however, could exist in the free-trade republic of Radical dreams fully as much as in the oligarchical England of 1834. And anyway emancipation was not going to be achieved without the utmost tenacity of purpose. Yet the workers had shown themselves incapable of sustained zeal; by their immorality and drunkenness they were rotting their moral fibre. For awhile they would be enthusiastic, then lapse into apathy once more, leaving the field to their oppressors: 'For three years I have been trying to help you, and you will not help yourselves. . . . Your undaunted friend Oastler has done so in a still greater degree, and even he is disheartened.' So Bull in his bitterness announced he would take no further part in such a hopeless cause.

Peter Bussey, the militant left-wing publican of Bradford (who was later to become a member of the Chartist Convention) sent a copy of this onslaught to the radical *Leeds Times,* asking the editor to publish it in full. 'It is true,' he said, 'and we only wish it were not so.'

¶ 5

These prophecies of failure came all too true. The hopes of the previous autumn vanished in sheer tragedy during the spring and summer of 1834. A series of disastrous strikes and lockouts brought down the Grand National in ruins, while the conviction and deportation of the Dorchester farm laborers spread panic among the workers. The National Regeneration Society was soon buried in the general wreckage. When Doherty's cotton spinners (the real driving force of the Society) presented their demands, they were simply ignored. A specially convened delegates' meeting hastily postponed the general strike from 1 March to 1 September, but long before then the movement had gone to pieces. In April the Oldham operatives made a feeble attempt to implement the plan, but within a week it had collapsed. In industry after industry the masters took the initiative, striking first and striking hard. Everywhere they presented 'the ticket.' The mill owners of the Leeds district, for instance, held a big meeting on 8 May whereat they entered into a compact not to employ any man who would not sign their pledge.[3] This led to many lockouts, vast protest meetings on the moors, and some rioting. Overseers refused poor relief to strikers; magistrates announced they would not renew licenses to public houses where trade-union lodges were known to meet. After that it was only a matter of time: hunger did the rest. In three weeks the men began to drift back, and in five it was all over.

[3] The wording of the Leeds 'ticket' was as follows: 'We whose names are hereunto subscribed do declare that from and after the 12th of May, 1834, we shall cease to be members of the Trades' Union, or have before disunited ourselves from that body, and that so long as we continue in the employment of ——, we will not be members of the Union or of any similar association.'

Nothing more was heard of Fielden's Society for Promoting National Regeneration. Oastler was left with the gloomy satisfaction of knowing that his estimate of that scheme had been substantially correct; but in the general collapse his own Factory Society had vanished as well.

CHAPTER XXII

The Problem of the Poor Law

OASTLER had celebrated his forty-fourth birthday during the recent Huddersfield by-election. He was now entering upon middle age in the fullness of his powers with the continuing satisfactions of a useful career in prospect before him. His work was congenial; he could continue with his participation in local politics; and, in spite of his gloom at the moment, he had not abandoned the hope that the Ten Hours cause would march to eventual success. That would be the crowning of his reputation.

Yet fate was to prescribe a course very different from the apparent certainty of all this. Once already, out of merest chance, it had completely altered his design for living. Now something similar was to happen again. But this time there would be no dramatic moment of illumination to mark the change. It would come out of the growing pressure of events, and already that pressure was in the making far beyond the range of his awareness. To understand it, however, one has to sense the drift of things in areas totally unconnected with the textile industries.

¶ 1

All the while Oastler and his friends in the north had been concerning themselves with problems arising out of the new industry, southern England had been preoccupied with another social problem no less grave: the inert and stagnant mass of pauperism in the countryside. From about the year of Oastler's birth onwards, rural pauperism had been increasing ominously, and by the time the Ten Hours Movement started, more than half the laboring population of the midland and southern farming areas was receiving some sort of parish relief. 'The economic and social conditions of the labourers in the rural districts,' write the

Webbs, 'notably those south of a line drawn from the Severn to the Wash, was in the first three decades of the nineteenth century, in the midst of greatly increasing national wealth, probably at its very lowest level since the Elizabethan Poor Law had been established.'

This tragedy is attributable to an intricate combination of circumstances varying in their intensity from one county to another. For one thing, much incidental misery resulted from the enclosure movement, which was gathering momentum from 1760 onwards. The transformation of the age-old system of communal cultivation into an individualistic economy of enclosed private farms shattered for hundreds of little cottagers the prescriptive rights and assured status that the ancient custom of the village had afforded them. Hitherto they and their forbears had had a place of sorts—albeit, perhaps, a marginal one—in an acknowledged corporate routine. Now they were left shelterless in a competitive scramble beyond their comprehension, and that at the very time when the growth of the great power mills in the north was depriving many of them of the little extra income their families had managed to make by domestic spinning. So while the more substantial men were benefiting from the new dispensation of compact farms and scientific methods, countless small folk who had lost their grazing and their gleaning rights on the common lands were left dependent solely upon the wages they could earn working for others.

But these wages were pitiably inadequate to meet the rising cost of living. Ever since the middle of the century prices had been steadily mounting. Then came the economic dislocations resulting from the twenty years' war with France, further complicated by the currency derangements of the period and a sequence of disastrously bad harvests after 1792. These things further caused the cost of living to soar to a height that spelled abject misery for the rural wage-laborer.

Subjected to the shock of all these stresses, the little hierarchy of the old country village steadily disintegrated. The larger men went up while the smaller went down. Two opposing classes thus tended to appear: on the one hand the capitalist farmers, and on the other a rural proletariat made up of the underpaid.

the unemployed, and the partly employed. Both during the war and in the depression that followed, the latter suffered cruelly. As Professor Trevelyan vividly puts it: 'hollow-cheeked, ragged, housed in hovels, the peasantry of England degenerated year by year under the eyes of men who were doubling and trebling their rents, and who tried to silence Cobbett as an "incendiary" because, when no one else dared, he pointed out the contrast.' The suffering was plain to behold. Unfortunately, however, the treatment of the malady proved to be as disastrous as the disease.

The general principles governing England's treatment of her indigent and unemployed had been set by the famous Poor Law of 43rd Elizabeth (1601). According to this statute, each of the 15,000 parishes in the country was responsible for the support of its own poor. Pauper children were to be apprenticed to useful trades, the sick and the aged were to be relieved at home, vagrants were to be punished, and the honest unemployed were to be given work to do. The cost was defrayed out of a 'poor rate' levied upon the householders of the parish. The general administration of the law was in the hands of the local Justice of the Peace, though the actual levying of the rate and disbursement of relief was done by the village churchwardens and specially appointed overseers.

The system worked satisfactorily enough for a relatively stable society supervised by a watchful and vigorous Privy Council. But with the decline of the monarchy, the Privy Council left matters pretty much to the discretion of the local authorities. Various experiments were tried in different parts of the country. One of the early horrors of the rising industrialism, for example, was the vicious practice whereby contractors disposed of pauper children to the Lancashire cotton mills for profit. As the eighteenth century advanced, the problem of pauperism grew continuously more acute, so that under the tremendous impact of new economic forces the system of relief was called upon to cope with a situation that the framers of the Elizabethan statute had never dreamed of. And worsening matters was a pernicious 'settlement' law, which prevented mobility of labor by providing that a man could get poor relief only in the parish to which he 'belonged.' This led to an enormous volume of litigation, as parishes sought to protect themselves from becoming chargeable with the maintenance of paupers that belonged elsewhere. In the process a new and sinister kind of serfdom was created.

Sheer necessity had led to a widespread tendency for local authorities to give the able-bodied unemployed some kind of 'outdoor' relief, that is to say without compelling them to enter a workhouse. Then came the notorious 'Speenhamland decision' of May 1795. That year prices were so high and distress was so acute that the Berkshire magistrates meeting at the village of Speenhamland (thinking the crisis was only temporary) adopted the policy of supplementing the laborer's inadequate wages out of the poor rates. The amount of relief given was to vary with the fluctuating price of bread and the size of a man's family. Magistrates elsewhere resorted to the same device and soon it was in general use throughout most of southern England. For the next 40 years it remained an essential feature of Poor Law policy for the agricultural districts.

Some such expedient was unavoidable in view of the tragic conditions in the rural villages. Canning was reported to have said in after years that it saved England from revolution during her life-and-death struggle with Napoleon. Nevertheless there can be no denying that the eventual results of this allowance system were appalling. The cost of poor relief went up enormously, of course, provoking continuous lamentations from rate-payers. It had been under two million pounds in the seventeen-eighties: by 1803 it had doubled; in 1831 it was nearly seven millions. But far worse than the monetary burden (which was most inequitably distributed over the total field of wealth) were the wider social consequences. The Speenhamland system produced a deplorable confusion between poor relief and wages and thus fatally blurred the distinction between the pauper and the independent laborer. The big farmer obviously had no reason to offer decent wages, since any pittance he might give would now be supplemented out of the public purse; and the laborer likewise had no inducement to work hard or to save, since he could not improve his condition however much he tried. An inevitable deterioration of morale resulted. The wretched peasant took his miserable parish dole as of right; even prudence no longer paid, since each child (whether legitimate or not) brought in an extra eighteenpence a week. And caught between the upper and the nether millstones was the small farmer who employed no hired help but ran the farm with his family only. He was now compelled to pay the rates that subsidized his bigger rival.

¶ 2

One Government after another had evaded tackling the problem in any comprehensive manner, but by 1831 it was scarcely possible to continue doing so any longer. The previous autumn there had been extensive rioting, which had been ruthlessly crushed with 3 executions and over 450 transportations. Now Lord Grey's new Whig Administration decided to act. But before attempting any clinical treatment of its own, the Government called in special consultants on the health of the body politic. In February 1832, within a few days of the appointment of Sadler's Factory Committee, it set up the famous Royal Commission on the Poor Laws.

To appreciate the temper of the Commission and the nature of the reform that followed, it is essential to realize how widespread in intellectual and upper-class circles was the conviction that poor-relief ought to be entirely abolished. Abolition, it was held, was an inescapable corollary of the teachings of the economists. The obsession of the age with the new political economy has already been noted; it colored man's thinking about every kind of social problem—charity and the poor law no less than trade unionism and factory reform. The natural laws regulating social life, it was believed, operated automatically and were not malleable to human purpose. The Tory *Quarterly* as well as the Whig *Edinburgh* repeatedly said just what the Factory Commissioners had written in their *Report:* that 'agitators' only throve upon the workers' ignorance of economic laws. In an article immediately following the suppression of the laborers' revolt, the *Edinburgh* attributed that uprising 'in the greatest part and immediately' to 'vulgar errors . . . which a knowledge of the natural laws that regulate the production and distribution of the wealth of nations alone can dissipate.'

And one of the most pernicious of the 'vulgar errors,' according to these analysts, was the idea that public charity could really benefit society. McCulloch and Senior made that clear by explaining the nature of the 'wages fund.' At any particular time, they taught, there is available only a fixed amount of wealth for the payment of wages. This sum being limited, each person's share will be determined by the number of people among whom it has to be distributed. Trade unions and strikes intended to force up the price of labor were thus essentially futile: at best they could only enable one group of workers to benefit at the expense of the rest; at worst they would put the employer out of business altogether. The only way in which there could be any ultimate improvement in wages was by increasing the fund through productive labor or by decreasing the number of workers who had to share it. And the teaching of Malthus seemed to reinforce this gloomy analysis by pointing out the inevitable tendency of population to outrun food supply unless kept down 'by vice or misery' or prudential restraint. Poverty was chiefly caused by over-population; misery was really thus part of nature's grand design to keep the population within bounds. So public relief of the poor stood emphatically condemned on two counts. It dangerously drained the wages fund while destroying the incentive to augment it; and at the same time it encouraged the reckless increase of a population foredoomed to live in the shadow of distress.

Nassau Senior, the Drummond professor of political economy at Oxford, who was one of the dominating figures on the Royal Commission, had already publicly stated that the poor laws ought not to be reformed but ought to be completely swept away. Henry Brougham, the new Lord Chancellor, was vehemently of that opinion too, and persuaded Harriet Martineau to write a special series of her popular didactic stories to show the reading public just how evil the poor laws actually were. ('Those who framed the Statute of Elizabeth,' Brougham smugly explained in the House of Lords, 'were not adepts in political science; they were not acquainted with the true principles of population. They could not foresee that a Malthus would arise to enlighten mankind.') Most of the Cabinet and a large part of the

House of Commons shared these same convictions. 'The system of poor relief,' Lord Althorp told the House, 'is contrary to the principles of political economy which even prohibit the exercise of private charity.' These instances might be extended indefinitely. 'Bear in mind,' Dickens satirically wrote to his friend Forster, 'that the *Westminster Review* considered Scrooge's presentation of the turkey to Bob Cratchit as grossly incompatible with political economy.' After a generation of hesitation, opinion had at last become favorable to drastic action.

The Commission presented its report in February 1834, after two years of investigation. It was a formidable document, eventually extending to 15 folio volumes. The main findings, however, compounded as they were from Senior's economic doctrines and Chadwick's philosophy of administrative reform, were forthright and clear-cut. The gist of the argument was that the Elizabethan Poor Law had been perverted to improper use through the allowance system, that this had sapped individual initiative, and that only by altering the purpose of the law so as to reinvigorate initiative and stimulate mobility could the disease be cured. All outdoor relief was condemned on principle. Expediency had to temper conviction, however, so it was not proposed to do away with relief altogether. But it was proposed to make this relief as unattractive as possible, at least for the able-bodied. One of the indictments the Commissioners brought against the prevailing system was that too many of the existing workhouses allowed the pauper to live in comfort.[1] The central principle of reconstruction must therefore be the institution of a rigorous workhouse test: either you come into the public workhouse on our terms or you stay out and get no relief. And to make this test effective, the offering in the workhouse must be 'less eligible' (i.e. more unpleasant) than the condition of the worst-paid laborer outside. The only sane policy, said the Commissioners, 'is to subject the pauper to such a system of labour, discipline and restraint as shall be sufficient to outweigh in his estimation the

[1] 'In by far the greater number of cases [the workhouse] is a large almshouse . . . and the whole body of inmates subsisted on food far exceeding both in kind and amount not merely the diet of the independent labourer but that of the majority of the persons who contribute to their support.' *Report,* pp. 53–4.

advantages which he derives from the bodily comfort which he enjoys.' This, of course, would entail a sweeping reform of existing workhouses, which were used chiefly for the aged and impotent. Workhouses must be made bigger and more numerous, and the areas they served must be larger and more economical than the old parish. And to prevent the system from lapsing into chaos again, a permanent and independent regulatory Commission ought to be established, with power to make general orders which should be binding upon all local authorities. For orphans, the aged, and the insane, separate institutions were recommended.

There can be no mistaking the accent of these recommendations; it had already been heard seven months before in the *Report* of the Factory Commission. The two documents, indeed, are but two applications of the same political philosophy, written largely with the same pen. Bentham's confident ex-secretary, Edwin Chadwick, had changed his desk for a brief while the previous summer to dispose of the factory question, and then had returned for the final drafting of the Poor Law Report. In each instance he was presenting the new Parliament with a manifesto of the higher radicalism: a creed that would restrain the wrongheadedness of philanthropy by the scientific application of the laws of self-interest while at the same time countering the inefficiency of democracy with the wisdom of a centralized bureaucracy.

Without delay the Government introduced a Poor Law Amendment Bill based upon these findings and hurried it on to the Statute Book in 16 weeks. The Commission had voiced the temper of the House with almost as much accuracy as the Factory Commission had done. The opposition, though militant, was very small: in no division did it muster more than 50. The country gentry had as much interest as anyone else in lightening the burden of the poor rates; so whatever the inspiration of the measure, the Tories were willing enough to support a Whig bill that they themselves had not had the courage to introduce. And the Government's clever handling of the matter made this all the easier, for the new scheme was presented as something essentially conservative, involving no new principles but creating a few new devices in order to relieve agriculture and restore the pristine intentions of the old Elizabethan law. Little could those who voted for it see that its administrative application would entail a governmental change of the utmost magnitude, destined to provide the rationale of Britain's poor-law policy for almost a century.

The essentials of this momentous Act were simple, apart from such technical matters as the alteration of the Settlement laws and the treatment of illegitimacy. Two new agencies were created, one central and the other local. The entire control of poor relief for the country was entrusted to a central Board of three Commissioners. This Board was given unprecedentedly extensive powers: it could appoint assistant commissioners who served· as its local agents, it might issue all manner of rules and regulations having the force of law, and it could order the appointment or dismissal of officials. New administrative areas were to be set up by combining parishes into 'unions.' Each union was to have a democratically elected Board of Guardians, which was to operate the Act (under the watchful eye of the Commissioners) in its district: that is to say, applying the regulations, levying the poor rate, and appointing the necessary officers. Basic to the whole plan was the power of the Commissioners to order these local Guardians to enforce the workhouse test.

On the face of it, nothing could have been simpler or more reasonable. The social revolution it wrought, however, was not to be seen in the wording of the Act itself, but would lie in the executive orders that the Commissioners were to issue. And that those would lack nothing in ruthlessness and uniformity was assured when the first Board was appointed and Edwin Chadwick became its secretary.

¶ 3

The reception accorded the new Act was to make a dramatic chapter in British social history, bringing Oastler to the front again in a new and more reckless role and eventually altering the whole tenor of his life. It was a reception, however, in no degree foreshadowed by the figures of the divisions in the House; moreover, circumstances as well as geography delayed the fullness of its fury for another two years, though ominous rumblings were to be heard long before the measure passed the Lords.

The early opposition was formless and dispersed, lacking both effective leadership and an alternative proposal. That was true at Westminster no less than in the country at large. Apart from their hostility to the new proposals, the small band that resisted the bill through Parliament had little in common. It was a strangely mixed company, which included Stanhope the patrician and Cobbett the champion of the common man; Phillpotts the die-hard Bishop of Exeter and Attwood the radical banker from Birmingham. Yet, few in numbers though they were, they spoke for wide constituencies of the spirit that were inadequately represented in the legislature. The humane were shocked by what seemed the heartlessness of the workhouse test; the devout were apprehensive about the ominous triumph of an atheistical creed.[2] The old-fashioned Tory resented the idea of bureaucracy butting into parish affairs; the unsophisticated Radical felt he had lost another battle in the intensifying class war. Northern operatives suspected the scheme was a device for providing employers with an ample supply of cheap labor; and some with no political pretensions at all simply felt there was an uncomfortable element of truth in Disraeli's remark to the Maidstone voters that the

[2] A clear declaration of this attitude is to be found in Frances Trollope's preface to her novel *Jessie Phillips:* 'The author is anxious to declare her detestation of the newly broached doctrine that the poor have no *right* to a sufficiency of necessary food to sustain the life that God has given them. She is far from denying that such a conclusion may be very logically deduced from the positions of dry, hard, utilitarianism and mere pounds-shillings-and-pence-counting political economy. But there is, it seems to her, an element in the question which is apparently not dreamt of in the philosophy of those who deny to the poor their right to a share in Nature's feast. She hopes and believes that there are still abundantly enough English hearts to join with her in scouting this doctrine as Unchristian.' The same opinion was voiced by Thomas Carlyle with a grim and subfusc irony in *Chartism* (1840): 'One sole recipe seems to have been needful for the woes of England: "refusal of outdoor relief." England lay in sick discontent, writhing powerless on its fever-bed, dark, nigh desperate in wastefulness, want, improvidence and eating care, till like Hyperion down the eastern steeps, the Poor Law Commissioners arose, and said, Let there be workhouses, and bread of affliction and waters of affliction there . . .' But even Carlyle thought that the new law, though 'heretical and damnable as a whole truth,' was 'laudable as a half-truth.'

new law was 'announcing to the world that in England poverty
is a crime.' To the unique Cobbett, who fought the measure tooth
and claw through every stage, and whose capacious and angry
heart embraced something of all these sentiments, it was an outright 'Poor Man's Robbery Bill': a repudiation of the right to
subsistence implicit in the very nature of society, and the last
episode in the Reformation swindle whereby the privileged had
despoiled the Church of the funds that had been dedicated to
charity. But Cobbett died before he was able to carry the fight
to the people.

The press was by no means unanimous in support of the new
scheme either, the Tory papers in particular being very critical.
Some, such as the *Standard,* had begun by approving and then
had reversed their stand. But the most consequential opposition
of all came from *The Times.* Until April 1834, the 'Thunderer'
had been a supporter of the general policy of the Whig Government, but that month it entered upon a violent and enduring
quarrel with Brougham, the Lord Chancellor. Thenceforth it
followed a policy of implacable hostility to the New Poor Law,
lasting for years. 'From that hour,' says Harriet Martineau in her
History, 'the virulence with which the leading paper pursued the
Lord Chancellor, the new poor law and the parties concerned in
its preparation, exceeded any hostility encountered by the Whig
Government from any other quarter, and certainly had no small
effect . . . in impeding the working of poor-law reform.' John
Walter its proprietor, who was Member for Berkshire, remained
one of the little group of intransigents in the House, and his
Letter to the Electors was one of the first pamphlets in the voluminous literature of denunciation that was to characterize the
next decade.

But for all this, the application of the new law during the first
two years proceeded smoothly enough and with remarkable
speed. The Commissioners started their reconstruction in the
southern counties, where the allowance system had been most
general. Soon they were claiming striking success and the extirpa-
tion of the worst abuses. In parish after parish men refused to go
into the workhouse; the numbers of able-bodied applicants for
relief fell off sharply; and the burden of the poor rates began to

lighten.[3] There were some turbulent meetings and a few sporadic riots; and a Cambridgeshire clergyman named Maberley toured East Anglia on a crusade of protest: but little came of it all. To begin with, at least, luck favored the new experiment. A couple of good harvests, a spell of business prosperity, and the boom in railway construction helped the absorption of surplus labor. The real trouble was to come when the Commissioners had finished with the agricultural south (for which the reform was primarily designed) and started applying their principles to the totally different conditions of the industrial north. That, by chance, was to happen at the onset of an acute depression.

Until the spring of 1834, Oastler had given hardly any thought to these matters. This was not simply because he was preoccupied with the factory question; it was mainly due to the fact that the problem of poverty in the northern industrial districts was something very different from what it was among farm laborers bound to their parish by the Settlement laws.

There was no 'crisis' of Poor Law administration in the West Riding; the Speenhamland system of allowances to supplement wages had never been general in those parts and the poor rate was less than a third of what it was in East Anglia. Poverty there was in plenty, but its causes were many and complex. There was no single sort of 'poor' man who could serve as an archetype for Miss Martineau's admonitory novelettes. Here it was a matter of mill hands being taken on and put off to the rhythm of the business cycle; of domestic workers living on the margin and fighting a collapse in the standards of craftsmanship; of shifting population, rapid urbanization, and casual labor; and many other things besides.

One of the tragic features of the New Poor Law lay in the simple fact that it was primarily devised to meet one set of conditions and got extended to another. In fighting the rural pauperism of a passing age it failed to take sufficient cognizance of the urban poverty of the age that was emerging. Indeed, the Royal Commission made no pretense of analyzing the general problem of poverty at all. Such things as sweating, under-employment,

[3] In 1832 they were £7.03 millions; in 1836 they had fallen to £4.71 millions.

and the technological displacement of labor found no mention in the famous *Report*. Yet they were the very things that forced themselves with painful insistence upon the attention of anyone living in the industrial districts.

Outdoor relief was a sheer necessity in the textile districts. Here it was not a matter of stimulating mobility and compelling men to work; it was a question of keeping men alive until work became available again. In its existing organization the industry demanded some such unemployment grant to maintain the necessary labor supply. If that was true for factory labor, it was even more obviously true for the handloom weavers in their cottages. Their standard of living was low enough in any case: during bad seasons their earnings fell even below subsistence level. According to one official estimate, 7 out of every 10 of them were driven to seek occasional relief from the parish.

On the moor edges around Fixby were many such cottagers whom Oastler had come to know well. 'Hundreds and thousands are there,' he wrote to the Duke of Wellington, 'living on a short allowance of water-porridge and potatoes, never tasting flesh meat.' These were the people who brought Oastler face to face with the Poor Law question in the lull that followed the factory agitation. For them the thought that the new law was soon to be applied in all its rigor was a prospect of unmitigated horror. To deny them parish assistance would spell starvation; to make them go into the workhouse would mean the irrevocable destruction of their independence.

¶ 4

William Duncombe, the Member for the North Riding who had supported the factory movement from the beginning, sent Oastler a copy of the Government's Poor Law Bill as soon as it was published. Oastler read it carefully and was astounded. 'The perusal of that document convinced me,' he wrote, 'that the Whigs were traitors to the poor by whose influence they had been elevated to power.' At once he called to Fixby a number of his friends, leaders of the Short Time Committees and others, and went over the bill with them, clause by clause, pointing out all its startling implications. Then and there he pledged himself to unrelenting opposition and to the use of every means in his power to prevent the scheme from going into effect, at least as far as the West Riding was concerned.

Whatever may be one's judgment upon Oastler's subsequent conduct in the fulfilment of this vow, his attitude is at least understandable in the light of his personal experience and general social philosophy. A more complete contrast it would be hard to imagine than that between Oastler's preconceptions and those of the men who formulated the Poor Law Report. He was thinking of an idealized past while they were thinking of the renovated State of the future. His picture of society involved benevolent paternalism and the feudal pyramid, theirs the new individualism and the 'unseen hand' of economic law. His immediate thought was of actual conditions around Huddersfield and Leeds, whereas those were merely subordinate considerations for the Commissioners. Above all, he looked upon poverty as essentially a challenge within the Christian way of life, not as a relentless device of Nature's to keep down the population to manageable proportions.

His condemnation of the Government's Bill, therefore, was complete and unqualified. In specific terms, the indictment was twofold: that the new scheme involved a grave departure from constitutional precedent, and that its ultimate effect upon national morale would prove to be calamitous. Both arguments, it is worth noting, were to be brilliantly elaborated by Disraeli in a famous speech in the House five years later.

Oastler saw the Act as destroying the old autonomies of county and parish, and upsetting the traditional balance between central and local government. 'Before this revolution,' he wrote when the law had gone into effect, 'England was an infinity of self-governing Republics under one, controlling, limited, constitutional monarchy.' Now the close bond between ratepayers and their dependents was to be severed, the influence of the country gentry was to be undermined, and the powers of the Justice of the Peace were to be taken away. In their stead was to be put a remote central authority with only indirect knowledge of local conditions: one, moreover, endowed with a power hitherto unknown under the British system to issue regulations having the

force of law. By delegating this power of subordinate legislation
to an independent Board having no accountable representative
in the House, Oastler believed, Parliament was forswearing one
of its sacred functions. It was an opinion, he was soon to learn,
shared by no less an authority than old Lord Eldon, the ex-Lord
Chancellor, who was as enraged as Oastler at such a constitutional innovation. All this Oastler expounded to his friends at
Fixby before the bill had passed the Commons:

I showed, that if that Bill were passed, the rate-payers would no
longer have any power over the poor rates; that all the parochial
officers would become servants of the Commissioners; that the paupers
would be their mere slaves; that it would be impossible to guess what
might hereafter become the law of England, seeing that the Commissioners, instead of the Legislature, would be empowered to make
laws for the government of the people. I denied the power of Parliament thus to transfer my allegiance, and resolved that I would never
yield to the unconstitutional power of the Commissioners.

But these constitutional consequences were not the only ground
for alarm. The principles underlying this bill were 'calculated to
destroy the British character,' he wrote a day or two after the
third reading, and to take away 'the birthright of every poor,
needy and industrious Englishman.' Society is held together only
by the moral bonds of mutual obligations; destroy those and it
disintegrates into an anarchy of warring atoms. And fundamental
to all else is the obligation to guarantee to even the humblest
the means to live a decent life: that is an ethical postulate inherent in the very fact of society itself. 'When the *rights* of the
poor to his share of the rent of the soil is taken away, it destroys
the rights of the landlord and everyone else, and the King in
signing [the Bill] will sign his own abdication.' So wrote Oastler
when the measure went up to the Lords. Terrible retribution
would inevitably follow any attempt to violate these eternal
principles: 'sure I am, if anything like this Poor Law Bill passes,
the nature of Englishmen will be changed, or we shall have a
revolution:'

If that law is enforced in the manufacturing districts, notwithstanding the intelligence and patience of the labouring classes, I am sure
the destruction of life and property will be the price the country will

have to pay for it. I know the feelings of the poor on this subject, and, thank God, they know their *Constitutional,* their *Christian,* their *Natural* Rights. . . . They know that if paupers have no right to parish pay, *no person in England has any right to any property whatever* . . . Oh that our rulers might at length learn that there is no benefit in robbing the poor.

¶ 5

Having to go to London at the end of June on business for Thornhill, Oastler took the opportunity to do some lobbying of his own against the Poor Law Bill. He reached town the day the third reading was carried in the Commons by a vote of 187 to 50, so all his efforts were spent upon members of the House of Lords.

His first call was upon the Duke of Wellington, with whom he had kept up a desultory correspondence during the previous two years. Although he had been sadly disappointed in his earlier expectations of the Duke, Oastler found it hard to believe that anyone with the Duke's political convictions could possibly bring himself to support this latest Whig assault on established institutions. Yet Wellington at the very start of the interview told Oastler he was already pledged to support the bill. Oastler pleaded and argued with the old gentleman, trying to convince him that this was 'a most cruel, dangerous, uncalled-for and unconstitutional measure,' but it made not the slightest difference. Wellington remained obdurate and replied, we are told, 'with considerable force and zeal.' For Oastler it was a painful hour: his lingering illusions about his former hero were irrevocably shattered. 'My failure was complete,' he afterwards confessed; 'I left him grieving that one whom I had so much revered should resolve to give his support to such an unjust and revolutionary measure.' A fortnight later the Duke gave the bill his blessing in the House of Lords and announced 'that the measure was the only plan he had ever seen that he approved of.'

Still Oastler persisted. From mansion to mansion he went bearing the Peers the same message: 'if they passed that law they destroyed their title to their property and their honours and undermined the throne of England.' Not all treated him as the

Duke had done; a few even received him enthusiastically. The Marquess of Salisbury, for instance, had him to breakfast, went over the bill with him in detail, and finally promised to vote against it. Lord Kenyon was already a declared opponent of the measure and greeted Oastler as a comrade in arms. But the man who gave him the most encouragement was the venerable Earl of Eldon, now in his eighty-fourth year. The former Lord Chancellor, whose very name has become a symbol of Tory effort to stand upon the ancient ways, was as shocked by the new proposals as he had been by the Reform Bill of 1832, though it was the legal and not the social aspect of the matter which troubled him. But he thought Oastler's labor profitless. 'It is sure to pass,' he said, 'for nowadays they will pass anything.' Yet his gloom did not prevent his launching into a tirade against the newfangled notions of bureaucratic authority and delegated power. 'The new Poor Law Bill is unconstitutional,' Oastler reported him as saying; 'there is no authority lodged in the legislature to pass such a Bill, nor any constitutional power, when it is passed, to enforce it. If matters have come to this, a Convention should be called.' Those were strong words. In Oastler's ears they sounded as a trumpet call to action. It was a call the northern workers were to hear repeated many scores of times in the years to come. Nothing, Oastler confessed long afterwards, more emboldened him to go on with his course than the reassurance Eldon gave him at this interview that his own judgment of the matter had been sound.

For nearly a fortnight he went about London in this way, interviewing likely opponents of the bill. But the aristocracy by no means took up all his time. Much of it was spent in the company of Henry Hetherington, who introduced him to a number of the other leaders of the metropolitan working-class movement. These men were all manhood-suffrage Radicals, principally engaged at the moment in a dour struggle against the fourpenny stamp duty on newspapers—the tax whereby successive governments of the previous nineteen years had sought to check the growth of a proletarian press and to stop the spread of 'subversive' ideas. Several of them, including Hetherington himself, had already suffered prison terms and fines for promoting unstamped journals in defiance of the law. They were all as bitterly opposed to the New Poor Law as Oastler was; to that extent, therefore, they could accept him as an ally. They knew of his efforts on behalf of factory regulation, of course, and they had Hetherington's assurances in regard to his popularity in the north. None the less they were greatly puzzled by Oastler's insistence upon his Toryism and by his unceasing claim that only through the establishment of a renovated Tory state could social welfare come.

Their bewilderment, however, did not lessen their cordiality. Hetherington invited Oastler to contribute to his illicit journal, *The Poor Man's Guardian;* Oastler was only too willing to oblige; and from that time forward articles from his pen appeared with increasing frequency in its columns. Later on he was asked to write for other journals of the same sort, which he gladly did. Some of his old Tory friends in Yorkshire began to get apprehensive about the development of these new associations. To them the Hetherington circle was little better than a gang of ruffians bent upon destroying the foundations of Church and State. But Oastler retorted with some asperity and went his way undeterred.

¶ 6

This visit to London gave Oastler the unexpected opportunity of pleading another kind of cause. He was suddenly called upon to give evidence before the Select Committee on Handloom Weavers then sitting under the chairmanship of 'the handloom weavers' champion,' John Maxwell, M.P. for Paisley. Ashley was one of the members of the Committee and it may have been at his suggestion that Oastler was invited to appear.

This matter of the cottage handloom weavers was another of those problems that had increasingly obtruded themselves upon his awareness as his efforts on behalf of the factory children had expanded in scope. The more he had mixed with the workers on the Ten Hours Committees, the more his eyes had been opened to the mass of squalor and misery that surrounded him on all sides. He thus came to realize that by no means all the evils arising from the progressive industrialization of England were concentrated in the mills. Suffering and frustration of a different kind, but every bit as distressing, he learned, was to be found in the cottages of the domestic industry he had been prone to romanticize. And since misery of any kind was always a stimulus to him, he had flung himself into the cause of these people with the same abandon he had given to his other crusades. More, perhaps, than any other social question except that of child-labor, the plight of the weavers compelled him to reconsider and refashion his entire political program.

Handloom weaving, which according to one of the official estimates still involved more than three-quarters of a million workers in the various textile industries, was certainly in a terrible plight. At one time—particularly during the halcyon years between 1795 and 1815 when weavers were in great demand—the trade had prospered exceedingly. Now it had fallen upon evil days and the lot of the cottage weaver had become sad indeed. Earnings had dropped catastrophically. 'Anything above 10s. per week can only be earned by the most skilful and steady hands,' reported a Commissioner in 1838; 'ordinary weavers seldom exceed 6s. or 7s., and any decay of power reduces the earnings of the worsted weaver below 6s.' Handloom weaving was, in fact, a doomed occupation, and the slowness of its passing constituted what Professor Clapham has called 'a crying national tragedy.' Year after year petitions poured into the House of Commons begging Parliament to act, and in the spring of 1834 the Government had appointed this Select Committee to consider what might be done.

There was little difference of opinion concerning the general nature of the tragedy, but the devising of a remedy seemed to be beyond the wit of contemporary statesmanship. The fact was that the industry was overmanned; and, in the deflationary era after Waterloo, that spelled inevitable disaster. Moreover, the fatal ease with which the craft could be learned continuously drew in newcomers, so that weaving became 'the last refuge of the unsuccessful.' The customary standards and safeguards of an ancient calling thus collapsed under the pressure of cut-throat competition; and the demand for bulk production, in which quality was sacrificed to quantity, only intensified the process. Even the Select Committee was horrified by the discoveries it made. 'The sufferings of that large and valuable body of men,' said the final *Report*, 'are not only not exaggerated, but they have for years continued to an extent and intensity scarcely to be credited or conceived, and have been borne with a degree of patience unexampled.' For men such as these, on the verge of want and despair, parish relief was an indispensable refuge in times of under-employment. It was the Government's threat to take away this refuge that led them to rally with such fervor to Oastler's great defiance later.

Fixby was situated in the heart of a handloom-weaving district where the men specialized in fancy goods, a trade peculiarly liable to wild fluctuations. When Oastler's father had first gone there, it had been an exceedingly prosperous region, but since Richard had been at the Hall the deterioration had been continuous. Wages had fallen, and the standard of living had drawn ever nearer to the level of destitution. The one-time independent weavers who had abounded in the district had more and more become mere employers' outworkers, doing jobs put out to them by merchant employers who themselves were frequently little more than agents for the large wholesale houses in London and elsewhere. The growing power of remote capital was every year becoming more apparent.

With his characteristic simplicity Oastler told his vivid story to the Committee. The King's Speech at the opening of Parliament had commented upon the industrial prosperity of the country; said Oastler,

The very day when I read the speech of the King to this House, in which he said, 'the manufacturing districts were in a state of prosperity'; on that very day, I met with several handloom-weavers, who were 'manufacturing operatives.' I questioned them very closely, and I found that on that day, when they were said to be in such a state of 'prosperity,' those men, and women, too, were carrying burdens (warp and weft) eight or nine miles, to fetch their work, they had to carry them back again (in pieces), and they were making from 4s.6d. to 5s.2d. a-week, clear wages. Those persons work from 12 to 14 hours a day. But I am speaking of weavers in constant work. I very often find them going home without work at all. I met a lot of them, the week before last (there were eight of them), and there were only three in the lot who had work. There are scores and hundreds of families in the district that I am now alluding to, to whom a piece of flesh meat is a luxury, it does not form a regular article in their daily consumption; they live generally on porridge and potatoes, and they do not know what it is, many of them, very many of them, to taste flesh meat from year's end to year's end, excepting somebody gives them some. Their children will sometimes run to Huddersfield, beg, and bring a piece in; it is quite a luxury when a piece is brought into their houses. But, as to their clothing, they are clothed in rags; and their furniture is such, as I am sure I cannot describe, but such as a convict ought not to have.

They cross-questioned him in regard to the remedy he proposed. He told them he wanted to see in each district a statutory Board composed of masters and men to fix wages and prevent sweating. He also wanted to see a legal limitation on hours of labor. Both devices, he explained, would help prevent the glutting of the market, which was having such injurious effects upon everyone concerned. The fierce competition of one British merchant with another in the foreign market led to ruthless price cutting. The only outcome of that was a cutting of wages which inevitably caused a glut in production, since the weaver was now driven to make more cloth in an effort to keep up his meager standard of living. Oastler then elaborated his favorite argument about underconsumption. If the standard of living could be raised, he said, the workers would have more to spend, the home market would expand and general national prosperity would result. At present, because of the irresistible power of the capitalists, the cycle operated in the opposite direction. Until that could be reversed conditions would get progressively worse. 'What we want principally,' he declared, 'is to cut the dreadful power of capital.'

He explained to the Committee what he called 'the slaughterhouse system' to show just what he meant by saying that capitalism was wrecking the industry.[4] Some big house in London or Manchester would contract to take the whole of a manufacturer's

[4] Oastler's use of the word 'capitalist' is liable to be misunderstood. He was referring to finance-capitalism only: 'Let me be clearly understood when I use the word "capitalist," ' he wrote; 'I do not mean a manufacturer or merchant or farmer who regularly employs his capital in his business. But I always allude to a few immensely wealthy "Money Dealers" who hover about trade like locusts, and very often effect great changes by their operations which are ruinous to the regular trader but profitable to themselves.'

output. For a while all would go well. Then the 'slaughter-house man' would postpone payment. The manufacturer operating with little capital on small margins could not afford a long wait for his money and would have to get an advance from a bank upon his bills. The first few times there would be no difficulty. But then the wholesaler would begin to find fault with the goods supplied to him: he would allege they were deficient or not according to specification and would demand a discount of five or ten per cent. The manufacturer with little to fall back upon could do nothing but agree; then his credit with the bank would be ruined. In this way the wretched manufacturer would get thrown helplessly into the hands of the 'slaughter-house man,' becoming a mere agent on his behalf and losing independence altogether.

A variant of this type was the man who made it his business to prey upon misfortune and literally to exploit adversity. He would find out which manufacturers were in distress or threatened with writs and then buy up their stocks wholesale at enormous reductions. These stocks could then be sold at big profits well below prevailing rates with disastrous consequences for the general price structure of the trade. The fair trader would thus be forced to cut his own prices and this in turn would mean the cutting of the wages of his work-people. These 'slaughter-house men' were thus a grave deflationary menace contributing in no small degree to the general collapse of the trade that had become increasingly apparent since the onset of the post-war depression.

Custom was breaking down—that was what Oastler saw with poignant clarity—and chaos was resulting. The concentration of capital and the growing intensity of competition were together destroying those old routines of manufacture and commerce that had been the accepted *mores* of generations, so that there now seemed to be no fixity anywhere. It was a sort of ethical version of Gresham's law that he was trying to convey to the Committee: just as bad money drives good from the market, so were low standards of commercial morality making impossible the maintenance of those that had been traditional. What Oastler was really seeking was some kind of institutional device to suppress the lower ethic. His proposals for wages boards and restriction of hours, he believed, would achieve just that. But in addition he urged that capital should be taxed directly. As things were, he pointed out, 'an enormous mass of capital has not a single six-pence of taxes to pay anywhere.' What the Government ought to do, therefore, was to abolish all indirect taxation and substitute a graded direct tax upon property of every kind.

But the Government must act quickly. Laissez-faire was not only resulting in a disastrous economic collapse for cottage weavers who were as helpless as their employers in the spreading tentacles of capitalism, but was also leading to an ominous moral collapse as well. 'The working class of society seem to have greatly fallen off in their allegiance to the Government of this country because they feel they are not protected.' Consequently they might easily become 'the tools of very designing men.' A new social policy was therefore imperative:

Government ought to give protection to Labour. I consider it the first, essential duty of Government to do it, and I do not think that the Government can claim on any ground the allegiance of the opera-tives when they see that *capital and property are protected and their labour is left to chance.*

Much of what Oastler said was amply corroborated by other witnesses. But though the Committee accumulated a great deal of information and presented it to the House in a *Report* that ranks as one of the great studies in industrial pathology of the nineteenth century, it was unable to agree upon a remedy. Trade Boards and a minimum wage system had both been suggested by others besides Oastler. 'As to the practicability and efficiency of these plans,' said the Committee as their final word, 'your Com-mittee do not feel warranted in giving any decided opinion; but they are impressed with a serious conviction that some legislative enactment is *imperatively necessary* for the removal of existing evils.'

Yet the House did nothing and Oastler's rage deepened.

Toryism Reconsidered

FOR nearly four years, almost without a pause, Oastler had lived in a state of high tension. Riding hither and yon organizing and speechmaking, lobbying and conferring, in Mayfair mansions and backstreet taverns, he had awakened the conscience of thousands to a quickened sense of social urgency. Now, with the conclusion of his visit to London, that chapter came to a sudden end. Unwanted leisure was forced upon him in which he could write of his ultimate dreams more prolifically than ever before; but for a while, at least, there was no immediate objective on which his restless energies could be set. A pervasive gloom engulfed him during the ensuing eighteen months. Each of the causes with which he had identified himself seemed to be a closed issue. The factory question had been temporarily settled by Althorp's Act and its reopening appeared to have been indefinitely deferred by the collapse of Fielden's project. The New Poor Law had gone on the Statute Book in the face of negligible protest and his lobbying against it had been merely a waste of time. With Baines in the House of Commons and Sadler irrevocably defeated at Leeds and Huddersfield, the hope of creating a new radical Toryism in the West Riding had proved an idle fantasy. And now the Committee on the Handloom Weavers was about to append to its voluminous evidence a page of barren aspirations by way of 'report' which the government would ignore completely.

There are hints, too, of a still deeper crisis in Oastler's inner life. His original naïveté had been subjected to shattering assaults over the past four years and the process had occasioned a pained bewilderment. Whether naïveté be an inborn quality of the personality or the result of social conditioning is an open question; in either case, the impact upon it of events that contradict its simple pattern of expectation is certain to involve grave emotional distress. And such distress is all too liable to seek its easement in the histrionic fancies of a martyr's reverie. That is clearly what was happening to Oastler. From his home and from Fulneck he had imbibed an evangelical optimism which had long been sorely strained. He had looked upon squalor and misery in the cottages and seen hunger and destitution shuffling through the streets; impotent poverty and blighted childhood had wrung his heart. All he had sought was to alleviate their pain. Yet his name had been traduced and his intentions distorted; the prosperous had seemed to block his way and the perpetrators of cruelty to thwart his efforts. It is not surprising, then, that during these months he was so often to be found identifying himself with those ancient laments to which he daily turned for consolation: 'the mouth of the wicked and the mouth of the deceitful are opened against me . . . they have compassed me about with words of hatred and fought against me without a cause.'

¶ 1

In the lack of any other outlet for his energies, he seized whatever opportunity offered to put his more general political ideas before the public through letters, articles, and pamphlets. Sometimes, to his obvious satisfaction, controversy was forced upon him. He was always considered fair game by the northern Whig journals: and when they took to belaboring him, as they did from time to time, a lusty passage of arms invariably followed. It was an age when controversial standards were by no means exacting, and Oastler never failed to take advantage of the latitude they afforded fully as much as his adversaries did. Such scuffles had little enduring significance, however, though they doubtless added to local entertainment. His more expository essays, on the other hand, reveal a consistent and expanding trend of thought of no little importance for the understanding of his larger intentions.

One thing particularly noticeable is Oastler's constant preoccupation with the theme of 'party.' Time had been, not so very long since, when he had hoped to find endorsement of all his aspirations on the Tory benches. It was the passage of the New

Poor Law that had brought the culminating disillusionment: the latest 'gift of party,' Oastler called it, whereby 'the vested rights of the poor have been bartered for the political interests of Whigs, Tories and Radicals.' Painfully he had come to learn that the values he cherished were not to be found within the limits of any one affiliation. There now followed an outraged contempt for the whole idea of party. What did the word 'Whig' connote, he asked, when it was applied alike to an enemy of the workers such as Poulett Thomson and to a proved friend like John Maxwell? Or the word 'Tory' when affixed to two such contrasted men as Sadler and Peel? Or 'Radical' as claimed by a ruthless individualist such as Hume and by a humanitarian like John Fielden? Only one thing mattered now—the *social question;* everything else was secondary. But party names and allegiances obscured that fundamental truth even to the workers, while all the time behind the scenes the scheming of the capitalist interests continued. And the pity of it was that as long as the common people let themselves be deluded by the slogans of faction, their conditions would continue to go from bad to worse. With a desperate urgency Oastler felt that they must be made to see these things if Britain were not to pass under the complete domination of the moneyed interests.

Precisely there lay the danger. As Oastler looked upon the outward situation, he seemed to see the whole social structure collapsing for lack of any public intention to preserve it. Money making, and not the preservation of the national patrimony, appeared now to be the universal objective. And the Government of the country seemed itself determined to forward the destruction of the very thing entrusted to its guardianship. Political economy, said Oastler, had become the new state religion of Britain with the Houses of Parliament for its Cathedral. Its votaries embraced the new fatalism with a fanatical devotion: 'they really believe that God Almighty made Capital first and then made Labour to bow to its bidding.' This was no mere party matter, either, since all parties were about equally corrupted. Brougham, Peel, and Hume were representative: 'there you have a Whig, a Tory and a Radical, all three political economists, enough to lead an angel astray.' The old truth that no man liveth unto himself seemed entirely forgotten. 'The Bible is put out,' he wrote in one of his articles, 'and Miss Martineau is come in.' The result was that a few prospered while the many suffered. And the end was not yet, for the evil masqueraded under many guises:

The Demon called *Liberalism* who is now stalking through the land scattering absolute want in the richest corn fields, and the deepest distress amongst the busy rattling of our looms—assuming first one name and then another: March of Intellect, Political Economy, Free Trade, Liberal Principles, etc., but always destroying the peace of the cottage and the happiness of the palace—this Demon will be found to have been the enemy of true religion and of the prosperity and well-being of man.

Who could wonder at the rapid headway infidelity was making among the working classes, he asked, when even parsons and professing Christians failed to raise their voices against the new blasphemy? Between the teachings of the economists and the gospel of fellowship there could be no compromise.

'The real cause of our general distress,' he wrote, 'may be found in our entire abandonment of the great principles of the Divine Legislator.' We must therefore return to the principle that we are members one of another: in other words, to the idea of an organic social harmony. That would entail the substitution of a positive conception of purposiveness for the learned rationalization of doing nothing. 'To secure real prosperity to this nation, the contentment and happiness of the labouring classes must be the very first object of government.' Oastler defined his position in a sentence when he declared: 'the object of Government ought to be to encourage as much as possible *the universality of competence*, not the absorption of all the means of national competency into a few hands.'

These are recurrent themes in his meditations at this time, developed over and over again in a variety of ways. But how were they to be put into effect? In an interesting and comprehensive essay published in installments in *The Agricultural and Industrial Magazine* during the winter of 1834–5 he outlined a practical program.

First and foremost, of course, there must be total repeal of the New Poor Law. That measure was the negation of social responsibility cast into the form of a statute—'the grand battery established by capital and property to ward off the claims of the poor.' Unless it were repealed, rebellion would surely follow and society disintegrate into anarchy.

Second only to that was the obligation that 'statesmen should devise plans to give labour a real value.' The only way in which this could be done would be by setting up a series of regional tribunals, the members of which were to be chosen jointly by employers and employed in each locality. It should serve as both a court of arbitration and an economic legislature: on the one hand settling disputes between masters and men with little expense, and on the other, fixing minimum wages, maximum hours, and general conditions for the industry concerned. And it would have the added advantage, Oastler believed, of being able to use its authority to prevent gluts by curbing the terrible evil of overproduction. In this way class animosities would be eliminated and the spirit of industry transformed. And still further to foster a positive sense of citizenship Oastler wanted to see National Orders established. Decorations and honors should not be limited to the upper classes: no one section of society contributed more to the community than any other. New orders of chivalry appropriate to the modern age ought therefore to be created: an Order of the Plough, an Order of the Loom, and so on, so that meritorious service in all walks of life might be publicly recognized and rewarded.

Thirdly, the Government ought to prosecute a vigorous policy for the establishment of peasants' small-holdings and the promotion of land resettlement. Reviving an old Tudor idea,[1] Oastler urged that to every cottage there be allotted a small plot of land so that the farm laborer might have some more substantial stake in his country than was provided by his miserable wages. The benefits to the nation at large that Oastler saw accruing from a broad-based system of peasant proprietorship seemed well nigh limitless. And along with that, he thought,

[1] The Statute of 31 Eliz. cap vii (1589) provided that every cottage (with certain exceptions) must have four acres of land attached.

should go a state-aided scheme for the reclamation of waste lands. When these extensive acres had been drained and conditioned, they could be leased to the unemployed. To Oastler it seemed the stupidest of follies to get rid of Britain's most vigorous manhood by encouraging emigration, as the Whig Government was doing, when with a little forethought rich use could be made of such human resources at home. The futility of the paradox had been sharply brought home to him only a few weeks before he wrote this article. He had had occasion to go to the Liverpool docks where he had seen two ships drawn up at the quayside. At the gangway of the one, emigrants from Yorkshire and Lancashire were taking a tearful farewell of their relatives, while from the other were disembarking unemployed Irish come to look for jobs.

As to general fiscal policy, he had a number of suggestions to make, all designed to preserve the home market and stimulate domestic consumption. But his pet notion, which he was to elaborate many a time in the years to come, was that all indirect taxes whatsoever should be abolished. In their place he urged the institution of a coherent scheme of direct taxation so that the burden might be placed on the shoulders best able to bear it. In particular he wanted to see a graduated tax on capital. From the beginning of fiscal history, land had been directly taxed; why, then, he asked, when huge fortunes were being made in commerce and industry, should not proper public levy be made upon these other sources of wealth as well? Sooner or later that was bound to happen, for the existing anomaly was too glaring to last; it was only a question of whether the adjustment would be effected reasonably and constitutionally or would be brought about by revolution. 'There is a debt due to Land and to Labour from Capital which *must* eventually be paid, or there will in the end be scrambling for it.'

More than economic measures would be required, however, if the enduring well-being of the masses was to be the goal of public policy. The problems of morale and education were just as pressing as the problem of the distribution of wealth. Under a system of laissez-faire, the evils of ignorance, intemperance, and frustration took their terrible toll of society unchecked.

Thus the vices of one generation created the milieu for the
next. Yet by a few simple and inexpensive devices, Oastler believed, this whole empire of vice might be overthrown. In every
town there should be set up 'places of rational and gymnastic
exercise.' These civic recreation centers would be library and
gymnasium combined: they would have reading rooms staffed
with advisers to help and encourage members, places for playing games, and facilities for teaching physical training. But it
was not only of the men Oastler was thinking when he contemplated the question of morale; to cater for them alone would be
to treat but half the problem. The operatives' wives and daughters
were just as much in need of help. As he had come to know cottage life more intimately, Oastler had been appalled to discover
what superstition and ignorance prevailed in these homes, even
concerning the most elementary facts of health and regimen. To
remedy this state of affairs, he urged that every community employ a staff of qualified matrons who would act as advisers and
confidants of the womenfolk. Such a corps of professional coun-
sellors, he was convinced, could speedily eliminate a vast amount
of unnecessary misery and might eventually be able to effect a
great transformation.

¶ 2

By no means all of Oastler's polemics were conducted on this
high plane of persuasive dignity, however. Indeed, one of the
puzzling things about Oastler is the suddenness and frequency
with which he slipped gear, so to speak, during his continuous
controversial journey. One moment he was making an impressive appeal to the constructive imagination of awakened pity,
while the next he was resorting to abusive personalities with all
the flagrant demagogy of a tub thumper. He could truthfully
claim that he never resorted to the tactics of abuse until he himself had first been attacked; but once the word-slinging had begun he showed that he had a repertoire of invective that not
even the great William Cobbett could surpass.

In August 1834, for example, the *Bradford Observer* made
some of his remarks in the London radical journals the occasion
for a bit of caustic Oastler-baiting. The *Observer* was a new

'liberal' paper which had recently been started by a group of nonconformist mill owners. Oastler was stung to fury by its comments and immediately gave vent to one of the most vitriolic pamphlets he ever wrote: *A Letter to those Sleek, Pious, Holy and Devout Dissenters, Messrs. Get-all, Keep-all, Grasp-all . . . the Shareholders in the Bradford Observer*. In it he accused the owners of the paper of the most outrageous hypocrisy, professing piety in their chapels while maintaining in their mills some of the worst conditions to be found in the Bradford district. The charges were all explicit and identifiable, challenging the reader to make his own verification.

Some weeks later, on the publication of the first reports by the new factory inspectors, the *Leeds Mercury* came out with an editorial commending the general excellence of factory conditions which those reports revealed, and condemning 'the gross delusions got up by Messrs. Sadler, Oastler, Bull and Co.' Oastler counter-attacked with venom, the Baineses replied, and for a short while the controversy raged again almost as fiercely as it had done four years before. Just before Christmas, Oastler brought it to a momentary climax with another pamphlet: *A Well-seasoned Christmas Pie for 'The Great Liar of the North,' prepared, baked and presented by Richard Oastler*. Even for Oastler the seasoning was hot, though that did not detract from its considerable popularity.

But it was in April 1835 that chance gave Oastler the fullest scope for venting his pent-up anger, and he seized the opportunity with a roar that echoed all over the north. In that month, a Huddersfield mill owner named Joseph Schofield was convicted of violating Althorp's Act and fined £5. Two charges were proved against him: that he had been employing children in his mill without the requisite age certificate, and that he had kept one little girl at work 13 hours continuously without even a break for meals. To Oastler, this first conviction of a local mill owner under the new law would have been particularly gratifying in any case, coming opportunely as it did after the recent press attacks. But there was cause for even richer satisfaction over the episode. This Schofield was noted for being a very 'respectable' figure; one of Huddersfield's most prominent dissenters—trustee and deacon of Ramsden Street Chapel, conspicuous in local 'liberal' politics, and prominent at all missionary gatherings. Ever since the Fixby Hall Compact, Oastler had known what conditions were like in the Schofield mill and many of his barbed innuendos about nonconformist hypocrisy had been directed at this particular individual. Now the man had actually been convicted in open court. Three lurid pamphlets came out of Fixby in quick succession,[2] all elaborating the same theme. Schofield had been found out, but he was only one among many hypocrites. There were plenty of others just as bad who had so far managed to keep clear of the law: men who made great parade of their chapel piety while piling up profits out of the exploitation of children. 'Cardinal legates from the Court of Hell,' Oastler called them, who for four and a half years had been reviling him personally while loudly denying that there was any need for Parliament to regulate their factories. Now that he had been given his chance, Oastler dropped all innuendo and lashed these pious enemies of social legislation with exultant savagery. One of this chapel set he singled out for special castigation—Moore, the Huddersfield postmaster. Here was another of Oastler's slanderers: another deacon, a friend of Schofield's, a man whose disgusting fornications could be proved, and one who would even betray his trust by tampering with the mail when it suited his purpose. In each succeeding pamphlet Oastler piled up the maledictions until he finally compelled Moore to bring a libel suit against him. That was just what Oastler wanted; but the denouement lay many months ahead and by that time the pattern of north-country politics was vastly altered.

¶ 3

During the spring and early summer, occasional factory meetings were held which Oastler was called upon to address. But though for a brief hour he could still fire his audience with fervor, nothing significant resulted. A heavy inertia seemed to have

---

[2] *The devil-to-do amongst the dissenters in Huddersfield* (1 June 1835); *The Huddersfield dissenters in a fury. And Why? Because the mask is falling* (18 June); *The Huddersfield dissenters stark, staring mad because the mask has fallen* (7 July).

the whole British working-class movement in its grip as though the workers were exhausted by the emotional orgies of the past four years—the Reform Bill hysteria, the Ten Hours crusade, the National Union extravagance, and the final disastrous gamble with direct action. 'If persevered in much longer,' Oastler wrote, 'it threatens to consign them to utter oblivion.' When in December 1834 he went to Norfolk for his annual visit to Thornhill, he found the same apathy there too. The Poor Law Commissioners were busily instituting the new workhouse system throughout East Anglia and the laborers seemed completely cowed. 'Could you have believed,' he wrote to Hetherington, 'that the people who four or five years ago frightened the King and Government out of their senses would in so short a time have laid themselves down and licked the feet of whole shoals of tyrants nicknamed Commissioners?'

The only thing left for him to do was to go on writing for the unstamped radical press in London. His articles in the *Poor Man's Guardian* had proved so popular that in June 1835 he was asked by John Cleave, the publisher of the *Weekly Police Gazette*, to write for that illicit journal as well. Other invitations of a similar sort followed, so that hardly a week went by without at least one of his articles appearing in some proletarian periodical. 'In this course,' says one commentator, 'Mr. Oastler was opposed by some of his dearest friends who were shocked at the thought of him, a churchman and Tory, writing in the papers of what they knew to be radical and revolutionary journals.' Oastler was pained but defiant, and more than once sought to justify his stand. 'I have tried the press,' he explained in one place,

pamphlet after pamphlet have I sent forth, full of mourning, lamentation, and woe, but the rulers of the land have turned a deaf ear. . . Now I will labour in another field, in it I will sow the seed, and harvest will come in its season. I want the aid of all parties, and must work on until I succeed. . . Knowing, as I do, that the working men and their families do not obtain the stamped press, and that the unstamped press is universally read by them, regardless of caste or party I have resolved to avail myself of the only medium through weekly periodicals in which I can effectually communicate what I know and think on subjects most important to the working men.

Some of his best writing is to be found in these forgotten journals. In a breezy, conversational style he elaborated his political philosophy even though he knew it would be distasteful to a good many of his new readers, and in the light of that doctrine he commented on the passing scene. But whatever the ostensible theme for the week might be, the underlying intention was always the same: to make his readers aware of the tragic reality of the social problem. It was because the moral will of so many of the middle classes was atrophied, he maintained, that social misery persisted. In some cases, this was due to ignorance; in others, to the timidity begotten of a craving for 'respectability' or to the slavish following of party banners. But whatever the cause, the consequences were plain for all to see; not until the public conscience was shaken out of its lethargy could there be any betterment. 'Perhaps the dry bones in these valleys of slavery may realize the prophet's vision,' he wrote to a friend, 'and a strong army of patriots may yet arise in the plains of England resolved to assert their rights and tear the laurels from the brow of Capital.'

But no moral revival could come without general acknowledgment of the three basic postulates to which Oastler reverted time and time again. First, that 'every man born in England has a natural right to live well in England'; 'the labourer has as much right to receive as much wages as will maintain himself and his family in plenty and comfort, by a fair and reasonable day's work, as any landlord or any fundholder or any creditor has to receive his rents etc.'; secondly, that British governmental institutions are intended to secure this right; and finally, that the denial of this right automatically destroys any claim to allegiance. When a government repudiates the obligations to the common man that these principles impose upon it, Oastler asserted, 'it has by its own act and deed put him without the pale of the Commonwealth, and he is morally justified in taking care of his own life and the life of his family.' This, he told Hetherington, may be treason according to the law of Malthus, but it is certainly not treason according to the law of God.

These weekly essays were both popular and influential. In many a public house and reading room men talked and argued

about them, with the result that from time to time a lively controversy developed in the correspondence columns. On one occasion the editor of the *Twopenny Dispatch* reported that a 'host of
letters' had descended upon him on account of the previous
article: so many, in fact, that there was not even 'room for a general analysis.' Common to every one of them, he added, was the
regret that 'so good a man as Mr. Oastler . . . with his ardent
zeal and universally admitted devotion to the interests of the
working classes' should go on calling himself a Tory and defending the Monarchy and the Church. In the Manchester Radical
Association the difference of opinion regarding Oastler became
so sharp that the society held a debate about him. One wing
insisted that no one who repudiated manhood suffrage could
possibly be a true friend of the people, while the other maintained that his labors were 'all excellent and well calculated to
release the working classes from their present miseries.' The
secretary was therefore instructed to get from Oastler a fuller
statement of his opinions on the suffrage question. But on that
Oastler remained as irreconcilable as ever; his new friends had
not changed his attitude in the least degree. 'My opinion on universal suffrage is,' he replied, 'that if it were the law of the land
next week it would in a very short time produce universal confusion and would inevitably lead to despotism.'

But that did not mean that he thought nothing could be done
to make Parliament more effective: quite the contrary. In that
connection one suggestion he put forward in these essays is specially worthy of note, both because of the discussion it provoked at the time and because of its anticipation of something
the Chartists were to attempt three years later. Briefly it may be
described as the establishment of a People's Lobby at Westminster. Recent events had proved what could be accomplished by
well-organized parliamentary lobbying, the textile manufacturers in particular having shown themselves conspicuously skilful
at the art. Why should not the workers profit by that lesson,
Oastler asked. What he proposed, therefore, was that there should
be set up a nation-wide League of Citizens operating through
democratically organized committees in village, town, and
county. These committees would gather facts, discuss problems,

and suggest remedies. A League newspaper would publicize the information and the National Committee would distil from it a workable program. At election time the League would examine the career and professions of every candidate, irrespective of his party label. Where it found a man whose principles coincided with its own, it would give him its support and work for his return. Where it found no such candidate, it would select one of its own and 'return' him as the 'real' representative of the people. Such 'real' representatives would engage a room somewhere near Palace Yard (just as the cotton manufacturers had done in 1833) and conduct themselves as a shadow Parliament. They would send formal addresses to the King, maintain close contact with well disposed Members of both Houses, and press appeals, arguments, and information upon the rest; they would memorialize the Government about current legislation; and during recesses they would tour the country to keep public opinion fully aroused and informed.

It was an attractive idea, though one that was destined to have greater applicability to the American system of government than to the British. The *Twopenny Dispatch*, when it was first mooted, was inundated with letters about it, and there was much argument about its feasibility. Oastler never pressed it very strenuously: even he succumbed to the prevailing despair before the year was out. 'Capital,' he lamented, 'will go on feeding on Industry, and Party on Patriotism until the end cometh.'

¶ 4

On top of all this despair came acute personal sorrow with the death of Michael Sadler. Sadler had never fully recovered from the illness that first showed itself during his chairmanship of the Select Committee. In the hope of building up his strength after his defeat in the Huddersfield by-election, he had retired to his estate outside Belfast; but the improvement that followed proved only temporary. His condition gradually worsened, and on 29 July 1835 he passed away in his fifty-sixth year.

His loss was a great blow to Oastler. For over twenty years these two had been the most intimate of friends: in fact, ever since they had walked the slums of Leeds together during the great cholera epidemic. Oastler's regard for Sadler amounted almost to veneration: 'that heaven-born man,' he called him, 'of whom this age has not had the like.' It was always to Sadler that Oastler had turned whenever he sought consolation and advice. Now that steadying influence was gone and nothing really took its place. Oastler had the strange fluidity of disposition that has to find its coherence and stability in male comradeship. Bull's friendship was precious and indispensable; but Bull was a younger man, more of a follower than the followed, and his counsel never had for Oastler the weight that Sadler's always carried. And as for the friendships that came later, vital though they were, most of them clearly had more of a dissipating than an integrating influence. Apart from the pain it brought, therefore, Sadler's passing was an event of the utmost consequence in Oastler's life.

The Christmas of 1835 was probably the unhappiest Oastler had ever experienced. He had begun the year in gloom; he ended it in blackest despair. Wherever he looked he could find not the least cause for hope.

As usual, he stayed with Thornhill in Norfolk over the New Year. Desultory rick-burning and ham-stringing were still going on at the same time that the landlords were complaining of dwindling rents. The 'county' folk he met at Thornhill's house parties seemed just as shortsighted as the Yorkshire manufacturers, approving the New Poor Law and endorsing the 'conservatism' that Sir Robert Peel had proclaimed in his Tamworth Manifesto.[3] To Oastler this was nothing less than a betrayal of their own order; for, as he saw it, 'conservatism' was but a device of 'that crafty stock-jobber' Peel to abandon Toryism and the old

[3] The 'Tamworth Manifesto' was an open letter Peel addressed nominally to his constituents in the borough of Tamworth, actually to the country at large, in December 1834. It purported to be a 'frank exposition of general principles and views' which would determine the policy of his Government. It was an appeal for the support of all 'moderates,' pledging Peel's acceptance of the Reform Act of 1832, declaring his intention to conserve existing institutions, but promising cautious reform as occasion demanded. It thus marked the beginning of modern Conservatism and the abandonment of Tory fundamentalism. Disraeli in his novels was to satirize the pronouncement for its 'unprincipled opportunism' as caustically as Oastler did, and in much the same terms.

social order in order to effect an alliance with the capitalist interests. Worse still was his discovery that even his employer seemed to be thinking along 'conservative' lines too. So another illusion was shattered. 'I had some hopes in the aristocracy,' he wrote on his return, 'now I have none.'

Sometimes in a fleeting mood Oastler had visions of a rejuvenated and revived Church of England leading the nation in a great crusade to Christianize the conditions of life for the masses and provide a way out of the moral impasse in which the country appeared to be caught. The Church would have to put its own house in order first before it could start rousing the national conscience: but was that really too much to hope for? In an open *Letter to the Archbishop of York* written in the new year, Oastler made an ardent plea that the Church should be purified and transformed into a true Church of the People. He had recently 'discovered' Latimer, and as he read *On the Plough* and the other classic sermons he responded with a fervor that spilled over into this pamphlet. Why could not the Church produce Latimers in these days too? The necessity was just as great as in Edward VI's time, and the social problem just as much of a religious issue. 'The factory question is indeed, My Lord, a soul question: it is souls against pounds, shillings and pence.' But the Archbishop made no response.

CHAPTER XXIV

The Third Rousing of the North

WHEN Althorp's factory act went on the Statute Book in August 1833, the leaders of the Ten Hours Movement had decided to discontinue their agitation until such time as the measure had proved itself unworkable. By the autumn of 1835 that time seemed to be at hand, for loud complaints about the law could be heard on every side.

Employers had originally hailed the eight-hour day for children with approval because it made possible relays of juvenile workers. In practice, however, the relay system proved much harder to operate than had been supposed. A sufficient supply of youngsters of the necessary age was just not available, and each stage in the progressive application of the Act brought out that fact more clearly—first when it was applied to the ten-year-olds in March 1834, and then when it was extended to the next age-group a year later.[1] The final inclusion of the twelve-year-olds would be certain to produce even greater difficulty and confusion. As March 1836 drew near, therefore, resentment against the Act steadily mounted. Discussion of the factory question once more became general, only this time it tended to center upon the particular problem of law enforcement rather than upon the wider issues that had been debated 5 years earlier.

Already there had been considerable evasion of the law, sometimes with the connivance of the very magistrates who should have enforced it. Employers resorted to various expedients. Some mill owners simply ignored the Act and defied the magistrates to penalize them. When, for instance, Charles Thornton of

---

[1] 'In large manufacturing towns it has been found utterly impossible to procure children enough for the execution of the relay system.' (The President of the Board of Trade, in the House of Commons, 9 May 1836.)

Wortley was prosecuted in September 1835 for working 4 boys 13 hours continuously without any break for meals, he told the Bench he would rather go out of business altogether than observe such a law, and the Bench sympathized to the extent of fining him only one shilling. Others were a little more subtle and used irregular relays: that is to say, while not exacting from the children more than the legal 8 hours of actual work, they broke up that work into spells so that by turning the youngsters out of the mill in between times they could spread the available supply of labor over the full length of the adults' working day.

But the simplest way to get round the law was by falsifying the ages of the children. In most cases there was no reliable record, since public registration of births did not begin until 1837. Parents lied glibly if they wanted to get their children into the mills. And when the Inspectors seriously attempted to enforce the clause requiring a doctor to certify that the child had the 'appearance' of the age specified, they found themselves confronted with all sorts of unexpected difficulties. Certificates were presented from dentists and quacks and cow-doctors; qualified physicians proved careless or complaisant; and families borrowed or even hired certificates from one another. It was the opinion of Mr. Clay, the appointed certifying surgeon for the Ashton district, that the attempt to put the Act into full operation would surely result in an enormous increase of perjury; he therefore resigned his charge rather than face the complications that it would bring.

If the age clauses of Althorp's Act were difficult to apply, however, its educational provisions requiring factory children to attend school two hours daily proved almost a dead letter from the start. These were the days before a national system of education had been established. Often schools were not available: and even where they were, the hours might not be convenient or the teachers might object to having grimy, ragged children from the mills forced upon them. Here again, therefore, many employers ignored the requirement altogether, while others gave it merely perfunctory acknowledgment by using any cellar as a 'schoolroom' and any available workman as a 'teacher.' A few of the bigger employers conscientiously tried to put the scheme into effect, but they were exceptions. In his first official report, Rickards, the Inspector for Yorkshire and Lancashire, bluntly declared that 'the utter impracticability of the schooling clauses being attended to by the masters is so obvious that . . . I trust I shall stand excused for dispensing with their observance.' His colleague for Scotland reported at the same time that not a single mill owner could be found observing the clauses in that area.

It should not be supposed, however, that it was only the employers who were complaining about the Act. Thousands of parents detested it because it kept their younger children out of the mills and thereby diminished the family budget. And many a spinner cursed it just as heartily for different reasons. In many mills the little 'pieceners' were hired and paid by the spinners under whom they worked. These workmen now found not only that 'pieceners' were harder to get but also that those who were available were demanding higher wages. Charles Hindley, the sympathetic M.P. for Ashton, considered this particular difficulty especially serious since it meant that any renewal of the agitation would find a considerable body of operatives openly siding with the employers.

For all these reasons, dissatisfaction with Althorp's Act was widespread by the end of 1835. Both sides were ready to cry 'I told you so': the majority of the mill owners because they said it all went to show how impossible it was to regulate economic matters anyway, and the Oastlerites because they had declared from the outset that the measure would create more problems than it solved. Little discernment was necessary, therefore, to see that the attempt to put Althorp's Act into full operation on 1 March 1836 would be certain to provoke a storm of some kind.

¶ 1

Although for two years there had been no organized agitation by the Ten Hours men, the opponents of factory legislation were far from inactive. There were ominously inconspicuous meetings of spinners and overlookers, for example, which became increasingly frequent as the year advanced. In one town

after another gatherings of operatives took place whereat it
was always voted by 'a large majority' to press for a twelve-
hour day for children; and invariably a resolution was carried
to communicate this decision to the employers. About the same
time, meetings of mill owners happened to be held at which
wondrously similar affirmations of policy got passed. From both
sources petitions were forwarded to Parliament asking for appropriate modification of the law. Some masters even brought
in attorneys to talk the men over. And the *Mercury* encouraged
the drift of things by advising workers to discuss the practicability of the existing statute, and then to inform Inspector Rickards of their conclusions at his next visit.

The surviving Ten Hours organization did what it could to
counter this drift, of course. The Bradford Short Time Committee put out a couple of effective manifestos disclaiming responsibility for Althorp's Act and reaffirming its conviction that only
a straight ten-hour day would obviate the growing difficulties.
Half a dozen meetings of protest were held in the larger towns
and a few new petitions collected. But little came of the effort.
Only in the latter part of 1835 did interest in the factory question really begin to revive. Once it had started, however, it
gathered momentum with such speed that it quickly developed
into the third big drive for a Ten Hours Bill.

The precise circumstances that gave rise to this new campaign are not now known, since all the papers relating to it
seem to have been lost. Yet one thing stands out clearly, namely,
that the initiative came from the cotton operatives of Lancashire under the leadership of John Doherty, the trade unionist,
and Philip Grant, the journalist. Not until it was well under way
were the Oastlerites of the West Riding involved. This undoubtedly accounts for the prominence given throughout the campaign to the demand for 'restriction upon the moving power'—
a demand that had distinguished the Lancashire agitation from
the beginning.[2] It may also have something to do with the
strange fact that Charles Hindley was asked to take charge of
the projected bill in Parliament in place of Lord Ashley. Probably several considerations led to the making of this change,

[2] See above, p. 149.

involving tactics in the House of Commons as well as in the districts. Hindley, the big cotton spinner, may have been deemed to have had a greater appeal for the House than Ashley, the big landowner. There was also the not inconsequential fact that Hindley was a local man speaking the Radical idiom, who, from his first association with the movement, had strongly insisted upon the necessity for regulating machine-hours as well as man-hours. Lord Ashley, on the other hand, had never even visited the industrial districts, and like Oastler was suspect in some quarters on account of his professed Toryism. But however necessary such a change in the parliamentary leadership may have seemed to be, it can hardly have been welcome to Oastler. Despite their common Fulneck background, Oastler had a deep distrust of Hindley, which he publicly and frequently expressed, and which he never lost.

The first hint that anything was afoot came with the convening of a delegates' conference at Preston on 23 August. The report shows that the Lancashire trade-union leaders had already been in consultation with Hindley and had received from him a promise to introduce a new Ten Hours Bill in the near future. This conference was a declaration of support. Two further conferences at Manchester drew up the detailed plans. The old Short Time organization was resuscitated, a fighting fund was opened under Fielden's treasurership, and a new Lancashire Central Committee was formed with the veteran James Turner as paid secretary. The idea was to begin the agitation about the middle of January 1836, a fortnight or so before Parliament was due to reassemble.

As preparations went forward, however, Hindley's attitude began to cause misgivings. Hindley was no crusader but a decent-hearted and public-spirited businessman whose whole approach to social problems tended to be cautious and pragmatic rather than defiant or enthusiastic. There seems no real reason for doubting his sincerity, though Doherty once told him in the course of a very frank talk that the operatives regarded him with 'a strong and rather growing feeling of distrust.' But he was inclined to look upon Parliament as a kind of glorified 'Royal Exchange' wherein deals were to be made and bidders could

not expect to clinch the bargain with their first offer. It was
characteristic of the man, for instance, that one of the first things
he did after accepting responsibility for the new Ten Hours
Bill was to bring about a round-table discussion on the subject
between the operatives' leaders and 7 of the Lancashire M.P.s.
Nothing positive came of the meeting, except a promise by the
Members to sound out the leading master spinners, yet it was
evident that Hindley would much prefer a bargain to another
battle.

That he by no means saw eye to eye with his colleagues became clear at the final Manchester conference of 2 January,
which completed the preparations for the campaign. Since Oastler was away in Norfolk, Bull attended on behalf of the West
Riding organization. There Hindley made a full statement of his
position. The immediate objective, he said, ought to be the
imposition of restrictions upon machinery rather than the enactment of any particular length of working day. He himself
heartily favored ten hours and would press for it; but that, he
considered, was essentially a matter for masters and men to fight
out between themselves. What he was primarily concerned with
was uniform and adequate law enforcement through control of
the factory power. If he could get that, he had no intention of
abandoning his bill however much it might otherwise be
amended. Ashley, he thought, had made a big tactical mistake
in yielding his bill to Althorp when the hours clause had been
defeated. Once control of the machines had been secured, efforts could be made in later sessions to carry the rest of the
program. He candidly confessed, however, to having qualms
about the effect of all such legislation upon foreign trade. On
that account he wanted to see the application of any new law
made in stages over a four-year period so that its results could
be carefully observed and checked.

Bull, of course, was immediately up in arms at this avowal.
Neither he nor Oastler considered Ashley had committed any
blunder in resigning the Ten Hours Bill to the Government
once its vital clause had been defeated, and he was distressed
to hear that Hindley intended to act differently. Insertion into
the new bill of a clause about the moving power was all to the

good, but to compromise on the Ten Hours issue would be a
gross betrayal of principle which the Yorkshire men could never
accept. Nor could he subscribe to the suggestion that regard
for the export trade should take precedence over humanitarian
considerations. And to drive home his argument Bull distributed a vigorous memorandum setting forth his position in detail.

The dispute was still largely academic at that stage, despite
the feelings it aroused. In the interest of unity, therefore, the
conference eventually postponed the matter for later consideration and passed on to more immediate questions. But the
episode did not enhance the general confidence in Hindley.

¶ 2

The 19th of January 1836 is not only the date of the big Ashton meeting that opened the new agitation, but also the day
on which there first appeared on a Ten Hours platform the
dynamic figure of Joseph Raynor Stephens, a man soon to be
as well known to the northern industrial workers as any of
their established leaders.

Stephens at this time was just 31. His father was a Wesleyan
minister who had become President of the Conference in 1827.
Deciding to be a preacher too, Joseph had been sent to the Wesleyan mission station at Stockholm, where he appears to have
been conspicuously successful on his preaching tours and to have
become a sort of unofficial chaplain to the British minister. Returning to England to be ordained in 1830, he had taken up
calls first at Cheltenham and then at Ashton-under-Lyne.
Wherever he went his remarkable oratorical power created a
deep impression, and everyone who heard him prophesied for
him a great future.

In 1834, however, he had fallen foul of the governing authorities in the Wesleyan Connexion by advocating the disestablish-
ment of the Church of England. At that time the Wesleyan
oligarchy was zealously seeking the credit of respectability, trying to assure the British ruling classes of the Society's political
innocuousness and its freedom from 'subversive' associations.
Stephens' outspoken criticism of the Establishment ill comported with that policy. When, therefore, he refused to give

an undertaking that he would abstain from such criticism in future, he was suspended from his ministry.

Thus excommunicated by the sect into which he had been born, he began a free-lance ministry of his own, backed by many admirers who provided him with a chapel at Ashton, where he could speak as he pleased. Independence and popularity matured his talents. Large congregations crowded on week days as well as Sundays to hear the new and eloquent evangelist, and rarely went away unmoved. For in some degree, at least, Stephens possessed the authentic qualities of the prophet: consuming ardor, a clear-cut apocalyptic message, and remarkable command of imagery. The gospel he proclaimed was anything but quietistic: it was a challenging call to the ethical sense. Sin and evil were real forces in the hearts of men, frustrating the fulfilment of divine intention; daily life was the field on which the cosmic struggle was fought out, so that only by the concrete affirmations of the regenerated will could victory come. It was a theme, it is to be noted, capable of being rendered in two keys. Until now, the rendering had been made chiefly in terms of the individual's inner life. With Stephens' joining of the Ten Hours Movement, however, and the wider contacts that followed, it became transposed into social terms and a new chapter in his life began. Poverty, hunger, and suffering were presented as the visible results of corrupt purposes; the struggle against them as the struggle against evil men, and the day of judgment as the day of reckoning. With but the slightest shift of accent, the call to arms could sound very like the call to the class war. Yet Stephens did not profess Radicalism. He had no faith in manhood suffrage as a panacea, and little, indeed, in political change of any kind. The available institutions were instruments enough for amelioration, he thought, would men but use them rightly. 'I do not wish to see the old English institutions destroyed,' he told one of his audiences. That was why he always called himself a Tory; but it was a strange and mystic Toryism beyond the grasp of party Tadpoles and Tapers, which seemed to find its inspiration in the Old Testament prophets rather than in the oracles of the Carlton Club.

His similarity to Oastler is at once apparent. In background and belief as well as in temperament the two had much in common. They had not yet met; but on the day they did come together, a few weeks later, they immediately recognized each other as warriors in the same army. There thus began a friendship of deepest intimacy which lasted to the end: one of the five enduring attachments that shaped Oastler's life.

From the night of the Ashton meeting, then, Lancashire as well as Yorkshire was to have the evangel of retributive Toryism preached to it with power and inflaming passion. The tempo of the campaign quickly accelerated; soon the newspapers were reporting meetings 'crowded to excess' with 'hundreds turned away.' Stephens was not the only big platform figure, of course: Turner, Condy, Grant, and Doherty were as tirelessly active as he was, and on the administrative side perhaps more so. But he alone brought to the campaign the revivalist fervor that whipped the audiences to frenzy.

¶ 3

Oastler came back from Norfolk to find the Lancashire agitation going at full strength. Bull reported all that had been happening while he was away, and together they drafted a powerful manifesto *To the Workers of Yorkshire and Lancashire.*

The immediate occasion of the appeal was the reassembling of Parliament at the beginning of February. By that time strange rumors were abroad to the effect that the Government was intending to repeal Althorp's Act altogether. Oastler's purpose, therefore, was to anticipate such a move by clarifying the situation for the northern industrial workers and presenting them with a realistic appraisal of the factory question as of the moment.

It was a lengthy document, sober and impressive; but its tone clearly betrays Oastler's alarm over the masters' maneuvers of the past twelve months and his fear that the operatives were likely to allow themselves to be duped into making a grave mistake. The argument was trenchant. Althorp's Act had failed, but the Ten Hours men were not responsible for that. The measure had been devised to please the masters and to fool the workers. Yet in order to capture a public opinion that Sadler and his movement had aroused, the Government had been forced to write into the law certain attractive features capable of being extended far beyond the original intention: in particular the eight hours' principle, the educational scheme, and the system of inspection. Badly though those devices were working at the moment, they might yet be made the basis of a sound industrial code. The forces militating against such a consummation, Oastler frankly warned, lay not only in the employers' ranks but almost as much in the ranks of the operatives themselves. While the masters were fuddling their brains with shortsighted selfishness, he declared, 'you are fuddling yours with drink,' distorting judgment, and confusing friend with foe. Whatever trap the Government was about to spring, then, the operatives must at all costs hold fast to the constructive principles already enacted:

Meet together in your different workshops and mills, and there discuss the best means of informing the legislature of your resolute determination to maintain the ground you have already gained. Let them know that it is your interest, that it is your wish, that no factories regulation act shall be passed which does not recognize these three great principles. Tell them that in addition to those clauses you wish for a clause to prevent all young persons between the ages of 14 and 21 from working more than ten hours a day in any factory—and that, to render these enactments more easy of execution you would wish them to restrict the moving power. Yes, let them know your mind on these subjects; but take care whatever you do that you part not with the three great principles of the present factories regulation act. . . *Stand firm* by these, and your emancipation is secured. None of your friends dare have asked for any of these great principles—the cowardice and hypocrisy of your enemies granted them. *See to it that you maintain them.*

In spite of his appeal, however, Oastler doubted that the workers really would stand firm. Clandestine meetings were being held in the factories all the time, as the *Mercury* had advised, and immense pressure was being put upon the operatives to declare themselves against Althorp's Act. Only a few days after the manifesto was published, Oastler's friend Duncombe, Member for the North Riding, wrote to say he had just encountered

Baines in the House and that Baines had boasted of having in his pocket a petition from nearly 400 Leeds overlookers asking for an eleven-hour day. Nor was Oastler alone in his fears. A day or two later Hindley sent an open letter to the Stockton Short Time Committee voicing the same apprehensions. The full application of the law on 1 March would be certain to call forth a vast volume of resentment, he warned. He suspected the Government would exploit that resentment to get the law altered, and feared the 'operatives would help this plot.' Only if the men resolutely banded themselves together in a firm fighting organization could the move be defeated. Hindley was worried and openly admitted the doubts he had about his suitability for the leadership in such a situation.

Meanwhile the reconstituted Ten Hours organization was pressing as vigorously as it could the plans drawn up by the various conferences. Public meetings continued, new committees were started, and Stephens along with six other Lancashire delegates went to London to undertake lobbying on behalf of the bill Hindley was about to introduce. In contrast to all the earlier campaigns, this one was being fought manifestly on two fronts: in Parliament, to consolidate and extend the gains already won, and in the districts to prevent such large-scale defections among the operatives as might destroy the chance of any substantial factory bill at all.

¶ 4

For a while Oastler was not able to take any active part in this new agitation, except with his pen, because he was busy preparing for a law suit which was due to come up at the next York Assizes. William Moore, the scurrilous Huddersfield postmaster whom Oastler had so ferociously attacked in his pamphlets on the *Huddersfield Dissenters*, had at last brought a libel charge against him, claiming £1,000 for defamation.

The case really had its origins earlier than the abusive pamphlets, going back as far as the Huddersfield by-election of January 1834.[3] In the course of that contest, Moore had put out a venomous placard raking up the old Foster controversy

[3] See above, pp. 255 ff. and 300.

and accusing Oastler of peculation in the matter of the factory fund. Oastler scorned to answer with a libel suit, though he might easily have brought one; but if Moore wanted to engage in a slanging contest, Oastler was more than ready to oblige. He therefore plastered the town with a poster equally spirited, in which he accused the postmaster of opening and reading the correspondence of his political opponents. To this the subsequent pamphlets added the charges of obscenity, cheating, and lewd living.

The case came before Lord Denman and a special jury on 20 February 1836. Local interest was great, both on account of the parties involved and the nature of the charges; and not a little piquancy was added by the fact that Moore had engaged as his counsel Blackburne K.C., Sadler's victorious Whig opponent in the by-election, whereas Oastler conducted his own defense.

Oastler's plea was fair and justifiable comment, and he took a posse of witnesses to York to substantiate it. According to every surviving account, his handling of his case was superb. The cross-examination of Moore was annihilating and all Blackburne's efforts failed to save his client from the ignominy that Oastler inflicted. By the time the wretched postmaster left the box his reputation had been ruined and his charges of peculation torn to tatters. It scarcely needed Oastler's own witnesses and the brilliant two-hour speech at the end to finish the rout. Everyone present was impressed by the display. Even the judge was moved to commendation and his summing up was overwhelmingly in favor of the defense. The result was that the jury found Oastler justified on one count (concerning Moore's bad moral character) but technically guilty on the other, and awarded the plaintiff one farthing damages instead of the £1,000 he asked for.

It happened that there was sitting in Court all through the trial Sir Francis Doyle, a Fellow of All Souls who was later to become Professor of Poetry at Oxford. In his *Reminiscences* Doyle has left us a little snapshot of the affair. Oastler, he says, 'made [Moore] so odious to everybody that the Queen's Counsel wrestled with their unlearned opponent in vain and could extract for their client nothing better than a farthing damages. His perora-

tion I recollect perfectly; it was grandly conceived and grandly
delivered. . . Oastler strode out of court in a blaze of glory.
Considering the toughness of a Yorkshire jury, and the real ability of the men whom he encountered and overthrew on their
own ground, I do not remember a greater rhetorical victory.'

The Tory press of Yorkshire as well as the unstamped press
of London hailed the verdict with delight. There seems little
doubt that it enhanced Oastler's reputation and dispelled any
unspoken suspicions that may have lingered from the Foster
episode. Henceforth his opponents were noticeably more cautious in the style of criticism they employed. Exhilarated by his
triumph, Oastler was now ready to throw his energies into the
developing struggle.

¶ 5

The campaign of northern meetings was continuing enthusiastically and the house-to-house canvassing of Members in London was proceeding smoothly when the whole pattern of factory
politics was suddenly changed. Until then, it was the Ten Hours
men who had held the initiative, since it was they who were
making the demand for more legislation, their tacit assumption
being that they were going to build upon the foundations Althorp had already laid. Now, overnight, the Government seized
the initiative for itself with a proposal that would destroy much
of the substance of Althorp's law and put back the factory issue
almost to where it had been in the spring of 1833. For on 16
March 1836, Poulett Thomson, President of the Board of Trade
(and a strong opponent of regulation), announced a ministerial
amending bill to the effect that the eight-hour day should henceforth apply to *no child above eleven years of age*. In other words,
the twelve-year-olds were now to be classed as 'young persons'
with a twelve-hour working day, meal times, of course, excluded.

The effect was astonishing. From Leeds to Glasgow, the operatives 'rose in a mass,' says Philip Grant, 'as if ignited by spontaneous combustion,' for the Government's proposal would not only
defer indefinitely the chance of a ten-hour day, but also make
permanent the relay system with all the consequences the operatives feared. New Short Time committees sprang into being, old

ones were quickened, and night after night demonstrations of protest were held. Petitions against the bill poured into the House of Commons. The Yorkshire organization, which had been somewhat lagging with its agitation until this moment, now became frantically active. Fourteen mass meetings followed in the Riding in quick succession, including one that packed Christ Church, Bradford, to the aisles. Oastler at last had an outlet again for all his pent-up energies, going from platform to platform pouring out his indignation with unsurpassed eloquence. Day after day Bull followed in his train, denouncing, organizing, and planning. Bull even tried to get a Memorial to the Queen asking her to intervene against the bill; but the Lord Chamberlain wrote to say that the Queen must adhere to her rule not to interfere in politics 'which, as a female, Her Majesty feels she has neither the right nor ability to discuss.'

Not since the Royal Commission left the north had there been such an explosion of anger. No longer did the operatives call themselves 'petitioners' in their appeals to the public: now they were 'remonstrants.' And a good many were coming to think that the Glasgow *Liberator* was right when it said that the days for agitating were over and the hour for a general strike had come.

The accompanying newspaper controversy reached a new pitch of bitterness. All the old arguments from both sides were bandied back and forth once more as they had been in the autumn of 1830, and all the old personal abuse as well. The *Mercury* renewed its denunciation of Oastler as a mischief maker and a revolutionary, and informed its readers that the workers had at last seen through his Tory machinations and were asking for an eleven-hour day. The satellite journals echoed these observations. Oastler came back with a sizzling retort. Why, he asked, had Baines advised against public meetings to air the question, and resorted to 'hole and corner' gatherings in the mills, if he was so confident that public opinion now repudiated the ten-hour demand? And who was Baines, of all people, to protest against violence when 'that consummate hypocrite' himself, not four years since, had openly urged citizens to intimidate the Government by refusing to pay their taxes?

A dozen other personal brawls swirled like the eddies in a flood torrent. Bull in particular came in for more contumely than he had ever before received, and none trounced him more roundly than did a brother parson from Halifax, named Gilmour, who called him a 'declaimer' consorting with the rabble and a participator in 'riotous assemblies and Bacchanalian orgies.' Every week fresh pamphlets, placards, and open letters appeared on the streets, and in issue after issue the journals lashed one another. The *Manchester Advertiser* barely deviated from the general standard when it characterized the *Manchester Guardian* as 'the common heap in which every purse-proud booby shoots his basket of dirt and falsehood . . . foul prostitute and dirty parasite of the worst portion of the mill owners.'

¶ 6

The crucial debate on the second reading of the Government's bill took place on 9 May. The President of the Board of Trade made an unconvincing showing, for his task was to repudiate one of the central affirmations in the Royal Commission's *Report* which had made possible the ministerial victory in 1833.[4] The *Report* had declared that 'nature' set the age of 13 for the beginning of adulthood, and upon that revelation Althorp's Act had been posited. Now Thomson strove to show that economic interest required childhood to end at the age of 12 and hence that economics superseded nature as a legislative guide.

The debate was long and comprehensive: so comprehensive, in fact, that the report of the 25 speeches could serve as a manual of current economic doctrines. Three years earlier, the findings of the Royal Commission had proved so compelling that a negligible margin had been left wherein persuasion might operate on the floor of the House. But this repudiation by the Government of part of the findings it had so recently extolled created a situation of considerably greater fluidity. The resulting discussion may be likened to a fugue of ideas in which pragmatism, prophecy, principle, and prejudice served as recurrent themes upon which the various speakers extemporized in turn, albeit not without many a discord. The four themes were sharply articulated. Poulett

[4] See above, p. 244.

Thomson opened with the argument that the full labor of the thirteen-year-olds was a practical necessity both for industry itself and for working-class families, and that 'sixty-nine hours of labour per week would not prove injurious to children above the age of twelve.' Dr. Bowring, Bentham's friend and biographer, prophesied disaster to Britain's overseas trade if the Government persisted in interfering with the self-regulating processes of economic life. (This was the speech in which that ideologue hailed the smuggler as 'a public benefactor' for promoting free trade.) Bennett of Wiltshire raised more fundamental issues by asking whether a consideration of human resources ought not to be included in any calculation of national wealth, and whether the principles determining public policy were to be restricted to the mathematics of an accountant's audit. To which Charles Villiers replied with the dictum that 'there is no necessary connection between wisdom and benevolence.' Most of the speakers expressed disquiet concerning the flouting of the law. The facts were fully admitted: but both sides cited them as the clinching argument for their own case.

Thomson carried the reading by a mere 2 votes—178 against 176. An excited Oastler in the gallery lifted up his hands and cried: 'O God, they are conquered!' And they were, for the embarrassed Government interpreted the nominal victory as a virtual defeat and immediately dropped the bill. 'With wondering incredulity,' said the Reverend William Hill of Bradford, 'will posterity receive the story.' At least one unhappy member of the Cabinet felt much the same way. 'The debate was, to me at least, very disagreeable,' wrote Sir John Cam Hobhouse in his memoirs. 'We carried Thomson's motion only by two: a cruel measure.'

¶ 7

The Ten Hours men were enormously encouraged by this result, for they had hardly dared to hope for such an outcome. Oastler, at least, had been firmly convinced that the opposition could not get within 100 of the Government's muster. But now that the apathy had lifted and the old fighting spirit was revived, it was agreed that the movement must press forward towards its final objective with every possible effort. The campaign of meetings was continued without pause, therefore, and the work of the committees sustained at full tension. 'This is probably the last tug we shall have to make,' Oastler told one of the gatherings. And in a powerful manifesto vibrant with the new resolve the returned delegates endorsed that opinion. 'We have come back victorious,' they declared, 'in spite of open foes and rotten friends; but we have not got, and they say we never shall have, the Ten Hours Bill. We say we will have either *that*, or something else a great deal more and a good deal better. And what say you?'

It was this militancy—growing rather than diminishing with the passing weeks—that distinguished the campaign of 1836 from any that had gone before. A new spirit was now working in the ranks of the northern industrial workers. Oastler was always responsive to the operatives' mood, and his speeches at this time plainly register the change.

A fortnight after the division in the House, more than 5,000 people assembled before the Court House at Bradford to resume the agitation. Walker and Rand, the promoters of the first Talbot Inn meeting, were there as well as Fielden and Bull and Oastler. The suggestion of direct action was unconcealed. 'Will you support me,' asked Fielden, 'in saying that if you cannot get a Ten Hours Bill by act of Parliament you will *in another way?*' And the shout that went up left no room for doubt. After such encouragement, of course, Oastler developed the theme with the diapason stop out. The time for pleading was past and the hour for deeds was at hand, he told the audience: 'if they don't give us a Ten Hours Bill quietly, we will *strike and do better.*'

At Leeds the following evening he continued the adjuration before another huge crowd:

I said at Bradford I would have a strike among the little ones, and I will too. . . If they don't give us a Ten Hour Bill the children shall not work: that is all. . . I will petition no more; I will reason no more. I am tired of reasoning. I am King of the Factory Children, and I can and will do it. . .

Oastler had now completely resumed his old domination of the platform. Halls and market places were thronged at his every appearance. By midsummer 1836, there was no longer any doubt that he had really abandoned the tactics of moral suasion for the advocacy of direct action. But to suppose that this transition was peculiar to him alone would lead to a radically false perspective of the times. There was an enhancement of belligerency all round. It was as marked in Lancashire as it was in Yorkshire, and as discernible in the comments of Fielden as in the outpourings of Stephens. When delegates from all the manufacturing districts conferred at Manchester on 16 June to consider the next step, they unanimously resolved to demand the Ten Hours Bill immediately, under threat of the workers taking the law into their own hands by limiting the working day for themselves. Nor was violent talk limited to one side. Though employers expressed the utmost abhorrence of the operatives' pronouncements, they too, in a good many instances, were provocatively militant. A large number of mill owners considered they had every right to circumvent a law that interfered with their business. The violence of the operatives' language was in large measure a response to this attitude. After Thomson's amendment had been defeated, the newspapers reported sundry meetings whereat masters openly discussed what steps they would next take to destroy Althorp's Act; and a big gathering of Halifax spinners in August voted to consider a scheme 'to stop every mill in England three months, and thus to force the Government to alter the law.' That was the spirit against which the continued campaign was being directed.

Whether the Government's recent discomfiture really led the Ten Hours men to expect they could get their bill carried on its next introduction is not certain. Hindley at any rate was under no such illusion, as his repeated pessimistic warnings made clear. But he had promised to bring forward the measure at the earliest opportunity and he intended to keep his word. When, however, a week after the Manchester conference he moved for leave to introduce the bill, his reception by the House as well as by the Government was so unsympathetic that after hurried consultation with Ashley, Fielden, and the other leaders he decided to withdraw his motion. Lord John Russell, the Home Secretary, gave a pledge that Althorp's Act would be more vigorously enforced in future, and for the moment that had to suffice. Back in the districts, therefore, the Short Time Committees gave their chief energies to watching and reporting on the observance of the law by the mill owners in their locality, and to continuing their propaganda in preparation for another effort the following session.

¶ 8

For Oastler there was no pause: with letter, speech, and pamphlet he continued feverishly throughout the summer and autumn. He quarreled with the Leeds Operatives' Conservative Association for its lukewarmness towards factory legislation; he castigated his old friend Sir John Beckett for voting in support of Thomson's amendment; and he denounced the wiles of the law-evading mill owners. In a powerful pamphlet entitled *The Unjust Judge* he showed up the flagrant bias of the Leeds Bench. A local mill owner who admitted to having grossly violated the law had been let off with a caution; but a local printer named Hobson, caught publishing an unstamped journal, had been given a six months' sentence. It was a theme not unsuited to Oastler's range of epithets and he took full advantage of the opportunity it offered. But the outstanding feature of these months was his obsession with the idea of direct action, an obsession that seemed to feed upon his new-found friendship with Stephens.

These two made their first public appearance together at the end of August on the occasion of a pageant organized by the Ashton Short Time Committee in Oastler's honor. As a spectacle it almost equaled the Factory King's triumphal entry into Manchester 4 years before. Oastler was met by the Committee on the outskirts of the town and led in procession, with bands blaring, through streets festooned with streamers and packed with cheering crowds. Before him was carried a banner bearing a verse that Stephens had written for the occasion:

> Receive, great Oastler, all that we can give.
> You in our own and children's hearts shall live.
> On your behalf shall many a prayer arise:
> Your fame shall fill the circle of the skies.

With two such masters on the hustings together, and an audience abandoned to them in advance, it was certain that Ashton

would be given an oratorical exhibition of a rare kind. But the
meeting stands out in the history of the working-class movement
for a more significant reason. In the House of Commons, law
evasion had been a matter for well-bred concern, but in the
shadows of the mills it became a cry to release more explosive
emotions. That night, in making his public declaration of fealty
to Oastler, Stephens for the first time enunciated the social escha-
tology that was later to lead him into strange paths:

We will have every one of them that dares to break the law sent to
the treadmill. And if that will not do, we will have them sent to Botany
Bay. And if they ever come back, we will have them sent to Lancaster
Castle and there hung by the neck. No more drivelling mill owners;
no more of your big words and scowling looks and frightening speeches.
We don't care for you. . . The King has allowed me to touch his hand,
and I have sworn allegiance to Richard, the Factory King. . .

Three weeks later, in the most notorious speech of his career,
Oastler abandoned all remaining restraint and threw down his
supreme challenge to the mill owners. It happened at Blackburn.
The Short Time Committee had organized a big demonstration
to be held in the town theater and had invited Oastler to attend.
When he arrived he found the Committee all agog about an
episode that had just occurred at the local petty sessions which
they wanted him to deal with in his speech. The Blackburn
magistrates were known to be shamefully lax in their application
of the Factory Act, and whenever they conveniently could they
refused to take any information laid before them. On this particular occasion, not only had they declined to hear the case but
one of their number had also been fool enough to say openly:
'That is Oastler's Law: we have nothing to do with that. Take
your complaints to him.' Oastler got the story corroborated and
then went on to the platform in fighting anger.

As was invariably the case when Oastler was billed to speak,
the place was packed to capacity. Even some of the local mill
owners had made reservations, and with them in one of the boxes
were several of the offending magistrates. For sheer dramatic
opportunity the occasion was unique, and Oastler rose to it with
an effectiveness that was to be talked about for many a day to

come. He began quietly enough in his usual conversational style. He told over again the story of the struggle for shorter hours. As his narrative unfolded the tempo quickened and the tension heightened. He spoke of setbacks and disappointments and the partial victory of Althorp's Act: with adroit transition he passed on to the subject of law enforcement and the gravity of the issues it raised. Then he repeated what the Short Time Committee had just told him. Turning to the magistrates in their box he asked if the report were true. But they only laughed. Slowly, impressively, he repeated the question and again they only laughed. He paused. The audience began calling out: 'It is true; they know it; it is true.' He let the cries subside, then moving across the platform he declared to the Justices before him:

Your silence, after my public appeal to you and after the declarations of your neighbours in your hearing, convinces me that I have not been misinformed. You say that the law is mine. I say that it is the law of the land which you have sworn to enforce. If you do not regard your oaths, and if the King of England has not the power to enforce the law, why, then it becomes my duty to explain in your hearing how you stand before the law. You are regardless of your oaths. You are persons holding property, your only title being the law of the land. Now, if the law of the land, intended to protect the lives of the factory children, is to be disregarded and there is to be no power to enforce it, it becomes my duty as the guardian of the factory children to enquire whether, in the eye of the law of England, their lives or your spindles are the most entitled to the law's protection. If the King has not the power to enforce the factory law I must and I will strive to force even you to enforce that law.

Suddenly swinging back to the tense audience he went on

If after this your magistrates should refuse to listen to your complaints under the factory act and again refer you to me, bring with you your children and tell them to ask their grandmothers for a *few of their old knitting needles* which I will instruct them *how to apply to the spindles* in a way which will teach these law-defying mill owner magistrates to have respect even to 'Oastler's law' as they have wrongly designated the factory law.

It was the most daring thing he had ever said in public. Incitement to sabotage!

Throughout the industrial counties the news of this challenge created an immense sensation. The respectable classes were unspeakably shocked, for the vista of possibilities conjured up by Oastler's grave declaration were frightening in the extreme. Under the leadership of the *Manchester Guardian* the 'liberal' papers turned upon him with rage. Making no mention of the magistrates' repudiation of the law, the *Guardian* extracted Oastler's challenging sentences for citation and appended its expressions of horror. It had heard 'nothing so atrociously wicked'; a man who could say such things was 'either a madman or a most hardened and desperate villain'; either his friends should put him under restraint or 'the law should interpose to check the career of wickedness which he seems disposed to run.' Of course Oastler answered all this; but the *Guardian* in printing his reply merely added another onslaught, accusing him of insanity. His subsequent rejoinders it refused to print at all.

Thereupon Oastler turned the speech, the correspondence, and his comments into a pamphlet called *The Law or the Needle,* which he publicized by every means at his command. Not a word would he retract; in fact he made his position more explicit than ever. If you sabotage the law, we will sabotage your machines; if you respect the laws protecting children, we will respect the laws protecting property. The choice is yours and the initiative is yours. But if you persist in violating the law—

I will in that event print a little card about *Needles* and *Sand* and *Rusty Nails,* with proper and with very explicit directions, which will make these law-breakers look about them and repent that they were ever so mad as to laugh at the Law and the King. These cards of mine shall then be the catechism of the factory children. I will take care to have every factory child well instructed in the art of self-defense, and I will make the factory masters bow to the Banner of the Needle.

This outspoken defiance, of course, only exacerbated the bitterness he had provoked. But it was not only the mill owners who were shocked. Many of his dearest friends were profoundly upset, and some of his acquaintances broke with him completely. Ashley announced he was 'exceedingly grieved,' and terminated their correspondence. Hindley angrily proclaimed he would never appear on a platform with Oastler again. Even the loyal Bull was distressed and publicly dissociated himself from the policy of sabotage. But the bitterest pain Oastler had to endure came from the permanent rupture of his friendship with John Wood, the very man who had first opened his eyes to the factory question. Wood's anger was not the kind to vent itself before the public eye, but it was deep and lasting. Oastler's extravagances of the past few months may already have strained affection beyond continuance: we do not know. The fact remains that after the publication of this pamphlet the two men never communicated again. Thus in little over a year Oastler had lost the friendship of both Wood and Sadler, two of his dearest companions. The anguish these two events caused him, however, is beyond the reach of biographical assessment.

Not everyone fled. Stephens still stood by him, endorsing everything he said, and at a spectacular evening demonstration in Huddersfield, in a setting of torchlights and banners, proclaimed as much with blazing rhetoric. What brought deepest solace, however, was Fielden's unshaken loyalty. Until now, the factory magnate and the Factory King had had little intimacy outside the committee room and the meeting hall, but in this hour when Oastler most needed it, Fielden gave reassurance and friendship without stint. Nothing more selfless or more gracious than this gesture is recorded in the whole of Fielden's career.

At Oldham, on 11 November, the campaign of 1836 was brought to a perfervid close. Fielden, Stephens, and Oastler appeared on the platform together, and, despite the fact that all seats had to be paid for, there was not even standing room available when the meeting began. Fielden made one of the greatest speeches of his career—a vehement philippic against the foreign-competition argument and a passionate defense of Oastler. Describing what he personally knew of the Lancashire magistrates' deliberate efforts to frustrate the application of the Factory Law while at the same time employers were straining every legal resource to smash the men's unions, he declared 'it was not possible for men to use language more violent than such conduct merited.' What the workers must do was to build up a penny-a-week strike fund and then at the end of a year 'come out' for a

month. If they did that, he said, 'depend upon it they would
obtain a Ten Hours Bill before the termination of the month's
holiday.'

Oastler's speech defies analysis; and in any case the hour and
the mood lent it those overtones of significance that escape recap-
ture across the years. Never had the man been more angry or
more overwhelming. His hearers were shaken out of their self-
control; they shrieked and they wept; and when he sat down
after one of the most grandiloquent perorations of his life, they
went on cheering until exhaustion alone brought cease. Giving
visible evidence of how deeply he himself had been moved,
Fielden in closing the meeting called it 'as important a speech
as was ever uttered.'

In more senses than one, that speech ended a chapter. It closed
not only the year's campaign but also a definite phase in the
factory agitation. Never again was the movement to be resumed
in quite the same form or with quite the same élan. New resentments and new objectives were about to complicate the pattern
of British working-class politics, permanently altering both Oastler's role and the quality of his appeal. In a personal sense, too,
a chapter ended at Oldham. The strain of the past few months
and the emotional crisis of recent weeks had evidently taxed
Oastler beyond his strength. Suddenly he had a complete breakdown. For nearly two months he was incapacitated, and could
not even make his annual New Year's trip to Norfolk. When he
did get about again, it was to find the overture to the new phase
already beginning.

CHAPTER XXV

The North Repudiates the New Poor Law

FEAR—widespread and primitive fear—was the dominant emotion in the new chapter of proletarian politics that so plainly began in January 1837. Without a full appreciation of this fact there can be no proper understanding of the turbulent happenings of the ensuing three years, for throughout that period the working classes of the industrial districts were in the grip of a demoralizing terror which vented itself in all the manifestations of blind defiance.

What they were afraid of was the workhouse and the New Poor Law. For over two years the Poor Law Commission had been prodigiously active in rural England, getting the new system started, cutting off relief to the able-bodied poor, and setting up workhouses. Resistance had been negligible and the task was now practically finished. In January 1837, therefore, the Commissioners turned their attention to the industrial districts, and their field officers descended upon Lancashire and the West Riding to make the necessary arrangements for putting the law into operation there too. Much had to be done. The old, autonomous parishes had to be surveyed and grouped into the new Unions; Boards of Guardians had to be elected; officers had to be chosen; and workhouse accommodation had to be provided. Not until all these preliminaries had been attended to would it be possible to transfer the powers of the existing Overseers to the new authority and to start applying the workhouse test. But, as was indicated earlier, applying the Act to industrial regions for which it had not been primarily designed was a very different undertaking from applying it to the southern countryside. The tradition of thrift in the north was old and strong, and people prided themselves on not going to the parish for help until they had to.

What little money was spent on poor relief was a sheer necessity to tide men over trade depressions: an essential element, in fact, in a well-established social pattern which kept the labor supply more or less stabilized. And the more acute the oscillations of the trade cycle became, the more essential some such relief was.

Into such a situation came the officers of the Poor Law Commission, proposing to establish a new dispensation. For months apprehension had been mounting among the workers: now their alarm quickly became frantic. To them it seemed as though a cruel and wanton attack was about to be made upon their independence, and, indeed, upon their very livelihood. They knew little about the technical details of the new law. What they did know was that its general intention was to deprive the able-bodied poor of their customary out-door relief, and to give the poor man the choice between going into a wretched workhouse or getting no parish assistance at all. They knew, too, that the Lord Chancellor of England had openly declared that any poor relief was a violation of the laws of nature and the laws of economics. But for tens of thousands of men in the textile districts, to take away parish assistance was to take away the very prop that did sustain their house. Once such men were shut up in a workhouse, segregated from their families, what chance was there of ever finding employment again? No wonder the new scheme hovered over their imaginations like a malignant threat, filling them with blind terror. And as always happens when fear is dominant, rumor fed the emotions out of which it sprang: in this case, grotesque and prolific rumors about barbarities practiced in the newly established southern workhouses. Apart from that, however, enough silly menaces were being uttered by middle-class dignitaries to increase tension anyway. 'Our intention is to make the workhouses as like prisons as possible,' said one of the Assistant Commissioners at a public meeting, 'and to make them as uncomfortable as possible.' Mr. Mott, another of these officials, frankly told Oastler in the course of an argument that 'the object in building these union-houses is to establish therein a discipline so severe and repulsive as to make them a terror to the poor and prevent them from entering.' Statements just as blatant were being made all over the country.

Yet these were by no means the only grounds the workers had for alarm. The Act of 1834 empowered the Poor Law Commissioners to transfer superfluous paupers from districts where they were not wanted to districts where labor was in demand. In their first two annual reports, the Commissioners made much of the success which, they claimed, had attended their efforts to promote migration into Yorkshire and Lancashire. Advertisements proclaiming the advantages of migration had been inserted in country newspapers and an office had been opened in Manchester to distribute the immigrants. Some of the southern Guardians were even employing traveling agents of their own to arrange for the removal of the unemployed from their areas. Such a scheme, of course, in the absence of adequate administrative machinery, lent itself to all manner of abuse, and many were the harrowing stories that were told about cruel frauds perpetrated upon whole families of those deluded unfortunates. But however admirable the intentions of the Commissioners may have been, the already fearful operatives in the factories saw the plan as nothing but a scheme to smash their trade unions and force down wages by a flood of non-union labor. Thus another count was added to the indictment these men brought against the New Poor Law.

And aggravating the whole situation came an acute trade depression, beginning in the latter weeks of 1836 and deepening as the new year advanced: a depression which brought thousands of homes to the verge of starvation. The handloom weavers were the first to be engulfed, but the mill workers were soon involved too. In March 1837, the Prime Minister was warned in a civic petition from Birmingham that 'unless remedial measures be immediately applied, a large proportion of our population will be thrown out of employment.' Four weeks later the *Manchester Times* reported that 'in this town and its neighbourhood many of the factories are working only four days a week, and some thousands of the handloom weavers have been discharged.' And so it went in one industrial center after another. Before many weeks had passed there was hardly an industry that was not in a critical condition, so that the numbers of those caught up in the panic dread of the workhouse swelled to enormous dimensions.

The Government made no effort whatever to allay the workers' fears. No public reassurance was uttered and no hint given that the rigors of the new law would be tempered in any way to meet the crisis. On the contrary, the Assistant Commissioners went to work on their task conscientiously, inflexibly, and (as their reports show) with a superb conviction regarding the fundamental rightness of their mission.

The result was inevitable. The workers struck back with all the resources available in a fierce effort to prevent the new machinery from being set up. Step by step they fought the application of the Act with guerrilla tactics of every kind. First they tried to carry the local elections and pack the Boards of Guardians with members pledged to frustrate the scheme. Then they tried to prevent the necessary officials from being appointed. When these methods proved inadequate they resorted to demonstrations, intimidation, and rioting. And when the Government still continued unshaken in its course, the leaders of resistance openly began talking of civil war and their followers started to lay in stores of arms and ammunition.

All this brought Oastler to the fore again in a new and passionately aggressive role, for since Cobbett's passing no man in England was more completely the embodiment of opposition to the hated law than he. To him resistance did not appear as the undertaking of a new mission, but rather as the continuance of the old one under another banner. As he saw it, the promotion of the New Poor Law and the simultaneous refusal of a Ten Hours Law were but complementary items in a uniform social policy which the Government was bent on pursuing at all costs. Both were inspired by an economic philosophy that put regard for untrammelled capitalist enterprise above all other considerations and thus treated the laborer as but an animate instrument to be bought and sold in the market like any other commodity. Furthermore, he was convinced that once the new scheme had gone into full operation, effective factory regulation would be quite impossible. Some years afterwards, in justifying his stand, he summarized his position this way:

The two questions were, are, and ever must be inseparably connected. It was in evidence that the New Poor Law was intended to be used to perpetuate slavery in factories. The Ten Hours Bill was intended to destroy that slavery. It was in evidence that the New Poor Law was intended to decrease the wages of the factory operatives. The Ten Hours Bill was, as I always believed and maintained, calculated to increase those wages. It was in evidence that the New Poor Law was, by the introduction of the families of agricultural laborers into the factory districts, intended to increase the competition for labor in factories. The Ten Hours Bill was intended and calculated to decrease that competition. For those and for other very weighty reasons we resolved, as I think, most wisely, and I am sure, as Ten Hours Men most consistently, to resist. . . Under my convictions it would, in myself, have been worse than cowardice had I otherwise acted.

This explains not only why Oastler again assumed leadership of the West Riding in such commanding fashion, but also why opposition to the law was so well organized almost from the start. It was the old Ten Hours organization that provided the cadre for resistance. Many of the old Short Time Committees were still in existence, despite the upheavals of the past three years; the Central Committee was still operating from Bradford under Parson Bull's guidance; and most of the men who had led the demonstrations against the Factory Commission in 1833 were still active in the local lodges. A proved and efficient fighting machine was thus already to hand. At the call of Oastler and the other leaders the Ten Hours Movement assumed a new objective. Wherever the Short Time Committees were strongest, therefore, there the struggle was fiercest. So while a uniform strategy was discernible throughout the campaign, there was considerable tactical variation between the different districts under their different leaders. The full story would have to cover innumerable local episodes. But in the last analysis three areas would stand out conspicuously alike for their practical and their symbolic importance. Those three are Huddersfield, where Oastler led the fight; Bradford, where Parson Bull was in command; and Todmorden, where operations were directed by John Fielden.

¶ 1

On Tuesday, 10 January 1837, Alfred Power, Assistant Poor Law Commissioner, came to Huddersfield to have his first meeting with the local Poor Law Overseers. This was the same Power that had made the West Riding survey for the Factory Commission four years before and been given such a rough reception. The reception he met with this time was even less cordial.

Tuesday was Huddersfield's market day, so the town was crowded with folk come in from the surrounding villages. For them Power's visit was a bigger attraction than the traveling entertainers performing in the market square. They were bent on seeing the fun, and a good many were determined to share in it as well. As the hour for the meeting drew near, therefore, they began drifting towards the George Inn, where Power had invited the local officials to meet him. By the time he arrived, conference room and corridors were packed and a large crowd was hanging around outside. To clear the place was manifestly impossible, so Power decided to hold the meeting despite the incursion. Tactfully explaining that there was no immediate intention of putting the new law into force there, but that the Commissioners merely wanted to set up the administrative machinery necessary for applying the Registration Act,[1] he went on to describe the plans for incorporating Huddersfield and its 33 adjacent townships into a single Union. Soon the meeting became lively. Heckling started and men began telling Power what an iniquitous law it was. Power lost his temper and told the gathering he had come to apply the law, not to hear it criticized. Whereupon a certain Christopher Tinker shouted that 'if all the labourers were of his mind, they would mark their names on a bit of lead, put it into a rifle, and send it through the first man that at-

[1] Power used this argument continually. A national system for the registration of births, marriages, and deaths had been enacted by Parliament the previous year. The administration of this Act was to be in the hands of the local Boards of Guardians, who were to divide their areas into registration districts. The Clerk to the Guardians was to be the Superintendent Registrar for the Union, and was to assume the duties of that office the following March. The opponents of the New Poor Law regarded this scheme as a mere trick. 'Your petitioners have seen with scorn and disgust,' said one Lancashire protest, 'the same disregard to moral principle evinced in the low cunning and deceit with which the Commissioners, under the pretext of having no object in view but to carry into effect the Act for the Registration of Births, Marriages and Deaths, have attempted to foist the New Poor Law on those manufacturing districts in which there exists a general conviction that its enforcement will be destructive of the peace of society, and of the security of life and property.'

tempted to put the law into force.' That caused an uproar which made further business impossible. Power angrily snatched up his documents and withdrew, announcing that if he could not get local co-operation he was going ahead with his job anyway.

A mandate for the establishment of the Huddersfield Union was thereupon issued, fixing the election of the Guardians for 10 February, and ordering the new Board to hold its first meeting at the George five days later for the purpose of electing its clerk and other officials.

As soon as the newly elected Board met, the tactics of the opposition were revealed. There had been much irregularity and confusion in the balloting (so much so, indeed, that a month later the Central Commissioners were to order new elections for both Huddersfield and Leeds). Taking advantage of this fact, one of the ex officio members of the Board—a Tory magistrate named Joseph Armitage, who was a close friend of Oastler's—moved that all business be adjourned until 3 April. A long wrangle followed in which several Whig manufacturers vehemently fought Armitage's proposal, but in spite of this the motion was carried. So the meeting broke up with no clerk appointed. During the next few weeks various communications arrived addressed to 'The Clerk of the Huddersfield Guardians,' but, as the Tory journals gleefully reported, 'since no official of that kind can be found, the epistles of the Honorable Commissioners remain in sealed repose.' Other Boards were urged to follow the same tactics. 'We cannot sufficiently commend the excellent and providential arrangements of the Huddersfield Guardians,' said one Halifax newspaper, 'sincerely wishing their laudable and sagacious example had been generally followed.'

Resistance inside the board room, however, constituted only a part of the campaign. From the day of Power's arrival opposition out of doors rose steadily, receiving a tremendous fillip with the appearance of the latest idol of the discontented, the genial and belligerent Feargus O'Connor.

O'Connor, now in his forty-third year, came from an Irish landed family which for many years had been associated with various kinds of revolutionary activity. Educated at Trinity College, Dublin, and then called to the Irish Bar, he had been returned to the House of Commons in the 1832 election as one of the followers of the 'Liberator,' Daniel O'Connell. He had voted for Ashley in the Ten Hours divisions and had been one of that miscellaneous band which had opposed the New Poor Law to the end. After a fierce quarrel with O'Connell (and sooner or later he quarreled with almost everyone with whom he had personal dealings), he was unseated in 1836. For awhile he lived at Hammersmith and participated in metropolitan radical movements. Then in August 1836 he set out on a tour of Scotland and northern England to exploit the seething discontents of the industrial areas.

Almost immediately he won an astonishing popularity. He was a born orator with a rich voice and consummate mastery of all the tricks of the platform. For all the personal animosities in which he was continually getting himself involved, he had a remarkable gift for capturing the loyalty and affection of men in the mass. He had the temperament as well as the talents of the demagogue; yet beneath the obvious appeal of his wit, blarney, and scalding invective, there was a genuine impulse of pity for suffering wretchedness. Within four months of the start of his peregrinations he was being hailed everywhere in the north as a leader.

He reached Huddersfield on the Saturday following Power's arrival. His fame, of course, had long preceded him; the local Radical Association therefore made elaborate preparations to give him a magnificent reception and asked Oastler to attend as well. A huge concourse went out at dusk to await the coming of his coach. He was put into an open carriage drawn by four horses and led by torchbearers, bands, and banners to the steps of the Cloth Hall, where (according to one hostile account) more than 8,000 people had assembled. After receiving an Address from the Radicals of Huddersfield, accompanied by numerous fulsome tributes to his genius, he returned thanks with one of his long, spicy orations on 'the glorious principles of Radicalism,' which had captured the crowd at every stopping-place on his tour.

Oastler came onto the platform while O'Connor was speaking and as the two men met a mighty roar went up from the throng. This was Oastler's first appearance since his illness and he was still in a very nervous condition. The speech he gave when O'Connor had finished had an hysterical tone not to be found in even the most denunciatory of his previous harangues. It was one passionate plea to the people to do all in their power to prevent the New Poor Law from ever going into operation at Huddersfield.

I ask not whether all these things are as Christ would have them be. But I come to tell you that if the diabolical Poor Law Act . . . is about to be thrust on these districts, *I will resist its introduction—I will resist its workings—I will not submit to it! It is an act of* Treason *against the constitution, against Christianity, against the State, and against the King, as well as against the Poor.*

At one point he broke down completely, betraying a loss of mastery that is itself indicative of the severity of the strain he had undergone in the past three months. Incomparably inferior though it was, however, to the great speeches of the earlier campaigns, it made an excellent pamphlet when revised and expanded. Published by Henry Hetherington under the title *Damnation, eternal damnation to the fiend-begotten, coarser-food New Poor Law,* it served as a general handbook of revolt and became one of the best known of Oastler's writings.

Everywhere in the Riding it was the same story: fear turning into anger as Power went from place to place to set up the new administrative machinery, and anger turning into class war as more and more men were thrown out of work by the spreading depression. The Ten Hours leaders were incessantly active, stiffening the will to resist. Chapels and public houses in remote villages rang to the denunciation of itinerant speakers while Oastler and Bull, Stocks and Pitkeithley led demonstrations in the larger towns. There was nothing haphazard about any of this: it was all carefully planned, and as the weeks went by the organization became more efficient.

At the beginning of March, a little-publicized but highly important conference of Yorkshire delegates was held at Bradford. Ostensibly it was called to consider the advisability of launching a new Ten Hours demand, since the Manchester Committee had already decided the time was ripe for such a step. Actually, how-

ever, it turned into a conference for the more effective promotion
of Anti-Poor Law efforts. The outcome was far reaching. The
delegates unanimously decided to establish committees of resistance in every village. These were to be co-ordinated by larger
committees in every Union, and these again by a new county
Central Committee, with headquarters in Bradford, under the
chairmanship of Oastler's friend William Stocks, the radical
Chief Constable of Huddersfield. In addition it was decided to
open a campaign fund and to have paid organizers constantly on
circuit through the Riding. Considerable secrecy veiled the operation of this scheme, just as it had veiled the staff work for resisting the Factory Commission in 1833; all that the public saw were
the outward results. But there can be little reasonable doubt that
the events of the next 18 months were largely shaped by the
calculated intentions of this new organization.

Thereafter, towns and villages vied with one another in the
militancy and tactics of their opposition. At Keighley matters
became riotous. There a vigorous Committee under the Ten
Hours veterans Wildman and Weatherhead made advance preparations for giving Power the same sort of attentions they had
given him when he came about the factory business in 1833.
Knowing that a few days earlier a false report of his arrival had
brought a huge crowd into the streets to make a demonstration,
Power slipped unobtrusively into the town and went to the
Mechanics Institute, where local officials were assembled by
arrangement. One of these officials, however, was an active member of the Short Time Committee and gave the plan away.
Within a very short time a throng was outside the Institute clam-
oring to be admitted. So threatening did the crowd become that
the conclave within judged it unwise to refuse the demonstrators
admittance. As soon as the doors were unlocked the place was
overrun. The presiding magistrate appealed to the men to withdraw and let the business proceed, but they refused to move;
instead, they started heckling Power and telling him what they
thought of the Act. Wildman announced that they were determined never to allow 'a Poor Law Bastille' to be built in Keighley,
and all Power's attempts to reply were drowned in catcalls and
hisses. Then Weatherhead took from his pocket a pamphlet that

he insisted on reading aloud giving 21 reasons why the New Poor Law was 'unscriptural, unconstitutional and atheistical.' Power tried to stop him, but that only made the crowd more ugly, so he had to submit. To punctuations of wild applause, Weatherhead read the indictment through to the end and then announced that it came from Richard Oastler's *Damnation, eternal damnation.* By this time a huge throng was surrounding the building waiting for Power to come out. Only slowly could he make his way to the hotel, according to one eyewitness, 'amidst the most deafening shouts, groans and execrations of the populace.' They jostled and pushed him and tore off his overcoat; and when he finally mounted his horse they 'hooted him out of town at the gallop.'

During the course of the following week, the newspapers reported, every one of the thirty-odd townships in the proposed Huddersfield Union held meetings to plan the steps to be taken next, for Power was due to come to Huddersfield for the adjourned meeting of the Guardians on 3 April.

This second meeting of the Huddersfield Board ran to much the same pattern as the first and proved just as abortive. Once again a turbulent crowd surrounded the hotel and forced its way into the conference room in defiance of all Power's appeals. They did not intend, one of their spokesmen told the Commissioner, to have 'their liberties as ratepayers legislated away in a hole and corner manner.' They wanted to keep an eye on the proceedings and make sure that none of their elected representatives betrayed them by succumbing to the blandishments of the man from London. The moment a chairman had been chosen (he was a Whig business man named Swaine), someone moved that the Board adjourn for another two months. All morning the wrangle went on with the onlookers freely participating, and not a scrap of business was transacted. The mob outside grew impatient and after the dinner interval tried to rush the building. The police barely held them, and only a magistrate's threat to read the Riot Act prevented matters from getting out of hand. Throughout the afternoon the abuse and execrations continued. At last, as dusk was falling, Power decided to put the crucial resolutions. The decision to adjourn was carried by 19 votes to 11, with 9 abstaining. And despite all Power's persuasions and threats, the even more important resolution to appoint a clerk to officiate in the interim was defeated by 21 to 19. 'So the law is a dead letter for two months longer,' a local paper reported. For once the *Mercury* and the *Intelligencer* were in agreement when they said it was going to be a difficult job to get the Act started in Huddersfield at all.

¶ 2

With his strength returning, Oastler flung himself into the fray with abandon. Friends of his, such as the Tory magistrate Armitage, sat on many of the Boards of Guardians, so he was kept fully informed of all that went on in the different Unions and could direct the resources of the Central Committee accordingly. His public appearances were invariably spectacular as he went about the Riding on his missions of incitement, and wherever his coming was announced people flocked to hear him. Always it was the same message he gave: the simple story of a happier England that once had been, when the recognized ties of mutual obligation bound men together into a commonwealth—a tacit contract sealed by the old Poor Law of 43 Elizabeth, which the capitalists for their own evil purposes were now seeking to abrogate. The Government was avowedly being conducted in the interests of these upstarts, he kept saying; what the people had to do was fight for the preservation of the ancient principles and the ancient ways.

This sort of talk gravely displeased Oastler's employer. Thornhill had once been persuaded to overlook his steward's embarrassing defiance of a neighboring landlord,[2] but open resistance to the Government was a very different matter.

The first hint of strained relations came early in April. On their own initiative, the parishioners of Fixby decided to oppose the New Poor Law by refusing to elect a Guardian from their township, and wrote to their landlord notifying him of their determination. Oastler knew what risks they were running by making such a gesture and warned them plainly. Thornhill was just as much of an autocrat over his own tenants as Sir John Ramsden was in Huddersfield, and if the whim took him would not hesitate

---

[2] See above, p. 191 ff.

JOSEPH RAYNER STEPHENS

Richard Oastler

RICHARD OASTLER, 'THE FACTORY KING,' AFTER HIS DISMISSAL FROM HIS
STEWARDSHIP

to evict those who opposed his wishes. Immediately he received the statement from the Fixby villagers, therefore, he sent Oastler a notice for circulation, commanding the tenants to appoint a Guardian. Accompanying the order was a curt note to Oastler himself saying,

I am sorry to have received the determination of the Fixby tenants. What appointing a guardian has to do with the merits of the bill, I know not. You will forward the enclosed to them.

Oastler at once replied:

I have this day received yours of the 11th inst., with your letter to the Fixby tenants. The letter I will deliver tomorrow. I have not, nor shall I read it, although it is unsealed. I know not what the tenants wrote to you, nor will I, in any way, interfere in knowing anything about it. I can only forfeit everything, even life, if needful, rather than, in any way, sanction the diabolical New Poor Law in any shape. The landlords may think it a good joke; but I know that it will, if enforced, put an end to rent days. I may be thought insane, but time will prove who are in their senses. . .

I have done my best for years to inform you of the real state of these districts. You have real property here, and I conceive that the present measure is making it nil. As for my own cast in the die, I care not one rush; but I do care for the aristocracy and the institutions of this my native country. If this accursed law is to be countenanced, then away with rents—I am sure of it. The 'appointing of guardians' is sanctioning the law, and my determination is, to lose life before I will do that. I fancy that I see you smile—but I know what I say.

What the tenants may do, I know not; but I shall indeed regret, if after all, their landlord should frighten them into the surrender of their rights, to the base and hateful three Commissioners. But it is of no use my writing about these matters—you cannot understand me. My living is in your hands—my conscience is my own.

That was the nearest Oastler had yet come to defying his employer, and it was only the beginning of the dispute. Month after month the correspondence continued, with Oastler striving to make the Squire see things from his point of view and the Squire (who knew nothing of local conditions and had not even been in the Riding for over 20 years) remaining obdurate. An open rupture seemed inevitable. Yet opinionated and irascible

though he was, Thornhill could not act too precipitately. Oastler
had become too big a public figure to be treated as a mere
servant: the backing he was getting from the local Tory gentry
as well as from several members of the House of Lords was by
no means inconsiderable; and as the months went by the support
he received from the London *Times* became increasingly enthusiastic. On top of all that, while resentment against the New
Poor Law was still rising, came a further enhancement of his
position with an invitation to stand as a parliamentary candidate.

¶ 3

The borough of Huddersfield was plunged into another by-
election by the sudden death of the sitting Whig Member, Blackburne, who had defeated Sadler in the memorable struggle three
years before.

By this time, the disposition of political forces in Huddersfield
was pretty accurately known. First created a parliamentary constituency by the Reform Act of 1832, it had since then experienced
three electoral contests and returned a Whig each time. In all 3
cases the voting had been remarkably uniform, with the Whig
vote varying from 241 to 263 and the Radical from 108 to 152.
The Tory voter had evidently kept away from the poll in the two
straight contests, for in the only triangular fight held (when
Sadler had been the third candidate) the Tory poll of 147 had
made no appreciable difference to these figures. It was obvious,
therefore, that only by a coalition of the Tory and Radical parties
such as Oastler had always pleaded for could the Whig dominion
be broken; but the complications that had attended Sadler's candidacy showed how remote were the chances for such a union.

The Whigs found their candidate without any trouble. The
man they chose was Edward Ellice, the twenty-six-year-old
nephew of Lord Grey, the late Prime Minister: as sound a choice
as could possibly have been made. On the other hand, both the
Tory and the Radical committees had great difficulty in reaching
a decision. For several days there was feverish coming and going
as one prospective candidate after another turned down the invitation extended to him. Finally, after all the efforts of the Tory

committee had failed to find a candidate in the ranks of wealth and breeding, it was decided to offer the nomination to Oastler, the popularity of whose appeal was beyond question. And at almost the same hour, though entirely independently, the Radical Committee made the same decision.

On the morning of Wednesday, 26 April, therefore, two separate deputations went to Fixby to present their requisitions. They arrived at the Hall together and in a joint ceremony made their offer. Upon Oastler's acceptance, John Whitacre, the local Tory mill owner, pinned on his breast the blue rosette of Toryism, and William Stocks, the Chief Constable, affixed the white rosette of Radicalism. Oastler, of course, was in transports of delight. The fusion he had so long desired had really come about at last, and he himself was to be the embodiment of it. Perhaps, as he said, the Fixby Hall Compact might serve after all as the model for a still wider federation of effort.

At once he sat down to compose an election address summarizing his political principles. It was rushed to the printers before midday and by late afternoon was being paraded throughout the borough by sandwich men accompanied by bands. The same evening, after a preliminary parade of the town, he held his first election meeting outside the Druids Inn. According to the *Leeds Times*, more than 10,000 people turned out to hear him, the huge crowd packing the alleys and sidestreets far beyond the range of the speaker's voice.

Two days later the Radical Committee put out their own election manifesto. As a document it is even more revealing of the current mood and the quality of Oastler's appeal than is the candidate's own address:

Why do the Radicals support Mr. Oastler, who designates himself an Ultra Tory?

1st, Because he is a strenuous advocate for equal rights and equal laws, which are the very essence of the Radical creed.

2nd, Because he would be an efficient and practical member; and it is time to distinguish between words and deeds, promisers and performers, and to cling to honest, straight-forward friends, rather than shuffling time-serving adventurers, nicknamed 'liberals.'

3rd, Because he is our neighbour, and acquainted with the wants and wishes of the great majority of the inhabitants of the borough, and his previous conduct is to us a sufficient guarantee, that he would do his duty.

4th, Because he has worked many years with the Radicals of this Borough without fee, and indeed with great pecuniary and personal sacrifices, for the attainment of several measures, and is willing to work with good men and true of all parties, and we believe he will not desert us in Parliament.

5th, Because we wish to achieve the independence of the Borough, and rescue it from the degrading influence of mere Whiggery, and of peculating John of Canal-Due Notoriety[3] and Mr. O. is the man who will endeavour to break through the Whig Boroughmonger's magic circle, and give the parish two members, instead of the Whig Lord his truckling nominee.

6th, Because, after much deliberation among the Radicals themselves, they have found that neither of their former Candidates have the slightest chance, under present circumstances, of being returned; and therefore our choice has fallen upon Mr. Oastler as the likeliest man to obtain a majority of votes; or at once to throw ourselves into the hands of our declared enemies, who, with all their liberality, cry out 'beware of further organic changes,'—now that they can pass 'Coarser Food and Starvation Laws' and every way oppress the labouring man.

7th, Because he is our champion advocate for shortening the time of infant labour in factories. And

Lastly, Because he is the determined opponent of the New Poor Law *Amendment* Act, which declares the labourers to be 'surplus' and ought to be 'starved off': for which purpose they have created their hideous Bastilles, in which husband is to be separated from wife, child from parent, and fed upon *Fifteenpence-halfpenny* per week, a law which will destroy all gradation in Society:—and further to keep down population they have contrived the Bastardy clause for the purpose of

[3] A reference to the excessive canal dues which old Sir John had been charging on his Ramsden Canal. Oastler's exposure of this little scandal in 1835 had resulted in a lowering of tariff rates in conformity with the charter of incorporation.

throwing all the burden upon the weaker sex, while the villain seducer is allowed to chuckle on unscathed—(poor out-lawed woman!) such enactments having a clear tendency to produce the horrid crimes of female suicide and infanticide.

Therefore we support Oastler: for to support such a man, even expediency itself becomes the consummation of principle, being to all intents and purposes the wisest course open for our adoption.

Committee Room, King Street
April 28th, 1837

In other words, the Radicals of Huddersfield were not only taking to heart the lessons of the 1834 fiasco but were also going to make the contest part of their campaign against the New Poor Law.

Strangely enough, the Leeds Radicals disapproved of Oastler's candidature. It was a curious exchange of roles between the neighboring boroughs. In the case of Sadler, the Leeds Radical Association had enthusiastically supported the proposal for a Tory-Radical alliance in 1832, whereas the Huddersfield Radicals had disastrously repudiated a similar suggestion when it had been made to them twelve months later. Now with Oastler standing, the Huddersfield men were all for a popular front against Whiggery while Leeds talked loudly about the purity of political principles. True, Oastler was a kindly and well-meaning man whose labors were to be warmly commended, said the *Leeds Times*, but he was 'a fanatical Churchman and a Winchelsea Tory'; no lasting benefit could come to the working classes by sending such a man to Westminster, however benevolent his intentions.

The Huddersfield men remained unshaken by this reasoning, however. Support for Oastler rose to a feverish intensity. Night after night the wildest enthusiasm was shown at crowded meetings both in the town itself and in the outlying villages. A mass of literature poured from the presses. 'The walls have been literally covered with placards,' said the hostile *Mercury* in admitting that the bulk of the populace followed Oastler. Stephens toured the constituency telling his hearers to boycott all shopkeepers and publicans who showed any sign of succumbing to

Ramsden's landlordly persuasions. Workers' delegates were sent from 14 Lancashire towns to work on Oastler's behalf. The Whig papers abused Oastler as an incendiary, an assassin, and a madman, and reminded the voters of *The Law or the Needle*. Oastler responded in kind and went from meeting to meeting denouncing 'the bloody, base and brutal Whigs,' who had transported the Dorchester laborers, frustrated factory reform, and passed the iniquitous Poor Law Act, all in the interests of capitalism. As for Ellice, he could scarcely get a hearing anywhere, and more than once his gatherings were broken up in a shower of dirt and missiles. The *Mercury* devoted seven columns to the story, and told how gangs of working-class women were going from shop to shop threatening to withdraw their patronage if the proprietors would note vote for Oastler. Sixty special constables were sworn in to help keep order, and just before nomination day the Justices took the additional precaution of asking for a body of Dragoons to be moved near the town in case of untoward happenings.

Nomination day, 5 May, was an Oastler carnival. Bull and Stephens were with their leader on the platform, along with the local Short Time Committee and several Tory manufacturers. Below them was an enormous throng of people and a veritable forest of blue and white banners adorned with apposite slogans. The chairman of the Radical Committee made the nomination and the chairman of the Tory Committee seconded. Oastler in his reply rose to the fullest expectations of his vociferous supporters with as aggressive a fighting speech as he had ever given. By the time he had finished the crowd was so excited that it refused to let the Whig candidate speak at all until Oastler himself appealed for fair play. Young Ellice, who was rather a colorless figure anyway, thus found himself in a singularly unhappy position. And when he frankly declared himself opposed to the Ten Hours Bill and admitted he 'knew little' about the Poor Law question, even Oastler's appeals could not quell the uproar that resulted.

A stranger coming into the constituency and estimating the outcome of the contest merely on the basis of the visible manifestations of feeling would have thought Oastler's return was assured. Even the *Mercury* seemed afraid that Oastler had at least an even chance of winning. But most of those who had been tramping the streets in the daily processions and shouting themselves hoarse in the riotous meetings were not ten-pound householders and thus had no vote. Only some 700 of the 10,000 inhabitants of the borough qualified for the franchise, and they were not the sort of people to make themselves conspicuous in public demonstrations. Despite appearances, therefore, there could be no certainty about the result until the last hour: a fact that only served to sustain the tension.

Saturday, 6 May, was election day. From sunrise onwards the streets of Huddersfield were thronged with Oastler's supporters bedecked with favors and insignia. Bands blared, beer flowed, and the mob made merry with songs and horseplay. So great was the excitement that Oastler deemed it wisest to stay indoors and have hourly reports brought to him about the way the poll was going.

At half-past eight Ellice was leading by 21 votes; two hours later the lead had increased to 59; by midday it had dropped to 46, and during the afternoon it fell still lower. But at dusk it began to rise again and when the poll closed at nightfall Ellice had been returned by a majority of 50. The final figures were:

Ellice 340
Oastler 290
    Ellice's majority 50

Oastler had done remarkably well. He had polled more than the combined votes of Sadler and Wood in 1834: more, indeed, than any previously successful candidate. If only faction did not lift its head again, here was substantial cause for hope for the next contest. Unfortunately, however, in the bitterness of his disappointment Oastler was incapable of looking at it in that light and made a sad exhibition of himself as a loser. Speaking at great length and in very bad style when the result was formally declared the following Monday morning, he attributed his defeat both to the presence of the military and to the intervention of Sir John Ramsden, who 'forced his tenants with unfeeling words and faltering tongues to say "Ellice" when in Heaven their vote was registered "Oastler." ' Later on he got his friend Duncombe to present a petition to Parliament asking that the election be annulled, though nothing came of the gesture. Whereupon the *Mercury*, obviously relieved at the outcome, gave vent to one of the most ferocious onslaughts upon him it had ever made. The 'incendiary' who taught children to sabotage machinery had now got his deserts, it declared. He was 'a foul-mouthed and truculent railer' who needed to be kept in his place.

CHAPTER XXVI

Defiance Becomes Turbulent

FOR all that it meant to Oastler in a personal sense, the by-election was merely an episode in the campaign against the New Poor Law and its outcome in no way affected the course of that struggle. Even had Oastler won, the immediate objective would have remained the same, namely, to prevent the law from going into operation in the chief boroughs of the industrial districts. And that meant keeping popular sentiment at a pitch of militant determination the whole time.

The vast county meeting at Hartshead Moor near Bradford on Whitsun Monday, 15 May, was held solely to forward that purpose. It had been agreed upon at the Bradford delegates' conference a couple of months earlier,[1] the idea being to organize as spectacular a demonstration against the New Poor Law as the Ten Hours men had staged with their pilgrimage to York in '32. The delegates had wanted to make it the most comprehensive gathering of workers ever held in Yorkshire, and that is what it proved to be. Fielden and O'Connor were there, along with Oastler and Stephens; Hetherington and O'Brien and Robert Owen came up from London to stand side by side with Stocks and Pitkeithly and a host of local luminaries. According to the *Mercury,* there were assembled 'the most violent, perverse and wrong-headed men that could be collected together in England.' Every branch of the working-class movement was represented: trade unionists and Ten Hours men, Radicals and secularists, co-operatives and friendly societies. As always with these mass demonstrations, the journalists' calculations of the size of the gathering varied greatly. The Whig press put it at something under a hundred thousand, the Tory at a quarter of a million.

[1] See above, p. 339.

But no one denied it was the biggest thing the Oastlerites had yet undertaken.

For once the men had luck with the weather. The plan they followed was exactly the same as the one they had used for the march on York. From every village and town in the Riding, contingents set out at dawn to converge upon Bradford, and by midday all the divisions had assembled at their assigned places on the moor. For the next six and a half hours the torrent of oratory poured in full spate. The affair had been admirably organized and the day ended without the slightest untoward incident having occurred.

All the newspapers gave it publicity. The derisive sneers of the *Mercury's* report, however, greatly angered those who had taken part. During the course of the following week, therefore, the more militant committees directed this anger to the promotion of still more demonstrations. Effigies of Baines bearing Cobbett's designation, 'the Great Liar of the North,' were paraded through the various towns and then immolated. At York they rode him about the city on a donkey and ended up by shooting him with great ceremony; at Huddersfield they burnt him at the stake in the market place; at Heckmondwike they cremated him outside the house of one of the chapel deacons who was a local agent for the *Mercury*. It all helped to keep resentment mobilized.

In popular estimation, however, it was the fate of Huddersfield that was going to determine the outcome of the larger struggle. Huddersfield was Oastler's stronghold, and as such served as the supreme symbol of resistance. If the line broke there, there was little chance of its holding elsewhere. That was why each meeting of its Guardians was regarded as a major engagement on which the issue of the entire campaign might turn.

Twice already Power had been thwarted in his attempts to get a clerk appointed and to set up the necessary administrative apparatus. Now, three weeks after the Hartshead Moor demonstration, the third meeting of the Board was to be held with the same items on the agenda paper. That it would be another stormy affair everyone realized: the depression was deepening, the temper of the unemployed was getting uglier, and the attitude of the Poor Law Commissioners was stiffening. As 5 June drew

near, therefore, apprehension spread. Clear evidence of that is
seen in the application for military protection made to the
magistrates by certain prominent Whig citizens. But the magistrates turned down the request: most of them were Tories frankly
sympathetic to Oastler's stand on the Poor Law question, and
anyway it was arguable that to call in the soldiers at this stage
would worsen the situation instead of bettering it. The Whigs
were enraged by the refusal. One of their supporters on the
Bench wrote a secret letter to the Home Secretary, Lord John
Russell, complaining of what had happened. The Tories had
deliberately refused to provide the public with adequate protection, he said; instead, they had simply 'sent for their popular
man Richard Oastler who pledged his word for the peace of
the town, and so we are left at the mercy of the Mob . . . who
have all gone over to the Tory side in consequence of R.O. being so much against the Poor Law Amendment Act.'

¶ 1

The meeting of the Guardians was to be held on Monday
forenoon at the borough workhouse. Over the week end Oastler
had the town plastered with posters calling upon the people to
remain resolute and to assemble on the morrow outside Radical
headquarters. According to the *Mercury,* some 10,000 responded
to the call, drawn from all the outlying villages as well as from
the town itself. After a rousing speech by Oastler urging them
to temper their determination with caution, they marched in a
huge procession to the workhouse. Most of them were unemployed, we are told, and all were ragged and hungry.

By the time they reached the workhouse, the Board was already in session. Oastler sent in a note asking that a deputation
might be allowed to attend the meeting, but Swaine, the Whig
chairman, gave a curt refusal.

It was this refusal that touched off the explosion. All Oastler's
warnings of an hour before went for nothing: the resentment
of months came pouring forth. The crowd smashed open the
gates and stormed the building. When the doors withstood their
battering, they clambered in through the windows. They wanted
to get at Power, the personification of all their resentments, but

the Assistant Commissioner had slipped away through a back
door just in time. For an hour and more they ran berserk. They
smashed all the furniture, broke all the windows, and ransacked
the kitchen. Every scrap of food on the premises was disposed of,
and soon the place was a shambles.

Oastler was powerless and several times got knocked down
in the wild scramble. All his attempts to calm the mob proved
futile. 'Nay, it won't do, King,' someone cried out when he tried
to bring them under control, 'you're betraying us now'; and they
went on with their orgy. Finally he left them to it.

Power and the Guardians had meanwhile reassembled at the
Albion Hotel. Thither the rioters went, too, when they had
finished at the workhouse. By this time the whole town was
agitated and the streets were packed with milling crowds becoming increasingly riotous as the day wore on.

In an attempt to pacify the mob, Power and Swaine now decided to admit Oastler's deputation to the 'adjourned' meeting
at the Hotel. But from time to time during the afternoon stones
came hurtling through the windows of the conference room
as the bitter wrangle about appointing a clerk dragged on.
Despite these menaces and all the pleading of the Whig members, the Tory magistrate, Battye, refused to read the Riot Act.
He did agree, however, to go onto the balcony and appeal to
the crowd for order. This eased things for a while, and during
the lull the crucial resolution was brought to the vote once
more. More than half of the Board was too terrified to vote, but
14 stalwarts raised their hands against appointing a clerk and
only 11 dared vote in favor. Several of the 'antis' rushed to the
window and called out the result to the crowd below. A shout
went up, and wave after wave of cheering followed as the news
spread into the streets beyond. For the third time in 6 months
Huddersfield had successfully defied the Commissioners.

Later in the afternoon Oastler addressed the people from the
steps of the hotel and got them to move off peaceably. Throughout the evening, however, sporadic rioting went on in different
parts of the town. It was not until the men had made a bonfire
in the Market Place and had relieved their feelings by burning

effigies of Power and Swaine and sundry local notables that they finally dispersed.

A week later the Board had to meet once more. Upon receipt of Power's report on the situation, the Central Commissioners in London had issued new instructions to the effect that a clerk must be appointed without further delay, and that if this could not be done by the ordinary procedure any three Guardians were empowered to make the appointment. When news of this ukase got around, apprehension at once began to mount again. To comply with this order would be sure to provoke a worse explosion than before. A troop of cavalry was therefore moved to within a mile of the town for safety's sake.

Despite the preparations for trouble made by both sides, the day passed in unexpected tranquillity. Swaine and most of the dissident Whigs stayed away from the meetings, and of those that remained not three could be found willing to incur the risks that would be involved in obeying the Commissioners' orders. So for the fourth time Huddersfield held officialdom at bay. To underline its defiance, the Board drew up a strong petition against the law for presentation to the House of Commons, and then adjourned for a further 3 months.

¶ 2

But neither the following week nor for many weeks to come was there any appreciable lessening of public tension. 'The excitement caused by the attempt to introduce the New Poor Law is unprecedented,' the *Intelligencer* reported a fortnight later. And confirming this was the bonfire mania: a strange and ominous manifestation of social pathology. Night after night in the region around Huddersfield the burning of effigies went on, Baines and Power being the most usual objects of execration. All through June it continued until the magistrates, in alarm at the way the habit was spreading, put a temporary stop to it by issuing a ban against any further such demonstrations. Oastler had prophesied 'the dagger and the torch' if there were no easement of the workers' distress, and already the torch seemed to be becoming uncomfortably popular.

Not since the Reform crisis seven years before had the emotions of the populace been so seething. This time, however, the middle classes seemed powerless to control them and daily grew more alarmed. Letters, signed and unsigned, went up to Lord John Russell begging the help of the Home Office. 'You doubtless know of the excitement,' wrote George Tinker, one of the Whig minority on the Huddersfield Guardians,

but I believe your Lordship cannot be aware of the perfect state of organization into which the district has been put and the violent and unprincipled measures which are in operation to defeat the intentions of the Poor Law Commissioners. The people's feelings have been worked up to a state of madness. . . An association is formed having for its avowed object direct opposition to the Law. Delegates are appointed and contributions levied for the purpose of paying the wages of itinerant agitators and for securing the return of Guardians pledged to oppose the orders of the Commissioners. It has so far succeeded as to secure the return of a considerable majority of the Guardians who communicate with and act according to its instructions. In the present alarming state of the district it will be dangerous to put the Law into operation.

The whole district, he added, was terrorized by 'the violence of thousands of irritated persons who are under the command of ONE individual whose avowed object is direct opposition to the established law of the country.' Other correspondents wrote in the same vein. 'It is perilous to stir out in the villages,' one reported in mid-June; 'night after night effigies are burnt, individuals grossly insulted and shopkeepers actually prevented pursuing their business.'

To many it seemed that the Riding was on the verge of insurrection. The situation had passed entirely beyond the control of the local authorities, a neighboring J.P. informed Whitehall: 'when a systematic opposition to a law is set up, it is more the office of the Government than of a magistrate to order what shall be done.' Convinced that the worst was to come, the more timid of the Guardians one by one resigned.

That Oastler was the real cause of all the trouble none doubted. He was not only the soul of the resistance, but also the inventor and organizer of that union of Tory and Radical which the

Mercury denounced as 'the most flagrant and unprincipled political coalition of modern times.' Sutcliffe, one of the big manufacturers of the town, summed things up more or less accurately when he wrote to Russell:

> The plain truth is that Mr. Oastler and the Tories are making a political question of the poor law bill to gain popularity with the Radicals, and the magistrates are helping by all possible means in their power. They keep aloof from acting along with the Guardians, and will not do their duty as magistrates in an honourable and straightforward manner. . . [They all] gave their votes to Mr. Oastler and used all the influence they could to send him to Parliament, and Mr. O. being such a violent opponent of the Poor Law Bill even got the most violent Radicals and all the operatives on his side at the Election, and the Magistrates have no shame in associating with, and leaning towards, and being friendly with such as Hobson, the printer of unstamped publications. . .

These appeals to Whitehall brought no immediate result. The Home Office papers conclusively show, however, that the complaints about the conduct of the Tory justices were really being taken seriously. Various prominent Huddersfield manufacturers were busily intriguing to get themselves elevated to the Bench, and Russell was already making discreet enquiries concerning the fitness of these gentlemen for such an appointment. Once they were there, they gave him to understand, they would tolerate no more nonsense from the 'incendiary.'

The Guardians met twice more before the year was out. Each time trouble threatened, but on each occasion the affair passed off without any breach of the peace and with the defiance sustained. On the second occasion, 11 September, only 14 of the 42 members bothered to attend. Being all 'antis,' they forthwith adjourned themselves until the end of January 1838.

Thus for an entire twelvemonth the Board had been successful in its policy of administrative sabotage.

¶ 3

The accession of Queen Victoria to the throne on 20 June 1837 automatically brought about a dissolution of Parliament.

Throughout July and early August, therefore, all other issues
were subordinated to the General Election struggle.

In Huddersfield, thus to have its fifth contest in five years, the
campaign began almost as soon as the news of the old King's
death reached the borough. Both the Tory and Radical committees unhesitatingly adopted Oastler as their candidate again,
in view of his previous showing, and started working on his
behalf immediately. The Whigs, on the other hand, had to import a country gentleman named Stansfield in place of young
Ellice, who moved to a less boisterous constituency.

The surprising closeness of the vote eight weeks earlier had
heartened both wings of Oastler's supporters, so that this time
they started off with a fierce will to win and were first in the field
by many days. Even before June was out, women supporters had
organized themselves for house to house canvassing on an extensive scale and nightly meetings were being held in the surrounding villages.

The workers put forth prodigious efforts to secure Oastler's return. Shopkeepers were threatened with loss of custom if they
voted Whig; electors were canvassed and recanvassed; processions and demonstrations were held every day. Once again the
nomination meeting conclusively showed where popular sympathies lay. Stansfield received what the *Mercury* euphemistically
called 'a most ungratifying reception' and eventually had to
abandon his speech. Crowded round the hustings were wild
Oastlerites carrying long poles to the end of which were tied
chunks of bread and cheese—a day's workhouse ration—which
they pushed under the noses of any Stansfield supporters who
came near enough to the edge of the platform to be reached.
Only one Whig speaker brought a cheer from the crowd. That
was the local manufacturer William Brook, who admitted in the
course of his much-interrupted speech of nomination that the
New Poor Law was inapplicable to the manufacturing districts
and that 'this law can never be introduced among us.' When
'King Richard' came forward the greeting he got was tumultuous.
Even the *Mercury* had to admit that 'the cheering continued
several minutes' and that the formal show of hands was overwhelmingly in Oastler's favor.

That same afternoon there took place in Oastler's office a fateful meeting that was not reported until long afterwards. A dozen Roman Catholics from the Irish colony in Huddersfield came to call on the candidate personally. All were voters, and all in substantial agreement with Oastler's program. But they were troubled by his known anti-Catholic bias and by his declaration on the hustings that if he were returned to Parliament he would support any move for the repeal of the Catholic Emancipation Act. Would not Oastler reconsider his decision, they asked, or at least qualify his statement in some way? They wanted to vote for him, yet could not conscientiously do so if this really represented his last word on the subject. Compromise, however, was anathema to Oastler, especially on such a matter. He thanked them cordially for their good will, but said: 'If I enter the House of Commons, it shall not be by equivocation. What I stated on the hustings I shall perform if returned.' The consequences were seen next day.

From five o'clock on election morning Huddersfield streets were seething with excited crowds. Voting started at eight o'clock after a dozen Metropolitan police—specially brought from London to keep order—had taken up positions around the polling booth. This time Oastler went straight into the lead. By half-past eight he had 77 votes to Stansfield's 30. At nine o'clock he had 119 to 85. An hour later he still had a lead of 23 and had far surpassed Sadler's poll in the 1834 contest. Then Stansfield slowly drew nearer. As the parish church clock chimed the three-quarters the Whig went ahead with a lead of 6. But Oastler had already polled more votes than had sufficed to return Blackburne and there were still some dozens of his supporters to be brought in.

From midday onwards the two men were running neck and neck. For the unenfranchised Oastlerites massed around the polling platform, the suspense seemed unbearable. Then between three and four in the afternoon Stansfield clearly took the lead again. Just before four o'clock—when Oastler was 17 in arrears— the crowd started throwing stones and menacing the Whig late-comers. Becoming alarmed, the officials at once adjourned the poll, for the memory of the recent workhouse riot was much too vivid to permit risks being taken. This only made the crowd more angry, so the police drew their cutlasses and began a slow advance. A shower of stones met them and one of the constables was badly hurt. Against the continuing hail of missiles, however, it was impossible to make a stand: gradually the policemen were forced back into the polling enclosure and finally had to flee through some premises at the rear.

By this time the mob was in a thoroughly ugly mood. It looked as though another large-scale riot was imminent. The military were hastily sent for, and three-quarters of an hour later two troops of the 15th Hussars came galloping into the town. Advancing to the head of the troops, two of the local J.P.'s read the Riot Act and implored the people to disperse: but in vain. Another shower of stones was the answer. Only one thing was left to do: the trumpeter sounded the 'advance' and the cavalry began to move forward. Instantly all fight went out of the crowd. Dropping their weapons they fled in panic as though a second Peterloo were at hand. Together the police and soldiers then cleared the streets and the evening passed off peaceably.

Next day at eight o'clock the polling was resumed and continued for another hour. But during that time Oastler added only a single vote to his total, and at nine o'clock he conceded defeat. The final figures were:

Stansfield	323
Oastler	301
Whig majority	22

The victor did not appear to return the customary thanks, nor did anyone else on his behalf. Oastler, however, keenly disappointed though he was, came to thank his supporters for their help and to urge them to prepare for the next contest. If only he had tempered his opinions on Catholic Emancipation he might have won this one.

¶ 4

The borough contest had ended on Saturday. The following Monday, 31 July, nominations were to be made at Wakefield for the county election. Since the redistribution of seats in 1832, the

West Riding had formed a single constituency (the largest in England) returning two Members to Parliament on its own account. On this occasion there were only three candidates for the two seats, Wortley alone representing the Tories while the veterans Morpeth and Strickland represented the Whigs. This, too, was going to be a close fight. Morpeth was certain to head the poll, as everyone knew; but between the other two the chances for the second seat were reckoned to be about evenly divided.

Here, then, was a ready-made opportunity for staging another huge Anti-Poor Law demonstration, which Oastler had no intention of passing up. One more thunderous protest, he thought, coming on top of all the recent manifestations of local feeling, might convince the Government that its Poor Law policy for the north must be abandoned. He therefore drafted a militant poster urging all his followers to meet him at the hustings, where he intended to heckle the three candidates about their attitude to the question. The manifesto was distributed by special messengers to agents of the Anti-Poor Law Association all over the constituency, so that by Sunday morning there were few places in the Riding that had not received the challenge:

ARE YOU FOR HAVING YOUR TOWNS AND VILLAGES FILLED WITH METROPOLITAN POLICE, ARMED WITH TRUNCHEONS AND PISTOLS? AND GIRT WITH MURDEROUS SWORDS? . . .

WILL YOU OR WILL YOU NOT DECLARE TO THE IRISH SECRETARY, LORD MORPETH, AT WAKEFIELD NEXT MONDAY, THAT THIS HORRIBLE BASTILLE LAW *Shall Not Be Established Here* AND THAT YOU WILL NOT BE CONTENT TILL IT HAS BEEN *Uprooted Everywhere?* . . .

THE HUDDERSFIELD MEN WILL BE THERE, AND SO I TRUST WILL YOU. THEY HAVE ASSISTED ME LIKE MEN TO GAIN THE VICTORY OVER THE POOR LAW COMMISSIONERS, DESPITE OF THEIR BLUE JACKETS AND CUTLASS-ARMED POLICE . . .

MEN OF HUDDERSFIELD—ONE TUG MORE AND *We Will Give That Execrable Law Its Death Blow* . . .

TO WAKEFIELD!   TO WAKEFIELD!

As a result of this summons and of the active counter-measures taken by the Whigs over the weekend, an enormous crowd foregathered at Wakefield. All the morning, men were pouring in from every direction. They came on horseback and in processions, in hackney coaches and in farm wagons, decorated with every conceivable kind of party token. Oastler walked the 20 miles from Fixby protected by a special bodyguard of 400 Huddersfield stalwarts. By noon more than 30,000 people had assembled and the air was ajangle with the bells and bands they brought with them.

On the hustings which had been set up in front of the Court House were notables from every walk of life in the county. Their disposition made an eloquent tableau of the balance of local political forces. Supporting the Whig candidates were numerous big manufacturers (including the notorious Jonathan Ackroyd), leading Nonconformists of various denominations, and representatives of the Irish interests, besides both the Baineses. Wortley's party was even more assorted. In addition to Monkton Milnes, Beckett the Leeds banker, and Rand 'the father of the worsted trade,' it included Feargus O'Connor, Parson Bull, and Oastler himself, as well as the usual array of landed gentry.[2]

In the absence of adequate policing, the gathering of such a huge concourse at such a time made trouble practically inevitable. Emotions in the Riding were dangerously wrought up anyway, as a result of recent happenings: the occasion served both to reinforce them and to give them vent.

The details of what followed are complicated and were heatedly argued about for many weeks, but the general pattern of events is clear. The hustings stood at the end of a small square, one half of which was assigned to the 'yellows' and the other half to the 'blues.' The thronged streets leading into the square were supposed to be similarly assigned, though, of course, the further along one went the less orderly the arrangements were

[2] The banners brought by the various contingents to this meeting and massed around the hustings give an interesting indication of the operative symbols being used by the two parties at this time. From the various newspapers we learn that the commonest slogans were:

For the *Blues:* 'Victory or the Bastilles'; 'No Poor Law in the West Riding'; 'If the poor rates and the paupers are to be commissioned, so shall the Rents and the Landlords, the Funds and the Fundholders'; 'The Altar, the Throne and the Cottage.' For the *Yellows:* 'The Queen and Reform'; 'Justice for Ireland'; 'Reform of every Abuse in Church and State'; 'Civil and Religious Freedom.'

and the more turbulent the crowd tended to become. At first the meeting proceeded smoothly enough, but in the middle of Morpeth's speech there began the diversion that led to all the trouble. A gang of drunken 'yellows' armed with sticks and clubs came up from one of the back streets and tried to force its way through the main crowd. Fighting started immediately, and within a very short time a pitched battle was in progress. Roof-tops were crowded with men hurling stones, and the air was thick with missiles. At one point a side wall gave way: soon there was hardly a sign of it left, for the factions instantly used the brickbats as weapons. The notables on the hustings found them-selves forced to flee, Whig and Tory helping one another on to the roof of the Court House and thence through a skylight to safety. Meanwhile an urgent call for the cavalry had been sent to the nearest barracks.

As soon as the riot had started, Oastler had jumped down from the hustings to lead the 'blues' in the fray. He received some nasty cuts from flying stones and had a couple of fingers broken while he and his bodyguard were being driven back into a near-by inn. There for an hour or two they had to withstand a siege by infuriated 'yellows' shouting 'Death to Oastler.' Fortunately for him the doors of the building held, though every window in the place was smashed.

The fracas ended almost as suddenly as it had begun. When the violence showed signs of having worked itself out, the three candidates with no little courage came forth from their hiding place to appeal to their followers for order. They were un-expectedly successful. By the time the cavalry arrived, the town was already quiet. But two people lay dead in the street and many scores were injured.

Next day, nearly 36,000 voters went to the poll in a sober mood and both Whigs were returned:

Morpeth	12,576
Strickland	11,892
Wortley	11,489
Strickland's majority over Wortley	403

CHAPTER XXVII

The Mobilization of Protest

THE successful resistance by the Huddersfield Guardians had taught both sides a lesson. On the one hand the opponents of the New Poor Law had learned what could be accomplished by threats and mass action. But for 'the personal intimidation of the parties who were called upon to act,' Power said in his report to London, the law would undoubtedly have gone into operation. On the other hand, the Government had come to see that sterner measures than any yet employed would be necessary to break Yorkshire resistance. Local machinery for the maintenance of order had clearly proved itself inadequate to its purpose. Unless that situation were remedied, intimidation might continue indefinitely: indeed, there was every likelihood that it would spread. In many of the Unions, for instance, Guardians had been elected and their administrative officials duly appointed, but they had not yet received orders to assume their duties under the Act. With public opinion in the state that it was, it was still highly uncertain by the autumn of 1837 whether some of these Boards would obey the orders even when they were issued.

¶ 1

This explains why the Bradford struggle was so crucial and why everyone attached so much importance to its outcome. Here was the first opportunity for both sides to apply the lessons they had learned at Huddersfield. Were Bradford to follow Huddersfield's lead, several other towns were likely to do the same almost immediately, notably Dewsbury and Oldham, where defiance had already been carried to considerable lengths. In that event, a complete administrative collapse such as the Oastlerites had sought to produce was by no means an impossibility.

Bradford's Board of Guardians had been elected at the same time as Huddersfield's, and in due course had complied with the Commissioners' instructions to appoint a clerk and other officials. But it was not until mid-October that Power issued orders for the Board to take over the poor relief of its Union. The first business meeting for the purpose was fixed for 30 October, and it was then that the trouble started.

The Anti-Poor Law Committee sent out the town crier to warn the people of Power's coming and to urge them to assemble at the Court House in readiness. Once again, therefore, there was played out the same farce that had been enacted at Keighley, Huddersfield, and elsewhere. The mob demanded to be admitted to the meeting and Power refused; whereupon the crowd turned rowdy and business became impossible. The Board then slipped out by a back door and reassembled secretly for a conclave in Power's room at the Sun Inn. Here they were joined by Mathew Thompson, the J.P. who had been one of Oastler's first supporters in the factory movement.

Thompson had originally been an opponent of the New Poor Law but had come to change his mind, at least to the extent that he was now willing to give the Act a trial. He warned Power, however, that high-handed tactics would do more harm than good, and urged that the meeting be openly resumed at the Court House in the afternoon with representatives of the public attending. Power was loath to agree, but Thompson managed to persuade the rest of the Board to his way of thinking, so the Assistant Commissioner had to submit.

Thompson's earnest appeal to the angry crowd to give the Act a trial and abstain from violence did little good. 'Nothing could, in fact, exceed the confusion which prevailed during the meeting,' Power wrote in his report; 'the greatest possible exasperation was evinced against the law.' And when Power finally came forth, the crowd mobbed him all the way back to his lodgings. They pelted him with mud and battered him with anything at hand, without a single one of the local constables coming to his protection. That night, bruised and angry, he wrote an account of the day's happenings for Somerset House, telling the Central Commissioners that unless the Government provided more adequate protection for the next meeting, Bradford's Guardians would probably be intimidated into inaction as Huddersfield's had been.

And he was right: for when he returned to attend the next meeting a couple of weeks later the magistrates and others whom he consulted solemnly assured him that it would be highly dangerous even to attempt to bring the Guardians together. The Anti-Poor Law Association had spared no effort to whip up resentment in the interval; a militant call to arms from Oastler adorned all the hoardings throughout the Union, and the town was seething. The only thing to do, they told him, was to postpone the meeting another week and meanwhile ask the Home Office to provide military protection. With extreme reluctance, Power assented. In the course of the next few days, accordingly, 20 additional special constables were sworn in, half a dozen Metropolitan Police were brought up from London, and a troop of the 15th Hussars was moved over from Leeds.

On Monday, 20 November, at ten o'clock in the morning, the full Board of the Bradford Guardians met in the Court House. A huge crowd had gathered outside, but the soldiers were kept in readiness in another part of the town. On being denied admittance to the meeting, the crowd quickly became restive and then began attacking the building. It was soon apparent that the police were going to be overpowered: the Hussars were therefore summoned, and the Riot Act was read. That only inflamed the crowd the more. For 2 hours they continued the attack while the soldiers sought to hold them off with sabres. Even that seemed as though it would be insufficient, however, and a courier had to be sent post haste to Burnley to ask for more cavalry and a company of infantry. In the meantime the Board within went ahead with its business and did everything Power wanted it to do.

The climax came some hours later, while the soldiers were escorting the Guardians back to their respective homes through the thronged streets. The mob suddenly went wild and attacked the troops with the utmost recklessness. The cavalry had to charge to clear a way for themselves, but time and again the crowd surged back. Then the infantry started to shoot. It was an ugly business, but eventually the mob was cowed. 'Many persons have been seriously hurt, both by sabre and gunshot wounds,' Power had to inform London; but by some miracle no one was killed.

That the Government was now determined to bring the northern situation under control by every means at its disposal was shown by the extensive troop movements of the ensuing fortnight. A further meeting of the Guardians had been fixed for 4 December. Before then, two companies of the 97th Regiment had been stationed at Bradford along with the Hussars; reinforcements were moved up to Burnley, Rochdale, and Leeds in case of further trouble; and plans were made to bring in the 4th and 7th Dragoon Guards should it prove necessary.

Evidence of the high state of public tension is seen in the wild rumors that spread throughout the Riding. According to one such report that gained general credence, Oastler was planning to march on Bradford with 5000 of his armed followers. In anticipation of trouble, many shops remained closed, insurance offices refused to issue policies, and a further 200 special constables were sworn in. Over the weekend soldiers were posted on all the roads leading into the town to bar Oastler's approach.

All these fears came to nothing, however. With soldiers patrolling the streets, the day passed quietly and the Bradford Board of Guardians completed all its unfinished business. Short of organizing outright insurrection, there was little that the Anti-Poor Law Association could do. The following week the Oddfellows Hall was packed to hear Oastler, Bull, and O'Connor denounce 'the bayonets and bullets of the base, bloody and brutal New Poor Law Whigs.' But this was only futile mouthing. None could deny that, for the time being at least, the Commissioners and the Home Office had triumphed.

¶ 2

Yet if the close of the year saw a conspicuous stiffening of the Government's attitude, it also saw a remarkable extension of the Anti-Poor Law organization. The months following the setback at Bradford were marked by a fury of planned activity exceeding anything that had taken place since Power had come to Yorkshire.

The West Riding Association had come into being in March 1837. Eight months later, while Bradford was in the midst of its troubles, a new organization with identical aims was founded on the other side of the Pennines. This South Lancashire Anti-Poor Law Association, as it called itself, owed little if anything to Oastler and Bull for its inception. The moving spirit behind it was a certain Reginald John Richardson, who forthwith became its full-time secretary. A central office was taken in Manchester; missionaries went forth to stir up opposition and enroll members; and local lodges were set up. Liaison was maintained with the West Riding men, and joint conferences were held from time to time to co-ordinate the efforts in the two counties.

The energy shown by Richardson and his Lancashire followers was prodigious. Deputations from the parent body visited every town of any size, held meetings night after night and got local Committees started. Each Committee pressed its opposition according to local circumstances. At Preston, for example, the opportunities were exceptional: no fewer than 24 of the 26 Guardians were members of the resistance committee. The surprising thing about this new movement was the speed with which it caught on. Soon it was spreading in Cheshire and a few weeks later had taken hold of the Staffordshire potteries as well. By early February more than 77 meetings had been reported in the London press, and the establishment of over 50 branches. 'The formation of the Anti-Poor Law Association,' said *The Times* in a cordial editorial, 'and the rapidity of its ramifications and spreading throughout the country, ought to convince Lord John that Englishmen will not tamely submit to oppression, and still less when it is attempted to be enforced by the bayonet.'

Shortly afterwards the Yorkshire organization launched another drive of its own patterned exactly upon the first great Ten Hours campaign which had roused the north six years earlier. The result was that before spring had come there was hardly an industrial center from Newcastle to Chester that had not received the fiery gospel of protest and had not had a committee for resistance set up in its neighborhood. While itinerant missionaries and local leaders dealt with the smaller places, Oastler, Stephens, and O'Connor concentrated on the key towns. Sometimes separately and sometimes together, they swept from one huge demonstration to another lashing their listeners into a furor.

Oastler was now at the zenith of his power and men came in their hundreds to receive the message he had to give. And always it was the same: that privilege is a trust held on behalf of the entire community and that certain fundamental obligations are implicit in the very fact of community itself. The cardinal postulate of an orderly social life in England, he said at one of these meetings, was

that every man has a right to his liberty and his subsistence; that the Crown guarantees those rights; that failing therein it has no constitutional claim to our allegiance; that all private property is held under the Crown on that condition; and, failing in that, that all private property must revert to the Crown for the good of all or be taken perforce by the needy.

The Whigs' repudiation of that principle in the name of 'individualism,' he invariably went on, could lead only to anarchy. 'There are certain bounds limited by the Constitution,' he said on another occasion, 'beyond which the Three Estates cannot travel and at the same time retain the present order of society or maintain the present ownership of property.' The bigger the audiences grew, the more menacing did his elaboration of the theme become. 'I tell you Churchmen, I tell you Dissenters,' he declared at Rochdale, 'before I would submit to such an Act I would see the whole Kingdom in a blaze.' Stephens was even more explicit. 'If it were right to confiscate the property of the people by abrogating the 43rd Elizabeth,' he said from the same platform, 'it is right for the poor to take a dagger in one hand and a torch in the other and do the best for themselves.'

Never in the years from Waterloo to today was there put forth in England such a volume of sustained and outspoken sedition as was heard during the five months of this whirlwind campaign against the New Poor Law. Wild talk about 'the assassin's knife' could be heard at every meeting. In this respect there was nothing to choose between Oastler, Stephens, and O'Connor. It was almost as though they vied with one another in the vehemence of their incitements. The best known of all these speeches, though

it was in no way exceptional, happens to be the one Stephens
made at a monster meeting at Newcastle on New Year's Day
1838. Oastler was not present on that occasion, but O'Connor
was, and James Cobbett and many of the other leaders. To the
accompaniment of thunderous acclamations from hundreds of
Tynesiders, Stephens went to the utmost limits of seditious oratory:

> If the people who produce all the wealth could not be allowed ac-
> cording to God's word to have the kindly fruits of the earth they had
> in obedience to God's word raised by the sweat of their brow, then war
> to the knife with their enemies who were the enemies of God . . .
> If the musket and pistol, the sword and the pike were of no avail,
> let the women take the scissor, the child the pin or needle; if all failed,
> then the firebrand—aye, the firebrand—the firebrand, I repeat. The
> palace shall be in flames . . .

¶ 3

The campaign had remarkably strong press support; a fact
that may in some measure account for the immunity these tem-
pestuous orators enjoyed.

First and foremost it had *The Times* sympathetically behind
it and reporting it fully. John Walter, the proprietor, had broken
with the Government over the Poor Law before that measure
had even reached the statute book in 1834. Thenceforward the
'Thunderer' remained the implacable critic of the Commissioners.
As the operation of the Act was extended, it exposed all the weak
points of the measure, publicized the harshness of the administration, and week by week gave considerable space to the stories
of cruelty and suffering that the movement uncovered. At one
northern meeting after another operatives and unemployed gave
throat to their gratitude for this support with cheers and resolutions of thanks. And eventually Walter himself came on to the
Anti-Poor Law platforms.

Along with the backing of *The Times* must be mentioned the
equally consistent support given by the *Standard, Sun, Herald,
Dispatch,* and *Metropolitan Conservative Journal,* as well as by
innumerable Tory journals in the provinces that followed the lead
of these London dailies: papers such as the *Manchester* and

Salford Advertiser, the *Liverpool Mail*, and the *Leeds Intelligencer*. As long as the Anti-Poor Law Movement remained independent—that is to say, until its program became entangled with other demands—Oastler and Stephens could always rely on this powerful backing.

But the most vigorous support of all came from the *Northern Star*, a new paper unique in British history to that date. We have already noted [1] how Feargus O'Connor, the imperious Irish megalomaniac, had worked for two years in the London working-class movement, how he had been unable to find therein the dominance that his consuming ambition demanded, and how in the latter part of 1836 he had set out on his northern tour to exploit the seething discontent lying between Trent and Clyde. That tour had been astonishingly successful and within a very few weeks O'Connor had pushed his way into the front ranks of proletarian leadership alongside Oastler, Stephens, and the rest. In the autumn of 1837 he confirmed this position by a masterly stroke of business.

While the northern troubles had been developing, a small group of Leeds Radicals had been planning the establishment of an independent newspaper with a wide popular appeal. The two promoters of the scheme were William Hill, an ex-Swedenborgian minister, and Joshua Hobson, a publisher who had produced much of the Ten Hours literature and had already served two prison sentences for circulating 'unstamped' periodicals. They had got as far as forming a committee and issuing a few shares when O'Connor came along and took over the enterprise. Persuading the committee that it would never be able to get together the necessary capital, he undertook to pay the interest on the few hundreds already subscribed and to find the rest out of his own pocket. The Committee agreed; Hill was made editor and Hobson publisher, and on 18 November 1837 the first issue of the *Northern Star* appeared at Leeds.

Its success was immediate. Though selling at fourpence-halfpenny a copy its circulation quickly exceeded that of the *Mercury* and rose for a time to as much as 30,000 a week. Two main reasons account for this, apart from its capable editorship. One was

[1] Cf. above, pp. 337 ff.

that it cleverly caught the mood of the ale house and the mass meeting, thus becoming in fact the first experiment in yellow journalism of the nineteenth century. The other was that it gave to northern Radicalism an organ: it reported any and every meeting of the cause, publicized the speakers and all the little local leaders, and by putting them 'in print' made the participants in the merest pot-house gathering feel that they were actors in a mighty drama.

From the outset the *Northern Star* gave the amplest publicity to the activities of the Anti-Poor Law Association. Its columns, too, were open without restriction to Oastler's untiring elaboration of the doctrine of social paternalism, which he presented over the next few months in a series of 'open letters' to various men of eminence. Thus flanked by the old 'Thunderer' in London and the new thunderer in Leeds, the Anti-Poor Law Movement awaited the coming year with dour hope.

¶ 4

As the tempest in the north mounted in fury, *The Times* began to urge the opponents of the New Poor Law to consider yet a further extension of their activities. Until now, both the Home Office and the Central Board of Commissioners had ignored the movement or treated it with contempt. The main reason they had been able to do so, *The Times* suggested, was 'the absence of systematic co-operation among the enemies of the Bill.' What was proposed, therefore, was that a huge national society should be set up 'for collecting authentic evidence in regard to the appalling evils [the Act] has engendered and aggravated, for counteracting the arbitrary powers and proceedings of its administrators, and for dragging into daylight those cases of hardship and tyranny which the reports of packed committees and paid commissions have found it expedient to conceal.' Such a society, it was believed, could achieve substantial amendment if not total repeal of the hated law. It would not supplant the existing associations but would incorporate them in a nation-wide effort. In some respects the scheme was not unlike the proposal for a 'people's lobby' that Oastler had put forward some years before, only this would be limited to a single objective. Indeed, there is reason to suppose the idea actually did originate with Oastler, since it had been first mooted by Lord Stanhope some months earlier and Stanhope had been in close touch with Oastler all the time. But it was not until John Walter took up the idea in December 1837 that anything serious was done about it.

After careful preparatory work, the London Central Anti-Poor Law Association was formally brought into being at a big meeting in the Freemasons Tavern on 19 February 1838. Delegates from the northern lodges attended as well as representatives of metropolitan resistance and most of the nationally prominent figures. The plan was unanimously approved and a four-point program agreed upon; Stanhope was elected chairman of the society, Fielden his deputy, and John Walter treasurer. An executive committee of 7 was appointed to assist these 3 in the formulation of policy.

It was a grandiose conception. Judging by the fanfare with which it was greeted and the enormous amount of space accorded to it in *The Times* (Oastler's speech alone took up four columns), one might reasonably have supposed that it would lead to big things. But as matters turned out, it came to very little. Indeed, the rest of its history proved a sad anticlimax: a fact only properly to be understood in the light of the dramatic change of direction that came over the entire proletarian movement in the course of the next few months.

The truth is that even while this new machine was in the making, the mood of the northern operatives was altering rapidly in a manner that neither Stanhope nor Walter appreciated. For more than a year, protest against the New Poor Law had continued and enthusiasm had been sustained. But all the recent efforts were beginning to seem futile as the misery of the depression continued and no prospect of alleviation was discernible. The rank and file were getting impatient with mere propaganda: what they wanted now was effective action, and that quickly, for, apart from the sporadic riots around the person of Power, the enemy had not even been brought to the encounter.

Unmistakable evidence of this rising mood was forthcoming at a Delegates Conference held at Manchester only 3 weeks after the London meeting. What was necessary, all the speakers agreed, was something spectacular which would shake the public out of its complacency and really frighten the Government. Various suggestions were considered and rejected. Then, in a passionate speech that swept the meeting off its feet, Stephens induced the delegates to approve a totally new expedient. This was that the unenfranchised and unemployed should demand to have their representatives heard at the bar of the House of Commons. A 'cabinet council' had been held at Huddersfield, he reported, whereat he and Oastler and a few of the other leaders had come to the conclusion that this was the only remaining constitutional step for them to take. Unanimously the meeting approved the idea. Oastler, O'Connor, Stephens, Bull, Condy, and John Cobbett were the representatives designated. Specially convened public meetings were to be asked to endorse the nominations; and John Fielden was to put the request before Parliament.

¶ 5

But Huddersfield still held out, though Oastler did not conceal his disappointment that more towns had not shown equal resolution. Had they done so, he told one of the Lancashire conferences, the prospects for the coming year might have been very much brighter. As matters stood, it was highly problematical whether Huddersfield could go on indefinitely resisting alone; the more so since, with the new year, the Central Commissioners were giving serious attention to the question of bringing the town into submission once and for all.

At its previous meeting, the Huddersfield Board had adjourned itself until 29 January 1838. As that day drew near, everyone began expecting trouble in view of the recent happenings at Bradford. None of the inns would take Power as a guest, and the proprietor of the Albion refused to allow another Board meeting to be held in his establishment. Oastler, of course, scattered his customary threats. 'We will all be there,' he wrote to Lord John Russell, 'and die rather than be enslaved.'

Two troops of the Hussars, however, aided by a bitter snowstorm that continued for hours, kept the town quiet while inside the heavily guarded Court House the Whig chairman Swaine resorted to high-handed tactics. The motion for the appointment of a clerk was put and defeated as before. But this time, in accordance with the instructions he had received from London, Swaine simply ignored the negative vote and declared elected a local solicitor named Floyd. That done, he went ahead with the rest of the long-deferred business despite all protests.

Clearly the 'antis' had been outwitted, but they were in no way disheartened. The annual election of the Guardians was due at the end of March and the 'antis' had every hope of being able to carry a majority of the wards as they had done the year before. Then they would be able to undo all that Swaine had just done. During the next few weeks, therefore, no effort was spared to make sure of an electoral victory. Delegates from the various townships of the Union met to concert their plans, and the Radical and Tory leaders agreed upon a slate of candidates to prevent the Whigs getting in on a divided vote.

As a result, the election proved to be an extremely spirited affair. The validity of a number of the returns was challenged and the bitter wrangle to which that gave rise was not settled for several weeks. So uncertain was the situation, indeed, that both parties claimed to have won a majority. None could doubt, therefore, that Huddersfield's new Board of Guardians would have just as stormy a course as its predecessor; and so it proved.

At the first meeting of the new Board held on 9 April the 'antis' quickly discovered that in several respects they were in a considerably weaker position than before. For one thing, tired of the struggle, three of the sympathetic Tory magistrates with ex-officio seats on the Board now absented themselves. For another, the Home Secretary had yielded to the persistent pressure from the local Whigs and had recently created two new magistrates, Sutcliffe and Starkey, both mill owners bitterly opposed alike to the Ten Hours Movement and the campaign against the Poor Law. Sutcliffe, it is to be remembered, was one of those who had been secretly complaining to Lord John Russell about Oastler's activities the previous year and had accused the Tory magistrates of 'not doing their duty in an honourable and straightforward manner.' He now took his seat fully determined to rectify that dereliction and to tolerate no more nonsense from those who would defy the law.

Right away, without nomination or any other formality, Sutcliffe put himself in the chair. When the question of the doubtful returns came up as the first item on the agenda, he brazenly assigned the 5 uncertain seats to his own Whig supporters merely on the authority of his *ipse dixit*. (Months later an official enquiry unseated them again.) In a similarly masterful manner he dealt with the rest of the business. For 6 hours the 'antis' fought and argued as best they could, but got nowhere.

There was still so much arrears of work to be attended to that another meeting had to be held a week later. This time the 'antis' seized the initiative. They took in with them a posse of Oastlerite townsfolk who resisted every effort to eject them. 'A complete bear garden was the result,' the *Mercury* reported. Catcalls and curses led to such disorder that even the imperious Sutcliffe found himself helpless. So he adjourned the meeting for a further 3 weeks.

This adjourned meeting of 7 May 1838 proved to be the culmination of Huddersfield's seventeen months of resistance to the New Poor Law. Both sides were set upon bringing the struggle to a decisive outcome, the 'antis' now fully realizing that if they lost this day they had probably lost the entire campaign.

When the hour of the meeting struck, only a dozen Whig members took their seats in the board room. Then the clerk started reading the minutes. As he continued, the sound of a distant rumbling began to be heard. It was the advancing crowd, several thousands strong, led by Feargus O'Connor and J. R. Stephens, specially brought in for the occasion and escorting the nineteen 'antis' who had become the heroes of the town. The constables outside were powerless to resist. The crowd surged into the building, packing the board room and filling the corridors. Those who could not squeeze in kept up a loud and continuous demonstration outside. This, the leader of the 'antis' announced, was going to be their own affair, and they were going to reconsider all the decisions the Board had taken under Sutcliffe's persuasions. The crowd roared its approbation as the 'antis' proceeded to elect a new chairman and to set to work on an agenda of their own.

Since the Whig appointees refused to yield the floor, pandemonium broke loose with each side trying to howl the other down. When the clerk tried to slip away, execrations turned to blows, as a free fight started for possession of his minute book. The Whigs were so hopelessly outnumbered, however, that they had not a chance. Once their minute book was captured they gave up the fight and withdrew. But only the vehement intervention of O'Connor saved them from a severe thrashing before their departure.

Thus left in sole possession of the meeting, the 19 'antis' speedily rescinded all the decisions taken since the Board's election and deprived Floyd of his clerkship. Then, having drawn up a new petition against the law for forwarding to Somerset House, they adjourned themselves for another 2 months.

The bastion still held. But a few days later, 6 of its defenders learned that they were going to be indicted at the York Assizes on a charge of 'tumultuous assembly.' So it was not yet certain who had carried the day after all.

CHAPTER XXVIII

The Farewell to Fixby

I T WAS probably during the spring of 1838 that Oastler reached the zenith of his popularity with the masses. Day after day he was addressing meetings, planning the Anti-Poor Law campaign, consulting with local lodges, writing to the newspapers. At the end of March, the *Northern Star* presented its readers with a large engraved portrait of him and published the first installment of his serialized biography. 'He is,' said the *Star* editorially at this time, 'the Father of the poor, the Defender of the oppressed, and the Dread of the tyrant.'

Suddenly—just when matters were coming to a head on the Huddersfield Board of Guardians—Oastler broke down. Of the details of the illness we know nothing. All we know is that he collapsed completely and was prostrate for several weeks. Stephens went to stay with him during his convalescence and was shocked to find a man so astonishingly changed in such a short time. Already, Stephens reported, 'traces of premature old age' were beginning to show.

And then, before he was able to get about again, his relations with his employer reached their breaking point.

¶ 1

Of Oastler's loyalty to Thornhill there had never been any question: he was utterly devoted to Fixby and all its interests, and between Squire and steward the happiest relations had subsisted for many years. Long letters from his prolific pen had kept his master fully informed of local happenings; and when the factory agitation started Oastler had been scrupulously careful not only to tell Thornhill all about it but also to keep him supplied with all the newspaper reports and propaganda bearing upon the movement. Thornhill had fully approved the cause. He had sent a donation to the fighting fund and, what was even more valuable, had used his good offices to put Oastler in touch with the Duke of Wellington and other members of the House of Lords whose support he was seeking. In so far as the factory question was concerned, therefore, there was no issue between them.

Their financial relations had given rise to a certain amount of difficulty, however, though hardly of a personal kind. Oastler's salary was £300 a year and had remained unchanged since his appointment in 1820; but part of that sum had been spent in various ways upon the estate. That this had been the case was Oastler's own responsibility, as he freely admitted, and arose from his unusual interpretation of his responsibilities as steward. From the day on which he had first gone to Fixby he had firmly resolved so to conduct the affairs of the estate as to make up for the absence of its owner. He did not regard himself as the mere caretaker of an empty Hall and the rent collector for an absentee landlord. Wisely or stupidly, he considered it his function to live and conduct himself as though he were a *locum tenens* for his master. 'I do endeavour in everything that I am able,' he once wrote to Thornhill, 'to attach everyone to Fixby; and as much as is in my power I try to make up for this neighbourhood the great loss it must experience by your non-residence.' He entertained visitors who had business with Fixby, as well as the tenantry. He dispensed charity and relieved poverty. In fact, he behaved as though he were one of the family doing duty for a relative.[1] Thornhill knew all this and made no demur. Year after year matters drifted on in this way, and Oastler's personal moneys became increasingly entangled with those of his employer. At the annual visit to Norfolk explanations were given, the accounts

[1] 'I have no perquisites,' he once told Thornhill, 'no not a single farthing. While every other steward in the neighbourhood is getting rich, I am as poor as Lazarus. I never charged a tenant a single farthing. While other stewards regularly charge for everything they do for them in the way of looking after alterations, visiting and examining premises, and arranging with the landlord, I never would receive a farthing for those things. . . . The repairs of Fixby Hall cost me some hundreds of pounds besides what you allowed me; and if they had not been done, it would now have been in ruins.'

were balanced, and both parties seemed satisfied. Oastler's confidence in his master was complete, while Thornhill for his part did not seem to mind his steward's incurring debts towards the estate through such a manner of living.

After 14 years of this sort of haphazard arrangement, some kind of orderly adjustment had become imperative. By that time Oastler had got himself into technical debt with Thornhill to the extent of more than £2,700. Details are now lacking; but there was no suggestion of any strained relations between the two men. Oastler offered to resign if Thornhill desired, but the Squire refused to consider such a thing. They thrashed out the matter in December 1834, and came to a mutually satisfactory arrangement. On the one side, Oastler assumed responsibility for the debt, which he acknowledged with a note of hand and agreed to pay off in annual installments; and on the other, Thornhill admitted that Oastler's salary was not large enough in view of his administration of the estate, and raised it by an extra £200 a year. It was agreed between them that 'the expense of the stewardship had caused the deficiency.'

Thenceforward the financial muddle began to get straightened out. In the following year Oastler paid off more than £300 of the debt, and the year after a further £141. By July 1837 it had been reduced by nearly £1,000—almost twice the increase in salary Oastler had received during that period. So there seemed no reason to doubt that in time it would be liquidated entirely. Unfortunately other factors intervened to prevent this, and those other factors were purely political.

¶ 2

It was only slowly that Oastler and Thornhill came to loggerheads over politics. The first tiff had been over the Huddersfield by-election in 1832 when Sir John Ramsden had complained to the owner of Fixby about Oastler's activities and Thornhill had replied by assuring Ramsden he 'would not keep persons in his employ who supported Radical candidates.' On that occasion Oastler had vigorously defended himself, Thornhill was reassured, and the matter had been allowed to drop.[2] A couple of

[2] See above, p. 192–3.

years later, some local busybodies had written to Thornhill about Oastler's part in the factory movement and had suggested that he was neglecting his work at Fixby in consequence. Once again Oastler had completely satisfied Thornhill, and their relationship had continued as before.

But when Oastler went to stay at Riddlesworth in December 1835, something of a real difference in opinion began to be revealed. Thornhill had gone 'Conservative'; he had come to approve the New Poor Law; and his attitude to 'Radicalism' and to the 'masses' had manifestly hardened.[3] Thenceforward there are clear indications that Oastler was increasingly haunted by the fear that an outright clash with his master might develop.

It was the Poor Law question above all else that caused the tension between them. Oastler did all he could to persuade Thornhill to his point of view. He wrote letters of prodigious length explaining the reasons for his opposition to the New Poor Law; he described the sad conditions prevailing among the handloom-weavers around Huddersfield and pointed out what the consequences would be if the new law were strictly applied in the Riding. And even though he knew he might be offending his master, he would not temper in the least the vigor of his observations. 'It is singular that I should be maintaining my views in the very heart of the manufacturing districts, in the very soul of humbug and dissent,' he wrote in one of his letters, 'and that I should grieve an aristocrat. If any man ought to be supported by the Aristocracy and the Landlords, I am that man.' But Thornhill was not the sort of person to be moved by that kind of appeal.

As Oastler's campaign against the New Poor Law expanded into a great mass movement, local Whigs bitterly complained to Riddlesworth. That, of course, only added to the tension. And when Thornhill heard that the tenants of his own township of Fixby had actually refused to elect a Guardian he became extremely angry. Whether that by itself would have occasioned a breach it is impossible to say. But no less a person than Frankland Lewis himself—one of the three Central Poor Law Commissioners —began to work on Thornhill to get Oastler silenced. These two had known each other for many years, so it is possible that pres-

[3] See above, p. 305–6.

sure was being brought to bear upon the Squire over a considerable period. It would seem, however, that the final persuasion
was not effected until Thornhill was in London for 'the season'
of 1838. On 30 May Oastler received the following letter:

49 Berkeley Square
May 28, 1838

To Mr. Oastler.

Sir:

I am sorry you still continue unwell. I trust your illness will not last
long, as I wish you to bring the accounts to London as soon as you
conveniently are able. I wish to come to a *final settlement,* as I am
sorry to say I cannot employ you any longer as my steward. I do not
consider it worth while entering into the number of objections that I
have; but suffice it to say, when I was induced to permit your residence
at Fixby, you explained to me that no person could properly attend
to my property, and do me justice, unless he gave up his *whole time*
to it and lived upon the spot. I am certain, from what I see of my
various concerns, that you have not attended to them as I wish;
therefore we must part. I wish you well for your own sake and doubly
so for that of your father.

I have written to a person this day to find a steward for me, and I
shall reside myself at Fixby as soon as you move out.

I remain,
Your well-wisher,
THOMAS THORNHILL.

It would hardly be possible to exaggerate the shock that this
curt dismissal was to Oastler. For 18 years he had labored at
Fixby with devotion and happiness; and for 20 years before
that his father had done the same. Ever since childhood, therefore, Fixby had been the certain background of his life and
around it all his emotions had become set. Now suddenly, in his
forty-ninth year, he was to be torn from it by an ignominious
dismissal while still embarrassed by a personal debt to his master
of some £2000.

¶ 3

During the next ten weeks Oastler was busy getting ready to
leave Fixby. There was much to be done: accounts had to be put
in order, the new steward inducted into his duties, and so on.

To one in Oastler's weak condition the strain involved was very great.

Yet he abated nothing of his efforts against the Poor Law, but rather pushed himself to the limit. At the end of July he appeared with O'Connor before a capacity house in the Halifax Theatre, where he wrought his hearers almost to tumult. What so greatly excited the audience, and what made the speech so memorable, was Oastler's first open advocacy of arming: 'I would recommend you, every one, before next Saturday night, to have a brace of horse pistols, a good sword and a musket, and to hang them up on your mantelpieces . . . *They* will petition for you.' Petitioning had failed; this was the workers' last resort. There would not be any need to use the arms, he declared: the threat itself would suffice to make the Government yield.

The Whig newspapers were scandalized, and many of Oastler's personal friends, too. But that did not deter him. At Dewsbury, the next week, he said the same thing and won an equally enthusiastic reception. Five days later an ugly riot broke out in the town. The crowd dispersed a Guardians' meeting, thrashed a local J.P. and threw him into the churchyard, and then began menacing known supporters of the New Poor Law. In panic, the Justices sent for the military, but by the time the soldiers arrived the crowd had vanished. Efforts were thereupon made by the local Whigs to get Oastler arrested on the ground that his inciting speech had made him morally responsible for what had happened. Sworn depositions about the speech were sent to the Home Office, but Russell had the good sense to take no action.

In the meantime, Oastler continued writing for the *Northern Star*. Week after week, in a series of open letters to individual politicians or *To the People of England* (some of which were reproduced in *The Times* and other London papers), he expounded once more his creed of constructive Toryism. Some of these letters are among the best things he ever wrote. Although there was nothing new in them, they put in succinct form the essentials of his social philosophy—his hatred of laissez-faire, his contempt for party, his detestation of the new 'Conservatism,' and his demands for social security and social protection. And mingled with the pleading there recurred time and again the new *motif*:

Arm, ye sons of Britain, whose souls are in the Ark of the Constitution! Arm, and make the traitors pause and tremble. . . You will have no need to learn the use of arms. The fact that you are known to be possessed of them will be enough. It will teach Howick and Co. no more to laugh at your petitions.

¶ 4

Ever since the news of Oastler's dismissal had been known to the Riding, his friends had been active on his behalf. Realizing that their leader would soon be without employment and without income, they had formed two committees to promote a national appeal for providing him with a farm or an annuity so that he might be free of pecuniary worries for the rest of his life. One committee, headed by John Whitacre, a neighboring landowner, appealed to the Tory gentry and the few Tory manufacturers, while the other, presided over by the loyal William Stocks, appealed chiefly to Radicals and operatives. In aid of their cause they had an 'Oastler National Testimonial' medal struck, which was sold to the general public for the benefit of the fund. The tenants on the Fixby estate, meanwhile, were collecting to buy Oastler some silver plate as a farewell gift.

All his friends and admirers were agreed that Oastler's going-forth from Fixby must be made the occasion for a great pageant in his honor. For weeks before his departure, therefore, they were working on the plans. The festival of tribute they were going to hold should be worthy of one who for so long had himself been a master-organizer of public demonstrations. They would escort him on his last journey from the Hall in a huge procession, and conduct him to a mass meeting in Huddersfield, where the testimonials would be presented.

Thus it was that after nearly 18 years of residence Oastler left Fixby Hall on Saturday, 25 August 1838, never to return.

The procession was to leave at five in the afternoon. Long before that hour, however, men and women from the villages roundabout were making their way up the hillside towards the Park. Local gentry came on horseback and in carriages. Delegations from Short Time Committees and Anti-Poor Law Associations poured in from Cheshire and Derbyshire, Lancashire and the

Riding, each with its banners and flags and insignia. From as far afield as Manchester and Rochdale, Glossop and Dewsbury they came, all wearing the blue and white favors of Oastler's election campaign and as many as could afford it the Oastler Memorial Medal as well. A small cannon had been placed on one of the eminences in the Park, and as the various deputations arrived it boomed forth in salutation. Ten bands had been brought along by different townships, and all through the afternoon played songs and melodies appropriate to the occasion.

Shortly after five o'clock, Richard and Mary Oastler came on to the terrace. The servants of the estate were all drawn up outside and Oastler went down the line shaking hands with each in turn. Then he mounted an open barouche drawn by two greys; flags and banners were raised aloft; the cannon fired a last salute; the massed bands struck up 'See the Conquering Hero Comes'; and the procession moved off. It was nearly a mile long, and according to *The Times* reporter could not have included fewer than 15,000 people. At its head rode a number of gentlemen on horseback carrying white wands; gigs, carriages, and phaetons followed; then came the rest on foot, marching with their bands and banners.

The enthusiasm displayed all along the route was immense. By the time Huddersfield was reached nearly two hours later, the town was thronged to greet 'King Richard.' On the outskirts the procession paused while a choir of factory children sang one of the old songs of the Ten Hours Movement, then it wound its way through the main streets of the town. 'Throughout the whole line of road,' said an eyewitness, 'the windows and the housetops were crowded, and every inch of standing room on the causeways and elsewhere was occupied.' Wave after wave of cheering rolled forth as Oastler passed by.

The procession finally brought up at an open plot of ground near St. Paul's Church, where hustings had been erected. By this time, said *The Times*, there must have been more than 50,000 people assembled. Before such a concourse Oastler's friends—rich and poor, Radical and Tory—vied with one another in praise of the man and of the causes for which he had labored. Addresses and testimonials were presented by the delegates of the various organizations, and then Oastler came forward to reply. But he was far too deeply shaken to speak with his customary power. He got only a little way before he was completely overcome, so the proceedings were forthwith brought to a quiet close.

'Such a display was never before seen in the Town of Huddersfield,' declared the *Leeds Intelligencer*. 'We know of nothing in our experience which has equalled this expression of sympathy,' wrote Samuel Kydd, the historian of the Ten Hours Movement, 20 years later. And the *Mercury*, true to form, devoting two and a half columns to these events and a long abusive editorial to Oastler himself, called the affair an 'outrageous farce.'

¶ 5

This farewell demonstration had an unforeseen consequence which widened the breach between Oastler and Thornhill beyond any hope of mending.

Until just before Oastler's departure, Thornhill had continued friendly enough towards his old steward. There was no suggestion of vindictiveness. All Thornhill had wanted was to get rid of a servant whose conduct had become embarrassing. Certainly on Oastler's side there was no malice. He took the new steward into the Hall, entertained him as his own guest, introduced him to the tenants, and generally helped him to find his feet. Together they went over the books with the assistant steward and got the accounts in order.

Then appeared the unfortunate placard. The committee organizing the farewell celebrations published on their own initiative a poster calling for public support. But they injudiciously used in it phrases that cast aspersions upon the Lord of the Manor, particularly a remark about 'the shafts of malice thrown by an aristocratic absentee landlord.' Some evilly disposed person sent a copy of the poster to Thornhill, who immediately became enraged. Believing it was composed by Oastler himself, he wrote a bitter retort for publication in all the Riding newspapers, in which it duly appeared on the very day Oastler left Fixby. In fact two letters, both signed by Thornhill, were published side by side. The first had been drawn up some time earlier by Thornhill's lawyer and had evidently been composed with considerable care to defend the Squire in what was proving to be a highly unpopular action. This offered as the reason for the dismissal the allegation that Oastler had become so immersed in politics that he would never be able to repay the debt he owed his master. It was nonsense, of course, since Oastler had already paid off a substantial part of the debt, and to deprive him of his income was scarcely the best way of insuring he would repay the remainder. But the second letter, written by Thornhill in his anger without the knowledge of his lawyer, bluntly declared that Oastler was not being dismissed for his political activities at all, but because he had *converted moneys of the estate to his own use.*

This completely ruined any chance that the two men would come to some sensible agreement about their tangled finances. Moreover, it put Oastler in an awkward position. Up to the present, not the hint of an aspersion upon his integrity had been cast by his master. Now he was suddenly being accused of malversation and would have to defend himself. He consulted counsel at once, and was told he must not hand over any books or papers of the estate when he left, but must retain them until he had cleared himself of the preposterous charge. He was also advised not to have any meeting with Thornhill until the accusation had been withdrawn. It was in this unsatisfactory state of affairs, carrying the Fixby account books with him, that Oastler quit his old post.

¶ 6

When Oastler left Fixby he was far from having recovered from his illness. For the next 5 months, therefore, he took things more lightly than he had done for many years, staying with various friends and spending a restful holiday by the sea at Rhyl. He continued writing for the *Northern Star,* however, and his columns abated nothing of their militancy. He went on advising the masses to arm, despite the fact that such advice had already shocked friends as well as enemies. The London *Standard,* which had been enthusiastic in his support for so long, felt compelled to warn him that he was getting perilously near treason in some of his utterances, and 'entreated' and 'supplicated' him to modify his language. Many other admirers felt the same way and told him so openly. But he heeded nothing of their warnings:

Once more [he wrote in October] I solemnly urge every Englishman who loves his country and his hearth to ARM. . . The people of England are sound at heart; they are loyal; and it is they alone under God who will ever be able to roll back the stumbling block of innovation and restore the Constitution of our beloved country to its original splendour and beauty. It is because I believe this is the destiny of *the people* that I urge them to fast, to pray, and to arm.

For some while his relations with Thornhill remained at a standstill. Then in mid-October he received a letter from the lawyers demanding settlement of the debt. He was still in a bellicose mood, for Thornhill's public accusation had angered as well as wounded him. He did not for a moment deny the debt, of course; but he wanted the matter brought into open court, where Thornhill would be compelled either to prove his allegation or withdraw it. So he wrote to the lawyers defiantly:

If Mr. Thornhill claims the money directly, the best way will be to proceed by law. I shall not oppose the claim—I will take no measures to prevent him—I have no money now for lawyers—my body is at his service any day, and my property also, as soon as I can turn it into money. But if indeed it be true, as you say it is, that 'Mr. Thornhill is most anxious to allow any expense or other deduction that I may be fairly entitled to,' why then, my dear Sir, if this declaration of yours be truth and not fiction, then, as we say in Yorkshire, 'the boot will be on t'other leg'—Mr. Thornhill himself (when his anger is over) being judge.

A week later the writ for debt was served upon him.

To Oastler's chagrin, London was fixed as the venue of the trial. This he considered grossly unfair. The expense of taking witnesses to London would be altogether beyond his means: moreover he felt it would be quite impossible 'to make a London jury understand the nature of a rural steward's position.' So he sought to get the case transferred to Yorkshire before a special jury. But Thornhill objected. In a sworn deposition he declared that all Oastler wanted was 'to have an opportunity of calumniating and declaiming against the plaintiff among his tenants.' Furthermore, he said, a fair trial in Yorkshire was impossible because of 'the excited state in which a considerable part of that country has been thrown into of late by the defendant's agitation.' Oastler's motion was therefore dismissed.

Notice of the trial was served on 23 January 1839, but nothing happened. Six months later a second notice was served, and again nothing happened. And thus for many weeks the matter stood.

CHAPTER XXIX

Chartism

IN INDIVIDUAL no less than in collective life it sometimes happens that there are seasons when various trains of tendency converge with such obviousness and dramatic force as to induce the conviction that a turning-point of destiny has been reached. The old astrologers sought to convey that sense with their metaphors about the conjunctions of the planets. Looking back upon his career in the tranquillity of old age, Oastler always regarded the month of May 1838 as just such a turning-point both for himself personally and for the proletarian movement in general.

First there had been his nervous breakdown, which was to leave him, at least physically, a permanently weakened man. Then had come his dismissal from Fixby, with all the emotional havoc that wrought. And while he was prostrate, Huddersfield's resistance to the Poor Law Commissioners had reached a climax with the riot of 7 May and the ensuing indictment by the Government. That riot, moreover, served to underline the admitted fact that the whole Anti-Poor Law Movement had now reached something of a stalemate occasioned in part by deep-seated conflicts in its ranks concerning both immediate tactics and ultimate purpose.

Above all there came the great resurgence of proletarian effort known as the Chartist Movement, focusing the discontent of the masses upon new objectives and eliciting remarkable fervor. This was a nation-wide movement, which swept aside all local and more limited efforts and substantially altered Oastler's status in working-class endeavor. And the month of May 1838 was crucial in that process too.

¶ 1

The Chartist Movement has often been likened to a river into which many separate streams of social protest emptied themselves. But the two headwaters from which it principally derived were the London Working Men's Association and the Birmingham Political Union, which came together to make Chartism in May 1838.

The London Working Men's Association had been founded in the summer of 1836 by that able group of Radical artisans whom Oastler had first come to know while he was lobbying against the Poor Law Bill and to whose illicit journals he had been contributing ever since.[1] Henry Hetherington, William Lovett, John Cleave, and James Watson were its moving spirits. Their immediate aim was educational, but their ultimate purpose was to build up a working-class elite capable of forming the nucleus of an independent political party. At first, therefore, their activities were confined to research, discussion, and propaganda. 'Imagine,' said one of their manifestos, 'the honest, sober and reflecting portion of every town and village in the Kingdom linked together as a band of brothers, honestly resolved to investigate all subjects connected with their interests, and to prepare their minds to combat with the errors and enemies of society.' That was the goal they set themselves. Intensely distrustful as they were of the middle classes, however, they kept their organization extremely exclusive. Beginning with 33 members, they still had only about 200 by the spring of 1838. But they invited a chosen few of their bourgeois sympathizers to become 'honorary members,' among whom they included Oastler.

Gradually a new conception of their function took shape in their minds. They began to think in terms of more immediate objectives and to see themselves as leaders of the entire working-class movement. Accordingly, at their first big public meeting in February 1837, they put forward their specific demands for the famous 'Six Points,' which Parliament was to be asked to enact.[2]

[1] See above, p. 285.
[2] The 'Six Points' were: (a) manhood suffrage, (b) annual Parliaments, (c) payment of Members, (d) equal electoral districts, (e) abolition of property qualifications for Members, and (f) voting by secret ballot.

Shortly afterwards missionaries were sent out into the provinces to promulgate these ideas. The success these orators achieved was phenomenal and grew with the deepening of the depression. 'They thought they had lighted a candle,' says one writer, 'and it turned out to be a rocket.' Within a twelvemonth the new enthusiasm had spread throughout the land and more than a hundred affiliated associations had been established. No longer was it a movement of comfortably situated artisans: now it embraced workers of every kind, including the unskilled and unemployed, without distinction. What had begun as an educational mission had thus turned into a national agitation on behalf of a new Parliamentary Reform Bill based upon manhood suffrage. After consultation with a few Radical M.P.'s, Lovett and his friends drafted such a bill, which they published on 8 May 1838 under the name of *The People's Charter*.

During those same twenty-four months another movement had been steadily converging upon the same point.

A group of prominent middle-class Radicals in Birmingham— all of whom had been active in the struggle for the 1832 Reform Bill—had become seriously perturbed by the growing distress in their city and had formed themselves into an association for its relief. In their case, too, the original intention gradually expanded, as local effort gave way to the larger purpose of seeking a national remedy for what after all was a national disease. To this end they re-established the Birmingham Political Union, which had been dormant since 1832, and invoked the full co-operation of the working classes. The first panacea they advocated under the influence of their unorthodox banker Attwood was the abolition of the gold standard and the provision of 'cheap money' by the establishment of a managed paper currency. As a means of attaining this goal, as well as to rally wider support, they soon broadened their demands to include five of the Six Points for which the London men were working. These were cast into the form of an impressively sonorous *National Petition*, which the Radicals of England were asked to join in promoting. The London Working Men's Association responded immediately.

Propaganda was then intensified and from Birmingham a second group of missionaries went forth to spread the gospel of

democratic reconstruction. One of these agents, an eloquent working man named Collins, had particularly impressive success at
Glasgow, where the brutal crushing of a recent strike had left
the operatives in a mood of militant bitterness. In consequence
the whole of Clydeside was swept into the movement. Whereupon it was decided to stage there a huge mass demonstration as
the prelude to a series of similar meetings all over England. To
this Glasgow meeting on 21 May 1838 there came not only the
leaders of Scottish unionism and the leading men from Birmingham but representatives of the London Association as well. On
that day the Radicalism of the Midlands, the Metropolis, and
Scotland coalesced in a unanimous demand for the *Petition* and
the *Charter*. And at the same meeting the banker Attwood put
forward two further suggestions that were to influence the
movement profoundly. One was the proposal that a National
Convention of Radicals should be held to promote their aims;
and the other, that if they could not get what they wanted
through parliamentary means they should call a General Strike.

   With this May meeting Chartism really became a formidable
national movement. Plans for holding a Convention were put in
hand immediately.

¶ 2

   The bearing of Chartism on Oastler's career becomes apparent only after a consideration of its effects upon the Anti-Poor
Law agitation and upon his personal following.

   Chartism destroyed the Anti-Poor Law agitation. That it did
so was due as much to the limitations of the one movement as to
the superior appeal of the other. Stanhope's plan had been to
federate all the local organizations into one great national association pledged to repeal. But now that the organization had
been set up, there appeared to be little agreement about what
to do next in the face of the Government's adamantine attitude.
Members had already shown themselves impatient with a cautious petitioning policy, yet there seemed little likelihood of
getting more vigorous action from such a dignified body as the
London Committee. Furthermore, its demands were essentially
negative. Repeal would be all to the good, though it has to be

remembered that in many parts of the north the hated Act had
not even gone into operation. What the workers wanted, however, was some positive relief from their misery, and repeal
would not bring that. That is why Anti-Poor Law meetings became punctuated with increasing frequency by interrupters calling for universal suffrage.

Chartism offered the evocative hope and as a result the greater
enthusiasm swallowed up the less. This was but the repetition
of a pattern that had occurred several times before. The Grand
National Union had sapped the vitality of the Ten Hours Movement; Fielden's Regeneration Society had annihilated Oastler's
Reformation Society; the Anti-Poor Law Association had pushed
the factory question into the background; now it was the turn
of the Anti-Poor Law Movement to be absorbed.

But the relationship between the two agitations is not as simple as such an assertion implies. Among those who endorsed the
Chartists' aims, at least in London, were some who were very far
from condemning the New Poor Law, and who believed the
campaign against it was a pernicious and dangerous thing.
Francis Place, we are told, 'kept up even among the extreme
democrats a tiny minority of audible opinion in its favour'; and
when he co-operated with the Working Men's Association he
made its leaders promise they would keep off the Poor Law question in their agitation.[3] This, indeed, was one of the numerous
elements of disunity in the Chartist movement, making many of
the northerners intensely suspicious of the London men. Beaumont, in his paper the *Northern Liberator,* warned his Newcastle
readers that Place was 'the very head and chief, the life and
soul, of the Poor Law Amendment Bill.'

Others, even if they did not endorse Place's approval of the
Poor Law, were convinced that the repeal movement was nothing
but a trick of the Tories to fool the workers. (The same thing
had often been said of the Ten Hours Movement.) Editorially
The Chartist declared that:

[3] The first manifesto put out by the L.W.M.A. struck a compromise, with
the ambiguous warning: 'Fellow men! Do not be led away by promises of
repealing the detested Poor Law, or any of the other infamous laws which
Whig and Tory have united to enact—unless the promise be accompanied by
the Pledge of Universal Suffrage.'

in the hands of a red hot Tory like Earl Stanhope, the nephew and admirer of that base and bloody tool of tyranny, William Pitt, the Anti-Poor Law agitation becomes nothing more than a trick of faction, a trick by which the Tories hope to get hold of the places and salaries of the Whigs, with the intention of using their power when they get it in a much worse manner than the Whigs ever have or ever can use it [sic].

Conversely, there were many stalwarts in the Anti-Poor Law Movement who were just as strongly opposed to Chartism. These were mainly the philanthropists and humanitarian Tories such as Duncombe and Parson Bull, who became greatly disturbed at the frequency with which the suffrage question erupted into their meetings. Walter of *The Times* felt particularly embarrassed on this account. It seems that in his alarm at the rapid spread of the new sentiment he actually played down the Anti-Poor Law story in his columns during the autumn of 1838, though by the end of the year he had recovered from his fears and was advocating the cause as zealously as ever.

And adding to contemporary confusion on the matter was Sir Edward Lytton Bulwer's opinion, endorsed by the Radical-Whig *Morning Chronicle,* that Chartism was nothing but the Anti-Poor Law Movement in another form.

The truth is that the formulae of the charter induced an illusory sense of unity. Men supported its demands for widely differing reasons, each faction hoping that its own particular goal might thereby be attained: a fact that stood clearly revealed in the recriminations that followed failure. Even among Oastler's circle of intimates there were acute differences of opinion about the movement.

Most of 'Oastler's boys,' including all six who had made the Fixby Hall Compact, were ardent Chartists. Two of them were actually elected to the Convention. For them the New Poor Law was but one example of class legislation, further installments of which would be sure to follow under the dispensation of the 1832 franchise. So they saw nothing incompatible between their support of the Charter and their membership of Short Time and Anti-Poor Law Committees. And without doubt their attitude was typical of tens of thousands in the north. R. J. Richardson, the organizer-in-chief of the Lancashire Association, carried this attitude to the extreme when he publicly repudiated his own organization, declaring that there could be no hope of effecting repeal until the Charter was achieved.

Parson Bull, on the other hand, could not bring himself to believe in the relevance of constitutional change to the daily lives of those around him. He was appalled by the ignorance and squalor, the drunkenness and credulity he could see on every hand, and sincerely believed that to give the vote to men living in such conditions would be to invite disaster. Bull was essentially an empiricist; practical remedies for specific ills he would fight for with unrelenting tenacity, but abstract ideas and general schemes made no appeal to him. So, lionhearted though he had been on behalf of factory children and Poor Law reform, he would have nothing whatever to do with Chartist activities.

Stephens' attitude was different again. In contrast to Bull, he participated in Chartist demonstrations to the limit of his capacity and got himself elected to the National Convention as delegate for Ashton (though circumstances prevented his taking his seat). In sheer emotional power he was probably the greatest orator associated with the movement. Moreover none surpassed him in the recklessness with which he advocated the use of violence. Months before there was a Chartist Movement he had talked openly about using 'the dagger and the torch'; now he proclaimed himself 'a revolutionist by fire, a revolutionist by blood, to the knife, to the death.' He was soon to have the additional distinction of being the first of the leaders to be arrested. Yet in spite of all this, it is doubtful whether Stephens can really be called a Chartist at all. He always denied that he was one. Nor is there any evidence that he put much store by the Six Points; at his trial he called them 'a rigmarole in which I never had a share.' Were Chartism to triumph, he added, 'my blood would be the first blood that would have to flow for the olden liberties of England.' According to the autobiography of one who later joined the movement, 'his followers were not even known as Chartists, but were always designated Stephensites.'

Only by appreciating the fact that Stephens saw the movement purely as a social protest can one begin to understand him. It was he who coined the phrase, which has now passed into the history books, that Chartism was 'a knife and fork question.' His single aim was to arouse the masses to a sense of the social and economic iniquities that were crushing them, and he believed that a militant self-consciousness on their part would compel even a government of the privileged to establish minimum standards of social decency. He hated and feared the individualistic philosophy of the economists and sought to do everything in his power to frustrate its application. But just what positive steps he wanted taken is not very clear—apart from factory reform, wages boards, and the restoration of the old Poor Law. Throughout his career he considered himself to be fighting on the defensive against the triumphant advance of capitalistic individualism; and in that struggle, he believed, almost any weapon was legitimate.

Another of Oastler's collaborators who took up Chartism for social rather than political reasons was the Bury doctor, Matthew Fletcher, who serves to typify yet a fourth variety of Chartist. He, too, became a member of the National Convention, playing for a while a not unimportant part in its proceedings. Above all else Fletcher was a humanitarian reformer—warmhearted, aggressive, and impetuous. He had flung himself wholeheartedly into the Ten Hours Movement, then into the Anti-Poor Law campaign. Finally he got caught up in the procession marching behind the National Petition. Eventually, however, he grew disgusted with the whole affair on account of the personal animosities and confused purposes that were so blatantly confessed as the Convention stumbled through its dismal course in 1839. He even went so far as to say that he believed Chartism had really been put forward by the champions of the New Poor Law in order to divide and destroy the repeal movement when it was becoming too powerful—an opinion, it is to be noted, the precise opposite of that held by the editor of *The Chartist* cited above.[4]

[4] Fletcher is not the only one to have this belief. Elie Halévy, for instance, holds that the Radical O'Connell deliberately sought 'to help the Government and to break the redoubtable agitation against the Poor Law by putting forward in revolutionary circles the alternative programme of Parliamentary reform.' *A History of the English People:* vol. III, p. 299.

As for Feargus O'Connor, with whom Oastler continued on the most intimate terms all through, his role almost defies analysis. With his control of the *Northern Star* and his extraordinary platform power he achieved unquestioned supremacy in the north and came to dominate the movement completely. He was no man's vassal, however, but went his own way regardless of the pronouncements from London or Birmingham. At the beginning of 1838 he declared himself in favor of manhood suffrage though opposed to secret balloting, yet he continued unabated his onslaughts upon the New Poor Law. Soon he had added the demand for peasant proprietorship of 'two acres and a cow.' His advocacy of physical force to achieve these ends was continuous and extreme, though he showed remarkably little inclination to put his preaching into practice even when others had made a beginning. Nothing could have been further removed from the cautious parliamentarism of the London Working Men's Association than O'Connor's flamboyance. His neurotic drive to dominate led him to quarrel with almost everyone (Lovett publicly called him 'The Great I AM' of proletarian politics). By April 1839, he was claiming that he personally had created the reputations of Oastler, Stephens, and others. A few years later he became permanently insane.

¶ 3

Oastler's own attitude towards Chartism was determined by the general social philosophy he had been proclaiming in season and out of season for the past 7 years. The events of 1838 did not cause him to modify his position in the slightest.

Clearly Oastler was not a Chartist. No Church-and-King man could ever be that, and Oastler stayed a Church-and-King man right to the end. As in Bull's case, his realistic sense of the human material he was dealing with inhibited all sympathy with the demand for a democratic suffrage, though he was still prepared to accept the plan for a 'mixed' franchise, giving separate representation to both the propertied and unpropertied orders, such as Sadler had put forward in 1831. Like Bull, too, he ardently wanted to see certain specific reforms enacted, the immediate and tangible results of which would be visible in the form of a shorter

working day, minimum wages, and substantial relief to the unemployed. He was always afraid that the daily sufferings of ordinary inarticulate people might get overlooked in the absorbing
process of reforming the mere mechanics of politics; and none
could convince him that an extension of the franchise might not
lead to an indefinite postponement of social reconstruction. Ever
since his disillusioning experience in the Huddersfield by-election
of 1834, he had had the uneasy suspicion that it would be just as
difficult to get comprehensive social reform out of a Radical Administration as it was to get it out of the Whigs.

Nevertheless Oastler saw as clearly as Stephens did that there
was far more behind Chartism than a demand for the vote: that
as far as the northern workers were concerned it was in truth a
protest against hunger, misery, and frustration. But he had known
of these things long before Chartism ever appeared. Time after
time during the previous 10 years he had seen poverty-numbed
men surge forth out of cellar and hovel at the call of some new
gospel and then crawl back disillusioned and bitter. They had
come forth at the bidding of the Political Unions in 1831-2 and
had been cheated of their hopes; they had come out again when
Owen and Fielden promised them the eight-hour day and had
retired broken; they had foregathered in innumerable assemblies
in the back rooms of dingy inns while Maxwell was trying to
persuade Parliament to help the handloom weavers, and not even
a gesture of sympathy had they won; they had cursed Power
and the Poor Law Commissioners at tumultuous assemblies, and
the Government had relentlessly moved the Hussars closer. So
many times it had happened before and now it was happening
all over again, only this time they gave the play a different name.
And all the while thousands of families continued on the brink
of starvation, without even enough clothing to keep out the dank
cold of the northern winter.

That was how Oastler looked at it. What intellectual London
artisans said about education and the vote, and what Birmingham
businessmen said about inflation did not seem to signify much.
The immediate need was to make Parliament see that there were
limits beyond which the impoverished and the unemployed could
not be driven. The Government seemed to suppose that by the

very nature of things the unprivileged had an obligation to submit quietly to the ineluctable operations of economic law. The people must teach their rulers to think otherwise. They had appealed and petitioned time and again to no effect. Now they must act.

That was why Oastler told them to arm. He was not proposing an insurrection, and he was not advocating civil war. What he did say was that if the masses armed and disciplined themselves, the Government would have to do something for them and abandon its laissez-faire policy. At the back of his mind were notions he had picked up from his reading about bygone days when the peasantry of England, armed with bills and bows, had rallied to the call of their local Tylers and Ketts in defense of their rights. 'I am now convinced,' he told a Nottingham audience, 'that rights will only be granted to an armed host of freemen.' There was no need to threaten or bluster. The mere possession of arms would suffice to pull the Whigs up sharply, confronted by the new-found resolution of a suffering people. Let the operatives and the unemployed and the handloom weavers get pikes and guns, then, and get them openly. Let them practice military exercises, too—though without their weapons—so that they might induce a sense of solidarity and discipline among themselves and of apprehension among their enemies. 'The fact that you are known to be possessed [of arms] will be enough,' he kept saying. If the workers used discretion and fraternized with the soldiers whenever possible there would be no trouble.

After all, he kept reminding his audiences, had not the Whigs themselves resorted to much the same tactics when they were trying to overcome the Tories in 1832? Even young Baines, who now preached 'constitutionalism' to the Chartists in every week's *Mercury*, had taken an active part in 'physical force' demonstrations. What of the pikes and tricolors and groans for the Queen, for instance, at the famous Cloth Hall Yard meeting during the 'days of May'? (It was a point that Disraeli was to develop in the House of Commons some months later, and to cap with one of his best-known epigrams.[5]) If the middle-classes could

---

[5] 'In a country so aristocratic as England even treason, to be successful, must be patrician.'

legitimately use these tactics, he asked, why not the workers?

Those were the arguments Oastler was putting forward in letter, speech, and pamphlet months before the missionaries came into the northern shires from London and Birmingham. And he went on repeating them long after his dismissal and long after the Convention had assembled. But in all those months he hardly ever touched upon the franchise question or the Charter itself. He did once say, however, that he had been compelled to drop out of political activity for a while because the new movement had ruined his Anti-Poor Law agitation.

Yet though his attitude towards these things seemed intelligible enough to himself and his intimates, there was many a Chartist who could not but feel bewildered and chagrined by his stand. The men of Colchester were voicing the opinion of many beside themselves when they adopted a resolution 'reprobating the conduct of Stephens and Oastler for endeavouring to draw the working people from the duty which they owed to themselves and their country.' Oastler's leadership was clearly on the wane.

¶ 4

One can only speculate on what Oastler's role in the Chartist movement would have been had he not been dismissed from Fixby. As it was, his position was difficult enough, with some of his dearest friends strongly opposed to the movement, some participating in it wholeheartedly, and some joining with enthusiasm and then withdrawing in disgust. But he was spared any significant decision himself. For months after his breakdown he was unable to do much of anything, and hanging over him all the while was the expectation of his impending trial.

Then, two days after Christmas 1838, Stephens was suddenly arrested for seditious utterances.

Throughout the autumn, while Chartist fervor was spreading over the land and the elections to the National Convention were being held, Stephens had gone forward unceasingly with his campaign of prophecy and commination. For greater effect he had taken to holding his meetings by the light of torches and flares on the open moors outside the big towns; and every night his incitement reached its climax with a boast about arms in readiness. Five thousand of his Ashton men, he claimed, were already equipped for action. Rumor distended the threats to enormous dimensions, and innumerable stories were told about hidden caches of munitions and about smithies making pikes against the day of reckoning. The Home Office became alarmed as the fear of incendiarism mounted. Might not these hysterical meetings really portend the fulfilment of all those prophecies about 'the dagger and the torch'? So the authorities finally struck, taking him into custody after one of his characteristic speeches delivered at Hyde in Cheshire. He was committed for trial at the next Liverpool Assizes, but allowed bail in the interim. This prevented his taking his seat at the National Convention.

'The agitation caused by his apprehension was very remarkable,' reports the unsympathetic Place. Far from damping Chartist ardor, the Government's action only stimulated it, and all manner of demonstrations, meetings, and protests followed. A 'Stephens Defense Fund' was opened and met with a remarkable response. Before the trial took place the following August, nearly £2,000 had been collected.

Stephens' arrest roused Oastler to an amazing outburst of activity. The long holiday in North Wales seemed to have restored his old vigor so that he was chafing to get back into the battle again. In February, therefore, he set forth upon a campaign of public meetings in aid of the Defense Fund which indisputably ranks as one of the most remarkable performances of his career. His hearers became convulsed with emotion as he shook them with his denunciations and his prophecies. Time and again newspapers reported that 'the effect produced upon his audience was such as we never before witnessed.' It was as much a religious revival he conducted as a political campaign. Never had the accent of the old Hebrew prophets rung so clearly in his discourses: the ancient texts of warning and retribution welled up from the depths of his anger with immense power. *Thus speaketh the Lord of Hosts, saying: Execute true judgement and shew mercy and compassion every one to his brother; and oppress not the widow, nor the fatherless, the stranger, nor the poor. . . The Lord will be a refuge for the oppressed, a refuge in times of trouble. . . He shall judge the poor of the people, He shall save the children of*

the needy, and shall break in pieces the oppressor. . . Ye shall
know that I the Lord have poured out my fury upon you. . . 'I
have learnt my politics as well as my religious creed from the
Bible,' he kept declaring; 'obedience must ever be limited to
such laws only as are in accordance with the revealed will of
God.'

Several times a week he addressed these gatherings as he toured
Lancashire, Cheshire, and Derbyshire. And always he concluded
with the same theme: his vision of a creative Toryism and the
promise it held for the suffering masses. If matters were allowed
to go on drifting as they had been in the past few years, assuredly
the doom of the transgressor would overtake the British ruling
classes.

I hope the time will come when party differences shall be forgotten
[he said at Mansfield], and Patriot and Christian shall be the only
names known. Then it will be satisfactorily ascertained and acknowledged by persons of property that their only security to that which
they call their own is founded on universal justice, and that if they
dare to trample on the right of the poorest and weakest and most de-
fenseless, the widow and the fatherless . . . if they dare to do this,
Omnipotence will raise up a loud shout from the voices of Englishmen, and a cloud of witnesses arise ready for the fight to declare and
to maintain in the face of the proudest and richest that 'if we have no
right to live, thou hast no right to rule.'

Huge crowds flocked to hear this apocalypse. Hundreds who
could not get into the halls waited outside to cheer the prophet,
and local bands led him down the thronged streets.

But it could not last. The tremendous effort finally exhausted
all his reserves of energy and after six weeks he had to give up.
More than five years were to pass before he took part in another
campaign, and by that time he was a greatly altered man.

Through the eyes of one discerning observer we get a particularly interesting glimpse of Oastler at this moment in his career.
The novelist Fanny Trollope had recently become aware of the
factory question. Deciding to write a story about it in order to
bring the problem home to a larger public, she had obtained from
Lord Ashley letters of introduction to various Ten Hours leaders and, accompanied by her son Tom, had set out on a tour of

Yorkshire and Lancashire to pick up local color. They interviewed many people, including John Wood and Parson Bull, both of whom they found very pessimistic about getting any effective legislation in the near future. But the man who impressed them beyond all others was Oastler: 'the most remarkable individual with whom this journey brought us into contact,' said Tom. They talked with him on the factory question and borrowed from him his collection of pamphlets and scrap books from which they culled material clearly discernible in the novel. They also followed him round to some of his meetings, where they saw for themselves the dramatic power of his oratory in halls 'filled to suffocation, besieged by crowds around the door.' It was this first-hand experience that led Tom to call Oastler 'the Danton of the factory movement.'

Both of them went home deeply shocked by 'the horrors of uncivilized savagery and hopeless, abject misery' which they had seen. Their findings appeared next year in *Michael Armstrong*, the first novel of factory life. 'There was no exaggeration in the outline of the picture,' Tom said of his mother's book, searing though that is; 'what we are there described to have seen, we saw.'

¶ 5

For Oastler this stirring campaign brought to a close ten years of almost continuous participation in local and national politics. He had no share in the events that led to the climax and then to the collapse of Chartism; and the affair of the Huddersfield Guardians, of which he had been the leading spirit, moved to its culmination without him.

Stephens was brought to trial in August and sentenced to eighteen months' imprisonment. Oastler's own trial was still deferred. On receiving his second notice in June, he moved to Brompton to await proceedings, yet nothing happened. Month after month the suspense was drawn out. A third notice came in December and a fourth in mid-January, but still nothing happened. He began to wonder if anything ever would happen, and toyed with the idea of getting some kind of journalistic work.

In the meantime the Chartist bubble reached its maximum and

then burst. Amidst great excitement the National Convention had duly assembled in London on 4 February 1839. But soon the extravagant hopes of speedy action were dispelled and all the weaknesses inherent in the movement stood revealed. Personal antipathies, quarrels over tactics, and differences about ultimate objectives split the body into fragments. One by one the moderates withdrew and the rest became progressively more confused in regard to the course they ought to pursue. In May they adjourned to Birmingham. On 12 July (which happened to be the day on which Parliament formally rejected the National Petition), they decided to call a general strike; but ten days later they cancelled the decision. Dissension grew while sporadic rioting occurred. In the late summer with the backing of the Government, local authorities struck hard everywhere. Some twenty members of the Convention itself were arrested along with scores of lesser men all over the country—'physical force' and 'moral force' advocates alike. In the course of the winter more than three hundred men were sentenced to terms varying from a few months to transportation for life. Thus with all its leaders in prison or in retreat, Chartism as a national movement ceased to exist. It disintegrated into local groups, wherein the spirit of the Charter was kept alive against the day of some future revival of effort.

¶ 6

Effective resistance to the New Poor Law likewise ended when Chartism collapsed. Even Huddersfield, the last bastion of recalcitrance, was brought to an inglorious surrender.

Following the riotous meeting of the Board of Guardians on 7 May, the 'antis' had everything their own way for the rest of the year 1838, since an official investigation of the election returns gave them a clear majority by unseating three of the Whigs. For another year, therefore, the orders from Somerset House continued to be set at naught. 'Any device that could be started which was calculated to evade the bringing of the law into operation was seized upon and obstinately persisted in,' complained the *Mercury*, 'making the proceedings altogether one of the most complete farces ever acted by any body of men who claimed to

have been appointed to exercise executive power.' Several times
special constables had to be sworn in to guard the Court House,
and for one particularly threatening meeting on Christmas Eve,
troops of the 7th Hussars and the 1st and 3rd Dragoon Guards
had again to be moved into the town to keep order. Yet still the
Whigs could make no headway.

But as the year 1839 advanced, resistance gradually weakened.
For one thing, local exploits like those at Huddersfield received
less and less publicity in both the Radical and the Tory press
as public attention became increasingly concentrated upon the
Convention and other national matters. For another, most of the
leaders were too preoccupied with their own concerns to pay any
further attention even to Huddersfield. Oastler and Stephens
were both awaiting trial; Pitkeithley, Bussey, Rider, and Fletcher
were busy at the Convention; Richardson had abandoned the
cause. And those who were left seemed more reluctant to invoke
the mob than they once had been, six of them having to face
charges of 'tumultuous assembly' for the part they had played
in the fracas of 7 May. Nor, one suspects, were these the only
reasons for the weakening of resistance. There are hints that even
among the 'antis' there were some who could be won over to
acceptance of the law when they came to realize that the new
system would create a number of desirable offices which would
eventually have to be filled. Towards the end of the year an unsavory dispute arose on the Huddersfield Board concerning the
attempt made by a Guardian hitherto foremost in opposition to
secure one of these 'jobs' for himself.

The trial of the six riotous Guardians and the annual elections
for a new Board both took place in March 1839, and the two
events together ended the story of Huddersfield's long-drawn-out
opposition to the law. At the Assizes, the Judge intervened after
hearing a full account of the riot and its antecedents. Expressing
grave doubts regarding the legality of the magistrate Sutcliffe's
high-handed action, he persuaded the defendants to agree to a
verdict of *guilty*, both parties entering into recognizances to
keep the peace and conduct the business of the Union satisfactorily in future. At the elections which followed, the 'antis' were
overwhelmingly defeated. The new Board with its large Whig

majority was therefore able to start putting the law into operation without further delay.

Not that this victory at the polls immediately ended the Whigs'
difficulties. Sporadic local rioting still occurred from time to
time. At Kirkheaton, for example, there was a rising of the whole
district when the relieving officer came to the workhouse to
inaugurate the new dispensation. The mob seized and destroyed
his books and chased him literally 'like a fox,' we are told, over
fields and through hedges until he was out of the township. But
as time went by such incidents became fewer. The collapse of
the National Convention and the ruthless action of local authorities completely broke what remained of the Anti-Poor Law Movement.

The Anti-Poor Law Movement had been defeated, yet the agitation was not without result. It had helped to make the Central
Poor Law Board realize that in the northern manufacturing districts the administration of the law would have to be conducted
on lines somewhat different from those followed in the rural
south. The Commissioners thus found themselves compelled to
compromise. For the unions in Lancashire and the West Riding
they issued orders instructing the Guardians to continue giving
relief according to the Elizabethan and 'all other' Poor Law
statutes. This enabled local authorities to use their discretion
and even to maintain the old policy of their respective areas.
Some measure of the failure to carry out the Act with the rigor
that Henry Brougham and Harriet Martineau desired can be
found in the impressive fact that as late as 1848 the number of
paupers in the workhouses of England and Wales was just over
300,000 whereas more than six times that number were receiving
relief outside.

¶ 7

Sorrowfully Oastler watched from afar the dissipation of yet
another dream. His general interpretation of these affairs, however, received striking expression in an entirely unexpected quarter. In the parliamentary debate upon the National Petition held
on 12 July 1839, Benjamin Disraeli made what was conspicuously the most original of all the speeches, and that amounted

to a terse summary of Oastler's own philosophy. The similarity of ideas is so remarkable that anyone familiar with Oastler's utterances could parallel Disraeli's observations from them paragraph by paragraph.

Like Oastler, Disraeli could not accept the Petition; and though he spoke understandingly of its advocates he voted against their demands: 'I am not ashamed to say, however much I disapprove of the Charter, I sympathize with the Chartists.' Nor could he be convinced that political rights necessarily ensure social happiness; the movement was the expression of a far deeper malaise than the Six Points suggested. 'I believe,' he declared, 'the real cause of this movement is a sentiment on the part of the people of England that their civil rights have been invaded.' The close connection between Chartism and the New Poor Law he saw as clearly as Oastler did. 'The New Poor Law is an invasion of their civil rights. We cannot deny that we have based this New Poor Law upon a principle that outrages the whole social duties of the State—the mainstay, the living source, the robustness of the Commonwealth. . . We have taught the unfortunate labourer that he has no legal claim to relief.' Furthermore, Disraeli interpreted both this law and the protest against it as the outcome of something deeper still: namely, the political revolution that had been brought about in 1832. The reasoning he used was identical with Oastler's. Prior to the Reform Bill, he said, 'the old Constitution had an intelligible principle which the present has not.' The political rights enjoyed by the few under the old system had been entrusted to them on condition they performed certain public functions. But the Act of 1832 gave political power into the hands of a new class which had 'not been bound up with the great mass of the people by the exercise of social duties.' The only thing these new men wanted was power—without corresponding responsibilities, 'without any appeal to their pockets, and without any cost of their time.' Hence their demand for 'cheap government' as well as their demand that government should shoulder new burdens. But, said Disraeli in terms identical with those Oastler had been continuously using since 1835, 'I contend one cannot have a cheap and centralized government and maintain at the same time the civil rights of the people of England.' The New Poor Law was but one proof of this: others would soon follow. And what made matters worse was the fact that even the Tories had become corrupted by the new ideas. Now that they had recovered from the stupor of defeat, they too were beginning to think 'they should have a slice of the cake and fruits of reform.' Such a system, however, was bound to break down in the long run. Whiggery was deluding itself if it seriously supposed it could 'establish a permanent government on what is styled nowadays a monarchy of the middle classes.' Such a conception was alien to the character of the English people. 'I am convinced that if they persist in their present system of cheap and centralized government, they will endanger not only the national character but also the national throne.'

Those were not merely Oastler's arguments: they were some of his very phrases.

CHAPTER XXX

Trial

THUS the year 1839 dragged for Oastler to a futile close. By his fiftieth birthday he was as downcast and frustrated as he had been in the winter of 1834–5 after the defeat of the Grand National Union. For the second time in his life his own more limited efforts had been swept aside by a torrent of popular excitement that had accomplished nothing; but this time his own career was in ruins too. Most of what he held of value and graciousness in life had been torn from him. He was an exile from his own Yorkshire, living on charity and awaiting trial. Some who had been his friends for years now shunned him altogether, others were in prison. No one was left to carry on his work. Parson Bull remained loyal, though critical; but he, too, had left the Riding, having recently been appointed Vicar of St. Thomas's, Birmingham.

Until a settlement had been reached with Thornhill, Oastler could make no plans. Yet weeks went by and still Thornhill gave no indication of his intentions. Suddenly Oastler's hopes soared: in mid-December 1839, he received notification that Thornhill had withdrawn the record. He naturally supposed that his old master had at last relented and that some agreement could now be worked out between them. But a month later the cat-and-mouse game began again with Oastler's receipt of a fourth notice of the impending trial.

At the end of January 1840, there was a brief break in the monotony of waiting when he spoke on behalf of John Walter before enthusiastic Tory audiences in a Southwark by-election. This brought him additional notoriety, which incidentally revealed what a significant public symbol he still remained. The Whig press sneered at the proprietor of *The Times* for having 'called to his assistance the great Radical leader Oastler.' The Whig candidate inflamed supporters by reading to them some of the more lurid passages from Oastler's speeches. Abusive letters were sent to Oastler himself: 'You were lucky,' said one, 'in escaping being tarred and feathered in Southwark. It was resolved on, but you could not be found when all was ready.' Echoes were heard in a confidence debate in the House of Commons a few days later. Speaking in defense of the Whig Government, Sir George Grey challenged the Opposition with the inquiry: 'whether there had not been an unhallowed alliance between Tories and Chartists and Destructives, and if it was not a notorious fact that at an election which took place within these few days for a great metropolitan district the champion of Conservatism invited and received the aid of the incendiary Oastler?' Duncombe from the North Riding rose to defend Oastler, who nevertheless continued to be a target for Whig shafts. As leader of the Conservative opposition, Peel sought to disembarrass himself of the suggestion that he endorsed Oastler or welcomed his support, but that did not prevent Lord John Russell from repeating the charge at the conclusion of the debate. Oastler wrote vigorous and lengthy answers to each of these attacks and *The Times* published them in full.

Until June he was also occupying his time writing a series of long autobiographical letters *To the People of Yorkshire,* which appeared weekly in the *Northern Star.* They gave him another opportunity to restate his political philosophy and warn the workers of the expanding consequences of capitalism, but they do not appear to have attracted much attention. The workers were too numbed by defeat to be moved by such appeals now.

At last, after almost two years of waiting, Oastler was brought to trial on Friday, 10 July 1840.

The case came up before Chief Justice Tindal and a special jury in the Court of Common Pleas. It was described as 'an action on a promissory note for money had and received, and for the detention of certain books alleged to belong to the plaintiff.' Thornhill's counsel was the distinguished barrister Fitzroy Kelly Q.C.— later to become Attorney General under the Earl of Derby. Oastler conducted his own case with the help of R. B. Cobbett.

The trial lasted only a short time. Kelly first sought to show that the money was actually owing from Oastler to Thornhill and began to read the friendly correspondence between them to prove it. Oastler quickly interrupted, for he had expected something quite different. He had come prepared to defend himself against the charge of defalcation which Thornhill had made in the Yorkshire papers, whereas Kelly explicitly said in his opening remarks that he was going to refrain from introducing 'any other matter not bearing on the precise question before the jury.' If Kelly really meant this, Oastler declared, there was no need to waste the time of the court any longer. He unreservedly admitted an honorable debt to his former employer and expressed his willingness to 'submit to a verdict at once and place himself in Mr. Thornhill's hands.' He had merely resisted the action, he said, 'because he understood that it had been imputed to him that he had fraudulently detained the money.' The Judge assured him that 'there was no imputation whatever' upon his character. Oastler and Kelly thereupon conferred and agreed upon a verdict for Thornhill for £2,600, without prejudice to a counterclaim by Oastler for £500. Judge and counsel both expressed their satisfaction at this sensible outcome, and the case ended. Oastler was greatly relieved at the verdict. 'It was, I can assure you,' his solicitor R. B. Cobbett wrote to Stephens in prison, 'quite to my and my client's satisfaction; and I think the libellous tongues of our most libel-loving and respectable people will be tied on that subject.' The only reason Oastler had wanted a public trial was to have his personal honor vindicated and he felt that this had now been accomplished. All that remained to be done was to come to some arrangement with Thornhill about paying off the debt, and that ought not to be difficult.

For four more tedious months Oastler waited for Thornhill's next move. So long was the silence that he again began to think his old master had relented and that the rift between them might be healed. All his money had gone and he was living on anonymous donations. 'It is a fact,' he wrote to a friend, 'that the only money I have comes by letters—sometimes a five pound note, sometimes a ten, sometimes a twenty—but from whom, except in two instances, I know no more than you.'

But in November Thornhill's lawyer wrote to ask what proposals for settlement Oastler was prepared to make. There was little Oastler could suggest. He offered to hand over a proportion of all his future earnings, once he had got another post, until the debt was cleared. This failed to satisfy Thornhill, however. His lawyer replied saying he must have 'the debt and costs, or security for the payment of it by installments at reasonable periods, or execution must issue forthwith.' Of course it was impossible for Oastler to meet such a request. Whereupon a writ of execution was secured, and on Wednesday, 9 December 1840, at five o'clock in the afternoon, the gates of the Fleet Prison closed upon Richard Oastler, the one-time 'Factory King.'

❀ ❀ ❀

Thornhill's conduct towards his steward leaves much to be accounted for; yet no one has ever elucidated it satisfactorily. The old gentleman had been greatly angered by the farewell placard. But Oastler was easily able to explain that as none of his doing, and the most casual enquiry from respectable people around Huddersfield would have speedily confirmed him. Obviously something more lay behind all this. It is particularly unfortunate, therefore, that the Thornhill family papers were destroyed a few years ago, thereby preventing our learning the story that was never made public.

One can only guess what happened, and the likeliest surmise is that some of Thornhill's friends connected with the Government persuaded him to put Oastler out of the way. Thornhill had earlier admitted that Frankland Lewis of the Poor Law Commission had asked his co-operation in getting the Poor Law started in the Fixby area. (The connection between the two men was close: they had been at college together, and gossip had it that one of Thornhill's daughters was about to become Lewis's second wife.) It is thus not inconceivable that when the Anti-Poor Law fury mounted in the north, when Oastler openly talked of arming as Chartist enthusiasm was spreading, the Whig leaders should have suggested to Thornhill that he might render an even more conspicuous service to the cause of law and order and help ward off the civil commotion that many in authority believed imminent. Nor were those in Whitehall the only ones likely to have brought pressure upon Thornhill. Note has already been made of the virulent things that numerous prominent local citizens, such as the magistrate Sutcliffe, were secretly writing to the Home Secretary even in 1837. Thornhill must have been inundated with such communications as the fear of insurrection grew. Imprisonment for debt would cause far less of an outcry than arrest for sedition, and would have the added advantage of smearing Oastler's reputation as well. With his arrest none of the big northern leaders would be left at large. And that was just the situation on the afternoon Oastler walked into the famous debtors' prison.

CHAPTER XXXI

Life in Prison

BY THE PAYMENT of a fee of twenty-eight shillings and eightpence Oastler was put 'on the foundation' of the Fleet Prison: that is to say, he was entitled to rent a cell. And for a further seven shillings a week he could hire furniture. Having paid his fees, he was taken to number 12, Coffee Gallery, a small, dark cell groined with brick, close behind the Warden's House. Some weeks later, however, better and cheaper quarters became available and he took them.

When the turnkey at last left him, Oastler tells us, and he found himself alone, he knelt down and prayed for a long while —prayed for his family and the causes he had so deeply at heart, and even for his persecutors. Rising refreshed, he took out his Bible and turned to the 56th and 57th Psalms for consolation: 'Mine enemies would swallow me up all the day long: for they be many that fight proudly against me. What time I am afraid, I will put my trust in Thee . . .' A tranquillity slowly spread over him, and the peace that comes with acceptance. He filled his pipe, he says, and as he smoked fell into a reverie upon the strangely winding path that had led him from the Yorkshire dales to a London prison. There must be some inscrutable purpose behind it all, he felt. 'I could not help exclaiming: "How strange, how mysterious are the plans of God; truly His way is in the sea and His path in the great waters, and His footsteps are not known."'

But what of the future? Idleness was unthinkable. His heart still burned with indignation and pity for the unnumbered thousands whose misery his imagination could never escape. He was more than ever convinced that his own social philosophy alone provided the clue for betterment. There was only one thing he could do in the circumstances: he could conduct from prison a little magazine to spread his message among all classes of society in the hope that one day his convictions might bear fruit. He consulted his wife. They agreed to throw their remaining savings into the project; a publisher was found; a prospectus was issued; and three weeks later the first number of *The Fleet Papers* appeared.

¶ 1

It was an eight-page magazine cast in the form of an open letter to Thomas Thornhill. At the head of each issue were the four mottoes that epitomized his social principles:

> *The Altar, the Throne and the Cottage*
> *Property has its Duties as well as its Rights*
> *The Husbandman that laboureth must be first*
> *partaker of the fruits*
> *He shall judge the poor of the people, He shall save*
> *the children of the needy, and*
> *shall break in pieces the oppressor*

The covers (at first bright blue, then later changed to white) gave an additional four pages for communications, answers to correspondents, and a few advertisements.

These *Fleet Papers* are what today would be called 'news letters'—general comments upon the passing scene, expositions of a particular philosophy, and interpretations of men and movements in terms of that analysis. Oastler's propensity for letter writing thus found ample scope at last in a weekly medium controlled entirely by himself. There was a large autobiographical element in all that he wrote: not only in the sense that he frequently referred to the events of his past life but also in the sense that incarceration induced in him a curious self-dramatization which seemed to find relief in publicly serializing itself.

For this reason the *Papers* are extremely illuminating. They reveal (as the writings of extroverts so often do) far more than their author either realized or intended. In them we see depicted the man's deep emotional drives: his unshaken convictions, his profound prejudices, and his passionate repudiations. And equally clearly we can see his obvious intellectual limitations. There was a streak of naïveté in him which the *Papers* bring out clearly: a certain intellectual flaccidity contrasting markedly with his lusty fervors. To say that, however, is not to deny that he had a well-integrated scheme of moral values or to assert that he was lacking in intelligence. Quite the contrary. Implicit in everything he wrote and did was a coherent philosophy of life which went along with a practical shrewdness and an intuitive insight of no mean order. But this intelligence did not operate primarily on the analytical level. It is hardly surprising, therefore, that his literary style should have the characteristic tang that accompanies an idiom compounded of strong visual imagery and a preference for emotive words.

There is a strangely Dickensian flavor in these *Papers*. They abound in a robust pathos entirely foreign to our own age. The compassion is forthright and unabashed, unqualified by the hesitancy bred by sophistication. The drama of good and evil locked in mortal combat, which Oastler seeks to convey, tends to become a melodrama in which the chief villains are the factory system and the Poor Law, Chadwick and the Home Secretary. The magazine thus gets transformed into a weekly evangelical tract presented in a political form. Yet criticism is stilled as one reads on, for academic distaste is swept away by the torrential earnestness of the writer. One can no more cavil at the idiom of the man than one can cavil at the broad dialect of a slum missionary. Here from the prison cell comes the pleading of one who has looked into the eyes of suffering and cannot forget what he has seen.

¶ 2

Immediate success justified the risk Oastler had taken. The circulation of the first number was doubled by the second, and that doubled again by the third. Subscriptions came in from admirers all over the country. London and provincial newspapers published favorable notices and reprinted excerpts, so that Oastler's words and reputation spread to quarters they had never before reached. His old supporters—the *Leeds Intelligencer, Northern Star, Manchester Advertiser,* and *Halifax Guardian—*

gave him ample publicity as a matter of course. What is more noteworthy is the backing he received from papers in other parts of the country. A survey of the reviews shows that in the first few months alone he had the benediction of no fewer than 30 provincial journals,[1] while in London the *Times, Standard* and *Morning Herald* continued the support they had always given him.

Typical of the comments in these papers was that published by the *Planet* just after the prospectus for the *Fleet Papers* had been issued.

We have had the opportunity [it declared editorially] of seeing Mr. Oastler on some occasions of great political excitement, and we can say of him with perfect sincerity that we believe a more humane man, a more honest man, or a more able man there does not exist. We do not coincide with Mr. Oastler in his opinions, and we differ altogether from him in politics. We do not approve of the course which he has pursued on many occasions; but feeling and believing that he has always acted conscientiously, we are compelled to say that there is no one better entitled to the sympathy and the support of the public. If he is now a prisoner, it is because he has thought much of others and never of himself—that he is the victim of his own philanthropy, and therefore entitled to the aid which every honest man can tender him. There is no man has done more than Mr. Oastler to mitigate the operation of the New Poor Law. His opposition to it has been attended with a thousand advantages, and he has kept public feeling alive to whatever defects were to be found in the working out of its details. He has aided others—we hope that he is destined to discover that humanity in England can find not only thousands of admirers but millions of supporters. . .

¶ 3

If Oastler had expected that he was going to be lonely in prison, he was almost embarrassingly disillusioned. From the first day

---

[1] In addition to the newspapers mentioned above, the following published extracts and favorable notices from time to time: *The Planet, Oxford City and Country Chronicle, Liverpool Mail, Hull Packet, Lincolnshire Chronicle, Sheffield Iris, Cleave's Gazette, Worcester Journal, New Moral World, Nottingham and Newark Mercury, Morning Star, People's Magazine, Britannia, Shropshire Conservative, Leicester Journal, Birmingham Advertiser, The Satirist, Chester Courant, Salopian Journal, Suffolk Herald, Cumberland Pacquet, Exeter and Plymouth Gazette, Stockport Advertiser, Berwick and Kelso Warden, Monmouthshire Beacon, Dublin Evening Mail, Sheffield Patriot, Wakefield Journal, Newcastle Journal.*

of his confinement, friends known and unknown began to visit him. As the weeks went by they came in such a constant stream that he had to hold regular 'at home' days on Tuesdays, Thursdays, and Saturdays, and beg that he might be left to himself for the rest of the week since otherwise he would find the strain of entertaining too great. He was almost one of the sights of London, declared a surprised columnist. From breakfast until closing time an extraordinary assortment of people from all walks of life crowded into his cell on visiting days: some to cheer him and others to hear him discourse, some to bring gifts and others to beg help. It was, he said, a continuous levee. One Yorkshire journalist who went back home to write half a column on what he had seen in 'the old King's cell' reported that he met there in the space of an hour or two a Member of Parliament, a couple of Polish Counts, the son of a Peer, several mechanics, a French officer, two London and several provincial editors, as well as numerous miscellaneous callers.

It was great comfort to Oastler to be courted in this manner. And what particularly softened the shock of imprisonment was the fact that it brought about many a reunion with those who had broken with him in recent years. Even Ashley came to see him, though the two had not spoken since Oastler's notorious speech on 'the Law or the Needle.' The comment in Ashley's journal has a generosity that honors the writer as much as his subject:

July 13 [1841].—Called on Oastler today in the Fleet Prison. I broke off from him when he became ungovernably violent, and dealt in language and advice which must have issued in fire and bloodshed. Years have now elapsed; his fury has subsided, and his service must not be forgotten. No man has finer talents or a warmer heart; his feelings are too powerful for control, and he has often been outrageous because he knew that his principles were just. The factory children, and all the operatives owe him an immense debt of gratitude. It is difficult to assign him his due portion of all the service that was rendered in the beginning of this mighty question. His employer, Mr. Thornhill, has used him infamously.

Of course, his older friends were in a class apart: it was their more intimate visits that brought Oastler the richest easement.

Bull and Stephens, Walter and Fielden, Ferrand and Duncombe, as well as the men of the Fixby Compact, all stuck loyally by him and came with unfailing regularity to see him.

Equally unexpected was the steady stream of gifts that began coming in from all parts of the country. Folk in all walks of life who had never set eyes on him, including avowed political opponents, joined in this spontaneous tribute. Very soon Oastler had to start publishing what he called his 'Rent Roll' to make acknowledgment to his many benefactors, for never a week passed without its due quota of gifts. Pages could be filled listing them all: fruit, vegetables, clothes, cakes, groceries, books, tobacco, furniture, and sundries too numerous to classify: while his wealthier benefactors, such as Walter and Duncombe, provided him with a veritable wine cellar. In this way his ordinary wants were amply supplied throughout his prison term, so that from time to time he was able to give little lunch and dinner parties. But the gifts were not only in kind. Money came too with remarkable regularity, ranging from the sixpence of a handloom weaver to £5 from the American Consul. A computation from the donations listed in the *Papers* shows that in his first two years of imprisonment Oastler received well over £300 in cash, a sum that enabled his wife to live comfortably in lodgings near by.

Meanwhile, impressive homage of another kind came from the northern operatives when 'Oastler Committees' were formed out of the remnants of the old Ten Hours organization. Huddersfield, Manchester, Chorley, Bradford, and Keighley were the first towns to start such Committees, which began right away collecting money from workers in the factories 'in heartfelt respect' (as the Bradford operatives put it when forwarding their first £7) 'for the person and principles of their old King.' Other groups raised subscriptions as well, such as the Manchester Cotton Spinners Association and various co-operative societies. And sometimes where there was no local organization, individual workers went round the mills collecting a few shillings on their own initiative.

From time to time these lodges did things in a big way. Oastler had been in prison hardly a month before his 'Huddersfield Boys' held an 'Oastler Festival' in the Philosophical Hall. There was a high tea followed by a concert and dance attended by over 600

people. Special songs were written for the occasion, which closed
with a new version of the National Anthem beginning:

> God save our Factory King,
> Oastler the Brave, we sing;
> Long live our King.

A check for over £ 23 went to the Fleet as a result.

The Bradford society followed with a similar 'Festival,' organized entirely by operatives. Indeed it went one better by
hiring the band of the Royal Foresters. Their local poetasters, too,
were called upon to rewrite favorite hymns and songs, including
the Old Hundredth.

> Come, let us all together sing,
> May plenty crown our faithful King;
> For his endeavours for the Poor
> May Heaven reward him evermore.

So it went in other places, even in towns like Sutton-in-Ashfield,
where there had been no kind of Oastler society before.

The weeks thus slipped by with Oastler's days too full to allow
of much repining. There were the regular eight pages of the
Fleet Papers to be written before each Wednesday morning, and
the business connected with the magazine to be attended to.
Letters had to be sent to the newspapers and an extensive correspondence dealt with. Moreover, visitors became more numerous
instead of less. Yet in between times Oastler got a considerable
amount of reading done: government reports, Hansards, and current magazines were always strewn about his cell.

Politically, too, he was far from inactive; frequently he had to
serve as a sort of go-between for interested parties. Deputations
from the Short Time Committees came to consult him and make
plans for a new Factory Bill. The handloom weavers continued
to seek his help. Letters of introduction were sought. He even
had a hand in getting Walter adopted as candidate in the Nottingham by-election of 1841. Independently of one another, both the
Tories and Chartists of Nottingham had written to Oastler asking
for suggestions for a suitable candidate. Each group mentioned
the same requirements: its man must be a Ten Hours advocate

and an opponent of the Poor Law. By good chance it happened that Walter came to see Oastler the very day he received these enquiries. Oastler showed him the letters and urged him to consider the dual nomination; then he wrote to Nottingham pressing Walter's claims and suggesting that the two parties should collaborate. This they did; Walter duly received a joint invitation and was finally elected.

For four days in July there was a pleasant break in the routine when he made an unexpected trip to York. Thornhill was having a lawsuit with one of his tenants who subpoenaed Oastler as a witness. Oastler was therefore escorted north by train—the first train journey of his life—and taken to the Assizes (though eventually, much to his relief, his evidence was not called for). The journey had other pleasures, however, than the novelty of the transportation. He was allowed to receive various friends who traveled to York to meet him, and he was twice permitted to see Feargus O'Connor in jail. His warm regard for the Irishman had remained unshaken by the vicissitudes of the past three years. It was a real grief for him, therefore, to find how ill O'Connor had become during his solitary confinement.

The only other interruption came with the closing down of the Fleet Prison in November 1842. To his great disgust Oastler found himself transferred along with the 72 other inmates to the Queen's prison, under the jurisdiction of the Home Office. This transference to a common state institution he considered a humiliating indignity. But more than indignity angered him. His new cell proved to be filthily dirty and crawling with bugs, so that he had to spend £5 on having it cleaned and repaired. So loud were his complaints in the *Papers* that the Home Office sent an Inspector to verify his charges. The Warden confirmed them, and the Inspector was finally instructed by the Board of Works to reimburse Oastler for the expense to which he had been put.

Eventually he became reconciled to his new quarters, since they proved to have distinct advantages over the old. But he continued to show his resentment by addressing all subsequent numbers of the *Fleet Papers* to his 'new gaoler,' Sir James Graham the Home Secretary, instead of to Thomas Thornhill. As the months passed into years, however, hints began to appear in his writings that he was finding it more and more difficult to sustain his lofty mood of Christian resignation. A deep weariness with his lot becomes discernible, venting itself in occasional petulance and querulousness. Now and again a fellow-prisoner died, and Oastler began to wonder whether for him, too, death alone would open the prison gates.

CHAPTER XXXII

The Faith of a Tory

FOR the student of British public opinion a peculiar interest will always attach to the *Fleet Papers*. In them can be found not only a compendious statement of Oastler's personal convictions but also a remarkable anticipation of certain important ideas that other men were to make famous later. Here in popular form is the first draft of those articles of social faith that came to be known to the next generation as Tory Democracy. Appropriately enough, indeed, the earliest use of the phrase 'Democratic Tory' is found in an article about Oastler which appeared in the *Deutsche Allgemeine Zeitung* for 6 July 1843.

Oastler had a lucid and coherent theory of society, the formulation of which can be traced through all its stages. It began with a certain way of feeling about life. During the struggles over the Ten Hours Bill and the New Poor Law it was made progressively more explicit in speech and pamphlet. Finally, in the leisure that imprisonment brought, it attained definitive form. For the rest of his life Oastler was only rendering the same themes in a variety of keys.

It is important to observe, however, that he carried his ideas to a certain degree of elaboration and not beyond. He was no academic. He was seeking to instill a particular doctrine in men's minds as an incitement to action. His notions, therefore, clear and vigorous though they are, do not amount to a system. They have much the same relationship to a formal social philosophy as the gospels of Wesley and Simeon have to systematic theology. Everything he taught was capable of being developed more fully, but he had neither the training nor the inclination to undertake such elaboration himself. As one of the first in the century to expound the doctrine that Marx not unsympathetically called 'feudal so-

cialism,' he has obvious affinities with others that followed after,
notably the Young England group, John Ruskin, William Morris,
and even the 'Fourth Party' of Lord Randolph Churchill. Comparison with each of these could prove illuminating, though it
would be little more than an intellectual exercise. Oastler's ideas
are important not so much for any originality that may be claimed
for them as for the revealing light they shed on the sentiments
of the man himself and on the quality of his appeal as a public
figure.

The fact that he was the recipient of charity from people of
widely differing faiths in no way tempered the forthrightness of
his declarations. Week after week without compromise, he went
on developing the cardinal idea he had been proclaiming for so
long: that England was headed for disaster unless her rulers
reversed their present policy and implemented the principles of
Tory social reform. From one point of view that amounted to an
interpretation of history; from another, to a theory of politics.
But it matters little which way one chooses to consider this teaching, for the two lines of thought eventually converge upon the
same practical conclusions. The essential thing is that at the back
of his mind was the picture of a social harmony that had once
actually existed: an English Eden into which had crept the ser-
pent of laissez-faire.

¶ 1

There once was a time, he taught, when statesmen had conceived their main task to be the regulation of the multifarious
activities of society to the end that the general welfare of the
whole might be secured. Looking back upon that Golden Age,
said Oastler, 'we find that all [Britain's] institutions were guarded
by wise regulations which were intended and calculated to establish the security and promote the interests of all. Each was
permitted to occupy his own sphere—none was allowed to trench
upon or invade the rights of another; the whole system of the
British Constitution being a series of guards, checks and counter-
guards, intended to prevent competition and undue expansion.'
Now, on the contrary, in the name of 'freedom,' Britain's statesmen were deliberately abnegating that solemn responsibility. The

outcome was disastrous. 'Every step from the regulating, protective and restraining system of our ancestors towards the selfish and independent theories of modern times has, notwithstanding all the discoveries of science, been marked by more poverty, more misery and more wretchedness.' The inevitable result of abandoning the principle of general welfare in favor of the doctrine of struggle and survival was that a lucky few prospered at the expense of the degraded many.

Consider, said Oastler, some of the implications of the old system:

The ancient corporations and guilds were instituted for the express purpose of guarding the interests of the different grades of all crafts by apportioning the supply to the demand and thus preventing competition. The law of apprenticeship has also reference to the protection and upholding of the value, as well as apportioning the quantity of labour to be assigned to each craft or manufacture; nay, the constitutional legislation of our forefathers abounds with proofs that they deemed the right use of legislation to be the regulating and apportioning the quantity of the different products of our industry, by restraints, penalties or rewards. So tenacious were our bygone legislators of the character of our manufactures, that they not only legislated to prevent the undue competition of the covetous, but they also considered the Crown to be involved in the honour or dishonour of our manufacturers, and passed very stringent laws to prevent frauds in manufactures.

The labourers' wages were then also protected by statute, and the common foods of the working people . . . were prohibited from being made articles of speculation. Care was then taken that the labourer's hope of reward should not be cut off by the inordinate desire for gain in the capitalists.

The British social tragedy lay in the indisputable fact that this system of control had been abandoned at the very time when it was most urgently needed: at a time, that is to say, when expanding technology most obviously menaced the welfare of those least able to protect themselves. Having thus failed to control these new forces in their beginning, statesmen now found they were confronted with powerful vested interests opposed to any regulation whatsoever.

The policy of inaction had sundered society, with a class of wealthy exploiters on the one hand and a mass of exploited work-people on the other, the latter compelled by their very poverty and powerlessness to accept such terms as were offered:

This system of permitting the unlimited centralisation of manufacturing wealth has not only weakened the country but has tended to remove the blessings of the national laws from all the manufacturing operatives. They are no longer, as they used to be, sprinkled about in families working independently in their domestic circles, but thousands of them are now pent up in mills and workshops under one man:—he alone has the care and control of them—him only do they serve. His laws are their guide, and they are virtually removed from under the laws of the land. It is, in a great measure, to this source that much of the discontent and demoralisation of the country is attributable.

What Oastler pleaded for was the re-establishment of a system of regulation firmly grounded upon the welfare of the working classes. His own phrase for this ideal was *the social state*. Order must be its principle, and not the anarchy of laissez-faire:

God has appointed the proper stations and ranks for each. He has exhibited Himself in His Word and His works as the God of Order, and has thus left man without excuse if he should be in want and destitution. Why, then, should any starve who are surrounded by such means of acquiring plenty? It is solely, Sir, because the duty of our Governors is neglected—they refuse to take the power of apportioning the industry of the people to their wants—they resign the power which is vested in them by infinite Wisdom, and leave each one to think and work for himself; and thus they entirely neglect the great object for which they are appointed—to take supervision of the wants of the people, and the best means of providing for their comforts and necessities.

No assuagement of England's misery would be found until Government assumed its ancient responsibilities again and took as its guiding principle this conception of ordered liberty. It was because he held this conviction so deeply that Oastler persisted in calling himself a Tory. It was his way of advertising his undying hostility to the doctrine of individualism. John Ruskin,

whose social philosophy has so many striking similarities to
Oastler's, was to do the same thing later. 'I am a violent Tory
of the old school,' Ruskin declared. 'I am still an old-fashioned
Ultra-Tory,' Oastler wrote from prison. And he went on to
elaborate:

> A Tory is one who, believing that the institutions of this country are
> calculated, as they were intended, to secure the prosperity and hap-
> piness of every class of society, wishes to maintain them in their
> original beauty, simplicity and integrity. He is tenacious of the rights
> of all, but most of the poor and needy, because they require the shelter
> of the constitution and the laws more than the other classes. A Tory
> is a staunch friend of Order for the sake of Liberty; and, knowing that
> all our institutions are founded upon Christianity, he is of course a
> Christian, believing with St. Paul that each order of society is mutually
> dependent on the others for peace and prosperity, and that, although
> there 'are many members, yet there is but one body. And the eye can-
> not say unto the hand, I have no need of thee; nor again the head to
> the feet, I have no need of you. Nay much more, those members of
> the body which seem to be more feeble are necessary.' Sir, I am just
> such a Tory; or if you prefer it in my own words, as I once defined it
> to the Duke of Wellington when he asked 'What do you mean by
> Toryism,' you shall have it: I replied, 'My Lord Duke, I mean a place
> for everything, and everything in its place.'

In the light of such a conviction individualism becomes more
than a mistaken program: it becomes a grave moral error:

> Take but degree away, untune that string,
> And, hark! what discord follows; each thing meets
> In mere oppugnancy.

Yet 'degree' appeared to be weakening with every passing year.
Old ways were being challenged by the new temper of pertina-
cious questioning that Jeremy Bentham and James Mill had so
greatly fostered. Oastler was seeking a ground for the re-affirma-
tion of loyalties and a restatement of old principles. And none
could deny that Toryism was sorely in need of some such restatement if it was not to become a vanished dream, for the enuncia-
tions that Sidmouth and his like had given it had been obtuse
to an extent that exceeded caricature.

¶ 2

Behind such convictions was an implied theory about the
nature of social institutions.

Oastler's entire public life was a sustained protest against the
view that society was to be interpreted as an aggregation of
individual units. This was no mere scholastic doctrine reached
by pondering upon the philosophers. It was a living intuition
which was somehow integral to his temperament. To begin with,
he was hardly aware of the fact, as his speeches clearly show;
but the long-drawn-out struggle against a contrary mode of
thought induced in him the self-consciousness that made articu-
lation possible. Church and Crown, Quarter Sessions and professional guilds, and all the other venerable associations that make
up the complex of society he saw as more than administrative
agencies of the moment. They were incorporations of the living
past, enduring reservoirs of public energy. What has been said
of Disraeli is true of Oastler no less: 'by making his reckoning in
terms of the values created by history, he became the foe of all
doctrines which reckon in terms of bare units and majorities.'
He was thus as emphatically opposed to the reasonings of Chadwick and to the new bureaucracy as he was to the radical
atomism that derived from 'the principles of '89.' Society he regarded not as a mechanical contrivance but rather as a garden:
a garden in continuous need of being tended by wise gardeners
lest it become overrun by weeds and pests. Laissez-faire simply
amounted to an abandonment of the gardener's duties.

This led him to a theory of national character. Oastler's expositions abound in references to 'the character of Englishmen.'
The phrase was not a rhetorical flourish: it indicated a problem
which was worrying him acutely. Personal character, Oastler
considered, has to be regarded as a patterning of loyalties and
habits. Since of necessity such patterning can occur only within
and around institutions, to grow up in the midst of a given institutional complex is to take into one's personality something
distinctively national—a certain way of thinking and feeling and
a certain system of preferences. Change or destroy the institutions,
therefore, and you alter the character of men. In this conception

is to be found the explanation of Oastler's dread of the new industrial *mores,* as well as his hatred of the teaching of the economists. The dynamism of the new technology that was fast destroying the old way of life alarmed him because of the consequences it would have upon the quality of citizens. To interpret the purpose of life in terms of 'getting on,' without the counter-balancing influence of other standards, would literally be to change 'the character of Englishmen.' Social power, according to his view of the matter, was passing into the hands of crude, enterprising, and relentless men animated by just such an aggressive purpose and lacking in all tradition, while at the same time the less fortunate were breeding a new generation in the slums cut off from any redeeming influence whatsoever. And the popular social philosophy seemed to rationalize and justify the process. To Oastler, with his simple Christian standards, the spectacle was distressing in the extreme, for he considered it nothing less than blasphemy to suggest that enlightened selfishness would prove to be the fulfilment of the laws of nature.

Yet this latter idea was manifestly in the ascendant. It is not just a question of what scholarly economists wrote in their treatises and articles. It is something far more extensive than that, namely, what politicians and journalists and the educated classes generally thought the economists had taught. And what economists were thought to have announced was that the processes of both production and distribution must in all circumstances be kept free from any 'artificial' interference from outside. The dominant belief of the age was that under 'the obvious and simple system of natural liberty' social life was self-adjusting. Given freedom of trade, movement, and contract, economic law would operate to produce the greatest volume of wealth. Each participant would then get his proper share of the proceeds while at the same time the amelioration of ills would be automatically effected as a by-product of economic expansion. In such a philosophy there could be no place for collective purpose and social regulation since, as one historian of the doctrine puts it, 'the individual aims only at his private gain, but in doing so is "led by an invisible hand" to promote the public good which was no part of his intention.' One of the most brassy expositions of this thesis is to be found in Dr. Ure's *Philosophy of Manufacture* (1835); but the doctrine pervaded the age, begetting a welter of clichés and catchwords littering the columns of contemporary journalism as well as the pages of more substantial productions. 'Lawgivers are nearly always the obstructors of society instead of its helpers,' Buckle wrote in his *History of Civilization;* and when *The Economist* was started in 1843, its commentaries upon current affairs pointed the moral every week.[1]

Oastler passionately repudiated this manner of social thinking. With its avowed exaltation of selfishness, and the complacency of its fatalism in the face of human suffering, it amounted, he said, to an outright repudiation of the Christian revelation. It was, in fact, anti-Christ. But he nowhere made any attempt to refute it systematically. He contented himself with continuous denunciation and satire, and the boisterous reiteration of richer possibilities than political economy seemed to imply. A single instance of his method will suffice:

See the two systems in juxta-position, as propounded by an apostle of each creed:—

CHRISTIANITY	FREE TRADE
'The Husbandman that laboureth MUST be first partaker of the fruits.'	'To give capital a fair remuneration, the price of labour MUST be kept down.'
—Saint Paul	—William Huskisson

There I leave the two creeds to commend themselves to the hearts and understandings of all people of every rank, sect and party. Uni-

---

[1] Two citations will illustrate this attitude. The first, which appeared in September 1849, is from an article by Thomas Hodgskin, who was at that time on the staff of *The Economist*. The second, which appeared in May of the previous year, is probably from the same pen: 'Examined in detail and looked at under the most general aspect, all the great branches of human industry are found replete with order which, growing from the selfish exertions of individuals, pervades the whole. Experience has proved that this order is invariably deranged when it is forcibly interfered with by the State; and thus not *laissez-faire*, not the undirected exertions of merchants, manufacturers and farmers, but the interference of governments is anarchy. "Self-love and social are the same." '

'Suffering and evil are nature's admonitions; they cannot be got rid of; and the impatient attempts of benevolence to banish them from the world by legislation, before benevolence has learnt their object and their end, have always been more productive of evil than good.'

versal comfort, peace, plenty and happiness must result from one, whilst the track of the other cannot fail to be marked by uneasiness, discontent, want and wretchedness. It is the fruits of the latter on which England is now feeding.

A thousand times Oastler pointed this antithesis. How was it, he kept asking, that these allegedly immutable laws of economics operated so conspicuously in favor of the privileged and capitalist classes only, and not for equal benefit to the rest of society? Why was it that a cosmic destiny had singled out one factor in the productive process, Capital, for primary remuneration, rather than Labor? And in the same terms he continuously denounced the population doctrines of Malthus, which had had such a maleficent influence on the spirit of the age. Even supposing that Malthus's premise is true and that the production of food does increase only arithmetically while the population increases geometrically, why, he asked, should that be interpreted in the interests of a small privileged class to the detriment of all the rest?

The unchristian, unnatural, and, thank God, unconstitutional dogma 'that nature has only provided a table for the rich—that the poor have no right to sit down and eat at her banquet—and that the land is unable to support the people' has of late years infused itself into the hearts of our heartless statesmen of every party, and (with shame I confess it) some of our bishops are believers in that doctrine of devils which has produced a code of execrable and atrocious laws at total variance with every precept of our Holy Religion, every principle of our Constitution, and consequently every security to Rank and Prosperity. It is in vain to attempt to restore peace and stability until that most fatal heresy is entirely eradicated from the minds of our lawmakers.

Weekly the *Fleet Papers* fulminated against 'liberal' deductions from the Malthusian doctrines.

All this confusion and fraud and oppression and injustice arise from the adoption by the Government of the insane notions that there is no natural tie between the soil and the people, that property has no duties, that man has no natural *rights*, that there are too few acres and too many men.

This violent animosity towards political economy was determined not only by Oastler's dislike of the substance of the economists' teachings, but also by his thinking-habits. Throughout his life he saw society in concrete terms. He was therefore incapable of conceiving an 'economic man'; he could not separate the wage-getting and money-making activities of men from all the other drives that make up human nature. The processes of production, in his view, take place in a spiritual medium that includes loyalties and resentments, custom and hopes, and the promise of an eternal destiny. In other words, to the abstraction of the 'economic man' he opposed the affirmation of the soul. Assessment of policy was to be made, therefore, not by calculating consequences upon the plane of the market but by estimating them upon the plane of God's intentions. Whether one considers this kind of conviction to be merely naïve and silly, as the editorial writers of *The Economist* did, or to be the promising postulate for a richer social analysis, as both John Ruskin and J. A. Hobson maintained, it remains the key to all Oastler's thinking about economic matters.

Oastler thus stands out distinctively as one of the first men in the nineteenth century to affirm the relevance of Christianity for an industrial society. Others before him had preached benevolence or taught the necessity of resignation; he, on the contrary, sought to make the New Testament ethic an imperative for change. Wilberforce had invoked Christian principles to combat slavery; John Howard and Elizabeth Fry had invoked them to promote legislation for remedying the horrors of the prisons. But these were specific reforms of age-old evils. Oastler was doing something different. He was striving to proclaim general principles that should condition the operation of the entire economic process; and this, he saw, would involve a drastic modification of the prevailing conception of the triangular relationship between State, Industry, and Church. In all simplicity he took as a divine command the dictum that the husbandman should be the first partaker of the fruits; and he interpreted the growing proletariat as the husbandmen. He did not want them to be 'resigned.' The egregious Archdeacon Paley had written a notorious book called *Reasons for Contentment addressed to the Labouring Part of the British Public*. Oastler's expository writings might not inappropriately be entitled *Reasons for Discontentment* addressed to the same public. From beginning to end they are a sustained protest against the social fatalism of the early economists,[2] and a militant declaration that the public relationships of mankind, no less than the private, have to be judged by the ethical standards given by the Christian revelation.

This latter fact has to be borne in mind when one is considering Oastler's professions of Toryism, too. His vindication of existing institutions covered no tolerance of exposed abuses and involved no assertion that 'whatever is, is right.' On the contrary: he was as assiduous as any Radical in uncovering and denouncing the corruptions of Church and State. These things also, just as much as economic arrangements, have to be gauged by the standards of righteousness, which means that they must be measured in terms of their effect upon the total membership of society and not upon one class only. Liberalism he condemned because he saw it as advancing the interests of only the bourgeoisie, and Conservatism because it was calculated to benefit only the privileged. Toryism—that is to say, the platonic Toryism he had in mind—was synonymous with the well-being of the whole. 'I am a loyal subject of the Queen,' he wrote in one of his letters to Lord John Russell just before going into prison. 'I am the friend of the aristocracy and have sacrificed much on their account; I revere the national Church and have always told the people so. But,' he continued,

if the Church, the Throne and the Aristocracy are determined to rob the poor man of his liberty, of his wife and of his children, then is the Church no longer that of Christ;—then is the Throne no longer that of England;—then are the nobles no longer safeguards of the people. Then are they worse than useless. Then with their bitterest foes would I cry, *Down with them, Down with them all to the ground.*

---

[2] An observation by J. E. Cairnes, one of the later classical school, indicates the spirit Oastler was combating: 'No one can have studied political economy in the works of its earlier cultivators without being struck with the dreariness of the outlook which, in the main, it discloses for the human race. It seems to have been Ricardo's deliberate opinion that a substantial improvement in the condition of the mass of mankind was impossible.'

¶ 3

What Oastler was asking for was a system of social organization purposely calculated to assure men freedom from want, and providing them at the same time with those institutions of fellowship that alone make possible the fulfilment of human capacities which is character. But though he pleaded for ordered liberty, nothing was further from his mind than a scheme for centralization. To him centralization was synonymous with despotism: it meant the assumption of power by a remote London oligarchy claiming the right to interfere in local affairs about which it knew nothing. To his way of thinking, centralization dehumanized relationships, destroyed local vitalities, and became the breeding ground of 'jobs' for the supporters and dependents of unscrupulous politicians. There was a lusty provincialism in Oastler's make-up which he deliberately flaunted. He had all the countryman's suspicion of the big city and all the northerner's distrust of the men south of Trent. Over and over again, therefore, he denounced the unifying and standardizing tendencies of philosophic Radicalism. Should that flood rise much further, it would wash away forever all the old landmarks until there was nothing left but the monotonous sameness of fashion dictated by London. 'If there be any excellency in the Constitution of England over that of all other nations,' he declared, it is in this,—

that it leaves the inhabitants of every locality to manage their own affairs. It is, in fact, an *infinity of republics* under one head; which head is not intended to exercise any influence or control over the executive in different parts of the provinces, but is established to poise and regulate the whole by preventing the jarring which would otherwise be inevitably occasioned by the separate independencies. It is, in fact, the 'fly-wheel' of society, interfering with none of the intricacies of its machinery but regulating the movement of the whole.

That was one of many reasons why he hated the New Poor Law; and that was why he never really reconciled himself to the idea of a factory inspectorate. What he would have preferred was a straight Ten Hours Bill, leaving the responsibility for its enforcement to the localities. There was an apparent inconsistency in

Oastler's thinking here, for none had been more vociferous than
he in condemnation of the local magistrates' failure to execute
Althorp's Act faithfully. His answer to such a charge, however,
was obvious. The fault lay, he averred, not in the *principle* of a
local magistracy but in the type of man—the middle-class *nouveau
riche*—deliberately promoted to the Bench by a commercially
minded Whig Government.

✻　　　✻　　　✻

Such were the doctrines he promulgated and elaborated week
by week and got reproduced in numerous local Tory newspapers.
In terms of these ideas he commented on passing events. The
depression had worsened since he left Fixby, and England had
passed into that terrible phase of distress known to historians as
'the hungry forties.' The shadow of that suffering lies dark across
the pages of the *Fleet Papers*. This, Oastler kept iterating, is the
due nemesis of 'utilitarianism' and Whiggery: this is the result
of freer trade, of unrestrained capitalism: this comes of struggling
to capture world markets and of letting industry and commerce
usurp the primacy that belongs to agriculture: this is the result
of deliberately throwing overboard the idea of national self-
sufficiency and admittedly abandoning the principle of collective
social purposiveness. Unceasingly he fired his broadside at the
Anti-Corn Law League, now quickly gathering momentum,
accusing it of fostering economic anarchy in the interests of an
industrial oligarchy. The men prominent on the platforms of the
League were the very men who had wrecked the efforts to get
a decent factory bill passed. Now they were using the prevalent
misery as an argument on behalf of their own interests.

When the Whigs went out of office in September 1841, and
Peel formed a new Government, Oastler was at first elated and
actually dared to hope that the Whig trend of policy would be
reversed. But elation quickly gave way to disillusionment and
then to anger as his worst fears about 'Conservatism' became confirmed. 'My heart grieves sorely when I find that we have still a
Whig ministry with a mere change of name,' he wrote. Men like
Ashley and Beckett, whom Oastler had hoped to see in office,
were conspicuously excluded, while Graham—who had swallowed

in their totality the baleful doctrines of economic fatalism—was at the Home Office ably seconding Peel's progressive conversion to free trade. For both of them Oastler developed an intense dislike. And when they both openly repudiated the Ten Hours demand and then disavowed their intention of repealing the New Poor Law or doing anything about the handloom weavers, Oastler's disgust was complete. Thenceforward he attacked the disguised Whiggery that went by the name of 'Conservatism' as vehemently as he attacked Whiggery itself. In an analysis of the political situation submitted to the Prince Consort in 1854, Baron Stockmar averred that genuine Tories were an extinct species, and that 'the race which in the present day bears their name are simply degenerate bastards.' Here from prison, 13 years earlier, Oastler was saying the same thing in language just as pungent in every week's issue of his *Papers*.

The only act of the Peel ministry Oastler endorsed, and that wholeheartedly, was the imposition of the income tax. He called it 'the most legitimate, the most wise, and the fairest tax which can be imposed upon our domestic resources.' It would put the owners of machinery on the same footing as owners of real property, making them all contribute on equal terms to the national necessity. For many years he had advocated some such device and had been laughed at by the northern manufacturers. Now his hopes had at last been realized. Apart from that, the fruits of the Tamworth Manifesto brought him no consolation. The social policy of Peel and Graham seemed to Oastler in no wise different from that of Grey and Melbourne.

CHAPTER XXXIII

'The Ransomed Patriot'

OASTLER had just returned from church one Sunday morning in June 1841 when a servant in livery entered the cell carrying a case of wine from his master, who was waiting in a carriage outside. Having deposited the case on the table, the servant handed his master's card to Oastler, who read thereon, to his astonishment, the name of Fitzroy Kelly Q.C., Thornhill's counsel in the lawsuit. The gesture was as unexpected as it was magnanimous and excited Oastler no end. He rushed off to the Warden to get permission for Kelly to be allowed inside the prison (for the rules forbade Sunday visiting), the Warden consented and Kelly came in.

The conversation that followed did more to cheer Oastler than any single happening since he had entered that gloomy building 18 months before. Kelly had come entirely on his own initiative to tell Oastler how much he regretted this imprisonment. When their case was ended in court, he said, he had fully supposed an amicable settlement between master and steward would follow as a matter of course. Since matters had turned out otherwise, however, and he believed Oastler was being treated with undue harshness, he now offered to act as mediator between the parties. 'If you will accept of my services as your adviser and friend,' Oastler reported the lawyer as saying, 'and will communicate to me the particulars of your own case as you would have explained them to the court had you not stopped me and consented to a verdict, I will to the best of my ability endeavour to persuade Mr. Thornhill to grant your release. I am already fully acquainted with Mr. Thornhill's case, and am sure there is not any reason why you should suffer imprisonment.'

Oastler accepted the offer with delight. It was agreed that he should prepare a full statement of his case and that Kelly should come back later in the week to go over it in detail. This was accordingly done. Kelly made himself thoroughly familiar with Oastler's position and claims, and then wrote to the irascible old gentleman at Fixby interceding on the prisoner's behalf to effect a settlement.

Nor was Kelly alone in his intercessions. Over the next few weeks various other appeals of a similar kind were made. Walter, of *The Times,* for instance, went to the trouble of going up to Yorkshire in person to plead with Thornhill. And deputations of Oastler's friends from Dewsbury, Huddersfield, and Bradford likewise called on the Squire of Fixby for the same purpose. But Thornhill remained adamant. He would not consent to Oastler's liberation, the newspapers gave out, without full security for the debt. On that he took his stand, and none of the press publicity these efforts were given succeeded in shaking him; an attitude that *The Age* editorially called 'as gross as the man himself.'

Yet Kelly's intervention was by no means profitless. The fact that the distinguished counsel against him had championed the prisoner's cause went a long way towards dispelling from the public mind the suspicion that there· was some culpability on Oastler's part in the matter of the debt. Moreover the relations between the two men did not end with this episode. Kelly continued sending gifts to the Fleet, a mutual regard ripened, and in the years to come Oastler found the lawyer 'a constant, faithful friend and benefactor.'

¶ 1

Since their hopes for securing his release by an appeal for clemency had foundered upon Thornhill's stubbornness, Oastler's more intimate friends decided that the only thing left for them to do was to raise a public subscription and pay off the debt themselves. At the beginning of October 1841, the newspapers friendly toward Oastler began commending the plan. The season seemed propitious, for a recent warm eulogy by Ferrand in the House of Commons had just evoked a new outburst of publicity, and a vigorous editorial in the *Standard* had set its tone.

Public gratitude is due to Mr. Ferrand [declared that paper] for his generous and manly acknowledgement of the inappreciable services of the excellent and cruelly persecuted Richard Oastler . . . It was honorable and worthy of all praise in Mr. Ferrand to render justice to such a man. For ourselves, we can never think of Mr. Oastler's services, and of their reward, without a sense of shame for our party and for ourselves—of shame for the party that neglects such a champion and benefactor, shame for ourselves upon the reflection that with all our efforts, and with the enjoyment at least of our liberty, we have not—no, nor all the Conservative press put together—done so much for the promotion of Conservative principles, for the cause of peace and religion, as this one gentleman has effected from his cell in the Fleet prison, the debtor of a Conservative, too, who knows that his victim is unable to pay and whose conduct must therefore be purely vindictive.

As already noted, an earlier appeal to provide Oastler with a life annuity had been launched at the time of his dismissal from Fixby. Something over £500 was raised, almost all of it from his wealthier neighbors, but then the project had collapsed. All sorts of other 'victim funds' for Chartist prisoners and their dependents had drained the generosity of the benevolent, not the least impressive of them being the fund of nearly £2,000 which Oastler himself had raised for Stephens. But by the autumn of 1841 circumstances seemed to be favorable for another appeal.

Negotiations of an informal kind went on all through the winter. William Atkinson, a city businessman who had recently become very friendly with Oastler, was the leading spirit, and he and William Duncombe (now elevated to the peerage as Lord Feversham) worked out the plans together. As a beginning, it was agreed that Atkinson should tour the manufacturing districts to talk matters over with the committees of the Oastler societies. This he did, visiting a dozen of the biggest towns and finding enthusiastic support everywhere. At the same time he enlisted the co-operation of the various local newspapers. His report was so encouraging that a general appeal seemed justified. An address was issued, trustees were appointed (Lord Feversham, Sir George Sinclair, John Walter, John Fielden, and Busfield Ferrand, with Atkinson as secretary), and an inaugural meeting was held in the British Coffee House, Cockspur Street, for the formal launching of the campaign. Even before the meeting was held subscriptions amounted to £550.

But though the appeal got off to a vigorous start and was given extensive backing by the press, it quickly flagged and then collapsed. No adequate explanation was forthcoming, either then or afterwards; yet during the next twelve months donations hardly came in at all. Oastler's hopes, which for a while had risen dangerously high, were rudely dashed. The inevitable reaction followed. Both physically and mentally the strain of imprisonment began to tell so that it became increasingly difficult to sustain the role of patient resignation, and a mood of heavy despair slowly settled upon him.

¶ 2

In the late summer of 1843, however, just two years after the original proposal had been mooted, the scheme was again revived with even heavier advance publicity than before. On 23 September *The Times* carried an enthusiastic article about Oastler and his *Papers*, in the course of which it declared: 'It is high time to do justice to Richard Oastler. With him originated the factory question and those ameliorations which have taken place . . . Why, if Oastler with his trenchant blade had not hewn his way through the positive mountains of obstruction which were raised to it in the early stages of this brilliant advance of humanity and justice, Lord Ashley would never have had a standing place.' Correspondents wrote endorsing the article; other journals reproduced or commended it, and for the next four weeks local papers all over the country were again extolling Oastler's merits and calling for his release. This sympathetic publicity was by no means confined to the Tory press. Cordial support came from many papers that at one time had been among his bitterest critics. Even the *Bradford Observer*, which had been so vitriolic in 1835, now called for his liberation 'for the sake of humanity.'

Encouraged by all this editorial approval, Oastler's friends convened a meeting at the Yew Tree Inn, Roberttown, for 15 November 1843, where, with the co-operation of delegates from all the textile centers, new plans were worked out for the final accomplishment of their purpose. An 'Oastler Liberty Fund' was to be instituted, a series of public meetings on the pattern of 1832 was to be undertaken, and local collecting committees were to be established. William Beckett, M.P. for Leeds, was to be the treasurer, and Lawrence Pitkeithly the secretary, while the indefatigable Ferrand undertook to conduct a month's speaking tour on Oastler's behalf.

The scheme was made public a week later before a cheering audience that filled to capacity the largest hall in Huddersfield. John Fielden presided; Walter came up for the occasion, and a galaxy of philanthropic factory owners and workers' leaders crowded the platform. One after another they joined in warm tribute to the man they were championing, all of them stressing the remarkable changes that had already come over the manufacturing districts largely as a result of Oastler's efforts. In fact the gathering virtually became another Ten Hours meeting, reminiscent of the great days of '32. Before it closed a Central Committee for Yorkshire had been set up (on which all the men of the Fixby Compact were included), and an additional £139 collected.

The same week a Central Operatives' Committee was established in Manchester with Thomas Daniel, the old Ten Hours secretary, as chairman, to organize the three counties of Lancashire, Cheshire, and Derbyshire. And shortly afterwards a similar committee was formed in London with Matthias Attwood M.P., as treasurer and a central office at 424 Strand.

Thus by the end of November, with the Ten Hours organization revived under another name on both sides of the Pennines, everything was ready for the final effort. And right at the outset the Leeds operatives scored a resounding success, the publicity value of which was inestimable: they sent a deputation to plead with the elder Baines and got from him a donation of £ 5! He took care in a covering letter to guard against misinterpretation by avowing himself as strongly opposed as ever to Oastler's doctrines. Nevertheless, as he fully realized, his gesture on behalf of their 'humane object' (as he called it) was calculated to have 'an influence beyond the mere amount of that subscription': and it certainly did. The Yorkshire press, including the *Northern Star*, hailed the gift with loud delight.

In the course of the next 5 weeks 20 big meetings were held in the larger towns between Liverpool and Hull. They were remarkable demonstrations. As one reads the numerous reports, one is struck by the enthusiasm displayed and by the co-operation of so many people for such an unusual purpose. But behind the cheers and the adjectives there stands out clearly something even more significant. Almost every surviving characterization of Oastler from his thirtieth to his sixtieth year pays tribute in one way or another to a certain lustihood and resoluteness fundamental to the character of the man. Even his enemies acknowledged it by their choice of abusive epithets. All the speeches of this campaign recur to that central integrity: it is the unanimity of their testimony in this regard that makes them so impressive.

It was the least likely of men who most succinctly voiced the general feeling—Captain Wood of Sandal, the man who had stood against Sadler in the Huddersfield by-election. Before an audience of over a thousand in the Wakefield Court House he paid chivalrous respect to Oastler with an unexpected perceptiveness. Replying to the disparagement of critics that Oastler was given to invective and recklessness, Wood humorously observed: 'As to *invective*, I might perhaps as much as any other complain, if so inclined; for he visited my political offences with a goodly octavo volume of his richest and most characteristic vituperation.' But such an attitude would betray only a narrow pettiness of spirit, he went on to say:

Let us not forget that Richard Oastler, to his own worldly loss and detriment, was the volunteer champion against the rich and powerful of the land of the most helpless creatures in existence; and let us estimate his merits and claims on our support not by those failings to which poor human nature is subject, but by his hatred of oppression, his ever-active philanthropy, and his unwearied exertions in the cause of those whom, under the existing factory system or the new poor law, he considered the victims of the most unjustifiable selfishness and cruelty.

Such encomiums were by no means limited to the platform. An outstanding feature of the campaign was the sustained press support that accompanied it. Metropolitan and provincial papers alike now treated Oastler as 'news' and gave ample publicity to the efforts being made to secure his release. *The Times,* of course, was unflagging in his support; so was the *Standard,* which carried a long biographical article early in December. The *Morning Post* called him 'a man of genius' and warned the Tories in no uncertain terms of the danger of leaving him in prison. Even the Peelite *Morning Herald,* which dissociated itself entirely from his philosophy and criticized his attacks on Conservatism, nevertheless gave sober praise to 'the first man who directed public attention to the wrongs and crimes of the factory system' and demanded his release in the name of 'justice, honour and good example.' The *Literary Gazette* observed that the imprisonment of such an 'able, consistent and truly philanthropic man' was a caustic commentary on the atrocious law of debtors, while the *Church Intelligencer* declared it would be a disgrace to Anglicanism if such a loyal and humane champion were left in prison any longer. 'The loss of the services of such a man,' said the *Liverpool Standard,* 'is a national calamity.'

From Cardiff to Kelso, from London to Carlisle, papers backed the drive, reporting the speeches and featuring articles on Oastler's career. Irrespective of party, they joined in impressive homage to the man of whom the Conservative *Courier* of Manchester not unhappily observed 'in him alone there has, in fact, been one whole party . . . [which] has conferred benefit upon us all.'

Only from two quarters was opposition forthcoming. The Whig *Globe* was bitterly critical, remarking that Oastler had been rightly incarcerated for 'very large defalcations,' and complaining that 'most of the Tory journals have opened their columns to articles addressed to the passions of the labouring classes' on Oastler's behalf. To this the *Standard* made an appropriately pungent reply. In the north another Whig journal, the *Liverpool Mercury,* also threw cold water on the movement and published a series of extracts from Oastler's 'violent and seditious speeches.' This, too, received its due answer, so that in neither case did the attack seem to do much harm.

All through December and most of January the campaign went on, with the inexhaustible Ferrand as its chief standard-bearer. Ferrand's energy was prodigious. His days were spent in personally soliciting the eminent, his nights in addressing meetings. From late November onwards there was hardly an evening in the week when he was not attending some gathering. Everywhere he went he received astonishing ovations which often continued for minutes at a time. And he exploited his opportunities to the limit by denouncing the New Poor Law and the Anti-Corn Law League and turning every speech into a full-blooded plea for the principles of Tory Democracy which would emancipate the workers from the exploitation of the capitalists.

¶ 3

By the end of January 1844, the Oastler Liberation Fund amounted to some £2,000. Accruing interest, however, had now increased the debt to about £1,200 more than this sum. Nevertheless Oastler's friends decided to wait no longer before taking action. The 'old King's' health had been clearly failing of recent months, so it was deemed unwise to allow him to stay in prison a day longer than necessary.

On 6 February, therefore, the Central Committee agreed to borrow the rest of the money in the hope that the Fund would eventually be able to repay the loan. Twelve guarantors were found, the necessary arrangements were quickly made with Beckett's Bank in Leeds, and within a week Thornhill's solicitors had received a cheque in final discharge of the debt.

So on Monday, 12 February 1844, after three years and two months of confinement, Oastler walked out of the Queen's Prison a free man again.

His Liberation Committee escorted him from his cell to the British Coffee House in Cockspur Street, where his friends had gathered for a lunch of celebration. Afterwards, shaking with emotion, he returned eloquent thanks to them for all they had done on his behalf and with moving simplicity dedicated himself anew to the cause of the weak and suffering.

Next day *The Times* carried a striking leading article on 'The Ransomed Patriot.' Defending Oastler with caution and good sense in the matter of the debt, it cited the cases of Pitt, Wilberforce, and Clarkson to show that 'not a few great and good men share with Mr. Oastler the infirmity of neglecting their private affairs in the zealous prosecution of a public cause.' But it was not the debt that was responsible for his incarceration, it added:

There can be no doubt Mr. Oastler would never have been shut up in prison—and once there, would not have been kept a single day—but for his persevering advocacy of the Ten Hours Factory Bill and resistance to the New Poor Law. Mr. Oastler's liberation, therefore, is a popular triumph and tells more than all he or we could write or say on these questions. His words now will have more weight than ever: this he will doubtless feel, and feel also more than ever the responsibility of a man so situated and so endued. We are not ashamed to declare our conviction that he is doing a great work. Of course it is easy enough for people who do not possess his feelings, or care for his objects, to criticize his manner of doing his work. Nothing is so easy as to sit still and find fault. For our own part, an active experience has long taught us, substantial errors apart, to take men and things more as we find them, and not to quarrel with the law of Providence which often consigns the statesman to final insignificance while it raises the simple child of nature into the architect or restorer of his country's fortunes. Mr. Oastler is the providential organ of the oppressed and suffering poor; and it is no wonder that his language and his measures are sometimes too close and lively an expression of what, after all, is the actual truth of the case. Those who do not see and know and feel what he does are not competent judges. If anybody thinks the work can be done better, let him come forward and try to do it.

All in all, that still remains the best vindication of Oastler yet penned.

¶ 4

Oastler's Yorkshire friends were naturally eager to hold some big pageant in honor of his return to his native county. Obviously it must take place at Huddersfield; and the date, too, fixed itself just as easily, for the Factory Act prescribed a half-holiday for workers on Shrove Tuesday, which this year fell on 20 February. During the intervening week, therefore, the Central Committee was extremely busy making all the necessary preparations.

Oastler had gone from London to stay with his sister at Leeds for a few days' rest. He was to be met off the train at Brighouse (for Huddersfield did not as yet have a station of its own) and then conducted into the town for the ceremonies. But at the last moment he changed his mind. He felt it would be too much of a strain to begin the great day with a tiring railway journey, so he went to Brighouse overnight and put up at the Railway Hotel, where he remained in seclusion until the proceedings began. The hotel was crowded with personal friends and committeemen from the various Oastler Societies. As the morning wore on, emotions rose. Then at the appointed moment Parson Bull led in the Factory King. 'The scene will never be forgotten,' wrote one reporter, 'old men, weather-beaten hardy veterans, were overpowered. They strove, but in vain, to restrain their feelings, and at last, fairly overcome, they burst into tears. The young and more susceptible had not waited for the infection, and for a while the ransomed captive gazed silently upon his friends and deliverers and then sank into a chair overcome by his feelings.' When calm had been restored, a formal address of welcome was read, Oastler replied, and everyone set about getting ready for the procession.

The affair turned out to be as spectacular as any of the old Ten Hours pageants. Throughout the morning bodies of operatives were arriving from the surrounding townships, and bands played to while away the time. By one o'clock there was a crowd of several thousands outside the hotel, including hundreds of factory children carrying small white flags inscribed with the jingle

> Our King is released, the Captive is free,
> Long may he live, and blest may he be.

When all the deputations had assembled, the procession accompanied by its four bands set off on the march to Huddersfield. Halfway to the town it was joined by another procession that had come out with three more bands to meet it. A halt was made while the line was re-formed; a body of horsemen took the lead; the banners were unfurled; and then the cavalcade advanced for the last stage of its journey. All along the route ballads and souvenirs were being sold by street hawkers among the throngs of sightseers. 'The immense assembly was an impressive sight,' wrote the reporter of the *Wakefield Journal*; 'no conqueror,

ancient or modern, ever had a more glorious triumph . . .
Crowds were congregated in every window, on every wall.' It
was, said an eyewitness in the *Birmingham Advertiser*, 'a day
which, it is certain, will be named to generations yet to come,
and by fathers to their children.'

Altogether it took two hours to cover the four miles from Brighouse to the hustings off the Halifax Road, where a crowd of over
10,000 had gathered. There Oastler was ceremoniously presented
with another Address from 'the inhabitants of Huddersfield and
of the various towns and districts in the West Riding of Yorkshire.' He made a gracious and characteristic reply, extolling the
glories of the Elizabethan constitution, after which proceedings
quietly ended. In the evening the operatives held a high tea and
dance of their own to complete the celebration.[1]

Other parties of welcome were held at Leeds and elsewhere
in the course of the next few days. When Oastler had seen all
his old friends and had made his personal thanks to those who
had so loyally stood by him, he went off for a holiday to his
nephew's place at Wold Newton Hall in the East Riding, where
he hoped to be able to get back his old vigor again.

Without doubt Oastler had now become a national figure. A
seal had been put upon the fact not only by the dedication to
him of a leading article in *The Times* but also by the inclusion
of his picture and biography in an interesting series of 'Parliamentary and Popular Portraits,' which the new fashionable journal, *The Illustrated London News*, was then running. It was an
honor he shared with a galaxy of representative Englishmen that
included Queen Victoria and Richard Cobden, Dr. Pusey and
Benjamin Disraeli. The comprehensive opening paragraph justifying his inclusion in such a gallery made a garland of commendation fitting to this hour of general esteem:

Mr. Oastler is in all respects a remarkable man and therefore entitled to a place in our gallery of national portraits. He is remarkable
for his talents—for his habits—his physiognomy—the expression of his
countenance—his principles and firm adherence to them—his persever-

[1] Even the *Leeds Mercury* devoted two columns to the pageant. The
paper not only refrained (for the first time in 14 years) from abusing Oastler,
but also called him a 'gentleman' throughout the article.

ance—his energy—his courage—his moral and political position; for his vigorous oratory, and especially for the extraordinary control which he exercises over the minds of great assemblages of working men, the secret of which is his long-tried honesty and his disposition and ability to promote the real interests of the poor and the oppressed. His motto is: *The Altar, the Throne* and *the Cottage*. In no instance of an active life has he been known to deviate from it.

MR. FERRAND.

CHAPTER XXXIV

The Ten Hours Movement Revives

OASTLER had returned to Yorkshire at a particularly opportune moment, for a new Ten Hours Movement was just getting under way. With a prestige enormously enhanced by his 'martyrdom' and the nation-wide publicity of recent months, he was thus able to step straight into his old role of leadership after almost six years of absence from the public platform.

¶ 1

Since the start of the Anti-Poor Law agitation in the spring of 1837 there had been no sustained campaign for factory reform. The operatives' energies had gone elsewhere. Had it not been for the dour pertinacity of Lord Ashley and a few of his friends in Parliament, the cause would have fallen as dead at Westminster as it had in the provinces.

Ashley had labored valiantly indeed, despite lack of support from the manufacturing districts and the Government's indifference. Knowing that it was useless to press for a new Ten Hours Bill at the moment, he had concentrated his attention upon the matter of law enforcement. The Inspectors' reports showed that Althorp's Act was still working badly despite the Home Secretary's promise that it would be enforced more rigorously. False age certificates were still being extensively used; fines for violation of the law were often farcically inadequate; and many of the old abuses were still being practiced, such as tampering with the factory clocks and denying the children time off for meals.[1] All

---

[1] In a pamphlet published in 1842, Sir Charles Shaw, Superintendent of Police for Manchester, declared that since so many mill owners were Justices of the Peace 'it was vain to make a complaint against a master, as all the masters were either directly or indirectly bound together.' An operative who won a favorable decision, he added, was a doomed man.

these things Ashley sought to publicize by such means as he could, and each year he introduced resolutions calling for their reform. Occasionally the debates became lively, as when the Irish leader Daniel O'Connell made his notorious *volte face* and announced himself opposed to any further interference with industry; but nothing positive was accomplished.

A measure of success Ashley did achieve in 1840, however: he persuaded the Government to institute two new investigations. A Select Parliamentary Committee was set up to enquire into the working of Althorp's Act, and at the same time a Royal Commission was appointed to investigate the employment of children in industries outside the scope of that Act, particularly coal mining. The Select Committee reported the following year with findings that made it impossible for the Government to continue evading the issues raised. But just as Ashley was in hopes of getting effective amendment at last, Melbourne suddenly called for a General Election. The Whigs were decisively defeated at the polls after more than ten years in office, whereupon Sir Robert Peel, as leader of the Conservatives, was called upon to form a new Administration in September 1841.

It was at this juncture that the Short Time Movement began to show signs of renewed vitality. Despite all the happenings of the past four years, something of a Ten Hours organization had been preserved. In a few towns the local lodges had managed to hold together, even though they were unable to do anything effective; and at both Bradford and Manchester the Central Committees were still intact. Nevertheless not a single workers' delegate had been sent to London to help Ashley with his various efforts. After Chartism had been smashed, however, the operatives gradually turned back to the old Short Time demand as they slowly recovered from the shock of the 1839 repression. The formation of the 'Oastler Societies' was one indication of the revival, and others were soon to be seen. Significantly enough, Mark Crabtree, who had lately been doorkeeper and messenger for the Chartist Convention, was now made paid organizing secretary of the West Riding Central Ten Hours Committee.

To foster this revival as well as to strengthen his own hand, Ashley set out upon a tour of the manufacturing districts at the end of July 1841. It was the first real contact he had ever had with the operatives and the experience was a revelation to him. The distress he saw on every hand shocked him profoundly; the indifference of the clergy to the suffering by which they were surrounded provoked his contempt ('cowed by capital and power,' he described them); the enthusiastic receptions he was given and the touching faith in his leadership which the operatives displayed moved him deeply. 'What a sin it is to be ignorant of the sterling value and merit of these poor men!' he wrote in his diary; 'I see and feel the truth of Oastler's observations, "they are neither infidels nor Jacobins; they love the Monarchy and they love religion." It is most correct, though they have been denied the blessings of the one and excluded from the benefits of the other.'

This triumphal progress of Ashley's greatly alarmed the Lancashire mill owners, who forthwith began to gird themselves for another fight. At a meeting of master cotton spinners in Manchester it was resolved to offer uncompromising opposition to any amending bill that might be brought forward when Parliament assembled. Ashley saw at once that such determination might well prove fatal to his intentions for, like Oastler, he had very little faith in the social sympathies of the new Prime Minister. 'I now can guess what Peel will do,' he wrote after hearing the news; 'he will succumb to the capitalists and reject my factory bill.' Despite this expectation, when Peel offered him a minor post in the Government, Ashley made an attempt to get from the Prime Minister a pledge on behalf of factory reform. Peel refused to give any such promise, saying that 'his opinions on the factory question were not matured.' Whereupon Ashley declined the invitation to enter the Administration.

Evidently the replacement of the Whigs by the Conservatives was going to make very little difference to the prospects of the cause, and the same old battle would have to be fought over again with the same weapons and maneuvers as had been used so many times before. As a beginning, the northern operatives decided to appeal to the new Ministers in person. At the end of October 1841, five of the Yorkshire Central Committee went to London and had lengthy interviews with various members of the Government. Oastler in prison helped them with the preparation of their case and published a full account of the discussions in the *Fleet Papers*. Matters seemed to go satisfactorily, the deputation returning home well satisfied with its reception and full of hope. But the hopes proved ill founded. Peel took most of the winter to get his opinions on the factory question 'matured' and then announced himself definitely opposed to a Ten Hours Bill.

That blocked any further efforts for another year. Furthermore, interest in the factory question soon waned with the sudden worsening of the depression. The year 1842 was one of commercial panic, mutiplying bankruptcies, and increasing unemployment. In Leeds, it was reported, a fifth of the inhabitants had to go on the poor rates. An immense resurgence of Chartist activity resulted, along with a wave of strikes against drastic wage reductions. But this second effort collapsed as ignominiously as the first had done: 1,500 arrests and 79 transportations effectively put an end to the feverish hopes that had inspired it.

Even a wary Conservative Administration, however, could not go on indefinitely postponing some action upon the factory question: the reports of the Government's Inspectors as well as the findings of the Select Committee made that impossible. Already the horrifying revelations of the Royal Commission had given a profound shock to the public conscience and had led to the speedy passage of Ashley's Bill to regulate the labor of women and children in coal mines. By March 1843, in spite of his intense dislike of 'restriction,' Sir James Graham, the Home Secretary, felt compelled to introduce an amending factory bill as well.

This bill of Graham's had certain distinct merits. But it was quickly wrecked by the inclusion of a well-meant though ill-devised scheme for the compulsory education of factory children under the auspices of the Church of England. This provision caused such an uproar among the various Nonconformist bodies that Graham had to abandon the entire measure. Not until the latter part of the year did the Ten Hours Movement begin to pick up again.

¶ 2

A week before Oastler came out of prison the Home Secretary
introduced a second bill without the controversial education
clauses. Admittedly it represented some advance on the existing
law. It accorded to women of whatever age, for example, the
same protection of a maximum working day as was provided
for 'young persons' (i.e. those between 13 and 18 years old),
and it attempted to abolish the relay system for children. Sundry
administrative reforms suggested by the Inspectors were also
included. Nevertheless, it remained in essence a twelve hours'
bill, since both Peel and Graham were convinced that any lower
minimum would have disastrous commercial and social reper-
cussions.

Yet even this cautious modification of the law went too far
for the northern manufacturers, and their opposition to it, the
Leeds Mercury reported, was 'intense.' Numerous conferences of
mill owners were held to plan resistance and organize petitions,
and delegates were sent to London to lobby against the measure.
This immediately provoked the Ten Hours organization into full
activity. All the familiar counter-measures were taken by the
Short Time Committees in the districts, while workers' representatives in London continued canvassing Members of Parliament
on behalf of the Ten Hours amendment that Ashley was intending
to introduce.

The story of the fantastic parliamentary situation that arose
during the progress of this bill has been told so many times by
historians and biographers that it needs no detailed recapitulation. There were two sections of the bill dealing with actual
working time: clause 2, which defined the night hours during
which the protected categories might *not* work, and clause 8,
which defined the day hours when they *might* work. The two
clauses were, of course, complementary. On 15 March 1844, in
the first of the two crucial debates, Ashley at long last carried
his amendment to clause 2. Thus, after fourteen years of struggle,
the factory reformers had actually induced Parliament to vote
their Ten Hours demand even though only by a bare majority of
8. The delight of the Ten Hours men was unbounded. But they

had reckoned without the pertinacity of the angry Home Secretary. Instead of accepting the vote and amending clause 8 to accord with it, Graham determined to fight on and to move the clause just as it stood. To everyone's astonishment his tactics succeeded. After a bitter debate on 22 March, Graham's proposal for a twelve-hour day was defeated by 3 votes, but immediately afterwards Ashley's Ten Hours substitute clause was rejected by 7. In a single evening therefore, the House had declared both for and against a ten-hour day. This obviously made nonsense of the measure; so to straighten out the resulting confusion the Government had to withdraw the bill and promise a new one in its place.

¶ 3

The excitement which these events aroused in the north was prodigious. Such enthusiasm was scarcely to be expected after the heavy indifference of the past few years. Yet the fact remains that in a very short while a fourth factory agitation was under way, closely modeled upon the great campaigns of '32, '33, and '36 and every whit as frenzied.

At first the Short Time Committees had limited themselves to lobbying at Westminster. But when it became clear that the masters would make no compromise and were going to fight the bill to the last, the Ten Hours men resolved to make their own appeal to the public. Bradford started the campaign on 5 March; Huddersfield followed; and on 9 March, after six years' absence, the 'old King' himself went on to the platform at Leeds amid scenes of the greatest fervor.

This was but a beginning. When the House of Commons got itself into the mess over Graham's Bill, the north suddenly awakened to a full realization of the situation. What had been a breeze of hope now developed into a gale of anger. The Central Committee went over to Wold Newton Hall to consult with Oastler, extensive plans were made for a series of huge mass demonstrations in the old style, and at Leeds on 8 April the real battle began.

It proved to be the biggest campaign the Ten Hours men had ever conducted, even surpassing in scope and intensity the one that had culminated in Althorp's Act of 1833; and this time it had the additional advantage of vigorous support by *The Times*. Walter, Fielden, Ferrand, and most of the old leaders threw themselves into the struggle with all their energy, but always it was the rising of the white-haired 'old King' that brought each meeting to its climax. Night after night he was addressing huge audiences. Frail though he was, in the month of April alone he spoke before 22 such assemblies. Wherever he went, effusive demonstrations greeted him. Crowds would go out along the turnpike to welcome his entry into the town; factory children would escort his carriage in procession through the crowded streets; church bells would be rung, or the town band would play him to the meeting hall. In one factory town after another it was the same: Halifax and Keighley, Preston and Blackburn, and the rest. Time after time the newspapers reported the place was 'crowded to suffocation'; the *Mercury* itself admitted the facts. And even Bolton's experiment of charging sixpence admission to swell the fighting fund did not prevent the hall from being 'crammed,' with hundreds turned from the doors.

At every gathering Oastler used the same arguments and made the same kind of appeal. The scathing gibes and the racy sallies that had so delighted his earlier audiences were now excluded entirely. Imprisonment had done more than sober him; it had permanently altered his plane of discourse. The social prophet in him had supplanted the fighting leader. As he stood before his hushed audiences pleading for a measure of the hour, his eyes seemed to be scanning the wider horizons of the years ahead; and as he sought to tell the things he saw, his words took on a new compulsiveness. That machinery might be controlled so as to become a blessing to all people; that labor might be organized so that neither unemployment nor overwork would break the spirit of men; that the collective purpose might direct itself to the achievement of an economy of abundance—this was the evangel to which his pleading was now consecrated; and these were the dreams to which his audiences were really responding with their prolonged ovations.

There were many other meetings besides those Oastler attended, in the big towns as well as in the villages. By every showing it was a remarkable phenomenon the significance of which *The Times* underlined in two impressive editorials. 'Strangers have been astonished to witness with what entire forgetfulness of personal fatigue and discomfort thousands, after standing twelve hours at the spindles, could go on standing in rooms crowded to suffocation till midnight that they might leave nothing unheard or unsaid by which they might understand and declare their cause.'

The Government introduced its promised new bill while the campaign in the north was at its height. It was still in substance a twelve hours' measure, so once more the decisive struggle would come when Ashley moved his Ten Hours amendment.

All the old arguments were traversed again, not a single idea being advanced that had not been developed during the famous newspaper controversy of 1830–31. The only notable features of the debate were the 'conversions' of both Lord Macaulay and Lord John Russell to the Ten Hours party, and the declaration by John Bright that a Ten Hours Act would be feasible only when the Corn Laws were repealed. The factory reformers never allowed this uncompromising champion of laissez-faire to forget he had made that pronouncement. Time and again in later controversies it was to be thrown back at him with vehemence.

The debate made no difference to the fate of the measure. This time the Government was determined to put an end to all the shilly-shallying and to push the bill through Parliament at any cost. To accomplish this purpose the Prime Minister told the House bluntly that if he were overridden in regard to the Ten Hours amendment he would resign. That settled the matter. In vain did Ashley stigmatize such a threat as 'despotism'; the Home Secretary retorted by saying that coercion of the Executive by the Legislature would be 'tyranny.' The party waverers were thus effectively brought to heel, so that Ashley's motion was overwhelmingly defeated by 138 votes. The bill then had an uneventful passage to the Statute Book. Only Brougham's last-ditch stand in the Lords caused any further liveliness when he denounced even such a bill as the product of 'misplaced and perverted humanity,' and described social regulation as a flagrant violation of 'the order of Nature and the directions of Providence.'

The Ten Hours men were profoundly disappointed that after coming so near victory they had again been defeated. Nevertheless in several respects the Act did represent a substantial gain for the cause of social decency. It was an appreciable advance, for instance, that women of all ages should now be included in the protected categories. This meant that they were prohibited from working at night and that, as with 'young persons,' their day work would be restricted to 12 hours of actual labor between five-thirty in the morning and eight o'clock in the evening. No less a gain was the further limitation of work by children (i.e. those under 13 years) to six-and-a-half hours a day, though this was somewhat offset by allowing them to go into the mills at the age of 8 instead of 9. Other good features were the provisions for fencing dangerous machinery and the various administrative improvements designed to make inspection more efficient. Philip Grant was thus justified in claiming that 'the memorable campaign of 1844, the greatest parliamentary struggle upon this subject on record' had really resulted in some worth-while changes.

CHAPTER XXXV

Interlude of Misfortune: 1844–6

FROM the day *The Times* had seriously taken up the question of his release from prison until the final enactment of Graham's Bill 8 months later, Oastler had lived in a state of continuous exhilaration. Once the fight was over, however, he found himself at a loose end. His situation was thus much the same as it had been 11 years earlier after Althorp's Act had been passed. Continuation of the factory agitation was out of the question and there was nothing else to absorb his energies. This time he had not even the anodyne of a daily routine. And to add to his unhappiness came a succession of misfortunes that sorely tried his faith.

Financial affairs continued to be a great worry. His release from prison had been made possible through the generosity of the 12 guarantors who had underwritten the outstanding portion of the debt. The Liberation Committee was hoping that contributions to the Release Fund would continue coming in at the same rate as before, so that the deficit might be made good and something be left over for the purchase of a small annuity on his behalf. To this end a second appeal was launched immediately after Oastler was freed. The Committee was reconstituted, a fresh brochure was issued, and the 'Oastler Testimonial and Annuity Fund' was opened. But the project failed dismally. For a few weeks donations trickled in: then they stopped altogether. When the Committee published its final report late in April 1844, a deficit of £1,100 was still showing, which the guarantors eventually had to make good themselves.

. This was a painful blow to Oastler's pride. And it hurt the more because of his failure to establish his counterclaims against the Thornhill estate. From the day of his dismissal Oastler had been very insistent about maintaining these claims. Not only did they constitute a substantial off-set to the debt: they also served as a balm to his wounded dignity throughout the months of humiliation. In spite of the good offices of Fitzroy Kelly, however, Thornhill had refused to give them any consideration until his own debt was disposed of. Unfortunately the old Squire had died shortly after that account was settled. But the Liberation Committee would not let the matter drop. Time after time they sought to take it up with young Thornhill, only to have their letters ignored. Finally they threatened legal action: whereupon Thornhill announced that if the case were brought into court he would plead the statute of limitations. To that, of course, there could be no answer, and the claims had to be abandoned.

The full measure of Oastler's disappointments was by no means yet told, however. Upon his release from prison he had unreservedly put himself in the hands of his Liberation Committee. Since they were assuming all his liabilities, they naturally felt they had a right to exercise some degree of control over him until he was able to stand on his own feet again; otherwise they might find themselves indefinitely saddled with responsibility for his future. They had therefore obtained a promise from him (which he readily made) to accept whatever advice they might give concerning his public activities. Only with their permission had he taken part in the recent campaign. But when that was over the Committee drafted a letter at its final meeting telling him in gentle yet unmistakable terms to withdraw from public life and find himself a job.

That such advice was deeply mortifying to him is obvious. Ever since his release Oastler had been hoping that the Committee would somehow be able to find him a position of consequence in which he would be able to continue his agitation on behalf of social regulation and Tory Democracy. This letter destroyed all such hopes. Keenly disappointed though he was, however, he wrote a gracious acknowledgment to the guarantors. 'Having placed myself entirely in the hands of my friends,' he told them, 'I received this letter as an intimation of the Divine Will; and in humble reliance on the guardian care of that God whom I desire to serve, I retire into that privacy from which I departed for the sole purpose of propounding those truths which I believed, and do still believe, essential to the best interests of every class of the community.'

Among other things, this meant he had to give up his *Fleet Papers,* which had been such a consoling hobby for so long. But their abandonment was made necessary largely in consequence of a stupid editorial policy. For the first three years the *Papers* had been eminently successful and widely circulated. But in the fourth volume their character had completely changed. Each issue was given over to long reports of meetings on behalf of the Liberation Fund or the factory campaign, and to little else. Inevitably they lost their appealing personal quality. It was a foolish mistake to make, yet Oastler persisted in it, despite the warning complaints of readers and the fact that he fell badly in arrears with his monotonous reports. (In July he was still giving accounts of April meetings.) Month by month the circulation fell until, on 7 September 1844, publication had to cease with Oastler owing his printers something over £100. Once more, therefore, he had to beg help from his unfailing friend, William Walker of Bradford, who had already given him several hundreds of pounds during the past five or six years. Walker consulted Fielden and Wood about it, and the three of them eventually paid the bills themselves. Oastler was indeed being made to drink deeply of his cup of humiliation.

Thenceforward for a while he passed into complete obscurity. Just how complete may be gathered from the fact that not a single document bearing upon his activities seems to have survived from the next two years. All we know is that he was living for part of that time at Headingly, outside Leeds, and that (according to a casual reference in a friend's letter) he was 'in business.' But what that business was or how he passed his days we do not know.

One event did occur during this period, however, that left a scar upon him for the rest of his life: that was the death of his wife on 12 July 1845. Something of what Mary had meant to him has already been indicated.[1] Two separate word-pictures of her have been left by men who knew her well, giving us a

[1] See above, p. 141.

glimpse of a singularly gracious personality. Both represent her as deeply religious, with an exquisite gentleness, and an unshakable faith in the guiding hand of Providence. Both suggest, too, a firm will beneath that gentleness, exercising a moderating influence upon Richard's impetuousness. She was wholeheartedly behind him in all his undertakings, encouraging, soothing, and tending him; and when enemies vilified and friends deserted, hers was the consolation on which he chiefly relied for renewal of fortitude. He had come to depend upon her perhaps more than he realized. Her passing in his fifty-sixth year, after almost 29 years of married life, was therefore a great shock: so great, indeed, that one acquaintance used to say he never quite recovered.

Shortly afterwards he was offered a job in a London stockbroker's office. With a heavy heart he said goodbye to his Riding friends and along with one of his unmarried nieces moved to a villa in Fulham. His days of action seemed clearly over.

CHAPTER XXXVI

Triumph at Last: 1847

THERE was no popular activity of any kind on behalf of the
Ten Hours cause during the two years of Oastler's eclipse.
Apart from the impossibility of starting another campaign so
soon after a new factory bill had been passed, there was the
additional reason that the public was much too preoccupied with
other matters. These were the months of the all-absorbing
cheaper-food agitation when, after years of intensive campaigning, the Anti-Corn Law League was making its last great drive
by every propagandist device known to the age to bring about
the abolition of the ancient tariff on corn. Final victory for the
League came by a vote of the House on 25 June 1846. That same
night Peel's Conservative Government was defeated on another
issue, and shortly afterwards Lord John Russell formed a Whig
Administration in its place.

Despite the lack of public support, Ashley had introduced a
new Ten Hours Bill on his own initiative the previous January.
Immediately afterwards, however, he had resigned his seat over
a matter of conscience. The suffering he had seen had convinced
him that it was necessary to have the Corn Laws repealed. Yet
he had been returned to Parliament as the protectionist Member
for an indisputably protectionist constituency. For weeks he
was torn by this conflict of loyalties, until he resolved it by the
brave renunciation that ended 20 years of continuous service in
the House.[1] He was to come back a year later, but in the interval

---

[1] Ashley's diary vividly reveals the struggle that was going on inside him:
'If I remain an M.P. I shall vote for it [i.e. repeal of the Corn Laws] in all
its parts and throughout all its stages; but can I remain so? Though no
pledges were given or asked, was there not between the electors and myself
an "honourable understanding" that "Protection" of some kind should be
maintained? If this be the case, I may not vote in direct contradiction of the

the factory question was to be brought to its climax without him.

The sponsorship of the Ten Hours Bill was taken over by John Fielden, who moved the second reading on 29 April. Three days of debate ensued; but in spite of the endorsement of Lord John Russell and a magnificent speech in its favor by Macaulay, the measure was again defeated through ministerial influence—this time, however, by a mere 10 votes in a House of 400.

The narrowness of the margin so heartened the factory leaders that they seriously began considering the advisability of bringing their cause before the public once more. Then came the change of Ministry in June and on a sudden the whole Short Time organization sprang into feverish activity. For the first time since the movement had started, a convert to factory reform held the Premiership: one, moreover, who only six weeks before had made an unequivocal declaration in favor of a ten-hour day. Hopes soared. Surely an all-out effort would bring victory this time! Fielden consulted with Oastler and the district leaders, and it was agreed to start campaigning immediately.

¶ 1

What followed was an exact repetition of the happenings of fifteen years earlier, now, however, with the initiative coming mainly from the cotton district west of the Pennines instead of from the Riding. The Lancashire Central Committee decided to revive the whole apparatus and strategy that the Yorkshire men had used in the great campaign of 1831–2. Everything was carefully worked out. Mass meetings were to be held in the principal towns; pledges of support were to be taken; new branch committees were to be organized and old ones enlarged; and missionaries from the larger centers were to go on circuit through the surrounding villages. To defray expenses, a fighting fund of £1,000 was called for. The only new feature of the campaign

---

principle; neither will I vote for it. Public necessity and public welfare both demand the repeal of the Corn Laws. I could justify such a vote before God, because I am convinced that it would be for the very best for every material and moral interest; but I have entered into relations with men, and I must observe them, though it be to my own detriment.' (Hodder II, p. 127.)

was to be the establishment of an official weekly organ. Philip
Grant was chosen as editor, and on 26 September 1846 the first
number of *The Ten Hours Advocate* appeared.

History was to repeat itself in other ways too. The factory
owners realized as clearly as the operatives did that the change
of government might well lead to a change in the law. Before
any of these plans had been put into effect, therefore, many of
the masters had already begun taking the familiar counter-
measures. Once again the Halifax employers won notoriety by
their initiative under the leadership of the Ackroyd family. During the late summer, workers in the Halifax mills were being
asked to sign the 'document' which their masters presented to
them:

> We the undersigned prefer working 12 hours per day or 69 hours
> per week with the present rate of wages, rather than 11 hours per day
> or 64 hours per week with wages in proportion to the shorter time of
> running.

The tactical significance of the reference to 11 hours instead of
10 is obvious. But the trick did not weaken the operatives' determination. On the contrary: it was widely publicized and denounced, the local Short Time Committee putting out a particularly able pamphlet exposing the underlying fallacy.[2]

From mid-August the agitation was in full swing throughout
Lancashire and Cheshire. Shortly afterwards the Yorkshire men
decided on their own campaign. At a meeting of delegates from
all the West Riding Committees held at Brighouse late in October, a strong desire was reported from the districts to have
Oastler lead them in the fight. An invitation was accordingly
sent to him, and further plans were deferred until his answer
had come.

Oastler accepted with alacrity, to the delight of everyone con-

---

[2] The gist of the pamphlet was that it was entirely beyond the power of
the masters to fix wages. 'Time for labour may be fixed, wages cannot.' And
even if an agreement on wages could be temporarily reached, there was no
relying upon the masters to keep it. Prosecutions by the Government's inspectors showed that many of the masters would not even observe the
12-hour day fixed by Statute. The 'document,' declared the pamphlet, was
therefore mere hypocritical bluff.

cerned. 'Our friends in Lancashire as well as Yorkshire,' wrote Philip Grant, 'will rejoice to learn that our old King, Mr. Oastler, has consented, at the urgent request of his own subjects, to attend the whole of these meetings. In his hands our cause is safe. He will hold no communion with anyone who would persuade the people to accept eleven hours as a compromise. His motto has ever been "Ten Hours and nothing less." We know of no man better able to fight the battle out of the House than himself.' Nor did he disappoint those expectations, for by every showing his campaign of the next few months was as triumphant a success as any he had ever achieved.

He came north the first week in November and opened the drive with a stirring rally of his old Huddersfield constituents. During the next three weeks he toured the entire Riding, addressing nine more great meetings. Everywhere he aroused the same perfervid demonstrations he had called forth two years earlier. Hundreds were turned away from halls packed to the last foot of standing room; and under the spell of his still remarkable power audiences again became shaken with the emotions he evoked. Never again was he to attain the mastery he displayed in those weeks. 'The zeal and enthusiasm which has been everywhere manifested,' wrote Grant, 'demonstrates how dearly he is beloved by his old subjects and how deeply rooted is the love for King Richard in every true Yorkshire heart.'

The Lancashire Committee was inundated with requests for Oastler to address meetings in the cotton towns too. But this outpouring of energy had severely taxed his strength. The speeches represented only a fraction of the demands made upon him; there were committees to attend, plans to be worked out, interviews to be given or sought, and innumerable letters to be written. It was not surprising, therefore, that the strain began to tell. 'We fear the labour is too great for any human being to accomplish,' *The Ten Hours Advocate* announced, 'but we hope God will give him health and strength to overcome the difficulty.' So numerous were the invitations, however, that the Lancashire secretary felt obliged to ask Oastler to address at least a few demonstrations west of the Pennines if he possibly could. But

again he had to decline in order that he might take a brief rest
before starting on the tour that the Scottish Central Committee
had already arranged.

¶ 2

On 10 December he began his three weeks' tour of Scotland
with a meeting in the Glasgow City Hall, which was 'crowded to
overflowing.' Thence to Paisley; and afterwards to Dundee where
his speech was received, we are told, with 'rapturous and enthusiastic cheering.' At Edinburgh a public breakfast was given
in his honor and two meetings were held, the second of which
was described by the local press as 'perhaps the most numerous
and respectably attended meeting ever held in Edinburgh.'

This tour seems to have been just as successful as the one
through Yorkshire, even though the audiences Oastler had to
deal with were very different. At every meeting he had on the
platform with him numerous clergy and local gentry as well as
representatives of the manufacturing interests, yet never once
did he strike a jarring note that might have alienated sympathy.
The plea he put forward was purely humanitarian, the deep
evangelical tone of his supplications appealing particularly
strongly to the Presbyterians who crowded to hear him. None
other but Ashley could have used that idiom so effectively. Both
the Scottish and the English committees were delighted with
the results. 'It far exceeds our most sanguine expectations,' the
Advocate declared.

There was one success, however, which surpassed all the rest,
and that was the winning-over of the eminent divine, Dr. Thomas
Chalmers. The Ten Hours men were desirous of getting Chalmers'
support for many reasons. He was, beyond doubt, the outstanding
figure in Scottish national life of his generation. His opinions
carried no little weight with the middle classes, and his writings
on social matters had already exercised much influence on liberal
thought. As soon as Oastler reached Edinburgh, then, he made
a special point of securing an interview with the great man.

When the campaign was over he wrote from memory an account of the talk they had. The reporting may not be literally

accurate; nevertheless it has interest in showing the sort of appeal Oastler was making at this time.

Chalmers had asked him to breakfast. When the meal was finished Oastler was invited to state his case. He had not gone far, however, before his host cut him short:

'I see,' he said, 'this Bill is contrary to the principles of Free Trade.'

'Decidedly,' Oastler replied. 'If Free Trade be right, the Ten Hours' Bill is wrong.'

'I am a Free Trader, and cannot support any measure that is opposed to it,' Chalmers rejoined.

'That is very strange,' Oastler said. 'I thought you were a Christian.'

'And so I am.'

'What!' exclaimed Oastler, 'a Christian and a Free Trader? You surprise me.'

'How so?' Chalmers asked.

'Why, Dr. Chalmers, it was from you I learned that Free Trade was anti-Christian. When a youth I read your *Astronomical Lectures,* and in one of them you treated on the responsibility of the rich . . .'

'What has that to do with Free Trade?' the divine interrupted.

'Everything,' said Oastler.

There you taught that God would require of every man a true account of the use of his wealth; and if it had not been used in accordance with His laws, you said, the punishment on the offender would be most dreadful. Now the doctrine of the Free-trader is, that no law is given—no responsibility is incurred! That wealth cannot (when its owner is seeking for its increase) be misapplied. That Christianity does not concern itself with the modes adapted to increase Capital! That even the most covetous and cruel person cannot err, so long as his aim is his own aggrandisement. That then he must, of necessity, be a benefactor to society. The Free-trader, therefore, laughs at the idea of Christian laws interfering with him. He rejects the interposition of the Almighty; he is an independent agent. He cannot be a Christian. Every Christian believes that man has fallen from perfection, that he is selfish, covetous, and that he needs the unerring teaching of the Almighty. The Christian must require that all human law shall be founded on the laws revealed in the Word of Truth—'Do unto others

as you would they should do unto you'; not 'Take advantage of another's poverty or ignorance, forcing or coaxing him to sell cheap; and
when he is a buyer, using the same means to make him buy dear' . . .
not 'get money any how, even at the cost of limb and life to those employed in his aggrandisement'; for 'love worketh no ill to its neighbour.'

The Christian will never forget [he continued], the Free-trader will
never remember, that the head and the eye must never be permitted to
invade the rights of the hands and the feet. The Christian knows that
Society is one compact body, each individual member being dependent
on the rest, each requiring the protection of all. The Free-trader, on
the contrary, persuades himself that each member is a separate piece
of independence, an isolated self.

Oastler went on to develop the argument for 'regulation' along
these lines, quoting (from a memory now richly stored with such
things) some of the more uncompromising pronouncements of
the economists to show the contrast between the Gospel of Christ
and the newer gospel of M'Culloch and Senior.

Then he clinched the argument by telling his host what he
knew from personal experience of factory conditions. Eventually
Chalmers announced himself convinced. He promised his support and gave Oastler a letter of introduction to various friends
who might prove useful. Oastler called on them all, reasoned with
them as he had done with Chalmers, and finally persuaded them
to join the operatives in establishing Edinburgh's first Ten Hours
Committee.

¶ 3

Meanwhile the movement in Lancashire and Yorkshire had
been rapidly gathering momentum as the two Central Committees kept exhorting the local lodges to ever greater efforts.
The close division in the House the previous May had shown just
what the disposition of parliamentary sentiment actually was.
Realizing, therefore, that right up to the last hour this was going
to be a hard struggle for the marginal vote, the Committees
sought to mobilize public opinion in such a manner as to bring
the fullest pressure to bear upon the largest possible number of
Members. To this end they urged the forwarding of petitions to
Parliament from every workshop and factory in the north, as

well as from every trade and profession that could be won over; and they advised each branch committee to aim at raising a separate local fund for sending its own delegate to Westminster to help with the heavy task of lobbying that Fielden was undertaking. Regional and county conferences were periodically held to review the agitation and plan new undertakings; an appeal for support was issued *To the Nobility and Gentry of England;* and all the various counter-measures taken by the factory owners were immediately exposed and denounced. An incredibly ill-timed 'compromise' proposal for an eleven hours' bill, which the faint-hearted Hindley brought forward, had to be promptly quashed.

As the day for the opening of Parliament drew near, this activity grew more intense. Twice Ashley toured the northern counties. Scores of meetings were held every night; petitions circulated by the dozen. Meanwhile Oastler had gone back to London to help Fielden with the work at that end and during January wrote various 'open letters' on the factory question to sundry men of eminence. Bright attacked him smartly in a speech at Manchester, accusing him of deluding the workers by leading them towards a cut in wages and thus destroying 'all chance of self-improvement.' Oastler replied with equal asperity and challenged Bright to a public debate in the Free Trade Hall at Manchester; but the champion of laissez-faire refused to take up the gage.

One good debating point Oastler never tired of making during these weeks, which all his fellow-workers kept echoing. This was to show the gross inconsistency towards the factory question displayed by the promoters of the Anti-Corn Law League. During the course of their agitation, Ashworth, Greg, and the other manufacturers had repeatedly said from their platforms what Bright had previously said in the House during the debate on Graham's bill: that the Corn Laws in effect 'added two hours' to the working man's day. But now that repeal of those laws had been effected, these same men were as hostile to factory legislation as ever. Was any further proof needed, Oastler kept asking, of the selfish hypocrisy of these 'liberal' capitalists, who for so long had used the humanitarian argument to bolster their

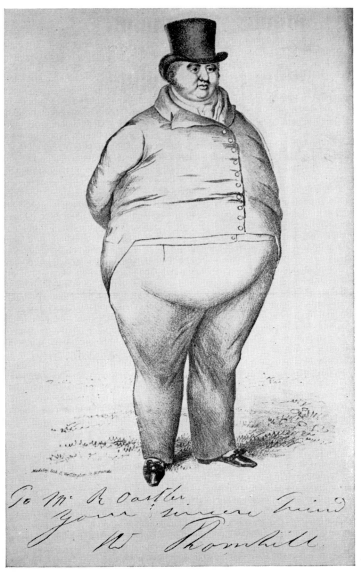

OASTLER'S EMPLOYER: THOMAS W. THORNHILL, SQUIRE OF FIXBY

demand for 'cheaper bread'? Did it not plainly show that their sole concern was for lower wages and greater profits?

¶ 4

Never before had the Ten Hours men prepared for the struggle with such elaborate care. They had rented an office off the Strand to serve as headquarters, and there, until the final vote was taken in the House, a staff of voluntary workers was kept hard at work. A dozen delegates came down from the north to assist. Every day they went in deputations to plead with Members and Ministers, while Fielden, Oastler, Wood, and the rest continued their own lobbying independently. Before the big debate began there was not a Member of the House who had not received a personal letter of appeal. Before each critical division, the office sent out a whip imploring all pledged supporters to be sure to be in their seats; and from time to time speakers' notes were issued, summarizing arguments that might be used and setting forth the refutations of points made by the opposition. This time nothing was left to chance.

The second reading was carried by an unexpectedly large majority—195 votes to 87. This by no means implied the safe passage of the bill, however, for the Cabinet itself was acutely divided on the question, and anything might happen in the Committee stage. Charles Wood—Member for Halifax, friend of the Ackroyds, and Chancellor of the Exchequer—had voted against his own chief; Sir George Grey, the Home Secretary, had voted for the reading but had intimated that he would move an eleven hours' amendment later. The Ten Hours men thus realized that victory would not be won until the last division had been taken. Though news of the second reading caused great excitement in the north, therefore, there was no relaxing of effort. Every Short Time Committee drew up a memorial to Lord John Russell expressing its gratification at the success to date but begging him to prevent mutilation of the bill in Committee. Extra delegates were sent to plead with the Prime Minister personally, and additional petitions were gathered in from the clergy.

The motion to go into Committee was carried by only 19 votes. The crucial division on the eleven hours' amendment was awaited with acute anxiety. Contrary to all expectations, however, the amendment was rejected by a large majority—146 to 68—because Peel and his followers abstained from voting. Thenceforward the bill had a comparatively smooth course. Both Russell and Grey accepted the vote with a good grace and gave the measure government support for the rest of its journey. So while an agitated delegation waited nervously in the Lobby, the third reading was carried easily by a majority of 63.

Next day, 4 May, Fielden took the bill to the House of Lords. Accompanying him were some 20 other Members, including Disraeli, Lord John Manners, and the veteran Ferrand. Only one division was taken in the upper House and that was convincing. At long last, therefore, on 8 June 1847, the Ten Hours Bill received the royal assent. When the two Central Short Time Committees in the north heard the news, they knelt in a prayer of thanksgiving.

¶ 5

On 12 June *The Ten Hours Advocate* was thus able to end its short life in triumph. In its last issue appropriate editorial tributes were paid to the little band of men whose efforts, extending over so many years, had alone made this success possible: to John Wood who, though never in the limelight, had 'made more pecuniary sacrifices than any man living' for the cause; to John Fielden, Lord Ashley, and the other parliamentarians who had borne the brunt of the battle at Westminster; and to Richard Oastler—'Oastler, who had been justly styled the *King*, and still lives to see the successful termination of his herculean labours.'

Included in the same festival issue was a letter from Parson Bull eulogizing Michael Sadler and his fellow-workers of years gone by, who had sowed the seeds that had made this harvest possible. But the deepest gratitude of all must be reserved for the 'old King.'

Oastler! Forget him? Nay, Oastler, I cannot write of thee—my friend, my fellow-labourer, my fellow sufferer, I cannot write of Oastler, nor yet of *her* whose prayers were thy support, whose smile was thy solace. No, Oastler! our hearts are too full. We know it, we feel it, we are gratified. Let that suffice. I cannot write of thee, nor need I, for thou my friend art known and read of all men.

Oastler's own feelings as he looked back upon the seventeen years of vicissitudes that had begun with that dawn dedication in the autumn of 1830 can well be imagined. The struggle had begun with his writing of a letter. He now wrote another to close the chapter. It was to be his *nunc dimittis;* and as his pen moved forward the piety of Fulneck spilled on to the page:

To THE YOUNG PERSONS AND CHILDREN EMPLOYED IN THE FACTORIES
OF THE UNITED KINGDOM.

My Dear Friends,

Praised be God! He hath not broken the bruised reed. He hath not quenched the smoking flax. He hath sent forth judgment into victory! He has answered our prayers, He has blessed our exertions, He has given us the Ten Hours Bill!

We were ridiculed and contemned, traduced and persecuted! We were poor and weak contending against the wealthy and powerful, enthroned in high places. We were ignorant and abhorred, resisted by the learned and honourable—we were of no party, and were opposed by all parties.

You were suffering, but the prejudices of habit and custom closed the ear of philanthropists to your cry. You were disregarded by those on whose aid you had calculated. Your moan was heard in 'a money-getting age.' You were the instruments of its production and, it was thought, at whatever sacrifice of physical, social, and moral and religious privileges, the produce of your killing toil was needed to uphold the nation's greatness; and thus your case was passed by as hopeless. Philanthropy flew to other climes for the exercise of its benevolence, and charged on your labours an enormous debt to rescue the degraded sons of Africa from British chains!

Still we persevered—through scorn and reproach and untold sufferings. We have witnessed an age of conflict, and thank God we can calmly survey the path in which we have been led and, appealing to our enemies, say: it is not stained by one unlawful act; though here and there a martyr lies whose memory is embalmed in our heart of hearts!

Year by year our ranks have been strengthened by influential supporters—in like proportion our opponents have dwindled—until the

Ten Hours Bill has been carried in the House of Commons by repeated majorities of nearly 3 to 1; and in the House of Lords in one division by almost 5 to 1, and afterwards without the slightest opposition.

It is the Lord's doing, it is marvellous in our eyes. Well, then, the conflict ended, the prize obtained, use it to His glory. We will forget all injuries, forgive all opponents, and prove to our friends that we are worthy of their support.

You have gained two hours daily. Devote them to the service of Almighty God, the improvement of your minds and hearts, to domestic duties and domestic pleasures. Strive to become good men, good women—useful members of society.

Eschew anger, wrath, malice, jealousy. Let love be without dissimulation; abhor that which is evil, cleave to that which is good.

In your last moments pray for

Your sincere and affectionate friend,

London, June 7th, 1847.   *Richard Oastler.*

As an indication of some of the basic traits in Oastler's character this is a revealing document. As an explanation of the political forces that led to the triumph of 1847 it is scarcely adequate. That there had been a substantial shift of opinion regarding the desirability of protecting children and women in factories no one can deny. Nor can there be much doubt about the honor due to the men responsible for this awakening of the national conscience. But the moment and the mood must be considered by the historian in casting up his final account, no less than the men. And in that regard it cannot be gainsaid that there was a large element of luck in the timing of Fielden's Bill. The recent resounding victory of the capitalists in the matter of the Corn Laws had outraged the country gentry and disposed them to take vengeance upon the manufacturers. Disraeli's revolt had split the Conservatives and put the Peelites in an ambiguous position. The continuing economic depression had already forced many factories on to a part-time schedule and was compelling the closing of numerous others, so that few concerns anywhere were working 10 hours a day. All these factors help to account for the curious division lists, with their significant abstentions and their equally significant conversions. It was, indeed, what the *Man-*

chester Advertiser described as a 'fortuitous conjuncture of events.'

Nor can the marked change in public sentiment be left out of the reckoning, for opinion concerning social problems had altered considerably in the years since Oastler had begun his campaign on behalf of the factory children. The public was now much better informed about what Carlyle called 'the condition of England question' than it had been in 1830, and the national conscience was obviously troubled as the literature of the 'forties abundantly proves. Oastler himself had inestimably contributed to that change by his unceasing efforts, but he was only one of many to whom the new social sensitivity has to be credited. Dickens was extending the range of middle-class sympathies with every book he wrote. Disraeli in *Coningsby* (1844) and *Sybil* (1845) had opened the eyes of people to the existence of 'the two nations' living side by side in the same country. Fanny Trollope had caused the tears to flow with her tales of the sufferings of *Michael Armstrong* (1840) in the mills and *Jessie Phillips* (1843) in the poor house, and various lesser storytellers had emulated her. Elizabeth Barrett had created a sensation with the outpouring of her passionate indignation in *The Song of the Factory Children* (1843), characterized by a recent writer as 'a blue book in verse.' And, in a different medium, a score of more substantial and analytical works had added to the uneasiness: Carlyle's writings, for instance, particularly *Chartism* (1839) and *Past and Present* (1843); Vaughan's *Age of Great Cities* (1844); and Mrs. Tonna's *Perils of the Nation* (1843), which was distributed by the evangelical Christian Influence Society and went through three editions in a few months. To these must be added the continuing stream of pamphlets and the reports of official investigations sponsored by the Government. (Parliamentary papers first began to be sold in 1835.) The cumulative effect of all this upon the public mood was immense, making it difficult (as one of Oastler's friends wrote in the late 'fifties) for those who came after to imagine what the dead-weight of indifference had been like when Oastler first embarked on his mission.

That, of course, in no wise detracts from the credit due to the men who had led the cause with such unflagging devotion and were thus in a position to make an ally of circumstance when the opportunity offered. And it is particularly gratifying that it should have been two manufacturers—Fielden and Brotherton—who finally piloted the bill through the House, backed in the Lobby by a small group of generous-hearted masters that included Walker of Bradford, Cooper of Preston, Kenworthy of Blackburn, and Taylor of Oldham. Their motives were surely beyond the suspicion of political coloring; for after all, had the prophecies of disaster so confidently made by the opponents of factory regulation come true, it was these men who would have lost their all. Of course, no such disaster befell. But more than 10 years were to pass before the gloomy Graham was to admit the falsity of his prognostications.

¶ 6

For weeks to come celebrations of the victory were being held in the industrial districts with each Short Time Committee organizing its local festivities. The rejoicings, we are told, 'were such as had never been known before.' There were teas, banquets, services of thanksgiving, and gala doings of all sorts. Addresses of gratitude were presented to the local and national leaders and a medal of commemoration was struck.

From all these rejoicings, however, Oastler was absent. One of his sudden collapses had overtaken him almost immediately after the bill had passed, and for more than a month he was unable to move from his room. There was another who was absent too. John Walter had fallen ill during the summer, and on 25 July passed away at the age of 71. His death profoundly grieved Oastler, who had come to have for him a reverence scarcely less than he had had for Michael Sadler. In spite of his weakness, Oastler insisted on attending the funeral. When all was over and the mourners had left, he went back alone into the crypt and kneeling by the coffin of his champion prayed earnestly and long for the triumph of those principles for which they both had fought so strenuously.

For the next year and a half he was living in obscurity at Fulham, with ill-health still periodically troubling him. One spell of sickness was so acute that for several weeks his doctor would allow him no contact whatever with the outside world. When he got about again it was to learn that the firm for which he had been working had gone bankrupt.

From time to time he still wrote for the newspapers, denouncing the class bias of a bourgeois Parliament and setting forth his own schemes for social reconstruction, but these effusions attracted little attention. A new medium was opened to him when his friend Stephens started an interesting little weekly magazine, the *Ashton Chronicle*, dedicated to the promotion of Tory humanitarianism. All the while, however, despite his diminished strength, Oastler was fretting for something more active to do. He tried to get Fielden and other friends to sponsor his old project of a People's Lobby, but none of them considered circumstances were propitious for such an undertaking. Oastler steadily grew more gloomy.

CHAPTER XXXVII

The Struggle for Law Enforcement

THE Ten Hours Act had been in operation barely eighteen months when, to the astonishment of the Government as well as the general public, the factory question was reopened with bitter intensity. An oblique attack upon the law, which the promoters of the measure had entirely failed to foresee, suddenly threatened to reduce to a nullity the central principle that had been so hardly won. Oastler chafing in retirement quickly came north to do battle once more, and before long a struggle was under way as fierce as any in the past nineteen years.

The underlying cause of the trouble was the business revival that succeeded the appalling depression of the early 'forties. Trade began to pick up just about a year after the Ten Hours Bill had gone onto the statute book. With orders steadily increasing, mill owners naturally wanted to operate their plants at the maximum so as to recoup their losses of the past few years. Not until then did the inconveniences of the new labor restrictions fully reveal themselves. The aggressiveness of the employers consequently grew with their sense of frustration: so did their ingenuity. Nor was it only the masters who were liable to be irked, as Hindley repeatedly pointed out. Thousands of operatives who had been on part-time or had had no job at all in recent months were only too glad of the chance to make extra money from longer hours and thus get rid of the crushing burden of debt so many of them had incurred during the depression. After bleak years of wretchedness the length of the working day seemed—at least for the moment—a secondary consideration in comparison with the immediate prospect of a welcome sufficiency for themselves and their families.

It was hardly surprising, therefore, that the increasing pressure of these forces should have put a great strain upon those barriers against overworking which the 'fortuitous conjuncture of events' had made possible. Evasion of the law was the first result; a powerful movement for its amendment followed. Out of such a situation there gradually developed in the Ten Hours ranks a confusion of purposes and a conflict of judgments that threatened to destroy the recent gains altogether.

¶ 1

The trouble started over the matter of relays. A vivid little letter published in the *Ashton Chronicle* in January 1849 shows how the issue broke upon the consciousness of the northern workers. The correspondent had been walking past one of the mills in the town when he saw a number of the operatives coming out. He stopped one of the women to ask whether a strike had started or a breakdown of machinery had occurred:

'No,' said she, 'it is something a good deal worse than that.' 'Why, what's up,' said I. 'There is plenty up,' she replied. 'They have begun a new trick this morning. They are working us in gangs now; our master is doing all he can to plague us out of our lives and get us to curse the Ten Hours Bill. We are working *shifts*. We all begin the first thing in the morning; the *first* gang goes out at seven o'clock and comes in again at half-past nine; and then *another* gang goes out and comes in at half-past eleven; and then *another* gang goes out and comes in at half-past two; and then we work on till half-past seven. Thus, you see, we are kept at it, backwards and forwards, here and there, from half-past five until eight o'clock. We can make no use of this time, but make it away as we can. There are some who are a good way from home that walk up and down anywhere, or go with a friend to their house. Others harbour with neighbours or shelter in beer houses. We are forced to skulk about and put the time in the best we know how, some one fashion and some another.'

As the depression lifted, the temptation to evade the Act in this way increased. With alarming rapidity the relay system spread in the cotton area (though curiously enough not among the woolen and worsted mills of the West Riding), so that in his next report the Inspector for the Manchester district was complaining that 114 mills in his territory had already resorted to it.

How was it, people began asking, that employers were allowed to go on with such practices when the intentions of the Act were so obvious? The answer is to be found in the faulty draftsmanship of the law, the ambiguity lying not so much in the recent statute as in the one passed three years before.

Fielden's Act had not repealed Graham's Act of 1844: it had merely supplemented and amended it. Now the Graham Act had provided that the work of protected operatives should *begin* simultaneously. But neither that statute nor the one amending it had declared that the hours specified should be worked *consecutively*. The less scrupulous masters were quick to seize upon this flaw, with the kind of result depicted by the Ashton correspondent. The protected operatives were not kept at actual work for longer than the permitted 10 hours. But their time was spread out so as to cover the entire working day: generally, said Inspector Horner, a matter of 13½ hours, but sometimes as much as 15. Between their working spells the operatives were just turned outside the factory gate, however distant their homes and whatever the weather. Ashley told the House he had been assured by one manager that 'the factory law had never worked so oppressively' as it was doing in consequence of this practice.

Three of the four factory Inspectors resolutely set their faces against this kind of evasion and fought it as strenuously as they could. Repeatedly they prosecuted offenders. But their assiduity only increased the confusion instead of lessening it, because magistrates gave conflicting decisions, some holding that the relay system was illegal while others maintained it was clearly compatible with a strict interpretation of the Act. Administrative chaos resulted. The Inspectors complained of the confusion and begged for a Home Office ruling on the problem. The Home Secretary, however, was disposed to connive at relays, and even went so far as to issue a circular advising the Inspectors to curb their zeal and not to prosecute unless the workers concerned had been 'actually employed for a longer period than that sanctioned by law.' Despite this, the Inspectors went on prosecuting, though with very indifferent results.

¶ 2

All parties to the controversy were divided, even the Ministry itself. Sir George Grey, the Home Secretary, was at heart an eleven hours' man and his notorious circular was partly an expression of his own preferences and partly the result of the enormous pressure that northern manufacturers brought upon him. On the other hand, both the Attorney General and the Solicitor General gave their opinions in favor of the Inspectors. Even the factory owners themselves were sharply divided. There was not only the conspicuous difference between Yorkshire, where the Act was almost universally observed, and Lancashire, where evasion was commonest, but also in Lancashire itself there was much local variation. At first it had looked as though there were going to be a complete failure of law enforcement west of the Pennines. Closer investigation showed, however, that it was really only a minority who were defying the Act there. On that, Oastler and Fielden, Ashley and Stephens all came to agree.[1] Yet the discovery of this fact did nothing to ease the situation. The masters who decently observed the law became strongly resentful of the unfair competition of their rivals, who sought to undercut them by evasion. Might it not be better, some of them began to ask, to amend the Act somewhat; to have, say, a ten-and-a-half or even an eleven-hour day, but to make its enforcement strict and uniform? By the end of February 1849, the *Manchester Examiner* had made itself the spokesman for this point of view, and before a year had passed the London *Times* had adopted it too.

As for the operatives, they were probably more bewildered than at any time since the movement started. The choice they had to make, it appeared, was one between higher wages and shorter hours. With the help of his assistants, therefore, Inspector Horner of the Manchester district organized a survey of public

---

[1] 'The great body of the mill owners are keeping the law,' declared Oastler. 'I did not know this until I came into Lancashire. I thought that the whole of the cotton masters were breaking the law . . . I would have it known to the Government and to the people and to the legislature and to the Queen that it is only an insignificant fraction of mill owners who are causing this hubbub in the factory district.' Ashley, too, called them 'a small, thank God, though powerful minority.'

opinion by the sampling method in order to find out just what they really wanted—one of the first such surveys, it may be noted, ever undertaken in England. An examination of more than 10,000 male workers revealed that approximately 70 per cent preferred a ten-hour day, even if that should involve a reduction in wages. But when the women were questioned they showed themselves almost evenly divided, nearly 50 per cent voting for the chance for a bigger wage.

In their bewilderment, many of the surviving Short Time Committees turned to Oastler and Fielden for advice. Protest meetings were already being held and militant placards issued when the Manchester Committee invited Oastler to come north again to help them. He accepted the invitation, though he was not at the moment disposed to urge any fresh campaigning. His belief was that once public opinion had clearly expressed itself against relays, the Government could be trusted to see to the enforcement of its own act. Numerous interviews which he had with mill owners, clergy, teachers, and others only served to confirm this belief. So in the Manchester Corn Exchange on 1 February, at Ashton a week later, and again at Staleybridge, he told the men to show a calm unanimity and abstain from resorting to strikes to achieve their goal, but to be ready to spring into action if any overt move for an eleven hours' bill should be made. Fearing to alienate moderate opinion or to make the Government hostile by anything that might be interpreted as agitation, he declined all the many other requests to address meetings of protest.

On his return to London he called upon Ashley to beg him intercede with Ministers for a speedy settlement of the question; then he sent the *Morning Post* a long report, which was widely reproduced in other journals. He was convinced as a result of his tour, he said, that 'the vast majority of factory masters are lending their aid to the well-working of the new system.' It was only 'a small band of cruel and despotic, mercenary and selfish masters, aided by brother rebels on the bench of justice' who were responsible for the growing chaos. Of these few the Government appeared to be afraid. 'If these transgressors are not restrained and punished, it is feared the disease will spread—that disaffection will ensue, and strife, revenge and anarchy will follow.' He confessed that he feared the consequences of another agitation 'in the present temper of the people.' (People were still tense and apprehensive after the various continental revolutions and the last Chartist flare-up of the previous year.) But if the private efforts of Ashley and Fielden should fail, he was prepared to advise the Short Time Committees to launch a new nation-wide campaign:

If agitation we must have, we will strive that it may be peaceable; but in the present state and circumstances of the people—the shop-keepers rapidly declining, the agricultural population on the brink of ruin, and the manufacturing 'hands' justly enraged—none can tell where agitation may end. Our motto will be The Law and No Sur-render. Our object is security, by removing oppression; the triumph of justice over tyranny, of law over rebellion. If there be cause for blame, it will rest with that Government which refuses to enforce the law.

Weeks went by and the operatives grew restive, but the Government took no steps to clear up the confusion. By the beginning of April a new Ten Hours Movement was plainly in the making. 'In almost every town they are mustering like men and setting themselves in order for the battle,' the *Ashton Chronicle* announced. Several conferences were held, at one of which the Bradford delegates reported that 'never in the height of the old agitation was there shown an equal amount of zeal and combination of purpose.' Petitions were sent to the Government; the Ashton clergy despatched a Memorial to the Queen appealing for her intervention; deputations from the Committees went up to Whitehall. In reply to a question in the House by Charles Hindley, the Home Secretary again promised to bring in a bill to settle the issue. Yet May came and still no move was made.

John Fielden had been too ill all that spring to take any part in the public protests. Nevertheless, on 24 May he got up from his sick bed and went along with seven other mill owners and Lord Ashley to plead with Sir George Grey in person and to present a petition against relays signed by 605 firms engaged in the textile industry. The following week end he published his *Advice to the Ten Hours' Men*. In substance it was a powerful plea for moral force tactics such as he had been recommending for months past to the Committees that had sought his counsel. Let the workers in each factory be firmly united on a Ten Hours demand, was the gist of his advice, and let the managers and foremen go in a body every week or two to try to persuade their recalcitrant masters to observe the law. If persisted in and publicized, such tactics would soon shame the law-breakers into compliance. At first there might be some victimization; let a victim fund be started, then. If every worker subscribed a halfpenny a week, a sum of £60,000 could be raised, which would be ample for its purpose. 'It would not require one tithe of this fund to support the dismissed managers and overlookers,' Fielden declared, 'for the masters would soon cease to dismiss them from the difficulty of supplying their places by suitable men—more especially when they saw that they were supported elsewhere.' Like Oastler, he emphatically warned the operatives against resorting to strikes; direct action, he felt, would only weaken their position and alienate sympathy. If the good will of the public could be sustained, he concluded, victory was assured.[2]

That was Fielden's last effort on behalf of the factory workers. Ten days later he was dead.

¶ 3

The death of their parliamentary leader just when his Act was being subjected to the most damaging assaults was a serious blow to the Ten Hours men. But worse was to follow.

A week after Fielden's funeral, the Home Secretary received a deputation of Lancashire mill owners who had come to plead for an eleven-hour day. At that interview (according to the *Manchester Guardian*, which was the only paper to carry the story) Grey promised he would introduce legislation to legalize the relay system. This was just what the Short Time Committees had been fearing all along; but it was not the only piece of bad news. Two members of the delegation, it was said, had later called on Lord Ashley and after a friendly talk had received his assurances that he would support a ten-and-a-half hours' amendment if the

---

[2] In some places strikes had already broken out. The Manchester newspapers reported strikes in progress at two mills in Staleybridge during April.

operatives would agree. Indeed, the *Guardian* declared, he was even willing to concede a further half-hour.

This report caused utter consternation in the Ten Hours ranks. The roundabout way in which the news reached them, coupled with the Government's long silence on the whole question of law enforcement, induced the operatives to believe that much more had been going on behind the scenes than they knew anything about, and that their betrayal was imminent. John Wood, William Walker, Samuel Fielden (John's son), and a number of other mill owners rushed up to London to protest to the Home Secretary, but were coldly received. Then they went on to see Ashley and made it plain to him that they would stand for no such concessions as he was willing to consider. This, and the loud outcry in the north, convinced Ashley; for the time being he said no more about 'compromise.'

The fact was (as he complained in various letters to the press) Ashley's position had been somewhat misrepresented. It was true that he wanted to see 'a satisfactory adjustment of this great question.' It may even have been true that he was beginning to get impatient with the intransigence of Oastler, Walker, and the rest, and would have been willing to accept a 'practical' solution of a problem that had been draining his energies for 16 years. But on three provisos he had been emphatic: one was that in no circumstances would he agree to an eleven-hour day for children; the second, that he would not accede to the ten-and-a-half hours' compromise unless the operatives themselves accepted it; and the third, that the masters must give a *quid pro quo* by shortening the total working day so as to make relays impossible. That was a reasonable enough attitude, certainly. The mistake had been in the manner of his publicizing it without any sort of consultation with his former colleagues. In spite of his explanations, many operatives continued to regard him with suspicion, thereby adding further to the confusion. These suspicions only deepened when both Hindley and Brotherton shortly afterwards declared themselves in favor of some sort of 'compromise' too. Hindley had blown hot and cold alternately all through the controversy, just as he had done during every previous crisis in the history of the movement. And some weeks later he complicated matters still more when (in spite of Ashley's published denials) he informed a Lancashire gathering that 'his Lordship recommends a compromise to ten-hours-and-a-half.' Oastler was shocked and bewildered. 'I have not seen that recommendation,' he wrote to a friend, 'neither have I read any disavowal from his Lordship of Mr. Hindley's charge.' To him it seemed nothing less than fantastic that with the Ten Hours Act safely on the statute book, with the Inspectors doing their utmost to enforce it and being backed in their efforts by the Law Officers of the Crown, with all Yorkshire and many of the Lancashire mill owners decently trying to observe it, Ashley at the last should be willing to betray the cause simply because the recalcitrance of a minority had made law enforcement more difficult than had been anticipated.

In view of all this muddle, the Ten Hours men came to the conclusion that the best thing for them to do was to make a fresh appeal to the public. Local committees had already been holding occasional meetings during the summer. Now it was planned to conduct a regular campaign throughout Lancashire and Cheshire. Fielden's eldest son Samuel was asked to take his father's place, Oastler was called north once more, and Stephens was invited to join them. All three accepted, and by mid-July the new campaign was in full swing. This time an exceptional amount of support was forthcoming from the local clergy.

Enthusiasm steadily rose as the mass meetings followed in quick succession at Manchester, Oldham, Burnley, Preston, and the other large towns. Stephens proclaimed it 'a holy war,' as he thundered forth with something of his old fire and denounced the 'compromisers' with characteristic vehemence. Sam Fielden, with his two brothers John and Joshua, gave the audiences practical common sense. Oastler made his own distinctively patriarchal appeal. He was not strong enough to address all the gatherings; but for five weeks he kept up with the campaign at the rate of three meetings a week. A picturesque figure with his long snow-white hair and his still impressive presence, he played the veteran's role with an easy skill. There was nothing fiery in his oratory this time. Two serious illnesses and the warnings of his doctors had induced a somber gravity, making his discourses read more like secular sermons than campaign oratory. All his

pleading centered upon the moral issues involved and upon the
relationship of law enforcement to civilized progress. 'It behoves
a man standing in my position,' he declared, 'who does not expect to live, to guide the coming storm, and before I leave this
world to prove to all men, for myself and for those who have
confided in me, that this quarrel is not of our seeking.' That was
his theme for every speech, and judging by reports it proved extremely effective. 'Expediency, cabal and cowardice fly from the
ground on which that rare old fellow stands!' wrote one of his
admirers. 'He is indeed a King of men. He leads the present
agitation.'

The results of the campaign delighted its promoters. Its moral
effects appeared to be considerable: the factory Inspectors began
to get more convictions, the public was impressed, and the hostile
magistrates seemed to have had their complacency shaken. 'Never
since we took any interest in this righteous cause,' said the *Ashton Chronicle*, 'did we see so much practical benefit accrue to it
in so short a time. Indeed, friends as well as foes stood astonished
at the almost universal favour which the labours of Messrs. Oastler and Fielden received from the general public.'

¶ 4

Unfortunately, the success of the campaign was partly offset
by a deep and growing disunity in the ranks of the operatives
themselves. For a long while the public knew nothing about this;
but by autumn the differences had become so acute and personal
animosities so bitter that it was impossible to keep them concealed any longer. The details are far from clear, since much of
the evidence has not come to light even yet; but at least the
outlines of the quarrel can be traced.

By the summer of 1849 the Ten Hours organization was tending to break up into three hostile groups. First there were the 'no
surrender' men who followed the leadership of Oastler and Sam
Fielden. To them any talk of compromising on the Ten Hours
principle seemed nothing less than betrayal. They believed they
had public opinion behind them and an unshakable moral case,
and they heartily approved the tactics that John Fielden had
recommended from his death bed. Numerically they were prob-

ably in a majority, though the loss of Walter and Fielden had considerably lessened their effectiveness. Secondly, there were the 'compromisers' who were prepared to bargain: some because they were sick of the long-drawn-out struggle and others because they honestly believed that this was the only way to end relays. Charles Hindley, M.P. for Ashton, was their leading spokesman. A few of the Short Time Committees, notably the one in Hindley's own constituency, had become completely dominated by this group. Even while the big publicity campaign was in progress, the *Chronicle* complained, a secret correspondence was going on between these committees and certain of the 'compromising' Members of Parliament, 'by means of which, as well as by other private and clandestine arrangements, the safety of the Ten Hours Act has been seriously endangered.' It was principally these men that employers were using for getting up petitions in favor of an amending Act. Thirdly, there was a strange group, mainly in the Manchester district, which was following a devious line of its own under the leadership of a man named Mawdesley. Professing to be thorough-going Ten Hours men, they advocated 'a general turn-out' to compel employers to observe the law. It was at these men, apparently, that Fielden's emphatic warnings against direct action had been aimed. The available evidence suggests, however, that their real concern was not with the hours' question at all but rather with the question of wages, and that they were making use of the factory movement for their own purposes. Industrial discontent was rife in Lancashire that summer: numerous strikes were in progress or preparation, so that it was inevitable that the activities of Trade Unions and Short Time Committees should have become entangled and the course of one struggle judged in terms of its effect on the other. Anyway, whatever their ultimate intentions may have been, these men completely controlled the Manchester body that called itself the Lancashire Central Committee, with results that proved extremely unfortunate for the whole movement.

The schism started when this third group called an 'urgent' delegates' meeting at Manchester on 26 August 1849. No general notice of the meeting was sent out; none of the national leaders was invited, though Oastler, Stephens, and the Fieldens were all in the vicinity at the time; and no explanation was given of the alleged urgency. Apparently the conference was being packed so that its two organizers, Thomas Mawdesley and Philip Grant (who was not even a member of the Committee), could be sure of having things their own way. The outcome of their deliberations was the publication of a militant manifesto *To the Workers of Lancashire* couched in singularly ambiguous terms and calling upon the workers to 'take matters into their own hands' by offering 'passive resistance to all masters who are violating the law.' If this meant anything at all, it would seem to have meant a call to strike. At any rate that was the interpretation put upon it by the newspapers as well as by the Ten Hours men, and the strangely furtive way the meeting was summoned appeared to bear that out.

At once the three Fieldens and the other leaders became alarmed. A strike at this stage of the controversy, they felt, might well lead to the loss of the Ten Hours principle altogether. Various disclaimers and protests were immediately issued, but by far the most important of them was Oastler's *Manifesto to the Workers of England, Ireland and Scotland,* which was widely reproduced in the London and provincial papers. It amounted to a dignified plea for the continuance of moral-force tactics in order to retain public support; and though firm in tone it treated the Manchester men with scrupulous courtesy. A number of people later reported that its effect had been considerable and that in no small degree it had been responsible for the dropping of the strike plan. However that may be, there was little talk about direct action afterwards. But the Manchester group was incensed. Mawdesley sent a bitter, rambling letter of denunciation to the newspapers, accusing Oastler of being 'ungenerous and unjust' to the Central Committee and of seeking to gratify his 'vanity and ambition' at the expense of the workers. Apart from the venting of his anger, however, it is difficult to see the purpose of Mawdesley's letter, for while he repudiated any intention of fomenting strikes, he continued using language which unmistakably implied their desirability. The *Ashton Chronicle* immediately retorted with a blistering denunciation of what it called 'this infamy of heaping coarse contumely and insult upon the head of the most heroic, self-devoted and suffering champion of the cause they profess.' By warning the workers against a policy that would have led to irretrievable disaster, it went on, Oastler had 'saved the situation.'

¶ 5

This ignominious squabble might never have occurred had the old Ten Hours organization been kept intact, which unfortunately it had not. A great burst of enthusiasm for the Ten Hours Bill; the establishment of a fighting machine; the climax at Westminster; and then the gradual disintegration of the organization, leaving behind only a few groups of local stalwarts—five times that cycle had occurred since 1830, the last time being in connection with the successful effort of 1847. The result was that the movement now had no settled constitution; consequently the little clique of twenty Manchester men calling themselves the Lancashire Central Committee had no defined responsibility to anyone and could do pretty much what they liked.

The sudden revival of interest in the factory question led to the same demand for more efficient organization as had characterized all the previous revivals. This time, however, there was a slight variation in the recurring pattern. The recent campaign of protest meetings had resulted in the spontaneous formation of local vigilance associations designed to promote the enforcement of Fielden's Act. They were not confined to operatives; doctors, parsons and businessmen joined, as well as trade unionists and co-operators—anyone, in fact, who agreed with the general purpose. The Todmorden Association, it was reported, soon had a subscription-paying membership of over 2,000. Interchange of ideas and plans naturally followed, and proposals for better co-ordination of efforts began to be made. At the beginning of September the leaders of these various bodies came together and agreed to federate into a county-wide 'Association for the Protection of John Fielden's Ten Hours Act.' A prospectus was issued explaining the aims of the Society; the scheme met with general approval; and at Bury a fortnight later a conference of elected delegates formulated a constitution.

With the possible exception of the old West Riding organization of 1833, this proved to be the best-planned scheme the Ten Hours men devised. To give it orderliness and to foster a sense of responsibility, the Bury meeting made it a membership organization. A penny was charged for the admission card, and a halfpenny a week as contribution to the 'victim fund' in accordance with John Fielden's original recommendation. Democratically elected representatives from the lodges met in periodical conferences and chose the permanent Executive. This Executive, all the members of which were operatives, had the responsibility of investigating victimization cases reported to it and of allocating the 'victim fund.' Sam Fielden was made president. His chief coadjutors were William Mallalieu as vice-president and Charles Howarth as financial secretary, both important in the history of the British working-classes for the prominent part they played in founding the Co-operative Movement.

The Association—its name was soon shortened to 'The Fielden Society'—caught on rapidly. By the time the first general conference was called early in November, a dozen lodges from the principal towns had joined. The same week Stephens replaced his local *Chronicle* with another weekly called *The Champion,* designed for a wider public. Its purpose was the same—the promulgation of a Christian political philosophy; and the 'old King' continued his regular contributions. But what gave the journal its chief market was the fact that the Fielden Society adopted it as an official organ and used it both to report the activities of the various lodges and to publicize the numerous factory scandals they were continually uncovering.

It was rather with an eye to future use than in expectation of immediate benefits that such elaborate care was taken over the details of organization. The first and urgent purpose the promoters of the Society had set themselves was to bring a case before the High Court to test the legality of the relay system. Since the Government had shown no intention of dealing with the question itself, this was the only way in which the confusion could be cleared up. To that end the delegates' conference had named a council to handle the matter. Included on it besides Fielden, Mallalieu, and Howarth were William Cobbett's lawyer son John, Matthew Fletcher the ex-Chartist doctor from Bury,

J. R. Stephens, and a well-known philanthropic manufacturer from Crompton named William Taylor.

The outcome was awaited with acute anxiety by all parties in the north. The crucial judgment was given by Mr. Baron Parke in the Court of Exchequer on 8 February 1850, shattering all the hopes of the Ten Hours men. Reasoning from 'strict construction' of the Statute of 1847, and buttressing his argument with the contention that a contrary interpretation would deprive mill owners of 'the full control of their capital,' the Judge found relays to be entirely legal whatever the intentions of Parliament may have been when enacting the law.[3]

The result was, as *The Times* rightly said in a critical editorial a column and a half long, Fielden's Act had been reduced to a nullity at one stroke.

[3] See Appendix E for the text of the judgment.

CHAPTER XXXVIII

The Fight for a Declaratory Act

THE Parke judgment legalizing relays caused great excitement in the northern counties—an excitement made up of
bewilderment, disappointment, and anger. To the ordinary worker
who knew nothing about legal interpretation and 'strict construction,' the whole business seemed incomprehensible. All he knew
was that for nearly 20 years this struggle for a reasonable working day had been going on, and that time after time as it seemed
to be on the verge of success it had somehow or other been
thwarted. Intrigue, select committee, royal commission, and threat
of resignation had all in turn been used to prevent the enactment
of a straightforward ten-hour day: and now, after such an enactment had actually reached the Statute Book, 'judicial interpretation' had erased it. No wonder there was what one paper called
'such a sensation in the manufacturing districts of Lancashire,
Yorkshire and Cheshire as the oldest living person cannot remember!'

It was not only the loss of the ten-hour day that caused the
'sensation,' however. As the operatives immediately realized, various other serious consequences followed from the Exchequer
decision, consequences about which the ordinary southerner knew
nothing. Sam Fielden tried to point out some of them in a realistic
letter to *The Times* written as soon as the judgment was known.
There was the problem of fines, for example. The imposition of
fines for bad or mutilated work was a universal practice in the
textile industries, and one that readily lent itself to all manner of
abuse by unscrupulous managers or masters. The relay system
which the Court had now legalized would complicate this practice seriously. 'When there is everlasting changing and shifting
throughout the day,' said Fielden, 'no man can tell which weaver

493

it was that spoilt the work, and the consequence is that the abatement must be made in the wages of *all* the weavers who work at any time during the day at the looms where the spoilt work occurs. Conceive the injustice of this, and the heartburnings it must occasion among the hands!' Then there was the question of 'speed up.' Obviously, when one relay of, say, a third of the workers in any given mill was turned off the premises for an hour or two, the remaining two-thirds would have to work more intensively to keep the machinery going. The strain of factory work would thus become greater than ever. Unfortunately such factors were beyond the awareness of most people unconnected with the industry. Inspection would be made more difficult, too. Ten hours was still the maximum working time allowed for young persons, and six-and-a-half hours for children, even though under the Parke judgment these might be spread out over a full day of 14 or 15 hours duration. But how could the Inspectors possibly check the actual hours worked under such a system? Juggling with the shifts could make it virtually impossible for them to do so. 'I assert with confidence,' Fielden wrote, 'that under this system now declared legal by the judges, I could deceive the Inspectors even if one of them stood at the door of every mill that I am connected with.' Some of the more belligerent employers had openly boasted of doing this very thing long before the Exchequer case was started.

¶ 1

How was the new situation to be met? That was the question the bewildered operatives everywhere were now asking. Every town in Lancashire was active and agog, *The Times* reported, and night after night meetings were being held in taverns and reading rooms to debate the problem. Innumerable conferences of managers, foremen, clergy, and others were convened. Big public gatherings took place at Oldham, Bolton, and elsewhere, each of which sent up a petition for a 'clear and intelligible Ten Hours act.' The rural deanery of Bradford protested against the consequences of the Court decision, and the clergy of the Calverley district sent a memorial against relays to Queen Victoria. So the storm raged for several weeks.

The Times came out squarely on the side of the Ten Hours men, calling upon the Government to do the courageous and decent thing. There was no need to reopen the whole question, it said; clarification of the existing law was all that was necessary. Let the Government bring in a simple declaratory bill to get rid of the ambiguities of phraseology and so make relays impossible. That was the position the Fielden Society took also. But some people in the north went further and tried to revive both of the demands that had provoked such sharp controversy seventeen years before: the old Lancashire demand, namely, that there should be a 'restriction of the moving power' in addition to regulation of hours, and Oastler's demand that a drastic penal clause should be added. Stephens was particularly vigorous in urging these two things. 'The engines must cease running when the day's work is done,' he wrote. 'This point we hold to be absolutely indispensable. Everywhere the people are agreed that without this all the legislation in the world is absolutely worthless . . . Nor is it possible to have an Act that will work together honestly, unless it contain a stringent punishment clause. A twenty-shilling fine is a mockery of justice . . . It is a farce to pretend to have a law which is powerless in the enforcement of obedience.' For the moment, however, there were more pressing matters to be dealt with before these proposals could be taken up.

First in importance was the question of leadership: who was to take John Fielden's place in the coming parliamentary struggle? Ashley would have been the obvious choice if confidence in him had not been so seriously undermined by his compromising interview with the mill owners the previous June. But the doubts raised by that episode had by no means all been dispelled. The three Fielden brothers, as well as both the Cobbetts, William Walker, and many others prominent in the movement, had come to distrust him profoundly. It is a puzzling fact, though one that Ashley's biographers have tended to gloss over. The unfortunate interview does not entirely account for it: but the significant thing is that the distrust persisted. Later events were to provide a strange commentary.

If Ashley was not to be asked to be leader again, however, who was? It was this question, ostensibly at least, that brought to a head all the antagonism that had been growing during the past six months between the so-called Manchester Central Committee and the new Fielden Society. Unfortunately it is just at this point that documentary evidence is most lacking. The only sources we have are the reports of the controversy as it developed in public, and those, of course, give us little help in understanding the intangibles involved.

¶ 2

In brief, what happened was that the Manchester group led by Mawdesley and Grant suddenly began to espouse Ashley's cause vigorously and to oppose the Fielden Society's activities at every turn, carrying their opposition even to the sorry length of an open rupture, which not merely weakened the Ten Hours cause but eventually contributed to its defeat. Why they did this remains a mystery, and one the more puzzling since it was these same men who only recently had been urging direct action and bitterly assailing Oastler for espousing moral-force methods.

The elements of a quarrel were already present, as the events of the previous autumn had shown. But it was the big conference of delegates held at Manchester on Sunday, 17 February, that brought matters to a head.

This important conference was called by the Lancashire Central Committee. An earlier meeting of delegates, called by the same group just before the Exchequer decision, had agreed that if action should become necessary in consequence of the court verdict, this should be taken only after a full conference of 'old and trusted friends' of the cause had thoroughly surveyed the situation. The Manchester gathering was the outcome.

Mawdesley wrote to Ashley telling him about it and inviting him to attend a preliminary meeting of leaders. Ashley could not come, but he sent a vigorous letter which was given considerable publicity, exhorting the operatives to stand firm by the Ten Hours principle and to press on with their propaganda and their lobbying. As things turned out, it was extremely unfortunate that Ashley did not attend. Had he done so, perhaps the later unhappy episode, which seems to demand such lengthy apologetics from his biographers, would never have occurred.

The preliminary meeting duly took place with newspaper reporters excluded. The leaders of both the Central Committee and the Fielden Society were present, as well as veterans such as old John Wood (who had specially come up from Hampshire) and William Walker. They surveyed the entire situation and tried to formulate a series of resolutions for recommendation to the full conference. But on one issue the gathering remained irreconcilably divided, and that was the question of Ashley's leadership. The meeting therefore had to adjourn without reaching any agreement.

The conference next day was the biggest ever assembled in the course of the Ten Hours Movement. Never before had more than 90 representatives come together. This time there were 220, drawn from all the factory districts of Yorkshire, Lancashire, and Cheshire. At meetings of this sort one never knew just how many towns were going to answer the summons; but on this occasion the response was so unexpectedly large that the gathering had to adjourn to the hall of the near-by People's Institute after a public roll call had been taken to verify the delegates' credentials.

As soon as the proceedings started, Oastler rose to explain his position. It was his first platform appearance since Mawdesley's ungenerous attack upon him four months before, and the dignified statement he made was intended as a reply to those reckless charges. He was present, he said, only because he had been invited by both the Central Committee and the Fielden Society, and because his friends had urged him to come. It was against his inclinations, for he wanted the delegates to reach their own conclusions without any interference on his part. (Mawdesley had accused him of seeking to 'dictate' to the workers.) He was therefore going to withdraw. The meeting pressed him to stay and even passed a resolution begging him to do so; but he refused. He did reply, however, to a question from the floor asking whether he would abide by the decisions of the conference and give them his support. He had no desire, he said, to be 'a clog or an impediment to the advancement of the cause.' If the delegates decided for a Ten Hours Bill he would co-operate to the utmost: that principle he would never abandon. 'And whomsoever you select as your parliamentary leader,' he added, 'shall have my support.' Then he retired.

The meeting lasted all day. A resolution calling for a simple Ten Hours Declaratory Act passed without demur; but a proposal to try for restriction of the moving power gave rise to such a long and inconclusive wrangle that it was finally shelved. Then the question of leadership was brought up. After much argument, a compromise was eventually reached by which the conference agreed to entrust the proposed bill to *three* members jointly— Ashley, Lord John Manners, and George Bankes. This seemed to satisfy all parties, and the meeting was then able to get down to planning the tactics for the coming struggle. After these had been agreed upon, someone raised the question of the recent behavior of the Central Committee. A protracted and stormy debate followed, at the end of which a resolution was unanimously carried, calling for the complete reorganization of the Committee so as to transform it from a purely Manchester group into a real county association representative of operative opinion in all the districts. The reorganization was left in the hands of the Committee itself.

When the business was over, Oastler was sent for and given a great ovation. He responded with a rousing speech surveying the long road the Ten Hours Movement had traveled during the previous 20 years, and bidding his hearers stand firm as worthy inheritors of the cause that Sadler and Fielden had bequeathed to them. Then the conference dispersed. The impressive thing about it, said the next issue of *The Champion,* had been the fact that none of the public leaders of the movement had taken any part in the proceedings but had 'left the discussion and decision of the question with the working men themselves.'

It thus seemed that the schism was ended. This, however, proved not to be the case. To the general astonishment, the Manchester group under Grant and Mawdesley called a second conference for the following Sunday. Admission was by ticket only and the 30 delegates that came were carefully selected. The reasons given for this extraordinary action were that 'an insult had been offered to Lord Ashley,' and that people who had no right to be there had attended the previous meeting. These are extremely questionable reasons. The Central Committee itself had called the original conference and its own chairman had presided. The credentials of every delegate had been publicly checked and not a single protest had been voiced. And according to the statement that the Committee itself had issued to the press afterwards, all the vital decisions had been reached unanimously. Furthermore (as the same report shows) studious care had been taken to say nothing that might hurt Ashley's feelings; and Philip Grant himself had proposed the compromise solution regarding the three parliamentary sponsors. It is apparent, therefore, that more was involved in the maneuver than we are aware of, though our lack of sources prevents our now knowing just what this was. All we know is that the rump 'conference' was held; the earlier resolutions were rescinded; nothing was done about reorganizing the Central Committee; and Ashley was called upon to assume sole charge of the proposed bill.

Sam Fielden at once circularized the Short Time Committees asking them to send delegates to yet another meeting on 3 March. Over 150 representatives attended and a day of lively debate followed. The Central Committee was declared to have forfeited the confidence of the workers; resolutions were passed reaffirming the original decisions of a fortnight earlier; and R. B. Cobbett, the solicitor, was asked to draw up the necessary declaratory bill for introduction into Parliament. A provisional committee of five was appointed to start the new campaign and to deal with the necessary business until such time as a popularly elected Central Committee should have been formed.

No time was lost in carrying out this program. All through March the campaign was vigorously pressed along the familiar lines. Big meetings were held in all the important towns. Circulars, addresses, and manifestos were put out by the Short Time Committees. Petitions were forwarded to Westminster. Delegates went up to London to help Rand, Walker, and a few other Ten Hours manufacturers plead with Ministers and Members. Oastler was not strong enough to attend the demonstrations, but he wrote numerous 'open letters' and got them widely publicized.

¶ 3

Meanwhile, new and unsuspected difficulties had developed
in London over the drafting of the declaratory bill.

When R. B. Cobbett had taken over the legal business on
behalf of the Fielden Society, he had instructed his brother John
(who had been handling prosecutions on behalf of the Factory
Inspectors for the past two years) and Barnes Peacock Q.C.[1] to
prepare the bill. This they did, and Cobbett then sent the draft
to Ashley for his approval. Ashley, however, sent neither comment nor acknowledgment but went ahead with a bill of his own.
When Cobbett eventually saw a copy of it he was greatly perturbed, for it seemed hopelessly inadequate on several counts.[2]
So he wrote to Ashley a second time, asking for an interview to
discuss the matter. Ashley replied admitting the shortcomings of
his draft and promising to eliminate them; but when the alterations came they still did not satisfy Cobbett or his colleagues
either. He therefore wrote a third time, begging a conference,
and eventually (through the persuasion of Manners and Bankes,
who both concurred with Cobbett's criticisms) Ashley consented.

At this meeting, Ashley, Bellenden Ker, and the two Cobbetts
finally agreed upon a bill to secure a ten-hour day and avoid
relays.

Ashley, however, was very unhappy about it: not because he
disagreed with the principles the draft embodied, but because
in the process of being made proof against evasion, it had become
transformed into something more than a mere declaratory bill.
Yet he had solemnly told the House, when asking for 'leave to
introduce,' that his bill would contain no new matter whatever.

He wrote to explain his dilemma to Mawdesley, virtually leaving the final decision in the hands of the northern operatives.
But a delegates' meeting at Manchester called specially to con-

---

[1] Barnes Peacock (knighted in 1859) subsequently became Chief Justice of Calcutta, and later a member of the Judicial Committee of the Privy
Council.

[2] Bellenden Ker, the parliamentary draftsman who had previously helped
Ashley, was reported to have said of this bill that he hoped it would not be
ascribed to him because 'it was enough to ruin the character of any man.'

sider the quandary unanimously pledged itself to an uncompromising Ten Hours position and voted to go ahead with the new bill. Ashley bowed to this decision and took the necessary steps to introduce the measure.

¶ 4

The issue seemed straightforward. A Ten Hours Act had been put on the Statute Book; bad draftsmanship had defeated its purpose; an amending bill to restore that purpose was therefore about to be introduced. Surely no hitch could occur now?

But within ten days all the workers' hopes had been blasted.

In the course of their interviewing in London, four of the Lancashire men called upon the proprietor of *The Times*, the third John Walter, to solicit his support. An amicable discussion ensued, during which Walter suggested that the operatives might do well to compromise on ten-and-a-half hours—a proposal his father had denounced in season and out for fourteen years. Shortly afterwards, with a curious timeliness, there appeared in bold type in *The Times* a letter signed 'A Manufacturer,' urging just this solution.

The effect of this letter was amazing. A tornado of protest swept the manufacturing districts. Within a few days, and without any pre-arrangement, meetings in vehement condemnation of the plan had been held in every sizable town on both sides of the Pennines. The West Riding was even more bitter than Lancashire, if that were possible, because the Yorkshire masters had been obeying the Fielden Act almost to a man and the net result of the new proposal would simply be to add a clear half-hour on to the Yorkshire working day. The Riding Central Committee therefore told Ashley in the most outspoken terms what its attitude was. Even the factious Manchester clique was caught up by the militant mood, and bade Ashley press on without surrender.

Thenceforward the situation developed with great rapidity. The letter from 'A Manufacturer' had appeared on 25 April. Eight days later, on 3 May, the Home Secretary announced that the Government had accepted the ten-and-a-half hours' compromise. To meet this sudden move, Oastler immediately wrote a vigorous denunciation, which appeared in *The Times* on the 6th. The workers' case, he said, was morally unassailable: 'against such a Ministry as this a less experienced man than Lord Ashley could not fail to triumph.' But Ashley did more than fail: he sold the pass. Three days after Oastler's pronouncement, there appeared in *The Times* a letter from Ashley to the Short Time Committees of the north, counseling them 'to accept forthwith the propositions made by Her Majesty's Government as the only means of solving the difficulties in which we are now placed.' And *The Times* editorially put itself behind the advice.

It was an astonishing *volte face*, and the shock to the workers was not lessened by the fact that the communication had been made indirectly through the columns of a newspaper instead of directly to the committees themselves. Ashley, of course, had his own good reasons for accepting the compromise. He believed that the success of Fielden's Bill had been due to a lucky political situation, which could not be repeated; he thought the odd half-hour too trivial to fight about; and he felt that the final ending of the relay system was well worth the small sacrifice of working time the scheme entailed. Impressed by his piety and the beneficence of his prodigious labors, therefore, his admirers have repeatedly stressed these considerations.

The fact remains, however, that without any warning he had dramatically gone back on his word. For most of seventeen years he had been considered the parliamentary Ten Hours leader. As such, he had become the trustee of a cause and the focus of faith for tens of thousands of simple people. He had thereby incurred moral responsibilities extending far beyond his own nicely objective calculations of the immediate situation, and it was these responsibilities he was abandoning. Moreover, the suddenness of his change was almost as distressing as the change itself. Ever since the Exchequer decision he had been telling the workers in the most unequivocal terms to 'hold fast' to the Ten Hours position; and only a few days prior to his *volte face* he had written to the Lancashire Committee asking for its instructions. Then came his abrupt declaration: 'I am bound to act as your friend and not as your delegate.'

Once before, four years earlier, he had found himself confronted by a similar spiritual dilemma in connection with the free-trade question. On that occasion, too, he had had to choose between his loyalty to personal convictions and his loyalty to the protectionist constituents who had elected him. In January 1846 he had chosen loyalty to his constituency, and had resigned his seat. This time, however, he was forsaking a far wider constituency.

He expected vituperation and he got it. The delegates in London recorded their conviction 'that the factory workers will never consent to any variation from the limitation of ten hours per day,' and the men back home echoed it with a mighty shout. The West Riding Central Committee emphatically repudiated Ashley and asked Lord John Manners to take his place. A conference of the Fielden Society did the same in even more militant terms. Had not their distrust now been amply justified? Even the Manchester Committee withstood the pleadings of Philip Grant (who approved the compromise) and decided to support Lord John Manners, who had promised to move a Ten Hours amendment to the Government's bill.

Oastler was roused to an anger he had not felt since the days of the Anti-Poor Law Movement, and in every way possible joined his voice to the general protest. He interviewed Members of Parliament, he sent an *Address* to every Member of the House of Lords, and he wrote fiery letters to the newspapers. Then he went north to join the fray there. On 27 May, at a big Manchester demonstration organized by the Fielden Society, he blazed forth with all his old passion. The whole question of the relationship between Capital and Labor would be opened up, he declared, if the Ten Hours Act were destroyed.

This speech provoked *The Times* to wrath. Perhaps Walter was getting a little alarmed by the vehemence and unanimity in the north: anyway, the attitude of his paper perceptibly hardened from that moment. In an aggressive editorial Oastler was denounced as 'despotical' and 'fanatical' because of his refusal to compromise. His language could not have been more extreme, said the writer, if the Government had proposed a fifteen-hour day; and after all, the worker's lot was not as bad as that of the

conscientious Member of Parliament who worked harder and
had less leisure than the average factory operative.

With that editorial there ended a definite chapter in the history of *The Times,* which the second John Walter had begun 18
years before. To Oastler it was a blow hardly less severe than
Ashley's change of front.

¶ 5

The rest is a sorry tale. What with the defection of their
leader, the loss of *The Times'* support, and the determination of
the Home Secretary to push his measure through, the Ten Hours
men were beaten from the start. And that in spite of the fact
that the overwhelming majority of factory owners were decently
observing the existing law.

Lord John Manners duly introduced his Ten Hours amendment and was decisively beaten by 181 votes to 142. But that
was not the worst. The most shameful part of the business concerned the question of children's work.

The Government's bill dealt only with 'women and young
persons,' whose work was to be limited to ten-and-a-half hours
between six in the morning and six at night. It thus left un-
touched the work of children under thirteen, whose work had
earlier been restricted to six-and-a-half hours between five-thirty
A.M. and eight-thirty P.M. It was immediately obvious, therefore,
that unless the working day for the two protected groups was
made the same, careful organization of relays of children would
enable the adult male operatives to be kept at work for the whole
fifteen-hour range just as before.[3]

Ashley tried to remedy this serious flaw by proposing a uniform
six-to-six day for all the protected categories, but the Home
Secretary would have none of it. Twice Ashley divided the House
on the issue and each time he was defeated. Disheartened and
disillusioned, he then washed his hands of the miserable affair.

After that the bill went through easily. In the Commons the
only high-spot had been Disraeli's brilliant attack on the Government, which put Oastler's position in a nutshell:

[3] The Inspectors' reports for 1850 showed that 257 mills were making use
of this device.

You take advantage of a flaw in an Act of Parliament and are about to deprive the people of an agitation of thirty years—of an Act of Parliament which they struggled for, which was ratified by the concurrence of the great parties of the state, and sealed by the approbation of the Prime Minister. You are about to rifle the people of this country of the consequences of that agitation and the legislation which followed—not on the merits of the case, but by acts which an attorney would despise. . . . I strip the question of all hair splitting. The working classes of this country imagine that when they gained the Act of 1847, they succeeded in restricting the hours of their labour to ten hours a day. When you tell them, in consequence of an Act which passed in 1844, they are virtually to be deprived of the fruits of their labours, exemplified in the Act of 1847, you enter into a mystification which they cannot comprehend, and which as clearsighted men, they do not wish to understand, and they ask you, will you stand tc the Act of 1847?

In the Lords, even Brougham protested against the trickery by which the workers had been deprived of the promises of 1847: but to no avail. The Bishop of Ripon's plea for a straight Ten Hours Bill was likened by *The Times* to the argument of 'a certain amiable incendiary'; opposition was easily overcome, and in August the bill became law.

They had called it a 'compromise' in order to force it through. 'It was in reality,' said Lord John Manners, 'a compromise of nothing but the rights of the people and of the honour of Parliament.'

❖   ❖   ❖

The new Act was at least an improvement on the Act of 1844. It fell considerably short of the intentions of Fielden's Act, however, and its importance has been strangely exaggerated by various writers. Thus, after 20 years of struggle, the regulation of factory labor resulting from the four piecemeal Acts of 1833, 1844, 1847, and 1850 amounted principally to this:

(1) Three 'protected' classes of workers had been established, namely children (between the ages of 8 and 13), young persons (between the ages of 13 and 18), and women. Adult males were unregulated.

(2) Children could not enter the factories until they were 8 years old, and their work was restricted to 6½ hours a day. But that spell might be taken any time between 5:30 A.M. and 8:30 P.M., and nothing prevented their being used in relays throughout that period.

(3) Women and young persons were classed together. Their labour was now restricted to 10½ hours daily (exclusive of meal times) taken between 6 A.M. and 6 P.M. on five days a week; but

(4) On Saturdays their work ended at 2 P.M., half an hour being allowed off for breakfast. This made a total working week of 60 hours.

(5) All this was supervised by regional Inspectors and their assistants who made quarterly reports to the Home Office.

CHAPTER XXXIX

Proclaiming Tory Democracy

A FIERCE agitation, the verge of success, and then the sudden shattering of hope leading to an acute emotional reaction: and after that nothing to do but wait for the gradual renewal of energies and the mobilizing of another effort . . . How often had Oastler passed through this cycle since his first awakening at Horton Hall 20 years before! And now in a few hectic weeks he had lived through it all again. This time, however, as he knew full well, there could be no renewal as far as he personally was concerned, and no lusty resumption of the fight. His best energies were spent, and his bodily frailty was plain for all to see. Yet his spiritual ardor was undiminished despite physical infirmity, and the consciousness of his mission was still heavy upon him.

¶ 1

There had been a time when Oastler had supposed that social problems were merely a matter of local maladjustment. But no sooner had he come to grips with one problem than another had revealed itself beyond. And as this sense of the regression of evils had grown upon him, he had become more and more persuaded that the fundamental issue was spiritual, not organizational, and that until by some means the hearts of men could be changed those evils would continue. The struggles in the market place were but the shadows cast by the forces struggling in the soul. The fight against manifest evil must go forward, of course; but at most that was but half the task. The other half must be the proclamation of a prophetic and constructive purposiveness to combat the 'infidel philosophy' which taught that social affairs should be left to the self-regulating processes of the competitive system.

After years of strife, Oastler had thus attained to the poignant vision of William Blake. He ached to make others share it until it had become the common mind of the nation. He could not cease from mental fight or let the sword sleep in his hand until the builders of the city had got busy. But the will to build was feeble: complacency and fatalism seemed to be paralyzing it. And sharpening his evangelical impatience was the consciousness that his own days were running out and that the final call might come at any moment.

He did what he could to further various causes that sought his support. He helped, for example, in the campaign Lord Robert Grosvenor was promoting to secure better working conditions for journeymen bakers; and from time to time he spoke at labor conferences and political gatherings in the London area. But all such efforts he now regarded as of secondary importance. What he most wanted to do was to proclaim to high and low the convictions that now obsessed him: to make men see the kingdom that might be theirs if they chose to enter into it. It was essentially a religious mission that he felt was laid upon him, and his sense of it was the stronger because his faith in the possibilities of Toryism as an organized political force had now almost vanished. The party, it seemed, was becoming increasingly entangled with commercial and industrial interests. Wellington had deliberately shut his eyes to the problems before him; Peel had sold out to the capitalists. Toryism, in fact, was rapidly ceasing to exist and was being replaced by an insidious 'Conservatism' begotten of a monstrous union between the capitalists' aspirations and a reactionary mood. Those who by inheritance should have been the leaders of the people had blatantly betrayed their trust and had allowed men of the new wealth to usurp their patrimony. That was how Oastler saw it. Nevertheless, in five open letters *To the Aristocracy of England* published in the spring of 1850, he made a last appeal to Tories to join in a crusade against 'the Manchester men,' whose doctrine of laissez-faire was the negation of creative purpose. But he scourged while he pleaded. 'The insatiable maw of these oppressors of the people opens to devour its numberless expected victims—and you are silent, inert, asleep . . . You who now are mesmerized under the deadly influence of an ignorant, an insane, an infidel philosophy!' No response was forthcoming, and only a few weeks later the House of Lords finally disposed of the ten-hour day.

There was one hope of Oastler's, however, to which he clung even when his expectations from Toryism had gone, and that was for the appearance of a heroic Leader who should sound the clarion that would call forth from the people a spontaneous movement for social reconstruction. It was a hope he cherished to the end as fervently as ever Carlyle did. It arose out of his early upbringing and his deep immersion in the Old Testament story, for it was the Bible, not Bentham, that had given him the categories for all his thinking. The Lord of Hosts had raised up prophets to recall His people to the path of righteousness in the days of old: surely in these latter days His arm was not shortened nor His strength stayed? Were not the missions of Wesley and Wilberforce, which had so profoundly determined his own life, to be reckoned as part of His uncovenanted mercies? 'A great Christian, constitutional mind is now required,' he wrote, 'to guide us safely over our present difficulties.' Years ago he had thought that Wellington was to be 'the man': but the Duke had spurned the invocation. Now Oastler was disposed to hope that in the person of the gracious and captivating Lord John Manners he had perhaps found the one who was to answer the beckoning of destiny.

Manners, the second son of the Duke of Rutland, was at this time (1850) thirty-two. Sensitive and generous by nature, he had fed his imagination since youth upon Scott's historical romances, Clarendon's cavalier *History*, and Kenelm Digby's idealization of the feudal spirit in *The Broad-Stone of Honour*.[1] These and other works of a similar tendency had developed in

---

[1] The spirit of this work may be indicated by the following passage: 'You are born a Gentleman. This is a high privilege, but are you aware of its obligations? It has pleased God to place you in a post of honour; but are you conscious that it is one which demands high and peculiar qualities? Such, however, is the fact. The rank which you have to support requires not so much an inheritance, or the acquisition of wealth and property, as of elevated virtue and spotless fame.'

him a romantic desire to revive the ancient glories of 'the good
old times' by renewing the principle of *noblesse oblige* and
transposing the code of chivalry for application to an industrial
economy. He had become deeply troubled in conscience by the
misery he found lurking in the shadows of the northern factories.
The awakening had occurred, as it had in the case of the Trollopes, during a tour through Lancashire which he took in 1841,
shortly after his election to Parliament from Sadler's old constituency of Newark. The following year Manners and his friend
George Smythe (afterwards Lord Strangford) formed the little
coterie of friends that came to be known as Young England. Their
aim was to sit and act together in the House and to seize every
opportunity that offered for pressing their ideas and policies for
social reform upon the Government, while promoting appropriate propaganda outside.[2] Scarcely a party in the ordinary sense,
and always small in numbers, Young England nevertheless created a considerable stir during the short period of its existence.
Busfield Ferrand was enthusiastically with them, for much of
what they were proclaiming he had been saying for years; Walter
of *The Times* gave them his support and let his home become
their informal headquarters; *Punch* scoffed; the *Illustrated London News* poked fun; the *Edinburgh* and some of the Whigs
grew a little apprehensive. Sir George Cornwall Lewis satirized
their teaching as a compound 'formed out of the doctrines of the
Catholic Church of the middle ages and the principles of the

[2] Later in life, in the preface to the collected edition of his novels, Disraeli summarized the basic tenets of the Young England group thus: 'They
recognised imagination in the government of nations as a quality not less
important than reason. They trusted much to a popular sentiment, which
rested on an heroic tradition and was supported by the high spirit of a free
aristocracy. Their economic principles were not unsound, but they looked
upon the health and knowledge of the multitude as not the least precious
part of the wealth of nations. In asserting the doctrine of race, they were
entirely opposed to the equality of man and similar abstract dogmas, which
have destroyed ancient society without creating a satisfactory substitute.
Resting upon popular sympathies and popular privileges, they held that
no society could be durable unless it was built upon the principles of loyalty and religious reverence.'
Marx characterized its doctrines as feudal socialism: 'half lamentation,
half lampoon; half echo of the past, half menace of the future; at times by
its witty and incisive criticism striking the bourgeoisie to the very heart's
core.'

modern Communists.' But after a couple of years or so the group began to break up, though not before Benjamin Disraeli, its oldest and most scintillating member, had conferred upon it lasting fame by his two memorable novels, *Coningsby* and *Sybil*, which dramatized its hopes and carried its message into thousands of middle-class homes. In the first of those books Manners figures in the character of Lord Henry Sidney.

More than any other man in Parliament, Manners seemed to fulfil Oastler's conception of what the ideal Tory leader should be if 'the Altar, the Cottage, and the Throne' were to be bound each to each in natural piety. Manners' political philosophy and Oastler's were practically identical. Both men were genuine humanitarians whose pity issued from a deep religious source; both drew inspiration from what they believed had been the merrier England of Elizabethan days; both wanted to see a revived and reformed Establishment become a true Church of the People. Each of them distrusted Peel, detested 'Conservatism' and the New Poor Law, and hated 'the infidel philosophy' of utilitarian economics. Both avowedly stood for hierarchy, social regulation, and national self-sufficiency. They both therefore advocated factory laws, wages boards, peasant proprietorship, and agricultural protection. And they were alike also in their conviction that the real problem facing the country was social rather than political: that the extension of the franchise would do little to fill the worker's larder but would assuredly allow the capitalist to go unhindered in his course.

It was not until Oastler came out of prison that he and Manners met. Manners had contributed to the Liberation Fund 'because,' as he wrote to Ferrand, 'in these days of philosophical cant Oastler has had the courage to fight the poor man's battle in the old-fashioned way.' His regard had been tempered by a certain caution, however, on account of reports he had heard about Oastler's 'incendiarism' during the Anti-Poor Law struggle. But his hesitancy was completely dispelled when he got to know the old warrior personally. They corresponded with some regularity, and Oastler found Manners a sympathetic listener for his various projects. The fight over the declaratory bill brought them still closer together. When his faith in Ashley was shattered, Oastler saw in Manners the man on whom Sadler's mantle was to fall. Manners for his part saw in Oastler a possibly useful instrument whom the Tory intransigents might use in the fierce rearguard action on behalf of Protection, which they were waging against the Peelites and the Whigs. 'Oastler is the one engine,' he wrote to the Marquis of Granby, 'by which the manufacturing districts can be worked, and I could wish Stanley sent him £10 with a few words of encouragement. Manchester and Leeds are not to be won by rosewater.'

Yet very little of practical significance came out of this mutual regard and community of hopes. The protectionist cause was already lost, and anyway Oastler was too frail for more than an occasional public effort. His services to Toryism had already been rendered, though the Tories themselves had been blind to the portent that he was. Manners, on the other hand, failed of Oastler's expectations for reasons of temperament. He was neither a Bismarck nor a Dolfuss. For all his appealing qualities and his deep convictions, he was totally lacking in the sustained aggressiveness that alone makes effective leadership possible. The Young England episode was his only experiment in daring. When that was over he was content to follow loyally whithersoever his more dazzling friend Disraeli should lead.

¶ 2

In the circumstances, there was nothing left for Oastler to do but embark upon some kind of propagandist work of his own against the day when, in the dispensation of Providence, the call to arms should sound again.

Ever since the winding up of the *Fleet Papers* he had hankered after another magazine to edit. He had been free to use the columns of Stephens' two journals, *The Ashton Chronicle* and *The Champion,* but he wanted a paper with a somewhat more general appeal as well as one he could control himself. For that, however, he must have backers. Obviously there would have to be some kind of guarantee fund, at least until the undertaking had become self-supporting. When the fight for the declaratory bill was finally over, therefore, he took up the idea in earnest and began the search for likely patrons. All the winter he was

actively canvassing, and by spring his fund amounted to nearly
£600. One could guess almost all the chief names in the subscription list without having seen them. Lord John Manners
heartily supported the scheme, as well as lesser Young Englanders; Lord Stanhope and the old Anti-Poor Law leaders;
Ferrand and other prominent protectionists; Feversham and the
Yorkshire Tories; and all the chief Ten Hours champions. Thornhill's counsel, Fitzroy Kelly, gave with particular generosity, and
went on giving. So did Pitkeithley and other of 'Oastler's boys'
from the West Riding.

With this substantial encouragement Oastler decided to wait
no longer. Agents were appointed in 22 towns (later, in 65); a
prospectus was issued; and on 3 May 1851, the first number of
The Home was published at the price of one penny.

It was larger than the *Fleet Papers,* each number consisting
of 8 double-column pages. The intention was to make it a family
magazine of the sort so common in mid-Victorian England, but
addressed primarily to working-class families and consecrated to
disseminating the message of Christian Tory Democracy. Oastler
himself wrote more than half of each issue which regularly consisted of an editorial, articles on current topics, poems, letters,
and a 'child's corner.' Of the other contributors the most frequent
was Samuel Kydd, a London lawyer who had been prominent
in the Fielden Society. He and Oastler were near neighbors at
Norwood and had now become the closest of friends.

The running of *The Home* filled all of Oastler's days. It was
his sole occupation and his constant delight, and as it prospered
with the passing months a tranquil happiness came over him.
The mellowness that comes with the resignation of age tempered
all the old ferocity and colored everything he wrote, so that those
who knew him only in his latter years could scarcely imagine
the imperiousness that once had been his power.

¶ 3

In the spring of 1852 a new Ten Hours agitation started. It
was the first for over 20 years in which Oastler had not participated; but he gave it full reports and his blessing in *The Home.*

The Fieldens and the Cobbetts were its chief promoters, aided as always by the constant Ferrand and the tireless Stephens. It began with a big gathering of delegates at Todmorden in March, and continued with public meetings and periodical conferences for sixteen months. The Fielden Society was revived: the old Short Time Committees were resuscitated; and all the techniques of the previous campaign were utilized once more. In spite of enthusiastic meetings and the presentation of numerous petitions, however, it never achieved the publicity or evoked the passions of the earlier crusades; nor did any striking personality emerge to give it the dramatic leadership that Oastler had formerly given. Yet it was not without results.

The aim was threefold: to publicize the still not inconsiderable evasions of the existing law, to revive the Ten Hours demand, and to secure restriction of the moving power. This would clearly mean direct statutory regulation of the labor of male operatives (in addition to that of women and children), as the promoters of the campaign frankly acknowledged. Perhaps it was the very flagrancy of this challenge to the dogma of the free labor market that accounted for the refusal of *The Times* to have anything to do with the movement. Only a single mention of any of the meetings was made in its columns, even though they were adequately reported in such Tory papers as the *Morning Advertiser* and *Morning Herald*. And when in July 1853 something of a climax was reached, *The Times* came out with a bitterly hostile editorial covertly attacking Oastler and declaring that there was 'an element of rank socialism' in the proposal to interfere with the freedom of adults.

On 5 July, with Oastler looking down from the gallery, James Cobbett again introduced the Ten Hours Bill, strengthened this time by the provision that no factory machinery should be allowed to run after half-past five in the evening. In an able speech he argued for the regulation and protection of every kind of manual labor in the interests of national well-being. But such flouting of orthodoxy was more than the House could stomach and the bill had to be withdrawn. Nevertheless the effort was not entirely fruitless, for it helped to stimulate the Government to action of its own which resulted in Lord Palmerston's bringing in a ministerial measure that speedily became law. Compared with Cobbett's intentions it was meager, yet it did eliminate the one glaring weakness of the Act of 1850. For the first time, a 'normal' and uniform working day was established in Britain for all three categories of protected workers. The stretching of the men's working day by the use of relays of children was thereby eliminated, since women, young persons, and children had all now to take their working time in the statutory hours between six in the morning and six at night.

What Ashley had supposed he was going to achieve by his unhappy 'compromise' in 1850, Palmerston thus accomplished three years later.

CHAPTER XL

The Closing Years

THE HOME' continued to run for five years, though increasingly beset by financial difficulties. The fare it provided and the appeal it made were too restricted for it ever to become the popular working-class magazine that Oastler had hoped it might be. Even the novels of Mrs. O. F. Walton do not surpass it in heavy piety; and the anti-capitalist distributivist economics it expounded sounded very much like a quaint anachronism in the days of the 'New Model' unions and the Crystal Palace Exhibition. There is little wonder, therefore, that the London workers did not take to it.

North of the Trent, however, there were a few circles that found in it the voice of their own aspirations, as Oastler's mail clearly proved, and these kept it going. In the summer of 1853 an effort was made to give them some sort of organization. Various prominent clergy, surviving Ten Hours men, and Young England sympathizers got together in Manchester under the leadership of Busfield Ferrand and established what they called 'The Labour League of Lancashire, Yorkshire and Cheshire.' They chose as their motto the famous dictum of Adam Smith:

> The property which every man has in his own labour, as it is the original foundation of all other property, so it is the most sacred and inviolable.

Committee rooms were taken in Stevenson Square; a campaign of meetings was undertaken; literature was put out, and The Home adopted as the official organ. The general aim was to promulgate the Oastlerite philosophy. In particular, the League worked for the establishment of local Trade Boards (such as Oastler had advocated before the Handloom Weavers Committee), the abolition of truck, the enactment of a ten-hour day, and the promotion of peasant proprietorship. It was just the kind of program that admirers of Disraeli's novels would support.

The scheme never came to much, however. After a year or so the League gradually faded away and no one has since thought to write its history. The circulation of *The Home* had been given a fillip: now that too started slowly to decline. From time to time appeals were made for a 'maintenance fund,' and by this means the paper was able to survive until 1855. But the last appeal in the spring of that year proved a failure, and in June Oastler had to stop publication.

He was sadly disappointed at the loss of his hobby, but he accepted it with resignation. He was too old and too weary to start anything fresh now, for though only in his sixty-seventh year, he was as frail as a man of 80. Nor could he longer blink the fact that the march of events had passed him by, leaving him out of touch with the things of the new generation. More and more, therefore, he tended to dwell upon the past and to live again in memory the days of his vigor.

Much of his time was taken up with correspondence. He had always been a prolific letter writer; now it was the chief happiness left to him to keep in touch with all his old fellow-warriors. All but one of the men who had made the Fixby Hall Compact were still alive and wrote to him regularly. Parson Bull was as devoted as ever; the Walkers, the Rands, the Fieldens, and literally dozens of others from high stations and low kept up their friendship with the old man with a remarkable and gracious constancy. From time to time some of them came to call upon him or to stay overnight; and all of them found ways of sending him gifts, as they had done when he was in prison.

Only once did he have anything more published. That was a pamphlet on his favorite theme, *Convocation: The Church and the People*, which he wrote while on a holiday at Conway in 1860. But it added nothing to what he had said many times before.

His pleasures and his needs were of the simplest kind. When *The Home* was ended he had moved to a little cottage outside Guildford, and there, with his niece to look after him, he found content at last. His daily rambles in the lanes around, the care of his garden, and the postman's coming set the routine of his days. On the shelves of his study stood all the records of his public work neatly bound and indexed. There were 24 volumes of pamphlets; innumerable press cuttings and blue books; letters, reprints, and papers; and even the posters of the big campaigns, which he had collected and kept. When his friend Samuel Kydd decided to write the history of the factory movement, Oastler put them all at his disposal. Kydd would come down for a day or two at a time, go over them with Oastler item by item, and take down notes of the old man's reminiscences.[1]

So the evening of his life slipped quietly by, without strain and without event, graced with the satisfaction of his knowing that largely through his labors the lives of thousands had been made more tolerable. The fullness of his hopes had been denied him. The ten-hour day was not to come until a Disraeli older than himself had attained to power in 1874; and reasonable treatment of the unemployed was deferred longer still. Even so, much had been accomplished, and the harsh dogmatism of earlier times had assuredly been modified. Oastler had been smeared with every epithet of abuse for pleading against the crushing mood of economic fatalism that dominated the 'thirties. Many who did not think his intentions evil at least believed his understanding weak. Happily, however, he lived to read some major recantations reported in the public press. None had more gloomily believed in the inexorable necessity of economic law, for instance, than his old enemy Sir James Graham. But even Graham modified his opinions. In the Commons on 8 May 1860, he frankly said:

I have a confession to make to the House. Experience has shown, to my satisfaction, that many of the predictions formerly made against the Factory Bill have not been verified by the result, as on the whole, that great measure of relief for women and children has contributed to the well-being and comfort of the working classes, whilst it has not injured their masters . . . By the vote I shall give tonight I will endeavour to make some amends for the course I pursued in earlier life in opposing the Factory Bill.

[1] Kydd's work was finally published in 1857 under the title *The History of the Factory Movement*. The author used the pseudonym 'Alfred' for reasons that have never become apparent.

In the summer of 1861 Oastler was overcome by a longing to meet all his old friends once more and to see again the Yorkshire vales he loved so well. For many years now he had been living in the south country, and his nostalgia for the north had become acute. With all the anxious thoroughness of age, he made his plans and counted the days. To lessen the fatigue of the journey, he proposed to stay at Harrogate overnight and go on to Bradford next day.

But as the train neared Harrogate he collapsed with a heart attack. They carried him to a hotel and sent calls by the electric telegraph to William Walker and Parson Bull. Neither got to him in time. As dawn was breaking on Thursday, 22 August 1861, Richard Oastler quietly passed away in his seventy-second year.

Newspapers in the north and in London honored his passing in editorials which themselves betoken the change in opinion his labors had helped to bring about. In that respect none was more significant than the judgment of the *Leeds Mercury* (which, report said, young Edward Baines had written himself):

His name was once a household word in every working man's abode throughout Yorkshire and Lancashire . . . We believe he has died without an enemy, and that the news of his death will be received with tears in many a poor man's dwelling. There can be no doubt that the factory operatives' condition is now vastly superior to what it was in 1830, or that to Mr. Oastler (after all drawbacks are made) this happy change is in no small measure due. He was a man of large heart whose story may perhaps point a moral, but will certainly excite much admiration for the purity of motive, the energy of character, the indomitable perseverance with which ends he believed to be right were pursued throughout a long and most chequered career.

This was from his fiercest opponent. The journals that had supported him from the beginning were, of course, even more laudatory. *The Times* was speaking for former foe and friend alike when it declared that the name of Oastler had been 'a tower of strength to the oppressed, both young and old.'

He was buried at St. Stephen's, Kirkstall, just outside Leeds, in the grave where his wife and children lay. They brought him from his beloved birthplace in a mighty cortege, for thousands turned out to join his last procession. Representatives of Short

Time Committees from the whole of northern England came, and friends from every class of society. The churchyard and the roads leading to it were thronged. Whigs and Tories, Radicals and Young Englanders, manufacturers and Trade Unionists came together that afternoon in a final gesture of respect to one whose simple cause had been the welfare of the common people. The men who had made with him the Fixby Hall Compact 30 years before carried him to his grave, and Parson Bull performed the committal.

A few years later the Trade Unions and Short Time Committees of Yorkshire and Lancashire decided to erect a national memorial in perpetuation of his memory. The money was easily raised. The sculptor Bernie Phillips was commissioned to do a bronze statue. And on 21 May 1869, Ashley (by then become Lord Shaftesbury) went to Bradford to unveil it. A hundred thousand people, it was estimated, gathered for the ceremony. 'Their enthusiasm knew no bounds,' wrote Shaftesbury in his diary. It was the final mammoth rally.

Then, as the men who had known him passed away one by one, England gradually forgot the strange story of her 'Factory King.'

Acknowledgments

TO the many who have helped me collect material for this book I desire to express my gratitude.

In particular I have to thank Mr. W. H. Barraclough and Mr. R. W. Parsons of the Bradford Central Library; Mr. R. J. Gordon of the Leeds City Library; Mr. Reginald Rye, Librarian of the University of London, and his colleagues in charge of the Goldsmiths Collection of Economic Literature; and the Reverend J. N. Libbey, of the Moravian Church House, London. In addition to helping the researches of the moment and guiding me through the records of which they are the respective custodians, all went to the further trouble of writing from time to time to draw my attention to new material as it came to light.

Mr. Philip Ahier, of Sheepridge, Huddersfield, generously put at my disposal his extensive knowledge of local history and topography.

To Miss M. G. Moore, M.A., of Bexleyheath, Kent; to Dr. William Armstrong of Sheffield University; and to Mrs. Margaret Van Houten, M.A., formerly of the Yale Graduate School, I am greatly indebted for collaboration in solving particular problems and for assistance in supplementary research.

Special thanks have to be given to Professor David Owen, of Harvard, who allowed me to use the material he has collected for a forthcoming biography of Oastler's friend John Fielden.

Numerous friends and colleagues have given help of all kinds while the work was in preparation, but three must be named with particular gratitude: F. J. C. Hearnshaw, Professor-Emeritus of the University of London; R. A. Jones of King's College, London; and H. L. Beales, of the London School of Economics.

C. H. D.

Notes

Abbreviations:

Alfred   for *History of the Factory Movement* (1857) by S. Kydd (pseud. 'Alfred')
Croft   for *Oastler and the Factory Movement* (1888) by W. R. Croft
Sketch   for *Sketch of the Life and Opinions of Richard Oastler* by J. R. Stephens
D.N.B.   for *Dictionary of National Biography*
U. of L.   for University of London, Goldsmith's Collection of Economic Literature

A.C.	for *Ashton Chronicle*	L.T.	for *Leeds Times*
B.L.P.	for *British Labourers' Protector* (Bradford)	M.C.	for *Morning Chronicle* (London)
F.P.	for *Fleet Papers*	M.G.	for *Manchester Guardian*
H.G.	for *Halifax Guardian*	M.S.A.	for *Manchester and Salford Advertiser*
H.H.E.	for *Halifax and Huddersfield Express*	N.S.	for *Northern Star*
I.L.N.	for *Illustrated London News*	P.M.G.	for *Poor Man's Guardian*
L.I.	for *Leeds Intelligencer*	T.D.	for *Twopenny Dispatch*
L.M.	for *Leeds Mercury*	W.P.G.	for *Weekly Police Gazette*
L.P.	for *Leeds Patriot*		

CHAPTER I

p. 5. Wesleyanism in the North Riding, and the Oastler family:
See John Ward, *Methodism in the Thirsk Circuit* (1860); *Letters of the Rev. John Wesley* (Standard edition, 1931), vol. 7, pp. 328–9. Cf. *Sketch*, pp. 1–2.
Wesley visited Thirsk 14 times between February 1747 and May 1790. Oastler described life on his grandfather's farm in *Home*, I, 100.

p. 6 ff. The Yorkshire Woolen and Worsted Industry:
William Wilberforce, one of the two members of Parliament for Yorkshire, described the industry to the House in 1800 thus: 'It is a domestic manufacture, not so much carried on in large factories where multitudes are collected together and children learn prematurely the vices of a more advanced age; but any industrious individual possessing credit for a capital of £10 buys therewith a pack of wool, works it up with the assistance of his wife and family, and brings it to the public market for sale, just as the little farmers bring their little articles of produce; the wealth thus acquired and diffused is not obtained at the expense of domestic happiness, but in the enjoyment of it.' (*Parliamentary History*, xxxv, p. 138.)
See especially *Report on the State of the Woollen Manufacture*, Parliamentary Papers, 1806, vol. III. The standard work on the Yorkshire industry

down to 1820 is Professor H. Heaton's *Yorkshire Woollen and Worsted Industries* (1920), to which this chapter is greatly indebted. See also E. Lipson, *History of the Woollen and Worsted Industries* (1922) and the same author's *Economic History of England*, vol. II. For Leeds, see W. B. Crump (ed.), *The Leeds Woollen Industry*, 1780–1820 (1931); and for Huddersfield see W. B. Crump and Gertrude Ghorbal, *History of the Huddersfield Woollen Industry* (1935).

On Yorkshire generally see T. Baines: *Yorkshire Past and Present* (1871), and the *Victoria County History* series. See also H. D. Fong, *Triumph of the Factory System* (1930). For the structure of the industry and the coming of machinery, see J. L. and Barbara Hammond, *The Skilled Labourer* (1920), chs. 6 and 11.

p. 6. Oastler's birthplace:
The exact location of this has twice been a matter of dispute in the local press. See the correspondence on the subject in the *Yorkshire Evening Post*, 29 Sept. 1913, and following issues; and ibid. 14 Aug. 1925 (with picture of the house), and 28 Aug. 1925.

CHAPTER II

p. 13. Home life and childhood:
Details are scattered throughout Oastler's writings: Cf. *Sketch*, pp. 1–9; *Home*, I, 29–30, 92; IV, 117.
Oastler was six years old when he first met Michael Sadler; see the delightful episode reported in *Home*, I, 173.

p. 15. Fulneck School:
For details of its history and curriculum see W. F. Waugh, *History of Fulneck School* (1909); W. G. Addison, *The Renewed Church of the United Brethren*, 1722–1930 (1932); Anon., *Celebration of the Centenary Jubilee of the Congregation of the United Brethren* (April, 1855); and H. Whittock, *The County of York*, vol. III. See also the informative article in the London *Times Educational Supplement*, 29 Jan. 1927, and letter from Miss D. A. Connor, 12 Feb., from both of which quotations in the text are taken. For further details I have been indebted to the Rev. J. N. Libbey of the Moravian Church House, Fetter Lane, London. Oastler frequently referred to his school days: e.g. *F.P.*, I, p. 5, and *Home*, I, pp. 21–2. On Steinhauer see *Home*, I, 21–2 and 37.

p. 17. Gig Mills and Shearing Frames:
See the Hammonds, op. cit.; and also F. O. Darvall, *Popular Disturbances and Public Order in Regency England* (1934). The latter work gives an excellent picture of public opinion in relation to machine breaking. The quotation from General Grey is taken from p. 62 of that work.

p. 20 ff. Philanthropic work:
The quotation is taken from the Rev. G. S. Bull's memorial lecture reported in *L.I.*, 7 Feb. 1863.
See also *Sketch*, p. 9; *F.P.*, III, 31–2; ibid., I, 235; *Home*, I, 277.

p. 23. Mary Oastler:
The description is based upon *Alfred*, II, 229, and P. Grant, *The History of Factory Legislation* (1866), p. 119, as well as upon remarks made by the

Rev. G. S. Bull, the Rev. J. R. Stephens, and others. Her background can be gathered from the biography of her mother: *Memoirs of Mrs. Tatham* (1842), by the Rev. Joseph Beaumont, M.D.

p. 23. Bankruptcy:
See *Sketch,* p. 5, and *L.M.,* 19 Feb. 1820.

p. 24. Robert Oastler's visit to New Lanark:
See Podmore's *Owen,* pp. 147–8, and also the report published by the deputation: *Mr. Owen's Establishment* (Leeds, Sept. 1819).

p. 24. Robert Oastler:
The account of Oastler's father given in this chapter is based upon public statements made by Edward Baines, senior; Richard's own numerous references; and *Sketch,* pp. 1ff. Robert's death was reported in *L.M.,* Sat., 29 July 1820. See also *F.P.,* I, p. 6; and *Facts and Plain Words,* pp. 9 and 59.

CHAPTER III

p. 25 ff. The Fixby estate:
The description is based upon the various local histories and topographical works, upon material supplied by the Huddersfield Public Library, and upon the various articles which have appeared in the local journals from the pen of Mr. Philip Ahier. *F.P.,* vol. I, abounds in items of interest concerning Fixby, e.g. pp. 98ff. See also Oastler's letter in *N.S.,* 7 Mar. 1840, and *Letter to the People of England,* in *L.I.,* 15 Sept. 1838. Cf. *Croft,* p. 98. For Oastler's appointment see *F.P.,* I, 6, and 201.

p. 33. The Halifax tithe dispute:
See reports in *L.M.* and *L.I.* (the former supporting Oastler and the latter condemning him), 22 Sept. 1827, to 21 Aug. 1828. Cf. *Vicarial Tithes* (1828) *passim;* and *Facts and Plain Words,* p. 52. As an instance of the new Vicar's fighting policy and his determination to get in all the dues he possibly could, whether from tithes or pew rents, the following may be cited: 'Mr. Joseph Fawthorp, surgeon, Halifax, occupied a pew in the Parish Church which Mr. Knight, the late Vicar, said he might enjoy rent-free. Mr. F. fitted it up and lined it. On the 29th of October, he received notice he was to quit. November 1st the lock and brass plate with Mr. F.'s name on it was taken off and sent along with the cushions and books to Mr. F., and another lock was put on. Mr. F. afterwards replaced his lock and plate. On the 3d. of November, Mr. F. was informed he must pay £50 a year if he continued to occupy the pew. On Sunday the 4th of November, the plate was gone and the door screwed up. On Sunday the 11th of November, the pew was filled with paupers, Mr. F. was obliged to leap over the side of the pew and pack in amongst the crowd as well as he could. On the three Sundays, November 18th, 25th, and December 2d, Mr. F. found the door fast and strong boards placed about ¼ yard above the seats so as to form a floor from side to side of the pew; still he continued to occupy it. The 25th of November was a Missionary Sunday; Mr. F. had again to leap over the side and, providing himself with a stool was very considerably elevated above the rest of the congregation and was compelled to assume the appearance of Chairman whilst the Vicar was depicting in dreadful colours the impious rites of heathen worship and proving the necessity of OUR endeavoring to improve THEIR religious feeling and to show them how to worship God

aright!! On Sunday December 9th, the seats and floor had been taken up, the earth removed so as to form a kind of grave. In the excavation, two or three baskets full of human bones had been disinterred, and then a quantity of water was poured in to make a puddle in order effectually to prevent Mr. F. from occupying it. He, however, nothing daunted, leaped over and remained there during the service. On Sunday December 16th, Mr. F. found the pew covered over with sack cloth, but still determined to occupy it. Do we not wonder such proceedings are allowed?' (Oastler, *Vicarial Tithes*, pp. 159–60). See also *Facts and Plain Words*, p. 52.

CHAPTER IV

p. 39.   John Wood of Horton Hall, Bradford: 1793–1871:
See T. Baines: *Yorkshire*, ii, 303–4. There are some valuable details in a manuscript *History and Annals of Bradford* now in Bradford Public Library. The book was written in 1840 by one John Clark, whose father was in Wood's employ for 15 years. Wood started a school for factory children in 1832. In November 1833, he instituted the ten-hour day in his mills without cutting wages. In 1836 he built St. John's Church and endowed the incumbency. His factory was a showplace for visitors to the town: see *L.M.*, 1 Nov. 1834, and *Penny Magazine*, 16 Nov. 1833. Wood paid for the building of St. John's Church, Bradford, together with parsonage and school room.

p. 40.   Oastler's visit to Horton Hall:
See *Alfred*, i, pp. 96ff. One of several accounts given by Oastler himself is in *Home*, ii, p. 53.

p. 42.   The letter on 'Yorkshire Slavery':
This has been reproduced many times in source books and elsewhere (e.g. Bland, Brown, and Tawney, *English Economic History*, p. 592). It first appeared in *L.M.*, Sat., 16 Oct. 1830. For Oastler's expectation, see *Facts and Plain Words*, p. 10, and his *Letters to the People of Yorkshire*, 28 Mar. and 4 Apr. 1840. Oastler's words are almost identical with those of Jeremy Bentham: 'I supposed that they only wanted to know what was good in order to embrace it.' Bentham *Works*, i, 5.

CHAPTER V

p. 51 ff.   The newspaper controversy:
The following are the leading editorials and letters bearing upon the question: *L.M.*, editorial, 16 Oct.; Townend's letter (anti), 21 Oct.; 'Verax' and Anon. (anti), *L.M.*, 23 Oct.; 'X' (pro), *L.M.*, 30 Oct.; Oastler's second letter and the Baines editorial, ibid.; Wood's letter (pro), *L.M.*, 6 Nov.; W. Morgan, letter, 6 Nov.; Townend's second letter, *L.I.*, 11 Nov.; *L.I.*, first editorial (pro), 11 Nov.; Matthew Thompson's letter (pro), *L.M.*, 13 Nov.; John Halliley (pro), ibid.; R. Webster (pro), *L.M.*, 20 Nov.

CHAPTER VI

p. 58.   The Talbot Inn meeting:
The poster, with Wood's letter, is in the Goldsmith's Library in the University of London. Reports of the Talbot meeting are given in *L.I.*, 25 Nov., and *L.M.*, 27 Nov. 1830 (with editorial comments).

p. 60. Oastler's third letter:
L.M., 4 Dec.; Townend's retort in *L.I.*, 9 Dec.; Oastler's reply, *L.M.*, 24 Dec.

p. 64–5. Opposition meetings and the Halifax Resolutions:
The Bradford meeting is reported in *L.M.*, 5 Feb. 1831. For the Halifax meeting see *H.H.E.*, 5 Mar., and *Alfred*, I, pp. 109ff. A letter on the subject from R. Webster appeared in *H.H.E.*, 19 Mar.

p. 66–7. Hobhouse's Bill:
Summary in *L.M.*, 5 Mar., and *H.H.E.*, 12 Mar. Objections by the 'practical men' are given in *L.M.*, 12 Mar.; comments in *L.P.*, 19 Mar. The protest from owners of water mills was published in *L.M.*, 9 Apr.

CHAPTER VII

p. 72. Oastler's fourth letter:
The expurgated version appeared in *L.M.*, 19 Mar. 1831. The full version, with covering letter and editorial comment, appeared in *L.I.*, 24 Mar. The attack by *L.M.* was published 26 Mar. The *L.P.* declared for Oastler on 26 Mar.
The 'Vindex' attack on Webster appeared in *H.H.E.*, 26 Mar. The same writer's other letters appeared in *L.M.*, 12 Apr., and *H.H.E.*, 19 Apr.

CHAPTER VIII

p. 82. Short Time Committees:
The information about these Committees is scattered. The account given in this chapter is based upon material in Oastler's papers, incidental remarks made in speeches and newspaper reports during the course of the controversy, and reminiscences made subsequently. It has to be stressed, however, that the Short Time Committees underwent many changes between 1831 and 1850; care must therefore be taken not to read back into the earlier years features characteristic of the organization in the 'forties.
The earliest newspaper discussion of these Committees is to be found in the Yorkshire journals for late November and December, 1831. On 26 Nov., *L.M.* expressed fears that the Huddersfield group was trying to get up an 'illegal convention.' Oastler replied, *L.I.*, 1 Dec., and an editorial reply also appeared in the *Intelligencer* the following week. An important letter from James Brook, Chairman of the Huddersfield Committee, was published in *L.M.* on 3 Dec. In it Brook stated that his Committee disregarded party differences, and implied that its first meeting had occurred just after the introduction of Hobhouse's Bill. See also *Croft*, p. 28. Additional details were given three months later in Oastler's open letter to John Doherty; see *Poor Man's Advocate* (Manchester), 24 Mar. 1832. It is difficult to understand why Mr. R. L. Hill should suggest in his admirable monograph, *Toryism and the People*, ch. IV (B), that Sadler was 'circumspect' about admitting the existence of these Committees. No secret had been made of their existence. On the contrary, no procedure could have been more open, as the text and subsequent notes show. To cite but two or three instances: it was common knowledge that the Committees had sent delegates to help Hobhouse with his bill (see Hobhouse's letter, p. 96); the Huddersfield Committee had invited local firms to a conference on the factory question as early as September 1831; the open letter from John Leech 'To the Friendly Societies and Unions' (see above, p. 102) had been broadcast over the

Riding, so had the booklet, *Humanity Against Tyranny*, which gave a good picture of Committee activities. Moreover, the great campaign of public meetings (ch. xii) had been organized by the various Short Time Committees, and numerous posters and placards pasted on the hoardings had been signed by one or other of the local Committee secretaries. All this was long before Sadler's Committee had been appointed. So vigorously had the Short Time Committees publicized themselves that there was no need for 'circumspection' on the part of anyone.

p. 83.   Memorandum of the Leeds Short Time Committee:
This was written on 25 Mar. 1831, and published in *L.M.*, 2 Apr. The covering letter from John Hammond, secretary, explained that the Committee, composed of representatives 'appointed by the operatives of the chief Leeds factories,' had been formed to promote the passage of Hobhouse's Bill.

p. 84.   First public meetings:
Meeting of Bradford overlookers in Fleece Inn, Monday, 11 Apr. The meeting of Leeds delegates took place on 14 Apr., and the second Bradford meeting on the 18th. See *L.I.*, 14 Apr., and *L.M.*, or *L.P.* for 16 Apr.; also same journals a week later. The figures for the petition are given in *L.M.*, 23 Apr.

p. 85.   The first Ten Hours manifesto:
See *L.I.*, 28 Apr., and *L.P.*, 30 Apr.

p. 86.   Huddersfield Short Time Committee:
According to D. F. E. Sykes, *Huddersfield and Its Vicinity* (1898), pp. 320–21, the following were the original members of the Committee: Armitage, George and William (cloth finishers), Beaumont, George (weaver), Bolland, Job (cloth finisher), Brook, James (furniture dealer), Earnshaw, Charles (cloth finisher), Glendinning, Samuel (cloth merchant), Hanson, John (fancy weaver), Hirst, John (co-operative store manager), Hobson, Joshua (weaver), Holt, William (cotton twister), Johnson, Thomas (weaver), Kitson, William (cloth finisher), Leech, John (general dealer), Pitkeithly, Lawrence (general dealer), Rawson, John and William (cotton spinners).

p. 88.   The Fixby Hall Compact; Sun., 19 June 1831:
The date can be fixed from James Brook's letter to *L.I.*, 26 Nov. Accounts of the meeting are given in *Croft*, pp. 28ff.; *Alfred*, p. 123; *Home*, vol. ii, pp. 77 and 85. Joshua Hobson's account is in his speech reported in various newspapers and in *F.P.*, iii, p. 447. See also *Sketch*, p. 8. There are numerous other references.

p. 88.   Joshua Hobson (1811–76):
See Sykes, op. cit. p. 301. Began as a joiner, then became a handloom cotton weaver. Wrote revolutionary articles for various Radical journals in Lancashire; became a local publisher and printed a number of Oastler's writings; fought the tax on newspapers and was twice imprisoned for distributing unstamped periodicals. Subsequently edited the *Huddersfield Chronicle* and then the *Huddersfield Weekly News*.

CHAPTER IX

p. 90.   Hobhouse's Second Bill:
The details of this measure were first given in *L.I.*, 11 Aug. 1831. Discussion followed in the correspondence columns.

p. 91.   The Huddersfield petition against Hobhouse's bill:
Details are given in *Croft*, p. 32ff., and in *Humanity Against Tyranny*,
where all the relevant documents of the episode are cited.

p. 93.   Sadler's letter:
A copy is to be found in Oastler's papers in the Goldsmith's Collection. It
is also quoted in *Alfred*, I, p. 129.

p. 94.   The Passing of Hobhouse's amended bill (1 & 2 Willm. IV, cap. 39):
The reports of the debates are extremely fragmentary: see Hansard for
30 June, 18 July, 30 July, and brief notices in local newspapers.
A Lancashire manufacturer named Kirkman Finlay declared in a pamphlet
entitled *A Letter to Lord Ashley* (1833): 'so little were the laws on this
subject ever regarded in these districts, that I assert without fear of contradiction, the provisions of the Acts of Sir Robert Peel and Sir John Hobhouse were till lately unknown to many and disregarded by a great proportion of the spinners and manufacturers in them' (p. 16). This pamphlet,
which is in Oastler's collection, is further quoted above, p. 218.
George Strickland told the House of Commons (20 Mar. 1833) that 'it was
the limitation of this bill . . . which had excited a great part of the present discontent.' This only confirms what one may gather from the contemporary accounts of the subsequent agitation. Halevy's comment is in *History
of the English People*, III, p. 110.

p. 95.   Controversy over the emasculation of Hobhouse's bill:
See Oastler's letter in *L.I.*, 10 Nov.; the Oastler-Hobhouse correspondence is
in *L.I.*, 24 Nov.; see also *Alfred*, I, pp. 138ff. For Strickland's letter and
editorial comment, see *L.M.*, 19 and 26 Nov.; Oastler's reply to this, with
the 17 questions is in *L.I.*, 1 Dec. Morpeth's letter appeared in *L.M.*, 5 Nov.,
and a lengthy editorial in same issue.

CHAPTER X

p. 102.   Address to the Friendly Societies and Unions:
This was printed in *L.P.*, 5 Nov. It was also turned into a broadside (see
U. of L. Broadsides, 526 [1]).

p. 103.   'Slavery in Yorkshire': Oastler's sixth letter:
First appeared in *L.I.*, 20 Oct., then in *L.P.*, 22 Oct.; was reprinted numerous times and in various forms.

p. 108.   The Sadler-Watson Controversy: Sept.–Oct. 1831:
Watson's letter to the Reverend John Anderson was written from London
on 16 Sept. 1831, and was first published in *L.M.*, 24 Sept. The full corre-
spondence as it developed in the various local journals is to be found in
Oastler's album on *White Slavery* in the University of London Library.
On Methodism at this period see especially E. B. Taylor, *Methodism and
Politics, 1791–1851*, and citations therein; and also E. E. Kellett, *Religion
and Life in the Early Victorian Age*.

p. 114.   The Address of the Huddersfield operatives to M. T. Sadler:
        Nov. 1831:
The report of the deputation, the Address and Reply are given in *L.I.*,
10 Nov., and *L.P.*, 12 Nov.
The *Address to the Working Classes* is in the Oastler collection.

CHAPTER XI

p. 118. The Debate with the Baineses: 10 Dec. 1831:
See U. of L. Broadsides, No. 519; also *L.I.*, 15 Dec. and *L.M.*, 17 Dec.

CHAPTER XII

p. 129 ff. The Campaign of Public Meetings:
The narrative in the text is based mainly on the material in Oastler's guard-book in the University of London collection. See also *Alfred*, i, pp. 220ff.; *Croft*, pp. 47–8, and reports in all local newspapers. The dates of the meetings were: Huddersfield, 26 Dec.; Bradford, 27 Dec.; Leeds, 9 Jan. 1832; Keighley, 30 Jan.; Dewsbury, 6 Feb.

p. 133. Parson Bull:
See *Bradford Antiquary*, N.S., III, 207; *History of the Parish of St. John, Bierly* (in Bradford Library); J. H. Dickon, *Bibliotheca Bradfordiensis*, p. 21; and *Gentleman's Magazine*, Nov. 1865.

CHAPTER XIII

p. 140. Oastler's collection of documents:
For details, see bibliography, Section I, below, p. 563.

p. 141. Mary Oastler's assistance:
The quotation is from *Alfred*, i, p. 229. Various comments made later by Parson Bull were in like vein; e.g. see p. 472 above. From letters in my possession I am able to confirm what is said by *Alfred* concerning the striking similarity of their handwriting.

p. 143. Kinds of publicity:
These are revealed in the Oastler collection in the University of London. The organization first employed press releases after the great meeting on 1 July 1833: see note below concerning page 239.

p. 145. The Leeds General Committee:
The papers referred to are in one of Oastler's bound volumes of documents.

p. 145–6. The London Society:
See *Times* of 2 Apr. 1832; Public Notices column; *M.C.*, 5 Apr., and *M.G.*, 7 Apr.; also note below concerning p. 216. A circular describing the aims of the Society is in University of London broadsides, 554(7).

p. 146. Financial organization of the movement:
This has been reconstructed partly from the documents in the Oastler collection and partly from the details that came to light in the course of the unsavory public controversy with Foster during the autumn of 1832 (see ch. XXI). See especially: *M.C.*, 25 Sept. 1833; 27 Sept.; 2 Oct.; 3 Oct.; 11 Oct.; 22 Oct.

p. 147. The Lancashire Movement: Jan.–Apr. 1832:
See *M.S.A.*, 1832: 25 Feb., 10 Mar., 17 Mar., 31 Mar.: *M.G.*, 10 Mar., 24 Mar.; and Doherty's journal, *The Poor Man's Advocate* (Manchester) *passim*. Various broadsheets of the Lancashire campaign are in the University of London. The author possesses part of Oastler's correspondence with Thomas Daniel of Manchester. Holland Hoole's pamphlet, *Letter to*

the Rt. Hon. Lord Viscount Althorp (12 Mar. 1832), gives the viewpoint of the Lancashire cotton masters. On Doherty, see Cole, *Common People*, p. 231, and Webbs, *Trade Unionism*, p. 117.

CHAPTER XIV

p. 154 ff. The Pilgrimage to York: 24 Apr. 1832:
The placards announcing the meeting and posters giving the detailed plans are in the collection of broadsides in the University of London. Accounts are in *L.I.*, 26 Apr.; *L.M.*, 28 Apr., and other journals. See also *Croft*, 59ff. and *Alfred*, I, 236–52. According to Croft, the resulting Petition to Parliament was 2,322 feet long and carried 138,652 signatures. The meeting cost £1500 (see *M.C.*, Foster's letter, 7 Sept. 1833).

CHAPTER XV

p. 164. Sadler's Speech and the Debate:
See *H. of C.*, 16 Mar. 1832: *Parl. Deb.*, 3rd series, XI, pp. 340ff.; also *Times* and *M.C.* (with editorial) for 17 Mar.
'The Committee,' Lord Morpeth told the House in 3 Apr. 1833, 'was forced on Mr. Sadler much against his will. He protested against it at the time, and consented to it only when he saw that there was little probability of carrying his measure without it.' (*Mirror of Parliament*, 1833, p. 1198.)

p. 168–9. Preparations made by the northern committees:
The details can be gathered from Oastler's papers which include the memoranda sent to local committees and some of the broadsides.

CHAPTER XVI

p. 178 ff. Leeds Demonstration, 14 May 1832:
For detailed account see special edition of *L.M.*, Tues., 15 May, entitled *Leeds Mercury Extraordinary*. Also *L.I.*, 17 May. An account of the affair appeared in *N.S.*, 5 Jan. 1837; the following week readers of that journal were presented with an engraving of the scene.

p. 180. Huddersfield Reform Meeting:
See *Facts and Plain Words*, p. 46. Oastler many times dealt with the franchise question in speech, article and pamphlet. One of his clearest statements is in his letter to Peter Bussey, published in *W.P.G.*, 5 Mar. 1836. The Reform Bill, he said there, 'just admits the very class of voters who fancy they have an interest in keeping down the people' . . . 'I should rejoice to see the suffrage extended upon the *ancient* and *varied* plan, because then no *one* class would be able to rule all the others.'

p. 181. Oastler's letter:
In Hist. MSS. Commission: Laing MS., II, p. 778.

p. 183 ff. Leeds Riot, 15 June 1832:
Accounts in *L.I.*, 21 June; *L.M.*, 23 June. A special brochure (8 pp. of three columns each) describing the episode was published by *L.I.* See also *F.P.*, I, 185–6.

p. 186. Radical Meeting at Huddersfield, 19 June:
L.I., 21 June: other papers of same week.

p. 188. Oastler's visits to Wellington and the Duke of Sussex:
These were described by Oastler many times. The most accessible accounts
are in *F.P.*, ɪ, 11, and Introduction to *Letters to the Duke of Wellington*.
See also *Alfred*, ɪ, 321, and *Croft*, 85.

p. 189. Oastler's evidence:
See *Parliamentary Papers*, 1831–2, xv, pp. 454–63.

CHAPTER XVII

p. 191. The Tiff with Thornhill:
Thornhill's note was not made public until 8 years later. See Oastler's letter,
N.S., 25 Apr. 1840. For Oastler's reply, *F.P.*, ɪ, 54–5. For Sadler's letters,
ibid. 56. For Thornhill's attitude to the factory question, see *F.P.*, ɪ, 204.

p. 194. Sadler's northern tour:
For Fixby meeting, see *L.I.*, 30 Aug. and special pamphlet in Oastler's collection. The two letters to Daniel are in the author's possession. For Manchester demonstration, 25 Aug., in addition to local press accounts, see
Alfred, ɪ, 254ff., and *Home*, ɪ, 189; also descriptive pamphlet in Oastler collection (vol. vɪ, no. 4).

p. 200 ff. Leeds Election Contest:
Posters, broadsides, etc. referred to are in the U. of L. collection. See also
local press, *passim*, August to December, 1832. Cf. G. O. Trevelyan's
Macaulay, ch. v.

p. 203. Oastler and the County Contest: Dec. 1832:
See *Facts and Plain Words, passim;* Oastler's election address is cited in *F.P.*,
ɪ, 166.

CHAPTER XVIII

p. 208. Baines's comment on the Sadler *Report:*
See *L.M.*, 12 Jan. 1833. Cf. also *L.M.*, 9 Feb.

p. 209. The Bradford Conference of Delegates, 11–14 Jan. 1833:
The papers are in the Oastler collection. See also *B.L.P.*, pp. 137ff. (18 Jan.).
The *Address* first appeared in *L.I.*, 24 Jan.

p. 212. Ashley's assumption of leadership, 6 Feb., 1833:
For Bull's account, see *Ten Hours Advocate*, 1847, p. 299; for Ashley's,
Hodder's *Shaftesbury*, ɪ, 148 and ɪɪɪ, 112; Ashley to Oastler, *Alfred*, ɪ, 347.

p. 213. Morpeth's motion and Oastler's attack:
See Hodder, op. cit.; Oastler's letters in *B.L.P.*, 8 Feb.; *L.P.*, 9 Feb.; *L.I.*,
23 Feb. For estimates of Morpeth, see *I.L.N.*, 15 Oct. 1842, and 24 Mar.
1855; also *Gentleman's Magazine*, N.S. xvɪɪɪ, 1865, p. 99, and G. H. Francis,
Orators of the Age (1847).

p. 215. Campaign of public meetings:
See *B.L.P., passim*, and *L.I.*, for Feb. and Mar.; also various pamphlets in
Oastler collection.

p. 216. Meeting in City of London Tavern, Sat., 23 Feb. 1833:
Verbatim report issued as pamphlet (Vol. vɪɪɪ, no. 5, Oastler collection);
see also *Alfred*, ɪɪ, 2ff. and *Croft*, 92–5.

p. 216. Oastler's Lancashire Campaign in March:
Oastler spoke at Charlton on 19th; Bolton on 20th; Chorley on 21st; Preston
on 22nd; Manchester on 23rd.
See *B.L.P.*; also *Alfred,* ɪɪ, 24; *L.I.*, 25 Mar. and 6 Apr.; and local press;
also special pamphlets in U. of L.

p. 219. Debates on Petitions, and Project of a new investigation:
Between the opening of Parliament (29 Jan.) and the carrying of Patten's
motion (3 Apr.), 73 petitions were presented in favor of the Ten Hours
Bill. Discussions took place on 26 Feb., 28 Feb., 6 Mar., 14 Mar., 20 Mar.,
25 Mar. and 27 Mar. The first petitions in favor of a new investigation were
presented on 27 Mar. See also Clokie and Robinson, *Royal Commissions of
Enquiry,* 105ff.

CHAPTER XIX

p. 222. Public Meetings:
Posters and pamphlets are in the Oastler collection. See also *L.T.*, and *L.I.*
for April, and *B.L.P.*, *passim.*

p. 223. Manchester Conference, 21 Apr. 1833:
The account is based entirely upon Oastler's papers which include minutes
of the conference. The *Address* can be found in Hodder's *Shaftesbury,* ɪ, 159.

p. 228 ff. Reception of the Royal Commission:
See *Alfred,* ɪɪ, 35ff.; *Croft,* 85; various University of London broadsides;
L.I., 18, 25 May, and 1–22 June; *Times,* 22 May and 10 June; *P.M.G.*,
1 June; and corresponding issues of other newspapers. Also numerous
pamphlets in Oastler's collection, and posters among the U. of L. broadsides.

CHAPTER XX

p. 237. Maneuvers of Master Cotton Spinners: mid-June 1833:
The meeting was reported in the local press. The resolutions concerning
alternative solutions were put before the public in various ways; e.g. see
broadside 565 (11) in University of London collection. For comment on
resolutions see *L.I.*, 29 June. The reaction of the operatives can be gathered
from the numerous broadsides and pamphlets put forth during these weeks.
The resolutions passed at the masters' meeting at Manchester on 9 July
were published in the Public Notices columns. Cf. *F.P.*, ɪ, 270.

p. 239. Wibsey Low Moor meeting, 1 July 1833:
The general summons took the form of a poster put out by the Central Committee from their headquarters, Yew Tree Inn, Roberttown, Bradford, on
24 June. This document summarized the situation to date. See U. of L.
broadsides, 565 (22). Other posters supplemented this and gave directions.
See *Alfred,* ɪɪ, 60ff.; *Croft,* 89–91; special pamphlet (Oastler's collection, vɪ,
no. 7); *L.I.*, 6 July; editorial comment in *Times,* 28 June and report 5 July.
A unique feature characterized the organization of this demonstration. This
was the first time (as far as is known) that the Central Committee sent out
its own lithographed press release to the newspapers. See document xv
in volume entitled *Oastler and the Factory Movement* (University of London). On page 1 was the note: 'Sir, I hope you will favour our Cause by

the insertion of the following paragraph. Yours obliged . . .' There followed
a summary report of the meeting, the list of resolutions, and the petitions
to be forwarded to both Houses.

p. 240. W. B. Ferrand:
No biography of Ferrand has been written. There are two articles on him in
I.L.N., viz.: I, 101 and IV, 292. See Boase, *Modern Biography* (supplement).
For additional information see Monypenny and Buckle, *Disraeli*, and Whib-
ley, *Lord John Manners*. Cartoons of Ferrand appeared in *Punch* VI, 190
and X, 130.

p. 245. Ashley's Bill in the Commons:
For the crucial debate on 18 July 1833, see *Parl. Deb.*, XIX, 913; also Hodder's *Shaftesbury* I, 164ff., and Hammonds' *Shaftesbury*, 32–3. For *Report*
of Royal Commission, see bibliography: comments in *Times*, 2 and 3 July.
For John Wood's attitude to the *Report* of the Royal Commission, see the
correspondence between Wood and Power that appeared in the *Standard*
and *Times* and was reproduced in *L.I.*, 20 July 1833. Ashley's letter to Oastler is given in one of Oastler's pamphlets (dated 14 Mar. 1835) in his collection, IX, no. 13.

p. 249. Protest Meetings:
These were reported in *L.I.* (e.g. 10 Aug.) and in various proletarian journals (e.g. *Glasgow Liberator* and *Voice of the West Riding*), and some of
the reports were turned into pamphlets also. The Conference of delegates
at Leeds was reported in *L.I.*, 3 Aug. The Preston Short Time Committee
circularized the Clergy (Oastler collection, V, 15). A final conference of delegates held at Birstall on 28 Oct., put out a pamphlet (Oastler's collection III,
21) defining its attitude towards the new Act; a broadside (University of
London, 565 [9]) was also issued.

CHAPTER XXI

p. 251 ff. The Foster Controversy:
See final issue of *L.P.* (16 Feb. 1833) for editorial giving reasons for the
journal's demise. The libel case is reported in *L.I.*, 20 Sept. 1832. The controversy began with an advertisement from Foster inserted in *L.M.*, 29 June.
Comments in that journal from that date to 4 Jan. 1834. The main letters
are: Foster in *M.C.*, 7 Sept. (reproduced in *P.M.G.*, 28 Sept.); Oastler's
reply, *M.C.*, 9 Sept.; Foster in *M.C.*, 16 Sept.; Oastler in *M.C.*, 25 Sept.;
Foster in *M.C.*, 27 Sept.; Oastler in *M.C.*, 2 Oct.; Foster in *M.C.*, 3 Oct.;
Jane Firth in *M.C.*, 11 Oct.; Foster in *M.C.*, 22 Oct. Editorial comments,
7 Sept. and 11 Oct.; *P.M.G.* comments 28 Sept.; 12 Oct.; 2 Nov.; *L.I.* comments, 14, 21, 28 Sept., and 12 Oct. See also *L.T.*, 19 Oct., for Oastler's
speech answering all this. Grant's comment in *P.M.G.*, 23 Nov. (p. 379);
Hetherington's change of attitude, *L.I.*, 21 Dec. and other journals.

p. 255 ff. Huddersfield By-election:
This is a difficult story to unravel. The narrative in the text was composed
by collating the accounts in *L.T.*, *L.I.*, *L.M.*, the election posters in the
U. of L. collection (especially no. 563 [3]), and the 6 controversial pamphlets, viz.: *The Pearking* (by Oastler), *Intercepted Letter* (by Wood),
Papal Bull (by Oastler), *Intercepted Mandate* (by Wood), *Penny Bellowing*
(by Oastler), *Twopenny Extreme Unction* (by Oastler).

p. 261 ff. The Eight Hours Movement and the S.P.N.R.: Nov.–May 1833–4:

See the radical journals *Crisis* and *Pioneer,* and the organ of the movement, *The Herald of the Rights of Industry,* as well as Cobbett's *Register,* vol. LXXXII; *M.C.,* 7, 8, 11, and 18 Dec. 1833, and 23 Jan. 1834; and *P.M.G.* The *Catechism* of the Society and some of its propaganda material can be found in Oastler's papers. Cf. Halevy, *History,* III, p. 119; Podmore, *Owen,* 434–5; Cole, *Chartist Portraits,* ch. VIII, and *Common People,* ch. XXII; Hammonds, *Shaftesbury,* 36ff.

The Committee of the Society consisted of John Fielden, Joshua Fielden, Thomas Fielden, George Condy, John Doherty, Robert Owen, Philip Grant, and 15 others.

CHAPTER XXII

p. 269 ff. The Old Poor Law and the New:

See the standard histories by Nichols and the Webbs; also Halevy, *History,* I, 329ff. and III, 121ff.; Maccoby, *Radicalism,* ch. VII; Hammonds, *Age of the Chartists,* ch. VI; and Clapham, *Economic History of Modern Britain.*

p. 282. Oastler's opposition:

See *F.P.,* II, 221–2; *Sketch,* 11; *Letters to Wellington,* p. 72, etc.; his first published statement was a letter in the *Argus and Demagogue,* 8 Aug. 1834, republished as a pamphlet in Bradford. See also *Home,* II, pp. 76, 84, 101.

p. 285–6. Oastler's contributions to the unstamped journals:

The first 'letter' to Hetherington's *P.M.G.* is dated 1 July 1834. See the comments in *Alfred,* II, 84–5. Cf. note below at p. 301.

p. 286. Handloom Weavers Committee, 1834:

The *Report* is in Parliamentary Papers, 1834, x (Oastler's evidence is on pp. 278ff.). Oastler was examined on 10 July.

For a comprehensive analysis of the condition of weavers in the West Riding, see: *Handloom Weavers Commission, Report of Assistant Commissioners;* Part III (1840), Report on Yorkshire by H. S. Chapman, pp. 527ff.

p. 293. Oastler on 'party:'

Oastler's denunciations begin in the late summer of 1834: e.g. see first letter in *Huddersfield Argus and Demagogue,* 2 Aug. The quotation concerning 'the Demon called Liberalism' is taken from his article in the *Agricultural and Industrial Magazine,* reprinted in *Letters to Wellington,* p. 173. Cf. article in *P.M.G.,* 15 Aug. 1835.

p. 301. Oastler's contributions to the unstamped journals: 1835:

He wrote 18 articles for Cleave's *Weekly Police Gazette* which appeared between 20 June 1835, and 2 Apr. 1836; a second series started in *P.M.G.,* 15 Aug.; a third in the *Twopenny Dispatch,* 3 Oct. A fourth series of 17 articles published in the *London Dispatch,* beginning 18 Dec. 1836.

p. 303. Scheme for a People's Lobby:

This was developed in *T.D.,* 14, 21 Nov.

CHAPTER XXIV

p. 307 ff. Operation of Althorp's Act:

See the reports of factory inspectors in Parliamentary Papers, 1834–7 (references in Bibliography). In parliamentary debates on subsequent proposals for legislation considerable light was shed upon the operation of the Act, by both opponents and proponents of the measure. For a discussion of the educational clauses see the admirable monograph by Dr. A. H. Robson, *The Education of Children Engaged in Industry* (1931), pp. 15ff. According to the Reports of the Factory Inspectors published at the beginning of 1836, the following were the numbers of operatives engaged in the textile industries at this time:—

	Cotton	Wool	Silk	Flax	Grand Total
Total (male and female)	220,134	71,274	30,682	33,283	355,373
Numbers between the ages of 8 and 13	28,771	13,322	9,074	5,288	55,455 (i.e. 15%)

Factory offences: according to a computation made in the *Morning Post* (19 Mar. 1836), the following were the figures for prosecutions in the areas named:

$£ - s - d$

Manchester   area : 52 persons and 74 convictions : fines = 247–12–6
Leeds   area : 72 persons and 85 convictions : fines = 272– 5–6
Macclesfield area : 17 persons and 35 convictions : fines = 117– 0–0
Huddersfield area : 35 persons and 62 convictions : fines = 268– 0–0

In the West Country there were only 21 convictions (with fines amounting to £65); for Scotland, Ireland and the four northern counties there were only 8 convictions.

p. 309 ff. The Factory Question; Jan.–June 1835:
Leeds flax operatives voted for full time for children 10 years old, at a meeting on 18 Feb.; two meetings of Bradford overlookers the same week voted three-to-one for an eleven-hour day at 10 years; a similar Huddersfield meeting was reported in *L.T.*, 21 Feb. Such meetings recur thenceforward. Counter-meetings then began to be organized by the Short Time organization, starting with those at Keighley, 3 Mar., and Oldham, 14 Mar. Contemporaneously gatherings of mill owners voted for repeal of Althorp's Act, beginning with meetings at Dewsbury and Gomershall in the week ending 28 Feb. The Central Short Time Committee, Bradford, published its first *Protest* on 19 Feb.; a second followed on 12 Mar. entitled *Ignorant Stupidity Corrected.*

p. 310. Lancashire preparations for a new campaign: Aug.–Dec. 1835:
Delegates meeting at Preston, 23 Aug.; manifesto published in *W.P.G.*, 26 Sept. (Francis Place issued an answer, to which Turner replied in *Manchester Advertiser;* letter dated 28 Oct.)
See also *W.P.G.* for 24 Oct. and 5 Dec.
Delegates meeting at Manchester, 17 Oct.; report in *W.P.G.*, 7 Nov.
Conference of M.P.'s and operatives: *M.S.A.*, 5 Dec. (with editorial).
Doherty's comments on Hindley reported in *M.S.A.*, 12 Dec.
Delegates meeting, Manchester, 2 Jan.; report in *M.S.A.*, 9 Jan. 1836.
See also *Alfred*, II, 87–8. Oastler's manifesto *To the Factory Operatives* was published in the newspapers of 20 Feb. 1836. On Hindley, see Boase, *Modern Biography,* and *Examiner,* 5 Dec. 1857.

p. 313.   J. R. Stephens:
See *D.N.B.;* Cole, *Chartist Portraits;* Holyoake, *Life of Stephens,* and the standard works on Chartism cited in the bibliography.

p. 317.   Oastler's libel suit: 20 Feb. 1836:
Report in *L.I.,* and other journals, 5 Mar. Also full report in *T.D.*
See F. H. Doyle, *Reminiscences and Opinions* (1886), pp. 190–92.

p. 321.   Poulett Thomson's Amendment: 9 May 1836:
See Hammonds, *Shaftesbury,* pp. 42ff.; Hutchins and Harrison, *Factory Legislation,* p. 58; Hodder, *Shaftesbury,* I, ch. 5; and Hansard for 9 May 1836. The circular letter sent by the seven Short Time delegates in London to every Member of Parliament is in Oastler's papers and was printed in *W.P.G.,* 2 Apr.
Comments on Thomson's proposal in *Morning Herald,* 18 Mar., and 5 Apr.; *L.I.,* 26 Mar.; *Christian Advocate,* 28 Mar.; *Standard,* 8 Apr.; *Morning Post,* 13 Apr.; *W.P.G.,* 16 Apr.; etc.
The Rev. W. Gilmour's attack on Bull appeared in *H.G.,* 9 Apr., and Bull's answer on 21 Apr.
Northern newspapers abound in reports of the protest meetings.
The *M.S.A.'s* attack on *M.G.* is to be found in the editorial column for Sat., 21 May.
For Hobhouse's comment see Broughton, *Recollections,* v, 53.

p. 323 ff.   Oastler's militancy:
See *M.S.A.,* 27 Aug., for Ashton meeting; Oastler's pamphlet of 2 Sept., entitled *The Factory Question.*
On the Blackburn speech see all northern newspapers; *M.G.,* 24 Sept., 28 Sept., 1 Oct., and 5 Oct.; also, *Croft,* 101–3, and *Alfred,* II, 108–9; citations, etc. in *F.P.,* II, 310 and 324; the Oldham meeting was fully reported in the newspapers and the report was turned into a pamphlet of 50 pages.

CHAPTER XXV

p. 331.   Resentment against the New Poor Law in the north:
For general surveys see Hovell's *Chartism,* ch. v; Maccoby's *Radicalism,* ch. x; the Hammonds' *Age of the Chartists,* ch. XIV; Nicholls and Mackay, *English Poor Law,* III, chs. XI and XII.
The quotation from the *Manchester Times* is taken from the issue of 23 Apr. 1837. Oastler's statement is quoted from *Alfred,* II, 79.

p. 336 ff.   Resistance at Huddersfield:
The two primary sources used for the main thread of the narrative in this and the succeeding chapters are (a) the report of the trial of 6 Huddersfield Guardians at York Assizes, 20 Mar. 1839, on a charge of 'tumultuous assembly,' and (b) the Annual Reports of the Poor Law Commissioners for 1837 and 1838 which give the letters exchanged as well as some of Powers' reports to London. With these two sources the ample newspaper accounts have been collated, and also the Home Office papers (see below, at p. 356).

p. 337.   Feargus O'Connor:
See the penetrating study in Cole's *Chartist Portraits;* also the numerous references to O'Connor in the various monographs on Chartism cited below, at p. 391.

p. 339. West Riding Delegates meeting, Bradford, 8 Mar. 1837:
See report in *L.I.*, 11 Mar., and cf. evidence in Home Office papers cited
below, p. 356. The first manifesto from the Central Committee appeared in
the *Times* on the editorial page, 21 Mar.
A letter from Patrick Bronte of Hawarth protesting against the New Poor
Law appeared in *L.I.*, 22 Apr.

p. 342. Thornhill and the New Poor Law:
The first Fixby meeting was reported in *H.H.E.*, 22 Feb.; a second meeting
followed on 11 Apr. (see version in *N.S.*, 2 May 1840).
See the correspondence in *F.P.*, ɪ, 209, 217; and ɪɪ, 45.

p. 344 ff. Oastler's first election contest: May 1837:
See detailed accounts in *L.I.*, *L.M.*, *H.G.*, *L.T.*, 29 Apr., and 6, 13 May.
Cf. *Croft*, 137–8. For Oastler's election address see *Morning Herald*, 1 May
1837. Lord Stanhope's letter in Oastler's support was published in *Times*,
9 May.

CHAPTER XXVI
p. 351. Hartshead Moor meeting, 15 May 1837:
See *L.I.* (5 columns) for 20 May, and other local papers; also London *Times*,
16 May, and editorial 19 May.

p. 353 ff. The Workhouse Riot, 5 June:
Detailed accounts in all local journals of week ending 10 June.

p. 356. Communications sent to Home Office: May–Aug. 1837:
These are to be found in the Public Record Office, London, in H.O., 52.35.
Tinker's letter is dated 8 June; Sutcliffe's, 7 June. Oastler's old enemy, Moore,
the postmaster, was sending reports too.

p. 358 ff. Oastler's second election contest, 28 July:
See *L.I.* and *L.M.* for 15, 22, 29 July, and 5 Aug.
Cf. *Croft*, p. 89; *Alfred*, ɪɪ, 200.

p. 361 ff. The Wakefield Riot, 31 July:
See the special *Supplement* on the subject put out by *L.M.* This contains
a street map of the zone where the riot occurred. Detailed accounts (differing in minor points) appeared in *H.G.* and *L.I.* See Oastler's pamphlet of
24 Aug., *West Riding Nomination Riot;* and his account in *Times*, 11 Aug.

CHAPTER XXVII
p. 364 ff. The Bradford Struggle:
See Nicholls, op. cit. pp. 253ff.; *L.I.*, 4 Nov., ff.; *L.M.*, 25 Nov.; and Powers'
account in Annual Report, op. cit. Accounts appeared in *Times*, 23–25, 28
Nov., 1, 8–9, 12, 13, 16, 18 Dec. An editorial on the riots appeared on
24 Nov. Matthew Thompson's opposition to the Law was vigorously expressed in a speech reported in *L.I.*, 11 Mar. His central theme on that
occasion had been that 43 Eliz. had given the poor man 'a *legal* claim to
support in need, in age, and in his infirmity'—a claim sanctioned 'by the Law
of Nature and of God.' His change of attitude apparently occurred in the
late summer.

p. 368 ff.   The Lancashire Association, Nov., 1837 ff.:
The first announcement of the Association in the London press appeared in
Times, 28 Nov. 1837. Thenceforward that paper has numerous reports of
the meetings and some indication of the underlying organization. The
quoted editorial appeared on 16 Dec.

p. 369.   The 'cardinal postulate:'
This quotation comes from Oastler's *Right of the Poor*, p. 14.

p. 370.   The support given to the Anti-Poor Law Movement by *The Times:*
This is so extensive that it well repays detailed study. In the first half of
1837, there are 14 reports of meetings in Yorkshire and nine of Lancashire
meetings, apart from reports of meetings in London and elsewhere, and
numerous other news items relating to the Poor Law. From November on,
reports of Anti-Poor Law activity are continuous until June 1838. During
that period nearly a hundred meetings were mentioned.

p. 371.   The *Northern Star:*
See Maccoby, op. cit. 177, and the various histories of Chartism cited below.

p. 372.   The proposal for a national association:
Times (22 Feb., 27 Feb., 14 Mar.) had reported meetings in London having
as their purpose cooperation among metropolitan parishes to resist the New
Poor Law. The vigorous activities of the London parishes was noted on
22 Dec. and more adequate co-operation was urged. This was when the first
proposal for a national organization was put forward. From that date the
idea was pressed until it culminated in the big meeting of 19 Feb. (reported
next day) establishing the association.

CHAPTER XXVIII

p. 378.   Oastler and the *Northern Star:*
The serialized biography ran from 31 Mar. to 21 Apr. 1838. It was written
by Joseph Rayner Stephens, and subsequently republished anonymously as
Sketch of the Life and Opinions of Richard Oastler. The Posselwhite engraving of Oastler was given to Yorkshire purchasers on 31 Mar. and to purchasers in Lancashire, Newcastle, and Scotland on 7 Apr.

p. 378.   Oastler's illness:
See *Sketch*, p. 16, and *L.I.*, 19 and 26 May.

p. 380 ff.   Oastler's relations with Thornhill:
See *Croft*, pp. 114ff.; *F.P.*, I, 204ff. and notes concerning Oastler's trial
(below, re p. 411).
Letter of dismissal is given in *F.P.*, I, 208.
Oastler's own account of the financial tangle is to be found in a letter of
two-and-a-half columns in *N.S.*, 15 Sept., and shorter letter of same date
in *L.I.*, 15 Sept.
See below concerning p. 386. The *N.S.* described the quarrel in detail on
22 Sept. Presumably Hill, the editor, had the details from Oastler himself.

p. 383.   Halifax meeting, 28 July:
See *N.S.*, 4 Aug., and corresponding issues of other papers.

p. 383.   Dewsbury Riots on 6 Aug.:
L.I. and *L.M.*, for 11 Aug.; editorials in *L.I.*, 18 Aug. and *N.S.*, same date.
See also Oastler's letter in *L.I.*, 25 Aug.

p. 383–4.   Oastler's letters in *Northern Star:*
Series of letters *To Lord John Russell,* Jan. 13ff.; *To Earl Fitzwilliam,* 16 June; ditto, 23 June; *To the Earl of Haddington,* 30 June; *To the Editors,* 7 and 14 July; *To the People,* 11, 18, 25 Aug., 15 Sept.; *To the Editors,* 13 Oct.–17 Nov.

p. 384.   Plans for a testimonial fund:
For this project see *N.S.,* 30 June; *L.I.,* 14 July; *N.S.,* 14 July (editorial, and appeal from G. R. W. Baxter, of Hereford). The only published subscription list is that appearing in *N.S.,* 15 Sept., and totalling £520. It was made up of individual donations from the Fielden Brothers, John Whitacre, John Wood, William Duncombe, William Walker, and 'the operatives of Messrs. Whitacres' mill.' The project was still being pressed in Nov.: see *L.I.,* 17 Nov.

p. 384–6.   Oastler's departure from Fixby: 25 Aug. 1838:
See London *Times,* 29 Aug.; *Alfred,* ii, 143; *F.P.,* i, 213ff. and 231–2; *Croft,* 118–20; *H.G.,* 1 Sept.; *N.S.* and *L.T.,* same date. Editorial comments in *L.M.,* 1 Sept.

p. 386.   Thornhill's letters of denunciation:
Published 25 Aug. in *L.I.* and other papers. The *Sun* and *N.G.* thereupon made violent attacks on Oastler. *N.S.* replied in an editorial of 1 Sept.

p. 387.   Appeal by the *Standard* for Oastler to be more moderate:
See *Standard,* Sept. 8.

CHAPTER XXIX

p. 391 ff.   Rise of Chartism:
See the standard works by Cole, the Hammonds, Hovell, West, Faulkner, Slosson, and Rosenblatt; Cf. Halevy, *History,* iii, 276ff., and Maccoby's *English Radicalism.*

p. 393 ff.   Attitude of Chartists to New Poor Law:
Beaumont's comment is to be found in *Northern Liberator,* 30 Dec. 1837. The citation from *The Chartist* is taken from the issue of 30 June 1839. Fletcher's suggestion that Chartism was promoted by opponents of the Anti-Poor Law Movement is in *N.S.,* 19 Oct. 1839. Note, also, the treatment of the subject in Lovett's autobiography. Cf. Halevy, op. cit. 304.

p. 403–4.   Mrs. Trollope's tour: Feb.–Mar. 1839:
Mentioned in *N.S.,* 2 Mar. 1839. See T. Trollope, *What I Remember,* ii, 7ff. Mrs. Trollope had her first interview with Oastler at Stalybridge on Mon., 24 Feb.

p. 405.   Collapse of Huddersfield's resistance to New Poor Law, spring, 1839:
The trial of the 6 Guardians was held at York on Wed., 20 Mar. 1839, before Baron Parke.
On 23 Mar., *L.I.* reported that the overseers and church wardens had received from the Central Poor Law Commissioners an 'extraordinary order' taking all management of the elections out of their hands and giving it to the Clerk, making him sole judge of persons proper to be elected. The ensuing election resulted in a complete Whig victory: *N.S.,* 6 Apr.

CHAPTER XXX

p. 411 ff.   Oastler's trial:
Report in *Times*, 11 July; reprint in *F.P.*, ɪ, 221. For subsequent events and Oastler's correspondence with Thornhill's solicitors see *F.P.*, ɪ, 226ff.

CHAPTER XXXI

p. 415 ff.   Prison Life:
The details are taken from *Fleet Papers*, and from the various accounts published in the cited provincial newspapers.

p. 418.   Comments in the *Planet*, etc.:
See that journal for 27 Dec. 1840. For similar comments see also *Oxford City and County Chronicle*, 26 Dec. and 6 Feb.; *N.S.* and *H.G.*, 26 Dec.; *Liverpool Mail*, 2 and 16 Jan.; *Hull Packet*, 8 Jan. and 12 Feb.; *Cleave's Gazette*, 23 Jan.; *New Moral World*, 4 Feb.; *Shropshire Conservative*, 13 Feb. and 10 Apr., etc.

CHAPTER XXXII

p. 425–6.   The 'Old System' of social regulation:
Quotation taken from *F.P.*, ɪɪ, 188.

p. 427.   Concentration of wealth:
Quotation taken from *F.P.*, ɪ, 315.

p. 427.   Order and 'Proper Stations:'
The quotation comes from *F.P.*, ɪɪ, 190. This entire issue of *F.P.* (11 June 1842) deals with the same subject.

p. 428.   Definition of Toryism:
The quotation comes from *F.P.*, ɪ, 39.

p. 431.   Oastler and the Economists:
The quotation comes from *F.P.*, ɪɪ, 58. A large part of this volume is devoted to the same theme.

p. 432.   Oastler and Malthus:
The quotation comes from *F.P.*, ɪ, 40.

p. 434.   'Down with them:'
This paragraph occurs in one of Oastler's letters *To Lord John Russell* in *N.S.*, 20 Jan. 1838.

CHAPTER XXXIII

p. 440 ff.   Movement for Oastler's release: 1843:
For the beginning of the movement see the *Times*, 20 Nov., 6 and 20 Dec.; *Wakefield Journal*, 27 Oct. and following issue; *N.S.*, 18ff. Nov.; *Bradford Observer*, 16ff. Nov.; *L.I.* and *H.G.*, 18ff. Nov.; *N.S.*, 2 Dec. (which also contains the letter from Edward Baines, senior). The reply of the *Standard* to the sneers of the *Globe* appeared on 15 Dec.

p. 445.   Oastler's release from prison: 12 Feb. 1844:
See *Times*, 9 Feb. and 13 Feb. (latter has report and editorial); *Morning Herald*, 13 Feb. Other accounts appeared in newspapers all over the country.

p. 448–9. Character study in *Illustrated London News:*
This appeared (with portrait) in the issue for 9 May 1844, p. 156. With
this estimate may be compared that written by Francis Place 17 months
earlier (B.M.: Add. MSS. 27820, 149–151):—'A man of great animal powers,
active, persevering, a ready writer and fluent speaker, of undoubted courage,
and entertaining the very best intentions to serve the mill and factory
workers, more especially the unfortunate and helpless children employed in
them. Withal, he was somewhat crazy, and of course greatly deficient in
judgment. Ever active, never still, writing and speaking incessantly, making
abundance of friends amongst the poor, and a like abundance of enemies
amongst those who employed them; and thus he put formidable impediments
in his own way.' In a letter written on 31 October 1835, Place had said:
'He is an odd fellow, but so is every man who thinks for himself—you are
odd—and so people say I am. Oastler calls himself a Tory, and in some
matters he and I differ very widely, but he does wish to serve the working
people in the way he thinks best, and we have a sort of bargain between
us that we will continue to disagree without quarrelling.'

CHAPTER XXXIV

p. 450. Ashley's efforts on behalf of factory legislation: 1838–44:
See the Hammonds, *Shaftesbury,* chs. v and viii; Hodder, *Shaftesbury,* i,
chs. viiiff. Bready, *Shaftesbury,* xiii; also *Alfred,* ii, chs. 8, 9, 11, 12.

p. 454. The absurd parliamentary impasse, 22 Mar. 1834:
In addition to the references just cited, see the well known passage in
Greville, *Memoirs* (v, 241) beginning: 'I never remember so much excite-
ment as has been caused by Ashley's Ten Hours Bill, nor a more curious
political state of things.'
Also Morley, *Cobden,* i, 302; *Alfred,* ii, 219ff.

p. 455. The new campaign: Spring, 1844:
This was by far the best-reported campaign since the start of the movement.
Moreover, the metropolitan press gave it fuller coverage than had been given
to any previous effort. *The Times* alone reported nineteen meetings in the
thirty days between 29 Mar. and 27 Apr. See *Alfred,* ii, ch. 14.

CHAPTER XXXV

For some of the important items in this chapter I am indebted to Professor
David Owen of Harvard University, who generously allowed me to see his
transcripts of letters passing between William Walker and John Fielden.
These materials will appear in Professor Owen's forthcoming biography of
Fielden.

p. 460. The Committee's letter (written by Wm. Underwood):
This, together with Oastler's reply, appeared in *F.P.,* iv, 493.

CHAPTER XXXVI

p. 464 ff. The Successful Campaign, 1847:
This story has been told many times; see the various biographies of Shaftesbury cited above, and *Alfred,* ii, ch. 16. The indispensable source is the
Ten Hours Advocate, which has been used throughout the chapter and
checked against Oastler's collection and the newspaper reports.

p. 467. Oastler's Scottish Tour, 1846–7 Dec.–Jan.:
The details are taken from the *Scotsman* and local papers, as well as the *Advocate*. Oastler's version of his interview with Dr. Chalmers is in *The Champion*, I, p. 151.

CHAPTER XXXVII

p. 479. Relays, and the ineffectiveness of the new Act:
Complaints begin to become general during Dec. 1848, and Jan. 1849. On 16 Dec. A.C. reported: 'in hardly a single mill (i.e. in Ashton) are the provisions of the Factory Act properly attended to.' The quoted letter is in A.C., 20 Jan. 1849. Twelve months earlier, however, Oastler had been receiving complaints. On 17 Dec. 1847, he wrote to Fielden: 'And so they are at work again! I gave them credit for more sense. Never mind: if we must have another tug, it shall, if I meddle, be for *Eight*.' Discussion in the press was general by the beginning of 1849.
See, e.g. *Times*, 9 Jan., 14, 22 Feb.; *M.G.*, 31 Jan., 14, 28 Feb.; *Manchester Courier*, 10, 17 Jan., 3, 10, 14 Feb.; *A.C.*, *passim*.
Oastler's letter to the *Morning Post* was reprinted in *H.G.*, 31 Mar. and A.C., 7 Apr.
On the whole problem see Hutchins and Harrison, ch. VI.

p. 483. Fielden's letter, 17 Mar. 1849:
This was sent to the Short Time Committees of Manchester and Burnley and was widely reported. See *Times*, 29 Mar.; *A.C.* and *M.A.*, 14 Apr.

p. 486. The New Agitation:
In addition to the various newspapers of the towns mentioned, see the article in *A.C.*, 21 July 1849. A few pamphlets of this new agitation survive in various public libraries.

p. 487 ff. The split in the ranks of the Ten Hours men, 1847:
This episode has not yet been properly elucidated; perhaps it never will be until additional manuscript material is discovered.
Strikes were reported in *Manchester Courier*, 11, 14 Apr. Grant told the Home Secretary that a delegates conference had considered a general strike (ibid. 20 June).
Hindley first opposed compromise (*M.G.*, 18 Apr.), then clearly indicated he favored it (*Courier*, 14 July) and associated Ashley with his position. Ashley later repudiated this (ibid. 28 July). Oastler attacked both Hindley and Ashley in an open letter (*A.C.*, 1 Sept.).
The Secretary of the Ashton Short Time Committee bitterly attacked the Manchester group in a letter to A.C., 8 Sept. Oastler's manifesto of 6 Sept. appeared in *A.C.*, 15 Sept., and elsewhere. Mawdesley's answer, ibid. 20 Oct. An illuminating letter from the Stalybridge secretary, A.C., 22 Sept., reveals considerable trouble in the Bolton area. A further attack on the Manchester group (? by Stephens) appeared in *A.C.*, 29 Sept. This has several items of information not found elsewhere. See also notes below at p. 496.

p. 490. The Fielden Society: Oct. 1849:
The rules (adopted at a Bury conference, 16 Sept.) were published in A.C., 3 Nov.

There is a revealing article on 'The old "Central" and the new Fielden Society' in *A.C.*, 20 Oct.
Mallalieu's *Address* on behalf of the society appears in the same issue. For the first full conference of delegates at Todmorden, 11 Nov., see *Champion*, pp. 27–8.
Press reports indicate that before the end of November, branches had been established at Todmorden, Wardle, Middleton, Clitheroe, Heywood, Hebden, Bridge, Stalybridge, Newton Moor, Rochdale, Burnley, Littleborough, Ashton. The Hammonds in their *Shaftesbury* (p. 138) make an obvious slip when they put the foundation of the Society six months later.

CHAPTER XXXVIII

p. 493.   Fielden's letter:
See *Times*, 18 Feb. 1850; *Champion*, p. 264.

p. 496 ff.   The three Conferences, Feb.–Mar. 1850:
For the conference of 17 Feb., see *Champion*, 251–6; *H.G.*, 23 Feb. For that of 24 Feb., see *H.G.*, 2 Mar.; *Courier* of 23 Feb. and 2 Mar.; *Champion*, p. 283; *H.G.*, 9 Mar.
On 24 Feb. a West Riding Conference was held at Bradford (see *L.M.*, 2 Mar.). Regret was expressed at Lancashire disunity and a resolution passed imploring 'all the delegates and factory workers of Lancashire to unite with each other most heartily for the speedy attainment of their common object.'
For a general survey of the struggle between the Fielden Society and the Manchester group, see *Champion*, I, 251 and 284. For Oastler's reply to Philip Grant's attacks, ibid. II, 350.

p. 500.   Difficulties in framing a Declaratory Bill: 1850:
See the *Champion*, pp. 383ff.; 392; 394–5. Cf. Hammonds, *Shaftesbury*, 139ff.
It is difficult to understand why Mr. and Mrs. Hammond should say in their *Lord Shaftesbury* (p. 139) that 'Oastler and his friends were quite unable to do justice to the legal difficulties involved' in drawing up a Declaratory Bill. In the first place, Oastler himself took no part in these legal discussions. He was at Broadstairs all this time, content to leave such matters in the hands of Cobbett, whom he trusted completely. In the second place, Oastler's 'friends' were probably far more qualified to appreciate the difficulties than Ashley. None knew better than Sam Fielden, Benjamin Rand, and William Walker the practical problems involved; and on the legal side, few lawyers had wider experience of factory law than Barnes Peacock, R. B. Cobbett, and J. M. Cobbett. The two former had taken the Exchequer case, while the latter (who was Bellenden Ker's junior) had been handling the prosecutions under the 1847 Act for two years past.

p. 502 ff.   Ashley's *volte face*: May 1850:
See the various biographies of Shaftesbury; *Times*, 25ff. Apr.; *Champion*, II, 27ff., 40, 53, 72, 168, 183; Oastler's letter appeared in *Times* on 6 May. Cf. *M.G.*, 27 Apr., 8 May, 11 May; *Courier*, 11, 18 May, 1 June. Cf. *The Home*, II, 57, and v, 189.

CHAPTER XXXIX

p. 509.   Lord John Manners:
See the biography by Charles Whibley. The quotations are taken from that work, vol. II, pp. 26–27. For Manners and 'Young England,' see vol. I, ch. 4; Cf. Monypenny and Buckle, *Disraeli* (Revised edition), I, 560ff. On Tory Democracy see, in addition, M. E. Speare, *The Political Novel* (1924) ch. III, and references there given; also R. L. Hill, *Toryism and the People, 1832–46* (1929).

p. 512 ff.   Oastler's later activities:
Work for the journeymen bakers; for speeches at Brighton, 2 Apr. 1850, and London, 2 May, see *Champion* II, 37.
Letters 'To the Aristocracy of England:' these were reproduced in various places, e.g. *Champion* I, 403; II, 30, 62, 85, 266.
Address to the London Trades Delegates, 20 Apr.: *Champion,* 378, 392.
Support for Ferrand's 'Wool and Flax League,' *Champion,* 291.
For various other activities see *Home,* vols. I–VI, *passim.* Oastler was once shouted down during a speech on behalf of tariff protection: see *I.L.N.,* 12 Jan. 1850.

CHAPTER XL

p. 516 ff.   Closing years:
See *Alfred,* II, ch. 16; *Croft,* pp. 139ff. Other details are taken from articles in *The Home.* See also the article 'Reminiscences of Oastler, the Factory King,' by William Walker's son, John, in *Yorkshire Daily Observer,* 17 Sept. 1904. Oastler spoke at the Tercentenary celebrations of Fulneck, 8 Apr. 1855; see the official report of proceedings in the British Museum; see also *Home,* 19 Apr. 1855.

p. 519.   Obituary notices:
See *The Times,* 24 Aug. 1861; *L.M.,* 24 Aug.; *Standard,* 23 Aug.; and Bull's three memorial sermons published as a pamphlet.

Appendices

A. *Resolutions* of the Master Worsted Spinners of Halifax: 5 Mar. 1831.
B. *Confidential Memorandum* used by the Short Time Committees: April 1832.
C. *Instructions to Local Short Time Committees* concerning the reception of the Royal Commission, issued by the Delegates' Conference at Manchester, April 1833.
D. *An Address . . . to all Ranks and Classes*, issued by the Delegates' Conference at Manchester, April 1833.
Protest of the Manchester Short Time Committee against the Royal Commission, 1833.
E. *The Judgment* of Mr. Baron Parke delivered in the Court of the Exchequer, 8 Feb. 1850.

APPENDIX A

RESOLUTIONS OF THE MASTER WORSTED SPINNERS OF HALIFAX

Passed unanimously at a meeting in the Old Cock Tavern, Halifax, Mr. James Ackroyd in the chair, March 5th, 1831.

1st. That this meeting views with alarm the measures proposed in the House of Commons, to curtail the hours of labour in mills and factories, and to limit the ages of children employed in the same.

2nd. That the condition of those employed in worsted mills does not warrant the conclusion that the present usages of the trade are injurious to the health and comforts of this class of operatives; and that the present term of labour (viz., twelve hours per day) is not attended with any consequences injurious to those employed, and is not more than adequate and necessary to provide for their livelihood.

3rd. That an enactment which will abridge the hours of labour, or limit the age of children employed in worsted mills, will produce the following effect:—1st. It will cause a proportionate reduction of the wages of this class. 2nd. It will materially cripple the means of those who have large and young families, who, in many instances, are the main support of their parents. 3rd. It will raise the price of goods to the consumers, which will affect the home trade considerably, and will produce the most serious effects

547

upon the prosperity of this district, by tending to foster the manufactures of foreign nations, our trade with whom depends upon the cheap and advantageous terms on which we now supply them with goods, and whose manufacturers would be enabled by an advance of price successfully to compete with the British merchant. 4th. It will throw out of employment and the means of existence numbers of children now beneficially engaged in worsted mills, and a corresponding proportion of wool-sorters, combers, weavers, and all those other classes necessary to produce the present supply of goods. 5th. The agriculturists will also feel the effects of the diminished consumption of wool in no slight degree.

4th. That the manufacture of worsted yarn is a much more healthy and wholesome employment than the preparing and spinning of cotton or flax, both as regards the material employed, and the temperature requisite for its advantageous manufacture, and that experience proves that the health and general comfort of the population employed in worsted mills is equal, if not superior, to that of any other extensive class of operatives.

5th. That the age to which it is proposed to limit those employed in worsted mills will be inefficient in securing the advantages which are desired, inasmuch as the period between fourteen and twenty-one is the most critical period in the life of those employed, and that those of the ages between seven and fourteen are more capable of undergoing long continued labour, than those of the ages before named. For confirmation of this opinion, we would appeal to all medical men of the district.

6th. That the character of the generality of master worsted spinners in respect to humanity, kindness, and considerate attention to those in their employ is unimpeachable, but that though there may be exceptions to this general and well-known fact, which this meeting is unacquainted with, yet that no legislative enactment can effectually protect innocence and poverty from the fraud and tyranny of the unprincipled, and from those evils inseparably connected with, and incidental to, all manufactures in the present state of society.

7th. That this meeting is impressed with a sense of the numerous hardships to which the labouring classes are subject, and that it declares it to be the bounden duty of all intrusted with the superintendence of mills and manufactories, to adopt every means by which the health and comfort of these classes may be best secured; but that so far from being justly chargeable with being the authors of the present protracted hours of labour, this meeting cannot submit to the imputation of avarice and injustice, and tyrannous conduct, whilst the fact is so notorious that it is *actual necessity* for voluntary and daily labour, to which the operative classes are subjected by the political and domestic circumstances of this country, *which alone* call for and demand the present long hours of application and labour.

8th. That until the burthens which now press upon the labouring classes are removed, all measures which tend to narrow the resources, obstruct or confine the industry, or reduce the rate of wages of the labouring classes have a positively injurious character, and ought to be deprecated and opposed by every humane and considerate individual.

9th. That when this meeting considers the present state and future prospects of trade at home and abroad, when it contemplates the rapid steps of foreign competitors in the various markets of the world toward perfection in manufactures—when it considers the condition of the people of this country, whose means to purchase worsted fabrics are most seriously diminished in consequence of the oppressive nature of taxes, monopolies, and restraints upon capital and industry, it cannot but feel convinced that every new impediment to the free exercise of industry and labour will be an additional grievance and hardship on their lot, and will be not less detrimental to the comforts and interests of the poor than to the enterprise and energies of their employers.

10th. That the British manufacturer is subject to a tax on corn, which operates as a heavy tax on labour, whilst rival manufacturing nations are exempt from this impost on trade; and that in addition to direct taxes on oil and soap, which are articles essential to the existence of the worsted manufacture, he is subject to the unjust influence of a monopoly, which denies him free access to our possessions in India, where there are millions of subjects who might rapidly become consumers of worsted fabrics.

11th. That such being the difficulties with which the manufacturer has to contend, it would be inflicting the most injurious effects upon this branch of industry (effects which are totally unwarrantable on the grounds of humanity and kindness to the labouring classes), to curtail the hours of labour, and limit the ages of children employed in worsted mills, unless the legislature shall at the same time fix the amount and rate of wages. That the impossibility of any legislative enactment to regulate these details is obvious, and that it cannot secure the labouring classes from the inevitable reduction in wages, which will be the consequences of shorter hours of labour, and of fluctuations of trade, whilst it will fetter their hands in times of brisk demand.

12th. That there are many worsted spinners in this district, whose manufactories are dependent on a due, and not excessive, supply of water, and that they have considerable interruptions to their trade in seasons of flood and drought; and that any restrictions upon the privilege hitherto enjoyed of working such mills in the wet season of the year, certain extra hours to compensate for the loss of time occasioned by the above casualties, would materially depreciate the value of such factories, and would be very injurious to the working classes, inasmuch as the proprietors would be unable to pay their operatives full wages, when the circumstances enumerated compel them to suspend their labour.

13th. That this meeting is convinced of the pernicious tendency and effects of all *legislative enactments*, whether protective or restrictive, which propose to regulate the details of trade and manufactures:—1st. Because they cannot equitably proportion the restrictions on industry to the circumstances of every individual case to which they apply, etc. 2nd. Because the consequences which they produce on the general interests of the trade affected by them, are more detrimental than the evils which they are intended to remedy.

14th. That a petition to both Houses of Parliament be drawn up, embodying these resolutions, and praying, that if on the balance of evidence tendered before a committee of the House of Commons, and on consideration of all the effects such an enactment will produce, it shall seem necessary to their honourable house to resort to interference with present established custom and usage in the worsted trade, that their honourable house would be pleased to adopt twelve hours per day, or seventy-two hours per week, as most fit, and least injurious term of labour, under present circumstances, to those employed.

APPENDIX B

CONFIDENTIAL MEMORANDUM

used by the Short Time Committees in the preparation of their evidence for the Parliamentary Select Committee, 1832.

MEMORANDUM. The local committees and others to whom a copy of these notes is entrusted, will take especial care that they are not shown to any but well-known friends. These notes apply solely to that branch of the evidence which must be got up by the Operatives themselves. A short minute of the general evidence has been previously communicated. The Committee will be pleased to consider it as absolutely necessary to attend to every particular head of evidence herein stated; to be very careful to ascertain as many facts under each head as they possibly can; and communicate them, with names of persons and places, to the Central Committee, at Leeds. It is essentially necessary and must always be borne in mind, that any pretended or assumed statements which cannot be fully and clearly substantiated by considerable evidence, would materially mar the cause.

OVERLOOKERS, OPERATIVES, and others who work, or have worked in Factories of various descriptions affected by the Bill. It is desirable that this class of Witnesses should be of various ages, and as far as can be, persons who themselves, or by their children, have been considerable sufferers by the system. They will have to give evidence from their own knowledge of

1. The general management, cleanliness and closeness of the Factories; the height of the rooms; the ventilation; the temperature, both as affecting the body and as ascertained by the thermometer; what difference there is in the different departments of the various manufactures; how far the inconveniences are unavoidable and how far they are produced by negligence; when are the necessary repairs done to the machinery; when is the engine cleaned.

2. Is there a regulation in some factories not to employ adults above a certain age, and what is that age?

3. The proportions of the persons employed under nine years of age, between 9 and 16 or 18, and those of greater ages; also, of males and females; the rates of wages; whether workmen by the piece are not obliged to turn off a certain quantity weekly; whether when the work is done by piece or by weight, the real quantity agreed to be returned by each overlooker or workman is not frequently greater than the nominal quantity without any extra allowance to the children: has not the overlooker in some cases an extra remuneration as an inducement to procure an increased quantity of work per week without any such allowance to the children; does the manager ever contract to do a certain quantity of work for a gross sum settled beforehand, and on such occasions is it found that any alteration is made in the hours of working when a large order is in hand; the youngest age at which children have been employed.

4. In the water-mills in your neighbourhood what is the average loss of time by deficiency or excess of water; how is that lost time made up; how far are the hours which the mills work regulated by their local situations in respect of water.

5. The hours of work at the factory; whether children are for any purpose compelled to attend earlier than the nominal hour of beginning, or later than the nominal hour of closing; in this respect what is the case on Saturdays; are the hours longer or shorter on Saturdays; are they ever extended to twelve at night; do they ever commence at twelve on Sunday night; how is the time reckoned and by what clocks.

6. What interval is allowed for breakfast, dinner, and afternoon refreshment; if none, what opportunity have the children of taking the food whilst at work; do they seem to have an appetite for such meals; is the food liable to be spoiled by dust and flue; can the food be covered whilst a child is eating at its work; do the children generally eat all that is sent them; when the threads break more than usual can the piecers find time to eat at all.

7. What interval is allowed for dinner; whether the children are or are not allowed to leave the factory for that purpose; how much of that interval is taken up with cleaning the machinery; do the children get any extra wages for cleaning the machinery out of hours; whether in any factories children have no time allowed for dinner.

8. If the children come too late are they not excluded till breakfast time, let the state of the weather be ever so bad; what fines, deductions, and other punishments are there for coming late, for going out during working hours or other offences, and how much do they sometimes amount to in a week; how are the fines applied.

9. What occupation are the children employed in before they go to the factory, and after they return from it.

10. On what parts of the work are children employed, such as piecers, scavengers, sweepers, carders, etc.; is not piecing a laborious employment on account of the reaching over; how is it with the other employments of children; do the children's fingers bleed at their work; does their work cause such bleeding; have they not to eat their meals whilst their fingers are in such a state; at what employments may they relieve themselves occasionally by sitting down; whether children have to work at night, and how long; is there any inducement in the way of pocket-money or the like to make children satisfied with working over hours, or at nights; when lost time is to be made up, are they not dismissed if they refuse to work over-hours; is not that particularly exhausting.

11. Are accidents frequent; from what do they generally result; are they more common towards the latter end of the day.

12. Are the children much fatigued; do they ever fall asleep at their work; is it necessary to beat them to keep them to their work; does this happen most towards night; with what instrument are they beaten; is the fatigue such as to take away the appetite; do the children ever faint; do they ever fall asleep in the factory when they ought to be going home; after ten hours actual work do children seem fit to work any longer.

13. Whether in the earlier part of the day and of the week, more work is not done in a given time; are not the children more spirited and active then; would a reduction in the number of hours of work cause a

proportionate reduction in the amount of work done; would not more work be done in a given time; when the hours are long is there not so much loss by sickness and fatigue, that it seems probable quite as much work might be done in a shorter time; have not some persons found it so; is there not a great waste of material when persons work in a state of over-fatigue; are there not considerable extra expenses attendant upon night-work.

14. Are not the children who are employed in factories generally speaking, necessarily strong and healthy when they are first selected; is there not soon a perceptible difference in the state of their health; do not many of them sooner or later become deformed, crooked, or crippled; when they are sick does the master afford them any assistance; is there any regular medical attendant paid by the master for attending to the factory; when the children become sick or crippled are they kept on, or are they turned off and thrown on their parish; are their settlements commonly in the parishes where they work.

15. Do children frequently die in consequence of illness acquired in factories; is not the health of factory persons generally very poor; is it not worse than that of persons in other commercial employments, such as hand-weavers, etc.; is there any difference in the health of children of the same family between those who are, and those who are not in factories; is not the eyesight of children affected in damp or hot employments; are they not liable to consumption, scrofula, cotton fever, asthma, complaints of the chest, rheumatism, weakness; when they have been removed to other employments, has not their health improved; have they ever to take vomits on account of the flyings; do not many parents refuse to send their children to factories on account of the long hours; do not the children stand their work much better when the hours are shorter.

16. Have the children regular opportunities of going to school; are they exposed to immoral communications at the factories, or in going and returning; are there not some factories where the treatment of females is particularly corrupting; what generally becomes of females brought up in factories.

17. How long do children brought up in factories continue to work there; what becomes of them afterwards; how many in the hundred stay there till they are thirty; in a hundred persons employed, how many are of the respective ages of 20 to 30, 30 to 40, 40 to 50, and upwards; are they not generally superannuated at forty, and turned off as being worn out; when they are turned off at that age are they fit for any good employment, or do they die soon, or are they thrown on their parish; whether those who enter factories at more advanced ages do or do not stand it better and longer before they become superannuated.

18. What changes have the masters voluntarily made since the first agitation of the question, or since Mr. Hobhouse's Bill was first talked of; when that Bill was done with, did they return to any of the old practices, and have they become more considerate again since the agitation on Mr. Sadler's Bill; has there been any examination of the factories and the work-people by Physicians, Surgeons, etc., on behalf of the masters; on any such occasions was everything just as usual, or were the lams, etc., kept out of sight, or the temperature lower than usual.

19. Are the parents desirous for the legislature to interfere to shorten the hours of their children's labour; do they wish the hours to be reduced in

proportion; would they, if they had the opportunity, send their children to mills which work short hours.

20. It is desirable that the local committee should as soon as possible return to the Central Committee the names of witnesses, and the substance of what each will be able to prove.

21. It must be borne in mind that the supporters of the Bill will have to make out a distinct case for every separate branch of manufacture affected by it.

22. It must also be an object with the local committees to guard against unnecessary expense by generally selecting such witnesses as from their own personal knowledge can depose to the greatest variety of facts; particular instances of an extraordinary nature will form an exception from this observation.

APPENDIX C

INSTRUCTIONS CONCERNING THE RECEPTION OF THE ROYAL COMMISSION
issued to local Short Time Committees by the Manchester Delegates' Conference, April 26th, 1833.

PRIVATE AND CONFIDENTIAL

Sir,

The Delegates' Meeting earnestly beg, that your Committee will *very carefully* consider *every* Particular of the following Instructions, and hope you will do your best to put them all into execution without a Moment's Delay.

Your obedient Servants,
G. HIGGINBOTTOM, Chairman
G. S. BULL, Secretary

Manchester, April 24th, 1833.

INSTRUCTIONS TO THE SHORT TIME COMMITTEES

Of England and Scotland, with Reference to the Commission

Forasmuch as the Commission has been *sued out* as it is believed, on the *false* pretence of insufficient and untrue Evidence, and with a view to the gratification of the Masters of Factories, and to the delay or defeat of the Ten-Hour Bill, and because it is plain that any voluntary recognition of such a Commission would preclude our privilege of Rejoinder, and also because this course is most unjustifiable, as proposing to try the Cause of the Rich before one Tribunal, and that of the Poor before another; it is therefore recommended by the Delegates to the Short-Time Committees, and to all our friends,

I. That on the arrival of the Royal Commissioners in every Town or District, a written Protest shall be presented by the Short-Time Committee of such Town or District, in a body or by their Secretary, protesting against the proceedings of the Commission as unnecessary, partial, and delusive, agreeably to the Form (to be forwarded), or otherwise expressed as the said Short-Time Committee may see good.

II. That each Short-Time Committee shall select two or more intelligent, and discreet, and inflexible men of good character, to watch the proceedings of the said Commissioners, from their arrival in, to their departure from, any place to which they may proceed. The duty of which Select Committee shall be, most accurately to observe and note the proceedings of the said Commissioners: the Mills or places to which they proceed, the persons whom they shall examine: distinguishing whether they are employers, overlookers, or operatives; and whether the latter are selected by or examined in the presence of, their masters or overlookers: and also to notice the time such Commissioners remain in each Mill or Factory they profess to inspect, and the number of hands employed; and also the persons whom they principally consult, or with whom they associate or visit; and also their conduct and proceedings in every particular, all which they shall as far as possible observe and record.

III. That as we apprehend that the Questions and Enquiries of the Commissioners will have a tendency to elicit Evidence favourable to an extension of actual labour to Eleven Hours, or longer, the said select Committee shall ascertain as far as it is practicable, the particular matters on which the witnesses shall have been examined; and also those points material to the subject, which shall be omitted in the examination. And also whether any part of the evidence contained in the Volume of Evidence of the select Committee, has been attempted to be controverted, and in what particulars, and by whom.

IV. That the said select Committee shall ascertain the names, connections, and relationships of the Clergy, of the Faculty, or other persons independent of the Factory System, who shall be consulted by the said Commissioners.

V. That the said select Committee shall inform themselves whether the Commissioners shall examine the Hospitals, Infirmaries, Poor-Houses, Sunday Schools, Lying-in Hospitals, and other charitable Institutions, as well as the Cottages and Cellar-dwellings of the poor, and ascertain as far as possible the nature and results of their several examinations.

VI. That the said select Committee shall ascertain as far as possible, any alteration which shall have been made in the Ages of the Children employed in Mills and Factories, their time of refreshment, hours of labour, or wages, or whether any extra painting, whitewashing, fencing off machinery, or other improvements in the management of said Mills or Factories, since the Bills for their regulation have been agitated, and especially since the Royal Commission has been known to be appointed: also to obtain as full and correct a list as possible of all the cripples and maimed in their neighbourhood, with their residences, etc.

VII. That the said Committee shall, if possible, inform themselves whether the infant, weakly, infirm, crippled or maimed hands shall have been removed, or the condition and temperature of the Mills, or the speed of the Engine, or the dress and condition of the Children altered and improved previous to the inspection of the said Commissioners.

VIII. That the said Committee shall inquire into, and record any cases of breaches of the existing law, gross instances of cruelty, or degradation and suffering which in the course of their duty now imposed upon them may fall under their notice, with a view to a further exposition of the state of factory labour.

IX. That any other observations of the select Committee regarding the character of the witnesses who shall be examined; their connection with or dependence upon their employers: or those Mill-Owners, being witnesses, who have been themselves notoriously law-breakers, shall also be recorded.

X. For the purpose of affording ocular demonstration in the persons of those employed in factory labour of the necessity for the limitation proposed by Lord Ashley, it be especially recommended to the fathers, mothers, and children of the operatives, peaceably and orderly, to assemble every evening, after the closing of the Mills, before the House or Inn, where the said Royal Commissioners shall remain, and state to them whether or not they wish to obtain the Ten Hours Bill.

XI. That a Book shall be kept by each Select Committee of all matters and things observed or done by them, agreeably to the above directions, and that a copy of the same shall be transmitted with all reasonable speed, by the Lancashire Committees to the Central Committee in Manchester, addressed to Mr. G. Higginbottom, 14, Larendon Place, Chorlton Row, Manchester; or by the Yorkshire Committees, to Richard Oastler, Esq. Fixby Hall, near Huddersfield. The Friends in Scotland have directed Communications to be sent to Dr. D. M'Aulay, 40, London-Street, Glasgow.

APPENDIX D

THE ADDRESS OF THE OPERATIVES OF ENGLAND AND SCOTLAND, TO ALL RANKS AND CLASSES OF THE LAND, APRIL 1833.

Fellow Countrymen—We appeal to you on behalf of the Ten Hours Bill, now before the House of Commons, and under Lord Ashley's care. Whatever may be the manifold causes of national distress, and of that poverty, in most cases, or that profligacy in some, which induces parents to submit their offspring to such ruinous toil, and whatever remedies it may be considered proper to apply, still, in the name of justice, let the law of England protect children without further delay from lawless and heartless avarice. We, who now address you, are operatives ourselves; we have heard and read discussion upon discussion on this humane and righteous measure, and after calm and deliberate reflection, we unanimously conclude that it will be favourable to commerce in general, to the honest master, and the industrious man, and to the moral and political health of society. At this moment we are called upon by the unjust and mercenary influence of the mill-owners in Parliament, to submit the case of the factory child to the investigation of a commission. Eighteen hundred pages of evidence have been collected from masters and men, the medical and clerical profession, and especially from the poor hapless victims of this cruel, money-getting system. But this suffices not. By a table appended to the evidence before the select committee, it is demonstrated, that more have died before their twentieth year, where the factory system extensively prevails, than have died at their fortieth year elsewhere. But this suffices not. Insatiable as death, the rich oppressor still asserts his right, to add to his blood-guilty store, by working the British Infant beyond the time of the soldier, the farmer, nay the adult felon, and the more fortunate child of British colonial slavery.

Fellow countrymen—This sort of oppression is not confined to our own generation, or our own country. It has been attributed to the corn laws: but when this system was yet in its infancy, and no corn law existed, the hours of labour exacted from children, were as bad or worse than now. It has been traced to taxation, which we feel to bear heavily and most unequally upon us. But in America, this, at all events, is not the cause of over-labour in factories, and there they work children in many cases longer than we do here. In fact, it is avarice which is the root of the evil—avarice which has not been content to supplant human labour by machinery, but now asserts, with bloody arrogance, its right to grind to the dust the helpless child, which it has obliged to take her father's place. Will you stand by and view this with cool indifference? Will you not unite your energies with ours, to protect the weak against the strong, and the indigent against the rich oppressor? See your country languishing—drooping its head under the chilly blasts of political economy—of grasping monopolies—of heartless calculation, which have blighted its fairest prospect. We know our agricultural brethren are sufferers from its horrid and pestilential breath as well as ourselves. The Ten Hours Bill is a sample in legislation favourable to us all. Sadler, than whom no man has been more beloved or hated, has stood like another Aaron between the dead and the living, with the fragrant incense of justice and benevolence in his hand, to stay the plague of political economy and all-engrossing covetousness. His senatorial mantle has fallen on a noble and illustrious successor, who fears God and regards man, but defies the scorn of the proud.

Let Lord Ashley's name be dear to Britain's honest labourers and oppressed factory children. Let his factory bill have your support. Our request is that you will use every lawful and constitutional means to promote its legislative adoption this session. Give them no rest—pour out your petitions for us and our children at the foot of the throne, and into both Houses of Parliament. Protest, as we do, against the mill-owners' commission. We will not, except by legal obligation, try our cause before it. We challenge such a jury, appointed as it is by those who have been arraigned at the bar of their country to try their own cause, or rather to cover their guilt from public view. Our gracious sovereign has been imposed upon; we acknowledge and revere his Majesty's authority, but we condemn unmeasurably the act of his advisers. Is it thus that justice can be attained, when the cause of the poor is tried in open court, and that of the rich in the secret chambers of guilt? We leave our cause in your hands, and implore our fellow-countrymen of every rank, to petition without delay for the Ten Hours Bill, and that it may be passed without reference to a partial, unjust, unnecessary, and delusive parliamentary commission, sued out on false pretences, to the abuse of his Majesty's royal prerogative, and to the hurt and grief of his loving and loyal subjects.

We address you as those who revere the constitution of our country. We honour the King—we respect the House of Commons; but we firmly believe that in the matter to which our present appeal refers, the influence of the interested and heartless mill-owners has misled the House of Commons, who were induced, by gross misrepresentation, to sanction the Commission by a majority of one!

Surely so important a question, decided only by a majority of one, might have caused his Majesty's confidential advisers to pause.

We believe his gracious Majesty has been imposed upon; and we have ventured to represent the same to our sovereign. We therefore protest—not against the exercise of his Majesty's royal prerogative, nor the authority of parliament—but we protest against the sordid influence by which both the one and the other have been so grossly imposed upon; and which influence seeks to rivet upon us and our children the chains of factory bondage.

Signed on behalf of the operatives of England and Scotland, in the manufacturing districts,

GEO. HIGGINBOTTOM, Chairman.

Manchester, April 25, 1833.

PROTEST OF THE MANCHESTER SHORT TIME COMMITTEE

To the Commissioners appointed by the House to inquire into the condition and sufferings of the Factory Labourers.

Gentlemen,—We, the undersigned, acting under the direction, and on behalf of the great body of factory labourers, in the town of Manchester, beg leave to present this our respectful remonstrance. First, however, we would declare our unfeigned loyalty and attachment to the King and constitution as by law established; next, we would express our no less sincere respect for yourselves, as well as for the authority under which you appear amongst us. Having premised thus much, we make bold to declare our unconquerable aversion to, and suspicion of, the effects of any inquiry so instituted; and our reasons are these which follow:—The evidence obtained before the committee on Mr. Sadler's bill, was called for on the suggestion of those factory masters, and their friends and dependents, who have avowed their heedlessness of the waste of infant life and strength, and the degradation in every way of the factory population, when put in competition with the profits of capital invested in steam mills. That evidence is now admitted, by the intelligent part of the public, to be conclusive proof of the fact that the factory system, as at present worked, does tend to deprave and degrade the labourers employed in it; and, what is our most especial cause of grief and despair, that it shuts out infancy from any chance of human instruction, dwarfs their bodies, twists and bends their tender bones, and deforms their figures. The numerical statements of deaths, deformities, and disease, furnished to parliament, leave no room for doubt upon these heads. That evidence taken before a competent and ordinary court of inquiry, is violently and without reason put aside, to make way for a mode of inquiry chosen by those whose interests are openly opposed to the physical and moral well-being of the factory labourers; and those very parties, as we perceive by the series of questions issued to them, are, in their own counting-houses, without the responsibility of an oath, or the restraint which would be imposed by a face-to-face examination, and the chance of a cross-examination, to give such answers as they think fit, which answers, as we cannot but suppose, are to be placed in opposition to the unanswerable body of evidence alluded to above. On the other hand, what are the labourers to do? Past experience has proved to them that there is no danger more directly threatening the very means of their existence than giving evidence of the facts as they exist. The minds of the masters must have undergone a complete revolution, if any such attempt on the part of the labourers will not only cause the loss of their places, but also the posting of their names in the entrance-hall of every mill far and near, for the purpose of insuring their exclusion from any such employment in any other place. For these reasons,—because the mode of inquiry is useless, its effects inevitably partial, its course unusual and unsatisfactory to the ends of justice; and one side of the evidence cut off by intimidation, expressed or implied, and in any case not to be given with impunity. We respectfully take leave to protest against any proceedings which may be taken in the course of your inquiries being used as counter-evidence to that taken before the committee on Mr. Sadler's bill.

APPENDIX E

JUDGMENT DELIVERED IN THE COURT OF EXCHEQUER FRIDAY, FEBRUARY 8TH, 1850.

'Ryder v. Mills'

Mr. Baron Parke,—'The question raised by this special case, by the agreement between the Crown and the defendant, is, whether it is an offence against the Factory Acts, or any of them, to employ a young person in a factory for ten hours and no more in one day, such ten hours ending at a period which is more than ten hours from the time when another child or young person first began to work in the morning of such day in such factory, if such last-mentioned ten hours are counted consecutively from that time, omitting only the meal times?

'This question depends entirely on the proper construction to be put on those acts, and more particularly on the 7th Victoria, cap. 15. These acts must be construed according to the established rules for the construction of statutes. In a court of law we have only to ascertain the meaning of the words used by the Legislature, and when that is ascertained we have to carry it into effect, and we are not to inquire whether the enactments are dictated by sound policy or not; that question is exclusively for the consideration of Parliament. We agree also with the Attorney-General, that though the immediate question in this case did relate to adult females, who are more capable of taking care of themselves, and of continued labour, than children, and consequently need less protection, and on whom the restriction from employing themselves as they may think best appears more of a hardship, the point to be decided is the same as if we were considering the case of children and young persons only, for the Legislature has clearly put all females on the same footing as they are. Indeed, the case as agreed on by both parties states that to be the question. Is, then, the owner of a factory liable to the penalty in respect to the employment of a child or young person in the manner stated?

'The act imposes a penalty, and therefore, according to the established rule, must be construed strictly; that is, a man is not to be restrained from the liberty which he has of acting as he pleases, and rendered liable to a punishment, unless the law has plainly said that he shall. It is not enough that we conjecture, even strongly, that it was the intention of the Legislature to have prohibited the act. There must be words indicating plainly and clearly that it has done so, and, applying this rule of construction, we do not think that there are words in the statutes sufficiently plain and clear to render the conduct of the defendant in the case above-mentioned liable to punishment.

'On the opening of the argument by the Attorney-General, we thought the defendant meant to contend that the time limited by the 26th section of the 7th Victoria, cap. 15, was to be calculated for each child or young person from the time that such child or young person first began to work in the morning; and that argument seemed to us to be altogether untenable, as being against the ordinary and grammatical sense of the words in that section.

'But such is not the construction contended for by the learned counsel for the defendant. He admits, and properly, that it is clearly the ordinary meaning of the words in that section, that the period from which the time is to be reckoned for all children and young persons working at the factory is that time when the first child or young person that was employed therein began to work. Both sides are agreed upon this limit of time, and there can be not the least doubt about it. So, also, it is perfectly clear that the times for meals for all young persons must all be at the same period of the day, according to the plain words of the 36th section, which may be explained by the convenience of all the women and children and young persons having their meals prepared at the same time.

'But it is contended for the defendant, that the other limit—the end of the time of working for all children and young persons—has not been prescribed, and that it has not been enacted that the time for the cessation of labour for all should be that when the first ceased labour. Certainly this has not been done in express words and nothing was more easy than to have said, in the 26th section, that the 12 hours—reduced to 11 and 10 by the subsequent statute, the 10th Victoria, cap. 29—should end when any one had worked that time; or to have said, in the 36th section, that all young persons should have the time for labour as well as for meals at the same period of the day.

'We must, then, consider whether, in the absence of express words to this effect, we can collect from other parts of the act that this was the meaning of the Legislature so clearly and unequivocally as to call upon us to give effect to it, and punish the defendant.

'Undoubtedly if there was such an enactment it would have the effect of securing to the children and young persons, whom it was most certainly the object of the Legislature to protect against their own improvidence, or that of their parents, the more effectual superintendence and care of the inspectors. Without question it would more effectually prevent them from being overworked, and secure to them more completely the benefit of some education in public schools which the Legislature meant them to enjoy; it would advance the intended remedy. But then this result could only have been obtained by a larger sacrifice of the interest of the owners of factories, and we cannot assume that Parliament would disregard so important a consideration.

'At any rate, a court of justice cannot render a man liable to a penalty merely because it might think that it would better promote the supposed object of the Legislature than the provisions of the statute according to their ordinary construction.

'The words used must plainly and clearly show that the act complained of is punishable. On the part of the prosecution it was contended that the intention of the Legislature could be clearly collected, partly from the words in the act itself, and partly from the schedules. Some reliance was placed upon the term "reckoned," in the 26th section, as meaning that it was to be continuously reckoned from the time when any one should begin to work; that is, that the next 12 hours after the time (with the intervals mentioned in the 36th section) should be the only hours of work; but we think that such is not the ordinary construction of that word; it means only that the computation of time shall then begin. It does not state when it shall end.

'An argument was also drawn from the wording of the 52nd section, which provides, it is said, for the beginning of work, and therefore the 26th section must have been intended, and ought to be constructed to mean, to provide for the whole time—the beginning and ending, otherwise that section would be unnecessary. But the 52nd section provides only for the evidence of the time of commencement—no more.

'The principal reliance was placed on the schedules which are required to be adopted by section 28, as showing the intention of the framers of the act, that the times of all should begin and end simultaneously; for, in the first form, it is clear that no names are intended to be mentioned. In the last, where particular individuals are to be named, the form expressly provides that it shall be so.

'It cannot be denied that the forms appear to have been constructed on the supposition that all would work the same time, but they are capable of being reconciled with the other supposition, for there seems certainly to be nothing expressly to forbid the blanks from being filled up so as to provide for the time of part ending at one hour, and that of the other part at another.

'Indeed, if it were not so, no factory-owner could employ some young persons for four hours, some for five, some for nine (which he unquestionably may): for the schedules, if they are to be filled up strictly according to the forms, stating all as beginning and ending at the same time, are not adapted to such a case, and they must, therefore, undergo some alteration.

'On the other hand, some argument in favour of the defendant was deduced from the peculiar language of the 28th section, which requires notice of the "times" of beginning and ending daily work of all persons, as if they might end at different times, and as if in such a case the act required each to be named with his allotted time in the notice. But the distinction between the use of the term "times" instead of "time" is by no means satisfactory to our minds, and we do not at all rest upon it.

'The ground upon which we proceed is, that though the act of Parliament (taken in conjunction with the 10th Victoria, cap. 29) does distinctly forbid the employment of young persons, and therefore all females, for more than ten hours, and those to be taken between half-past 5 in the morning and half-past 8 at night; though it distinctly requires that the time of all is to begin to be computed from the beginning of the first to work, and that an hour and a half shall be allowed for meals, and for all at the same time, it has not imposed in sufficiently clear terms any other restriction on the employment of young persons, and they are therefore at liberty to agree together for working for less than for the whole of that time within the limits before-mentioned, ending at half-past eight, or any previous time that they please, and with any intervals of leisure that may be thought convenient.

'Mr. Baron Alderson.—I have no doubt that that was the meaning of the word "reckoned," that it was to distinguish the hour at which the first person began to work from the half-past five o'clock, which was the limit of all. Instead of reckoning from half-past five, you must reckon from the time when the first person began.

(A true copy.)

'Whitehall, Feb. 18th, 1850.

G. CORNWALL LEWIS.'

Bibliography

I. OASTLER'S PAPERS.

II. OASTLER'S OWN WRITINGS.

III. MANUSCRIPT SOURCES.

IV. PRINTED OFFICIAL SOURCES.

V. CONTEMPORARY BOOKS AND PAMPHLETS.

VI. PERIODICALS.

VII. PREVIOUS BIOGRAPHIES OF OASTLER.

VIII. MONOGRAPHS, BIOGRAPHIES, AND OTHER STUDIES.

BIBLIOGRAPHY

I. OASTLER'S PAPERS

Oastler accumulated a considerable amount of material in the course of his public life (see above, ch. XIII). This collection went after his death to his friend Samuel Kydd. Upon the latter's death it was sold. Eventually the bulk of it found its way into the private library of Professor Foxwell, of St. John's College, Cambridge, and thence into the University of London Library, where it is at present. The rest was bought by Professor E. R. A. Seligman and is now in Columbia University Library. This material may be classified as follows:

(a) ALBUMS:

Two large volumes of press cuttings and comments covering the period 1830–36. (These are the two volumes shown in the portrait of Oastler reproduced in the frontispiece of this work.)

(b) DOCUMENTS:

A guard book of documents of various kinds bearing upon his campaigns.

(c) BROADSIDES:

Two large volumes of bills, posters, placards, etc. These are catalogued and summarized in the printed *Catalogue of Broadsides,* published by the University of London.

(d) PAMPHLETS:

These were bound in uniform format. Eighteen volumes, with index, are in the University of London, six in Columbia University. (The individual items in these volumes are separately listed below in Section v, and indicated by an asterisk.)

II. OASTLER'S OWN WRITINGS

(a) PAMPHLETS (written by Oastler or compiled from his speeches):

Vicarial Tithes, Halifax: A True Statement of Facts and Incidents. Halifax, 1827

Exposition of the Factory System. Mr. Oastler versus The Leeds Mercury. Leeds, 1831

A Letter to Mr. Holland Hoole. Manchester, 1832

Mr. Oastler's Speech at Huddersfield, on his Return from London. Leeds, 1832

To the Electors of the North-Riding of the County of York. York, 1832

Facts and Plain Words on Every-day Subjects. Leeds, 1833

Infant Slavery. Preston, 1833

Mr. Oastler's Reply to Mr. Gisborne, and Account of his Visit to Manchester. Manchester, 1833

Public Protest Against the Factory Commission. Leeds, 1833

Slavery in Yorkshire. Leeds, 1833

Speech Delivered in the Primitive Methodist Chapel, Bowling-Lane, Bradford, on Monday, the Fourteenth of January, 1833. Leeds, 1833

Speech Delivered at a Public Meeting Held in the Market Place, Huddersfield, on Tuesday Evening June 18, 1833. Leeds, 1833

A Speech Delivered by Richard Oastler, at a Meeting Held in the Manor Court-Room, Manchester, on Wednesday Evening, April 27th, 1833. Manchester, 1833

A Few Words to the Friends and Enemies of Trades' Unions. Huddersfield, 1834

Huddersfield Election. The Pearking, or (if you will have it so) The Biter Bit; in answer to the question who is to blame? Huddersfield, 1834

A Letter to the Editor of the 'Argus and Demagogue' on the Validity of Sir J. Ramsden's Title to the Sums of Money he Claims for Canal Dues, and on Other Subjects. Huddersfield, 1834

A Letter to those Sleek, Pious, Holy, and Devout Dissenters Messrs. Get-all, Keep-all, Grasp-all, Scrape-all, Whip-all, Gull-all, Cheat-all, Cant-all, Work-all, Sneak-all, Lie-well, Swear-well, and Company, the Shareholders in the Bradford Observer, in Answer to their attack on Richard Oastler, in that Paper of July 17, 1834. Bradford, 1834.

A Papal Bull, from Pope Gregory XVI to King Joseph, the Deluder, Companion of the Society of the Jesuits . . . the Wood-Be-Radical, and Sometime a Pensioner on the Half-pay List of the King of England. Huddersfield, 1834

A Penny Bellowing and Goring, Published for the Especial Benefit of the Deluded Followers of King Joseph. By Richard Oastler, 'The Fixby Mad Bull.' Huddersfield, 1834

A Serious Address to the Millowners, Manufacturers, and Cloth-dressers of Leeds, who have organized themselves into a 'Trades Union' to compel their workmen to abandon a RIGHT which the Laws of Britain Grant, to every subject . . . Huddersfield, 1834

Three Hundred to One! The History of the Yellow Dinner Ticket, No. 128, published for the express purpose of giving the Whigs an appetite for their Grand Dinner, on Friday, the 4th of April, 1834. Huddersfield, 1834

A Twopenny 'Extreme Unction,' Administered to King Joseph, by a Priest of his Making. Huddersfield, 1834

A Well Seasoned Christmas-Pie for 'The Great Liar of the North,' Prepared, Cooked, Baked and Presented by Richard Oastler. Bradford, 1834

Eight Letters to the Duke of Wellington: A Petition to the House of Commons: And a Letter to the Editor of the Agricultural and Industrial Magazine. London, 1835

Slavery in Yorkshire. Monstrous Barbarity . . . to E. Baines. Leeds, 1835

Yorkshire Slavery. The Devil-To-Do Amongst the Dissenters in Huddersfield: a letter addressed to E. Baines. Leeds, 1835

The Huddersfield Dissenters in a Fury. And Why? Because the Mask is Falling. A third letter addressed to E. Baines. Leeds, 1835

The Huddersfield Dissenters Stark, Staring Mad Because the Mask Has Fallen: the fourth letter to E. Baines. Leeds, 1835

Mr. Oastler's Three Letters to Mr. Hetherington. London, 1835

Richard Oastler on the New Poor-Law Act. Bradford, 1835

The Factory Question and the Factory Agitation Calmly Considered in a Letter to Those Millowners Who Are . . . Endeavouring . . . to Obey the Present Factories' Regulation Act. London, 1836

The Factory Question. The Law or the Needle. London, 1836

A Letter to the Archbishop of York. Huddersfield, 1836

A Letter to Those Millowners Who Continue to Oppose the Ten Hours Bill, and Who Impudently Dare to Break the Present Factories Act. Manchester, 1836

Letter to a Run-a-way M.P. Huddersfield, 1836

More Work for the Leeds New Thief-Catchers: a Letter to G. Goodman. Huddersfield, 1836

The New Poor Law and the Ten Hours' Bill. A Letter Addressed to the Right Honourable Sir Robert Peel. Bradford, 1836?

The Rejected Letter, with a Dedication to the Man Wot Would not Have it Read. Leeds, 1836

The Unjust Judge . . . A Letter to G. Goodman . . . on his Refusal to Imprison a Criminal under the Factories' Regulation Act. Leeds, 1836

Damnation! Eternal Damnation to the Fiend-begotten, Coarser Food, New Poor Law. A Speech. London, 1837

West Riding Nomination Riot: A Letter to Viscount Morpeth. London, 1837

A Letter to the Bishop of Exeter. Manchester, 1838

The Right of the Poor to Liberty and Life. Liverpool, 1838

Richard Oastler's Letter to the Nobility, Clergy, Farmers and Shopkeepers of the County of Nottingham. Nottingham? 1839

Brougham versus Brougham on the New Poor Law. With an Appendix Consisting of a letter to Lord John Russell. Dedicated to the Duke of Wellington. London, 1847

Free Trade 'not proven' in Seven Letters to the People of England. With an Introductory Address to Richard Cobden. London, 1849

Richard Oastler's Reply to Richard Cobden's Speech at Leeds, 18th December, 1849. London, 1850

Factory Legislation . . . (Introduction by W. Walker). London, 1855

Convocation: The Church and the People. 1860

(b) MAGAZINES:

Oastler edited two journals:

    The Fleet Papers: 1841–4 (4 volumes);
    The Home: 1851–3 (8 volumes).

(c) CONTRIBUTIONS TO CONTEMPORARY JOURNALS:
    (i) Oastler contributed regularly to the two journals edited by his
        friend J. R. Stephens:
                The Ashton Chronicle, 1848–9;
                The Champion, 1850.
   (ii) Throughout his life he also contributed to various daily and weekly
        newspapers, especially:
                The Times; The Morning Post; The Leeds Intelligencer; The
                Leeds Mercury; The Northern Star; The Poor Man's Guar-
                dian; The Twopenny Dispatch; The Weekly Police Gazette.
        No bibliography of these essays and letters has ever been com-
        piled, but sources used have been indicated in the notes above.

III. MANUSCRIPT SOURCES

(a) HOME OFFICE PAPERS (in the Public Record Office, London):
H.O. 40 (14); H.O. 40 (35); H.O. 40 (40); H.O. 41 (12); H.O. 52 (35);
H.O. 52 (38).
(b) THE PLACE PAPERS: (British Museum, Additional Manuscripts, espe-
    cially 27,820).
(c) LETTERS WRITTEN BY OASTLER (in the possession of the author):
A few other letters from Oastler's pen have survived and are to be found
scattered in various collections of documents as indicated in the notes.

IV. PRINTED OFFICIAL SOURCES

(a) REPORTS OF INVESTIGATIONS:
1. *Reports from the Select Committee on the Bill for the Regulation of
    Factories, P.P.,* 1831–2, xv.
2. *First Report from Commissioners appointed to collect information in the
    manufacturing districts, relative to the employment of children in fac-
    tories; with Minutes of Evidence and Reports of District Commissioners,
    P.P.,* 1833, xx;
        Second Report, P.P., 1833, xxi;
        Supplementary Reports, P.P., 1834, xix; *Part* ii, 1834, xx.
3. *Reports . . . on Hand Loom Weavers' Petitions, P.P.,* 1834, x, *and*
    1835, xiii.
4. *Reports from each of the Four Factory Inspectors on the educational
    provisions of the Factory Act, together with a joint report, P.P.,* 1839, xlii.
5. *Reports from the Assistant Handloom Commissioners, P.P.,* 1839, xlii;
    1840, xxiii, xxiv; 1841, x.
6. *Reports from the Select Committee on the Act for the Regulation of
    Factories, together with Minutes of Evidence, P.P.,* 1840, x; 1841, ix.
7. *Report of R. J. Saunders upon the Establishment of Schools in the Fac-
    tory Districts, in February* 1842, *P.P.,* 1843, xxvii.
(b) REPORTS OF INSPECTORS OF FACTORIES:
P.P., 1834, xliii; 1835, xl; 1836, xlv; 1837, xxxi; 1837–8, xxviii & xlv;
1839, xix; 1840, xxiii; 1841, x; 1842 (Sess. 2), vi; 1842, xxii; 1843, xxvii;
1844, xxviii; 1845, xxv; 1846, xx; 1847, xv.
(c) POOR LAW COMMISSIONERS: *Annual Reports,* 1837–40.

(d) STATUTES:

    1819: 59 *Geo.* III., *c.* 66
        An Act for the Regulation of Cotton Mills and Factories.
    1831: 1 & 2 *Will.* IV., *c.* 103
    1833: 3 & 4 *Will.* IV., *c.* 103
        An Act to Regulate the Labour of Children and Young Persons in Mills and Factories.
    1844: 7 & 8 *Vict., c.* 15
        An Act to Amend the Laws Relating to Labour in Factories.
    1847: 10 & 11 *Vict., c.* 29
        An Act to Limit the Hours of Labour of Young Persons and Females in Factories.
    1850: 13 & 14 *Vict., c.* 54.
        An Act to amend the Acts relating to Labour in Factories.
    1853: 16 & 17 *Vict., c.* 104
        An Act further to regulate the Employment of Children in Factories.

(e) HANSARD: Parliamentary Debates.

V. CONTEMPORARY BOOKS AND PAMPHLETS

N.B. 1. Those marked with an asterisk (*) were in Oastler's collection.
    2. It is impossible to list individually the numerous broadsides put out by Oastler and his friends. They may be found summarized in the printed *Catalogue of Broadsides,* published by the University of London.

'Alfred' (i.e. S. Kydd): *History of the Factory Movement.* London, 1857

* Allin, T.: *The Immortality of the Soul. A Sermon.* Hanley, 1823

* Atkinson, W.: *Lecture Upon Home Colonization,* etc. Leeds, 1832

* ——: *Popery Unmasked, and her Supporters Exposed.* . . Leeds, 1828

* Atwood, T.: *Distressed State of the Country.* Birmingham and London, 1829

Baines, E.: *History of the Cotton Manufacture.* London, 1836

——: *History, Directory and Gazetteer of the County of York.* Leeds, 1822–23

——: *Robert Oastler; J. Cawood: Mr. Owen's Establishment at New Lanark a Failure!* Leeds, 1819

Baines, E., Jr.: *The Social, Educational, and Religious State of the Manufacturing Districts.* London, 1843

——: *Life of Edward Baines.* London, 1859

* Baines, P. A.: *A Remonstrance, in a Third Letter, Addressed to Charles Abel Moysey, D.C.* n.p. 1824

Baines, T.: *Yorkshire Past and Present.* 3 v. Leeds, 1871

* Barnett, A.: *The Poor Laws and their Administration,* etc. London, 1833

Baxter, G. R. W.: *Book of the Bastilles.* London, 1841

Beaumont, J.: *Memoirs of Mrs. Mary Tatham.* Nottingham, 1842

* Beverley, R. M.: *A Letter to His Grace the Archbishop of York.* Beverley, 1831

* ——: *A Speech by R. M. Beverley, Esq.* . . . *agreeing to a petition against the Catholic claims.* Beverley, n.d.

——: *The Tombs of the Prophets, a Lay Sermon on the Corruptions of the Church of Christ.* Beverley, 1831

* Birley, J.: *Sadler's Bill, Cotton Branch.* Manchester, 1832

Bischoff, J.: *A Comprehensive History of the Woollen and Worsted Manufacture.* London, 1842

* Blakey, R.: *An Exposure of the Cruelty . . . of the New Poor Law Bill as Exhibited . . . by the Board of Guardians of the Morpeth Union.* Newcastle, 1837

* Bowen: *New Poor Law; The Bridgewater Case.* n.p., 1839

Bowring (M.P.): *Hand-Loom Weavers Speech.* London, 1835

* Brougham, H.: *Speech . . . House of Lords . . . March 20, 1838, on New Poor Law.* n.p., 1838

* Brown, J.: *A Memoir of Robert Blincoe.* n.p., 1832

* Bull, The Rev. George Stringer: *Letter and Prayer.* n.p., 1831

——: *An . . . Appeal to the Inhabitants of . . . Bradford on Behalf of the Factory Children.* Bradford, 1832

* ——: *The Evils of the Factory System, Illustrated . . .* Bradford, 1832

* ——: *Letter to Inhabitants . . . Byerley.* n.p., 1832

* ——: *Reply to the Leeds Mercury's Remarks on the Letter of Rev. G. S. Bull to Thos. B. Macaulay, Esq.* n.p., 1832

——: *A Respectful and Faithful Appeal to the Inhabitants of the Parish of Bradford . . . on the Behalf of the Factory Children.* Bradford, 1832

* ——: *To the Candidates, for the Borough of Bradford.* Bradford, 1832

——: *To the Inhabitants of the Agricultural Districts of the United Kingdom.* Ipswich, 1832

* ——: *To Inhabitants of Byerley Chapel.* n.p., 1832

* ——: *To Thomas B. Macaulay, Esq.* Leeds, 1832

——: *Factory Children.* n.p., 1833

* ——: *Speech of the Factory Children Concerning the Ten Hours Bill.* n.p., 1833

——: *Meeting of the Children Took Place.* Bradford, 1833

——: *Printed Letter: Calling for Petitions after Ashley's Motion to Renew Sadler's Bill.* n.p., 1833

——, (et al.): *The Proceedings of a Public Meeting of the People of Bradford . . . with the Address of the Rev. G. S. Bull.* Bradford, 1833

——: *Another 'Reverend Friend' for the Poor Curate of Byerley.* Bradford, 1834

* ——: *The Church Her Own Enemy.* Wakefield, 1834

——: *The Duty of the Ministers of the Gospel to Plead the Cause of the Industrial and Injured Labourers of Their Country.* n.p., 1834

* ——: *The Entire Demolition of Trade Unions by the Recent Discharge of an Old Rusty Parchment Blunderbuss, etc.* n.p., 1834

* ——: *Examples of Prayer, etc.* n.p., 1834

* ——: *The Gospel of Christ Recommended to Coal Miners.* Bradford, 1834

* ——: *A Lecture, delivered at the Friends' Meeting-House, Bradford . . . to the Benefit or Relief Societies . . . upon Certain Moral and Financial Evils . . . of Conducting the Business of those Useful Institutions.* Bradford, 1834

——: *A Lecture upon the New Poor Law Act, falsely called 'the Amendment,' etc.* Bradford, 1834

* ——: *A Letter to the Rev. T. R. Taylor, and Mr. Henry Forbes, of Bradford, Yorkshire.* Bradford, 1834

* ——: *The Poor Law Act, etc.* n.p., 1834

* ——: *The Poor Law Act. To the Inhabitants of Bradford and the Neighbourhood.* Bradford, 1834

* ——: *Remarks upon the Character of the Working Class*, etc. n.p., 1834
—: *The Sins of the Poor and of the Great Men Exposed*, etc. Huddersfield, 1834
* ——: *The Substance of a Lecture upon the New Poor-Law Act*. Bradford, 1834–5?
* ——: *To Coal Miners. 'Be ye also Ready.'* Bradford, 1834?
* ——: *To the People of Bradford, including the Unrepresented.* Byerley, 1834
* ——: *The Cause of Industry.* n.p., 1835
* ——: *The Farthing Candle.* n.p., 1835
* ——: *Morpeth, the friend of the Oppressed!* n.p., 1835
* ——: *Remonstrance (against scriptural profanity in a recent election at Bradford).* Bradford, 1835
—: *Horrors of the Whig Poor Law!* n.p., 1837
—: *The Poor Law Inquisitors and the Rev. G. S. Bull.* Bradford, 1837
—: *The New Poor Law, Shewn to be Unconstitutional,* etc. n.p., 1838
* ——: *The Oppressors of the Poor, and the Poor Their Own Oppressors!* Bradford, 1839
* —— and P. Bussey: *To the Friends of the National Regeneration Society.* n.p., 1834
* Bullock: *On Mending the Times.* n.p., 1833
* Bulmer, J.: *Letter . . . Mischief Likely to Arise from Too Great a Use of Machinery and Importation of Free Corn.* York, 1826
* Bulwer, E. L.: *The Present Crisis.* London, 1834
* Butler, W. J.: *New Poor Law. A Friendly Letter Addressed to R. Oastler,* etc. London, 1838
* Cayley, E.S.: *The Currency. Speech . . . in the House of Commons.* London, 1833
* ——: *Free Trade—Corn Laws. Speech . . . in the House of Commons.* London, 1834
Clark, John: *History and Annals of Bradford.* Manuscript in Bradford City Library. (1840).
* Clarke, W.: *A Reply to an Appeal to Members of Parliament and the Working Classes on the Ten Hours' Factory Bill.* Ashton-under-Lyne. 1838?
* Clayton, J.: *Statistical . . . Statement Concerning Wages.* n.p., 1832
* Close, F.: *Pauperism Traced to its True Sources.* n.p., 1839
* Cobbett, W.: *Cobbett's Poor Man's Friend . . . ; Defence of the Rights of Those Who Do the Work and Fight the Battles,* etc. n.p., 1826
* Cobbett, W., *et al.*: *The Flash in the Pan; or Peel in a Passion.* London, 1833
* ——: *Popay the Police Spy; or, a Report on the Evidence Laid Before the House of Commons,* etc. London, 1833
Condy, G.: *An Argument for Placing Factory Children Within the Pale of the Law.* London, 1833
* Cort, R.: *Rail-road Impositions Detected; or, Facts and Arguments, . . .* London, 1834
Couling, S.: *Our Labouring Classes: Their Intellectual, Moral and Social Condition Considered.* London, 1851
* Crabtree, G. *A Brief Description of a Tour through Calder Dale.* Huddersfield, 1833
* ——: *A Dialogue Between Tummus and Mary.* n.p., 1835

570   BIBLIOGRAPHY

* Crawford, S.: *Discourses on the Deity of the Son.* London and Leeds, 1835
* Cruttwell, R.: *Catholic Emancipation, Not Calculated to Relieve the Starving Peasantry of Ireland!* Halesworth, 1829
* ——: *Letter to the Right Honourable Lord Althorp* . . . Halesworth, 1831
* ——: *Petition to His Majesty the King, on the Currency, or standard of Value, as Connected with Taxation.* Halesworth, 1827
* Denison, W.: *Abstract of Evidence . . . to Inquire into the Operation and Effect of the Poor Law Amendment Act,* etc. n.p., 1837
* Detrosier, R.: *An Address Delivered at the New Mechanic's Institution.* Manchester, 1829–30?
* ——: *An Address Delivered at the Opening of the Banksian Society.* Manchester, 1829
* Dibb, R.: *The Factory Girl (a poem).* n.p., 1836?
* Dickenson: *Hymns for Factory Children, Original and Paraphrased.* Leeds, 1831
Dodd, G.: *Days at the Factories, or the Manufacturing Industry of Great Britain Described.* London, 1843
Dodd, W. ('A Factory Cripple'): *The Factory System Illustrated.* London, 1842
* Doherty, J.: *A Letter to the Members of the National Association for the Protection of Labourers.* Manchester, 1831?
* Downs, G.: *Copy of a Letter Received by the Chairman of Col. Williams' Committee, Ashton-under-Lyne.* Leeds, 1833
Doyle, F. H.: *Reminiscences and Opinions.* London, 1886
* Doyle, J.: *A Letter to the Duke of Wellington on the Catholic Claims.* Liverpool, 1828
* ——: *A Reply to the Charge of Dr. Elrington.* London, n.d.
* Eagle, W.: *A Legal Argument Shewing that Tithes are the Property of the Public and of the Poor.* London, 1831
* Edmonds, G.: *G. E.'s Appeal to the Labourers of England: An Exposure of . . . Machinery of the Poor Law Murder Bill,* etc. n.p., 1836
* Emerson, W.: *Friends and Fellow-Workmen . . . (inviting delegates to a meeting at Birstall to discuss the case of the Dorchester labourers).* Leeds, 1834
Faucher, L.: *Manchester in 1844: Its Present Condition and Future Prospects (Translated from French).* London, 1844
* Fenton, J. C.: *The Woodites' Forget-Me-Not.* Huddersfield, 1833
* Fidget (ps.): *A Letter to the Mayor and Citizens of London Respecting the Introduction of the New Police.* n.p., 1838
Fielden, J.: *Curse of the Factory System.* London, 1836
* ——: *The Mischiefs and Iniquity of Paper-money, and of the Present System of Banking and Funding.* London, 1832
* ——: *Speech . . . in the House . . . on Seconding . . . Motion for an Enquiry into the Working of the Poor-Law Act,* etc. n.p., 1837
* Finlay, K.: *Letter to . . . Lord Ashley on the Cotton Factory System and the Ten Hours Factory Bill.* Glasgow, 1833
* Firth, B.: *Church versus Dissent; or, Tory Spite and Virulence Overshooting their Mark.* London, 1835
* Fitton, W.: *National Regeneration.* London, 1834

* Fitz-John, W.: 1829; or, The Present Times: a Poem. Huddersfield, 1829
* Fry, J. S.: A Concise History of Tithes. n.p., 1820
  Gaskell, P.: Artisans and Machinery. London, 1836
  ——: The Manufacturing Population of England. London, 1833
* Gatliff: Report of the Sayings and Doings at Grand Yellow Dinner in a Wool Warehouse . . . Huddersfield. n.p., 1834
  Giffen, R.: Progress of the Working Class in the Last Half Century. London, 1884
* Gould, N. and others: Information Concerning the State of Children Employed in Cotton Factories. Manchester, 1818
* Gower, S.: What Are Poor Laws For? n.p., 1837
  Grant, P.: The Ten Hours' Bill. The History of Factory Legislation. Manchester, 1866
* Green: Arguments in Favour of M. T. Sadler's Bill. n.p., 1833
* Greeves, J. W.: A Reply to Mr. Geary's Appeal to the Weavers of Norwich. Norwich, 1830
  Greg, R. H.: The Factory Question and the Ten Hours Bill. London, 1837
  ——: The Factory Question Considered, etc. London, 1837
* Greg, W. R.: Enquiry into the State of the Manufacturing Population and the Causes and Cures for the Evils Therein Existing. n.p., 1831
  Grindrod, R. B.: The Wrongs of Our Youth: An Essay on the Evils of the Late-Hour System. London, 1843
* Hall, W.: Vindication of the Chorley Spinners. n.p., 1825
* Hanson, J.: Humanity Against Tyranny. Leeds, 1831
* ——: View Extraordinary of Sir John's Menagerie. n.p., 1837
* Hart, J.: The Cause of the Widow and the Fatherless defended by the God of the Bible. n.p., 1839
* Heaton, G.: A Letter to R. M. Beverley, Esq. on . . . the 'Present Corrupt State of the Church of England.' Doncaster, 1831
  Helps, A.: The Claims of Labour: An Essay on the Duties of the Employers to the Employed. London, 1845
* Higgins, G.: Address to the Electors of the West Riding of the County of York. Hackney, 1832–3?
* ——: A Letter (Being No. 1) to a Friend in the East Indies, Giving an Account of the State of Europe for the Last Two Years. London, 1832
  Hoole, H.: A Letter to the Right Honourable Lord Viscount Althorp . . . in Defence of the Cotton Factories of Lancashire. Manchester, 1832
  Horner, L.: On the Employment of Children in Factories. London, 1840
  ——: The Factories Regulation Act Explained, with some Remarks on its Origin, Nature, and Tendency. London, 1834
  James, J.: History of the Worsted Manufacture in England. London, 1857
* Jowett: Factory Question; Sayings and Doings of D. O'Connell, Esq. n.p., 1836?
* Kay, J. P.: The Moral and Physical Condition of the Working Classes Employed in the Cotton Manufacture in Manchester. London, 1832
  ——: The Social Condition and Education of the People in England and Europe. 2 v. London, 1850.
* Kennedy and Bowring: Copy of Correspondence Concerning Handloom Weavers. n.p., 1835
* King, W.: An Important Address to Trade Unions. n.p., 1832?
* Lillingston, C.: An Extract from a Speech. Birmingham, n.d.

Marshall, L.: *A Letter, Addressed to the Right Honourable Lord Althorp, Upon the Subject of Infant Slavery.* London, 1833

* Marcus: *Book of Murder: Vade Mecum for Commissioners and Guardians of the New Poor Law.* n.p., 1839

* ——: *Child Murder!* n.p., 1839

Matthews, W.: *Sketch of Principal Means Used to Ameliorate the Intellectual and Moral Condition of the Working Classes.* n.p., 1830

* Maunsell, R.: *A Letter, Address to the Rev. Sydney Smith.* Bristol, 1828

M. R. C. S.: *Appeal to M.P.'s and to Working Classes Concerning the Ten Hours Bill.* n.p., 1836

* Montrose: *Letter to Lord Althorp on the Factory Bill.* n.p., 1833

* Morgan: *Brief Review of the British Labourer's Protector and Factory Child's Friend.* Leeds, 1833?

* Napier, J.: *Address, Delivered before the Dublin Historical and Literary Society.* Dublin, 1828

* National Political Union: *On Pledges, to be Given by Candidates to the Electors of the United Kingdom.* No. 15. (Signed by R. Detrosier.) n.p., 1832

* ——: *Taxes on Knowledge. No. 13.* Southwark, 1832

* Nelson, J.: *The Farmer's Friend: Containing a Variety of Valuable Directions . . .* Leeds, 1820

* Nicholson, J.: *The Factory Child: a Poem.* n.p., 1831

* ——: *The Factory Child: a Poem.* (Another edition.) n.p., 1832

* ——: *The Factory Child's Mother, the Voice of True Humanity: a Poem.* Leeds, 1832

* Oastler, Mary (wife of Richard Oastler): *Song of the Factory Children.* n.p., 1832

* O'Connell: *Letter to the Members of the National Political Union.* Manchester, 1832

* O'Connor, F.: *A Series of Letters . . . containing a Review of Mr. O'Connell's Conduct during the Agitation of the Question of Catholic Emancipation, etc.* n.p., 1837

* Ormrod: *The Cry of the Poor (a poem).* n.p., 1837

Osborne, S. G.: *Replies of Sir Charles Shaw to Lord Ashley, M.P., regarding the Education and Moral and Physical Condition of the Labouring Classes.* London?, 1844

* ——: *A Word or Two about the New Poor Law.* n.p., 1837

* Osburn, W.: *Mr. Macaulay's Claims.* n.p., 1832

Parsons, E.: *History of Leeds, etc.* Leeds, 1834

Paul, W.: *A History of the Origin and Progress of Operative Conservative Societies.* Leeds, 1839

* Perceval, J. T.: *A Letter to Mr. J. Bowen (on the New Poor Law).* n.p., 1838

* ——: *Observations on the New Poor Law: Its Injustice, etc.* n.p., 1838

* Philips, C.: *The Queen's Case States.* London, 1820

Phillips, G. S.: *Walks Round Huddersfield.* Huddersfield, 1848

* Place, F.: *Improvement of the Working People: Drunkenness; Education.* n.p., 1834

Porter, G. R.: *The Progress of the Nation.* 3 v. London, 1836.

* Richardson, C.: *An Address to Working Classes of Leeds and West Riding.* n.p., 1831

BIBLIOGRAPHY

* ——: *Day-Dream; or, A Letter to King Richard (i.e. R. Oastler), containing a vision of the trial of Mr. Factory Longhours, at York Castle.* Leeds, 1832
* ——: *The Factory System.* n.p., 1831
——: *Speech Delivered April 19, 1833, before the Short-Time Committee* . . . Leeds, 1833
* Roberts, S.: *A Defense of the Poor Laws, with a Plan for the Suppression of Mendicity.* Sheffield, 1819
* ——: *England's Glory; or, The Good Old Poor Laws,* etc. n.p., 1836
* ——: *Letter to the Working Classes (anti New Poor Law).* n.p., 1838
* ——: *Lord Brougham and the New Poor Law.* n.p., 1838
* ——: *The Peers, the People, and the Poor.* n.p., 1838
* ——: *A Solemn Appeal to Ministers of the Gospel of Every Denomination on the Subject of the Poor Laws.* n.p., 1837
* Robinson, M.: *A Letter to R. M. Beverley, Esq.* London, 1831
* Ross, J. [an operative of Leeds]: *The Factory Child's Father's Reply to The Factory Child's Mother* [a poem by J. Nicholson]: *a Poem.* Leeds, 1832
* Royle, V.: *The Factory System Defended,* etc. Manchester, 1833
* Sadler, J. H.: *The New Invention of Double and Quadruple, or British National Looms,* etc. n.p., 1831
* Sadler, M. T.: *The Distress of the Agricultural Labourers Illustrated by the Speech of M. T. S.,* etc. Leeds, 1831
——: *Factory Statistics.* London, 1836
——: *Mr. Sadler and the Ten-Hour Bill.* Leeds, 1832
* ——: *Speech . . . On Moving the Second Reading of the Factories Regulation Bill,* etc. n.p., 1832
* ——: [On the Corn Laws—an extract or reprint from] *Ireland; Its Evils, and their Remedies.* n.p., n.d.
* ——: *Protest Against the Secret Proceedings of the Factory Commission in Leeds.* Leeds, 1833
* ——: *Reply to the Two Letters of John Elliot Drinkwater, Esq., and Alfred Power, Esq., Factory Commissioners.* Leeds, 1833
——: *Sadler's Speech in the House of Commons, Friday, March 16.* London, 1832
* ——: *Speech of Michael Thomas Sadler, M.P., on General Gascoyne's Motion.* London, 1831
* ——: *The Speech of Michael T. Sadler, Esq., M.P., on the State and Prospectus of the Country.* London, 1829
* Sandwith, H.: *An Apology for the System of Wesleyan Methodism.* London, 1825.
* Scrope, G. P.: *Plan of a Poor Law for Ireland.* n.p., 1834
* ——, Bull, and Oastler: *Political Economy versus the Hand-Loom Weavers: Two Letters . . . to the Chairman of the Central Committee. . . . With their Answer to the Same.* Bradford, 1835
Senior, N. W.: *Letters on the Factory Act.* London, 1837
* Shortreed, A.: *Observations on the British Constitution.* Edinburgh, 1831
Slaney, R. A.: *State of the Poorer Classes in Great Towns.* London, 1840
* Smith, Sydney: *A Sermon on Religious Charity.* York, 1825
* Smith, T. H.: *Hints to the Church-Wardens, Overseers, and Rate-Payers* . . . Nottingham, 1834

* Smithson, J.: *Speech at Public Meeting in Leeds Court House.* n.p., 1830
* Stanhope, Earl: *New Poor Law. Letter from Earl Stanhope to Mr. Richard Oastler.* London, 1837
* ——: *Speech at the Crown and Anchor Tavern.* n.p., 1837
* ——: *Speech on the New Poor Law,* etc. Leeds, 1837
* Stephens, J. R.: *The Political Preacher.* n.p., 1839
* ——: *Three Sermons Preached in London.* n.p., 1839
* Taylor, R.: *To the Editors of the 'Leeds Mercury'* (on the Ten Hours Bill). Leeds?, 1832
* Taylor, W.: *The White Slave's Complaint; or, The Horrors of Cotton Factories . . . : a Poem.* Stockport, 1836?
——: *Factories and the Factory System.* London, 1844
——: *Notes of a Tour in the Manufacturing Districts of Lancashire.* 2nd ed. London, 1842
Thackrah, C. T.: *The Effects of the Principal Arts, Trades, and Professions on Health and Longevity.* London, 1831
* Torrens, R.: *Address to the Farmers of the United Kingdom.* London, 1831
Trollope, T. A.: *What I Remember.* 3 v. London, 1887–9
Tuckett, J. D.: *A History of the Past and Present State of the Labouring Population.* 2 v. London, 1846
Ure, A.: *The Cotton Manufacture of Great Britain.* 2 v. London, 1836
——: *The Philosophy of Manufactures.* London, 1835
Verax (ps): *The Letters of Verax on the Currency.* Manchester, 1829
* Veritas (ps): *The Present Degraded State of Trade: Its Cause and Effects Considered in a Letter,* etc. London, 1829
* Vincent, G. G.: *Letter to Mr. J. Bower . . . Exposing the Unprincipled Nature of the New Poor Law.* n.p., 1838
Von Gagern, Baron: *England Rebuked by Germany.* n.p., 1833
Wade, J.: *History of the Middle and Working Classes.* London, 1834
Wakefield, E. G.: *Householders in Danger from the Populace.* n.p., n.d.
* Walker, J. K.: *On the Late Population Returns of the Manufacturing Districts.* n.p., 1831
* Walker, W.: *Poetical Strictures on the Factory System and Other Matters.* Leeds, 1832
Wallis: *Plans for Employing and Relieving the Labouring Poor.* n.p., n.d.
* Walter, J.: *A Letter to the Electors of Berkshire, on the New System for the Management of Poor.* n.p., 1834
Ward, J.: *Methodism in the Thirsk Circuit.* Leeds, 1860
* Wellbeloved, C.: *The Large Extent of the Subjects of Knowledge.* York, 1828
Wesley, The Rev. John: *Letters of the Rev. John Wesley.* (Standard edition.) Vol. 7. London, 1931
* Whiteley, H.: *Three Months in Jamaica.* n.p., 1833
* Whittle, J.: *An Address on the State of the Cotton Trade to the Master-Spinners and Weavers of Lancashire.* Manchester, 1829
Wilson, and Stuart: *Factory Commission. Correspondence between Mr. Wilson, Secretary to the Central Board of Factory Commissioners, and Mr. Stuart, One of the Commissioners.* London, n.d.
* Wilson, W. C.: *Remarks on Certain Operations of the New Poor Law,* etc. Kirkby-Lonsdale, 1838

Wing, C.: *Evils of the Factory System.* London, 1837

Wood, J.: *Autobiography.* (A MS. in Bradford Public Library.) Bradford, 1877

* Wood, Joseph: *Intercepted Letter of an Archbishop of the Church by Law Established.* Wakefield, 1834

* ——: *An Intercepted Mandate, from an Archbishop of the Church, by Law Established, to Silence the Bellowings of the 'Fixby Mad Bull.'* Huddersfield, 1834

* ——: *Proposals for the Immediate Reduction of Eight Millions and a Half of Taxes.* London, 1830

* ——: *Right of Labour to Legislative Protection Demonstrated: with remarks,* etc. Huddersfield, 1832

ANONYMOUS BOOKS AND PAMPHLETS:

* *Account of Deaths from Starvation . . . in Altingham Union.* n.p, 1839

* *An Address to the Christian Proprietors and Freeholders of Great Britain.* London, 1830

* *An Address to the English Nation Against the New Poor Law.* n.p., 1839

Address to the Friends of Justice and Humanity, in the West Riding of York. Bradford, 1833

* *Address of the United Delegates from the Factory Districts throughout the Kingdom.* Manchester, 1836?

* *Answer to Certain Objections Made to Sir R. Peel's Bill for Ameliorating the Condition of Children.* Manchester, 1819

* *Appeal to our Rulers and Ruled, in Behalf of a Consolidation of the Post Office, Roads, and Mechanical Conveyance.* London, 1834

* *An Authentic Report of the Trial of Michael Stocks, Esq.* Huddersfield, 1815

* *Brief View of Medical Evidence and Opinion . . . on the Factories Regulation Bill . . . 1832.* n.p., 1832

* *British Taxes Dissected . . . by one of the Council of the National Political Union.* London, 1833

* *Catechism of the Society for Promoting National Regeneration.* Bradford, 1833

* *Causes of the Distress of the Agricultural Population Considered.* n.p., 1831

Celebration of the Centenary Jubilee of the Congregation of the United Brethren. Fulneck, 1855

* *The Church of England and Dissent.* London, 1830

The Commission for Perpetuating Factory Infanticide. n.p., 1833

* *The Commercial Career of Sewell and Cross,* etc. n.p., 1838

* *The Condition of the West Indian Slave.* n.p., n.d.

* *A Dialogue Between Two Non-Electors.* n.p., 1836

* *The Difference between Protestantism, and Catholicism, misnamed Popery, Fairly Stated . . .* Manchester, n.d.

* *A Discussion of Parliamentary Reform.* London, 1831

* *Exposition of the Factory Question.* Manchester, 1832

The Factory-Child, A Poem. London, 1832

The Factory Girl's Last Day. n.p., n.d.

* *The Factory Lad; or, The Life of Simon Smike.* n.p., 1839

* *The Factory System.* n.p., 1833

A Few Arguments in Favour of Mr. Sadler's Bill, . . . by a Member of the Huddersfield Political Union. Huddersfield, 1833

* *Four Years of Liberal Government.* London, 1834

* *A Full and Accurate Report of the Trial of William Cobbett, Esq.* London, 1831

* *Give It a Fair Trial* (a skit on the New Poor Law). Huddersfield, 1837?

An Inquiry into the Destitute Condition of the Working Classes (particularly the cotton trade). n.p., 1829

The Justice, Humanity, and Policy, of Restricting the Hours of Children and Young Persons in the Mills and Factories . . . Leeds, 1833

* *Legalised Murder, or Killing No Crime.* n.p., 1823

* *Letter on the Coronation Oath.* London?, n.d.

Letter to the Right Honourable Lord Ashley, on the Cotton Factory Question, and the Ten Hours Factory Bill, by a Lancashire Cotton Spinner. Manchester, 1833

* *Letter . . . to . . . Parliament on the Distresses of the Hand-Loom Weavers.* Bolton, 1834

* *Letter to Sir J. C. Hobhouse . . . on the Factories Bill,* etc. n.p., 1832

* *A Letter to the Working Classes and H. G. Ward . . . addressed to R. Oastler. By a Sheffielder.* Sheffield, 1838

* *Letters to J. E. Gordon, Esq., M.P.* London, 1832

* *Most Blessed Amendment of the Poor Laws by the Dear Whigs.* Leeds, 1834

* *Noctes Old-Cockneyanae.* No. XLII . . . Halifax, 1832

* *Nottinghamshire Working-Men's Association. Address . . . to the People of England on the New Poor Law,* etc. n.p., 1838

* *Observations, etc., as to the ages of Persons Employed in the Cotton Mills of Manchester* . . . Manchester, 1819

* *Observations on Power-Looms and their Effect on the Hand-Loom Weaver,* etc. Glasgow, 1826

* *On the Factory System.* n.p., 1833?

* *Plain Words addressed to the Electors of The United Kingdom. By a Reformer.* London, 1834

* *The Poor Law Bill Exposed.* n.p., 1837

* *Principles, and not Men. A Dialogue between Tom and Jerry; . . . By a Chip of the Old Block.* Leeds, 1831

* *Prospects for Old England! Hints to the Duke of Wellington, and the New Ministry.* London, 1834

* *The Schoolmaster Abroad.* n.p., n.d.

* *The State and Prospects of Toryism.* London?, 1834

* *Statistics for the People.* No. 1. n.p., 1832

* *The Tables Turned: A Reply to 'Common Sense' by 'Common Honesty.'* n.p., 1832

* *To the Electors of the Borough of Manchester.* Manchester, 1832

* *To the Farming Labourers of Great Britain and Ireland* (on the Poor Laws; signed, A Freeman of Exeter). n.p., 1837

* *Trades Triumphant! or, Unions' Jubilee!!* n.p., 1834?

* *Voice from the North of England on the New Poor Laws: Ought We to Have Them, or Ought We not?* n.p., 1837

* *Whig Fraud and English Folly! The Bill not the Bill, nor any Thing like the Bill* . . . London, 1831

* *Who are to be the New Members for Leeds?* Leeds, n.d.
* *Word Addressed to the Wool-Sorters . . . and Others . . . on the Subject of the Ten Hours Bill.* Halifax, 1832
* *A Word to Electors: Letters on the Unrestrained Use of Modern Machinery.* Norwich, 1832

REPORTS OF MEETINGS:

* *Examinations, Taken in the Case of Maria Sleddin; published by order of the Committee of the Leeds Workhouse Board.* Leeds, 1823
* *Tenth Report of the General Committee of the Association for the Suppression of Mendicity in Dublin. For the year 1827.* Dublin, 1828
* *The Great Brunswick Meeting, on Penenden Heath.* Liverpool, 1828
* *Free Trade. Report of the Speeches . . . at the Dinner of Freeholders at Saddleworth, on Free Trade, Civil and Religious Liberty, Parliamentary Reform, Taxes on Literature,* etc. Manchester, 1830
The Ten-Hour-Bill. Report of the Proceedings of the Great Leeds Meeting to Petition Parliament in Favour of Mr. Sadler's Bill for the Regulation of the Hours of Children's Labour in Factories. n.p., 1831
Report of the Proceedings of the Huddersfield and Bradford Meetings, Held on the 26th and 27th of December, 1831. Speeches by Richard Oastler et al. Leeds, 1831
The Ten-Hour Factory Bill. Keighley Meeting, Monday, January 30, 1832. n.p., 1832
Report of Dewsbury Meeting on the Factory Bill . . . February 6, 1832. n.p., 1832
Mr. Sadler's Factory Bill. Report of the Proceedings of a Public Meeting, held . . . Tuesday, March 6th, 1832. Leeds, 1832
A Brief View of Medical Evidence and Opinion, Given before the Select Committee on the Factories' Regulation Bill, Appointed March 16, 1832. n.p., 1832?
* *Report to the County of Lanark, of a Plan for Relieving Public Distress and Removing Discontent . . . By Robert Owen.* London, 1832
Report of a Public Meeting to Consider of a Petition to Parliament, in Support of Lord Ashley's Factory Bill . . . April 8th, 1833 . . . Halifax, Yorkshire. n.p., 1833
Great Meeting in Leeds, on Thursday the 16th of May, 1833, of the Factory Children, to Present their Protest to the Commissioners Appointed through Mr. Wilson Patten's Motion for Further Enquiry, etc. Leeds, 1833
* *Extracts from the Minutes of Evidence before Select Committee of the House of Commons Connected with the Woollen and Fancy Trades, of the West-Riding of Yorkshire.* Huddersfield, 1833
The Great West Riding Meeting on the Present State of the Factory Question, on Monday, July 1st. Leeds, 1833
Great Meeting of the West-Riding in Support of the Ten-Hour Bill. Leeds, 1833.
Proceedings of a Public Meeting Held at Habden-Bridge, in the Parish of Halifax, Yorkshire, on Saturday Evening, August 24th, 1833. Huddersfield, 1833

* A Report of the Proceedings and Speeches of a Public Meeting Held in
. . . Oldham on . . . March 14th, 1835. Speeches by Richard Oastler et al. Oldham, 1835

* Authentic Reports of the Two Great Protestant Meetings Held at Exeter
Hall, London, on Saturday, June 20, and Saturday, July 11, 1835.
London, 1835

* Report of the . . . Proceedings of a Public Meeting Held in . . . Oldham on . . . the 11th of November, 1836, on the Subject of Shortening the Time of Labour . . . Oldham, 1836

* Poor Law Act: Public Meeting at Bradford, etc. n.p., 1837

* Great Meeting at the Crown and Anchor (Strand) on the Inhuman Poor-
Law Act: Report Taken from the 'Champion' Newspaper. n.p., 1838?

VI. PERIODICALS

Argus and Demagogue (Huddersfield)
The Ashton Chronicle
The Bradford Observer
The British Labourer's Protector and Factory Child's Friend (edited by
G. S. Bull)
Cobbett's Political Register
The Crisis
The Globe
The Halifax Guardian
The Halifax and Huddersfield Express
The Herald of the Rights of Industry
The Hull Packet
The Illustrated London News
The Leeds Intelligencer
The Leeds Mercury
The Leeds Patriot
The Leeds Times
The Liverpool Mail
The Liverpool Standard
The Manchester Advertiser
The Manchester Guardian
The Morning Chronicle
The Morning Herald
The Morning Post
The New Moral World
The Northern Liberator (Newcastle)
Northern Star
Oxford City and County Chronicle
The Pioneer
The Planet
The Poor Man's Guardian
The Sheffield Courant
The Sheffield Mercury
The Shropshire Conservative
The Standard (London)
The Ten Hours Advocate

The Times
Twopenny Dispatch
Wakefield Journal
Weekly Police Gazette (London)

VII. PREVIOUS BIOGRAPHIES OF OASTLER

Bull, G. S.: *Lecture on the Character and Career of Richard Oastler, Esq.* Leeds, 1861

Cole, G. D. H.: *'Richard Oastler' in* Chartist Portraits (ch. III). London, 1941

Croft, W. R.: *The History of the Factory Movement; or, Oastler and His Times.* Huddersfield, 1888

Gibbins, H. de B.: *English Social Reformers.* London, 1902

Greenwood, A.: *Richard Oastler, the Factory King.* Huddersfield, 1913

Hewins, W. H. S.: *'Oastler' in D.N.B.*

Stephens, J. R. (published anonymously): *Sketch of the Life and Opinions of Richard Oastler.* Leeds, 1838

VIII. MONOGRAPHS, BIOGRAPHIES, AND OTHER STUDIES

Addison, W. G.: *The Renewed Church of the United Brethren.* London, 1932

Beales, H. L.: *The Industrial Revolution.* London, 1928

Bowden, W.: *Industrial Society in England Towards the End of the Eighteenth Century.* New York, 1925

Bready, J. W.: *Lord Shaftesbury and Social-Industrial Progress.* London, 1926

Buer, M. C.: *Health, Wealth and Population in the Early Days of the Industrial Revolution.* London, 1926

Cecil, Lord Hugh: *Conservatism.* London, 1912

Christie, O. F.: *The Transition from Aristocracy, 1832–1867.* London, 1927

Clapham, J. H. *An Economic History of Modern Britain.* Cambridge, 1927

——: *The Woollen and Worsted Industries.* London, 1907

Cole, G. D. H., and Raymond Postgate: *The Common People, 1746–1938.* London, 1938

Crump, W. B.: *The Leeds Woollen Industry, 1780–1820.* Leeds, 1931

——and Gertrude Ghorbal: *History of the Huddersfield Woollen Industry.* Huddersfield, 1935

Darvall, F. O.: *Popular Disturbances and Public Order in Regency England.* London, 1934

Davis, H. W. C.: *The Age of Grey and Peel.* London, 1929

Dunlop, O. J., and R. D. Denman: *English Apprenticeship and Child Labour.* London, 1912

Edwards, H. W. J. (ed): *The Radical Tory.* London, 1937

Engels, Frederick: *Condition of the Working Classes in England in 1844.* (Translated from the German by Florence K. Wischnewetzky.) London, 1892

Faulkner, H. U.: *Chartism and the Churches. A Study in Democracy.* New York, 1916

Fay, C. R.: *Great Britain from Adam Smith to the Present Day.* London, 1928

——: *Life and Labour in the Nineteenth Century.* Cambridge, 1920

Feiling, K.: *The Second Tory Party, 1714–1832.* London, 1938

——: *What Is Conservatism?* London, 1938

Fisher, Mrs. H. A. L.: *Then and Now: Economic Problems after the War a Hundred Years Ago*. London, 1925

Fong, H. D.: *Triumph of the Factory System*. Tientsin, 1930

Gamage, R. G.: *History of the Chartist Movement*. Newcastle, 1894

Glover and Andrews: *History of Ashton-under-Lyne*. n.p., 1884

Gray, A.: *The Development of Economic Doctrine*. London, 1931

Gray, K.: *History of English Philanthropy*. London, 1905

Gregory, Rev. J.: 'Richard Oastler and the Ten Hours Factory Movement,' in *The Bradford Antiquary*, New Series, Part xv, October, 1911.

Halevy, E.: *A History of the English People: 1815*. London, 1924

——: *A History of the English People in 1815–30*. London, 1926

——: *A History of the English People in 1830–1841*. London, 1927

Hammond, J. L. and B.: *The Age of the Chartists*. London, New York, 1930

——: *Lord Shaftesbury*. London, 1923

——: *The Rise of Modern Industry*. London, 1925

——: *The Skilled Labourer*. London, New York, 1919

——: *The Town Labourer*. London, New York, 1917

——: *The Village Labourer*. London, New York, 1911

Heaton, H.: *Yorkshire Woollen and Worsted Industries*. Oxford, 1920

Hill, R. L.: *Toryism and the People, 1832–1846*. London, 1929

Hodder, E.: *The Life and Work of the Seventh Earl of Shaftesbury*, 3v. London, 1886

Holyoake, G. J.: *The Life of Joseph Rayner Stephens*. London, 1881

Hovell, M.: *The Chartist Movement*. London, 1918

Hutchins, B. L., and A. Harrison: *A History of Factory Legislation*. London, 1926

Hutt, W. H.: 'The Factory System of the Early Nineteenth Century,' in *Economica*, No. 17, March 1926. London, 1926

International Labour Office: *Factory Inspection: Historical Development and Present Organisation*. Geneva, 1923

Jephson, H. L.: *The Platform, Its Rise and Progress*. London, 1892

Jerrold, D.: *England*. London, 1935

Kebbel, T. E.: *History of Toryism: From the Accession of Mr. Pitt in 1783 to the Death of Lord Beaconsfield in 1881*. London, 1886

Kellett, E. E.: *Religion and Life in the Early Victorian Age*. London, 1938

Knowles, L. C. A.: *The Industrial and Commercial Revolutions in Great Britain During the Nineteenth Century*. London, 1921

Lever, T.: *The Life and Times of Sir Robert Peel*. London, 1942

Lipson, E.: *Economic History of England*. Vol. ii. London, 1934–5

——: *The History of the Woollen and Worsted Industries*. London, 1921

Ludlow, J. M., and Lloyd Jones: *Progress of the Working-Class, 1832–67*. London, 1867

Maccoby, S.: *English Radicalism*. London, 1935

Marston, M.: *Sir Edwin Chadwick*. London, 1925

Menger, A.: *The Right to the Whole Produce of Labour*. (Translated by M. E. Turner, with an introduction and bibliography by H. S. Foxwell.) London, 1898

Morris, G. W., and L. S. Wood: *The Golden Fleece: An Introduction to the Industrial History of England*. London, 1922

Neff, Emery: *Carlyle and Mill: An Introduction to Victorian Thought*. New York, 1926

Neff, W. F.: *Victorian Working Women*, 1832–1867. New York, 1929
Nicholls, Sir G. (continued by T. Mackay): *A History of the English Poor Law*. 3v. London, New York, 1898, 1904
Ostrogorski, M.: *Democracy and the Organization of Political Parties. Translated*. London, 1902
Parker, C. S.: *Life and Letters of Sir James Graham*. 2v. London, 1907
——: *Sir Robert Peel*. 3v. London, 1899
Penty, A. J.: *Towards a Christian Sociology*. London, 1923
Pinchbeck, I.: *Women Workers and The Industrial Revolution*, 1750–1850. London, 1930
Plener, E. V.: *English Factory Legislation. With an Introduction by A. J. Mundella*. London, 1873
Podmore, F.: *Robert Owen: A Biography*. London, 1906
Ramsay, A. A. W.: *Sir Robert Peel*. London, 1928
Redford, A.: *The Economic History of England, 1760–1860*. London, 1931
——: *Labour Migration in England, 1800–1850*. London, 1926
Robson, A. H.: *The Education of Children Engaged in Industry in England*. London, 1931
Rosenblatt, F. F.: *The Chartist Movement in Its Social and Economic Aspects*. New York, 1916
Rothstein, T.: *From Chartism to Labourism*. London, 1929
Slater, G.: *Poverty and the State*. London, 1930
Slosson, P. W.: *The Decline of the Chartist Movement*. New York, 1916
Smith, F.: *The Life and Works of Sir James Kay-Shuttleworth*. London, 1923
Spence? ('A Man of Leeds'): *Memoir of Eminent Men of Leeds*. London, 1869
Stamp, J.: *The Christian Ethic as an Economic Factor*. London, n.d.
Stewart, N.: *The Fight for the Charter*. London, 1937
Sykes, D. F. E.: *History of Huddersfield and Its Vicinity*. Huddersfield, 1898
Taylor, E. R.: *Methodism and Politics, 1791–1851*. London, 1935
Taylor, R. W. C.: *History of the Factory System*. London, 1886
Tillyard, F.: *The Worker and the State*. London, 1923
Turner, J. H.: *The History of Brickhouse, Rastrick, and Hipperholme*. Bingley, 1893
Walker-Smith, D.: *The Protectionist Case in the 1840's*. London, 1933
Wallas, G.: *The Life of Francis Place, 1771–1854*. London, 1898
Walpole, S.: *Life of Lord John Russell*. 2v. London, 1899
Warner, W. J.: *The Wesleyan Movement in the Industrial Revolution*. London, 1930
Waugh, W. T.: *History of Fulneck School*. Fulneck, 1909
Wearmouth, R. F.: *Methodism and the Working Class Movements of England: 1800–1850*. London, 1937
Webb, S. and B.: *English Poor Law History, Part I, to 1834; Part II, The Last Hundred Years*. London, 1926–1929
——: *History of Trade Unionism*. London, 1894
——: *The History of Trade Unionism. With bibliography*. (Revised edition.) London, 1920
West, J.: *History of the Chartist Movement*. London, 1920

Whibley, C.: *Lord John Manners and His Friends.* Edinburgh, etc. 1925
Wilkinson, W. J.: *Tory Democracy.* New York, 1925
Woods, M.: *A History of the Tory Party in the Seventeenth and Eighteenth Centuries.* London, 1924
Young, G. M., and others: *Early Victorian England.* London, 1934

PORTRAITS OF RICHARD OASTLER

1. Engraving by William Barnard, after the painting by Thomas H. Illidge. (Published at Leeds, 1832.)
2. Painting by Benjamin Garside. (Now in Huddersfield Public Library.)
3. Engraving by J. Posselwhite, after the painting by B. Garside. (Published at Leeds, 1838.)
4. Lithograph by Edward Morton, after the painting by W. P. Frith. (Published at Leeds, 1838.)
5. Lithograph by G. E. Madeley, 1840. (Published as frontispiece to *Fleet Papers,* vol. 1, 1841.)
6. Photograph, c. 1860. (Reproduced in *The Bradford Antiquary,* October, 1911.)
7. Statue in bronze, by J. Bernie Philip. (Now standing in Rawson Square, Bradford.)
8. Two medals, 1838 and 1869. (See below under *Memorials.*)

MEMORIALS TO RICHARD OASTLER

1. *Medal:* cast on the occasion of Oastler's departure from Fixby. On one side is the head of Oastler, with the words: 'The Oastler National Testimonial, 1838.' On the reverse is depicted a cottage in a rural setting; above are the words: 'Dwell in the land and verily thou shalt be fed;' beneath, 'Live and let live.'
2. *Bronze statue,* Bradford, by J. B. Philip. This statue was first erected in Foster Square, 1869. In 1920 it was removed to its present site in Rawson Square.
3. *Medal:* commemorating the unveiling of the Bernie Philip statue at Bradford. On one side is Oastler's head and the words: 'Richard Oastler. Born at Leeds Decr. 20, 1789. Died Augt. 22, 1861.' On the reverse are the words: 'To commemorate the inauguration of the OASTLER MONUMENT AT BRADFORD YORK on Whit Saturday May 15, 1869.'
4. *Stained glass window,* erected in 1864 in St. Stephen's Church, Kirkstall, Leeds. Inscription: 'This window is placed here out of dear affection and sincere gratitude to the beloved memory of Richard and Mary Oastler by their adopted daughter, A. M. Tatham. Not unto us, O Lord, but unto Thy name be the glory.'
5. *Monument* in the churchyard of Christ Church, Woodhouse, near Huddersfield. Inscription:
'The memory of Richard Oastler lives in the hearts of thousands. He was a true patriot, loyal to his Sovereign, faithful to the Church of his country. The oppressed, the friendless, and the poor (above all the hapless factory workers) found in him an able and fearless advocate. He died August 22nd 1861 and was buried at Kirkstall, near Leeds. In Christ was his hope, and with Him he rests in peace!'

6. *Monument* erected at the entrance to the 'Richard Oastler Memorial' playing ground, Greenhead Park, Huddersfield. Inscription: 'This playground has been provided by public subscription in memory of Richard Oastler of Fixby Hall, "The Factory King," who laboured and suffered for poor children, 1789–1861.'

Index

Aberdeen, Charles, 175, 176
Ackroyd, family, 465
  Jonathan, 362
  William, 64, 165
Address to All Ranks and Classes of the Land, 224, 555
Address to the Friends of Justice and Humanity, 260
Address to the Working Classes of Leeds and the West Riding, 116
Advice to the Ten Hours Men, 483
Agnew, Sir Andrew, 212
Agricultural and Industrial Magazine, The, 295
Althorp, Viscount, 166, 220, 238, 242, 245, 275
Althorp's Act (1833), *see* Factory Legislation
Anti-Corn Law League, 436, 463, 470
Anti-Poor Law Movement, attitude of press to, 370; destroyed by Chartism, 393, 394; collapse of, 405; achievements of, 407
  Lancashire, 368, 373, 374
  London, 372ff.
  Yorkshire, 335, 336ff., 339, 340, 351, 352, 365, 366, 367
Anti-slavery movement, 13, 19
Armitage, Joseph, 337, 342
Ashley, Lord, asked to sponsor Ten Hours Bill, 212; first letter to Oastler, 213; defines position to Morpeth, 215; public inauguration as parliamentary leader, 216; 217, 218; resigns factory bill into Althorp's hands, 245; 249; on Handloom Weavers Committee, 286; replaced

as leader by Hindley, 310, 311, 324; breaks with Oastler, 328; introduces Frances Trollope to Ten Hours leaders, 403; visits Oastler in prison, 419; persistent in advocating factory reform (1838–44), 450, 451; tours manufacturing districts, 451, 452; bill to regulate the labor of women and children in mines (1842), 453; impasse over Ten Hours amendment, 454, 455; Ten Hours amendment defeated, 457; resigns seat in Parliament, 463 and n.; tours northern counties (1847), 470; tribute to, from *Ten Hours Advocate,* 472; reported to have agreed to 10½ hours, 484, 485; attitude to question of extended day (1849), 485, 486; distrusted by Ten Hours men, 495; 496, 498; difficulties over Declaratory Bill, 500, 501; advocates 10½ hours, 502, 503, 504; unveils Oastler statue (1869), 520
Ashton Chronicle, 477, 479, 483, 487, 488, 489
Association for the Protection of John Fielden's Ten Hours Act, 490, 491; *see also* Fielden Society
Atkinson, William, 440
Attwood, Matthias, 278, 392, 393, 442

Baines, Edward, 24; early career, 45; political and social policy, 45, 46; receives Oastler's letter

Baines, Edward—(*Continued*)
on 'Yorkshire Slavery,' 46; 55; founds Leeds Liberal Association, 63; comments on Hobhouse Bill, 67; endorses Reform Bill, 68; asks Hobhouse to explain curtailment of his bill, 96; denounces Tory-Radical alliance, 115; public debate with Oastler, 118ff.; breaks with Oastler, 142; 'Great Liar of the North,' 161, 162n.; 178; at Leeds election riot, 184, 185; hopes for 11 hour bill, 219; 234; attends London meeting of textile manufacturers, 237; invited to arbitrate Oastler's dispute with Foster, 254; returned as M.P. for Leeds, 259; promotes 11 hour petitions, 317; effigy burnt, 162, 352, 355; at Yorks county election (1837), 362; contributes to Oastler liberation fund, 442

Edward, Jr., 24, 46; attitude to Oastler, 72; on curtailment of Hobhouse's Bill, 95; denounced by Oastler, 98; debate with Oastler, 118ff.; at Leeds reform demonstration, 179; 203; comments on Report of Sadler Committee, 208; 320, 400; final editorial on Oastler, 519

Bankes, George, 498

Beckett, Sir John, 112n., 259, 325, 362

William, 442

Benbow, William, 262

Birmingham Political Union, 391, 392; *see also* Chartism

Blackburne, Charles, K.C., 256, 259, 318, 344

Bradford Observer, 298, 441

Bright, John, 457, 470

Brook, James, 87n., 195

William, 358

Brotherton, Joseph, 149, 476, 485

Brougham (Henry) Lord, 274, 457, 505

Bull, Rev. George Stringer ('Parson Bull'), temperance campaign, 50; entry into Ten Hours campaign, 133; pamphlets, 143; pilgrimage to York, 157ff.; evidence before Select Committee, 174; helps Sadler in London, 187; accompanies Sadler on northern tour, 196, 197; denounced by *Leeds Mercury*, 201; 202; Bradford conference, 209, 210; visits London to find successor to Sadler, 212, 213; announces Ashley's promise of support, 213; campaigns for Ten Hours movement, 215; 216; protest against Royal Commission (1833), 224, 231, 235; 249; opposition to National Regeneration Society, 266; disagrees with Hindley's policy, 312, 313; tries to submit Memorial to Queen (1836), 320; denounced by Rev. Gilmour, 321; publicly dissociates himself from Oastler's violence, 329; opposition to New Poor Law, 335, 339, 367, 374; helps Oastler's election campaign, 348; at Yorks county election (1837), 362; opposition to Chartism, 395, 396; interviewed by Trollopes, 404; removes to Birmingham, 410; visits Oastler in prison, 420; attends Huddersfield celebration of Oastler's release, 447; eulogy of Sadler in *Ten Hours Advocate*, 472; conducts Oastler's funeral service, 520

Bulwer, Sir Edward Lytton, 395

Bussey, Peter, 267

Cairnes, J. E., cited, 434n.

Carlyle, Thomas, cited, 278n.

Chadwick, Edwin, 226, 275, 276, 277

Chalmers, Dr. Thomas, 236n., 467, 468

Champion, The, 491, 498

Chartism, ch. xxix *passim;* relation to Anti-Poor Law movement, 393, 394; Bull's attitude to,

395; Stephens' attitude to, 396; Oastler's attitude to, 398, 399, 401; collapse, 405; resurgence in 1842, 453

Child labor, 38, 47, 52, 53, 56, 59 and n., 104, 105, 122, 171–4, 208, 243 and n., 244; statistics of, in 1836, 536; see also Select Committee, Report (1831), Royal Commission, Report (1833)

Church Intelligencer, 444

Cleave, John, 301, 391

Cobbett, James, 370, 513ff.
  John, 374, 491, 500
  R. B., 411, 499, 500
  William, 50, 161, 162n, 262, 263, 278, 279

Condy, George, 148, 230, 263, 374

Conservatism, Oastler's attitude towards, 305, 436–7

Convocation: The Church and the People (1860), 517

Crabtree, Mark, 451

Damnation . . . to the . . . New Poor Law, 339, 341

Daniel, Thomas, 148, 195, 442

Declaratory Bill, problem of, 500, 545

Deutsche Allgemeine Zeitung, 424

Devil-to-do . . . in Huddersfield, The, 300n.

Dickinson, Joseph, 20–22

Discontent in northern factory districts (1831–2), 125, 126

Disraeli, Benjamin, on New Poor Law, 279; support for Oastler's opinions, 407–9; 472; attacks government for its 10½ hours plan (1850), 504, 505; on Young England, 510n., 511

Doherty, John, 148, 210, 237, 261, 263, 310, 311

Downs, George, 224

Doyle, Sir Francis, 318

Drinkwater, John, 228–31, 234–6

Duncombe, Hon. William (Viscount Feversham), 160, 281, 316, 350, 395, 411, 420, 440, 513

Economics, see Political Economy

Economist, The, 431 and n., 433

Edinburgh Review, 273

Eldon, Earl of, 283, 285

Ellice, Edward, 344, 349

Elliott, Ebenezer, cited, 182

Factory legislation, (1819) Peel's Act, 59 and n., 149; (1831) Hobhouse's Act, 94, 95, 149; (1833) Althorp's Act, terms, 245, 246; working of, 307–9; proposed amendment defeated (1836), 322; difficulties of application, 450; Select Committee to inquire into (1840), 451; prosecutions under, 536; (1844) Graham's Act, 457, 458, 480; (1847) Fielden's Ten Hours Act, 472; (1850) the 10½ Hours Act, 504; summary of achievements 1833–50, 505, 506; (1853) Palmerston's Act, 514, 515; statutes 1819–53 listed, 567

Factory Reformation Society, 260, 265

Fenton, Captain, 256

Ferrand, William Busfield, character and background, 240 and n., 241; visits Oastler in prison, 420; eulogy of Oastler, 439, 440; campaign on behalf of Oastler Liberty Fund, 442, 444, 445; supports 4th Ten Hours campaign, 456; 472; supports Young England, 510; 513; assists new Ten Hours agitation (1852), 514; founds 'Labour League,' 516, 517

Fielden, John, supports Ten Hours movement in Lancashire (1832), 149; promotes eight hours movement, 261–3; becomes treasurer of Lancashire Ten Hours campaign, 311; 323; stands by Oastler when others desert, 329; speech at Oldham (1836), 329; anti-Poor Law activity, 335, 351, 373; 374; visits Oastler in prison, 420; supports

Fielden, John—(Continued)
Oastler Liberty Fund, 442; supports 4th Ten Hours campaign, 456; helps defray debt on *Fleet Papers*, 461; sponsors Ten Hours Bill in Parliament, 464; lobbying for Ten Hours Bill, 470; tribute from *Ten Hours Advocate*, 472, 476; takes part in new movement, 483; *Advice to the Ten Hours Men*, 483; death (1849), 484

Samuel, continues father's work (1849), 485, 486; leads 'no surrender' group, 487; president of new Ten Hours organization, 491; letter to *Times* on Parke judgment, 493, 494; calls 3rd conference, 499; Ten Hours agitation of 1852, 513ff.

Fielden Society, 490; urges Declaratory Bill, 495; Manchester conference, 497; 503; revived (1852), 514

Finlay, Kirkman, 218

Fixby, 18, 25–9, 33; opposition to New Poor Law at, 342, 343

Fixby Hall compact, 88, 395, 420

Fleet Papers, The, 416–18, 461

Fletcher, Mathew, 397, 491

Floyd, H., 375

Foster, John, 116n.; quarrel with Oastler, 251ff.

Fulneck school, 15, 16, 149

General strike, 262, 393

Gig-mills, 17 and n., 18n.; *see also* Wool and worsted industry

Glendinning, Samuel, 87n., 157

Globe, The, 444

Graham, Sir James, 422, 453, 455, 518

Graham's Act (1844), *see* Factory Legislation

Grand National Consolidated Trades Union, 263ff.

Grant, Philip, 147; defends Oastler against Foster, 254; supports eight hours movement, 263; leads new Ten Hours campaign in Lancashire (1835–6), 310; 319, 458; edits *Ten Hours Advocate*, 465; and schism in Ten Hours movement, 489; opposes Fielden Society, 496; approves 10½ hours proposal, 503

'Great Liar of the North,' 161, 162n., 299, 352

Grey, Sir George, 411, 471, 481

Halévy, Elie, cited, 397n.

Halifax Guardian, 417

Halifax Resolutions, 65, 66, 547

Halifax tithe dispute, 33–5, 525

Halliley, John, 56, 171

Halliwell, William, 210

Hammond, John, 119

Handloom weavers, 287, 288, 289

Hanson, John, 87n., 157

Hartshead moor demonstration, 351, 352

Herald of the Rights of Industry, The, 265

Hetherington, Henry, endorses Ten Hours movement, 231; supports Foster, 253, 254; apologizes for criticism of Oastler, 254, 255; introduces Oastler to London radicals, 285; persuades Oastler to write for *Poor Man's Guardian*, 286; anti-Poor Law activity, 351; and London Working Men's Association, 391

Hey, William, 135, 255

Hill, William, 322, 371

Hindley, Charles, at Fulneck school, 149; supports Lancashire Ten Hours movement, 149; 195; fears operatives may betray Ten Hours principle, 309, 317; asked to take charge of Ten Hours Bill in Parliament, 310, 311; distrusted by Lancashire men, 311, 312; withdraws Ten Hours motion, 324; breaks with Oastler, 328; makes proposal for 11 hours bill (1846), 470; 483; willingness to compromise on Ten Hours principle, 485, 488; 543

Hobhouse, John Cam, 62, 79, 94, 96, 97, 170, 207, 322
Hobhouse's Act (1831), see Factory legislation
Hobhouse's factory bill (first), 65, 66, 67, 72, 79, 80; (second), 90, 94
Hobson, J. A., 433
Joshua, 87n., 88, 325, 371, 528
Hodgskin, Thomas, cited, 431n.
Home, The, 513, 516, 517
Hoole, Holland, 175, 176
Hope, J. T., 167
Howarth, Charles, 491
Huddersfield Board of Guardians, election of first board (Feb. 1837), 337; 1st meeting, 337; 2nd meeting, 341; 3rd meeting: workhouse riot, 352ff.; 4th meeting, 355; 5th and 6th meetings, 357; 7th meeting, 374, 375; new board elected (1838), 375; tumult at meetings, 376; members indicted, 377; weakening of resistance, 406
Huddersfield dissenters in a fury . . . , The, 300n.
Huddersfield dissenters stark, staring mad . . . , The, 300n.
Huddersfield parliamentary elections (1832), 186, 187, 202; (1833), 255ff.; (May 1837), 344ff.; (July), 358ff.
Huddersfield Radical Committee (1837), 345–7
Huddersfield Short Time Committee, see Short Time Committees
Huddersfield Union; burning of effigies in, 355; Home Office informed of Oastler's influence in, 356; resistance to New Poor Law in, see Anti-Poor Law Movement, and Huddersfield Board of Guardians
Humanity against Tyranny, 105, 106

Illustrated London News, The, 448, 449
Inglis, Sir Robert, 170

Keighley, 151, 340
Kellett, E. E., cited, 110
Kelly, Fitzroy, Q.C., counsel for Thornhill, 411, 412; visits Oastler in prison, 438; supports The Home, 513
Kenyon, Lord, 285
Ker, Bellenden, 500, 500n., 544
Kilham, Alexander, 14, 109
Kydd, Samuel, 162, 513, 518, 518n.; acquires Oastler's papers, 563

Labour League of Lancashire and Yorkshire, 516, 517
Lancashire, demand for regulation of machinery, 149, 311ff.
Lancashire Cotton Spinners Association, 59
Law of Population, 108
Law or the Needle, The, 328
Leech, John, 87n., 92, 103, 157
Leeds, expansion and prosperity (c.1780), 9, 10; Free Trade Resolution (1799), 10; Guardians of the Poor, 24; Liberal Association, 178, 183, 259; Radical Union, 199, disapproves Oastler's candidacy (1837), 347; Short Time Committee, see Ten Hours Movement; typhus epidemic at, 20
Leeds Intelligencer, rivalry with Mercury, 10; attitude to Halifax tithes dispute, 35; 46, 50; reaction to Oastler's 1st letter, 51, 52; corroborates Oastler's 2nd letter, 55; tribute to Oastler, 60; endorses Hobhouse Bill, 69; publishes Oastler's 4th letter, 74, 75; comment on Oastler's 4th letter, 76; 77, 84, 92; on Hobhouse's failure, 95; supports Sadler against Watson, 108; issues pamphlet on Oastler's debate with Baineses, 124; 137, 145, 158, 162, 186, 241; endorses appeal for Foster, 252; 355; anti-Poor Law movement, 371; on Oastler's farewell to Fixby, 386; publicizes Fleet Papers, 417

Leeds Mercury, 10, 13; attitude to Halifax tithes dispute, 35; general policy of, 45, 46; anticipatory editorial on Oastler's letter, 46; publishes Oastler's 1st letter, 47; controversy over Oastler's letter in, 51, 53; Oastler's 2nd letter to, 53; editorial on Oastler's 2nd letter, 54, 55; publishes letters in support of Oastler, 56; tribute to Oastler, 60; Oastler's 3rd letter in, 60; comments on Hobhouse's bill, 67, 68; endorses parliamentary Reform Bill, 68; Oastler's 4th letter in, 72; position on Oastler's 4th letter, 77; quandary over franchise and factory questions, 77, 78; attitude to Hobhouse's Bill, 80; 84; concern over limitations of Hobhouse's Act, 95; states Hobhouse's position, 96; controversy with Oastler over Hobhouse Bill, 98; Watson-Sadler controversy in, 108; condemns Radical Tory fusion, 115, 356, 357; new controversy over Ten Hours Bill, 119; 135, 142; exploits fear of radicalism, 145; calls Oastler 'king,' 156; mob demonstrations against, 161; and Reform Bill excitement, 178, 179; attacks Sadler's Ten Hours Bill, 194; discredits Sadler, 200; denounces Bull, 201; comment on Sadler Report, 208; urges 11 hours bill, 219, 320; 247; publicizes Foster's attacks on Oastler, 253, 254; continues controversy with Oastler, 299; urges operatives to reconsider factory regulation, 310; reports Huddersfield by-election, 347, 348; 350, 386; denounces anti-Poor Law policy of Huddersfield guardians, 405; modifies attitude to Oastler, 448n.; reports 4th Ten Hours campaign, 456; final tribute to Oastler, 519

Leeds parliamentary elections (1832), 107ff.; (1834), 259
Leeds Patriot, declares for Oastler, 78; urges public meetings for factory reform, 84; 92; supports Sadler against Watson, 108; endorses Radical-Tory fusion, 115; 162, 251, 252
Leeds Times, 267, 347
Letter to the Archbishop of York, 306
Letter to those Sleek, Pious, Holy and Devout Dissenters . . . , A, 299
Lewis, Frankland, 381, 413
Literary Gazette, The, 444
Liverpool Mercury, 444
Liverpool Standard, 444
London Society for the Improvement of the Condition of Factory Children, 216
London Working Men's Association, 391, 392, 394, 394n.; *see also* Chartism
Louden, Dr., 228ff.
Lovett, William, 391
Luddites, 22, 23

Maberley, Rev., 280
Macaulay, Thomas B., invited to stand for Leeds, 107; in fracas at White Cloth Hall Yard, 184, 185; election meeting, 197, 199; attitude to factory regulation, 199n.; attacks factory reformers, 200, 201; returned for Leeds, 202; vacates seat in parliament, 259; converted to Ten Hours cause, 457; speaks for Ten Hours Bill, 464
McCulloch, J. R., 207, 274
Mackintosh, Sir James, 242
Macturk, Dr., 133
Mallalieu, William, 491
Malthus, T. R., 274, 432
Manchester Advertiser, 148, 263, 321; supports Anti-Poor Law Movement, 370; publicizes *Fleet Papers,* 417
Manchester Cotton Spinners Association, 420

Manchester Examiner, 481
Manchester Guardian, 321, 328, 484
Manchester Times, 333
Manifesto to the Workers of England . . . , 489
Manners, Lord John, 472, 498, 503, 504, 505; character and social philosophy, 509–11; relation to Oastler, 511, 512, 513
Marshall, John, 63, 106n.
  John, Jr., 107, 114, 135, 184, 185, 197, 202
Martineau, Harriet, 171, 274, 279
Marx, Karl, 510n.
Mawdesley, Thomas, favors strike action, 488, 489; denounces Oastler, 489; opposes Fielden Society, 496; 500
Maxwell, John, 286
Methodism, *see* Wesleyan Methodism
Michael Armstrong, 173, 404
Milnes, Monckton, 362
Moore, William, 300, 317–9
Moravian Church, 15n.
Morning Advertiser, 514
Morning Chronicle, 208, 253, 255, 264, 395
Morning Herald, 207, 418, 444, 514
Morning Post, 142, 444, 482
Morpeth, Lord, 60, 62, 91, 95, 170, 182, 203, 209, 212–5, 220, 361, 363
Musgrove, Rev. Charles, 33–5; *see also* Halifax tithes dispute

National Association for the Protection of Labour, 148
National Convention of Chartists, 393, 404, 405
Northern Liberator, 394
Northern Star, 179, 371, 372, 378, 383, 387, 398, 411, 417, 442

Oastler, Mary (Tatham), 141, 385, 461
Oastler, Richard: Life:
  (1789–1830) birth, 4; childhood, 15; schooldays, 15, 16; architect's apprentice, 19; sympathy enlisted against Negro slavery,
19; as commission agent, 20; early philanthropy, 20–22; marriage, 23; bankruptcy, 23, 24; appointed Steward of the Fixby estate, 25; life at Fixby, 27ff.; becomes a Tory, 29ff.; leads Halifax tithe war, 33–5; opens land agent's office, 35
  (1830–36) first learns of factory conditions, 40, 41; letter to *Leeds Mercury* on 'Yorkshire Slavery,' 42–4; effect of letter, 50; 2nd letter on Yorkshire Slavery, 53, 54; praised by manufacturers, 60; 3rd letter on Yorkshire Slavery, 60, 61; castigated by Bradford mill-owners, 64, 65; 4th letter on Yorkshire Slavery, 71–4; attitude to Reform Bill, 71; anger at *Mercury's* cutting of 4th letter, 74; comments on Halifax Resolutions, 74–6; attitude to opponents of factory regulation, 81, 85; first statement of Ten Hours principle, 85; 'Fixby Hall Compact,' 86–9; learns of Huddersfield petition against factory regulation, 92; maintains contact with Sadler, 93; asks Hobhouse for explanation of his failure, 96; replies to Hobhouse's letter, 97, 98; controversy over Hobhouse Bill, 98; prepares campaign for new factory bill, 101ff.; 6th letter on Yorkshire Slavery, 103–5; beginnings of Tory Democracy, 111, 112; helps organize Sadler's election campaign, 113; leads operatives' delegation to Sadler, 117; public debate with Baineses, 118ff.; first campaign of public meetings, 129ff.; extends contacts among poor, 132; pamphlets, 143; personal fund for Ten Hours campaign, 146–7; pilgrimage to York, 154ff.; first called 'king,' 156, 157; preparation for Select Committee, 168, 169; attitude

Oastler, Richard (*Continued*)
to parliamentary Reform Bill,
180, 181; efforts to get pledges
from candidates, 182, 183ff.;
interviews Duke of Wellington,
187–9; evidence before Sadler
committee, 189, 190; trouble
with Thornhill begins, 191,
192; organizes Sadler's election
campaign, 194ff.; attends election meeting at Wakefield, 203;
summons Bradford conference
to organize new campaign,
209ff.; denunciation of Morpeth's tactics, 214; 2nd campaign to rouse the north, 215ff.;
Lancashire campaign, 216, 217;
organizes northern resistance to
Royal Commission, 222ff.; interviews Commissioners at
Leeds, 230; fans resentment
against Commissioners, 231;
protests to Commissioners, 232,
233; at Wibsey Low Moor rally,
239, 240; reaction to passage of
Althorp's Act, 246; quarrel
with Foster, 251ff.; role in Huddersfield by-election (1834),
257–9; founds Factory Reformation Society, 260; attitude
to Fielden's National Regeneration Society, 263, 265; opposition to New Poor Law, 281ff.;
2nd interview with Duke of
Wellington, 284; contributes to
unstamped press, 286, 301–3;
evidence before Select Committee on Handloom Weavers,
286ff.; publishes practical program (1834–5), 295–8; manifesto for 3rd Ten Hours campaign, 315–16; libel suit by
Moore, 317–9; campaign to
prevent amendment of Al-
thorp's Act (1836), 322ff.;
growing militancy, 323; public
entry into Ashton, 325; incitement to sabotage, 326, 327;
deserted by friends, 328; Oldham speech ends campaign of
1836, 330

(1836–40) opposition to New
Poor Law, 334ff.; first meets
O'Connor, 338; anti-Poor Law
agitation, 342; letters to Thornhill on Fixby guardian, 343;
receives joint nomination for
candidature, 345; first election
contest, 347ff.; leads Huddersfield struggles against New
Poor Law, 352ff.; second election contest, 358ff.; organizes
anti-Poor Law demonstration
at Wakefield, 361; helps anti-
Poor Law campaign at Bradford, 367; illness, 378; financial
relations with Thornhill, 379;
disagreement with Thornhill
on New Poor Law, 381; dismissed from his stewardship,
382; urges workers to arm, 383,
384, 388, 400; assisted by
friends, 384; leaves Fixby, 384,
385; accused of malversation,
387; served with writ for debt,
388; relations with London
Workingmen's Association, 391;
relation to Chartism, 398, 399,
401; campaigns for Stephens
Defense Fund, 402, 403; temporary end of active campaigning, 403; awaiting trial, 404;
helps John Walter at Southwark, 410, 411; series of open
letters, 411; trial, 411, 412
(1840–44) enters Fleet prison,
413; life in prison, ch. xxxi
passim; publishes *Fleet Papers,*
416; Oastler committees, 420;
Oastler Festivals, 420, 421;
helps Walter get Nottingham
nomination, 421; journey to
York, 422; transferred to
Queen's prison, 422; opposition
to Anti-Corn Law League, 436;
attitude to Peel ministry, 436,
437; appeals made to Thornhill
on his behalf, 438, 439; plan for
public subscription to defray
debt, 439–441; newspapers call
for his release, 441; Liberty
Fund started, 441, 442; re-

leased from prison, 445; Huddersfield celebration in his honor, 446, 447 (1844–50) leads 4th Ten Hours campaign, 455ff.; financial position after liberation, 459; forced to retire from public life, 460; leaves Yorkshire, 462; accepts invitation to lead new Ten Hours campaign, 465; new platform campaign, 466; tours Scotland, 467; converts Chalmers to Ten Hours cause, 467, 468; helps Fielden in London, 470; open letters to men of eminence, 470; exposes fallacious arguments of Anti-Corn Law Leaguers, 470; closing letter of 1847 campaign, 473, 474; illness, 476; invited north by Manchester Central committee, 482; reports on status of law enforcement, 482; campaign to fight compromise proposal, 486; 'no surrender' group, 487; manifesto against strike tactics, 489; contributes to *Champion*, 491; demands penal clause in Bill, 495; at Manchester delegates' conference, 497; denounces 10½ hour proposal, 502, 503; renews struggle in north, 503 (1850–61) shift of emphasis in his speeches, 507; faith in Toryism wanes, 508; last appeal to Tories, 508; turns to Manners, 509, 511, 512; *The Home*, 513, 517; declining years, 517–18; last pamphlet, 517; return to Yorkshire, 519; death, 519; burial, 519, 520
Personality:
character, 20, 47, 247, 417, 443 estimates, by Captain Wood, 443; by Francis Place, 542; in *The Planet*, 418; in *Standard*, 440; in *The Times* 441; in *Illustrated London News*, 448, 449; in *Leeds Mercury*, 519

physical characteristics, 126–8
Social and political ideas:
general theory of society, 282–4, 292ff., 302ff., 424ff., 429 on the need for a great leader, 188, 189, 509; on Whiggery, 192, 193; on Tory Democracy, 203, 204; on capitalism, 289, 290; on party, 293, 294; on social rights, 369; on the consequences of laissez-faire, 425; on a regulated society, 426, 427; on the British constitution, 425, 435; on national character, 429, 430; on political economy, 430ff.; on Malthus, 432; on Christianity in an industrial society, 433
Writings, listed, 564–6
Oastler, Robert, family background, 4, 5; embraces Methodism, 5; life at Thirsk, 5; becomes a cloth merchant, 6; philanthropy, 13; his 'liberalism,' 14; abandons cloth industry, 17; death, 24
Oastler, Sarah (Scurr), 13
Oastler societies, 451
O'Brien, B., 351
O'Connell, Daniel, 216, 451
O'Connor, Feargus, 337, 351, 362, 367, 368, 371, 374, 376, 398, 422
Oglesby, Rev. Richard, 130
Osburn, William, 145, 176, 210
Owen, Robert, 24, 59n., 216, 261, 263, 351

Parke judgment, 492, 558
Parliamentary Reform Bill (1831–2), 68 and n., 85, 90, 100, 126, 178ff.
Patten, Wilson, 219, 220, 221
Peacock, Barnes, Q.C., 500 and n.
Peel, Sir Robert, 305 and n., 411, 451, 452, 453
Perring, G., 116n., 195
Petition against Hobhouse Bill by Huddersfield firms, 91
Phillpotts, Bishop, 278

Pitkeithly, Lawrence, 87n., 157, 159, 339, 351, 442, 513
Place, Francis, 394, 402, 542
Political economy, 226, 247, 248; obsession of the age with, 273; Oastler's attitude to, 294, 295, 430ff.
Poor Law, problem of, ch. xxii *passim;* Report of Royal Commission on, 275; Amendment Bill, 276, 277; Commissioners tour Lancashire and Yorkshire, 331ff.
Poor Man's Guardian, 231, 253, 254, 286, 301
Power, Alfred, 228ff., 234, 235, 236, 335ff., 339, 341, 352, 354, 355, 364, 365, 366, 374
Propaganda, by Ten Hours movement, 143

Quarterly Review, 273

Radical Union (Leeds), 184, 199, 201
Ramsden, Sir John, 191–2, 346n., 349
John, 186, 187, 191
Rand, John, 40, 58, 132, 362
'Ransomed Patriot,' article on Oastler's liberation, 445, 446
Registration Act (1836), 336 and n.
Relay system, 214, 238, 308, 479, 493, 494, 558
Report of Factory Commission, 242
Report of Select Committee on Handloom Weavers, 291
Report of Select Committee on Sadler's Bill, 170ff., 207
Richardson, Cavie, 116, 229
Reginald J., 368, 395
Rickards, Inspector, 309
Robinson, G. R., 220
Royal Commission on factory conditions (1833), 225ff.; efforts of Ten Hours organisation to thwart, 223ff., 228ff.; Report, 242
Royal Commission on the Poor Laws, 273, 275, 275n.

Royal Commission on . . . children in mines (1840), 451
Ruskin, John, 425, 428, 433
Russell, Lord John, 68, 324, 353, 356, 383, 411, 434, 457, 464

Sadler, Michael Thomas, philanthropic work in Leeds, 20, 21; efforts on behalf of Hobhouse's factory bill, 93; invited to be Tory candidate at Leeds, 107; controversy over Watson's letter, 108; as candidate of Tory-Radical fusion, 113; receives *Address* from Huddersfield Short Time Committee, 114; asked by Short Time Committees to be parliamentary champion, 116, 117; 124, 135, 139, 153; pilgrimage to York, 155ff., Ten Hours speech in Parliament, 164, 165; chairman of Select Committee on Ten Hours Bill, 170, 174, 176; letter of consolation to Oastler, 193, 194; election campaign at Leeds (1832), 194ff.; tour of northern cities, 195–7; helps Bull seek successor, 212, 216; protest against Royal Commission, 225; hostility to Royal Commission (1833), 229, 234; traduced by Foster, 253–5; election contest at Huddersfield (1834), 256ff.; declines invitation to stand for Leeds, 259; death, 304
Salisbury, Marquess of, 285
Schofield, Joseph, 299, 300
Scurr, Sarah, 5
Select Committee on factory conditions (1831), 170ff.
Select Committee on Handloom Weavers (1834), 286ff.
Select Committee on the working of Althorp's Act (1840), 451
Senior, Nassau, 274, 275
Sharp, Dr., 133
Shaw, Sir Charles, 450n.
Short Time Committees: *Activities:* origins and membership, 82; attitude to Hobhouse Bill, 90;

100, 101; ask Sadler to represent their interests in Parliament, 116, 117; plan campaign of public meetings, 118; canvass mills for support, 124; use of propaganda, 143; work of, 143, 144; finances, 146; formed in Lancashire, 148; plan pilgrimage to York, 155; preparation for Select Committee, 168, 169; continue working throughout Reform Bill crisis, 181, 182; work for return of Sadler to Parliament, 198, 199; Bradford conference of (Jan. 1833), 209; list of (Feb. 1833), 209, 210, 210n.; reorganized, 210, 211; receive news of Ashley's leadership, 213; new groups started (1833), 215; Manchester conference to discuss Royal Commission, 223, 224; oppose the Royal Commission, 223ff., 228ff.; fear establishment of relay system, 238; bewildered by passing of Althorp's Act, 249; Birstall conference of West Riding delegates (1834), 260; delegates' conferences at Preston and Manchester, 311; work for law enforcement, 324, 325; fight New Poor Law in north, 335; send deputation to Oastler in prison, 421; revival (1844), 454; send appeal to Lord John Russell, 471; call on Oastler and Fielden for advice, 482; revived (1852), 514; erect memorial to Oastler (1869), 520; sources of information about, 527; confidential memorandum used by (Apr. 1832), 550

Central committees: Lancashire, 148, 195, 196; problem of organization, 490; Yorkshire, 144, 155, 156, 168, 169, 211n., 235

Local committees: Ashton, 325; Blackburn, 326; Bradford, 84, 310; Edinburgh, 469; Halifax, 137, 465; Huddersfield, 82, 86, 87, 92, 102, 114, 130, 190, 194, 528; Leeds, 82–4, 89, 117–19, 135, 183, 186, 198, 201, 228–30, 231, 234; Manchester, 152, 175, 176, 216, 218

'Slaughter-house men,' 289, 290

Smith, Dr., 160, 162

Southwood, 226

Smythe, George, 510

Social distress (1830), 49; (1837), 331ff.

Social movements in the West Riding (1830), 50

Society for Improving the Condition of Working Children, 145

Society for Promoting National Regeneration, 264ff.

Speenhamland system, 272

Spinning, *see* Wool and worsted industry

Standard, 137, 142, 279, 370, 387, 418, 439, 440, 444

Stanhope, Earl, 278, 373, 393, 513

Stansfield, 358, 359

Starkey, 375

Steinhauer, Henry, 16 and n.

Stephens, Joseph Rayner, character and social philosophy, 313, 314; lobbying at Westminster, 316; first public appearance with Oastler, 325; stands by Oastler when others desert, 329; helps Oastler's election campaign, 347, 348; anti-Poor Law activity, 351, 368–70, 374, 376; visits Oastler after illness, 378; attitude to Chartism, 396; arrest for sedition, 401, 402; Defense Fund for, 402; sent to prison, 404; visits Oastler in prison, 420; starts *Ashton Chronicle,* 477; threatens 'holy war,' 486; starts *The Champion,* 491; on council of Fielden Society, 492; urges restriction on moving power, 495; helps new Ten Hours agitation (1852), 514

Stockmar, Baron, 437

Stocks, William, 256, 339, 340, 345, 351, 384

Strangers' Friend Society, 21 and n.

Strickland, George, 160, 170, 182, 203, 220, 361, 363

Sussex, Duke of, 146, 189

Sutcliffe, 357, 375, 376, 406, 414

Swaine, 341, 374, 375, 353–5

Tamworth Manifesto, 305n.

Tatham, Mary, 23

Taylor, Ralph, 121, 145, 492

Ten Hours Advocate, The, 465, 466, 467, 472

Ten Hours Movement, begins, 85; first pamphlet of, 105; Sadler asked to introduce bill, 116, 117; social ferment giving rise to, 125, 126; first campaign of public meetings, 129ff.; Bill introduced into House of Commons, 139; becomes involved in party politics, 142–3; literature of, 143; organization expanded, 145–6; finances of, 146, 152; Lancashire movement, 147–50; masters' meetings in opposition to, 151; pilgrimage to York, 154ff.; 2nd reading of bill, 164; prepares evidence for Select Committee, 168–9; opposition exposed, 175; supports Sadler's election campaign, 194; influence of Select Committee's Report, 207–8; Bradford conference plans new campaign, 209; Ashley becomes parliamentary leader, 212–13; Yorkshire central committee transferred to Bradford, 211n.; 2nd campaign of public meetings, 215ff.; Royal Commission appointed, 220–21; Manchester conference plans resistance to Royal Commission, 223–4; efforts to thwart Royal Commission, 223ff., 228ff., 553; appeal to nation, 555; fear lest relay system be established, 238; Ten Hours clause defeated (1833), 245; confusion after defeat of Ashley's bill, 249; overwhelmed by Fielden's eight hours movement, 265; quiescence (1833–5), 300–301; third

campaign, 310ff.; campaign intensified, 322ff.; close of third campaign, 329–30; turns into Anti-Poor Law Movement, 335; in abeyance (1837–41), 450; begins to revive (1841), 450; 4th campaign, 454ff.; interest wanes (1845–6), 463; Bill again defeated, 464; 5th campaign begins, 464ff.; extends to Scotland, 467; Ten Hours bill enacted, 472; reasons for victory analyzed, 474, 475; law enforcement problem (1847ff.), 478ff.; new campaign, 482, 486; Fielden advises against strikes, 484; dissension in ranks, 487; establishment of Fielden Society, 490, 491; judgment in favor of relays, 492; quarrel over leadership, 495, 496; delegates' conferences, 498–9; passage of 10½ hours Act, 504; new agitation (1852), 513ff.; Palmerston's Bill passed, 514–15; see also Short Time Committees

Thackrah, Dr. C. T., 73, 135, 136

Thompson, Matthew, 40, 56, 58–60, 365, 538

Thomson, Poulett, 96, 170, 245, 319, 321, 322

Thornhill, Thomas, 18, 25–9, 187, 191–3, 305–6, 342–4, 378ff., 380–1, 382, 387–8, 411–14, 416, 419, 422, 439, 460

Times, The, attitude to factory question, 142, 164, 167, 208, 213–14, 227, 234, 245, 456–7, 481, 492, 493–5, 501, 502, 514; attitude to New Poor Law, 279, 344, 368, 370, 372–3, 395; attitude to Oastler, 383, 385, 411, 418, 441, 444–6, 502–4, 519; see also John Walter II

Tithes, Halifax dispute, 33–5

Torrens, R., 216

Tory Democracy, 69, 97, 111, 112, 115, 180, 203–4, 259, 424ff., 510

Toryism, analysis of, 30–2; defined by Oastler, 428, 434

To the Aristocracy of England, 508
To the Nobility and Gentry of England, 470
To the People of England, 383
To the People of Yorkshire, 411
To the Workers of Lancashire, 489
To the Workers of Yorkshire and Lancashire, 315, 316
To the Working Classes of the West Riding, 85
Townend, Simeon, 52, 59, 62, 64
Trevelyan, G. M., cited, 271
Trollope, Frances, 173n., 278n., 403–4, 475
Trollope, Thomas, 403–4
Turner, James, 175, 195, 210, 263, 311
Twopenny Dispatch, 303–4

Union of Operative Spinners of the United Kingdom, 148
Unjust Judge, The, 325
Unstamped journals, 81n., 285–6, 301–3, 391
Ure, Dr., 37, 431

Vicarial Tithes, 35

Wakefield Journal, 447–8
Wakefield riot, 362–3
Walker, William, 461, 485, 497
Walter, John, II, 279; support of Anti-Poor Law Movement, 370, 373; apprehensive of manhood suffrage movement, 395; Southwark election campaign, 410–11; visits Oastler in prison, 420; candidate for Nottingham, 421; intercedes with Thornhill, 439; supports Oastler liberation movement, 442; supports 4th Ten Hours campaign, 456; supports Young England, 510; death, 476
John, III, 501, 503
Watson, James, 391
Rev. Richard, 108
Weatherhead, A., 340
Webb, B. and S., cited, 269–70
Webster, Richard, 57
Weekly Police Gazette, 301

Wellington, Duke of, 187–8, 212, 284
Well-seasoned Christmas Pie, A, 299
Wesley, John, 5, 13
Wesleyan Methodism, 5, 13–14, 101n., 109–10, 523
Whitacre, John, 345, 384
Whitehead, Abraham, 174
Wilberforce, William, 19 and n., 140, 523
Wildman, J., 340
Wilson, James, 226
Wood, Charles, 471
John, 36; social attitude, 39–40; 41, 45; letter in support of Oastler, 56; organizes meeting of masters, 58, 60; 89; speech at Bradford meeting, 132; financial support of Ten Hours movement, 147; pilgrimage to York, 155ff.; prepares memorandum for Sadler, 165; lobbying at Westminster, 187; supports Sadler at Manchester rally, 196; opposition to Royal Commission, 223; 235; breaks with Oastler, 329; interviewed by Trollopes, 404; helps liquidate *Fleet Papers,* 461; lobbying (1847), 471; tribute in *Ten Hours Advocate,* 472; opposition to compromise proposals, 485; attends Manchester conference, 497; philanthropy, 526
Captain Joseph, 160, 186, 202, 256–9, 443
Wool and worsted industry, organization of domestic system, 6–9; beginning of large-scale enterprise, 11; gig-mills, 17 and n., 18 and n.; technical changes in (1780–1830), 36–8; problem of water mills, 67; Wilberforce's description of, 523; *see also* Select Committee (1831), Royal Commission (1833)
Wortley, S., 361–3

Yorkshire County Election (1807), 19; (1832), 203; (1837), 360ff., 363
Young England, 425, 510